LEGACIES OF TWENTIETH-CENTURY DANCE

Lynn Garafola

Wesleyan University Press
Middletown, Connecticut

Published by Wesleyan University Press, Middletown, CT 06459

Printed in the United States of America

5 4 3 2 1

LIBRARY OF CONGRESS CATALOGING-IN-PUBLICATION DATA

Garafola, Lynn.

Legacies of twentieth century dance / Lynn Garafola.

   p.   cm.

Includes bibliographical references and index.

ISBN 0−8195−6673−X (cloth : alk. paper)— ISBN 0−8195−6674−8
(pbk. : alk. paper)

1.   Dance—History—20th century.   2.   Dancers—Bibliography.

3. Ballet dancing—History—20th century.   4. Ballet dancers—

Biography.   I. Title.

GV1594.G37   2004

796.8′09′04—dc22   2004019057

Contents

Part IV: Staging the Past

Illustrations follow pages 118 and 246

Preface

All writing is ultimately autobiographical. In collating for publication the following essays, I have revisited older, other selves and questions that after twenty years as a scholar and critic of dance continue to excite me. I began to write under the influence of second-wave feminism. In dance, this called into question most of the verities of traditional criticism. It asked that we look at ballerinas not as goddesses but as artists and agents in their own right and as victims of a system of representation that idealized them and of male-dominated institutions that exploited them. It took a new look at the genesis of modern dance and the work of contemporary, feminist choreographers. The new writing did not ignore men—how could it? But the focus was to rescue from obscurity the legions of lost women in all fields of dance, and to understand why, in an art dominated by women, power was exercised overwhelmingly by men.

My first published article on a historical theme, "Lydia Lopokova and the Soirées de Paris," was written in 1981. Lopokova was a member of Serge Diaghilev's Ballets Russes, who left "Big Serge" not once but three times, tantalized Virginia Woolf, and married the economist John Maynard Keynes. Her papers resided at King's College, Cambridge, and they included a large cache of letters, the first by a ballerina that I had ever seen, breezy, first-hand accounts that became the basis of the article. I wrote the piece originally for *Dance Magazine,* which in those days, under the editorship of William Como, did wonderful portfolios about Diaghilev-era works and personalities. But before he could accept or reject the piece, Milo Keynes, who held the rights to the letters, asked if he could include my article in a book of essays about his remarkable aunt.

Much of the writing that follows was written for a general audience and published in the mainstream press. This accounts for the emphasis on clarity and the avoidance of the jargon that in the late 1980s and 1990s became the bane of scholarly writing in dance as in other disciplines. I spent the late 1980s and 1990s on the periphery of academia. I did not hold a teaching job. I lectured and wrote criticism. With the assistance of several generous grants, I continued to pursue research. I published book reviews and scholarly essays, edited several books, contributed to museum catalogues, translated the work of foreign colleagues, and curated my first exhibition. Balancing history and criticism, I thought of myself as a "public intellectual," although the public for dance seldom transcends the ghetto of the knowledgeable. And, of course, much of what I wrote was ill-paid, if paid at all.

My first book, *Diaghilev's Ballets Russes,* was published by Oxford University Press in 1989. The book was pivotal to my development as a scholar, a revisionist study of the Ballets Russes that plunged me into the many fascinating worlds of early twentieth-century dance in Europe. Mining primary and secondary sources, I made the transition from a budding literary scholar to a full-fledged historian. I discovered a passion for dusty archives and microfilm, and was rewarded by twilight strolls in London, Paris, and Monte Carlo after libraries had closed for the day. The notes and photocopies from those years remain the foundation of my personal "archive," and I am amazed, when I consult them, that I had the forethought to make them.

The research for *Diaghilev's Ballets Russes* and, more recently, for a biography of Ida Rubinstein that is my next major project, steered me to numerous sources and a host of forgotten dancers, male as well as female. It encouraged an abiding interest in the historical particular, the building block of a narrative generated dialectically from a fusion of the empirical and the theoretical, as opposed to the recent tendency to borrow theories from other disciplines and impose them uneasily on dance, regardless of their appositeness or applicability. It renewed my belief in the power of the written word and set me on a continued search for stylistic transparency. Finally, it led me to reaffirm the relevance not only of the feminism of my youth but also of the Marxian ideas of class and social difference bequeathed by the 1960s.

In recent years, class has dropped out of the "race, class, and gender" mantra, now ubiquitous in scholarly parlance, at least in terms of serious analysis. The word "elitism" is bandied about, without any real consideration of what it means in a particular circumstance. Broadway, Hollywood, and MTV are routinely invoked as "popular" forms of culture, although they are billion-dollar businesses and controlled by major corporate interests. So-called "high" culture is damned as elitist, yet its practitioners can only dream of the kind of contracts that pop singers, movie stars, and sports figures sign every day. Like the other arts (indeed, all human activity), dance exists within a network of social and economic relationships. It is no purer than Hollywood or professional sports; there is just a lot less money at stake. And because dance is female-identified, with an often blurry line demarcating professional from lay or amateur activity, it displays attributes of popular culture. In fact, throughout the history of ballet, the elite and popular have nourished and fed off one another. This is evident not only in the ballet lexicon and repertory of expressive forms, as these have developed over the centuries, but also in the extremely modest social origins of many ballet practitioners, especially in the past.

A deep current of anti-intellectualism runs throughout the dance world, a mistrust of scholarly analysis, of probing beyond the evident, of questioning the truthfulness of received wisdom. When *Diaghilev's Ballets Russes* was published in 1989, it was attacked by some for sullying ballet by subjecting it to the kind of intellectual analysis that is commonplace in other arts and disciplines. In what other field would the standard biography of an artist of the stature of George Balanchine be a book based on a series of *New Yorker* interviews published more than forty years ago? Dance scholars suffer from the wages of isolation more acutely than scholars in the other arts. For the most part, they labor in university departments where the emphasis is on studio rather than intellectual work or find homes in departments peripheral to their interests as dance scholars. At the same time, they are ghettoized by editors. Dance scholars are seldom asked to review a book not specifically about dance, yet scholars in every other field make free with dance material, mangling evidence and misreading cues, without anyone raising an eyebrow or suggesting that a dance expert review the manuscript. Well-received recent books like *Lucia Joyce: To Dance in the Wake* by Carol Loeb Shloss and *Natasha's Dance: A Cultural History of Russia* by Orlando Figes contain egregious errors that would be unimaginable if they involved any subject other than dance.

Over the years, I have continued to write performance criticism. For me, history and criticism are intimately connected. Only through the living art can one embark on the historian's imaginative journey into the past, even when the goal is humanist knowledge and discovery rather than the reconstruction of dance as performance. At the same time, criticism—because of the ephemeral nature of dance—is always historical, in the sense of being an act of remembering and reconstruction of an extinguished moment in time. The difference lies in context, in making sense of the signals, of reading the signposts. Writing about the past, one has many more gaps to fill, places to imagine, people to resurrect, and frames of reference to inhabit.

I was born and bred a New Yorker. The city made me what I am and gave me both a home and a subject. Several of the essays that follow are about New York—how its dance world came into being and how it changed over time, not once but many times over. Scholarship also changes over time. When I wrote "Dance in the City: Toward an American Dance," a piece commissioned for a volume on the arts in New York City from 1940 to 1965, I sought to integrate the left-wing story and the Broadway story into the larger narrative of the period. I wrote the essay in 1987, the summer before my daughter was born. Rereading it, I still consider it a strong essay. However, it leaves out the early years of African-American concert dance, a subject that since the 1990s a new generation of scholars—both African-American and white—has begun to elucidate and redefine. The old paradigm needs to be revised.

The book that follows is divided into four sections that reflect the preoccupations that have shaped my career as a scholar and a critic: "The Ballets Russes and Beyond," "Reconfiguring the Sexes," "Dance in New York," and "Staging the Past." Europe dominates the earlier sections, America the later ones. Yet many themes carry over, not only because the 1930s witnessed the return of many American artists from abroad and the arrival of the first wave of refugees from Nazi Germany, but also because institutions such as the New York City Ballet were at least partly descended from—and at least partly modeled on—European antecedents such as the Ballets Russes.

Diaghilev taught me about the visual. I became an armchair art historian and in time a curator. During the months of preparation for the 1999 exhibition, *Dance for a City: Fifty Years of the New York City Ballet,* I sometimes wondered what he would have done, what choices he would have made, when he would have nodded "Yes" or bellowed a defiant "No!" What pleasure there was in handling so many beautiful costumes, photographs, and other works of art, in working with so many creative people and especially with the exhibition designer, Stephen Saitas, who made me understand the real meaning of collaboration. The images in the "scrapbook" that follows have been chosen for different reasons. Some relate to the essays in this book, others to books I have written or edited such as *José Limón: An Unfinished Memoir,* with its luminous prose and passionate belief in art. Still others are simply pictures that I like. I am grateful to several rights owners for generously waiving or reducing their fees.

Thanks to my husband, Eric Foner, for his faith in me, to my editor, Suzanna Tamminen, for having the courage to publish serious books about dance, to my students at Barnard College/Columbia University for their enthusiasm, and to my daughter, Daria, for the many moments of beauty she has given me since first stepping into the world.

February 2004 L.G.

PART I

THE BALLETS RUSSES AND BEYOND

COMING HOME

DIAGHILEV IN PERM

For years, Perm was a "closed" city. In Soviet parlance, that meant off-limits to foreigners: tourists, diplomats, correspondents, and scholars. Not that many people itched to see this Urals capital. With its chemical plants and munitions factories, Perm was a city of smokestacks, gray, modern, and charmless. Until Gorbachev, moreover, it was a center of the Gulag. In the surrounding penal colonies, prisoners "of conscience" like the poet Marina Tsvetaeva had died or spent years at hard labor.

The last time I arrived in Moscow, I learned that, thanks to glasnost, Perm had been "opened." To get there, one had to be on "official" business, but for the first time since the 1930s, foreigners were welcome. I made up my mind to go, and a few months later, with an invitation from the Perm State Art Gallery, boarded the Aeroflot flight from Moscow. Two hours and two time zones later, I was in Perm.

My reason for going was curiosity. I wanted to see where Serge Diaghilev had grown up. I had written a book about him, and the geography of his life had become an obsession. I knew where he ate lunch in Madrid and ordered winter coats in London, where he recited Pushkin in Florence and "insulted" Ravel in Monte Carlo. I had walked the former English Prospect in Leningrad where he once lived and had stood in the lobby of the hotel in Venice where he died. And in Paris, Turin, Milan, and countless other cities, I had visited the theaters where his Ballets Russes performed.

Yet, like other Western scholars, I had never seen the city of his youth. Although Diaghilev was born in the province of Novgorod, he lived in Perm from the time he was two until he was eighteen. This upbringing set him apart from the friends and future colleagues he met in St. Petersburg when he settled there as a university student in 1890. One of these, Alexandre Benois, recalled his impressions of the young collegian in *Reminiscences of the Russian Ballet*: "[Diaghilev] was very much of a provincial when he first arrived in St. Petersburg and Valetchka [Walter Nouvel], Kostia [Konstantin] Somov and I were even shocked by his rather uncouth manners and primitive views, though this was only natural to one who had lived all his life in the depths of the Perm countryside."

This essay was written in 1990 and published several years later in *Ballet Review,* 24, no. 2 (Summer 1996). This is the original version.

On the drive from the airport, I learn that Perm today is an industrial city of one million. In Diaghilev's time, it was a mercantile and administrative center with only a fraction of the current population. In the taxi with me is Nadezhda Vladimirovna Beliaeva, director of the Gallery and my host, and Natalia Sergeevna Ginsburg, the museum's curator of foreign art, who is acting as my translator. We could be in the American rust belt. On both sides of the road are factories with peeling walls and corroded fittings. Although it's only eight-thirty at night, the streets are deserted.

At the hotel, a high rise on Komsomol Prospect, Nadezhda Vladimirovna outlines my program. It's a full one: talks, tours, performances, a visit to Diaghilev's house. Then she describes what the Gallery has done to "bring Diaghilev home." She begins with the 1987 exhibition "Sergei Diaghilev and Artistic Culture of the Late Nineteenth and Early Twentieth Centuries." Did I know this was the first show about Diaghilev since the Revolution? No, but it wasn't hard to believe. For years he had been a nonperson, and even today, eight years after the publication of Ilya Zil'bershtein's two-volume collection of documents, *Sergei Diaghilev and Russian Art,* he remains in the shadow of the artists he revealed to the West. Then, there was the three-day conference that dovetailed with the exhibition, and the volume of papers on topics ranging from Diaghilev's career as a student to his activities as a critic and historian of art. She talks about the 1987 show, rich in biographical materials and documents of life in old Perm.

The next morning, with Natalia Sergeevna, I get my first glimpse of the nineteenth-century city. It's just across the hotel's carless parking lot and beyond the steel-girdered "univermag" (Russian for department store). But it's another world entirely; taking leave of the Soviet present, you enter the Russian past. Within minutes, we reach a promenade. Below lies a river, serene and glassy in the morning light. This is the Kama; it winds north through the Perm oblast (district) and south past Kazan to the Volga. In Diaghilev's time, paddle-steamers traveled the river, discharging their passengers at the old boat station. This morning, a mist hangs over the water, and on the embankment remain patches of last night's snow. Above us rises a steeple. That's our Gallery, Natalia Sergeevna tells me. Before the Revolution, it was the Cathedral of the Transfiguration, attended by all the best people, including the Diaghilevs. In 1922, it became a museum. I later learn that of the dozens of churches that existed in Perm before the Revolution, few survived the 1930s.

At the Gallery, the curators are waiting. I am to give a talk, an informal one, and for once in my life I do it off the cuff. Today, I can't remember a word I said, but I know I will never have such an audience again or feel the reality of Diaghilev's life meshed with so many impossible dreams. Think of him: *barin,* patron, collector, captain for twenty years of an enterprise dedicated to beauty, a man who could move mountains to get what he wanted, and did, on three continents. He loved pleasure and found it everywhere, in good food, fine tailoring, rare books, handsome faces. He ate chocolates and cream puffs with gusto, without a care for his waistline or the diabetes that eventually killed him. If ever a figure was larger than life, it was Diaghilev.

Yet, in the faces around me that morning in Perm, I discern no irony, no sense of the incongruity between his privileged existence and their own. In this city of factories and housing projects, where people have forgotten the taste of chocolate and never known the feel of silk and where a trip to the West is an unimaginable luxury, Diaghilev gives leave to imagine another kind of world— a lost paradise of beauty, pleasure, and ease.

Significantly, my audience is all women. Warm, capable, with the toll of double-burdened lives showing on the older ones, they are typical Russian women, conjuring suppers from empty supermarket shelves and touches of elegance from drab, ill-fitting clothing. None has traveled abroad, and few have met a foreigner before. But they dream, finding in the past an escape from the present and in nostalgia a means of giving focus to their yearnings for a better life. For Diaghilev's admirers in Perm, the reality of his life pales before the liberating power of his myth.

That evening, I am taken to the Tschaikovsky Theater, where the Perm Ballet is to give *Don Quixote*. Before the performance, however, we have a date with the theater archivist. A jovial man with a passion for local history, he guides me through the exhibition on the gallery level of the theater. The show is about old Perm, and he happily points out the treasures: a ten-foot-long map of the Kama from its source all the way to Kazan, panoramas of the nineteenth-century city (in which I spot the Gallery's steeple), period photographs of notable buildings, including the Assembly of Nobles, the Meshkov mansion (a merchant palace on the embankment), and the Opera Theater. There are also pictures of leading citizens, including members of the Diaghilev clan.

Back in the office, he sits me down. You know, he tells me, it's not true what they say, that culture came to Perm with the Revolution. Not true at all. In the old days, this was a cultural center. All the best people made music; they gave concerts, they formed an orchestra, they organized benefit performances for charity. The Diaghilevs were very musical; they had a chamber group that was the pride of the city and performed several times a year at the Assembly of Nobles, just down the street from where the family lived. It was these same people, he continues, who built the opera house we're sitting in now. A subscription was taken up, and everyone pledged something; the Diaghilevs gave 5,000 rubles. That was in the 1870s. By the 1890s, touring opera companies, with dancers, were giving full-scale performances.

At intermission, his friend Galina, a designer at the theater, takes me backstage. In the left wing, she points out the remnants of an old wall, left standing as a souvenir when this part of the theater was rebuilt in the 1950s. Then, she relates a piece of old lore about Diaghilev. In his day, the theater was off-limits to students. But he used to sneak here anyway, roaming the corridors and getting into trouble for it. So this, I thought as we rejoined the crowd, is where it all started, in a theater his family helped to build. No wonder proprietorship came easily to him.

Like St. Petersburg, Perm is a city of white nights, and at eleven, when we leave the theater, it's still light. In front of us is Komsomol Square, the heart of what remains of the old town; people come here to stroll in the park, my guides tell me, because it gives them a sense of the past. Although it's hard to believe, until the 1930s the square was covered by a complex of shops. To my surprise, I learn that a Diaghilev had built this emporium; I hadn't realized that the family, apart from one vodka-producing maverick, was "in trade." Other sights are pointed out: the corner-wrapping building with a balcony where Dmitrii Vasil'evich Diaghilev, Diaghilev's great-grandfather, once lived, and across from it the former *gymnasium,* or preparatory school, that Diaghilev attended from 1883 until 1890, when he graduated. No wonder Nadezhda Vladimirovna is badgering the city fathers to rename this Diaghilev Square.

Among my guides is Evgeniia Ivanovna Egorova. A woman in her sixties, she grew up in the countryside, not far from the village of Bikbarda, where the Diaghilevs had an estate. To the south of Perm (today, about five or six hours by bus), Bikbarda was a beautiful spot, with flowering orchards and woods. In the summer, the whole Diaghilev family gathered there. As a boy, she adds, Sergei Pavlovich loved to swim, a piece of information I find astonishing given Diaghilev's later horror of crossing even the calmest waterway.

She also fills me in on the history of the clan. The first Diaghilev to settle in Perm was Pavel Fedorovich. He came from Tobolsk, in Siberia, where his boyar ancestors had been sent by Ivan the Terrible, and he died in Perm in 1767. His son, Vasilii Pavlovich, administered rural metalworks and, like most of the Diaghilevs, married into a merchant family. His son, Diaghilev's great-grandfather, was the Dmitrii Vasil'evich with the house on Komsomol Square. A musician, writer, and painter, he was the first Diaghilev to display the artistic proclivities that henceforth distinguished the family.

In a torrent of forenames and patronymics, the chronicle moves forward to Diaghilev's day. She tells me about Elena Valerianovna Panaeva, his stepmother, whose father built railroads and opened a theater in St. Petersburg for Italian opera that burnt to the ground in 1905; her sister, Alexandra Valerianovna, a singer who studied in Paris, performed in Milan, and married a nephew of Tchaikovsky. She tells me about cousins who painted and graduated from the Conservatory. And, leaping into the Soviet era, she tells me about nieces and grandnephews who carried on the family musical tradition.

I press Evgeniia Ivanovna for information about Diaghilev's immediate family. Did they remain in Perm? What happened to them during the Revolution? After Sergei Pavlovich left for St. Petersburg, she tells me, the house was robbed, and the family went to live in lodgings. Then, they moved to Poltava, a city in the eastern Ukraine, where Diaghilev's father resumed his military career. When

Pavel Pavlovich died in 1914 (on the day World War I broke out), Elena Valerianovna moved to St. Petersburg, where she died in 1919 at the age of sixty-eight.

There is pain on Evgeniia Ivanovna's face as she continues the story. Diaghilev's brother Valentin followed his father into the army. In 1917, when the Revolution began, he was a general and the father of four sons, two of whom perished in the Civil War. Then, in 1927, Valentin was arrested and sent to Solovki, a bleak island prison off Archangel, where he died two years later. His wife, Alexandra Alekseeva Peiker, was also arrested and sent to Siberia. The children were left to fend for themselves; Sergei was sixteen and Vasilii fourteen, and they had to sell off the family books and furniture to eat. As for Iurii, Sergei Pavlovich's other brother, he too was sent away, to middle Asia near Tashkent, where he died in 1957. (His wife, Tatiana Andreevna Lugovskaia, was a painter who participated in the early exhibitions of the *Mir iskusstva* group.)

As Evgeniia Ivanovna relates this sorry tale, I recall some letters I had read at the Dance Collection in New York. They were dated January 1928 and written by one Jean Herbette to Philippe Berthelot, a high-ranking official in the French ministry of foreign affairs. What the Dance Collection had were copies made for Diaghilev by his assistant, Boris Kochno. Their import was the following: In late 1927, presumably at Diaghilev's behest, the French approached Maxim Litvinov, the Soviet Commissar of Foreign Affairs, for information about the whereabouts of Valentin and his wife, Alexandra Alekseeva, both of whom had disappeared. An inquiry was made, but as Herbette reported to his superior, the secret police "found no trace of an arrest." The timing of the enquiry had always puzzled me. Now I understood. Diaghilev had lost his closest relations not in the Revolution, but in the first wave of Stalin's purges.

It is with Evgenia Ivanovna, too, that I finally lay eyes on Diaghilev's house. Located at the corner of Karl Marx and Pushkin streets, it is now elementary school number eleven. At first, I am struck by the modesty of the building; only one-story, it has neither the columns nor balconies of Perm's statelier monuments. Then I notice its elegance: the French windows, the classical cornices, and the rhythmic effect produced by their repetition. Today, the walls are pinkish-beige; the windows and cornices white. In Diaghilev's time, the façade was livelier, with loops and edgings painted in high contrast to the walls. We arrive a few minutes before ten. The principal, Raisa Dmitrievna Zobygeva, is finishing a science lesson. She motions us into the classroom and introduces us; "foreigner," I hear the ten-year-olds whispering as she writes out their assignment.

Raisa Dmitrievna shows us around. Except for the eighteen-foot ceilings and the windows that flood the administrative offices with light, little remains of the building's original layout. Only the parlor is intact, a huge corner room with a piano at one end, where today, as in Diaghilev's time, concerts are given. On the walls are blowups of family photographs: Diaghilev, in a high chair, with Elena Valerianovna, and as a *gymnasium* student, his right hand thrust Napoleon-style into his overcoat; his father, as a dashing officer; the three brothers, Sergei, Valentin, and Iurii, as children; the family's chamber music group. Though the chandelier, the pier glass, and all the old furniture are gone, it's not hard to imagine this room as the setting of Diaghilev's introduction to civilized pleasure. Or, on a grimmer note, to imagine that from the windows facing the Siberian Way, as Karl Marx Street used to be called, he had his first glimpse of prisoners setting off on foot to Siberia. The tsars had their Gulags, too.

In the journey from Perm to Paris, Diaghilev remade himself as a cosmopolitan. Yet, always, he remained deeply Russian, attuned to the ways and arts of a country that belonged fully to Europe only at its westernmost borders. This sense of Russia was surely a legacy of Perm; here, even the Westernized elite was surrounded by popular tradition. At the Gallery, behind what was once the iconostasis, I am shown a remarkable collection of icons "rescued" from abandoned churches in the Perm region. Few are as beautiful as icons I have seen in Moscow, but they display the robust imagination of genuine folk art, the "primitivism" that Diaghilev brilliantly exploited in works like *Le Coq d'Or*. Even more remarkable is the museum's collection of religious sculpture: polychrome saints and crucifixions unique to Orthodox churches of the Urals.

Although Diaghilev was not a religious man, he had a keen appreciation for Russian religious art. In the 1906 exhibition that marked his debut on the Paris art scene, he included no fewer than twenty-six examples of the successive schools of icon painting. Among the unrealized projects that occupied his thoughts in 1914 and 1915 was *Liturgie*, a cubo-futurist "mystery" inspired, in part, by the icon tradition of Russia's north. Doubtless, his first encounter with popular religious art came in the country churches of Perm.

Examples of these have been reconstructed at Khokhlovka, the Gallery's outdoor museum about forty kilometers from the city. Dark, wooden, crowned by a single onion dome, they are typical of the churches that once dotted the Russian countryside. What strikes me most about Khokhlovka, however, is the setting. Here is the Kama as Diaghilev knew it, sparkling, majestic, unpolluted. As far as the eye can see are timberlands of birch and pine, thick forests where people come in the fall to gather mushrooms and where I imagine the Dashas and Mashas of Russian fairy tales adventuring among the bears. The quiet and the boundless space are overwhelming. Only a will as titanic as Diaghilev's could survive the encounter with this nature undiminished.

Time and again, the Gallery curators who were my guides lamented their isolation within the larger Perm community. When it comes to dance, however, the city is far from a wasteland. Now the best of the country's regional troupes, the Perm Ballet began as a small ensemble in the 1920s. Until World War II, influence flowed from Moscow; then, with the arrival of the Kirov (now St. Petersburg) Ballet, which spent the war years in Perm, the technical and stylistic baseline was oriented to Leningrad. Kirov versions entered the repertory, while

Kirov teachers revamped the company's feeder school, training the teachers who have made the Perm Choreographic Academy (to give the school its full name) justly famous.

Today, Ninel Pidemskaia runs the school, and she kindly allows us to visit some classes. We begin with Ludmila Pavlovna Sakharova's, an advanced one for girls. Sakharova (who has taught at Oleg Vinogradoff's Universal Ballet Academy in Washington) is the school's most celebrated pedagogue, and in her newest crop of seventeen-year-olds you see the line, plastique, and coordinated use of the upper body that distinguishes the best Russian dancing. In Yelena Vladimorovna Bystritskaia's fourth-year class, I see how that coordination is achieved. She's working on an adagio, and after a few bars she stops the pianist. What's wrong with you today? she asks a blond girl in the tone of an offended lioness. No eyes, no head; you look terrible. The scene is repeated not once, but six times, with Yelena Vladimirovna pleading, threatening, cajoling, until the details of the preparation are correct.

Although he never abjured the technique of ballet, Diaghilev made his reputation as a promoter of choreographic experiment. How fitting, then, that the best of the handful of innovators on today's Russian dance scene should live and work in Perm. I meet Evgenii Panfilov in the tiny room of a local palace of culture that serves as headquarters of his Experimental Modern Dance Theater. We are not a ballet company, he announces straight off, and we're not subsidized by the state; the Perm Electrotechnical Plant, which sponsors us, gives us the studio down the hall where we rehearse and this room where we do everything else. Panfilov never went to ballet school. Deciding at nearly twenty to be a choreographer, he enrolled in the dance department at GITIS, a Moscow institute that specializes in training actors and directors. Returning to Perm before he graduated, he began to choreograph.

In the studio, he leads the company's dozen dancers through a typical warm-up. He has told me he doesn't have a "system," but all the exercises he gives work the torso, while encouraging freedom in the arms and upper bodies. I am impressed by the commitment of the dancers and by their diversity; one woman is black. After the warm-up, we repair to the auditorium for a run-through of Panfilov's most recent work, *The Armchair*. It's a dark piece, a succession of fantasies and deadly acts dominated by the image of a general in tsarist-style epaulets. Some of Panfilov's devices recall Pina Bausch, whose work, he says, he has never seen. But what distinguishes *The Armchair* from most examples of German dance-theater is the choreographer's commitment to dance; with Panfilov, movement is far more than the glue of a mixed-media collage. He does not eschew ballet, although he uses its steps selectively, assimilating them into an open-ended, idiosyncratic idiom that incorporates gesture, pedestrian movement, ritual, acrobatics, and occasionally speech.

I leave Perm on Tuesday afternoon. The morning is devoted to leave-taking, a last walk through the old streets, good-byes to the women of the Gallery who have become friends. In the hotel, waiting for the taxi, Nadezhda Vladimirovna sits me down. It's our custom, she says, when people leave, to keep a moment of silence. So, in the quiet, I sit, thinking of the city Diaghilev left and the benighted one he has come home to, and wondering, as I have so often these past days, at the spell of memory and its mysterious hold on the imagination.

THE DIARIES OF MARIUS PETIPA

Although he ranks among the greatest choreographers of all time, we in the West know surprisingly little about Marius Petipa. Of his ballets only a handful continue to be performed, even in doctored versions: *La Bayadère, The Sleeping Beauty, Swan Lake* (which he choreographed with Lev Ivanov), *Don Quixote,* and *Giselle* (which he exhumed long after it had vanished from the Paris stage). If to these full-length works are added the set pieces "Jardin Animé" of *Le Corsaire,* the "Grand Pas Classique" of *Raymonda,* and the "Grand Pas" of *Paquita,* the list of his extant dances is well-nigh complete. Yet Petipa's career as a choreographer spanned more than sixty years and witnessed the creation of close to one hundred ballets, dozens of dances in operas, and countless variations and pas de deux. For a choreographer whose fantasies in movement and visions of celestial harmony have decisively shaped our understanding of the "classical" in ballet, the survival of so small a fraction of his output is obviously a matter of regret. Of perhaps greater moment, in that it depends only partly on the survival of actual dances, is the paucity of literature addressing in any serious way the nature, scope, and background of his vast accomplishment.

By contrast, in Russia, where Petipa arrived from his native France in 1847, worked for more than a half century, and died in 1910, his art has given rise to an important body of scholarship. The foundation was laid in the decades before the 1917 Revolution, with the histories of Aleksandr Pleshcheev (*Nash balet* [Our Ballet]),[1] Konstantin Skal'kovskii (*V teatral'nom mire* [In the World of the Theater]),[2] and Sergei Khudekov (*Istoriia tantsev* [A History of Dances])[3] and with the appearance of a generation of critics, including André Levinson and Akim Volynsky, who not only opened the study of dance to aesthetic and theoretical issues but did so with intellectual acumen and sophistication.

Interest in Petipa did not abate with the Revolution. If anything, his legacy lay at the heart of the debate over the future of ballet, both its survival as an art form and its social identity, now that the autocracy that had supported it was gone. The historian Yury Slonimsky discovered ballet at the side of the young George Balanchine in the heady aftermath of the Revolution. By 1937, at the height of the Stalinist era, when Slonimsky published *Mastera baleta* (Ballet Masters),[4] making Petipa acceptable was no easy task. With socialist realism now

This essay was published as an introduction to *The Diaries of Marius Petipa,* a volume in the series *Studies in Dance History,* 3, no. 1 (Spring 1992).

official dogma and formalism a crime, Slonimsky argued that Petipa's monumental spectacles, with their multitude of mass dances, endless displays of virtuosity, and—beginning with *The Sleeping Beauty*—virtually meaningless plots, answered the expectations of a blasé public and the demands of the Imperial Court that employed him. Only then, having established Petipa's subordination (so to speak) to both audience and autocracy, does Slonimsky allow himself to speak of the choreographer's "great genius": his way of distributing dance material to increase the intensity of his plotless divertissements, his extraordinary command of the dance lexicon, the clarity of his plastic and emotional ideas, the exceptional simplicity in the choreographic design of his most complex dance combinations.[5] (By 1956, when Slonimsky published his study of Tchaikovsky's ballets,[6] the need for such political somersaults had considerably diminished.)

Several years Slonimsky's junior and fundamentally apolitical, Vera Krasovskaya relies on fact and chronology to anchor her two major works about the Petipa period, *Russkii baletnyi teatr vtoroi poloviny deviatnadtsatogo veka* (Russian Ballet Theater of the Second Half of the Nineteenth Century), and *Russkii baletnyi teatr nachala XX veka* (Russian Ballet Theater at the Beginning of the Twentieth Century).[7] At the same time, she invests Petipa's art with a peculiarly Soviet idealism; in Petipa's theater, she writes, "[the] world, raised above the everyday, could have its own dramatic collisions, its emotional experiences . . . enlarged and made more significant."[8]

Along with reinterpreting Petipa, Soviet scholars have also compiled important volumes of source materials. One such volume, edited by Mikhail Borisoglebskii,[9] dates from the late 1930s and is a treasure-trove of information, including visual material, about the history of the St. Petersburg ballet, ruled by Petipa for nearly a half century. Another, edited by Anna Nekhendzi and published in 1971, is *Marius Petipa: materialy, vospominaniia, stat'i* (Marius Petipa: Documents, Reminiscences, Essays).[10] This collection, the inspiration for the present infinitely more modest undertaking, includes the first translation, in any language, of portions of Petipa's diaries, a new edition of his memoirs, and several of his letters and interviews. Along with these primary sources, it contains essays and reminiscences by Fedor Lopukhov, Ekaterina Gel'tser, Nicolas Legat, Petr Gusev, Konstantin Sergeev, George Balanchine, Bronislava Nijinska, and Frederick Ashton—heirs of the Petipa legacy both in Russia and abroad—and a full list of Petipa's productions in Russia. This volume, which was translated into German and published in the former German Democratic Republic in 1975,[11] is a basic source for Petipa scholars.

Outside Russia, where the view of Petipa has been partly shaped by émigré memoirs of his last generation of dancers,[12] this Russian and Soviet literature is little known. There are notable exceptions: Slonimsky's chapter on Petipa from *Mastera baleta*, published in *Dance Index* in 1947, and Krasovskaya's essay on *The Sleeping Beauty*, published in *Dance Perspectives* in 1972. Although Petipa's own memoirs, translated by Helen Whittaker and edited by Lillian Moore, were not published until 1958,[13] already in the late 1930s, in his *Complete Book of Ballets,* Cyril W. Beaumont had included the libretti and in some cases also the original cast lists of eighteen of Petipa's ballets, most in English translation for the first time.[14]

Given the paucity of sources readily available outside the Soviet Union and in languages other than Russian, the publication of musicologist Roland John Wiley's *Tchaikovsky's Ballets* in 1985 and *A Century of Russian Ballet: Documents and Accounts, 1810–1910*[15] five years later were events of singular importance. Fluent in Russian and drawing on manuscript sources in that language both in Russia and in the West, Wiley has done more to fill the yawning gaps in our knowledge of Petipa than anyone else. Still, a full-scale biography of Petipa remains to be written, and most of his choreographic sketches have yet to be published. The man who more than any other defined the Russian school of ballet is only beginning to emerge from the shadows.

Hence, the importance of the diaries that follow. Written in French toward the end of Petipa's life, they come from the manuscript collections of Moscow's Central State Archive of Literature and Art (TsGALI) and are published here with the kind permission of the director, Madame N. B. Volkova.[16] Although excerpts from these diaries—in Russian translation—appeared in the Nekhendzi volume, little notice was taken of them in the West until the publication of the German version of the volume in 1975. This prompted a long and laudatory article by the critic Horst Koegler in the September 1978 issue of *Dance Magazine*[17] that quoted generously from the published extracts of the diaries, now translated (by Koegler) from German into English. (Obviously, things would have been easier all around if Petipa's French original had appeared alongside the first, Russian translation.) If readers of English were getting scraps of the diaries at three removes, readers of Russian were getting perhaps a third of what Petipa actually wrote. Heavily—and silently—edited, the published diaries offer but a partial view of the ballet master who emerges from the full text of the original.

It was in Moscow in the spring of 1990 that I first came upon these diaries at TsGALI. At my side was Elizabeth Souritz, that wise and generous historian of Russia's dance past. Not only had she alerted me to their whereabouts, but she had literally taken me by the hand to see them, getting me past the red tape and initiating me into the mysteries of using a Soviet microfilm reader. The reading room at TsGALI is large and airy. There, with mounting excitement, I first scrolled through the entries in the little notebooks where Marius Ivanovich Petipa, as he is known in Russia, had recorded the day-to-day events of his life.

The diaries begin on New Year's Day 1903 (Old Style) and run until 31 December 1905,[18] with two major interruptions: presumably the notebooks for the summers of 1903 and 1905, which Petipa mentions buying, have been lost. The diaries pick up again in mid-March 1907, when Petipa left St. Petersburg for Gurzuf in the Crimea, where he died in 1910, and end three months later. Apart from the diaries, the collection includes drafts of letters, miscellaneous notes, lists of dates and works, and draft pages from his memoirs: the opening of chapter 3 ("A Duel in Spain"),[19] all of chapter 4 ("My Arrival in St. Petersburg"), and most of chapter 5 ("An Insult to Andeyanova"). Although undated, the reminiscences were probably written in 1904.

Although these are the only diaries of Petipa to have come to light, they are almost certainly not the only ones he wrote. On the contrary, the unvarying form of the entries, their absolute regularity (the one time he misses a day—13 May 1903—he makes sure to note, "Forgot to write"), and the fact that they pick up *in medias res* leave no doubt that diary-keeping had long been a part of his daily routine. Each entry opens with the date (in Old and New Style), the temperature (in degrees centigrade), some remark about the weather and the state of his health. Then, he moves on to professional matters: rehearsals (what was rehearsed, by whom, with whom), meetings, performances (what was performed, by whom, the box-office take). After this, he mentions the day's unusual events: the arrival of a letter from abroad, a shopping excursion, calls paid or received, parties, a quarrel with his wife. And without fail he ends each day with a list of what he had spent: for toys, doctors, stamps, cabs, newspapers, tea. The entries are brief and matter-of-fact—the scaffolding of a life that made art not with words but in the wordless medium of movement.

Although the notes and diagrams preserved in Moscow's Bakhrushin Museum (a few of which are reproduced in the Nekhendzi volume) indicate that Petipa worked out the groupings and floor plans of at least some of his dances on paper, the diaries do not record his thoughts at the time of such explorations or explain the choices he ultimately made. On the other hand, they contain important information about the dating and evolution of certain works (including the completion, scene by scene, of the choreography), the collaborative method used to create them (who talked to whom and when), the backstage politics and administrative conflicts that attended their production, and their audience and critical reception. At the same time, the diaries provide a record of what was actually danced at the Maryinsky's twice-weekly ballet nights, and because Petipa frequently noted the box-office receipts and how many times a particular ballet had been given, they also document the popularity of individual works. With more than 200 performances by the start of 1903, Petipa's *Daughter of Pharaoh* was clearly the front-runner, with his newer *Sleeping Beauty,* at the 100 mark, a close second. Interestingly, *Swan Lake* was performed only twenty-nine times in the eight years following its premiere.[20]

Although the diaries cover only a brief period in Petipa's long career, that period was a significant one, for it witnessed the completion of his last two ballets (*The Magic Mirror* and *The Romance of the Rosebud and the Butterfly*) and his forced retirement from the Imperial Theaters. For Petipa this was not an easy time. *The Magic Mirror,* a four-act retelling of "Snow White and the Seven Dwarfs" that came to the stage on 9 February 1903, was generally regarded as a failure, an opinion that Petipa himself shared, though not for the reasons given by most of the critics. (They blamed him; he blamed the designs, by Alexander Golovin, and the score, by Arsenii Koreshchenko.) The premiere, a benefit performance for the ballet master attended by Nicholas II, the Empress Alexandra, and, in Petipa's words, the "entire Imperial family,"[21] was a glamorous occasion, even by the standards of the Maryinsky, where galas and grand dukes were commonplace. As one witness recalled:

> All seats in the theatre were sold out for the new ballet, about which people [had] talked for almost two years, the testimonial performance for the famous Petipa. Tales about the forthcoming novel spectacle interested everybody. The Imperial box was filled by members of the Imperial family. At eight o'clock sharp the dowager empress Maria Feodorovna and the czar with the young empress arrived. The ministerial box was also filled with invited persons of high society.[22]

"I was much feted," Petipa wrote after the performance was over, referring to the gifts and honors he had received as the evening's benefit artist, marking his completion of fifty-five years of imperial service. The ballet itself had quite a different reception. At the start of Act II, according to one account, the house exploded in whistles and catcalls. The newspapers were no kinder than the first-night public. Apart from the *Peterburgskaia gazeta* (Petersburg Gazette), which emphasized the ceremonial aspects of the occasion, the press subjected *Mirror* to what Alexandre Benois described as "coarse and absurd attacks."[23] Petipa's own assessment was equally damning. "The ballet is a fiasco," he wrote in his diary.

Despite his private misgivings, Petipa did everything possible to keep the work before the public. But the rechoreographing that occupied a considerable part of his energies in the autumn following the premiere only exacerbated the ballet's intrinsic weaknesses. Among the most scathing critics of the new version was Serge Diaghilev, editor of the art journal *Mir iskusstva* (The World of Art) and a proselytizer for new trends in painting and theater. In a letter to the editor of the *Peterburgskaia gazeta,* prompted by the premiere of the refurbished *Mirror* in December 1903, he wrote:

> Blame for the ballet's failure does not rest with the decorations or even with the unsuccessful, heavy music. One must look much deeper for it; it lies in the very enterprise of producing this ballet—unnecessary, boring, long, complicated, and pretentious. Let not the people who devised this production think that in this case they stand above the public, "which did not understand and appreciate their enterprise." The music, story, plan of action and all else in this ballet were not in the least for "comprehension only in the future"—the whole thing is perfectly comprehensible now, and appreciated according to its merits, as an utterly inartistic, un-balletic, and chiefly, an infinitely boring spectacle.[24]

This was not the first time a ballet of Petipa's had failed. As Yury Slonimsky has shown, the 1870s witnessed a string of Petipa failures as audiences deserted ballet for the frivolities of the operetta stage.[25] But because of his advanced age (he turned eighty-five two weeks after the premiere) and his strained relations with the newly appointed director of the Imperial Theaters, Vladimir Telyakovsky, *Mirror*'s failure proved tremendously costly. Only days after the premiere, rumors began to circulate about Petipa's resignation. In hostile circles, a new candidate was being discussed, and in the *Stock Exchange Bulletin* he was even named.[26] Within a year, Petipa was effectively given the boot, although thanks to the intercession of Baron Fredericks, Minister of the Imperial Court (of which the Imperial Theaters was a dependency), he remained on the company roster and payroll, with a yearly salary of 9,000 rubles for life.

The failure of *The Magic Mirror* was a decisive round in the bitter feud that began with Telyakovsky's appointment in 1901 to the highest post within the Imperial Theaters. As Petipa wrote of the former guards officer in his memoirs:

> Almost at once, I personally found M. Teliakovsky to be my bitterest enemy. He stopped at nothing. I was very soon to learn the direct strategy of this Colonel-of-the-Arts, for in fighting against people who did not please him, and whom, for some reason, he wished to discard, he was by no means scrupulous in his choice of weapons. He is a follower of the "new" school. Unfortunately, under his regime, works in which virtue triumphs, and evil is chastised, are completely forgotten. Now, on the contrary, evil triumphs viciously.[27]

Unsurprisingly, Telyakovsky did not look altogether kindly on the aging Petipa. He accused him of suffering from loss of memory, of constantly quarreling with his chief régisseur, of being under the thumb of Evgeniia Sokolova, who conducted the "class of perfection" and did her best to promote her own students. Especially irksome was Petipa's close relationship with the balletomanes:

> Certain balletomanes, particularly the well-known critic, Nikolai Bezobrasov, "put their oars in" over the casting of roles. Petipa was very friendly with the balletomanes and with the elderly editor of *Peterburgskaia gazeta,* [Sergei] Khudekov. Some balletomanes, with his permission, not only visited the wings and dressing-rooms, and attended rehearsals, but they also attended the Theatre School rehearsals. Sometimes they even sat in the studio by the mirror, next to Petipa, and together they chose dancers for various roles.[28]

Petipa's close relationship with Bezobrazov and his friendship with the "always charming" Sokolova[29] (his expression for the former ballerina with whom he arranged for his daughter Vera to study) are amply borne out by these diaries. Khudekov, however, is another matter. For though the publisher of the *Peterburgskaia gazeta* had contributed the libretti to *La Bayadère* and other

Petipa ballets of the 1870s and 1880s, by the early 1900s the former collaborators appear to have fallen out, given the consistently unflattering remarks about Khudekov ("the most miserable of men, faithless and without honor!!")[30] and his newspaper that appear in the choreographer's diaries.

In reconstructing the power struggle between Petipa and Telyakovsky, whom he almost always referred to in his diaries as "the director," it is far from easy to sift the truth from the protagonists' often conflicting accounts. Apart from issues of management and personnel, profound artistic differences separated Telyakovsky and his chief ballet master. Although he was indeed a former guards officer, Telyakovsky was not unacquainted with the performing arts, having previously managed the Moscow office of the Imperial Theaters. During his tenure in Russia's "second capital," he had done much to upgrade the quality of ballet at the Bolshoi. Under his aegis, Alexander Gorsky (the candidate mentioned as Petipa's replacement) staged his first productions, while Alexander Golovin and Konstantin Korovin, innovative designers associated with Savva Mamontov's Private Opera, received their first State commissions. In 1902, over Petipa's protests and at the risk of incurring his undying enmity, Telyakovsky brought Gorsky and Korovin to Petersburg to restage their updated Bolshoi version of Petipa's *Don Quixote* (among other novelties, it boasted a Serpentine Dance à la Loie Fuller). Petipa never forgave the enterprising director. "What . . . did M. Teliakovsky want?" he asked in his memoirs. "Plainly, what he wanted was for me to give up my place in Petersburg to this creature of his. He wanted M. Gorsky and his kind to stand at the head of the St. Petersburg ballet. What arrogance!"[31]

The following year, Sergei and Nicolas Legat, among the most talented of the company's excellent young generation of men, staged their first ballet, *The Fairy Doll,* with designs by another rising talent, Léon Bakst, who would achieve lasting fame with Diaghilev's Ballets Russes. None of these efforts by Telyakovsky to foster new talent earned much applause from Petipa. By all accounts (not least, the number of performances it received), *The Fairy Doll* was a success, but he called it a "fiasco" (7 February 1903) and wrote, after the premiere, that it was neither liked nor applauded (16 February 1903). Of Golovin's and Korovin's contribution, he was of one mind: their work was "appalling," "tasteless," and in the case of the opera *Ruslan and Ludmilla,* which they jointly designed, a "decadence."[32] A loaded word, this, in Russia in 1904. "Decadence is now the name for all that rises above triviality and lack of taste," wrote Alexandre Benois in his review of *The Magic Mirror,* alluding to the attacks that had rained on the painters of the World of Art and the poets associated with symbolism. The balletomanes took Petipa's side. At the premiere, Telyakovsky recalled:

loud concerted laughter broke out from the balletomanes in the parterre, catcalls and whistling, which momentarily grew into a veritable roar with exclamations of individual balletomanes: "Enough! What ugliness! It's time for this decadence to end!" One of the eldest balletomanes, General V[intul]ov, completely bald, cried out: "Get rid of Gurlya (my wife's name) and Telyakovsky! They will destroy the theatre with their novelties!"[33]

At eighty-five, Petipa had lost touch with his time.

Although it was easy enough to retire Petipa, removing him from the theater where he was still legally employed presented a problem for those who wanted him out. Beginning in the autumn months of 1903, Telyakovsky began maneuvering to that end, making life increasingly unpleasant for Petipa. Nikolai Aistov, the chief régisseur with whom Telyakovsky says the choreographer was always quarreling, was abruptly fired, only a few days after confessing to Petipa that he wanted to resign because "the bosses [were] on his back."[34] They must have been riding him hard, as they had already given his job to Nicholas Sergeyev ("that malicious régisseur Sergeyev," as Petipa would later call him),[35] best known in the West for his revivals of *The Sleeping Beauty, Swan Lake,* and *Giselle*—all this without consulting or even notifying Petipa, who heard the news from the now jobless Aistov.

Another source of annoyance was the "committee," as Petipa simply referred to it, set up by Telyakovsky and consisting of the choreographer and various administrators. Presumably aimed at curbing Petipa's still considerable authority in matters of repertory and casting, the committee drew Petipa's wrath even before it met. When it did assemble, he sat through two meetings, then resigned in high dudgeon. Around the same time, he announced that he would "no longer rehearse old ballets,"[36] thus inadvertently relinquishing a measure of the power he had otherwise guarded so jealously. Little did he imagine that an action intended to give himself time to work on new ballets would be used to keep him from rehearsing not-so-old favorites like *The Sleeping Beauty.*

What finally drove him from the theater was the fate of his last ballet, *The Romance of the Rosebud and the Butterfly.* In preparation since at least the spring of 1903,[37] *Rosebud* was scheduled to receive its first performance at the Hermitage Theater in mid-January 1904. With a libretto by Prince Ivan Vsevolojsky, director of the Imperial Theaters from 1881 to 1899, the ballet harked back to the "never-to-be-forgotten" years[38] of *The Sleeping Beauty, Swan Lake,* and *Raymonda.* For Vsevolojsky himself, Petipa had nothing but the highest regard. As he wrote in his memoirs:

> During the long years of Vsevolojsky's management, all the artists, without exception, adored their noble, kind, cultured director. This kindest of men was a real courtier, in the best sense of the word. I had the honour to work with him frequently, and in addition to everything else he possessed great talent for making sketches that were full of taste and intelligence, for operas and ballets. With what regret, with what pangs of the heart do I recall those happy days.[39]

Rosebud went into rehearsal in early December. By then, the dancers had been chosen, and little figurines, each representing a character from the ballet and labeled with the name of the dancer performing the role, had been handed over to Baron Kusov's production department. About one hundred people were in the cast, but with illness making the rounds, absences were high. Still, Petipa made good progress. By January 3, with most of the choreography apparently finished, Petipa pronounced the ballet "a little masterpiece." Then, strange things began to happen. The premiere was put off—from January 16 to 23.[40] Finally, with only two weeks remaining before the first performance, Petipa learned that the ballet had been canceled. No reason was given; Vsevolojsky was not even informed. "My work," wrote Petipa, "is wasted."[41]

The affair had the effect that Telyakovsky doubtless intended. In the ensuing months, Petipa absented himself from the studio with ever-increasing frequency. To the public humiliation of *Rosebud* were added small indignities. The weekly rehearsal schedule would fail to arrive; the promise of a carriage to fetch him would be forgotten; his name would be left off program credits; his request for tickets to a student performance would be ignored. And when rehearsals of *The Sleeping Beauty* got underway that winter, no one bothered to tell him. (Not that he long remained in ignorance of what was afoot; with his daughter Vera in the corps de ballet, news traveled fast.)

Through all this, Petipa retained both the desire and strength to choreograph. "I compose, therefore I am," he might have said in these last years of his life, as if each new dance were a talisman warding off the inevitable, a triumph scored against death itself. But even without the incentive of age or politics, it is hard to imagine him resisting the temptation of touching up a dance or redoing a variation. Choreography was in his blood, and dancers fed his imagination. Even after the scathing reviews that greeted his second version of *The Magic Mirror,* he kept on tinkering with the ballet, hoping against all odds to salvage at least some part of the unlucky work, which was given in truncated form on a mixed bill in 1904—with no greater success than its predecessors.[42]

In March of that year, despite painful swelling in his feet, he dragged himself to a rehearsal of *The Little Humpbacked Horse* with Julie Sedova, a favorite dancer who had asked him to come watch her.[43] The next day, swollen feet and all, he was back in the studio rehearsing Anna Pavlova in *Paquita* and composing, to new music by Riccardo Drigo, a variation for her forthcoming debut in the title role.[44] (A month later, with her debut only two days off, he composed still more variations.)[45] In April, he took the visiting Italian ballerina, Antoinetta Ferrero, through her role in *Coppélia,* even demonstrating parts of it, a feat that prompted him to write, "I am amazing,"[46] which at eighty-six he certainly was. Another, equally amazing feat lay ahead. As Petipa tells it: "In the evening, at the school, I composed for Mlle. Ferrero—in the ballet *La Fille Mal Gardée*—2 variations and 3 entrances in the coda—in one hour."[47]

He took special pains with his daughter Vera, who graduated from the Imperial Ballet School in 1903, going so far as to revive a pas from his 1875 ballet *The Bandits* for her to dance in the annual pupils' display. Even Mathilde Kchessinska, whom he thoroughly despised, enjoyed his bounty; her variation in the final pas de deux of *The Magic Mirror,* he wrote, was "very successful."[48] Fittingly, it was for Olga Preobrajenska, the most beloved of his ballerinas and a close personal friend, that in January 1905 he choreographed what he noted in the diary was his "last variation." It was for *The Traveling Dancer,* a one-act "episode" that he had first produced in 1865 and now, at her request, agreed to revive for her benefit performance.[49] With this last dance for "Preo," Petipa's long career as a choreographer came to an end.

This penchant for tinkering, amply documented in the pages that follow, raises a troubling question. What *was* a Petipa ballet if the text was always changing? To be sure, all dances change from performance to performance and from cast to cast, even when the steps remain the same. Often, however, these too will change, and within limits we accept those changes so long as the editing is not perceived to alter the spirit and general form of the choreography. (Typical of such changes are the "adjustments" made by a choreographer to accommodate the strengths and weaknesses of a dancer new to a role.) More rarely, a ballet may be rethought by its choreographer, thus giving rise to one or more alternate versions that may or may not be accepted as authoritative. When Balanchine, for example, eliminated the prologue from his 1979 recension of *Apollo,* although few denied his right to perform such radical surgery, most critics rejected the new version as a whim. By contrast, of the many variants of *Chopiniana/Les Sylphides* that Fokine produced over the decades, all are accepted as definitive. Indeed, in the twentieth century, the notion of a standard choreography slowly but surely has gained currency; however much the production of a ballet may change, its steps are expected to remain more or less the same. We have become sticklers for text.

In Petipa's time, the very opposite was true. Even if the results were criticized, no one questioned the right of a choreographer to redo or add to his own or anybody else's work. Thus, not only did Petipa routinely update choreography he deemed old-fashioned—thanks to his revisions, *Giselle, Esmeralda,* and *Le Corsaire,* forgotten elsewhere, gained a new lease on life—but he had no qualms about interpolating whole scenes, usually to new music, into preexisting ballets, for example, the "Jardin Animé" scene in *Le Corsaire* and the Grand Pas of *Paquita.* Obviously, for Petipa, the most fluid or unstable (although this was not a term he would have understood) element of a ballet was its choreography. Just as obviously, this openness of form was not perceived by him as being in any way problematic, except when management decided to replace his choreography with someone else's. In fact, Petipa was proud of his interpolations and protested vigorously if someone else, even the original choreographer, received credit for them. In a letter to Aleksei Suvorin, publisher of the St. Petersburg newspaper *Novoe vremia* (New Times), he insisted on his authorship of key dances in the last act of *Paquita,* first choreographed by Joseph Mazilier in 1846:

> I read in an unsigned article in your newspaper that the grand pas in the last act of *Paquita* is the composition of Mons. [Joseph] Mazilier.
>
> In 1847, in St. Petersburg, I staged and made my debut in the ballet *Paquita.* In the last act there was only a quadrille, a gavotte, and a pas de deux.
>
> When I restaged this ballet under the management of His Excellency Mons. I[van] Vsevolojsky, I composed the mazurka for the pupils of the school and a new grand pas. I left the quadrille and the gavotte.
>
> I have more than 50 witnesses.[50]

The choreographer's diaries document several instances of this typical Petipa practice. In April 1903, when *King Candaules* was revived with Julie Sedova in the starring role of Nisia, Petipa used the occasion to make numerous changes in the choreography. None of them was required by the production, which had been used since the ballet's premiere in 1868, but Petipa clearly felt the need to refurbish the dances, above all in the classical pas d'action of the second act. Thus, on March 1, he noted, "I recomposed the adagio of the Pas de Venus for Sedova and [Sergei] Legat"; on March 10, "I composed 3 variations for the 3 graces"; on March 22, "I composed the dance for the 4 nymphs, 4 satyrs, and Amour in the Venus pas"; finally, on March 30, only days before the premiere, he wrote, "I recomposed the bathing scene." Together, the replacements added up to a substantial amount of new choreography. But it was also substantive choreography that Petipa was replacing. The Pas de Venus, for instance, was the sensation of the original production; in it Henriette d'Or, for whom the ballet was created, executed five pirouettes on pointe, a tour de force that ensured the ballet's popularity.

Petipa's telegraphic entries do not tell us how the choreography was altered, only that it was. But in a set piece as celebrated as the Rose Adagio is today, no change is so small that it does not in some measure alter the character of the dance and the choreographic identity of the ballet. To Petipa and his contemporaries, textual fidelity was simply not an issue; revival was understood to be an act of revision, with old versions surviving like palimpsests in the new choreography (as did Perrot's dances for Giselle in Petipa's remake of the Romantic-era classic). Nor, obviously, was the identity of a ballet primarily or even largely derived from its choreography. Rather, what made *Paquita, Giselle, King Candaules,* and *La Fille Mal Gardée* what they were was the one thing that remained constant from version to version—the libretto. The score was a close second, although the tradition of specialist composers, which survived in Russia well into the 1890s, militated against the idea of musical integrity that became commonplace with Diaghilev. Indeed, few were the scores apart from those by Tchaikovsky and Alexander Glazunov that were not in some way altered or added to, usually without the composer's consent. Thus, if *The Sleeping Beauty* were performed one evening—as it was, "for the first time," as Petipa noted on 7 November 1904—without the Blue Bird pas de deux, the surgery was no more radical than anything Petipa had himself performed on a score of ballets. With no artistic grounds on which to lodge a complaint (and no copyright protection), all he could do was rail against Telyakovsky's "bad management."

Because the diaries date from the very end of Petipa's life, they make clear his formative influence on dancers of the early Diaghilev period. His great favorite, after Preobrajenska, was Pavlova. He rehearsed her, composed for her, attended her performances religiously, and in November 1904, long after he had stopped going regularly to the theater, took her through the mad scene in *Giselle*. Another favorite was Julie Sedova, a strong technician with a vivacious personality who, with her husband, was a frequent visitor to the Petipa home. Along with likes, the diaries record his dislikes, which were legion. Kchessinska, his prima ballerina assoluta, was "rotten," "spiteful," a "nasty swine" who refused to share her roles with deserving rivals like Preobrajenska.[51] Soloists and even pupils fared no better. "Mlle. Vaganova," referring to the great pedagogue of the Soviet period, was "dreadful" in *The Pearl;* Lubov Egorova was "very bad" as Pierrette in *Harlequinade;* in the Grand Pas of *Paquita,* Ol'ga Chumakova, Elena Makarova, and Ekaterina Ofitserova "were . . . a great fiasco"; the advanced girls in Klavdiia Kulichevskaia's class at the Imperial Ballet School were "all . . . bad."[52]

Toward Pavel Gerdt, the great premier danseur and hero of more than a score of his ballets, Petipa harbored feelings that were surprisingly ungenerous. At one point, he calls him "deceitful"; at another, he accuses him of "stealing my compositions" and says that he has sent him a letter to that effect.[53] What prompted this particular outburst was the revival early in 1905 of *The Blue Dahlia,* a two-act ballet choreographed by Petipa in 1860. Gerdt was in charge of the rehearsals and, whatever he was doing, Petipa hated it. Another outburst followed a few days later: "At 1, went to the Maryinsky to see the rehearsal of *The Blue Dahlia,* dreadfully mounted by that swine Gerdt. I wrote a letter to the Director to have my name removed from the program."[54]

Whether it was the idea of Gerdt tampering with his choreography or the choreography itself that upset him more is unknown. But, as the diaries make clear, this was not the first time since Petipa had withdrawn from active service that dances of his were tossed out and replaced by the work of former subordinates. Only three months before, for the Golovin/Korovin production of Glinka's *Ruslan and Ludmilla,* Petipa's lezginka, in service since 1886, was summarily replaced by a new dance choreographed by régisseur Aleksandr Shiriaev. According to Petipa, the result was "awful . . . something Spanish and something of the tarantella, but nothing of the lezginka."[55] (The *Russkaia muzykal'-naia gazeta* [Russian Musical Gazette], one of the few publications to mention the new dance, thought it "[had] acquired a more balletic character.")[56] How

Petipa gloated the day after the *répétition générale,* when Telyakovsky asked him "to correct the lezginka composed by Mons. Shiriaev"[57]—an invitation Petipa understandably declined.

In his memoirs, Petipa devotes two full pages to this incident, a measure of the rage that "induced [him]" to write his own account of the past,[58] an account that he hoped would vindicate him in the eyes of the public and expose the full evil of Telyakovsky. Thanks to the diaries, we can now date, with some precision, the genesis of these memoirs and resolve, with some authority, various claims about the method of their composition. In her introduction to the English-language version, Lillian Moore states her belief that they were dictated:

> Probably he dictated them (in French, doubtless, for after nearly sixty years in St. Petersburg he still had not learned to express himself fluently in Russian), for his tone, even in the Russian in which they were published, seems casual and conversational, and he often skips rather abruptly from one subject and one period to another, as one might do in talking. In the last pages, where he speaks of the new Director of the Imperial Theatres, Teliakovsky, who has taken away all his power over his beloved ballet company, one can almost hear the echoes of his furious trembling voice.[59]

Moore, it should be pointed out, never saw the original French. Nor, for that matter, did Helen Whittaker, who prepared the English version from the Russian translation, first published in 1906. Neither, moreover, was privy to the handwritten chapters included with these diaries. (Like many Soviet archives, TsGALI was until recently off-limits to foreigners.) Where Moore could only speculate, we (thanks to glasnost) can state with certainty: Petipa wrote, in his own hand, at least three of the early chapters of his memoirs. Moreover, it seems likely that what prompted him to set to work was the *Rosebud* debacle, not the "amiable testimony" of Telyakovsky to which he alludes in his memoirs. According to Petipa, Telyakovsky had told a newspaper reporter that he, Petipa, was "too old"; "today he forgets what he said yesterday, and tomorrow he won't remember what was said today." So, explains Petipa, with something less than total accuracy, "I thought of writing my memoirs; and without any notes, without any diary, I have remembered and recalled all the outstanding events of my life, beginning with eight years of age."[60]

As it turns out, the first mention of the memoirs occurs exactly eight days after *Rosebud* was to have received its premiere at the Hermitage. "I stayed home alone to write my memoirs. Week of madness."[61] In the ensuing months, if the evidence of the diaries is to be trusted, he laid them aside. Then, he set to work again. "Yesterday," he announced on September 21, "I began to write my memoirs. They positively must appear."[62] Throughout the autumn, Petipa continued to write. Unfortunately, the entries that mention the memoirs are all maddeningly telegraphic ("I worked on my memoirs").[63] All, that is, except the last one:

"I do not have the energy to take up anything or finish my memoirs. What a rotten end."[64]

During the next fourteen months, as Petipa grew increasingly ill, the memoirs apparently languished. Finally, at Christmas 1905, he returned to them, this time, however, with one Mlle. Louise, a French teacher who gave occasional lessons to his daughter Vera and now arranged to work with him at home on a regular basis.[65] Because the diaries break off at the end of the year, it is impossible to know how long and under what conditions the two collaborated and how much of the book remained for them to complete. My own guess is that the first nine chapters were written by Petipa, and that the last four, with their messy chronology, abrupt shifts in subject, and interpolated testimonials, were dictated to Mlle. Louise and pieced together with her less than skillful help.

With his retirement from active service and declining health, Petipa's life grew steadily more circumscribed. While he continued to receive the weekly rehearsal schedule, he seldom went to the studio and only rarely to performances, although with three daughters in the company and a wife who was a subscriber,[66] it was hard not to keep up with ballet gossip and politics. Still, the immediacy of the earlier entries is missing, and the life that Petipa now recorded was increasingly the inner one of an invalid. Only the national news seems to have broken through his isolation. When the Russo-Japanese War broke out in January 1904, he followed the bulletins avidly. "Wire," he wrote on February 12. "Victory at Port Arthur. The Japanese attacked during the night. They lost ships, torpedoes, etc., many drowned. A naval victory. Bravo!"[67] In the months to come, there were few occasions for Russians to rejoice. In mid-March came the "unhappy news" that "Admiral Makarov was hit by a torpedo and killed"; the navy was lost, and there were "masses of dead."[68] In December, Petipa learned that Port Arthur had been taken, a "calamity" that was followed two months later by the loss of the Manchurian city of Mukden.[69] In this first war to pit Japan against a major Western power, Russia would suffer a humiliating defeat.

The war in the Far East had serious repercussions at home, contributing to the unrest that culminated in the 1905 Revolution. Like most Russians, Petipa was alternately bewildered and appalled by much of what transpired—from the massacre of "Bloody Sunday," when troops gunned down peacefully demonstrating workers who had come to the Winter Palace with a petition begging the tsar to end the war, to the wave of strikes and popular violence that in the wake of "Bloody Sunday" cut off power, closed down newspapers, darkened theaters, shattered street lamps and shop windows, and led to the death of Grand Duke Sergei Alexandrovich by an assassin's bomb. "The city is in a state of siege," wrote Petipa after a night of rioting on the Nevsky Prospekt.[70] He missed his newspapers and lost patience when the lights went out. And he could not understand why factory workers did *not* want to work, when he had struggled so long not to retire. Petipa's mixed emotions toward these tumultuous events are clearly reflected in his diaries. On the night of "Bloody Sunday," which coincided with the benefit performance for Preobrajenska that included *The Traveling Dancer,* he wrote:

> No newspapers. The workers do not want to work. It's a very bad time for Russia. May God protect the Emperor! Huge brawl at the Alexandrinsky Theater. Half the performance given; money returned. Strike—people dead in the street. People who had paid for their seats did not come to the ballet . . . Preobrajenska—gifts, flowers, etc., etc. It's too much—here they're dancing and in the streets they're killing.[71]

The "huge brawl at the Alexandrinsky Theater," when a member of the audience shouted at the celebrated actor Konstantin Varlamov, "How can you act at such a time, when blood is spilling in the streets?" thereby prompting management to suspend the performance,[72] was not the only occasion when events in the streets had repercussions on life within the Imperial Theaters. Anonymous letters threatening Kchessinska, whose liaisons with grand dukes were well known, arrived at the Maryinsky Theater and induced such fear in the ballerina that she voluntarily turned a performance of *Swan Lake* over to Preobrajenska.[73]

Between March and October, the city was quiet. Then another wave of strikes hit, and with them the cry for autonomy that had rallied disaffected professionals throughout the country reached the studios of the Imperial Ballet. In an unprecedented move, the dancers went on strike. Their demands included bread-and-butter issues like higher salaries and a five-day work week. But the key issues were artistic—the right to choose their own régisseurs and the return to active duty of Petipa, his assistant Aleksandr Shiriaev, and teacher Alfred Bekefi, another dismissed Petipa loyalist.[74]

Needless to say, Petipa monitored these events closely, viewing them less as an assertion of autonomy on the part of the dancers than as a belated vindication of himself, although the two were clearly intertwined. "Bravo! I am avenged. The entire troupe met this morning to speak on my behalf against the Director," he exulted on October 15,[75] when 163 members of the ballet troupe, defying an order to leave, held an all-day meeting in the rehearsal room. Among the strikers were his daughters Marie, Nadia, and Vera, as well as dancers with close personal ties to him, including Preobrajenska and Pavlova. Pavlova, in fact, was on the strike committee, as were Fokine and Petr Mikhailov, who, together, called on Petipa, presumably to discuss strategy.[76] Nadia, in all likelihood, was also a member, as she not only spoke at one of the meetings (as her father notes) but accompanied Fokine to see Vsevolojsky about what could only have been a strike matter.[77] Although Petipa frequently saw Vsevolojsky at the former director's home, there is no indication that the Petipa children ever accompanied their father on such visits.

Not content to remain on the sidelines, Petipa wrote directly to the dancers, presumably to stiffen their resolve and warn them about Telyakovsky's spies. He knew whereof he spoke. By mid-October, rumors were flying, as management sought to intimidate the dancers and sow dissent within the previously united company. The dénouement was not long in coming. Under pressure, Sergei Legat removed his signature from the troupe's petition; the next morning, he committed suicide, slitting his throat with a razor.[78] His suicide, like the strike in general, touched Petipa personally. Not only had Legat been one of his finest dancers, he was also his daughter Marie's common-law husband. In recording the tragic episode, Petipa gave the facts as he must have heard them from his daughter: "Sergei Legat went mad, biting Marie; then, he killed himself."[79]

The incident took management aback. The next day the troupe was called together, a meeting attended by Telyakovsky and two of his handpicked underlings. "They are all afraid," gloated Petipa. "We have triumphed."[80] Alas, Petipa does not explain how the striking dancers had triumphed. In all likelihood, he succumbed to the passion of the moment, as other evidence suggests that in the aftermath of the strike they enjoyed anything but the spoils of victory. As Bronislava Nijinska recalled, "Many of the . . . artists involved were eventually dismissed without cause, or were not given the chance to dance good roles, or simply were not duly promoted."[81] For Petipa, this truth must have been a bitter pill to swallow. In the weeks following Legat's suicide, he retreated back into his private world.

In addition to documenting his life as a working professional, the diaries introduce us to Petipa, the family man. In his memoirs, he devotes only a few sentences to his second wife, the dancer Liubov' ("Louba") Leonidovna Savitskaia, and the great contentment that followed their marriage in 1876. His previous marriage, to the ballerina Mariia Sergeevna Surovshchikova, the muse of his first decades in Russia, had ended in a separation. He writes:

> I had aided greatly in the success of my first wife. I had done everything I could to help her attain the highest position on the ballet stage, but in our domestic life we were unable to live long in peace and harmony. Our differences in character, and perhaps the false self-esteem of both of us, soon made a compatible life impossible. My first wife died in Pyatigorsk in 1875, and in the following year I first learned what is meant by domestic happiness, and a pleasant family hearth. Having married Lubov Leonidovna, the daughter of the artist Leonidov, I learned the value of a kind and loving wife, and if I am lively and healthy today, in spite of my advanced age, I dare say that I owe it entirely to the love and care of my wife, who to this day gives me affection and attention and complete happiness.[82]

Liubov' was thirty-six years his junior, and even before they had exchanged vows, she had given birth to the first of their six children. With one surviving daughter from his first marriage and one surviving son from a previous liaison, Petipa stood at the head of a large and ever-growing family that by 1903 numbered more than a half-dozen grandchildren.[83] This domestic side of his life is wonderfully documented in his diaries. At holidays and name-day parties, we see him surrounded by a flock of relatives—children, grandchildren, in-laws. We see him buying presents—scent for his wife, a white scarf for Vera; toys, sweets, and Easter eggs for the little ones. We feel his pride when his son Marius passes exams and share his delight at the arrival of a new grandchild.

He was passionately devoted to advancing his daughter Vera's career as a dancer. On summer holiday in the Crimea, he gave her daily lessons and, when they returned to St. Petersburg, additional lessons in mime. For her first important role, the White Cat in *The Sleeping Beauty*, he sent her to work with Preobrajenska (who had created the part) and, swallowing his pride, asked Telyakovsky for permission for Vera to study with her.[84] Finally, when it seemed that his daughter's career was stagnating "as vengeance against me," Petipa implored Telyakovsky's superior, Baron Fredericks, to "speak in her favor."[85]

The dead were as close to Petipa as the living, and not a birthday would pass that did not find him bringing flowers to the graves of his beloved daughter Eugénie, who had died while still a teenager, his brother Jean, and his father Jean Antoine Petipa, both of whom had followed him to Russia and died there. Like all happy families, the Petipas had their share of domestic squabbles and problems, such as when daughter Nadia's marriage was faltering, and Louba, trying to patch things up, brought two of the five grandchildren to live with her and Petipa. The couple eventually made up.[86]

The Petipa of these diaries is old, very old. Born in 1818, he is eighty-four when they begin and eighty-nine when they end. Like most old people, he worried about his health and thought a great deal about his ailments, monitoring the aches and pains and colds meticulously noted in his diary. But as the entries make clear, Petipa's health really was failing. The victim of a skin disease that appears to have been a virulent form of eczema, he first mentioned the itching that was its chief symptom within days of the failure of *The Magic Mirror*,[87] suggesting that the illness may well have had a psychosomatic component. Certainly, the itches do seem to worsen with every slight, real or perceived, and every run-in with his various "enemies."

Whatever the cause, whatever the disease, one thing is clear: Petipa was often in pain. By 1904, he was seldom free of it; he counted as good a day when it was not altogether unbearable. His illness was not only physically painful, but mentally as well: an affront to his self-pride, to his vanity (even in his mid-eighties, he was meticulous about his wardrobe and personal grooming), and the pleasure he took in his body. Overnight, it seemed, his skin had turned old, his vigor had gone; a turn in the Summer Garden would leave him exhausted; he would doze off in an armchair; sometimes, he would spend whole days in his study "bored to tears."[88] ("Tedium is one of the worst things in life," he asserted on one occasion.)[89] Rarely was his sleep undisturbed. His thoughts often turned to death. "Take me, God!!" he wrote—not for the first time—on 28 August 1905. Many were the occasions when he feared that he would not live out the month. More than once he even planned his funeral:

> My last express wish for my funeral. A very simple ceremony. Two horses to carry my body. The newspapers. No letter of invitation will be sent, a notice beforehand taking its place.[90]

His depression deepened with the death of his sister Victorine in January 1905. A former opera singer, she was six years his junior and, since 1898 when their brother Lucien had died, Petipa's sole surviving link to the family of his childhood. Although he had made his home in Russia for over sixty years, the fact of her existence meant that he did not wholly belong to his adopted country: he still had people in France. The two corresponded regularly, and seldom did a letter leave Petersburg without a gift of ten or so rubles in the envelope. Now, with the death of his "beloved sister," he had only his Russian family. In the months following her death, his thoughts often turned to the roving tribe of his childhood. "All the dear relatives who adored me are dead," he sighed in August.[91] "Mother dear, you were the only one who loved me!" he wrote a few months later.[92] At the same time, he had his goddaughter Jeanne send him a portrait of his brother Lucien that was apparently in her possession all the way from Paris.[93]

As his pain and inactivity grew, Petipa's temper noticeably worsened, with those closest to him bearing the brunt of his spleen. When Louba or Vera went off to the theater, he accused them of neglect. They were "spiteful"; they didn't get along; they were all Russian; the grandchildren had "bad manners."[94] He could rage like a Lear, and did: "My wife detests me. Vera told me that she does not love me. Victor feels nothing for his father, nor does his brother Marius. The only one who loves her father is my dear daughter Louba."[95] Or, on another occasion: "My noble family does more harm to my disease than the disease itself."[96] Even as he lay (as he thought) at death's door, he remained a man of the theater.

Virtually all this personal detail is missing from the Russian version of these diaries. Also missing (perhaps less surprisingly) are his uncharitable remarks about Russians. When critic Aleksandr Pleshcheev failed to turn up for several days running, Petipa was incensed. "I am still waiting for Mons. Pleshcheev. That's the thoughtlessness of Russians."[97] His own family was not exempt. "Stayed home on my chair," he wrote around the same time. "No one came to keep me company. That's Russians for you."[98]

Although Petipa, by all accounts, never learned to speak Russian properly, over the years the language did seep into his consciousness. "Kristos voskres," he wrote in an Easter entry,[99] transliterating the phrase "Christ is risen," the traditional Orthodox greeting after Midnight Mass. "Beriguis" (for "beregis")—

meaning "take care" or "be careful"—was another phrase that Petipa apparently had incorporated into his daily vocabulary.[100] Prolonged contact with Russian gave an odd twist to certain words. Among these was "papier"—French for "paper"—which Petipa routinely used like the Russian "bumaga" to mean document or official paper. Sometimes, he translated a term exactly, so that in French it made no sense, unless one knew the meaning of the Russian original. One such example is his (mis)translation of "shveitsar," meaning "porter" or "doorkeeper," as "suisse," or Swiss, although this word in Russian is actually "shveitsarets." For "cab" or "cabbie" he sometimes used the French "cocher" and sometimes the obsolete Russian "izvozchik." Other Russian words that crop up from time to time are "ikra" (caviar), "dvornik" (caretaker, janitor), "storozh" (watchman, guard), and "kapel'diner," an obsolete term meaning a theater "usher" or "box-keeper." Still, Petipa never wrote in Russian. Instead, he relied on translators, usually his son Marius, or, in one instance, a "Mons. Dolinskii," to put into Russian what he had previously written in French.[101] And even though his correspondence with the administrative staff typically was conducted in French, out of sheer perversity he would occasionally send an answer in Russian "to teach those swine a lesson," as he put it on one occasion.[102]

Also missing from the Russian version are the lists of out-of-pocket expenses that typically ended his account of each day. Because no tip was too small, no purchase too trivial that Petipa did not note it down, these items are a fount of information, rich in the detail that elsewhere he stinted. Although he was a frugal man, he was generous toward those he loved, and rare was the day when he did not return home with some little treat—raisins, grapes, caramels, a pot of chrysanthemums, a cuckoo clock for the kitchen, smoked salmon. He was a great fan of French newspapers and illustrated magazines, and subscribed to several—*Le Gaulois, L'Illustration, Le Journal pour rire, Modes Chic*—in addition to the *Journal de Saint-Pétersbourg,* a French-language weekly published in the Russian capital. He was a smoker; he trimmed his beard and hair regularly; he looked after his own wardrobe, consulting tailors and buying just about everything he needed from ties and shirts to underwear and socks.

Although he was amply provided for, Petipa was far from rich. He lived strictly within his means, even if this meant forgoing certain comforts. Thus, when he traveled to Paris with his wife and Vera in the summer of 1905, it was Preobrajenska who paid the fare for the extra place in the sleeping compartment that allowed the trio greater privacy.[103] This is not to imply that Petipa was cheap or tight-fisted, only that as the son of itinerant dancers and as a sometime itinerant dancer himself, he had early learned the value of a dime. He knew, too, that money was finite; once spent, it was gone. On holiday in the Crimea, he complains at one point that they are spending too much on meals; the next day he cuts back, as though the proverbial wolf were already at the family door. At a break during one of the last rehearsals of *The Magic Mirror,* he "gave everyone lunch";[104] on the day of the premiere, he provided lunch for the orchestra and, in the evening, five bottles of champagne. "Expenditure quite heavy," he wrote afterward, noting the forty-ruble outlay such generosity entailed.[105] For Petipa, as for most Europeans of modest means of his day, frugality was not a choice, but a way of life.

In preparing this edition of the diaries for publication, certain cuts have been made to save space and to sustain the reader's interest. Eliminated are most of the entries for the summer months of 1904, when Petipa was on holiday in Gurzuf, and all entries that consist solely of weather reports, shopping lists, and medical bulletins. Within entries, too, most of the aches, pains, itches, sweats, dizzy spells, coughs, shivers, spasms, and other symptoms that Petipa routinely noted as part of his daily health report have been cut along with the creams, pills, ointments, mineral waters, tonics, and enemas with which he regularly doctored himself—although selective symptoms and remedies have been left to give a flavor of the original. After the first dozen entries, the weather reports have been eliminated and also the routine expenses. The purchases that remain have been kept either because they reveal something about Petipa (e.g., his penchant for going shopping after a run-in with Telyakovsky) or because they convey a sense of the period (e.g., the need to tip domestics when paying calls). Editorial notes, including those translated from the Russian version of the diaries, follow the entries to which they refer.

In transliterating Russian names, I have followed the Library of Congress system, although for individuals known in the West under a variant of their original names, I have chosen to use the familiar form: hence, Preobrajenska and Fokine, as opposed to Preobrazhenskaia and Fokin. In the notes, both Russian and Western versions are given the first time someone is mentioned, and both versions are listed and cross-referenced in the index. Wherever possible, the full Russian name—Christian name, patronymic, and surname—is given, both in the notes and in the index. For designers of the early decades of Petipa's Russian career, full names almost never appear on programs and rarely in most of the standard sources, a reflection of the era's prevailing view that the designer, who often doubled as a scene painter, was fundamentally an artisan, not an artist. Although the argument can be made that the scene designer did not really come into existence in Russia until the 1890s, as it is impossible to distinguish scene painters who designed what they painted from those who painted what someone else had designed, anyone who painted for the Imperial stage is identified in the index as a designer.

The list of ballets and the dances in operas that follows the diaries proper is based on the list in the Nekhendzi volume, although, wherever possible, information concerning earlier productions has been added, along with the names of performers. As it stands, the present list is the fullest chronology of Petipa's works in English. This said, it should be noted that the list is far from complete, omitting as it does all the works he created prior to going to Russia. Moreover, the Russian editors chose not to include the many *pièces d'occasion* created by

Petipa for Imperial weddings, state occasions, and performances at court theaters, apart from the Hermitage. In other words, this chronology falls far short of Harvey Simmond's exemplary *Choreography by George Balanchine;*[106] one can only hope that a similar volume will materialize in the future about Petipa.

Because these diaries were not intended for publication, Petipa paid little heed to the niceties of writing such as spelling, grammar, and punctuation. He was equally relaxed about names and titles, and his method of transliterating from Russian to French can only be described as creative. In the interest of clarity, I have silently corrected Petipa's mistakes and standardized the spelling of names and titles, but otherwise retained the vagaries.

Many people have helped make this volume possible. To Madame N. B. Volkova, the director of TsGALI, I am deeply grateful for permission to translate the diaries and for providing me with photocopies of the originals from which to work. To Selma Jeanne Cohen and Timothy J. Scholl I am indebted for looking over the bibliography and suggesting various titles; to Stephen Vallillo, for copying the photographs from the *Yearbooks of the Imperial Theaters* reproduced as illustrations; to my coeditor John Chapman, for his numerous editorial suggestions. A year in residence at the Getty Center for the History of Art and the Humanities eased the financial burden of the later stages of this project. To Elizabeth Souritz, a source of inspiration from the start, I dedicate this volume.

NOTES

1. Aleksandr Alekseevich Pleshcheev, *Nash balet (1673–1896): balet v Rossii do nachala XIX stolietiia i balet v S.-Peterburgie do 1896 goda* (Our Ballet [1673–1896]: Ballet in Russia until the Beginning of the Nineteenth Century and Ballet in St. Petersburg until 1896) (St. Petersburg: A. Benke, 1896).

2. Konstantin Apollonovich Skal'kovskii, *V teatral'nom mire: nabliudeniia, vospominaniia i rassuzhdeniia* (In the World of the Theater: Observations, Reminiscences, and Debates) (St. Petersburg: A. S. Suvorin, 1899).

3. Sergei Nikolaevich Khudekov, *Istoriia tantsev* (A History of Dances), 4 vols. (St. Petersburg: Peterburgskaia/Petrogradskaia Gazeta, 1914–1918).

4. I[urii] I[osifovich] Slonimskii, *Mastera baleta: K. Didlo, Zh. Perro, A. Sen-Leon, L. Ivanov, M. Petipa* (Ballet Masters: C[harles] Didelot, J[ules] Perrot, A[rthur] Saint-Léon, L[evj] Ivanov, M[arius] Petipa) (Leningrad: Iskusstvo, 1937).

5. Yury Slonimsky, "Marius Petipa," trans. Anatole Chujoy, *Dance Index*, 6, nos. 5–6 (May–June 1947), pp. 129–130.

6. I[urii] I[osifovich] Slonimskii, *P. I. Chaikovskii i baletnyi teatr ego vremeni* (P. I. Tchaikovsky and the Ballet Theater of His Time) (Moscow: Gosudarstvennoe muzykal'noe izdatel'stvo, 1956).

7. V[era] Krasovskaia, *Russkii baletnyi teatr vtoroi poloviny deviatnadtsatogo veka* (Russian Ballet Theater in the Second Half of the Nineteenth Century) (Leningrad: Iskusstvo, 1963); *Russkii baletnyi teatr nachala XX veka* (Russian Ballet Theater at the Beginning of the Twentieth Century), 2 vols. (Leningrad: Iskusstvo, 1971–1972).

8. Vera Krasovskaya, "Marius Petipa and 'The Sleeping Princess,'" trans. Cynthia Read, *Dance Perspectives*, 49 (Spring 1972), p. 21.

9. Mikhail Vasil'evich Borisoglebskii, ed., *Proshloe baletnogo otdeleniia peterburgskogo teatralnogo uchilishcha: Materialy po istorii russkogo baleta* (The Past of the Ballet Section of the Petersburg Theatrical School: Documents for the History of Russian Ballet), 2 vols. (Leningrad: Izdanie leningradskogo gosudarstvennogo khoreograficheskogo uchilishcha, 1939).

10. *Marius Petipa: materialy, vospominaniia, stat'i* (Marius Petipa: Documents, Reminiscences, Essays), ed. A[nna] Nekhendzi (Leningrad: Leningrad State Theater Museum, 1971).

11. *Marius Petipa, Meister des Klassischen Balletts: Selbstzeugnisse, Dokumente, Erinnerungen* (Marius Petipa, Master of the Classical Ballet: Testimonials, Documents, Reminiscences), ed. Eberhard Rebling (Berlin: Henschelverlag, 1975).

12. The most important of these are Alexandre Benois, *Reminiscences of the Russian Ballet*, trans. Mary Britnieva (London: Putnam, 1941); Michel Fokine, *Memoirs of a Ballet Master*, trans. Vitale Fokine, ed. Anatole Chujoy (Boston: Little, Brown, 1961); Tamara Karsavina, *Theatre Street: The Reminiscenes of Tamara Karsavina*, foreword J. M. Barrie (London: Heinemann, 1930); Mathilde Kschessinska (Princess Romanovsky-Krassinsky), *Dancing in Petersburg: The Memoirs of Kschessinska*, trans. Arnold Haskell (Garden City, 1961; rpt. New York: Da Capo, 1977); Bronislava Nijinska, *Early Memoirs*, trans. and ed. Irina Nijinska and Jean Rawlinson, introd. Anna Kisselgoff (New York: Holt, Rinehart and Winston, 1981).

13. Marius Petipa, *Russian Ballet Master: The Memoirs of Marius Petipa*, trans. Helen Whittaker, ed. Lillian Moore (London, 1958; rpt. London: Dance Books, n.d.). This is a translation of *Memuary Mariusa Petipa solista ego imperatorskogo velichestva i baletmeistera imperatorskikh teatrov* (The Memoirs of Marius Petipa, Soloist of His Imperial Majesty and Ballet Master of the Imperial Theaters) published in St. Petersburg in 1906. For Moore's own study of the Petipa family, see "The Petipa Family in Europe and America," *Dance Index*, 1, no. 5 (May 1942), pp. 72–84.

14. Cyril W. Beaumont, *Complete Book of Ballets: A Guide to the Principal Ballets of the Nineteenth and Twentieth Centuries* (London: Putnam, 1937). The libretti included were for *Le Marché des Innocents, The Daughter of Pharaoh, King Candaules, Don Quixote, Camargo, La Bayadère, Zoraiya, or The Moorish Girl in Spain, Night and Day, Le Talisman, Kalkabrino, Cinderella, Swan Lake, Halt of the Cavalry, Bluebeard, Raymonda, The Trial of Damis, or The Pranks of Love, The Seasons,* and *The Sleeping Beauty.*

15. Roland John Wiley, *Tchaikovsky's Ballets: Swan Lake, Sleeping Beauty, Nutcracker* (London: Oxford University Press, 1985); ed. and trans., *A Century of Russian Ballet:*

Documents and Accounts, 1810–1910 (London: Oxford University Press, 1990). Wiley his since added a biography of Lev Ivanov to the list. See Roland John Wiley, *The Life and Ballets of Lev Ivanov* (Oxford: Clarendon Press, 1997).

16. The full citation is TsGALI USSR, Fond 1945, M. I. Petipa, Opis' 1, Storage area 1, Diary notes of M. I. Petipa, 1866–1907.

17. Horst Koegler, "Marius Petipa: A New Perspective," *Dance Magazine* (September 1978), pp. 62–67.

18. Because Russia retained the "old style" Julian calendar until 1917, when the "new style" Gregorian calendar (in general use throughout the rest of Europe for several centuries) was finally adopted, a difference of thirteen days existed between New and Old Style dates during the period covered by the diaries. Thus, New Year's Day in Russia was January 14 and New Year's Eve, January 13. It should be noted that Petipa's dating was occasionally inconsistent.

19. This and the chapter titles that follow are from the English-language edition.

20. *The Daughter of Pharaoh* received its two hundred and third performance on 19 January/1 February 1903; *The Sleeping Beauty* its one hundredth on 13/26 April 1903; *Swan Lake* its twenty-ninth on 26 January/8 February 1903. *Raymonda,* which received its thirtieth performance on 10/23 October 1904, and *The Little Humpbacked Horse* its fifty-first on 4/17 April 1904, were other popular repertory items.

21. 9/22 February 1903.

22. Quoted in Slonimsky, "Marius Petipa," p. 126. The witness was Vladimir Telyakovsky, director of the Imperial Theaters.

23. The phrase is from Benois' review of *The Magic Mirror* published in *Mir iskusstva.* For his translation, see *Reminiscences of the Russian Ballet,* p. 223.

24. Sergei Diaghilev, Letter to the Editor, in Wiley, *A Century of Russian Ballet,* pp. 420–421. In the months preceding this second performance, Petipa created a number of new dances. At the same time, he requested changes both in the score and in the designs.

25. Slonimsky, "Marius Petipa," pp. 107–108.

26. The candidate was Alexander Gorsky. The announcement, which appeared in the chronicle column, read: "The ballet company will have to get used to a new ballet master, A. Gorsky. He will stage his own versions of 'The Humpbacked Horse' and 'Swan Lake.' He stages both ballets entirely differently and in a much more original manner." Quoted in Slonimsky, "Marius Petipa," p. 126.

27. Petipa, *Russian Ballet Master,* p. 67.

28. V. A. Telyakovsky, "Memoirs: Part 2," trans. Nina Dimitrievitch, *Dance Research,* 9, no. 1 (Spring 1991), p. 29.

29. 25 November/8 December 1904.

30. 2/15 November 1904.

31. Petipa, *Russian Ballet Master,* p. 78.

32. See entries for 1/14 February 1903, 9/22 February 1903, and 4/17 December 1904.

33. Quoted in Wiley, *A Century of Russian Ballet,* p. 419.

34. 24 September/7 October 1903. Petipa learned of the dismissal from Aistov on 30 September/14 October 1903.

35. 23 April/6 May 1905.

36. 14/28 October 1903.

37. The first mention of the ballet is on 9/22 March 1903: "Wrote out the small details for the music that Mons. Drigo will compose for *Rosebud and the Butterfly,* His Excellency Mons. Vsevolojsky's short ballet. At noon, Mons. Drigo came by for a minute to talk about this little ballet."

38. Petipa, *Russian Ballet Master,* p. 59.

39. *Ibid.,* p. 58.

40. 3/16 January 1904.

41. 9/22 January 1904.

42. Acts I and II and Scene 2 of Act IV were given with Scene 4 of *The Little Humpbacked Horse* on 14/27 April 1904. "Ballet warmly applauded," wrote Petipa that night. "Mlle. Preobrajenska and everyone else were very good, but the music is still appalling. I was recalled 5 times." Another performance, on 12/25 September 1904, teamed *The Pearl* with a truncated version that included Act III instead of Act II. This performance was not rehearsed by Petipa, but by the chief régisseur, Nicholas Sergeyev.

43. 4/17 March 1904.

44. 5/18 March 1904.

45. 28 April/11 May 1904.

46. 15/28 April 1904.

47. 23 April/6 May 1904.

48. 11/24 January 1903.

49. 4/17 January 1905.

50. A draft of this letter, undated, follows the concluding entries for 1907 on manuscript pages 477–478.

51. See entries for 20 February/5 March 1905, 14/27 April 1903, 13/26 April 1903, and 25 January/7 February 1904.

52. 27 February/12 March 1905; 17/30 October 1904; 24 October/6 November 1904; 1/13 May 1903.

53. 16/30 October 1903; 10/23 February 1905.

54. 18 February/3 March 1905.

55. 4/17 December 1904.

56. Quoted in Nekhendzi, *Marius Petipa: materialy,* p. 363, note 118.

57. 5/18 December 1904.

58. Petipa, *Russian Ballet Master,* p. 91.

59. Lillian Moore, "Introduction," *Russian Ballet Master,* pp. ix–x.

60. Petipa, *Russian Ballet Master,* p. 77.

61. 31 January/13 February 1904.

62. 21 September/4 October 1904.

63. 22 September/5 October 1904; 11/24 October 1904.

64. 18/31 October 1904.

65. 25 December 1905 2/7 January 1906; 26 December 1905/8 January 1906; 27 December 1905/9 January 1906; 28 December 1905/10 January 1906; 30 December 1905/12 January 1906.

66. Being a subscriber meant purchasing tickets for a substantial number of ballet performances. "My wife," wrote Petipa on 13/26 November 1905, "has taken out a new subscription for 20 performances."

67. 12/25 February 1904.

68. 15/28 March 1904.

69. 21 December 1904/3 January 1905; 26 February/11 March 1905.

70. 11/24 January 1905.

71. 9/22 January 1905.

72. *Marius Petipa: materialy,* p. 363, note 126.

73. 14/27 January 1905.

74. For an account of the strike in greater detail, see Lynn Garafola, *Diaghilev's Ballets Russes* (New York: Oxford, 1989), pp. 3–7.

75. 15/28 October 1905.

76. 18/31 October 1905.

77. 20 October/2 November 1905; 23 October/5 November 1905.

78. *Marius Petipa: materialy,* p. 365, note 146.

79. 19 October/1 November 1905.

80. 20 October/2 November 1905.

81. Nijinska, *Early Memoirs,* p. 155.

82. Petipa, *Russian Ballet Master,* p. 58. The ballerina Ekaterina Vazem, who starred in many Petipa works of the 1870s, offers quite a different view of Savitskaia in her reminiscences: "A very crude and loose-tongued lady, Savitskaya quite often quarrelled with her husband at rehearsals, during which she would at times shower him with the most vulgar abuse." Ekaterina Vazem, "The Balletmaster M. I. Petipa," in Wiley, *A Century of Russian Ballet,* p. 283.

83. For a list of Petipa's siblings, wives, children, and other relatives, see "Family of Marius Petipa" following this essay. Unfortunately, there is no information about any of the grandchildren, except those who achieved some eminence in the theater.

84. 22 September/5 October 1904; 25 September/8 October 1904.

85. A draft of this letter, undated but probably written in 1905, appears on manuscript page 43 of the diary materials. It reads in part: "In the last two years, my daughter Vera has made great progress; I vow to you, sir, that she has been left in the corps de ballet with only a small increase in pay as vengeance against me. Before dying, her old father Petipa implores you, Baron Fredericks, to speak in her favor . . . for without your help she will never advance."

86. See 1/14 September 1905, 3/16 September 1905, 5/18 September 1905, 6/19 September 1905, 7/20 September 1905, 9/22 September 1905, and 11/24 September 1905.

87. 15/28 February 1903. The premiere of *The Magic Mirror* took place on 9/22 February 1903.
88. 16/29 March 1905.
89. 1/14 March 1905.
90. This undated note, probably from 1904, appears on manuscript page 53 of the diary materials.
91. 25 August/7 September 1905.
92. 14/27 November 1905.
93. 26 September/9 October 1905.
94. 28 August/10 September 1905; 26 August/8 September 1905; 13 July 1907.
95. 14/27 November 1905.
96. 13 July 1907.
97. 4/17 March 1905.
98. 6/19 February 1905.
99. 27 March/9 April 1904.
100. 20 October/2 November 1904.
101. 12/25 September 1905. How well Petipa read Russian is a matter of conjecture. A number of entries refer to his wife reading him the Russian newspapers, which suggests that his knowledge of the written language was fairly rudimentary.
102. 8/21 September 1904.
103. 3/16 May 1905.
104. 1/14 February 1903.
105. 9/22 February 1903.
106. *Choreography by George Balanchine: A Catalogue of Works,* ed. Harvey Simmonds (New York: Eakins Press Foundation, 1983).

FAMILY OF MARIUS PETIPA

PARENTS

Jean Antoine Petipa (1787–1855), dancer/choreographer
Victorine Grasseau, actress

SIBLINGS

Joseph Lucien Petipa (1815–1898), dancer/choreographer
Elisabeth Marianne Petipa (b. 1816)
Victor Marius Alphonse Petipa (1818–1910), dancer/choreographer
Jean Claude Tonnerre Petipa (1820–1873), dancer
Amata Victorine Anna Petipa (1824–1905), opera singer

Mariia Sergeevna Surovshchikova-Petipa (1836–1882), dancer, mother of Petipa's oldest daughter, Mariia Mariusovna, and his second son, Jean Mariusovich

Liubov' ("Louba") Leonidovna Savitskaia (1854–1919), dancer, mother of Petipa's six younger children: Nadezhda Mariusovna, Victor Mariusovich, Liubov' Mariusovna, Marius Mariusovich, Evgeniia Mariusovna, and Vera Mariusovna

CHILDREN

Marius Mariusovich Petipa (1850–1919), actor (son of Marie Thérèse Bourdin, d. 1855)

Mariia ("Marie") Mariusovna Petipa (1857–1930), dancer

Jean Mariusovich Petipa (1859–1871?)

Nadezhda ("Nadia") Mariusovna Petipa (1874–1945), dancer

Evgeniia ("Genia," "Génie," "Eugénie") Mariusovna Petipa (1877–1892)

Victor Mariusovich Petipa (1879–1939), actor

Liubov' ("Louba," "Loubouchka") Mariusovna Petipa (1880–1917), dancer

Marius Mariusovich Petipa (Marius II) (1884–1922), actor

Vera Mariusovna Petipa (1885–1961), dancer/actress

OTHER RELATIVES

Lucienne Mendès, singer, niece of Marius Petipa

Jeanne [?], godchild of Marius Petipa, possibly a niece

Konstantin Chizhov, son-in-law of Marius Petipa, husband of Nadezhda Mariusovna Petipa

Nadezhda ("Nadine," "Nadinka") Konstantinovna Petipa-Chizhova (b. 1896), actress, granddaughter of Marius Petipa

Kseniia ("Xenia") Konstantinovna Petipa-Chizhova (b. 1905), dancer, granddaughter, and goddaughter of Marius Petipa

DESIGN AND THE IDEA OF THE MODERN

IN EARLY TWENTIETH-CENTURY BALLET

During the early decades of the twentieth century, the visual component of a ballet became to a very large extent the preeminent sign of its modernity. The great exception to the rule was *Le Sacre du Printemps* (1913). Here, in the dance work that more than any other seemed a declaration of modernity, the radical newness of Stravinsky's score and Vaslav Nijinsky's choreography was accompanied by sets and costumes by Nicholas Roerich that belonged stylistically to the nineteenth century. But *Sacre* was an anomaly. Beginning with Loie Fuller in the 1890s, the new dance that flourished in the opera houses and concert halls of Europe until the 1930s was identified not only by its choreography but also by the style of its scenography. Regardless of the subject, the music, and even the choreography, a ballet was modern if it looked modern. The sign was in the design, in the way the body was clothed (or unclothed) and presented; in the way the stage space was bared, framed, divided, or adorned. The American critic John Martin once defined the "modern dance" that emerged in the United States in the 1930s as a "point of view."[1] The new ballet that emerged in Europe in the early 1900s and remained a vital movement for the next thirty years was equally a point of view, even if the view it espoused was quite different. What defined the new ballet as opposed to its nineteenth-century predecessor was its embrace of the contemporary world and the living makers of high culture. Where ballet of the late 1800s had languished in a ghetto of cultural isolation or prospered as commercial entertainment, the "new ballet" was a full citizen of the artistic polity. It existed in the here and now, and its works embodied aspects of contemporary culture. Even in ballets of a retrospective nature or that made a point of employing the academic idiom or *danse d'école*, the goal was not to recreate the past but to present it within a modern framework.

In this movement to make ballet modern, no figure was more important than Serge Diaghilev. Born in Russia, he was a Napoleon of the arts, the founder and long-time artistic director of the company that made ballet a full partner in the adventure of European modernism. The Ballets Russes exploded on the

This essay was originally published in Spanish translation in *El Teatro de los Pintores en la Europa de las vanguardias* (Painters' Theater in Avant-garde Europe) (Madrid: Museo Nacional Centro de Arte Reina Sofía, 2000).

artistic scene in 1909, with its now legendary debut at the Théâtre du Châtelet in Paris. So great was its success that within two years Diaghilev had transformed it from a seasonal organization made up of dancers on summer holiday from Russia's Imperial Theaters into a permanent expatriate enterprise. The company quickly established itself at the forefront of the dance avant-garde, where it remained, despite the occasional challenge to its supremacy, until Diaghilev's death in 1929, when it collapsed. During those twenty years, the Ballets Russes initially created and subsequently largely defined what came to be known as "modern ballet" or the "new ballet." By this was meant a form of ballet that had broken with nineteenth-century musical, choreographic, and scenic conventions, even if its technical basis remained the *danse d'école*. Nowhere was this break more visible than in the new and widely imitated approaches to set and costume design put into currency by the Ballets Russes.

To be sure, the Ballets Russes was not the first attraction to link the new dance with new forms of scenic design. Both Loie Fuller and Isadora Duncan, American dancers who spent most of their adult lives in Europe, transformed the stage into a new kind of dance space, one that placed a premium on fantasy and challenged conventional images of the female body—Fuller, by her extraordinary use of light; Duncan, by the radical simplification of her vocabulary. More ambitious in scale at least were the experiments of Emile Jaques-Dalcroze at Hellerau, where students trained in his system of rhythmic gymnastics played a key role in such avant-garde milestones as *Orfeo* (1912) and Paul Claudel's *L'Annonce faite à Marie* (1913). Just as Duncan and Fuller inspired numerous imitators, so Hellerau left its mark on countless practitioners of the new dance.

Although the Ballets Russes certainly left an imprint on the dance avant-garde, its greatest impact was felt in the mainsteam of European theater dance. Within a generation, the practices of the previous century—even at such hidebound institutions as the Paris Opéra—were transformed, even as the physical appearance of the stage changed virtually beyond recognition. Like the artists and aesthetes who formed his early circle in St. Petersburg, Diaghilev came of age during the culminating era of Marius Petipa's dominion over the Imperial Ballet. He attended the premiere of *The Sleeping Beauty* (1890) and the most important premieres thereafter; he knew the company and its repertoire intimately, and was critical of both. Of *The Sleeping Beauty,* his friend, the future Ballets Russes designer Alexandre Benois, wrote: "The production . . . had all the usual qualities and shortcomings of the Imperial stage—great luxury and at the same time lack of taste in the choice of costumes—especially with regard to colours. The décors were technically perfect, but lacked any poetical quality."[2] Five scene painters were responsible for the sets, while the costumes were designed by yet another hand. This specialist tradition of scene and costume design was not confined to Russia; it existed throughout Europe and was a phenomenon both of the opera house and the music-hall stage.

This tradition Diaghilev rejected. Beginning with Léon Bakst and Benois, the artists most closely identified with the prewar Ballets Russes, he commissioned designs for both scenery and costumes from easel painters, bypassing professional scene painters and costumers entirely. Although some of these craftsmen had created marvels, as artisans they operated within a set of highly limiting conventions; indeed, at the Maryinsky Theater, according to Vladimir Telyakovsky (the last director of the Imperial Theaters), scene painters "were divided according to their painting specialties: architectural, forest, marine, and other types of décor." Scene painters never did costumes (or props), and several individuals frequently contributed to a multi-act work (hence the five who worked on *The Sleeping Beauty*), making it "impossible," as Telyakovsky noted "to gain a coherent impression from the entire production."[3]

Artistic coherence early became a Diaghilev trademark. Typically, only one artist was assigned to a production. But even in cases where a second or even a third was involved, their contributions worked together harmoniously. Diversity was another Diaghilev trademark. Ballets Russes designers spanned the stylistic gamut, from Bakst, the virtuoso colorist of fin-de-siècle fantasies, to Picasso, whose magnificent designs for *Parade* announced Diaghilev's conversion to modernism. Diaghilev did not invent a school of design or a formula to be applied universally (as some of his British acolytes seemed to believe). Rather, he treated design as a creative element, a way of making the imagination of the visual artist palpable and the dance space itself a privileged area of fantasy.

Dance, of course, was not the only realm of early twentieth-century performance to experience a design revolution. Operas such as *Victory Over the Sun* (1913), which had designs by Kasimir Malevich, and plays such *The Magnificent Cuckold* (1922), which was designed by Lubov Popova, exemplified the brave new world that could be glimpsed in "advanced" quarters of the European theater. But the revolution penetrated no other medium so thoroughly as dance. Movement was central to avant-garde performance. To many, it seemed innocent of history, unencumbered by convention, a language that was primitive in the sense that it had existed long before words and was thus truthful in a way that words were not; as Martha Graham once said, "Movement does not lie." And it was full of suggestion, tantalizing possibilities that did not have to be spelled out, that could be simply intuited and grasped, without the mediation of the intellect. Needless to say, ballet was far from innocent of the past and anything but free of convention. Its history stretched back to the Renaissance; its lexicon of movements were bound by a strict and formal grammar. But as remade by Diaghilev, it was an art reborn, salvaged from the ghetto of triviality and inconsequence in which it had languished in the West since the 1860s.

In varying degrees, the works that Diaghilev chose to produce broke with the dramaturgical and choreographic conventions associated with Petipa. He adopted the one-act ballet as his company's basic format, emphasized dramatic and formal consistency, and focused attention on the male dancer. He insisted that the movement style of a work reflect the subject, rather than the other way around, thus implicitly rejecting the notion of the *danse d'école* as an all-purpose Ur-language. In most instances, he eschewed Petipa's highly structured pas de deux, with its opening supported adagio, solo variations, and razzle-dazzle coda. He rejected the conventions of the bravura dance, along with show-stopping steps like fouetté turns and double tours en l'air. And although his dancers continued to perform their daily exercises with full turnout (or what was considered full turnout at the time), all his choreographers, beginning with Michel Fokine, experimented with modifying this most defining element of ballet technique and with using the parallel positions that were typically regarded as its antithesis.

But it was not solely that the technique of the *danse d'école* appeared in varying degrees to be modified in Ballets Russes productions. The body itself was reborn, not once but several times. The body celebrated by Fokine in the years before World War I was pliant, curved into expressive spirals, clad in soft-flowing tunics—natural and uncorseted, like Isadora Duncan, whose praises he sang in his memoirs. Nijinsky, who succeeded Fokine as Diaghilev's in-house choreographer, shunned nature, which as a dancer—a very great dancer—he embodied so well. In his path-breaking works for Diaghilev, he hardened the contours of the body; he celebrated the angle rather than the curve, movement across a two-dimensional plane rather than dancing in the round. In the years dominated by Léonide Massine, who choreographed his first ballet for Diaghilev in 1915, the dancing body was transformed yet again; this time, in keeping with the cubofuturist aesthetic that held sway during the war and post-Armistice years, it was shorn of nature, masked by layers of fabric, make-up, putty, and padding and reconstructed as a comic figure or human grotesque. By contrast, the ballets of Bronislava Nijinska, who followed Massine as Diaghilev's "house" choreographer, seemed populated by hapless girls and androgynes with the minds of men; the men themselves were peacocks, flamboyant and useless. Finally, there were the deco gods and goddesses of Balanchine's works, handsome, sleek bodies with the attenuated lineaments of athletes, Jazz Age neoclassicists.

From its earliest days, the Ballets Russes stood for erotic fantasy—homosexual, heterosexual, or indeterminate. But the pervasive sensuality of so many productions opened other imaginative vistas as well. In the early years, the exotic went hand-in-hand with the erotic; indeed, in ballets such as *Cléopâtre* (1909), *Schéhérazade* (1910), and *Thamar* (1912), which had famed temptresses of the East as their titles, the perfume of otherness made the expression of desire both permissible and overt. If Bakst's massive and all-encompassing forms invoked a society hostile to private expression, his spaces, yawning with the promise of secret pleasures, and his colors—hot, vivid, intense—heightened the emotionalism of the drama. Sometimes, however, the appeal to the eye had an intellectual goal, underscoring ironies and clashes of source and style. In *Le Coq d'Or* (1914), for instance, the Russian avant-garde artist Natalia Goncharova painted several curtains and backdrops that elided the colors and motifs of traditional Russian peasant art with the angular, two-dimensional forms of cubofuturism. In

Parade, the 1917 avant-garde landmark that had designs by Picasso and music by Satie, the popular entertainments and lore of old Paris fairgrounds were juxtaposed with décors in cubist style and costumes that looked like cubist sculptures.

Many ballets invited time-traveling as well as space-traveling. In the series of works initiated during the company's peregrinations in Italy during the First World War, period elements cohabited with the most up-to-date modernism, as in *Pulcinella* (1920), which featured characters from the commedia dell'arte, sets and costumes by Picasso, and music by Pergolesi "modernized" by Stravinsky. *La Boutique Fantasque* (1919), whose gaiety made it the most popular of Diaghilev's ballets just after the war, charmed audiences with its old-fashioned plot, tunes from Rossini, and the brilliant Mediterranean world evoked by Derain in his curtain and décors. In these works, one could return however briefly to a world that had vanished in the war. Fantasies of the Jazz Age abounded in ballets of the mid-1920s. In *Zéphire et Flore* (1925), the heroine's friends were flappers from the Champs-Elysées; in *Le Train Bleu* (1924), the Beautiful People doing calisthenics on the beach wore sportswear by Chanel and popped in and out of cabanas by the sculptor Henri Laurens. In *Les Biches* (1924), the most subtle of Diaghilev's ballets with a contemporary setting, Marie Laurencin's designs seemed to absorb Nijinska's flappers in a cocoon of feminine pastels. Here was the promise of sex and high life, glamor, style, and sensuality.

If anything, it was Balanchine, that most metaphoric of choreographers, who made the sex overt and the desire transparent. In his ballets of the late 1920s, the bodies of his protagonists stand revealed, the women—like the Siren in *Prodigal Son* (1929) or the protagonist of *La Chatte* (1927)—in tutus so short as to reveal the full line of the leg, the men in waist-cinching trunks or tunics. And in the two ballets that are still performed today—*Prodigal Son* and the 1928 *Apollon Musagète* (or *Apollo*, as Balanchine later preferred)—the choreography of the pas de deux, with its twining, sliding, even slithering bodies, leaves no doubt as to what is really taking place. The transparency of Gabo and Pevsner's clear plastic set for *La Chatte* seemed to presage the naked stage the mature Balanchine would make his trademark, just as the projections devised by Tchelitchew for *Ode* (1928), which Massine choreographed, anticipated his collaborations with Balanchine in the 1930s—works like *L'Errante* (1933) and *Orpheus and Eurydice* (1936) that were haunted by erotic mystery and infused with an atmosphere of surrealist suggestion.

The alliance of modern art and modern ballet forged by the Ballets Russes was emulated all over Europe and even in America. Within no time at all, thinly veiled imitations of the company's exotic specialties appeared on the music-hall stage, where they were typically mounted and performed by former Diaghilev dancers. A sophisticated adaptation of the Ballets Russes "method," although using different materials and a different stable of artists, could be discerned in a number of productions by Jacques Rouché's experimental Théâtre des Arts, including Louis Laloy's "Chinese drama" *Le Chagrin dans le Palais de Han* (1912), which had designs by René Piot and choreography by Léo Staats; and *Ma Mère l'Oye* (1912), Maurice Ravel's ballet, which had designs by Jacques Drésa and choreography by Jane Hugard.

In the 1920s, several new enterprises took the Ballets Russes as their model. The most influential was the Ballets Suédois, or Swedish Ballet, founded in 1920 by the immensely wealthy Swedish collector Rolf de Maré and disbanded by him five years later. Even more than the Ballets Russes, the Swedish company was a showcase for the Paris avant-garde, above all the composers known as "Les Six" (who were taken up by Diaghilev after receiving initial commissions from Maré) and painters of the School of Paris such as Léger (whom Diaghilev ignored despite his brilliant designs for *Skating Rink* [1922] and *La Création du monde* [1923]). More transitory was Comte Etienne de Beaumont's 1924 Soirées de Paris, which presented an ambitious program of plays and ballets, the latter choreographed by Massine for a company led by Ballets Russes veterans. With most of the other collaborators having worked at one time or another for Diaghilev, the dance part of the enterprise was little more than a knockoff of the Ballets Russes. More interesting was the company of singers and dancers organized by Marguerite Bériza, a one-time prima donna of the Chicago and Boston operas, who sponsored some of the more interesting experiments in lyric theater of the mid-1920s. The Théâtre Bériza produced not only opéras bouffes and miniature operas but also ballets, including *El amor brujo* (1925), to Falla's celebrated score, and *Sept chansons* (1925), to the opera by Malipiero; like most of the Bériza ballets, this was designed by the Hungarian artist Ladislaw Medgyès. Charles Cochran, whose sophisticated revues set the tone for London during the Jazz Age, not only hired Massine and featured numerous graduates of the Ballets Russes in his shows, but also incorporated into them miniature ballets founded on the one-act Diaghilev model. Meanwhile, throughout the 1920s, the venerable Paris Opéra, now under the enlightened direction of Jacques Rouché, called on several key Diaghilev artists, including Bakst and Benois (who designed the 1924 revival of *Giselle* that brought the romantic classic back to the theater where it originated), Nijinska, Ida Rubinstein, the mime star of Diaghilev's earliest seasons, and most importantly, Serge Lifar, the leading man of his last seasons, who ruled the Paris Opéra Ballet for decades. And in the nationalist quarters of British and American ballet during the 1920s and 1930s, variations on the Ballets Russes "recipe" abounded, albeit with different artists and an ideological slant that pitted the fledging companies against the "cosmopolitan" offspring of the Ballets Russes that inherited repertory, personnel, and a "Russian" point of view from the original Diaghilev company. In émigré ballet, as in émigré cabarets like the Chauve-Souris, the idea of "Russianness," diluted over time and commercialized, had become increasingly problematic.

Ballet's adventure with modern art lived on until the Second World War. After that, the relationship between the two broke down. Among the culprits was abstract expressionism, which Lincoln Kirstein and others could not accept because of its rejection of the figurative. Another was the move, epitomized by Balanchine, away from the use of painted décors in favor of lighting alone as a source of color, atmosphere, and emotional tone. Finally, there was the tendency to treat the scene designer as an illustrator of the choreographic subject rather than a creative partner, an artist whose vision was integral to the conception and identity of the work as a whole. This had been a foundation of Diaghilev's collaborative "method." Ironically, it was dance avant-gardists like Merce Cunningham, who routinely worked with painters like Robert Rauschenberg and Jasper Johns, who continued Diaghilev's collaborative tradition while rejecting both the goal of fusion and the presumption that this was both desirable and necessary—key Diaghilev ideas. Although ballet continues to honor Diaghilev as one of the most influential figures of its past, it is in contemporary dance that his vision of the dance stage as a meeting ground of the arts and a space for the expression of fantasy retains something of its original force.

NOTES

1. John Martin, *The Modern Dance* (New York: A. S. Barnes, 1933), p. 20.
2. Alexandre Benois, *Reminiscences of the Russian Ballet,* trans. Mary Britnieva (London: Putnam, 1941), p. 126.
3. Quoted in Tim Scholl, *From Petipa to Balanchine: Classical Revival and the Modernization of Ballet* (London: Routledge, 1994), p. 9. Diaghilev did not cease to employ professional costumers and scene painters; he used them, however, not as designers, but only to execute the designs of others.

DIAGHILEV'S MUSICAL LEGACY

"It is not an exaggeration," composer William Schuman once remarked, "to claim that the great patron of twentieth-century music has been the art of dance."[1] To be sure, Schuman was largely referring to modern dance. He himself had composed two scores for Martha Graham—*Night Journey* (1947) and *Judith* (1950)—and another, *Undertow* (1945), for Antony Tudor, the honorary modern among ballet choreographers of the period. Several of his Juilliard colleagues had also composed for modern dancers. Norman Lloyd, who, with his wife Ruth, had served as musical director of the Bennington School of the Dance and the Humphrey-Weidman company, had written the music for works by Graham (*Panorama*), Doris Humphrey (*Lament for Ignacio Sánchez Mejía*), and Hanya Holm (*Dance of Work and Play*). Louis Horst composed more than a dozen of Graham's early works, while Vivian Fine wrote for Holm (*They Too Are Exiles*), Graham (*Alcestis*), Charles Weidman (*Opus 51*), and José Limón (*My Son, My Enemy*).

Such largess was not unique to modern dance. The renaissance of ballet as an elite art that began in Europe on the eve of the First World War was as much a musical as a choreographic phenomenon. The new ballet created the need for new music, and the decades that followed witnessed a dramatic expansion in the repertory of music for ballet. In part, the new music that came into being from about 1910 until the outbreak of World War II was of recent vintage, works commissioned from living composers by ballet companies or their patrons. In part, however, the urgent need for new music was met by old or existing music, almost always conceived for the concert hall. In addition to adding to the musical literature and expanding the literature of music for dance, the new ballet of the early twentieth century significantly altered the relationship between composer and choreographer. This was partly a result of the enhanced status of dance relative to the other arts; for the first time, the dancemaker enjoyed something approaching parity in relation to the composer. But it also reflected a shift in what was thought to constitute the relationship of music and dance within the context of a ballet.

In this revolution, no figure was more important than Serge Diaghilev and no single company more important than his Ballets Russes.

Born in 1872, Diaghilev grew up in Perm, a provincial Russian capital on the

This essay is adapted from a lecture given at Skidmore College on 10 April 2000.

edge of Siberia, in a household where music was woven into the fabric of everyday life. He had a fine baritone voice, played the piano, and knew whole operas by heart. In 1890, he arrived in St. Petersburg to study law, the gateway to a position in the civil service. But his real goal was to be a composer, an ambition he gave up only when Rimsky-Korsakov pronounced his music "absurd."[2] Too proud to be third-rate, Diaghilev turned to writing. He became an art critic and a historian, discovered forgotten painters, and published a book on the eighteenth-century Russian portraitist Dmitry Levitsky. Full of vigor, with an energy as boundless as Russia itself, Diaghilev was an empire builder. He founded *Mir iskusstva* (World of Art), a journal that championed symbolism, neonationalism, *décadence,* and other new artistic currents. He organized numerous art exhibitions, including the mammoth Exhibition of Historic Russian Portraits of 1905, which brought together hundreds of old paintings from attics and ruined estates. For a time, he worked as an assistant to the director of the Imperial Theaters, editing its yearbook and doing the spadework for a production of *Sylvia* that was never realized but that anticipated the collaborative method of his future ballet enterprise and involved its key designers. And in the music by Léo Delibes, a composer "worshipped" by Diaghilev and his circle, there was a unity and high artistic quality unusual in ballet scores of the 1870s and 1880s that Diaghilev would later make commonplace.

Diaghilev grew up at the height of what musicologist Roland John Wiley calls the "specialist" tradition of ballet music. By this he means music "written to order," scores cobbled together to serve the needs of the choreographer (or ballet master, as he was called). It was the latter who designated the tempos and number of bars in a piece, who ordered scenes to be cut or abbreviated, variations to be added, and changes made in the composition of motives. "Music in ballet," wrote the Russian theater critic Konstantin Skalkovsky, "must complete in the imagination of the audience everything that is beyond the means of dance and its poses to express."[3] Melodious, rhythmic, and *dansante,* ballet music acknowledged the conditions of the stage and the composer's profound knowledge of choreographic structure. Cesare Pugni (who composed *Esmeralda, The Little Humpbacked Horse,* and *The Daughter of Pharaoh*) and Ludwig Minkus (who composed *Paquita, Don Quixote,* and *La Bayadère*), were the specialist composers par excellence of the ballets of Diaghilev's youth. In the 1890s, however, the specialist system was challenged by Tchaikovsky, whose *Sleeping Beauty, Nutcracker,* and *Swan Lake* were staged in rapid succession at St. Petersburg's Maryinsky Theater. In these ballets, the composer largely abided by choreographic convention, especially with regard to the structure and duration of the dances. But he also subordinated them to the larger whole, to the needs of narrative unity, and, especially in the so-called "white" acts or vision scenes, to the creation of an atmosphere suffused with poetry and emotional suggestion.

Like Benois and the other *miriskusstniki,* Diaghilev admired Tchaikovsky enormously, as he did Alexander Glazunov, who composed *Raymonda* just before the dawn of the new century. Nevertheless, with the exception of *The Sleeping Beauty,* which he revived in its entirety in 1921 (as *The Sleeping Princess*), and the partial exception of *Swan Lake,* which he revived in variously abbreviated versions, Diaghilev refrained from using the music these composers had written for ballet. In part, this was because he was interested in new blood. But to a far greater extent it was because the specialist tradition within which these scores were conceived had wed them to choreographic conventions that it was impossible to divorce. Once these conventions were thrown over, the need for new music became urgent.

In 1906, in conjunction with the Exhibition of Russian Art at the Grand Palais that marked his Paris debut as an impresario, Diaghilev organized a concert of works by a half-dozen Russian composers. So successful was the event, described by critic Robert Brussel as "an all too rare occasion to admire a group of composers who have had and will have the greatest influence on the evolution of contemporary music,"[4] that the following year Diaghilev returned to the French capital with a series of five "historical" concerts designed to present the full range of Russian music. Not only were all the major Russian composers represented; Diaghilev had also engaged an extraordinary roster of Russian vocal talent headed by Felia Litvinne and Fedor Chaliapin.[5] In 1908, Diaghilev returned yet again to Paris, this time with a magnificent production of *Boris Godunov,* the first time Mussorgsky's opera was seen in the West. Finally, in 1909, the last year his enterprise enjoyed the blessings of the Imperial government as well as an Imperial subsidy, Diaghilev offered Paris theater goers a veritable cornucopia—a half-dozen operas and several programs of ballets. To the amazement of the Russians, the ballets stole the show. Although Diaghilev produced a number of operas in the next twenty years, the die was cast. His destiny lay with the ensemble we know today as the Ballets Russes.

This company, which began as a summer touring ensemble and became a permanent organization in 1911, was conceived in part as a showcase for the ballets of Michel Fokine. Still shy of thirty, Fokine had been choreographing for benefits, school performances, and charity evenings since 1906. Unlike the multiact ballets that dominated the Maryinsky or Bolshoi repertory, his works (to use the language of the day) were "miniatures," that is, short ballets lasting well under an hour, in addition to solos and other dances that were complete in themselves (rather than being excerpts from a larger work). Although highly regarded as a dancer, Fokine met stiff resistance as a choreographer. The Maryinsky administration wanted no part of his "new ballet" (as critics were starting to call his controversial new works); he was accused of "Duncanism" (that is, of being unduly influenced by the American dancer Isadora Duncan), of destroying the formal beauties of the classical dance, of breaking with the conventions that had governed it for generations.

Although Fokine bristled at the accusation of influence, there is no question that Duncan, who gave her first Petersburg concerts in 1904, left a deep and enduring mark on his sensibility. Early on, Duncan had rejected the hack music specifically written for dance, especially on the music-hall stage. Instead, she danced to music from the concert hall, works by Brahms, Schubert, Strauss, and Rameau, the Bacchanale from Wagner's *Tannhäuser*, Gluck's *Orfeo*. In St. Petersburg, she gave an all-Chopin program that included many of the waltzes and mazurkas that Fokine would later use in *Chopiniana*, or *Les Sylphides*, as Diaghilev renamed the ballet for Paris. Thus, even before teaming up with Diaghilev, Fokine had liberated the "new ballet" from the program music that had served its predecessor. As he wrote in 1914, "the new ballet . . . in contradistinction to the older ballet . . . does not demand 'ballet music' of the composer as an accompaniment to dancing; it accepts music of every kind, provided only that it is good and expressive."[6]

Although dancers routinely appeared in the dance acts of Russian operas, music by Russian composers not written specifically for ballet was noticeably absent from the repertory of the Imperial Ballet. The upshot of this was an unofficial ban on the nationalist composers known as the "Mighty Five" who had dominated Russian music since the 1870s. Between 1909 and 1915, Diaghilev not only staged for Western consumption more than a half-dozen masterpieces of the Russian lyric repertory; he also presented nearly a dozen ballets to music by its outstanding nationalist composers. Among these works were *Schéhérazade* (1910), *Sadko* (1911), *The Golden Cockerel* (1914), and *Midnight Sun* (1915), all to music by Rimsky-Korsakov; *The Polovtsian Dances* (1909) to Borodin's music from the opera *Prince Igor*; *Thamar* (1912), by Balakirev; and three ballets, *Cléopâtre* (1909), *Le Festin* (1909), and *Les Orientales* (1910), to music by all the above plus Glinka and Mussorgsky.

This musical inheritance gave the Ballets Russes a good part of what was perceived as its national character and identity; it was a major ingredient of the recipe that by the 1920s and 1930s Swedes, Spaniards, Americans, and even Indians were appropriating in their quest for a national form of choreographic expression. But this nationalism was not the only imperative governing Diaghilev's repertory decisions, especially with regard to music. Like most Petersburgers, he was a thorough-going cosmopolitan and an ardent Francophile. Thus, even before the 1909 season was over, he was courting Debussy, whose *Masques et Bergamasques* was to be the first of the new company's French ballets. Nothing came of the project; instead, it was Debussy's *Prélude à l'après-midi d'un faune*, written in the early 1890s, that marked his debut on the Ballets Russes stage. It was followed in 1913 by *Jeux*, his only original work for Diaghilev, although, unlike *Faune*, which is still danced today, it quickly disappeared from repertory. More successful was Ravel's *Daphnis and Chloe*. Produced by Diaghilev in 1912, it was a luminous and sensual work that is still occasionally performed, albeit with different designs and choreography.

Preromantic music was another addition to the literature of ballet music that Diaghilev made. His interest in the music of Scarlatti, Cimarosa, and Pergolesi dated to the war years, when he found himself in Italy, with the time to rummage through libraries and manuscript collections. Another discovery of this Italian period was Rossini; from his music, Diaghilev wove together the sparkling score of *La Boutique Fantasque,* the "hit" of the company's 1919 season. In 1924, in Monte Carlo, for the Festival of French Music intended to transform the gambling haven into a major arts center, Diaghilev resurrected long-forgotten operas by Gounod and Chabrier, works that delighted connoisseurs but did nothing to further Diaghilev's ambitions. Like the early cycle of Italian ballets, the mounting of these French operas bore the imprint of his intelligence and the mark of his imagination.

Still, Diaghilev's fame does not rest on the old music he recycled for choreographic use, however much this expanded the literature for ballet. Rather, it rests on the new music he brought into being. Thanks to Diaghilev, ballet acquired a remarkable body of new music, music that was modern, equally at home in the concert hall and in the theatre. Just as the music of Russia's nationalist composers was a key source of the company's Russian identity, so the music commissioned from the era's most "advanced" composers was a key source of its modern identity. This, too, became an indispensable ingredient of the recipe so many companies of the interwar years sought to follow. From Argentina's "Ballets Espagnols" to Lincoln Kirstein's Ballet Caravan, the expression of nationality went hand-in-hand with the methods and styles of modernism.

Among the composers who owed their careers to Diaghilev, none was greater or more closely identified with the Ballets Russes than Igor Stravinsky. Plucked from obscurity by Diaghilev, he composed his first ballet for the company in 1910. This was *Firebird,* and it catapulted the young composer to international fame. Diaghilev called Stravinsky his "first son," and together, over the next two decades, despite ruptures, financial bickering, and grand Oedipal gestures, they sired nearly a dozen works: *Petrouchka* (1911), the great *Sacre du Printemps* (1913), *Le Rossignol* (1914), *Pulcinella* (1920), *Les Noces* (1923), *Oedipus Rex* (1927), and *Apollon Musagète* (1928), to cite only the most important. These works underscored not only the "Russianness" of the Diaghilev enterprise but also its commitment to modernism. With *Sacre,* the Ballets Russes moved to the forefront of the avant-garde.

Stravinsky's career as a composer for the dance stage was not limited to the Ballets Russes, nor did it end with Diaghilev's death. For Ida Rubinstein, he composed *Le Baiser de la Fée* (The Fairy's Kiss, 1928) and *Perséphone* (1934), a work that combined movement, song, and spoken text. For Balanchine, with whom he first worked in the 1920s, there were innumerable ballets, starting with *Jeu de Cartes,* which the choreographer staged for his 1937 Stravinsky Festival at the Metropolitan Opera. Thus began the second great collaboration of Stravinsky's career, a relationship as fecund as his earlier one with Diaghilev. Among the offspring was *Balustrade,* first choreographed in 1941 for the Ballet Russe de Monte Carlo to Stravinsky's Violin Concerto and rechoreographed thirty years later for the New York City Ballet as *Stravinsky Violin Concerto*. It was followed by *Orpheus* (1948) and *Agon* (1957), probably the greatest of the Balanchine-Stravinsky commissions, works that did as much to define the New York City Ballet as *Petrouchka* or *The Rite of Spring* had defined the Ballets Russes. There was *The Flood* (1962), an opera conceived for television; *Le Baiser de la Fée* (1937), *Danses Concertantes* (1944, 1972), *Duo Concertant* (1972), *Rubies* (1967), *Symphony in Three Movements* (1972), *Pulcinella* (1972), *Perséphone* (1982), and innumerable versions of their first collaboration together, *Apollo* (1928). Finally, there was the 1972 Stravinsky Festival, in the course of which the New York City Ballet danced more than thirty works to the composer's music. Even today, nearly twenty years after Balanchine's death, not a season passes when Stravinsky's music is unheard on the stage of the New York State Theater, something one cannot say of many concert series.

Diaghilev's "second son" was another Russian composer, Sergei Prokofiev. Prokofiev composed three ballets for Diaghilev: *Chout* (1921), *Le Pas d'Acier* (1927), and *Prodigal Son* (1929). *Prodigal,* which is still danced with Balanchine's choreography and the Rouault designs that Diaghilev originally commissioned, was a milestone in the composer's life. It was here that Prokofiev, the modernist, found his path as the maker of neotraditional narratives. Returning to the Soviet Union, he composed *Romeo and Juliet,* a full-length work that premiered in the late 1930s and, with Galina Ulanova as the heroine, dazzled audiences when danced by the Bolshoi on its first tours of the West in the 1950s. The scores that followed—*Cinderella* (1949) and *The Stone Flower* (1954)—were less successful, burdened with a narrative detail that seems to restrain the lyrical impulse and limit the free play of fantasy. In *Cinderella,* there are few scenes of pure dance.

Beginning with *Parade,* which had music by Satie, a theme by Cocteau, and cubist-style designs by Picasso, French influence on the Ballets Russes perceptibly increased. The ballet came to the stage only months before the Bolsheviks seized power in Russia, an event that turned expatriates like Diaghilev and Stravinsky into émigrés, forcibly severed from their homeland. If, before, Russia had been an ever-fertile source of ideas and talent, that role was now assumed by France, or more properly, Paris, the capital of the cosmopolitan polity that was the homeland of émigré ballet until World War II.

Satie was not the first French composer commissioned by Diaghilev. Before the war, both Debussy and Ravel had written ballets for him, as had Reynaldo Hahn, a composer of lesser stature. However, with Diaghilev's conversion to modernism, he lost interest in "Debussyism" (Cocteau's disparaging term for musical impressionism). In 1920, he turned down Ravel's *La Valse,* telling the composer that the work was a "masterpiece . . . but . . . not a ballet."[7] The French composers he now courted were members of the group championed by Cocteau and baptized "Les Six" (an echo of Russia's "Mighty Five"). The most important were Poulenc, Milhaud, Honegger, and Auric: all were under thirty, hungry for fame and fortune, with none of the contempt that "serious" composers had once had for the ballet stage. If anything, they reveled in it. All wrote ballets (although Diaghilev, for some reason, never gave Honegger a commission), and both Honegger and Auric became distinguished composers for films.

Although Diaghilev certainly was aware of their music by the late 1910s, he waited several years before offering them commissions. In fact, it was Rolf de Maré, the millionaire founder and artistic director of the Ballets Suédois, a company of Swedish dancers that was a knockoff of the Ballets Russes both in repertory and artistic approach, who launched them in the dance world. In 1921, five of the six contributed music to Cocteau's *Les Mariés de la Tour Eiffel* (The Newlyweds on the Eiffel Tower), a charming spoof of a French wedding lunch that was a direct descendent of *Parade;* the same year, Milhaud wrote *L'Homme et son désir* (Man and His Desire), a ballet inspired by Nijinsky. In 1922 and 1923, the company produced two of its greatest works—*Skating Rink,* which had music by Honegger, and *La Création du monde,* an African creation myth, which had a jazz-influenced score by Milhaud; both were designed by Léger. *Within the Quota,* an "American" ballet produced for the company's 1923 U.S. tour, had music by Cole Porter and a backdrop by Gerald Murphy that was a blow-up of the front page of a Hearst-style newspaper. *Relâche* (Canceled, or No Performance), the company's last ballet, had music by Satie, a set by Picabia consisting of hundreds of glaring headlights, and a film by René Clair, *Entr'acte,* that has since become a classic of French experimental cinema.

Even if Diaghilev had little sympathy for the more extreme experiments of the Ballets Suédois, he could not remain immune to its influence. Beginning in 1923, a number of artists associated with the Ballets Suédois received their first commissions from him. This group included Auric, who wrote no fewer than three works for Diaghilev: *Les Fâcheux* (1924), *Les Matelots* (1925), and *La Pastorale* (1926); Poulenc, who wrote *Les Biches* (1924); Milhaud, who wrote *Le Train Bleu* (1924); and Henri Sauguet, who wrote *La Chatte* (1927). Much of this music was dismissed by critics as inconsequential, "*musiquette.*" But in revivals of *Les Biches* and *Le Train Bleu,* one is struck by the freshness and gaiety of the music, by the fit between its unpretentious tunes and the depiction of everyday life, by the independence of the music in relation to the choreography.

In Fokine's 1914 letter to the *Times* laying out his choreographic principles, he insisted on the freedom and equality of the collaborators:

> The new ballet, refusing to be the slave either of music or of scenic decoration, and recognizing the alliance of the arts only on the condition of complete equality, allows perfect freedom both to the scenic artist and to the musician. . . . It does not impose any specific "ballet" conditions on the composer or the decorative artist, but gives complete liberty to their creative powers.[8]

In practice, however, such liberty eluded Diaghilev's artists until the 1920s. As the extensive correspondence among the various collaborators of *Petrouchka* makes clear, the prewar goal was *Gesamtkunstwerk,* the fusion of scenic, chore-ographic, and musical texts into a single theatrical gestalt. If this was perceived by collaborators as independence, it was almost certainly because so many of the time-honored conventions from Petipa's day had gone. No more pas de deux, no more waltzes, no more thirty-two-bar variations, no more mime scenes, no more acts, etc., etc. Overnight, the nineteenth-century forms had collapsed —totally and irremediably. In this void—for it was a void in terms of lacking any reliable signposts—the need for collaboration, the personal crafting of the individual work, grew exponentially. In a sense, the emphasis on fusion and col-laborative harmony reflected a need that would become less urgent once new parameters had been set and new conventions instilled, that is, once the "new ballet" or "modern ballet" (a somewhat later term) had established itself as a formal practice. One could argue that by the 1920s this had happened, thus al-lowing a looser weave in the assembling of the final product and greater artis-tic independence for the collaborators.

In the decades to follow, ballet was not alone in linking its identity with modern music. When Martha Graham and other pioneers of U.S. modern dance turned away from music tailor-made for the choreography (such as Louis Horst's scores for Graham, which were often composed after the dance was set), they looked instead to the European modernists brought into the dance fold by Diaghilev. By the mid-1930s, they were also beginning to commission works from modern American composers. The "American" dance, as they frequently referred to modern dance, needed music that was both modern and American. Copland's score for *Appalachian Spring* (1944), Graham's most luminous work, was probably the most felicitous of these collaborations.

Diaghilev's children were many, and their offspring legion. Indeed, even today, more than seventy years after Diaghilev's death, we are still living off his legacy. He brought new music to dance and commissioned some of its greatest scores, including works that were equally at home in the concert hall. He reared a whole generation of composers willing and able to write for the dance and to-tally revamped what was thought of as dance music. His influence was felt throughout Europe as well as in the United States, in modern dance as well as ballet. The literature of music for the dance would be much the poorer were it not for Diaghilev and his Ballets Russes.

NOTES

1. Quoted in Andrea Olmstead, *Juilliard: A History* (Urbana: University of Illinois Press, 1999), p. 203.
2. V. V. Yastrebtsev, *Reminiscences of Rimsky-Korsakov,* ed. and trans. Florence Jonas, foreword Gerald Abraham (New York: Columbia University Press, 1985), p. 90.

3. Quoted in Roland John Wiley, *Tchaikovsky's Ballets: Swan Lake, Sleeping Beauty, Nutcracker* (Oxford: Clarendon Press, 1985), p. 5.

4. Robert Brussel, "Concert de l'exposition de l'art russe," *Figaro*, 7 November 1906, p. 4.

5. For the individual programs, see Robert Brussel, "Un Festival de musique russe à Paris," *Figaro*, 16 April 1907, p. 2.

6. Michel Fokine, "The New Russian Ballet," *The Times*, 6 July 1914, p. 6.

7. Quoted in Arbie Orenstein, *Ravel: Man and Musician* (New York: Columbia University Press, 1975), p. 78.

8. Fokine, "The New Russian Ballet," p. 6.

In the year 1913 the twentieth century seemed to bid farewell to the Belle Epoque. In Paris, it was the year of *The Rite of Spring;* in New York, of the Armory Show; in St. Petersburg, of the futurist opera *Victory Over the Sun.* Among the artists of the avant-garde, a radiant new world lay on the horizon. For many it harbored dreams of utopian promise; for others new forms of artistic magic. A new day was dawning, and everything seemed possible, at least in the more enlightened centers of the West. Finally, it seemed, the world was becoming more civilized.

Or was it?

At the fabled premiere of *The Rite of Spring,* heads were bashed and voices raised in horror. The orchestra banged out Stravinsky's barbarous chords, and Nijinsky, the ballet's choreographer, shouted counts to the terrified dancers. "The genius of Igor Stravinsky," wrote composer Florent Schmitt, "could not have received more striking confirmation than in the incomprehension and vicious hostility of the crowd. . . . With a logic, with an infallibility, human stupidity demands its rights."[1]

With hindsight, it is tempting to see *The Rite of Spring* as a premonition of the brutal violence that in little more than a year would envelop Europe. But in 1913, despite intermittent skirmishes on the European periphery, few imagined that the world they knew would come so abruptly to an end with World War I. And none, certainly not the Russians who dominated the Ballets Russes, could have foreseen the 1917 Revolution, which left many of them stateless and severed the development of Russian ballet at home from that of the diaspora. No, the violence of 1913 was happily confined to theaters and galleries; it was a tempest in the teacup of Belle Epoque privilege.

Let us return then to that last year of peace before the déluge, and to the cities—Paris and Petersburg—that witnessed Nijinsky's greatest triumphs in the short span of his performing life. What dance did audiences see in the

This essay is based on a lecture given at the Bruno Walter Auditorium on 27 February 2003 under the auspices of the New York Public Library for the Performing Arts. It was subsequently published in the CORD *Newsletter,* 23, no. 1 (Spring 2003).

French and Russian capitals that fabled year? What was old? What was new? What was different? What was Russian?

The year 1913 witnessed the eighth "Russian Season" organized by Serge Diaghilev in the French capital. The first, in 1906, had been an Exhibition of Russian Art; the second, in 1907, a series of concerts of Russian music; the third, in 1908, the first production of the opera *Boris Godunov* outside Russia. Only in 1909 did Diaghilev organize his first season of ballet, although, unsure how Paris would take to it, he included several operas to be on the safe side. He needn't have worried. The ballets were a huge success; the operas (except for *Prince Igor,* with its Polovtsian Dances), a *succès d'estime.*

In the years that followed, Diaghilev returned each May to Paris with three or four premieres and a rapidly growing repertory of ballets. For the most part, these were newly minted works, or revisions of works choreographed by Michel Fokine for performances outside the regular Maryinsky repertory, what critic Valerian Svetlov had called "the modern ballet"—or *sovremennyi balet*—in his 1911 book of that title defending it. (It was translated into French as *Le Ballet contemporain.*) Although the "new" ballet clearly dominated, the repertory also included notable representatives of the "old." *Giselle,* which had vanished from the French stage in 1868, was presented in 1910 in Paris and the following year in London, on both occasions in Marius Petipa's revised Petersburg version. Other Petipa dances were included in the divertissement ballets that Diaghilev produced in 1909 and 1910: the Blue Bird pas de deux from *The Sleeping Beauty,* the Grand Pas Classique Hongrois and the Saracens dance from *Raymonda* in *Le Festin* and *Les Orientales* respectively. And in 1911, for London, Diaghilev produced the first of several versions of the Petipa-Ivanov *Swan Lake.*

In the years before World War I, it has been said, Diaghilev revealed Russia to the West. In fact, the Ballets Russes revealed many Russias, refracting them through a distinctly Petersburg lens. There was the eighteenth-century European city, with its neoclassical palaces and monuments, to which *Le Pavillon d'Armide* paid tribute and which Alexandre Benois recreated imaginatively in his paintings and designs. There was the old Russian city of shrovetide revels and carnival entertainments memorialized in *Petrouchka* and in poet Alexander Blok's play *The Fairground Booth.* There was the city enamoured of the commedia dell'arte, its masks and its artifice, the world of Diaghilev's ballet *Carnaval,* the paintings of Konstantin Somov, and the theater of Meyerhold in his guise as Doctor Dapertutto. There was the city that dreamed of the ancient world, evoked by Léon Bakst in his settings for *Narcisse, Daphnis and Chloe,* and *L'Après-midi d'un Faune.* There was the city fascinated by the riotous colors and pleasures of the Orient, brought thrillingly to life in *Cléopâtre, Schéhérazade,* and so many other ballets. Finally, there was the city that viewed Russia as the exotic or Eurasian other. Thus *Firebird,* a ballet pieced together from a half-dozen suitably Russian sources; the *Polovtsian Dances,* with its Golden Horde of real men; and the chilling, "Scythian" masses of *The Rite of Spring*. For Diaghilev and his fellow Petersburgers, there was no single way of being Russian or experiencing their own Russianness. The multiple aspects of the prewar Ballets Russes in part reflected this complex Petersburg identity.

Initially, the dancers who participated in Diaghilev's "Russian Seasons" came exclusively from the Imperial Theaters of St. Petersburg and Moscow. They danced in Paris over the long summer break, discovering a world that few Imperial dancers had seen. Most returned to Russia. Some, however, found the attractions of the West irresistible and resigned. The resignations increased dramatically when Diaghilev formed a permanent company in 1911. Nijinsky was among those who severed his ties with the Maryinsky that year, along with his sister, Bronislava, and Adolph Bolm. Many dancers, however, preferred to shuttle back and forth. They took frequent leaves, and so long as their requests were granted, they were happy to spend part of the year at home and part abroad.

It soon became evident that the Imperial Theaters could not satisfy Diaghilev's growing need for artists. By 1913, the company included more than a dozen Polish dancers and even a small handful of English ones, to say nothing of Russians trained outside the Imperial system. (Among them was Picasso's future wife, Olga Khokhlova.) Many more "outsiders" would join the Ballets Russes during and after World War I, even as Russians fleeing the Revolution would augment the company's diminished Russian contingent. The Russianness of the later Ballets Russes and its successor companies was not therefore a simple matter of ethnic origin. Rather, it represented a composite identity, at once cosmopolitan and parochial, international and émigré. On both counts, it clashed with the growing nationalism of institutions created in response to the Ballets Russes or reinvigorated by it.

In 1913, with *The Rite of Spring*, Diaghilev seemed to cast off his company's moorings in the Belle Epoque. No work would go further in rejecting the narrative and stylistic conventions of Petipa, to say nothing of elements such as turnout, ease, elegance, finish, refinement, grace, symmetry, and idealism that had defined ballet since the seventeenth century. Indeed, it is hard to imagine that Petipa's last four-act ballet, *The Magic Mirror,* a retelling of "Snow White and the Seven Dwarfs" described by Diaghilev as "unnecessary, boring, long, complicated, and pretentious,"[2] had premiered only ten years earlier. Petipa's ballets were compendia of different movement idioms, elaborated over time and coexisting within the framework of a single "grand ballet." The one-act ballets of Diaghilev's prewar repertory, by contrast, tended to explore these idioms individually, testing their expressive possibilities within a single work—the use of popular urban material in *Petrouchka,* classical dance in *Carnival* and *Le Spectre de la Rose,* pantomime (and "exotic" styles) in *Schéhérazade.* Thus, *The Rite of Spring* can be seen as testing the expressive boundaries of the "grotesque" dance, transforming this minor, even comic idiom (think of Carabosse and her train in *The Sleeping Beauty*) into a comprehensive vision infusing the Russian folk forms from which much of the ballet's movement derived. Musically, *The Rite of Spring* was just as path-breaking. Music critic Louis Laloy recalled the afternoon a few weeks before the premiere when Stravinsky had played a piano arrangement of the score with France's greatest composer, Claude Debussy: "We were dumbfounded," Laloy wrote, "overwhelmed by this hurricane which had come from the depths of the ages and which had taken life by the roots."[3]

Compared to Stravinsky's "hurricane," the season's other premieres were musically tame. The new ballets, in fact, were by French composers: *Jeux* had a commissioned score by Debussy, and *The Tragedy of Salomé* had music by Florent Schmitt originally composed for the dancer/choreographer Loie Fuller. Neither ballet left much of an mark. What did impress audiences were the operas that Diaghilev presented that season. One was *Boris Godunov*, with the great Russian basso, Fedor Chaliapin, in the title role, a reprise of the version Diaghilev had presented in 1908 but with new sets and costumes (the original ones having been sold to the Metropolitan Opera to pay off debts). The second was *Khovanshchina*, which was new to Paris and which, like *Boris*, had music by Mussorgsky. The productions were splendid, with sumptuous costumes, splendid singers, and a chorus from Moscow. Astruc later said they cost a half million francs, and the same again for the Ballets Russes.[4] No wonder he went bankrupt before the year was out!

During the prewar years, the Ballets Russes seldom performed on consecutive days, and, with three performances a week, the 1913 season was no exception. *Boris* and *Khovanshchina* filled in some of the gaps. Others were filled by Gabriel Fauré's "lyric poem" *Pénélope*, sometimes paired with Loie Fuller's multimedia staging of Debussy's *Nocturnes*. Preceding the season were several operas, including triumphant productions of Berlioz's *Benvenuto Cellini* and Carl Maria von Weber's *Der Freischütz*. (Weber's music for *Le Spectre de la Rose* could be heard throughout the Ballets Russes season). It was splendid company and identified the Ballets Russes with the blossoming of early twentieth-century lyric theater.

Diaghilev's early seasons in the French capital had taken place at the Théâtre du Châtelet, home of spectacle ballet and "high art" imports such as Richard Strauss' opera *Salomé*, and at the venerable Paris Opéra. In 1913, however, the Ballets Russes was among the attractions inaugurating Gabriel Astruc's splendid new theater, the Théâtre des Champs-Elysées. Just across the Seine from the Eiffel Tower, it was an homage to Art Nouveau and the Belle Epoque, a temple of the Muses, and a meeting ground of the international elite, which had contributed much of the money to build it. No expense had been spared. Advertisements for the theater promised "English comfort, German technology, and French taste."[5] It had wonderful acoustics, excellent sightlines, and the best equipped stage in Paris. And the theater was beautiful. Inside, frescoes by Maurice Denis covered the dome with scenes of music-making and dancing, ancient gods and barefoot nymphs. In one, a group from *Les Sylphides* appears; in another, Nijinsky holds Tamara Karsavina aloft. Nijinsky was also enthroned on the marble facade of the theater, dancing with Isadora Duncan, in a high relief by Antoine Bourdelle called "The Dance." "It is like a meditation," he later wrote. "At least, that is what I wished to create. Isadora moving and tossing back her lovely head, closes her eyes to dance inwardly in her pure emotion. . . . Nijinsky tear[ing] himself with a wild impulse from the marble that still holds him."[6]

Even more than Nijinsky, Duncan belonged to Paris. It was here that she had settled, refined her art, and achieved recognition as a uniquely American artist; it was here that she had met her Lohengrin, as she called Paris Singer in *My Life*, lived with him, fought with him, and given birth to their son, Patrick. In the last week of March, she presented *Orpheus* at the Trocadéro with students from her sister Elizabeth's school in Germany. There was music by the Colonne Orchestra, poetry, and even a lecture on Greek tragedy, all by distinguished French artistic figures. In April, the same week the Théâtre des Champs-Elysées opened, she moved to the Châtelet, where she presented *Iphigenia* to sold-out houses. And it was on April 19 that her children plunged into the Seine in a freak accident that killed them. "Nothing that has happened in a long time has so touched the hearts of Parisians," reported *The New York Times*. "All Paris is in mourning."[7]

However influential Duncan may have been, the Ballets Russes left a far deeper mark on the Paris dance world. The company inspired parodies and imitations as well as efforts to rejuvenate French ballet and to extend its visibility beyond the circle of Paris Opéra devotees. Ida Rubinstein, the exotic voluptuary of *Cléopâtre* and *Schéhérazade*, abandoned Diaghilev after the 1910 season, bored of "plastic movements, caresses, embraces, and stabbing herself."[8] She was rich and independent, and when the Italian poet Gabriele d'Annunzio announced that at long last he had found his St. Sebastian, she recreated herself as an actress and patron, returning to Russia only to raise funds for her multi-media extravaganzas. Her productions coincided with Diaghilev's; the two shared venues and artistic personnel, and competed for space in the same glossy magazines. *La Pisanelle, or The Perfumed Death*, a d'Annunzio play set in the High Middle Ages, opened at the Châtelet during the 1913 Ballets Russes season. With costumes and sets by Bakst, dances by Fokine, stage direction by Meyerhold, and with Rubinstein herself in the title role of the sinner-turned-saint, *La Pisanelle* recreated the St. Petersburg world of Diaghilev's earliest seasons. Like Duncan, Rubinstein was a personality, followed and photographed, caricatured and impersonated. One such impersonator actually appeared on the cover of *Le Théâtre* in 1913, in the exotic outfit she wore in the scene from a revue improbably set in a Boy Scout camp.

Rubinstein was not alone in appropriating or adapting elements of Diaghilev's "recipe." Natalia Trouhanova, another Russian transplant who made a career for herself in France as a concert dancer, challenged him on musical grounds. In 1912, only weeks before the premiere of *L'Après-midi d'un Faune*, she presented her most ambitious project yet—a series of ballets to modern

French music. Organized by Jacques Rouché, the founder of the innovative Théâtre des Arts (and future director of the Paris Opéra), the program included *La Péri*, which Diaghilev had inexplicably failed to produce; *Adélaïde, or The Language of Flowers*, to Ravel's "Valses nobles et sentimentales," now heard for the first time; Florent Schmitt's *Tragedy of Salomé*, which Diaghilev would use in 1913; and Vincent d'Indy's *Istar*. For M. D. Calvocoressi, a music critic who had worked closely with Diaghilev, Trouhanova had done what the impresario had only promised—serve the cause of modern French music.

Nationalism was indeed a theme of the Théâtre des Arts. Between 1910 and 1913, when Rouché was at the helm, it offered a Gallic antidote to the cosmopolitanism identified with the Ballets Russes. Rouché, wrote Maurice de Brunoff, was "an artist and friend of artists."[9] He produced works of exceptional artistic merit, designed by French artists and set to music by French composers. The repertory included dramas, as well as ballets, and long-forgotten hybrid genres—court ballet, lyric tragedy, opera-ballet—resurrected from the distant French past. Dance figured prominently in many works, including Ravel's *Ma Mère l'Oye*, which premiered in 1912 with choreography by Jane Hugard. Hugard had some connection with the Paris Opéra (although just what is impossible to say). Léo Staats, who had recently left the Opéra payroll, had a closer connection with the Rouché enterprise, "arranging" (as the phrase was) the dances in a number of productions. As for the dancers, a few were from the Opéra, and one, a very young Louis Aveline, may have been a student at its school. Mostly, however, the dancers hailed from the concert stage and commercial world, including the clowns Tommy and Georgey Foottit. Even if not all the fare was French in origin, the shaping and presentation of material conformed to notions of French elegance, artistry, and taste.

Meanwhile, the Paris Opéra Ballet was slowly stirring from its artistic slumber. In 1911, Ivan Clustine became the troupe's principal ballet master, succeeding Léo Staats and "Mlle. Stichel" (whose real name was Louise Manzini), one of the very few women to occupy this exalted post. Bolshoi-trained, Clustine brought to the Opéra choreographic experience both in his native Moscow (where Gorsky's rising star had overshadowed him) and in Paris, where he settled in 1903. He kept an eye on new trends and sought to accommodate them in his ballets for the Opéra. One, *Suite de Danses,* which premiered in 1913, had music by Chopin and evoked the poetic world of *Les Sylphides;* another, *Roussalka* (1911), had a distinctly Slavic ring. Although Mathilde Kchessinska and Nicolas Legat had paid occasional flying visits to the Opéra, its traditions remained intact. The corps was French, trained in the Opéra school; the étoiles were Italian. Carlotta Zambelli, who led the company in these years, was a ballerina of the old school whom even Diaghilev admired; he engaged her for the ill-fated Narodny Dom season in St. Petersburg that was destined never to materialize. Zambelli, wrote an enthusiast in 1913, "is the dance itself. She has lightness, grace, and art, that is, all the natural gifts combined with those gained through work."[10] The troupe's second ballerina was Aida Boni, whose much reproduced portrait by Frédéric Lauth was exhibited in the 1913 Salon of the Society of French Artists.[11]

From Paris the Ballets Russes went to London, which had now become its second most popular destination. Then, after a brief holiday, the company embarked for South America, its first overseas tour. Diaghilev stayed in Europe. He had no love of sea voyages, and there was much to attend to—ballets to plan, music by Bach, Monteclair, and Scarlatti to choose, designers like Benois to consult, composers, including Richard Strauss, to guide. He was in Venice when he heard the news of Nijinsky's marriage to Romola de Pulszky. He sobbed, shouted, and raged. He was jealous and his pride bitterly wounded. Diaghilev was never a man to accept defeat. He plowed on, making plans for Fokine to choreograph the new Strauss ballet and for Anna Pavlova to return. Autumn found him back in St. Petersburg, living at the Hôtel de l'Europe. He summoned Serge Grigoriev and ordered him to fire off a telegram to Nijinsky, dispensing with his future services. He then set off to woo Fokine. According to Grigoriev, it took a five-hour phone call for Diaghilev to accomplish this goal;[12] according to Fokine, he "made a most eloquent speech, trying to convince me that he was now wholeheartedly on my side, that his infatuation with his favourite was now long forgotten, and that it was only I who could now save the art of the Russian ballet . . . which now faced danger."[13] No one could be as persuasive as Diaghilev.

Now that he had dealt with personnel issues, Diaghilev set off with Fokine and Benois for Moscow. Here were the magnificent collections of contemporary art amassed by Shchukin and Morozov; here too were painters whose work lay at the forefront of the Russian avant-garde. Musically and choreographically, *The Rite of Spring* had broken new ground. In terms of design, however, it had remained loyal to the decorative aesthetic of *Mir iskusstva*. In Moscow, the three Petersburgers visited the studio of Natalia Goncharova, whose painting in 1913 and 1914 displayed the broad eclecticism of the prerevolutionary vanguard at its creative zenith: semi-abstract rayonist compositions; cubofuturist works; and a type of neoprimitivism that drew on Russian folk art. In August, she had staggered Moscow with a mammoth exhibition of 768 works, her entire output of the previous decade. Although Diaghilev could not have seen the show, he surely must have heard about it. In any event, he immediately enlisted Goncharova to design Rimsky-Korsakov's opera-ballet *Le Coq d'Or;* her brilliant palette and refined stylization of peasant motifs made it the one genuine success of the 1914 season. On that same trip, he also attended a performance at the Bolshoi, where he discovered the young man whom he would groom as a replacement for Nijinsky, both as a dancer and as a choreographer. This was Léonide Massine.

Not all avant-garde activity was centered in Moscow. In Petersburg that December, Russian futurism moved from the streets to the city's Luna Park. Here, among the merry-go-rounds and roller-coasters, the first futurist opera received its premiere. *Victory Over the Sun* was about a band of "Futurecountrymen" who set out to conquer the sun. The libretto was by the futurist poet Alexei Kruchenykh; the music by Mikhail Matyushin, and the sets and costumes by Kasimir Malevich, who in two years time would paint his first Suprematist—or wholly abstract—canvas. "A blinding light came from the projectors," Kruchenykh recalled. "The scenery was made of big sheets—triangles, circles, bits of machinery. The actors' masks reminded one of . . . gas masks. The costumes transformed the human anatomy, and the actors moved, . . . [to] the rhythm dictated by the artist and director."[14] "The theatre at Luna Park became a sort of Futurist salon," an enthusiast recalled. "Everyone came there: Futurist poets, critics and painters."[15] Although his presence remains unrecorded, it is easy to imagine Diaghilev among the crowds. In fact, *Victory Over the Sun* could well have been the catalyst of his futurist experiments of the war years.

Meanwhile, at the Maryinsky Theater, the "old ballet" held sway. We have no proof that Diaghilev attended any performances there, but given his wooing of Fokine and his always pressing need for dancers, one can safely assume that he did. In many respects, little had changed since 1909, when he had presented his first dance season in Paris. In 1913, between January 6 and April 28, when the season ended, the Imperial Ballet gave exactly twenty-one performances. The most popular works were Gorsky's version of *The Little Humpbacked Horse* with six performances; his *Don Quixote* with five, and Petipa's *Daughter of Pharaoh* with four. There were two performances each of *La Bayadère* and *Swan Lake*, one of *Paquita*, and one of a mixed bill, which included the only premiere of the period, Fokine's one-act *Les Préludes* (of which more later). It was a picture, duly recorded in the *Yearbooks of the Imperial Theaters*, of numbing sameness.

Things definitely perked up in the fall. Not only were there more performances (twenty-nine to the spring's twenty-one), but they offered greater variety. The season opened with *Raymonda*, with three additional full-lengths—*Don Quixote*, *Swan Lake*, and *The Nutcracker*—being given before the end of the year. (At this time *Nutcracker*, like *Giselle*, was routinely paired with a short ballet to fill out the bill; in this case the one-acts were Legat's *Fairy Doll* and Petipa's *Les Caprices du Papillon*.) What is astonishing, however, is the number of mixed bills—thirteen, or nearly half of the ballet performances between September and December. Among the works were *The Trials of Damis* and *The Seasons*, both choreographed by Petipa in 1900 for the Hermitage Theater; *Fairy Doll*, which the Legat brothers had choreographed in 1903; and no fewer than seven ballets by Fokine—*Le Pavillon d'Armide*, *Chopiniana*, *Egyptian Nights*, *Carnaval*, *Islamey*, *Papillons*, and *Les Préludes*. Versions of all these ballets existed in the West. *Islamey*, for instance, was a knockoff of *Schéhérazade*; *Egyptian Nights* and *Chopiniana* forerunners of *Cléopâtre* and *Les Sylphides*. *Les Préludes* entered the Maryinsky repertory less than three months after its premiere by the Pavlova company.

The sole new ballet produced at the Maryinsky in 1913, *Les Préludes* was inspired by Lamartine's *Poetic Meditations* and set to Liszt's tone poem. "The abstract ideas of this poem," explained Fokine to Cyril W. Beaumont in 1925, "were given symbolic form on the stage." Fokine defended his use of what he called "symphonic music." "Liszt was not thinking of ballet when he wrote his symphonic scene. Nor was Lamartine thinking about music when he wrote his philosophical poem." He then contrasted the premiere in Berlin, where the ballet was applauded by Richard Strauss and conductor Arthur Nikisch, to that in St. Petersburg, where the public was far less welcoming.[16]

Leading the attack was Fokine's nemesis André Levinson. He criticized just about every aspect of the ballet: the choice of music ("What vain vagary prompted [Fokine] to interpret . . . Liszt's romantic, pastoral and triumphant tone poem?"); the Duncan-inspired and Dalcroze-influenced choreography ("they join hands in a circle and rise on *demi-pointe* [Duncan's favorite motif] or . . . move in single file like a display of rhythmic gymnastics"); and the "vulgar symbolism" which reminded him of Leonid Andreyev's plays. He ended the diatribe by ascribing to Fokine "a vain wish to rival Dalcroze."[17]

Choreographer Fedor Lopukhov saw things a little differently. In *The Ballet Master and His Art,* published in 1925, he calls *Les Préludes* an early example of "dance symphonism," by which he meant that "the dances [were] based upon a thematic choreographic development that is strictly adhered to, without the addition of a single random movement."[18] Fokine was not alone in turning to Liszt at this time. In 1911, Diaghilev had toyed with the idea of using the Fourteenth Rhapsody. In 1916, Nijinsky was hoping to produce a ballet to Mephisto Valse, which his sister, Bronislava Nijinska, would stage in 1920, along with the composer's Twelfth Rhapsody.

Although the split between Russian ballet at home and Russian ballet abroad had widened by the eve of World War I, exchange between the two continued. The number of mixed bills and one-act ballets in the 1913 Maryinsky repertory reveals the impact both of the Diaghilev model and of Fokine's "new ballet," even if the "old ballet" continued to dominate (above all during the winter months). Many dancers shuttled back and forth, dancing abroad, without relinquishing their affiliation with the Imperial Theaters. This group included Fokine himself, who shared artistic direction of the Maryinsky troupe with the conservative Nicolas Legat. (The *Yearbooks of the Imperial Theaters* lists them in alphabetical order simply as "balletmasters.") Serge Grigoriev, Diaghilev's trusty *régisseur,* and his wife Lubov Tchernicheva, also remained on the Imperial payroll; whatever bad blood may have existed between Diaghilev and the director of the Imperial Theaters, Vladimir Telyakovsky, this did not preclude dancers taking regular leaves of absence. In any event, with ninety-four women and seventy-two men, plus guest artists, the troupe was hardly strapped for manpower. In fact many dancers joined the Ballets Russes on an occasional basis, eager, one imagines, to see the world and make some extra money. One of the few who never did was Agrippina Vaganova, the celebrated pedagogue, on whose watch as future director of the Leningrad company most of Fokine's works disappeared from repertory.

If there was a shortage, it was at the ballerina level. Kchessinska, for instance, made only one or two appearances a season. Pavlova paid a short visit to Petersburg, dancing her last performances—ever—at the Maryinsky in January and February 1913—a string of *Don Quixotes* and *Daughter of Pharaohs*, and, two days after the jubilee performance marking the three hundredth anniversary of the House of Romanov, *La Bayadère*. Audiences received her rapturously, and the Tsar made a point of receiving her on the two occasions when he attended her performances. Olga Preobrajenska danced several ballerina roles—Sugar Plum in *The Nutcracker*, Swanilda in *Coppélia*, the title role in *Raymonda*, Colombine in *Harlequinade*—as well as performing in several Fokine and one-act Petipa ballets. The busiest of the senior ballerinas was Karsavina, who appeared in most of the Fokine ballets as well as the "old" repertory, dancing Sugar Plum, Kitri in *Don Quixote*, Odette-Odile in *Swan Lake*, Nikiya in *La Bayadère*, the Tsar Maiden in *The Little Humpbacked Horse*, and the title role of *Paquita*. In spring 1914, she would add Giselle and Aurora to the list. Other ballerina roles were filled by Lubov Egorova, Elena Smirnova, and Vaganova, although none of them ever attained the unchallenged supremacy of a Kchessinska or Pavlova. Meanwhile, in September 1913, Olga Spessivtseva made her debut in *Raymonda*, while another debutante, Felia Doubrovska (or Dluzhnevskaia), appeared as Cleopatra in *Egyptian Nights*. A new generation of ballerinas was in the making.

In her essay "Mr. Bennett and Mrs. Brown," Virginia Woolf says that "on or about December, 1910, human character changed."[19] It is tempting to say that in 1913 something similar happened in ballet, that after Nijinsky's *Rite of Spring* nothing was ever quite the same. But reality, as always, is messier and more complicated than sweeping theories, however seductive. Nothing springs entirely from a void, and nothing ever completely dies. Old and new are locked in a symbiotic relationship. At no time was this clearer than in 1913, where in Paris no less than St. Petersburg, *The Rite of Spring* and *Victory Over the Sun*, radically new artistic works, erupted on the artistic landscape. Their impact was long felt, and *The Rite of Spring*, especially, became a symbol of the ephemerality of an art form that consumes its original in the act of performance. At the same time, the "old" world continued to thrive. Indeed, reading over the lists of ballets and roles in the *Yearbooks of the Imperial Theaters*, one is struck by how little has changed over the course of a century. Even if the choreography is different, the ballets are the same—*Raymonda, Swan Lake, Nutcracker, Bayadère, Giselle, Don Q, The Little Humpbacked Horse*. It's almost like being in a time warp. Institutions are an inherently conservative force. They don't promote change. On the contrary, they ensure stability. Thus, it is no accident that *Victory Over the Sun* came into being in an amusement park or that *The Rite of Spring* was born in a touring company. "In an itinerant theatre you risk something fundamental each minute," Benois wrote just after the premiere of *Petrouchka*.[20] With *The Rite of Spring*, Diaghilev took the biggest risk of all and scored his greatest triumph.

NOTES

1. Quoted in Vera Stravinsky and Robert Craft, *Stravinsky in Pictures and Documents* (London: Hutchinson, 1979), p. 101.

2. Sergei Diaghilev, Letter to the Editor, in Roland John Wiley, *A Century of Russian Ballet: Documents and Eyewitness Accounts, 1810–1910* (Oxford: Clarendon Press, 1990), p. 421.

3. Quoted in Edward Lockspeiser, *Debussy: His Life and Mind,* rev. ed. (Cambridge: Cambridge University Press, 1978), vol. 2, p. 181.

4. Gabriel Astruc, *Le Pavillon des Fantômes* (Paris: Grasset, 1929), pp. 286–287.

5. Quoted in Vera Krasovskaya, *Nijinsky,* trans. John E. Bowlt (New York: Schirmer Books, 1979), p. 248.

6. Quoted in Michel Dufet, "Bourdelle and the Dance," *Bourdelle and the Dance: Isadora and Nijinsky* (Paris: Arted, 1969), n.p. "The Dance" is reproduced in Plate 99. Maurice Denis' frescoes for the dome are reproduced in L. Dimier, "Le Théâtre des Champs-Elysées: Décoration par Maurice Denis," *Le Théâtre*, April 1913, II, pp. 4–17.

7. Quoted in Peter Kurth, *Isadora: A Sensational Life* (Boston: Little Brown, 2001), p. 297.

8. Prince Peter Lieven, *The Birth of Ballets-Russes* (London: Allen and Unwin, 1936), p. 119.

9. Maurice de Brunoff, "La Direction nouvelle de l'Opéra," *Comoedia Illustré,* 5 November 1913, p. 92.

10. Georges de Dubor, "Au Foyer de la Danse: Théâtre National de l'Opéra," *Le Théâtre,* September 1913, I, p. 16.

11. See, for example, the frontispiece of *Le Théâtre,* July 1913, II.

12. S. L. Grigoriev, *The Diaghilev Ballet 1909–1929,* trans. and ed. Vera Bowen (London: Constable, 1953), p. 92.

13. Michel Fokine, *Memoirs of a Ballet Master,* trans. Vitale Fokine, ed. Anatole Chujoy (New York: Little, Brown, 1961), p. 224.

14. Quoted in RoseLee Goldberg, *Performance: Live Art 1909 to the Present* (New York: Abrams, 1979), pp. 24–26.

15. Quoted *ibid.,* p. 24.

16. Letter to Cyril W. Beaumont, in M. Fokin, *Protiv techniia: vospominaniia baletmeistera, stat'i, pis'ma* (Leningrad: Iskusstvo, 1962), p. 503.

17. André Levinson, *Ballet Old and New,* trans. Susan Cook Summer (New York: Dance Horizons, 1982), pp. 88–90.

18. *Fedor Lopukhov: Writings on Ballet and Music,* ed. and introd. Stephanie Jordan, trans. Dorinda Offord (Madison: University of Wisconsin Press, 2002), p. 100.
19. Virginia Woolf, "Mr. Bennett and Mrs. Brown," in *The Captain's Bed and Other Essays* (New York: Harcourt Brace Jovanovich, 1950), p. 96.
20. Roland John Wiley, "Benois' Commentaries, Part VI," *The Dancing Times,* March 1981, p. 390.

DANCE, FILM, AND THE BALLETS RUSSES

On 29 December 1921, as *The Sleeping Princess* entered the second month of its run at London's Alhambra Theatre, *The Times* announced that a plan was afoot to film the ballet. Amazingly, the initiative came from the inveterately anti-populist Diaghilev himself. Impressed by the film version of *The Three Musketeers* that Walter Wanger was then presenting at Covent Garden to music "synchronized" by conductor Eugene Goosens, Diaghilev had come to the conclusion "that the same method might be applied to bring about the more general appreciation of classical *ballet*." "It has [also] been suggested," continued *The Times,* "that the film be done in natural colours in the same way as *The Glorious Adventure*, the next production to be shown at Covent Garden [and] the first British film of the kind to be carried out in colours. In this way the glories of M. Bakst's costumes would not be lost, and the whole action of the *ballet* would be materially assisted."[1] The scheme, as indicated by a follow-up article, was part of a larger undertaking to "produce original films built up on original musical scores and on the scores of a number of existing operas." The artistic side was entrusted to motion picture newcomers—the painters Augustus John and S. H. Sime—who were to "concern themselves with the settings," and the composer Josef Holbrooke, who was to "provide much of the music."[2] In other words, the plan was intended to appropriate the "cheap and rapidly breeding cinema," in T. S. Eliot's words,[3] for the purposes of "high art," the reason Diaghilev would have entertained the idea in the first place.

Neither *The Sleeping Princess* nor any other Ballets Russes production was ever filmed. Yet the cinema, which came of artistic age during the life span of the company, shadowed virtually every stage of its development. Diaghilev himself, with his deep-seated mistrust of mass culture and its allied forms of mechanical reproduction, had little use for film: in his mind, it belonged to the world of popular entertainment—to the music halls, for instance, where, by the late 1890s, biographs and "cinématographes" were sharing bills with clowns, acrobats, singers, mimes, comedians, cyclists, instrumentalists, and dancers of every variety, including ballet. Just as in his early days as an impresario he insisted on identifying his company exclusively with "high art" venues and audiences and dissociating it from the "popular" ballet tradition linked to music hall

This article was originally published in German translation in *Spiegelungen: Die Ballets Russes und die Künst*, ed. Claudia Jeschke, Ursel Berg, and Birgit Zeidler (Berlin: Verlay Vorwerk 8, 1997). It was subsequently published in *Dance Research*, 16, no. 1 (Summer 1998).

and spectacle shows, so he took pains throughout his career to restrict the use of film and cinematic borrowings. Indeed, in almost every instance where they do appear in Ballets Russes productions, they had already undergone an aestheticizing process that at least partly transformed their original identity and gave them currency as high art. At the same time, especially during the pre–World War I period, there are parallels between the two media that suggest the existence of a common source on which film and ballet equally drew, while in the years that immediately followed, film drew on approaches associated with the ballet stage and, in Russia especially, ideas put into currency by the "new dance." The rebirth of twentieth-century ballet coincided with the birth of film as an art form: never again would the two media be so close as during that period of genesis.

In 1914, Michel Fokine laid out the principles of his "new ballet" in an article published in the letter columns of *The Times*. Although the cinema is nowhere mentioned, his "rules" suggest a number of parallels between the "new ballet" and film. One is the emphasis on naturalism. "Dancing and mimetic gesture," he stated,

> have no meaning in a ballet unless they serve as an expression of its dramatic action. . . . [T]he new ballet admits the use of conventional gesture only where it is required by the style of the ballet, and in all other cases endeavours to replace gestures of the hands by [a] mimetic of the whole body. Man can be and should be expressive from head to foot.[4]

Fokine's revolt against the stylized pantomime and "conventional system of gesticulation" of the "old ballet" and his insistence that they be replaced by a more natural style of acting paralleled the changes in acting on the drama stage of the immediately preceding decades while coinciding with the requirements of silent screen acting. The contrast between the gestural histrionics of Sarah Bernhardt and the infinitely more subtle mimetic effects of Eleanora Duse—both preserved on film—sums up this shift, while revealing the obvious superiority of Duse's approach in exploiting the possibilities of the new medium.

Fokine's embrace of naturalism almost certainly had its source in the psychological realism of the Moscow Art Theater. He was in the audience for its first performances in St. Petersburg, and must have viewed its evocative reconstructions of character and place, especially in its performances of Chekhov, as a thrilling alternative to acting on the ballet stage, which, as he wrote in 1916, "essayed to express a psychological feeling by a fixed movement, or series of movements, which could neither describe nor symbolise anything."[5] The dancers formed under his aegis—Vaslav Nijinsky, Anna Pavlova, Tamara Karsavina, to name only the most celebrated—were all superb dancer-actors who changed personalities with their roles, "subordinat[ing]," as Pavlova explained it, the "physical elements to a psychological concept."[6]

In this process, rhythmic gesture played a crucial role. To be sure, as an action performed in time and generally to music, all dance gesture is in some measure rhythmic. However, where conventional ballet mime gestures were fixed in meaning and shape, Fokine's "expressive signs" were open-ended: their form varied, and they acquired meaning from the musical and dramatic contexts in which they appeared. In this sense, they closely resembled the "choreographed" gesture of silent film, where, as in the "new ballet," physical expressiveness was at a premium. Although the conventionalized gestures of a Bernhardt might enhance the words they accompanied, they could not make up for the absence of speech. As much as the "new ballet," then, the silent screen called for actors who embodied Fokine's "mimetic of the whole body." Discussing the progressive tendency of modern choreography to "eliminate the artificial dividing line between dancing and mime," the British music critic Edwin Evans insisted in *The Dancing Times* that the "point of intersection" between ballet and cinema lay in the "art of rhythmic movement . . . one and indivisible."[7] Serafima Astafieva, a former Diaghilev dancer, described the connection between the two media even more succinctly. "The cinema *is* mime," she told readers of the magazine in 1917.[8]

No wonder so many early Ballets Russes dancers were tempted by the cinema. In 1919, ten years after she had dazzled Paris audiences in the title role of *Cléopâtre*, Ida Rubinstein appeared as the exotic heroine of *La Nave*, a screen version of Gabriele d'Annunzio's play directed by his son. In 1921, at the height of her fame, Karsavina played a Belle Epoque Parisian dancer in a film dramatization of Arnold Bennett's *The Old Wives Tale*. Ever a pioneer, Anna Pavlova had taken the plunge six years earlier, appearing as Fenella in a cinematic version of the Auber opera *The Dumb Girl of Portici*. In this "straight" dramatic role (augmented with dances to satisfy her fans), she displayed the rhythmic subtlety, gestural expressiveness, and luminous facial expression of an ideal Fokine dancer who was equally at home in the new medium. Another fascinating experiment by a Diaghilev star was *The Dance of Death*, a film of Adolph Bolm's ballet *Danse Macabre* produced in 1922 by Dudley Murphy. (Two years later, Murphy collaborated with the painter Fernand Léger on *Le Ballet mécanique*, one of the earliest abstract films.) The first in a projected series of twelve "visual symphonies"— filmed dance interpretations of classical music—*The Dance of Death* was advertised as the first dance film to be synchronized with a sound score.[9]

The roster of Diaghilev's early seasons also included two dancers who eventually made long-term careers in film. One was Vera Karalli, a protégée of the Bolshoi choreographer Alexander Gorsky, who became one of the Russian cinema's first silent screen stars. Like Fokine, Gorsky had fallen under the sway of the Moscow Art Theater, and during the years he directed the Bolshoi company, he formed a brilliant constellation of dancer-actors. A dark-haired beauty, Karalli had the plasticity that Gorsky prized highly in his dancers, and he cast her in works, such as *Nur and Anitra*, influenced by the "free" dance style of Isadora

Duncan. Her screen credits included *Do You Remember?*, *Chrysanthemums*, *War and Peace* (in which she played the role of Natasha), and *The Dying Swan*. In *Chrysanthemums*, she performed a Duncan-style dance—choreographed in all likelihood by Gorsky—that ended with her dying on a bed of flowers.[10]

Even more amazing was the film career of Theodore Koslov, another Bolshoi dancer who came to the fore under Gorsky. Koslov left the Ballets Russes after the first season, long enough to "steal" Fokine's choreography of *Cléopâtre* and *Les Sylphides*, which, along with *Schéhérazade*, he restaged in New York for Gertrude Hoffmann's "Saison Russe." Eventually, he made his way to Hollywood and in 1917 went to work for Cecil B. DeMille. His screen debut as the Aztec leader Guatemoc in *The Woman God Forgot* was the first of many "exotic" roles he played as a member of DeMille's repertory company. "When I first saw Kosloff," wrote the director's niece Agnes de Mille of her future teacher,

> he was naked in feathers, leaning on a feathered spear. He had painted himself horned eyebrows in the Russian Ballet style, and his gestures were real classic pantomime, involving clenched fists and the whites of the eyeballs, a positive style which gave the camera something substantial to focus on. Here was passion and here certainly was sincerity in amounts. Every expression was performed with a force that could have carried him across the room and over the wall. I was awe-struck.[11]

During the 1920s, Kosloff was involved in almost every film DeMille made. He served in many capacities—actor, dancer, choreographer, technical art director, and unofficial advisor. A close friend of the director, Kosloff also acted as an aide-de-camp in staging the huge crowd scenes, often in the form of flashbacks and supplied with extras from his school, that were a trademark of DeMille's films. With their exotic backgrounds (ancient Babylonia in *Why Change Your Wife?*, ancient Rome in *Manslaughter*, ancient Palestine in *The King of Kings*) and fantastic orgies (the jazz dance in *Saturday Night* took place in a swimming pool), these scenes recalled not only the bacchanalias of Fokine's *Cléopâtre* and *Schéhérazade* but also the spectacular crowds of Gorsky's productions at the Bolshoi, especially *Don Quixote* and *Salammbô*, in which Kosloff had also danced.[12] Like Fokine's dances for the "Oriental" extravaganzas *Aphrodite* and *Mecca*, his first major commissions in the United States,[13] Kosloff's film work plundered an earlier style of European "high art" to entertain the American masses.[14]

Although Kosloff's career, like Karalli's, reveals a direct link between the new dance and film, it was Russia's theatrical culture that served as the major transmission point between the two media. Even before the 1910s, when choreography became what film scholar Mikhail Yampolsky has called "a metamodel for the performing arts,"[15] the Moscow Art Theater offered classes in expressive movement. Initially taught by Mikhail Mordkin, a Gorsky protégé, they were later taken over by Eli Kniepper (Rabanek), one of Duncan's early Russian followers: among her students was Alisa Koonen, who became a leading actress of Alexander Tairov's Kamerny Theater.[16] At St. Petersburg's Antique Theater, co-founded by Nikolai Evreinov in 1907, the dances were confided initially to Fokine and subsequently to Valentin Presniakov, a Maryinsky and sometime Ballets Russes colleague who also taught classes to the actors in "plastique."[17] Dance figured prominently in Evreinov's Crooked Mirror Theater, which offered hilarious parodies of *Giselle, Swan Lake,* and *Esmeralda* and impersonations *en travesti* of Duncan and Maud Allan by the company's in-house "ballerina" Nikolai Barabanov.[18] At the Liteiny Theater, another artists' cabaret, Boris Romanov choreographed *The Goatlegged,* a ballet that satirized the bacchanalia of Fokine's *Daphnis and Chloe* and had Anna Akhmatova's inamorata, Olga Glebova Sudeikina, as its sensational star.[19] Romanov also staged dances with "a touch of an orgiastic bouquet" (as Akim Volynsky later wrote) at another bohemian cabaret, the Stray Dog, where Karsavina herself occasionally performed.[20]

According to the choreographer Lasar Galpern, who served as ballet master and teacher of gesture at Moscow's Jewish State Theater from 1919 to 1923 and staged the first German *Rite of Spring* in 1930, it was Tairov who "first . . . made his actors real dancers."[21] Movement played an extensive part in Tairov's productions: Indeed, on the Kamerny stage, as John E. Bowlt has observed, "theatre once again became a kinetic rather than a literary or decorative experience."[22] Several of his actors had dance training—Koonen, Alexander Rumnev (who may have studied with Mordkin),[23] and Vera de Bosset (later Stravinsky), who had studied ballet at Lydia Nelidova's Moscow studio and later played the role of the Queen in Diaghilev's *Sleeping Princess.* While acting with Tairov, she became a well-known film actress, appearing in *War and Peace* and starring in a number of comedies opposite one of the sons of Marius Petipa.[24]

Tairov, in fact, was deeply enamoured of ballet. He admired Pavlova, adopted much from Fokine, and had worked with Boris Romanov. In a 1921 article, he called ballet dancers "the *only* actors in contemporary theatre who understand the significance of the corporeal in our art."[25] His productions, theater historian Konstantin Rudnitsky has observed, emphasized a "balletic coordination of movements," "beauty and purity of pose and gesture," and a "balletic method of organizing space," which "allowed the actors to demonstrate . . . their physical virtuosity." When rehearsing Koonen in the title role of *Sakuntala,* Tairov advised her to study Duncan, explaining that in her dancing "there is a kind of earthly gravitation which seems to make the gesture heavier, creating its volume."[26] In *Famira Kifared,* where he gave much thought to equalizing the status of body movement and speech, "the lightness and ease of the theatrical language," notes Rudnitsky, "was accompanied by a slow heaviness of movement and the deep, guttural singing by the tense excitement of the dance."[27] And he confided the design of this and other key productions to Alexandra Exter, whose interest in "'rhythmically organized space' pointed forward," as John Bowlt has said, "to her Constructivist designs for the movie *Aelita*,"[28] even as it coincided with the initial stage of her collaboration with choreographer Bronislava Nijinska.[29]

Meyerhold, too, viewed movement as integral to the stage, although, unlike Tairov, he had little use for ballet as such. Nevertheless, many of his experiments, from the slow, "signifying" movement, "inner rhythm," and "sculptural expressiveness" of his symbolist phase, to the use of commedia dell'arte devices in his studio work, and the "études" that were the embryo of his later system of biomechanics, resonated with certain aspects of Ballets Russes productions.[30] If anything, the post-Revolutionary development of biomechanics only enhanced the importance of rhythm. "Through biomechanics," writes Rudinitsky, "Meyerhold turned rhythm into a component of the performance which created form and also gave it content. The rhythmic organisation of a role entailed the impulsive reflexive link between thought and movement, emotion and movement, speech and movement. . . . Every movement, whether . . . intended . . . or not, acquired sculptural form and significance."[31] As a disciple of Meyerhold in this period, Sergei Eisenstein absorbed these ideas, which not only found their way into his early films but also were connected directly to his experience of dance. Recalling his fox trot lessons with Valentin Parnakh in 1921, he wrote: "in contradistinction to the dances of my youth, with their strictly prescribed patterns and rotation of movement, the fox trot was a 'free dance,' held together only by a strict rhythm, on the framework of which one could embroider any freely improvised movement. . . . Here . . . [was] that captivating free running line, subordinated only to the inner law of rhythm."[32]

Dance also figured prominently in Lev Kuleshov's theory and practice of montage. Like many pioneering Russo-Soviet filmmakers, he was deeply interested in Delsartian theories of gesture and Dalcrozian ideas of rhythm, especially as these were reinterpreted in the 1910s by Prince Sergei Volkonsky, the former director of the Imperial Theaters under whom Diaghilev had briefly served. Volkonsky himself taught briefly at the First State Cinema School, which was set up after the Revolution by Vladimir Gardin, as did Kuleshov and Nikolai Foregger, known in the 1920s for his "machine dances." The school maintained close ties with the Experimental Heroic Theater directed by Boris Ferdinandov, who had developed a Dalcrozian-inspired system known as "metro-rhythm." Kuleshov was especially close to this group, and two of his earliest montage experiments involved dance. "The question of dance," wrote Valentin Turkin in 1925,

> has a special significance for contemporary cinema and, in particular, for the mastery of film acting. The search for strict artistic form in cinema is moving towards the measured construction of the actor's movement on the screen and of the rhythmic montage of the film, i.e., towards the creation from the movement on

the screen of a kind of "dance" . . . Film drama is trying to immerse itself in the culture of dance, in rhythm, so that it actually becomes "dance," a sort of contemporary, realistic or, if you prefer, analytical or biomechanical ballet.[33]

For all the crossovers and parallels linking dance and film during the early years of the Ballets Russes, the cinema left no discernible mark on the company's aesthetic. With the First World War, this ceased to be the case. Diaghilev's discovery of the Italian futurists and embrace of Cocteau's "poetry of the everyday" prompted a sea change in his attitude toward film, which now made its appearance in Ballets Russes productions as a sign of modernity and as a choreographic strategy.

In September 1916, accompanied by choreographer Léonide Massine and a skeleton company of dancers, Diaghilev settled in Rome. By the following winter, three works were on the way—*The Good-Humoured Ladies, Fireworks,* and *Parade*—in which the influence of film was palpable. In Rome, Diaghilev renewed his contacts with the futurists that the company's American tour had interrupted. The year 1916 was a productive one for futurist cinema. No fewer than four futurist or futurist-inspired films were made that year—*Vita futurista, Il perfido incanto, Thais,* and *Il mio cadavere.* Of these, the most important for the Ballets Russes was *Vita futurista,* which involved several artists close to Diaghilev, including Filippo Marinetti, with whom he had briefly entertained the possibility of an "alliance,"[34] and Giacomo Balla, who would create the set and lighting design of *Fireworks.* Another futurist with an interest in cinema whom Diaghilev commissioned in this period was Fortunato Depero.[35] "It is necessary," Depero asserted in his 1916 manifesto "Notes on the Theatre," "to add to theatre everything that is suggested by cinematography." "*Why does cinematography triumph?,*" he asked. "It wins because it is fast, because it moves and transforms rapidly, . . . is varied and rich, improvised, and surprising. . . . Cinematography, removed from the assassin's hands of certain reconstructors of historical dramas . . . and of melancholy makers of banal human passions . . . will become a powerful means of artistic creation."[36] "The Futurist Cinema," a manifesto by Marinetti, Balla, and others published in November 1916, echoed these visionary ideas. The futurist cinema, proclaimed the authors, was "an alogical fleeting synthesis of life," "a school of joy, of speed, of force," a "polyexpressive symphony." At the same time, they singled out as attributes of the new cinema such techniques as "simultaneity and interpenetration of different times and places" and "unreal reconstructions of the human body."[37]

Such ideas left a deep imprint on Massine's developing sensibility as a choreographer. Beginning with *The Good-Humoured Ladies,* simultaneity and speed became preeminent features of his choreography. In seeming response to the futurist call for the "interpenetration" of time and place, he compressed Goldoni's play into one act, balancing the action simultaneously on both sides of the stage so as to retain all the complications of the plot. At the same time, he speeded up the dance gesture and used broken, angular movements to distort it; he stressed dynamism through continual movement, and strove for what he called a "synthesis of movement and form" or "choreography and plastic art."[38] He was fascinated by Charlie Chaplin and gave Niccolò, the waiter in *Ladies,* a "whimsical side-way shuffle" (as Cyril W. Beaumont described it)[39] that recalled the star's distinctive gait. And it was in Rome that Massine bought his first camera. "I take great interest in cinematography," he wrote to a Moscow friend, Anatoly Bolchakov. "I tried to shoot movies, but so far did not succeed."[40]

Of all the works produced by Diaghilev in this period, *Fireworks,* to Stravinsky's music of the same title, most closely approximated film. Balla's mise-en-scène for this short piece—a light show played on a setting of geometrical solids—epitomized the brevity, dynamism, and abstraction to which futurist theater aspired. "He filled the stage," critic Maurizio Fagiolo dell'Arco has written, "with disturbing crystalline forms, beams of colored light, coral formations, symbols of the infinite (spirals and running light-waves), emblems of light (obelisk, pyramids, rays of sunlight and sickle-moons), aerodynamic symbols (flights of swifts and firebirds). It was all projected onto a black backdrop, illuminated from behind with red rays."[41] The emphasis on light, the idea of phenomena in constant mutation, and the use of images inspired by the natural world suggest an influence on Balla even more powerful than futurism—that of Loie Fuller. Indeed, only a week before the opening of Diaghilev's last prewar season, she had presented her own version of the Stravinsky piece at the Théâtre du Châtelet, an "orgy of color, light, and sound,"[42] deploying, as critic Emile Vuillermoz wrote, "all her virtuosity and all her inventive genius."[43] Although Fuller herself is not mentioned in Depero's "Notes on the Theatre," her work certainly embodied the "plastic-magic phenomena" that he espoused in his "vast re-creation of mimicry."[44] Moreover, as Giovanni Lista has pointed out in his recent biography of the dancer, the "Dance of Geometric Splendor" in *Vita futurista* was actually an adaptation of Fuller's *La Danse de l'acier.*[45] By eliminating the human element, as her *Fireworks* had not, Diaghilev's chromokinetic experiment achieved the paradoxical status of an abstract film realized through the medium of the stage.

However intriguing this line of experiment may have been, Diaghilev did not pursue it. Indeed, as Bronislava Nijinska later noted, he had little sympathy for ballets "without libretti."[46] He found abstraction "foreign," and even in works such as *La Chatte* or *Ode* that made use of abstract elements, he insisted upon a libretto detailing the mimetic action. This is not to say that film as such vanished from the Ballets Russes repertory. However, with the exception of *Ode* (of which more later), its influence was circumscribed: it became a touchstone of the everyday, a sign denoting the pleasures of modern life.

In this, no one proved more influential than Jean Cocteau. His ballet *Parade,* produced by Diaghilev in 1917, was a paean to what he called the "music of everyday"—variety, circus, jazz, and cinema. Movies, especially America movies, fascinated him. He loved Westerns, and pictured himself in his letters as living in "Texas" or "a corner of the Far West."[47] And, like Massine—as well as Diaghilev, for that matter—he adored Chaplin, a "modern Punch [who] speaks to all ages, to all peoples."[48] Cocteau's notes for the ballet's "Little American Girl" are full of cinematic allusions, and even those for the Chinese Conjuror, a role partly inspired by the magician Chung Ling Soo, include a reference to the "silence of thunderous events in silent films."[49]

Movies were not simply a "popular resource"[50] in *Parade*. They were also a cornerstone of the American myth that now made its debut in Cocteau's work. "The United States," he wrote in 1919, "evokes a girl more interested in her health than in her beauty. She swims, boxes, dances, leaps onto moving trains—all without knowing that she is beautiful. It is we who admire her face, on the screen—enormous, like the face of a goddess."[51] Under Cocteau's tutelage, Massine's American Girl evoked the "reality" of her celluloid counterpart. "Wearing a blazer and a short white skirt," the choreographer wrote,

> she bounced on to the stage, crossing it in a succession of convulsive leaps, her arms swinging widely. She then did an imitation of the shuffling walk of Charlie Chaplin, followed by a sequence of mimed actions reminiscent of *The Perils of Pauline*—jumping on to a moving train, swimming across a river, having a running fight at pistol-point, and finally finding herself lost at sea in the tragic sinking of the *Titanic*. All this was ingeniously danced and mimed by Maria Chabelska who interpreted Satie's syncopated ragtime music with great charm and gusto, and brought the dance to a poignant conclusion when, thinking herself a child at the seaside, she ended up playing in the sand.[52]

Although *Parade* announced the modernism of Diaghilev's new aesthetic, his artistic "recipe" for the next several years pointedly excluded Cocteau's "gentrified" populism. Indeed, between 1917 and 1924, when *Le Train Bleu* came to the stage, allusions to film—and contemporary pastimes in general—were noticeably absent from the Ballets Russes stage. Ironically, it was during these same years that film discovered dance in a big way. In May 1922, the French monthly *La Danse* commended Pathé-Revue's new weekly feature of the best dances and dancers from leading Paris and foreign theaters. It also praised an "astonishing" new process—slow motion—that thanks to the Pathé Ultra Rapid Camera, the company had used in dance filming as early as 1919.[53] (In September of that year, *The Dancing Times* published a "specimen" of the new process—a still from "The Jigg.")[54] Many writers noted the educational aspect of the new technique, which opened up "interesting possibilities for analysing and demonstrating dance steps"[55] and led one French publishing house to "shoot . . . an entire series of modern dances," with on-screen explanations of how to do them.[56] *Dancing Grace*, filmed by Pathé in the early 1920s, shows Lydia Lopokova bounding across a lawn with gravity-defying lightness, a hint at the artistic effects that slow motion could generate. However, it was Loie Fuller, in her 1920 feature-length film *Le Lys de la vie,* who explored the new technique for poetic ends, creating fleeting, dreamlike images that "freed" the medium from "illusionism" and imbued it with fantasy.[57]

Cocteau was fascinated by slow motion. He used it in *Le Boeuf sur le toit,* presented in 1920 at the Comédie des Champs-Elysées, and in *Les Mariés de la Tour Eiffel,* produced the following year by the Ballets Suédois. Like freeze framing, another technique borrowed from the cinema, slow motion also appeared in *Le Train Bleu,* most notably in Scene 5, where the "tarts" and "gigolos" at play on a Riviera beach glimpse an airplane passing overhead. Cocteau's scenario contains many film allusions. In Scene 9, for instance, when the Tennis Champion and Golf Player come to blows, he writes: "The one who receives them should stoop; the one who delivers them should be carried away by the gesture into nothingness, turning in place, etc. . . . (Think of Ch. Chaplin's battles.) Tarts and gigolos shoot movies, take pictures, wind film, keep score, etc."[58] And in Scene 10, as Perlouse and Beau Gosse move to center stage for a final embrace, he adds, "like the end of adventure films."[59]

References to movies appeared in other ballets as well. *Within the Quota,* a 1923 Ballets Suédois offering, featured a Mary Pickford type ("The Sweetheart of the World"), who transformed the hero, a Swedish immigrant newly arrived in New York, into a movie star. With a jazzy score by Cole Porter that spoofed the plunkings of movie house accompanists, the ballet poked fun at Hollywood conventions—even as it imitated them. *La Pastorale,* which Diaghilev produced in 1926, aped such conventions as well. In fact, part of the action—devised by Boris Kochno—actually took place on a movie set. "The members of a film company arrive to 'shoot a scene,'" wrote Cyril W. Beaumont in his "annal" for 1926:

> The operators set up their cameras and the producer indicates what is to be done. The Star and two actors go through a scene. . . . The telegraph boy awakes and is amazed to find himself alone with the Star. They fall in love and stroll away. The producer and his staff begin an agitated search for the Star. . . . [T]he boy return[s] arm-in-arm with the Star, . . . the boy disappears. The members of the film company depart.[60]

With twelve scenes, a large number of rostrums and screens on wheels, the production was not only trite but also unwieldy.

Although Diaghilev toyed with film as a setting and a mimetic device, it was his rival Rolf de Maré who first made it part of the text of a ballet. Premiered in 1924 by the Ballets Suédois, *Relâche* was an event in the history of avant-garde performance. With a scenario by the painter Francis Picabia,[61] who designed the remarkable sets, the ballet included a cinematic interlude, *Entr'acte,* that has since become a film classic. *Entr'acte* was directed by René Clair, who had made his first on-screen appearance in Loie Fuller's *Le Lys de la vie* and his debut as a director in 1923 with *Paris qui dort*. *Entr'acte* had no story or narrative logic, and its images—a cannon dancing a gig, a runaway casket that exploded like a grenade—were treated as dynamic events, liberated (in Jacques Bourgeois's phrase) "from the obligation to convey meaning."[62] The action of the ballet—which included the dancers stripping from formal attire to tights and then dressing again, miming the words to Satie's music for "The Dog's Tail," and pouring water from one bucket to another—had little obvious connection to the film. Indeed, most of the staged action, a combination of mime and what today would be called "pedestrian" movement, was the antithesis of Clair's exuberant images and dynamic editing.[63]

In 1928, when film made its belated appearance on the Ballets Russes stage, it was over strong objections from Diaghilev. The result, however, was a deeply poetic work, one that, despite the incoherence of the scenario (by Kochno) and the mediocre music (by Nicolas Nabokov), was transformed by Pavel Tchelitchew's "phosphorescent kinetics" (in Lincoln Kirstein's phrase)[64] into a visionary integration of dance and film. In *Ode*, as Donald Windham later observed, "it [was] impossible to say . . . where the designer's work end[ed] and the choreographer's beg[an]."[65]

Tchelitchew's scenario, dictated to his technical assistant Pierre Charbonnier, describes the ballet's cinematic effects and equally remarkable lighting effects. Both recall earlier experiments by Loie Fuller and newer ones in "pure cinema" by filmmaker Henri Chomette (René Clair's brother) and the surrealist artist Man Ray. In the third tableau, Tchelitchew writes:

> A diffused sombre blue light is interrupted by the projection of a great hand on the white screen. . . . It halts and . . . a real box materializes from the screen. The illusive hand continues to descend, and La Nature, stepping forward, receives the box and places it on the ground as the hand fades. She opens it and from it springs (projected in brilliant white on a black screen) a large white oval (a seed) which expands, . . . becomes a stem and then a cluster. . . . Finally, as the box gives forth more seeds, a luminous tree develops. Magically, to right and left respectively, appear, all at once, a bouquet of flowers and various fruits.[66]

In the sixth tableau, the soloists danced under spotlights, while

> [p]rojected on the screen behind, as if in the midst of flames, is a pagan fete, a sort of bacchanal with nude men and women. The vision and the actual dancers mingle like one scene. The luminous arches, dimmed for the dances, return, becoming cascades. Lights jump about and tremble, multiply and turn into fixed signs of the heavens. Like a fireworks spectacle, stars, balls of fire, lightnings, spirals appear and play about. A general light now turns green, blue, yellow, orange,

red in quick succession; at last, a quivering white. In sudden changes, this alternates with red, which finally becomes incredibly bright, like fire, and remains. The background lights have been fading and now are bright, silvery reflections, all pulsating.[67]

Ten years after the premiere, the critic A. V. Coton still remembered the ballet vividly:

One's strongest remaining impression is of the unearthly beauty created in most of the scenes by a revolutionary use of light . . . —floods, spots, panoramic effects, projections against a screen and great bursts of light suggesting the sudden animation of pyrotechnical set-pieces, as the groups of dancers and static figures were bathed in pools of glowing illumination, swiftly dimmed and flooded again, almost imperceptibly changing colours . . . A projector shot enormous blossoms on to the backcloth whilst figures in the foreground complemented the pattern in a slow-tempo process referential to the opening and unfolding of flowers seen through the agency of the quick-time cinema camera. The final and furthest departure came when a white-clad and masked group danced within a geometric limitation of spaces bounded by cords which were passed from hand to hand, creating an infinite succession of Euclidean forms about which the figures wove a complementary notation of space-images, as they joined hands, linked arms, released, extended in slow arabesque and moved silently around this formalized stage-within-a-stage.[68]

In this mystical decor, Massine created his first semi-abstract choreography. By 1927, asserts his biographer Vicente García-Márquez, Massine's interest in abstraction "had become nearly all-absorbing." With the painters Sonia and Robert Delaunay, he began work on *Perpetomobile,* a ballet to Schubert consisting of "visions of rhythm and colour" or, as Sonia Delaunay put it, "pure dance for the senses and the intellect, without tricks, naked."[69] The project came to nought. However, in *Ode,* despite a scenario that was often at cross-purposes with the design, Massine's choreography attained something of this formal "nakedness" and "purity." Felia Doubrovska, who danced one of the female leads, later recalled that except for some of the architectural and geometrical configurations and the role danced by Serge Lifar, the choreography was poetic and classical, emphasizing long arabesques, développés, and a formal rhythmic beauty.[70] The classical line was accentuated by the white leotards and tights worn by the soloists, men and women alike. "It was the first time," wrote Alexandra Danilova, who danced the other female lead, "we didn't wear anything on top of our leotards."[71] It is unclear whether this particular idea was Massine's (as he claimed) or Tchelitchew's (as Danilova says), since there is no evidence of how the two collaborated.[72] That they did work closely together (at least on some sections of the ballet) is clear from Beaumont's description of one of the pas de deux, a kind of elegy,

> in which the dancers . . . [held], each with one upraised hand, a slender, horizontal pole, from the first and last third of which was suspended a length of gauze. . . . A number of beautiful effects were achieved when the dancers danced behind the gauze, which invested them with an ectoplastic quality, or else appeared alternately in the open space, so that a solid form danced with a shadowy one.[73]

And a little further on, speaking of the ballet's strange, celestial beauty, Beaumont adds:

> Those extraordinary designs, formed of ever-changing lines and triangles of cord, suggested animations of the diagrams illustrating Euclid's propositions; and yet always in and out of those corded mazes moved, crouched, leaped, and glided those beautiful unknown forms.[74]

After performances in Paris and London, *Ode* was dropped from the Ballets Russes repertory. Although British critics like Coton saw the work as prefiguring Massine's symphonic ballets and American critics such as Kirstein as presaging Tchelitchew's creations with Balanchine, none of these later works entailed the use of film. Indeed, within the realm of dance theater, few designers pursued this avenue of investigation until the advent of postmodernism. In the intervening decades, ballet (and modern dance, for that matter) shied from incorporating film into works conceived for the stage. This diffidence may well have been prompted by cost: film is an expensive medium. Other possible explanations include the divide between post-Diaghilev ballet and experiments in other media, and, in the United States especially, "highbrow" mistrust of a medium overwhelmingly identified with mass culture.

The Diaghilev era was rich in crossovers between dance and film. Diaghilev was not only aware of them, but also attracted in some measure to their possibilities, especially when they were associated with the avant-garde. However, on every occasion that he undertook a project in which cinematic elements appeared, he chose not to pursue the line of exploration beyond the individual project. In the case of *Parade*, it is easy to ascribe this failure to the antipopulism that colored all his attitudes. *Fireworks* and *Ode* are another matter, however. Both originated in trends within the avant-garde and embodied an experimentalism that was as essential to his art as tradition. Too much so, perhaps: In their embrace of abstraction, they entered a territory from which Diaghilev, the traditionalist, felt compelled to retreat. If Diaghilev declined to explore the possibilities opened by his encounters with film, ultimately it was because he could never abjure a notion of high art that the mere existence of the cinema threatened to destroy or countenance a form of theatrical representation that eliminated or dismembered the human figure. Above all, these roads not taken reveal the sway of tradition over Diaghilev's imagination even at its most experimentalist and the limits of his trust in the new.

NOTES

1. "A Film to Music: 'The Sleeping Princess,'" *The Times,* 29 December 1921, p. 6. The article, which was unsigned, was written by the newspaper's film correspondent.
2. "Films Based on Music: An Ambitious Scheme," *The Times,* 17 February 1922, p. 8.
3. T. S. Eliot, " In Memoriam: Marie Lloyd," *The Criterion,* 1, no. 2 (January 1923), p. 194.
4. Michel Fokine, "The New Russian Ballet," *The Times,* 6 July 1914, p. 6. Fokine's "letter" is reprinted in Cyril W. Beaumont, *Michel Fokine and His Ballets* (New York: Dance Horizons, 1981), pp. 144–147.
5. Michel Fokine, "The New Ballet," in Beaumont, *Michel Fokine,* p. 135. This article was originally published in the Russian periodical *Argus* in 1916.
6. Quoted in Valerian Svetloff, *Anna Pavlova,* trans. A. Grey (Paris, 1922; rpt. New York: Dover, 1974), p. 156.
7. Edwin Evans, "Ballet and Film," *The Dancing Times,* February 1922, p. 433.
8. Quoted in Martel Epique, "New Schools for Old: A Chat on Mime with Mme. Astafieva," *The Dancing Times,* May 1917, p. 244.
9. Suzanne Carbonneau Levy, "The Russians are Coming: Russian Dancers in the United States, 1910–1933," Ph.D. diss., New York University, 1990, pp. 321–322, 443, note 104.
10. For Gorsky and Karalli, see Elizabeth Souritz, "Isadora Duncan and Russian Dancemakers Before World War I," in *The Ballets Russes and Its World,* ed. Lynn Garafola and Nancy Van Norman Baer (New Haven: Yale University Press, 1999), p. 107.
11. Agnes de Mille, *Dance to the Piper* (Boston: Little, Brown, 1951), pp. 45–56. Unlike her uncle, who changed the spelling of his surname to DeMille, Agnes de Mille retained the traditional spelling of the family name.
12. For an extended discussion of Kosloff's film career, see Carbonneau Levy, "The Russians are Coming," pp. 137–162.
13. For a discussion of Fokine's contribution to these works, see Dawn Lille Horwitz, *Michel Fokine* (Boston: Twayne Publishers, 1985), pp. 41–50.
14. Agnes de Mille alluded to this in a 1938 letter to her mother. Calling Massine "the real Cecil de Mille [sic] of the dance," she described a section of his *Seventh Symphony:* "When in the allegretto a naked adolescent is brought in crucified and trundled around the stage for twelve minutes while Nini Theilade weeps and caresses him and John the Baptist dressed as Bella Lugosi has epilepsy at his feet, I realized I was watching the thing that Cecil has been waiting all his life to do, or maybe he has done it but in his case for the masses. . . . Massine will make a fortune out of it. I must see if I can't bring the two together" (quoted in Barbara Barker, "Agnes de Mille, Liber-

ated Expatriate, and the *American Suite, 1938*," *Dance Chronicle,* 19, no. 2 (1996), p. 129 note.

15. Mikhail Yampolsky, "Kuleshov's Experiments and the New Anthropology of the Actor," in *Inside the Film Factory: New Approaches to Russian and Soviet Cinema,* ed. Richard Taylor and Ian Christie (London: Routledge, 1991), p. 46.

16. Natalia Roslavleva, "Stanislavsky and the Ballet," introd. Robert Lewis, *Dance Perspectives,* 23 (1965), p. 23; Souritz, "Isadora Duncan and Russian Dancemakers."

17. Spencer Golub, *Evreinov: The Theatre of Paradox and Transformation* (Ann Arbor, Mich.: UMI Research Press, 1984), pp. 110, 127. During the 1910–1911 season, when Presniakov was brought into the company, the actors also studied Dalcroze eurhythmics (*ibid.,* p. 127).

18. *Ibid.,* pp. 149, 151. Barabanov, who worked by day as a clerk, danced under the stage name Z. F. Ikar. In addition to dancers, his repertory also included impersonations of singers and actresses, such as Sarah Bernhardt.

19. Elizabeth Souritz, *Soviet Choreographers in the 1920s,* trans. Lynn Visson, ed. Sally Banes (Durham: Duke University Press, 1990), p. 35; Solomon Volkov, *St. Petersburg: A Cultural History,* trans. Antonina W. Bouis (New York: Free Press, 1995), pp. 190– 191; *Dearest Babushkin: The Correspondence of Vera and Igor Stravinsky, 1921–1954, with Excerpts from Vera Stravinsky's Diaries, 1922–1971,* ed. Robert Craft, trans. Lucia Davidova (New York: Thames and Hudson, 1985), p. 5.

20. Volynsky is quoted in Souritz, *Soviet Choreographers in the 1920s,* p. 34; for Karsavina, see John E. Bowlt, "Constructivism and Russian Stage Design," *Performing Arts Journal,* 1, no. 3 (Winter 1977), p. 74.

21. Lasar Galpern, "Body Training for Actors," *Theatre Workshop,* January–March 1937, p. 44. In the 1910s, Galpern studied ballet with Nicolas Legat, character dance with the Bolshoi's Lev Lashchilin, body movement for actors with Prince Sergei Volkonsky, and eurhythmics at the Dalcroze Institute, Moscow. After leaving Russia, he danced briefly with Bronislava Nijinska, and in 1926 became the ballet master of the Cologne Opera House, where he staged *The Rite of Spring* four years later. In 1932, he was hired by Roxy to produce ballets for the Radio City Music Hall in New York. He remained in the city, where he directed the American Children's Theatre, taught dramatic art at the Group Theatre, staged *The Prodigal Son* for the Philadelphia Ballet, presented solo concerts (frequently on "Hebrew" themes), and worked as a staff choreographer for the WPA Federal Dance Project. In the 1940s, he settled in California. For his *Rite of Spring* and a discussion of his artistic views, see Susan Manning, "German *Rites:* A History of *Le Sacre du Printemps* on the German Stage," *Dance Chronicle,* 14, nos. 2–3 (1991), pp. 133–135; for a collection of his essays, including "Body Training for Actors," see Lasar Galpern, *Letters on the Theatre and the Dance* (New York: Polychrome Corp., 1942).

22. Bowlt, "Constructivism and Russian Stage Design," p. 69.

23. Rumnev was the stage name of Alexander Ziakin, a close childhood friend of Pavel Tchelitchew. As young men, notes Tchelitchew's biographer Parker Tyler, the two "nursed tendencies toward designing for the stage as well as dancing there" (*The*

Divine Comedy of Pavel Tchelitchew [New York: Fleet Publishing, 1967], p. 182). As a teenager, Tchelitchew had studied privately with Mordkin (p. 183). In his book, Parker reproduces a seminude photograph of Rumnev, whose musculature and well-developed instep reveal extensive ballet training.

24. *Dearest Babushkin,* p. 5. According to Robert Craft, she was cast as the Bride in *Les Noces* but was obliged to withdraw because of illness (*Igor and Vera Stravinsky: A Photograph Album 1921 to 1971,* ed. Robert Craft [New York: Thames and Hudson, 1982], p. 56, note 58). Given the ballet's neoclassical style and the fact that all the women danced on pointe, it seems highly unlikely that Nijinska would have cast her in the part. In any event, this is the only source in the considerable memoir literature about the ballet that mentions Vera as rehearsing the role.

25. Quoted in Konstantin Rudnitsky, *Russian and Soviet Theater 1905–1932,* trans. Roxane Permar, ed. Lesley Milne (New York: Abrams, 1988), p. 17.

26. *Ibid.*

27. *Ibid.,* p. 18.

28. John E. Bowlt, *Russian Stage Design: Scenic Innovation, 1900–1930* (Jackson, Miss.: Mississippi Museum of Art, 1982), p. 131.

29. For their collaboration, see Nancy van Norman Baer, *Bronislava Nijinska: A Dancer's Legacy* (San Francisco: Fine Arts Museums of San Francisco, 1986), pp. 18–21, 49–53. It is worth noting that Exter was only one of several Russian designers, including Boris Bilinsky, Yury Annenkov, and Alexandre Benois (who headed the design team for Abel Gance's *Napoléon*), who worked in ballet, drama, and film during the interwar years. The subject certainly deserves an in-depth investigation.

30. For some of these connections, see my *Diaghilev's Ballets Russes* (New York: Oxford University Press, 1989), pp. 29–32 (*Carnaval* and *Petrushka*), 53–55 (*L'Après-midi d'un Faune*), 70–71 (*Le Sacre du Printemps*), and 73–74 (*Till Eulenspiegel*).

31. Rudnitsky, *Russian and Soviet Theater,* p. 94.

32. Sergei M. Eisenstein, *Immoral Memories: An Autobiography,* trans. Herbert Marshall (Boston: Houghton Mifflin, 1983), p. 46.

33. Quoted in Yampolsky, "Kuleshov's Experiments and the New Anthropology of the Actor," p. 48. For Volkonsky's ideas and their dissemination, see pp. 32–37; for Kuleshov's montage experiments involving dance, pp. 45–46; for the Experimental Heroic Theatre, pp. 46–47.

34. Serge Diaghilev, telegram to Igor Stravinsky, [January 1915], in *Stravinsky: Selected Correspondence,* ed. Robert Craft, vol. 2 (New York: Knopf, 1984), p. 17.

35. Depero, in fact, received two commissions: to design the sets and costumes of *Le Chant du Rossignol,* scheduled for production in spring 1917, and the horse in "Bova Korolevitch and the Swan Princess," the second episode of *Contes Russes,* which premiered in 1917. For whatever reason, Diaghilev decided against using Depero's designs for *Le Chant du Rossignol,* which came to the stage in 1920 with designs by Matisse. Depero's horse suffered a similar fate. As Massine recalled in his memoirs: "The question of what to do about the knight's horse caused us much perplexity. Diaghilev had commissioned the futurist artist Fortunato Depero to design something

suitable, and eventually we were summoned to his studio on the outskirts of Rome. As we walked into the room the artist pointed proudly to his construction—a bulbous outsized elephant! We stood staring at it silently for a few moments until Diaghilev, in a sudden outburst of rage, smashed the papier-mâché animal with his walking stick" (*My Life in Ballet,* ed. Phyllis Hartnoll and Robert Rubens [London: Macmillan, 1968], p. 99).

36. Fortunato Depero, "Notes on the Theatre," in Michael Kirby and Victoria Nes Kirby, *Futurist Performance* (New York: PAJ Publications, 1986), p. 209.

37. Marinetti *et al.,* "The Futurist Cinema," *ibid.,* pp. 212, 213–214, 216. Another futurist film that Diaghilev may have seen and certainly knew about was *Drama v kabare futuristov No. 13* (Drama in the Futurists' Cabaret No. 13), directed by Vladimir Kasyanov and released in January 1914. The film starred Natalia Goncharova and Mikhail Larionov, artists who formed the nucleus of Diaghilev's wartime creative circle, and included a "futurist tango" as well as a tap dance, the latter performed by Goncharova. For a description, see Anthony Parton, *Mikhail Larionov and the Russian Avant-Garde* (London: Thames and Hudson, 1993), pp. 71–73.

38. Leonid [sic] Massine, "On Choreography and a New School of Dancing," *Drama,* 1, no. 3 (December 1919), p. 69. Another ballet choreographed during the months in Rome that employed simultaneity, although less successfully than *Ladies,* was the Baba-Yaga episode of *Contes Russes.* "In working out [the] finale," wrote Massine in his memoirs, "I allowed my imagination to run away with me and created such a variety of simultaneous movements, with the principal characters weaving to and fro among the *corps de ballet,* that each group overshadowed the next and it was imossible to see any of the movements clearly. The scene was so lacking in artistic coherence that instead of an exciting conclusion it was nothing but a frenzy of disconnected activity" (*My Life in Ballet,* ed. Phyllis Hartnoll and Robert Rubens [London: Macmillan, 1968], pp. 100–101).

39. Cyril W. Beaumont, *Complete Book of Ballets* (London: Putnam, 1937), p. 844.

40. Quoted in Vicente García-Márquez, *Massine: A Biography* (New York: Knopf, 1995), p. 398, note 16.

41. Maurizio Fagiolo dell'Arco, "Balla's Prophecies," *Art International,* 12, no. 6 (Summer 1968), p. 67.

42. Henri Quittard, "Les Concerts," *Figaro,* 9 May 1914, p. 5.

43. Quoted in Giovanni Lista, *Loie Fuller: danseuse de la Belle Epoque* (Paris: Stock-Editions d'Art Somogy, 1994), p. 500.

44. Depero, "Notes on the Theatre," p. 207.

45. Lista, *Loie Fuller,* p. 643, note 39.

46. Bronislava Nijinska, "Reflections About the Production of *Les Biches* and *Hamlet* in Markova-Dolin Ballets," trans. Lydia Lopokova, *The Dancing Times,* February 1937, p. 617.

47. Francis Steegmuller, *Cocteau: A Biography* (Boston: Little, Brown, 1970), p. 201.

48. Jean Cocteau, *Carte blanche* (Paris: Mermod, [1952]), p. 201. For Diaghilev's regard

for Chaplin, see Richard Buckle, *Diaghilev* (London: Weidenfeld and Nicolson, 1979), p. 316.

49. Quoted in Frank W. D. Ries, *The Dance Theatre of Jean Cocteau* (Ann Arbor, Mich.: UMI Research Press, 1986), p. 40. For Chung Ling Soo, see Deborah Menaker Rothschild, *Picasso's "Parade": From Street to Stage*, foreword Jeanne Thayer and Michael Iovenko (New York: Sotheby's Publications, 1991), pp. 76–79, 91–95.

50. Cocteau uses the phrase in the preface of *Les Mariés de la Tour Eiffel*. See Jean Cocteau, *The Infernal Machine and Other Plays* (New York: New Directions, 1963), p. 153. The translation is by Dudley Fitts.

51. Cocteau, *Carte Blanche*, p. 149.

52. Massine, *My Life in Ballet*, p. 104.

53. R. J., "La Danse et le cinéma au ralenti," *La Danse*, May 1922, n.p.

54. Theodore Curzon, "Film Dancing," *The Dancing Times*, September 1919, p. 563.

55. "Paris Notes," *The Dancing Times*, August 1922, p. 935.

56. "La Danse à travers le monde," *La Danse*, September 1921, n.p.

57. Lista, *Loie Fuller*, p. 535. Although filmed in 1920, *Le Lys de la vie* had its first public screening only in March 1921 (*ibid.*, p. 643).

58. The libretto of *Le Train Bleu* is reproduced in Erik Aschengreen, *Jean Cocteau and the Dance*, trans. Patricia McAndrew and Per Avsum (Copenhagen: Gyldendal, 1986), Appendix 5. Scene 9 appears on p. 272.

59. *Ibid.*, p. 273.

60. Cyril W. Beaumont, *Bookseller at the Ballet* (London: C.W. Beaumont, 1975), pp. 345–346.

61. The ballet was actually conceived by the poet Blaise Cendrars, who wrote the original scenario. However, after he left for Brazil, it was turned over to Picabia to "embroider." Although traces of the original scenario remained in the ballet, Cendrars himself ceased to figure in the production. For a discussion of Cendrars's contribution, see Miriam Cendrars, "Les Métamorphoses parisiennes d'un ballet suédois," *Continent Cendrars,* 1 (1986), pp. 12–23.

62. Jacques Bourgeois, *René Clair* (Paris: Roulet, [1949]), p. 28.

63. For a description of the staged action, see William Canfield, "Dada Experiment: Francis Picabia and the Creation of *Relâche*," in *Paris Modern: The Swedish Ballet 1920–1925*, ed. Nancy Van Norman Baer (San Francisco: Fine Arts Museums of San Francisco, 1995), p. 132.

64. Lincoln Kirstein, *Tchelitchev* (Santa Fe, N.M.: Twelvetrees Press, 1994), p. 28.

65. Donald Windham, "The Stage and Ballet Designs of Pavel Tchelitchew," *Dance Index*, 3, nos. 1–2 (January–February 1944), p. 9.

66. Quoted in Tyler, *The Divine Comedy of Pavel Tchelitchew*, p. 331.

67. *Ibid.*, p. 333.

68. A. V. Coton, *A Prejudice for Ballet* (London: Methuen, 1938), pp. 86–87.

69. Quoted in García-Márquez, *Massine*, p. 199.

70. *Ibid.*, p. 201.

71. Alexandra Danilova, *Choura: The Memoirs of Alexandra Danilova* (New York: Knopf, 1986), p. 93.

72. Massine, *My Life in Ballet,* p. 174; Danilova, *Choura,* p. 93. Although Tchelitchew's scenario, as quoted in Tyler's *The Divine Comedy of Pavel Tchelitchew,* does mention leotards, this may be the author's own rendering of a less precise term in the original French. Massine makes only brief mention of Tchelitchew, crediting him with the "row of puppets in period costume" that formed the background of one of the scenes and with the "irregular framework of white cords . . . used to enclose the action" (*My Life,* p. 174). Tyler, in a chapter replete with unascribed conversations, simply identifies Massine as the ballet's choreographer (*Divine Comedy,* p. 330). Nicolas Nabokov, the ballet's composer, is also silent on the subject, merely saying that when he arrived in Monte Carlo he was told by Boris Kochno that "Tchelitchew had invented marvelous sets for *Ode*" and that "Massine liked them" (*Bagázh: Memoirs of a Russian Cosmopolitan* [New York: Atheneum, 1975], p. 153).

73. Beaumont, *Bookseller at the Ballet,* p. 383.

74. *Ibid.*

FORGOTTEN INTERLUDE

EURHYTHMIC DANCERS AT THE PARIS OPÉRA

Late in the summer of 1917, Jacques Rouché, the director of the Académie Nationale de Musique et de Danse, better known as the Paris Opéra, sent a letter to dancers of the ballet troupe. Did they, he asked, care to take class in the eurhythmics section he was about to establish or would they rather study with their usual teacher, the former ballerina Rosita Mauri, who conducted the class of perfection? Although the file copy of Rouché's letter seems to have disappeared, a number of responses to it have survived at the Archives Nationales in Paris.[1] Letters from dancers tend to be rare, and this group, amounting to some twenty items, is especially valuable because it deals with an episode that is little known even among scholars of the period. Moreover, because this episode occurred at the start of a modernization process that in time transformed every aspect of ballet at the Opéra, the teaching practices alluded to in some of the letters suggest reasons for the deteriorating performance standard that led many to dismiss the company as second-rate.

Jacques Rouché, who served as director of the Opéra from 1915 to 1944,[2] was already a familiar figure in Paris theater circles at the time of his appointment. Born in 1862, he began his career as a diplomat, worked in the perfume business, and in 1907 became editor of *La Grande Revue*, an intellectual journal with extensive coverage of the performing arts and a roster of regular and sometime contributors that included M.-D. Calvocoressi, Camille Mauclair, Jacques Copeau, Henri Matisse, Emile Jaques-Dalcroze, André Dunoyer de Segonzac, and Louis Laloy (who wrote not only about music and opera, but also about dance).[3] Although Rouché had dabbled in theater production as early as the 1890s, it was only in the years prior to the First World War that it became his life's work. By then, he had become fascinated by the new theater movement that throughout Europe was challenging both the aesthetics of naturalism and the conventions of nineteenth-century stagecraft. Rouché's interest in theatrical developments outside France, which he investigated on a study journey that took him to Germany, Italy, and Russia, prompted his only extended piece of writing, the magnificent volume *L'Art théâtral moderne*.[4] First published in 1910, the year that he assumed direction of the Théâtre des Arts, the book laid

This article was originally published in *Dance Research*, 13, no. 1 (Summer 1995).

out the theoretical principles underlying the innovative approaches that he now sought to put into practice in the several dozen plays, operas, and ballets mounted by the new venture. His efforts were rewarded. Between 1910 and 1913, when he accepted the Opéra appointment, the Théâtre des Arts won high praise for the imagination of its programming, the taste and artistic quality of its productions, and the talented young artists—many of whom would go on to distinguished careers at the Opéra and elsewhere—enlisted as collaborators. An important episode in the history of early twentieth-century French theater, the enterprise was a laboratory for Rouché's later activities at the Opéra.

Unlike Lugné-Poe's Théâtre de l'Oeuvre, which staged some of the earliest French productions of Henrik Ibsen, Maurice Maeterlinck, August Strindberg, Maxim Gorky, Emile Verhaeren, and other modern playwrights, Rouché's enterprise offered not only dramatic works—the French premiere of George Bernard Shaw's *Mrs. Warren's Profession* (1912), Jacques Copeau's adaptation of *The Brothers Karamazov* (1911), Henri Ghéon's "popular tragedy" *Le Pain* (1911), Saint-Georges de Bouhelier's *Le Carnaval des Enfants* (1910)—but also works of lyric theatre that stood outside the tradition of French "grand opera." Some of these came from the eighteenth-century repertoire—Jean-Philippe Rameau's opera-ballets *Les Fêtes d'Hébé* (1911) and *Pygmalion* (1913), for example. Others, like Jacques Offenbach's one-act operetta *Mesdames de la Halle* (1913), Léo Delibes' opéra-bouffe *Les Deux vieilles gardes* (1912), and Emmanuel Chabrier's *Une Education manquée* (1913), although of more recent vintage, had long ceased to be performed. Still others, including Maurice Ravel's *Ma Mère l'Oye* (1912), were new.

To design these works, Rouché called upon a group of French painters, including Maxime Dethomas, Drésa, and René Piot, who had contributed in various ways to *La Grande Revue*. None had worked previously for the stage: Piot, for instance, was best known for his frescoes.[5] Modernist in orientation, all three artists would follow Rouché to the Opéra, where they would contribute significantly to the new look of postwar productions. Design, in fact, played a key role in Rouché's earliest reform efforts. "At that time," he later told an interviewer referring to his tenure at the Théâtre des Arts, "I was rather keen on returning the theatre to the painter, without, however, giving him the dominant role. . . . Already I was seeking a way to fuse the arts without distorting them, to combine and enrich them."[6] The collaboration of nonspecialist stage painters, announced a reviewer for *Comoedia Illustré*, "decidedly marks a new tendency in France, which Monsieur Jacques Rouché has encouraged and supported with success."[7]

However new in terms of French theater, Rouché's approach to design was clearly indebted to the fusionist ideology and post-symbolist aesthetic of the Ballets Russes. His interest in dance, especially new dance, also owed a debt to the Russian enterprise, even if in France (unlike Italy), ballet had remained an integral part of opera throughout the second half of the nineteenth century.

Under his aegis, the Théâtre des Arts gave unusual prominence to dance, which was featured not only in lyric works like *Pygmalion* and *Les Fêtes d'Hébé*, but also in plays like Louis Laloy's *Le Chagrin dans le Palais de Han* (1912), an adaptation of Ma-Tcheu-Yuen's fourteenth-century Chinese drama, and Molière's comedy-ballet *Le Sicilien, ou l'Amour peintre* (1910), with music by Jean-Baptiste Lully. Rouché also produced a number of full-fledged ballets, including Laloy's *Les Folies françaises, ou les Dominos* (1911), to music by François Couperin, and *Dolly* (1913), to music by Gabriel Fauré; Catulle Mendès' *L'Amoureuse Leçon* (1913), to music by Alfred Bruneau; Gilbert de Voisins' *Le Festin de l'Araignée* (1913), to a score by Albert Roussel; and Ravel's *Ma Mère l'Oye* (Mother Goose), adapted by the composer from his original piano suite. It was Rouché, too, who organized at the Théâtre du Châtelet in 1912 the dance concert starring Natalia Trouhanova that offered premieres of Paul Dukas' *La Péri* and Ravel's *Adélaïde, ou le Langage des fleurs* (based on the "Valses nobles et sentimentales" with an argument by the composer), in addition to reprises of Vincent d'Indy's *Istar* and Florent Schmitt's *La Tragédie de Salomé*—all of which Rouché would later produce at the Opéra.[8]

Apart from the Trouhanova works, which were choreographed by the former Bolshoi ballet master Ivan Clustine, and *Ma Mère l'Oye,* which was staged by Jane Hugard,[9] the dances in these productions were entrusted to Léo Staats, another Théâtre des Arts alumnus who would follow or, more correctly, return with Rouché to the Opéra. Staats had studied at the Opéra school under Louis Mérante, graduating into the company in 1893, the same year he choreographed his first ballet, *Ici l'on danse*. In 1908, when André Messager and L. Broussan assumed the management of the Opéra, Staats was appointed ballet master, producing during his two-year tenure new versions of *Namouna* (1908) and *Javotte* (1909).[10] With the reopening of the Opéra late in 1915 (it had closed at the beginning of World War I), he returned to the house, both as a choreographer and, after a stint in the army, as its principal ballet master, a post he held from 1919 to 1926.

The dancers who worked under Staats at the Théâtre des Arts were an eclectic group. In *Le Festin de l'Araignée,* for instance, the mantises were played by the clowns Tommy and Georgey Footitt, while the spider was played by the exotic Sahary-Djeli, a music hall celebrity and sometime Salomé known for her extreme suppleness.[11] Similarly, in *Nabuchodonosor* (1911), a drama with musical interludes, the role of the Young Dancer was performed by Trouhanova, a soloist who specialized in exotic and "Greek" styles (although she did not disdain to don pointe shoes on occasion). Although several of the dancers had studied with Staats (like most Opéra ballet masters of the time, he gave private classes in addition to teaching at the Opéra) and although at least two of them (including the future *premier danseur* Albert Aveline)[12] were members of the Opéra troupe, most lacked the well-rounded training of the professional ballet dancer. Caryathis, the *nom de théâtre* of Elise Toulemon, who later published several volumes of reminiscence under her married name, Elise Jouhandeau, was one such student. Having run away from home and settled in Montmartre, she announced to her friends that she intended to be a dancer. One of them took her to the studio where Staats gave private classes to the Opéra's *"grands sujets."*[13] Although she was only a beginner, Staats agreed to teach her.

Before long, however, she discovered Jean d'Udine, a "dissident apostle" (in André Levinson's phrase)[14] of the Dalcroze system, whose Ecole Française de Rythme, located on the Avenue de Ternes, attracted pupils such as Comtesse Etienne de Beaumont and Rouché's own daughters, one of whom, Madame Barbey-Rouché, later became the director of the most important Dalcroze school in Paris.[15] D'Udine's method, Caryathis later wrote, "was of great help to me in creating my musical interpretations," an allusion to the choreographic career that began at the Théâtre des Arts, where, at the urging of Staats himself, she composed the first of her own dances—the "red dance" before the Emperor in *Le Chagrin dans le Palais de Han.*[16] Pleased with her performance, Staats introduced her to Ravel and gave her the role of the Serpentin Vert in *Ma Mère l'Oye.* It was only after these experiences, if her memoirs are to be believed, that Caryathis discovered "the Attic art . . . and poetry of perfection" of Isadora Duncan and presented her first recital.[17]

After auditioning unsuccessfully for a character dance position at the Opéra in 1915 (a move that her lover, actor Charles Dullin, strongly opposed and probably worked behind the scenes to defeat),[18] Caryathis appeared in ballets by Debussy and Florent Schmitt and in 1919 in the "Fête nègre" organized by the art dealer Paul Guillaume and the poet Blaise Cendrars at the Comédie des Champs-Elysées.[19] She choreographed erotic dances (with titles like *Bacchanale, Dionysienne,* and *Volupté*),[20] Spanish-style dances,[21] and in 1921, at the Théâtre Colisée, the dances to Satie's "La Belle Excentrique"[22]—offerings that in their use of parody and jazz anticipated, according to Levinson, works such as *Les Biches* and *Against the Quota.*[23] She also appeared in Francis Picabia's 1924 New Year's Eve spectacular, *Ciné-Sketch,* at the Théâtre des Champs-Elysées, along with Marcel Duchamp, Jean Borlin, and the entire Ballets Suédois company.[24]

Caryathis was not the only dancer at the Théâtre des Arts influenced by various currents of the era's new dance. Her close friend, Ariane Hugon, although a member of the Opéra company, had fallen under the spell of the Greeks. Photographs show her prancing in tunics and sandals with the pliant upper body of early Ballets Russes dancers. Hugon did not actually reject the technique of the *danse d'école.* She approved, for instance, of its limbering and stamina-building exercises and its method for inculcating the art of harmonious gesture. But she believed in instinct and "beautiful emotions," and in dances with titles like *Vision antique* she presented herself to the public as a Duncan-style dancer, even while remaining on the Opéra payroll and performing featured roles in several Théâtre des Arts productions.[25]

Djemil-Anik was another Théâtre des Arts dancer with an unconventional background who, like Caryathis, went on to a career as a soloist. Born in Martinique of mixed race,[26] Djemil was the Good Fairy in *Ma Mère l'Oye* and one of the dancers in *Le Chagrin dans le Palais de Han*. She boasted many friends among the avant-garde, including the painter Kees Van Dongen, who arranged for her to dance at Guillaume's "Fête nègre," where, according to Baron Mollet, Apollinaire's former secretary, she appeared "completely nude and painted from head to feet" by the artist himself.[27] Unlike Caryathis, who specialized in ironic vignettes to contemporary music, Djemil made her mark as an exotic dancer. At a 1922 concert at the Comédie Montaigne that Levinson reviewed, she performed an "Egyptian triptych," in addition to Javanese, Japanese, and Chinese dances.[28] Later recitals added Indian, African, and West Indian numbers to this repertoire—a *tour de monde* worthy of Ruth St. Denis and her American progeny.[29]

However interesting some of the Théâtre des Arts dancers may have been as individuals, the company as a whole left much to be desired. In a letter written in 1911 after attending a performance of the Ballets Russes, René Piot, who had no qualms about speaking his mind, complained to Rouché about the "cows" [veaux]—a favorite word of his—"imposed on us by Staats."[30] In another letter, the artist refused to apologize for an outbreak of temper inspired by the "disorderly habits" of the troupe, which no one, apparently, was able to control:

> I reacted with anger because these women are such cows that someone has to make them understand what they are, and the language I used was the only one they understand. Obviously, I do not speak of your little actresses, who are very nice, or of dancers like Anik or Zourna, who are fine: but Staats has given us real shits [des excréments].[31]

Piot complained that the dancers failed to appear for rehearsals, ruined his costumes by sitting on the skirts, chattered in the wings during performances—behavior that he contrasted with the exemplary discipline of the Ballets Russes, which he had visited backstage with designer Léon Bakst.[32] On one occasion, he advised Rouché to contact an agency in Milan for dancers. "You can find . . . what you want for as little as *70 francs a month!!*. . . The school of Milan, although based on old principles, is perhaps the best in the world. Technically, their dancers appear to be of the first order."[33] On another occasion, he asked whether he could replace Staats' "sluts" [roulures] with dancers engaged by designer Maxime Dethomas. On still another, he mentioned to Rouché one Mademoiselle Negri,[34] who had a small troupe that performed at private gatherings. "If you take her as première danseuse, you could perhaps ask for her dancers, if they are good. In any case, they can't be worse than what Staats gets us."[35] Obviously, neither Rouché nor his close advisors had a clue as to what should be done to form a disciplined dance unit, although all were agreed upon its necessity and the need for it to be modern, whatever this might mean.

As the first decade of Rouché's tenure as Opéra director would prove, being modern meant many things. It prompted him, for instance, to engage the Ballets Russes in 1919, 1920, and 1922,[36] and Loie Fuller and her company in 1920 and 1923. It led him to invite Michel Fokine to stage *Daphnis and Chloé* in 1921 and Bronislava Nijinska to choreograph *Les Rencontres* in 1925; Ida Rubinstein to appear in *La Tragédie de Salomé* in 1919 and Anna Pavlova to dance *La Péri* in 1921. The same impulse prompted him to revive eighteenth-century opera-ballets like Rameau's *Castor and Pollux* (1918) and Lully's *Le Triomphe de l'Amour* (1925); to stage ballets like *Les Abeilles* (1917), to music by Igor Stravinsky, and *Adélaïde, ou le Langage des fleurs* (1917), to music by Ravel, composers new to the Opéra; to produce Enrique Granados' opera *Las Goyescas* with the Spanish dancer Amalia Molina (1919); and to present a troupe of real Cambodian dancers in 1922. It prompted him to hold open auditions in 1916 for character and "*plastique*," or expressive dancers to augment the existing in-house company,[37] and, in 1917, to appoint Nicolà Guerra, a respected Italian choreographer and teacher, as its ballet master. And, finally, it led him, again in 1917, to establish a full-fledged eurhythmics department under the direction of Jane Erb, a Dalcroze instructor who had taught the method in Switzerland and was on the staff of the oldest "official" Dalcroze school in Paris, the Ecole de Rythmique.[38] As Rouché wrote in an article published after the Second World War, on assuming his post as director of the Opéra, he had a "strong desire" to institute both a system of primary education on the Russian model and a "Dalcroze class in rhythmic solfège." The latter, he added, was inspired by his observations at Hellerau, which he had visited in either 1913 or 1914.[39]

From the start, the class was a source of contention. Although poets like Paul Claudel and composers like Arthur Honegger may have shared Rouché's enthusiasm for the Dalcroze system,[40] which received extensive coverage in the post-Armistice press,[41] devotees of the "old ballet" were openly hostile to it. As Léandre Vaillat wrote in his *Ballets de l'Opéra de Paris,* "the conflict was no longer between the Italian school and the French school, nor between the French and the Russian schools, but between the academic and the eurhythmic."[42] Not unexpectedly, few of the dancers queried by Rouché were willing to abandon the "traditions of the house" that had bred them.[43] As he later wrote: "Unfortunately, dancers . . . count time in their own way, which is not that of the composer; indifferent to the sequence of sounds, they seek, in the paradoxical formula of Serge Lifar, an extra-musical dance musicality."[44] Still, some of the dancers did express an interest in expanding their horizons, in "keeping up," as soloist Olga Soutzo put it, "with the new methods advocated" by Rouché. She, for one, asked to be enrolled "in the school of rhythmic dance," in addition to taking three or more classes a week with "Mademoiselle Mauri."[45]

A much admired *étoile* who had danced at the Opéra from 1878 to 1898, the Spanish-born Mauri was well equipped to pass on the traditions of the house. Trained in France and "finished" at La Scala, she created the ballerina roles in Louis Mérante's ballets *La Korrigane* (1880) and *Les Deux Pigeons* (1886), his divertissement for Jules Massenet's opera *Le Cid* (1885), and Joseph Hansen's ballet *La Maladetta* (1893). Her repertoire also included the title roles in Mérante's *Sylvia* and *Yedda*, ballets created for Rita Sangalli in 1876 and 1879, respectively. As Yvonnette in *La Korrigane*, wrote François Coppée, the ballet's composer, Mauri was "dancing personified":

> To the trials of rehearsal . . . [she] brought a kind of physical enthusiasm, a kind of joyous delirium. You felt that she loved to dance for nothing, from instinct, for the love of dancing, even in a dark and empty theatre. She whinnied and darted like a young foal; she soared and glided in space like a wild bird; and, in her sombre and somewhat wild beauty, there is something of both the Arab steed and the swallow.[46]

After retiring from the stage, Mauri remained at the Opéra, where she taught the class of perfection. However, her conduct of this class, at least by the mid-1910s, was anything but satisfactory. Although most of the dancers chose to continue studying with her (the classes, after all, were free), several were sharply critical of her teaching methods. Wrote Jeanine Laugier:

> I have just received your letter asking whether I plan to attend the Mauri dance class at the Opéra; I respond as you ask; yes, Monsieur, I will take my lessons as in the past, that is, on a regular basis. But I must point out to you that we cannot continue the classes as they are given by Mademoiselle Mauri, who no longer gives us the same hours as before the war or works with us on the repertoire that you program.
>
> I am sorry to have to write you this, but Mademoiselle Mauri takes us only from 10:30 to 11:20; there is no longer time for all of us to work. Moreover, she has ceased to rehearse the variations we have to perform.[47]

At fifty minutes, the class was little more than a warm-up.

Camille Bos, a soloist promoted to *première danseuse* in 1920, not only re-iterated Laugier's criticisms, but also threatened to withdraw from Mauri's classes unless Rouché took action to improve them:

> In response to your letter I cannot tell you my intentions on the choice of a teacher.
>
> I hesitate to work with Mademoiselle Mauri, and if the lessons ressemble those of last year, that is, if she does not work with us on our variations for the repertoire, I shall be forced to look for another teacher.

Consequently, I count on you, Mr. Director, to do what is necessary with Mademoiselle Mauri in order to do what is best for our common interests.[48]

Jeanne Schwarz, another soloist, went even further than Bos: She flatly refused to work with Mauri, her teacher of eight years:

> In response to your letter . . . on the subject of lessons, I have the pleasure of advising you that I will not be attending Mademoiselle Mauri's class.
> If this class were really a class of perfection, I would make it my duty to attend, but lessons like these, which I have had for the past eight years, I prefer not to take.[49]

In 1920, Mauri finally retired, and the class of perfection passed to Carlotta Zambelli, the Opéra's much esteemed *étoile*.

Not all the dancers were as conscientious as this group of letter writers. In the aftermath of the 1920 strike, when Rouché was forced to make sharp cuts in personnel, he drew up a list of expendable artists, with information based partly on their answers to an earlier questionnaire.[50] Of the twenty-five dancers who were dismissed, all but one (a *coryphée*) were in the lowest ranks of the corps de ballet, and the nature of their infractions, coupled with the fact that more than half the group had passed the age of thirty, indicates that poor teaching alone did not account for the company's sorry state. Discipline was at low ebb. None of the dancers attended class on a daily basis; some, in fact, never went to class at all. Many came late to rehearsals, or even skipped them; others missed entire performances. Some returned weeks late from holiday, spoke insolently to superiors, refused to obey instructions, forgot their entrances, disrupted rehearsals, created disturbances in the wings and onstage. One was continually drunk. Another was pregnant. To Rouché, the company must have seemed ungovernable.

Morale, too, was low. For many dancers, a job at the Opéra was just that, a way of making a living, of supporting the children and the sick and elderly parents whose existence depended on their relatives' income. And what an income: 275 to 400 francs a month, *L'Humanité* reported on the eve of the strike that closed down the Opéra in January 1920—a "derisory" sum.[51] Moreover, for those in the second *quadrille,* the company's lowest rank,[52] there was little chance for advancement. Most had entered the company at fourteen or fifteen (although some were actually as young as eleven or twelve), which meant that their training was rudimentary: a turn or two on pointe, an entrechat quatre were all they were expected to do.[53] Promotion came quickly or not at all. By the age of twenty, if a dancer was still in the *quadrille,* her career was effectively over. For such dancers, the "décor props" of the company in Jane Hugard's phrase,[54] there was nothing to do except bide their time until retirement. Unsurprisingly, many did as little as possible in the interim.

By comparison with this jaded, semi-skilled proletariat, Rouché's newcomers were models of professional pride. They came to the Opéra not as *petits rats* deposited at the school by their mothers, but as adults committed to careers as artists. Much to the chagrin of traditionalists like Vaillat, eurhythmic dancers were cast in most of the Opéra's new productions of the late 1910s and early 1920s. These included operas like *Castor et Pollux* (1918), Ernest Reyer's *Salammbô* (1919), Antoine Mariotte's *Salomé* (1919), Vincent d'Indy's *La Légende de Saint Christophe* (1920); Francesco Malipiero's *Sept chansons* (1920), Hector Berlioz's *Les Troyens* (1921), Gabriel Dupont's *Antar* (1921), Massenet's *Hérodiade* (1921), Giuseppe Verdi's *Falstaff* (1922), Massenet's *Grisélidis* (1922), his *Esclarmonde* (1923), Albert Roussel's *Padmâvatî* (1923), Charles Tournemire's *Les Dieux sont morts* (1924), Alexandre Georges' *Miarka* (1925), and André Bloch's *Brocéliande* (1925), as well as dance works, such as *La Tragédie de Salomé* (1919), *Maïmouna* (1921), *Petite Suite* (1922), *Artemis troublée* (1922), *Fresques* (1923), *Concerto* (1923), and *Istar* (1924).[55]

Obviously, no account of the Opéra in these years can fail to take account of the much disparaged eurhythmic section. Its dancers turned up nearly everywhere, even in ballets like *Sylvia* and *Les Deux Pigeons,* the most traditional of the Opéra's dance offerings, where "crossover dancers"—of whom more later—performed the roles of Diane and the Queen of the Gypsies. In less traditional works, classical and eurhythmic dancers often shared the boards, although only occasionally, to judge from the programs, did they appear in the same numbers. Thus, in *Castor et Pollux,* the divertissements were performed by classical dancers (led by ballerina Aïda Boni), while the Furies and Demons in Act III were played by eurhythmic dancers (led by Yvonne Daunt). In *Hérodiade,* the divertissements were again danced by classicists, as opposed to the Sacred Dance, which was interpreted by "eurhythmicians." In *Antar,* the two "schools" were similarly juxtaposed, with ballerina Camille Bos and a classical corps of "flowers" symbolizing the refreshments of the oasis, and Daunt embodying the thirst of the desert. To traditionalists like Vaillat, this division of labor suggested anything but parity. Referring to Ida Rubinstein, who headed the mixed casts of *La Tragédie de Salomé, Artemis troublée,* and *Istar,* he wrote that her presence alone "confirmed the triumph of *la rythmique.*"[56]

Like the casts, choreographic assignments were sometimes shared. In *Les Troyens,* the divertissement in Scene 6 was by Staats, while "La Chasse royale" in Scene 5 was by Rachel Pasmanik, an early Dalcroze follower and prize-winning student at the Conservatory of Geneva,[57] and Jessmin Howarth, a graduate of the Dalcroze school in London and a former instructor at the New York Dalcroze School.[58] The same troika also shared the choreography of *Hérodiade.* Whatever Staats may have thought privately of his eurhythmic colleagues, publicly he accepted their collaboration with grace: as a veteran of the Théâtre des Arts and of numerous music hall engagements, he had worked closely with artists of many different backgrounds and performance styles. Indeed, in *Sept chansons, Miarka,* and *Brocéliande,* nearly all his dancers came from the Opéra's eurhythmic section. Nicolà Guerra, by contrast, refused point blank to share choreographic duties with Jane Erb, that section's original head. "I have just learned," he wrote in outrage to Rouché in 1918, "that you have assigned Act III of *Castor et Pollux,* that is, the dances for the demons and the furies, to the teacher of the eurhythmic school. If this is true and if you remain of the same mind, allow me, Mr. Director, to state in all frankness that I withdraw as of now from the composition of this work."[59] Despite the ballet master's threats, Rouché stood his ground: Erb stayed on the production, as did Guerra.

Sometimes, too, eurhythmic works appeared on the same bill with classical ones. In 1922, when Rouché organized a season of French ballet and scheduled the first all-dance nights presented at the Opéra in decades, the two "schools" figured pretty much equally on the bills.[60] Thus, on 11 July 1922, the second night of the "French" season, he offered *Sylvia* (with Zambelli in the title role), *Artemis troublée* (featuring Ida Rubinstein), and *Petite Suite* (1922), a work to Debussy choreographed by Pasmanik and Howarth;[61] the following night, *Namouna,* "La Chasse royale" from *Les Troyens, La Péri,* and *La Maladetta* (in a new version by Staats starring Zambelli and Jeanne Schwarz);[62] a few nights later, *Maïmouna, Artemis troublée,* and "La Chasse royale";[63] a week or so after that, *La Tragédie de Salomé, Artemis troublée,* and *Sylvia.* Other works presented in the course of the season were *Coppélia,* the ballet from Charles Gounod's opera *Roméo et Juliette,* Fokine's *Daphnis and Chloé,* Staats' *Frivolant* (1922), and his extremely popular *Taglioni chez Musette* (1920). Obviously, the nationality of the composer had more to do with identifying a ballet as French than the nationality of either the dancers or the choreographers.[64]

Castor et Pollux appears to have been Erb's only contribution to the Opéra repertoire. Pasmanik and Howarth were more prolific. In addition to choreographing *Petite Suite,* they supplied the dances for at least three operas: *Les Troyens, Hérodiade,* and *Falstaff.* Clara Brooke, a Dalcroze disciple who had taught at Hellerau and in the United States and participated in the Dalcroze demonstrations at the Salle Gaveau in 1920,[65] was another woman from the eurhythmic section who choreographed for the Opéra in these years: her credits included the operas *Esclarmonde* and *Les Dieux sont morts.* The only male choreographer among the "eurhythmic sisterhood" (to borrow a phrase from René Piot)[66] was Plácido de Montoliu, a Spaniard from Barcelona who had taught at the Dalcroze Center in Hellerau and, beginning in 1913, in various cities of the United States.[67] According to Vaillat, Montoliu conducted the eurhythmic section's "class of perfection" (a term, needless to say, that Vaillat employs with irony). Presumably, this was during the 1922–1923 season, when Montoliu choreographed the "Dance of the Spirits" in Act II of *Grisélidis* (dismissed by Vaillat as "a trifle") and two dance works: *Fresques* and *Concerto.*[68] With the possible exception of Howarth, none of these choreographers appears to have performed at the Opéra.

In fact, apart from the names of the productions they choreographed, the tenure of these choreographers at the Palais Garnier is a mystery. How they worked, what they taught, why they were hired in the first place—on these and other questions the literature is silent. The few authors who mention the episode at all do so only to rue that it came to an end (the view of Dalcroze biographer Irwin Spector) or that it was undertaken at all (the case of Opéra historian Ivor Guest).[69] A rare glimpse into the eurhythmic studio comes from P. J. S. Richardson, the editor of *The Dancing Times*, who visited one of Howarth's classes on a tour of the Opéra in 1921:

> I had a peep at Miss Howart's [*sic*] Rhythmic Class, where the Dalcroze Eurhythmics are taught. Here I saw about half a dozen girls—some "grands sujets," others merely "petits sujets"—moving round the room, keeping perhaps common time with their feet, whilst their arms beat triple time, and their bodies softly swayed from side to side. I believe it is a debateable point even at the Opera as to whether these exercises are of real value in the dancing curriculum. I should mention that in the ballet classes all are dressed alike in white, but in the Rhythmic Class regulation swimming costume is worn.[70]

Who were the dancers Richardson might have seen? Among the "grands sujets" the most important were Yvonne Daunt and Yvonne Franck. Both joined the company during the war years—Daunt in 1918, Franck in 1917—and were quickly cast in major roles of the eurthythmic repertoire. Of the two, the English-born Daunt was probably the more interesting dancer: by 1920 she was already an *étoile*. Richardson spoke with admiration of her performance as the Spirit of Fire in *Antar,* noting her abandon and calling her a "brilliant exponent of barefoot dancing."[71] A. t'Serstevens, introducing an album of dry points by Louis Jou that depicted Daunt in various roles, referred to her as a "Doric" dancer—"grave, severe, and full of wisdom."[72] In 1922, when she replaced Ida Rubinstein in the title role of *La Tragédie de Salomé,* Levinson (who thought that Daunt was miscast) described her as a "queen of the Amazons":

> She has . . . a vigorous run that in three leaps allows her to cross the stage on a diagonal. For her are the big bravura steps, those series of grand-scale pirouettes; why not fouettés en tournant? Her training is solid; her technique honest. I like seeing her straight back as her foot lowers, its pointe strictly vertical, the coup de pied prominent. For the developpés of the adagio, aplomb is visibly wanting; the lineaments are perhaps too robust. . . . But whatever is traveling or dynamic and greedy for space—that is for her.[73]

As Levinson's description makes clear, Daunt had strong classical training behind her. So, too, did Franck. The day before seeing *Antar,* Richardson actually watched the two of them take a private class with Madame Blanche d'Alessandri, a highly respected ballet teacher. "These *étoiles* of the Opera are enthusiasts," he wrote, "and are not content with the classes at the Opera itself. The success and grace of Mlle. Daunt's barefoot work could now be traced to its origin—her strength and accuracy in the technique *à la barre.*"[74]

Other dancers praised by the ballet brotherhood were Alice and Juliette Bourgat, who joined the Opéra in the early 1920s. Reviewing the 1922 revival of *La Péri,* Louis Laloy singled out Juliette for her "vigorous bounds and expressive mime" in the title role, rechoreographed now by Staats.[75] The same year, in *Petite Suite,* which Levinson dismissed as a "trotting of bare feet all around the music," it was her sister, Alice, who caught the critic's eye and actually caused him (as he put it) to "applaud the *adversary.*" Four dancers were in a boat:

> One of them, at the prow, looks ahead, fascinated; two others, pensive, observe the wake, their eyes lowered, while in the middle, a fourth, Mademoiselle [Alice] Bourgat, leans with a slow and curved movement over the invisible oar; the swaying of the skiff causes her supple body to undulate in its tunic. This imaginary crossing lasts some moments; under the baton of [Camille] Chevillard, a vision of the landscape seems to rise from the orchestra, fluid as a canvas of Corot. There is nothing that is not essential here, only four young women in lamé tunics sitting on the bare stage hearing the music vibrate in themselves. Everything is suggested, nothing is realized. It is the spectator's imagination, stimulated by the magic bow, that *creates.*[76]

Vaillat praised both sisters for their contribution to *Concerto.* Since this is the only time he had anything good to say about any eurhythmic dance or dancer, his remarks are worth quoting, even if his mistakenly credits Montoliu's choreography to Alice Bourgat:

> To [Sammartini's] exquisite music . . . Mademoiselle Alice Bourgat has arranged a pas de deux, or more correctly, a *pas* for two dancers, herself and her sister Juliette, which they execute in an identical manner, each doubling as the shadow of the other, and both wearing the same costume—a short fringed tunic of silk and a little Hindu diadem—designed by René Piot with that sure sense of orientalism that is his. Here was a composition based on eurhythmic methods, but one that was refined in personality and musicality: the arms, the legs, the entire body truly danced.[77]

Levinson, for his part, praised the "decorative sense" revealed by Montoliu in *Fresques:* he especially liked how the choreographer distributed the groups of dancers onstage and the "elegance with which he chained them in a kind of farandole."[78] And for all Levinson's complaints, he felt that Montoliu's treatment of Sammartini's music was a "revelation," leaving the spectator "free to recreate the spectacle in the inner theatre of his mind."[79]

In a real sense, the best of the Opéra's *rythmiciennes* were what might now be termed "crossover" dancers. Although, officially, they belonged to the eurhythmic section, they also appeared in classical works, even if they did not necessarily dance on pointe (although, judging from photographs, Daunt sometimes did).[80] Thus, in Staats' ballet *Frivolant* (1922) and in his dances for the opera *Padmâvatî* (1923), both Daunt and Juliette Bourgat performed alongside leading Opéra classicists, as did Yvonne Franck in the choreographer's production of *Cydalise et le chèvre-pied* (1923), and the two Bourgat sisters in his *La Nuit ensorcelée* (1923). All four dancers remained at the Opéra after the eurhythmic section was abolished in 1925, indicating the degree to which they had integrated themselves into the repertoire at large. Obviously, technical ability was a factor in this assimilation: all were proficient in classical work. However, this was not the only reason. Many roles of the period did not call for all the refinements of classical dancing. Some were character roles (in fact, Richardson, at one point, describes the choreography for Daunt as a Fury in *Castor et Pollux* as "character work").[81] Others demanded strong mimetic talents (throughout this period the Opéra made regular use of "mimes" like Georges Wague); still others, that dancers, including classical dancers, perform barefoot, as in *Les Troyens,* the first time, as a shocked Vaillat noted, that this had happened at the Opéra.[82] Moreover, apart from the principal dancers and soloists, it is unlikely that the standard of classical technique was very high, especially with regard to pointe work. In many photographs of the period, the appearance of the shoes worn by Opéra dancers suggests that they were only lightly blocked; in some instances, they also seem to lack a stiffening shank. What they resemble are the so-called "demi-pointe shoes" manufactured today by Freeds and used chiefly by British dance students. Because of their construction, these slippers give very little support to the foot. Indeed, in such shoes, the multiple turns and jumped steps on pointe associated with the Italian bravura technique of the late nineteenth century are all but impossible to execute.[83] This would tend to suggest that at the Opéra in the 1920s the difference between a crossover dancer like Daunt and the average ballet dancer was considerably less than might be expected.

More dramatic than the technical divisions between the two categories of dancers was the fact that several women of the eurhythmic section choreographed, even if they seldom had the opportunity to present their work at the Opéra. Daunt was among this group, and in 1921 she invited Richardson to a recital of dances at her studio before an audience of hand-picked guests:

Mlle. Daunt appeared with bare feet in soft Greek draperies, and gave a selection of about a dozen numbers. Here was something utterly different from the so-called Greek dance of to-day. Mlle. Daunt has conceived the idea that the technique which she has learnt à la barre is just as much the basis of bare foot dancing as it is of dancing sur les pointes in the conventional ballet. She put this to the test, and absolutely proved her point. Combining the soft arms which one associates with the neo-classic school, with the clean and accurate leg work of the operatic school, the result was a true poem. Her dances were both grandiose and humorous—her interpretation of the idea "Poland in Chains and Poland Free," in which she made use of a magnificent Chopin polonaise, was an excellent example of the former, in which her remarkable elevation was given free play. A dainty "Menuet," by Lully, was most expressively treated in a humorous vein, and her art was so great that one forgot the incongruity of the menuet being danced with bare feet, but time prevented her making the necessary changes between each number.[84]

Levinson, by contrast, was so distressed by the recital that he devoted an entire column, "Lettre à Mlle ***, de l'Opéra," to exhorting the wayward Daunt to come to her senses, forget the "outmoded childishness of Duncanism," and accept what she was—"a remarkable classical dancer."[85]

Yvonne Franck and Alice Bourgat were other members of the Opéra's eurhythmic section who choreographed as well as danced. Already in the mid-1920s, Franck had shown her work on a concert program shared with Daunt.[86] Now, in 1927, she and Bourgat teamed up on a project using students from the Opéra school. "One day," writes Odette Joyeux in her charming memoir of life as a *petit rat* in the 1920s, "I found my way to the eurhythmic studio. Although similar to ours, it was four times smaller; brown linoleum covered the floor. . . . Two young women were talking to us. . . . I didn't listen to what they were saying. I had vaguely understood that it was about a *cachet,* a fee."[87] The women, it turned out, were Franck and Bourgat, and although they belonged "to that other race" (as Joyeux thought of the *rythmiciennes*), they were going to stage a children's ballet. The title, the girls learned, was *L'Eventail de Jeanne;* it had music by Ravel, Jacques Ibert, Francis Poulenc, and a half-dozen other composers, and had been commissioned by Jeanne Dubost, a well-known hostess and music patron, for a private party. Joyeux seems to have been especially taken with Franck:

> Mademoiselle Franck was very tall. Her slender silhouette carried with elegance the masculine suits that became her better than the suggestive frocks of courtesans. . . . Under her pale blond hair, she offered an intelligent and ruddy face, and she wore a pearl necklace that I was astonished to see around her neck. She owned a beautiful convertible that she drove in an offhand way, and the luxurious modernism of her dressing room was surprising in a labyrinth where everything seemed to be of another age, another world.[88]

Joyeux's own dance, to Poulenc's "Pastourelle," pleased her immensely:

> The music attacked; I waited a few measures, then jumped onstage. Straightaway, I became a little girl on a stroll, a capricious little girl who nonchalantly hoisted herself on pointe, then, weary from the effort, dropped to the floor. The little girl

sighed, stretched, . . . played with her hat, and, without knowing why, recommenced her stroll, interspersed with leaps and pointes. The little girl whirled, then deliberately turned her back, and waddled off. Flirty and provocative, she returned, laughed, stuck out her tongue, and bounded out.[89]

Despite the resounding success of *Jeanne*, which, exceptionally, was taken into the repertoire of the Opéra although only in 1929, there was little in-house demand for these choreographers' services. The two continued to dance: Franck led the ballet (choreographed by Nijinska) in the 1926 and 1928 revivals of Gluck's *Alceste* and appeared in Nijinska's dances for the 1927 production of Philippe Gaubert's opera *Naïla*, in which Bourgat also performed. At the premiere of Jacques Ibert's opera *Persée et Andromède* (choreographed by Staats) in 1929, Bourgat was one of the Furies; at that of Maurice Emmanuel's opera *Salamine* (choreographed by Guerra) a few months later, Franck was the Danseuse Mariandyne. The following year, the two appeared in the divertissement by Staats for Raoul Brunel's opera *La Tentation de Saint Antoine*. With Serge Lifar's appointment as the Opéra's principal ballet master late in 1929, however, their careers waned. After *Tentation*, their names disappear from the cast lists of new productions (although both appeared in the 1931 revival of *Padmâvatî*), leading one to assume that they were either dropped from the company or pushed aside. The Opéra's eurhythmic adventure was over.

By 1930, however, the *classe de rythmique* itself was long gone. Five years before, adopting the tone of a necrologist, Levinson had announced to *Comoedia* readers—with what pleasure one can easily imagine—that the class was "no more."[90] Its death marked a turning point in the "reclassicization" of ballet, a call to order analogous to the conservative trend that appeared in French painting and music in the years after World War I. Just as Picasso had turned to Ingres and Stravinsky to a slew of composers past, so the Opéra began to take stock of its heritage. In 1924, *Giselle* returned to the repertoire after an absence of more than a half century; the following year, *Soir de fête*, a one-act work by Staats based on Delibes' music for *La Source*, invoked the forms and spirit of one of the Opéra's most popular ballets of the 1860s and 1870s. Other works, from *La Nuit ensorcelée* (1923), by Staats to a libretto by Bakst and music by Chopin, to *Le Triomphe de l'amour*, a reconstruction of Lully's seventeenth-century *ballet royal* with choreography by Staats, looked resolutely backward. Well might Levinson write in 1925 that "in one season, the Opéra ballet had won back much lost ground. . . . The revivals of *Le Triomphe de l'Amour, Giselle*, and *La Source* . . . signify a deliberate return to French tradition. . . . The choice of works implies a recognition of the *danse d'école* as the basis for all true renewal. Embracing the beautiful cadences of classicism, the Opéra rejects the idioms of Geneva and pidgen-French exoticism."[91] So strong was the prevailing spirit of reaction that by 1925 even Nijinska, whose studio in post-revolutionary Kiev was linked in the general mind with Dalcroze experimentalism,[92] insisted to

Rouché that were she to teach at the Opéra, she would have nothing to do with eurhythmic dancers.[93]

The upshot of all this was to close off an important channel of dance experimentalism. By contrast with Germany and the United States, where elements of the Dalcroze system, like elements of Duncanism, Denishawn, and other movements, seeped into the richly textured fabric of *Ausdruckstanz* and modern dance, in France the experimentalist impulse failed either to penetrate the "high" dance mainstream or to establish institutional alternatives to ballet, even if certain expressions of that impulse—such as Djemil-Anik's exotic dances or Caryathis' avant-gardist ones—found a temporary berth on the music hall or concert stage. In a country where the production of art was totally centralized, where the state played a critical role in funding, and where the prestige conferred by a single institution was the coin of cultural acceptance, rejection by the Opéra of dance experimentalism was tantamount to willing its artistic death.

The disbanding of the Opéra's *classe de rythmique* in 1925 marked the beginning of the end of the experimentalist dance movement born in France in the first decade of the twentieth century from the combined influences of Duncanism, aestheticism, exoticism, eurhythmics, and the Ballets Russes. All had come together in the Théâtre des Arts, not well perhaps, but in a way that proved sufficiently inspiring to turn several dancers into choreographers. Like Denishawn, the Théâtre des Arts was a crucible of "modern" dance talent, with the added distinction that, like the Ballets Russes, it was also a meeting ground for painters and composers of high order. When Jacques Rouché signed the order disbanding the troupe he had founded and defended at great cost, did he think back to the days when the new was an idea haloed with possibility, rather than a betrayal of the great tradition? When the exploration of techniques outside the *danse d'école* was not always condemned as a pastime for dilettantes? When works like *Le Sacre du Printemps* shook the world? One would like to think he did, if only for a brief and passing moment.

NOTES

1. The letters are filed in AJ13/1206 (II), Archives Nationales (Paris).
2. Although named to the post in 1913, Rouché did not actually take office until 1915 because of the outbreak of World War I.
3. See, for instance, Laloy's reviews of Léo Staats' version of the ballet *Namouna* ("La Musique," *La Grande Revue,* 10 April 1908, pp. 608–611); Isadora Duncan ("La Musique," *La Grande Revue,* 10 March 1909, pp. 184–188); Michel Fokine's ballet *Le Pavillon d'Armide* and Diaghilev's production of Alexander Borodin's opera *Prince Igor* ("La Musique," *La Grande Revue,* 10 June 1909, pp. 607–610); Olga Preobrajen-

ska's two-act version of *Swan Lake* at the London Hippodrome ("Le Ballet Russe à Londres," *La Grande Revue*, 25 June 1910, pp. 864–866). For Matisse's "Notes d'un peintre," see *La Grande Revue*, 25 December 1908, pp. 731–747; for Emile Jaques-Dalcroze's "Le Rythme au Théâtre," *La Grande Revue*, 10 June 1910, pp. 539–550. Drawings by André Dunoyer de Segonzac accompanied the articles by Jaques-Dalcroze and Laloy (on Duncan), as well as the review by "Toulet" of Diaghilev's 1910 season ("La Saison Russe à Paris," *La Grande Revue*, 25 June 1910, pp. 867–873).

4. Jacques Rouché, *L'Art théâtral moderne* (Paris: Cornely, 1910). A new edition appeared in 1924.

5. For Piot's double career as a fresco painter and a designer, see Rodolph Rapetti's "René Piot et le renouveau de la fresque" and Martine Kahane's "René Piot. Décors de théâtre," in *René Piot, 1866–1934*, catalogue of an exhibition presented at the Musée d'Orsay, 26 February–27 May 1991.

6. "Mise en scène en crise, ou crise de mise en scène? Ce que j'ai fait au Théâtre des Arts. Ce que je fais et veux faire à l'Opéra," *Excelsior*, n.d. Dossier d'artiste (Jacques Rouché), Bibliothèque de l'Opéra (Paris) (hereafter BN-Opéra).

7. "Au Théâtre des Arts," *Comoedia Illustré*, n.d. [1913], p. 655. Valentine Hugo Collection (hereafter Hugo Collection), Folder 25, Theatre Museum (London).

8. *Adélaïde, ou le Langage des fleurs* was staged by François Ambrosini at the Opéra in 1917; *La Tragédie de Salomé*, by Nicolà Guerra, in 1919; *La Péri*, in a new version by Clustine for Anna Pavlova and Hubert Stowitts, in 1921; *Istar*, by Léo Staats, in 1924. *Ma Mère l'Oye* was produced at the Opéra in 1915.

9. Of Hugard's contribution, and that of the ballet's other collaborators, Ravel had nothing but high praise. In a letter dated 1 February 1912, he wrote to Rouché: "Your idea of mounting *Ma Mère l'Oye* enchanted me from the very beginning. For a long time, I have dreamed of writing a work for the Théâtre des Arts, whch is the only theater in France today that brings us something new. However, I didn't dare hope for the total joy, so delightful to a composer, of seeing a work for the theater realized exactly as he had conceived it. The sumptuous and delicate harmony of Drésa's décor and costumes, whose theatrical logic is so fresh and personal, seem to me the most perfect commentary for my musical fantasy. Madame Hugard also proved to be an intelligent and fine collaborator, who took it upon herself to observe my tiniest instructions, and to realize them in an elegant and sensitive manner. All of my interpreters, including the children young and old, brought to their roles, large and small, an artistic integrity which delighted me and touched me profoundly. . . . Above all, dear Monsieur Rouché, I wish to express to you my pleasure at having met an artistic director whose constant concern is to respect the composer's ideas, while assisting him with the kind of intelligent advice that comes from a gentleman of taste" (*A Ravel Reader: Correspondence, Articles, Interviews*, ed. Arbie Orenstein [New York: Columbia University Press, 1990], pp. 129–130). At this time, Hugard was probably a dancer at the Opéra; in 1932, she was definitely on the payroll, although presumably as a teacher or régisseur. A fluent writer, she contributed an essay on the Opéra, "Du

Ballet classique," to the volume *Les Spectacles à travers les ages: musique, danse* (Paris, Editions du Cygne, [1932]), pp. 193–212, and the preface to Gaspard Maillol's album of woodcuts of Opéra dancers, *Danseuses* (Paris: La Presse à Bras, [1932]). She is identifed in the Maillol album as "Jane Hugard de l'Opéra."

10. *Namouna* was produced at the Opéra in 1882 by Lucien Petipa; *Javotte* received its Paris premiere at the Opéra-Comique in 1899 in a choreography by Madame Mariquita.

11. For photographs of her in *La Danse prohibée*, see Jean Codak, "Sahary-Djeli: The 'Mysterious One,'" *Arabesque*, November–December 1986, pp. 12–13, as well as the cover of the same issue.

12. In 1913, for instance, he partnered Ariane Hugon, another Opéra dancer, in *L'Amoureuse Leçon*.

13. Elise Jouhandeau, *Joies et douleurs d'une belle excentrique: L'Altesse des hasards* (Paris: Flammarion, 1954), pp. 13, 19.

14. André Levinson, *La Danse d'aujourd'hui: Etudes, Notes, Portraits* (Paris: Duchartre et Van Buggenhoudt, 1929), p. 456.

15. A prolific writer, d'Udine was the author of *Dissonance*, a "musical novel" (Paris: Editions du Courrier Musical, [1901–1902]); *Gluck* (Paris: Henri Laurens, 1906?); *Qu'est-ce que la Danse?* (Paris: Henri Laurens, 1921), *Qu'est-ce que la peinture et les autres arts plastiques?* (Paris: Henri Laurens, 1929). Levinson, in *La Danse d'aujourd'hui* (p. 456), mentions two other titles—*La Géométrie rythmique* and *L'Art et le Geste*—neither of which I have been able to locate. D'Udine's real name was Albert Cozanet. I am indebted to Selma Odum for the information about Madame Barbey-Rouché.

16. Jouhandeau, pp. 37 and 63. According to Caryathis, Staats had the other dancers in the cast compose their dances as well (p. 62).

17. *Ibid.,* p. 101.

18. *Ibid.,* p. 227. Caryathis writes that Dullin managed to "circumvent" Rouché, who engaged one of her friends instead.

19. *Les Mémoires du Baron Mollet* (Paris: Gallimard, 1963), p. 134. "La Fête nègre," which took place on 9 June 1919, was organized in tandem with Guillaume's "Première Exposition d'art nègre et d'art océanien" at the Galerie Devambez, 10–31 May 1919. For Guillaume's various activities and the interest in African art among the Paris avant-garde, see Colette Giraudon, *Les Arts à Paris chez Paul Guillaume 1918–1935*, catalogue of an exhibition at the Musée de l'Orangerie, 14 September 1993–3 January 1994; Paul Guillaume, *Les Ecrits de Paul Guillaume* (Neuchâtel: Editions Ides et Calendes, 1993); Katia Samaltanos, *Apollinaire: Catalyst for Primitivism, Picabia, and Duchamp* (Ann Arbor, Mich.: UMI Research Press, 1984), especially chapter 2, "Apollinaire and Primitivism."

20. "Dans les Théâtres," *Le Gaulois*, 2 April 1919, p. 4.

21. "Le Deuxième Spectacle de *L'Oasis*," *Comoedia*, 25 June 1921, Hugo Collection, Folder 21.

22. Ornella Volta, *Satie et la danse* (Paris: Editions Plume, 1992), pp. 45–50.

23. Levinson, *La Danse d'aujourd'hui*, p. 469.

24. "Petites nouvelles théâtrales," *Comoedia*, 16 December 1924, p. 2. A rehearsal photograph of Marcel Duchamp and Bronia Perlmutter, both nude, in a scene from *Ciné-Sketch* is reproduced in Billy Klüver and Julie Martin, *Kiki of Montparnasse: Artists and Lovers 1900–1930* (New York: Abrams, 1989), p. 137.

25. André Arnyvelde, "Ecoles de beauté," *Je sais tout-Nöel*, n.d., pp. 612–613, Hugo Collection, Folder 49.

26. Baron Mollet describes her as a "black *martiniquaise*" (*Les Mémoires du Baron Mollet*, p. 134). However, photographs of the period indicate that she was of mixed blood, closer in coloring to *café au lait*, as Levinson described her "beautiful . . . torso," in a 1922 review ("Classicisme et exotisme," *La Danse au Théâtre* [Paris: Bloud & Gay, 1924], p. 136). For photographs, see Levinson's *La Danse d'aujourd'hui*, pp. 299 and 306, and his *Les Visages de la danse* (Paris: Grasset, 1933), p. 247.

27. *Les Mémoires du Baron Mollet*, p. 134.

28. Levinson, *La Danse au Théâtre*, p. 136.

29. In *La Danse d'aujourd'hui*, Levinson took Djemil to task for precisely this aspect of her work: "Each of her exotic images has an atmospheric value. . . . Their ports of call . . . lead her through Shanghai, Angor-Wat, Delhi, and Baalbek, from the banks of the Sumida to the quays of Algiers; no sooner has she landed than she embarks for the perfumed Antilles. . . . I admire the intelligent will, the robust and beautiful body, the application of this individual artist, who searches relentlessly and continually adds to her creations. But I judge her method with extreme skepticism. . . . Mademoiselle Djemil-Anik never ceases to hide her true face under masks rejected as soon as they are donned. . . . She gives herself over to pastiche, taking figurative monuments as points of departure. It is a mistake to seek counsel from stones; . . . the conventions that determine their unchanging forms are utterly opposed to saltatory flight. . . . The squatting Bodhisatva whose hieratic pose Mademoiselle Djemil reproduces at the beginning of one dance waits impatiently to return to his initial pose" (p. 307).

30. René Piot, letter to Jacques Rouché, n.d. [1911]. Fonds Rouché, Th. des Arts, R8(4), Pièce 15(7), BN-Opéra.

31. René Piot, letter to Jacques Rouché, n.d. [1911?]. Fonds Rouché, Th. des Arts, R8(4), Pièce 15(9), BN-Opéra.

32. René Piot, letter to Jacques Rouché, n.d. [1912?]. Fonds Rouché, Th. des Arts R8(4), Pièce 15(19), BN-Opéra.

33. René Piot, letter to Jacques Rouché, n.d. [1912?]. Fonds Rouché, Th. des Arts R8(4), Pièce 15(28), BN-Opéra.

34. Probably Teresina Negri, a dancer at the Opéra-Comique.

35. René Piot, letter to Jacques Rouché, n.d. [1912?]. Fonds Rouché, Th. des Arts, R8(4), Pièce 15(24), BN-Opéra.

36. Although the Ballets Russes appeared at the Opéra in 1910 and 1914, most of its prewar seasons were given at the Théâtre du Châtelet and the Théâtre des Champs-Elysées.

37. "Courrier des théâtres," *Figaro*, 19 September 1916, p. 4.

38. Irwin Spector, *Rhythm and Life: The Work of Emile Jaques-Dalcroze* (Stuyvesant, N.Y.: Pendragon Press, [1990]), pp. 82, 224, 230.

39. Jacques Rouché, "La Danse en Russie (Impressions de voyage, hiver 1914)," in *L'Art du Ballet des origines à nos jours* (Paris: Editions de Tambourinaire, 1952), p. 100.

40. For Honegger, see Spector, pp. 254–257; for Claudel, see his article "Sur la Musique," *L'Opéra de Paris*, no. 2 (October–November 1950), p. 4. Claudel wrote in part: "I must confess that I have the greatest sympathy for the ideas of Jacques [sic] Dalcroze. Many years ago I attended a performance of Gluck's *Orphée* staged by him that was full of beauty. When a true school, as yet nonexistent, is established for the training of actors, the doctrine of Jacques [sic] Dalcroze will play a fundamental role in that undertaking. No step or gesture of the actor can be made without heeding a certain inner ear open to the bar."

41. See, for instance, Emile Jaques-Dalcroze, "Le Rythme, les races et les tempéraments," *Mercure de France*, 1 April 1919, pp. 408–422; "Rythmiciennes," *Femina*, 1 August 1919, pp. 27–30; Marius Boisson, "Le Mouvement discipliné par le rythme des sons. M. Jaques-Dalcroze fait une démonstration de sa méthode intégrale d'eurythmie, "*Comoedia*, 13 February 1920, p. 1; Fernand Vandérem, "Rythmique," *Femina*, April 1920, pp. 2–6; W. Berteval, "L'Enseignement de la Musique par la Méthode Jaques-Dalcroze: la gymnastique rythmique," *La Grande Revue*, 1 July 1923, pp. 119–132. In 1921 and 1922, *La Danse* devoted a number of articles to teachers and choreographers associated with the eurhythmic movement. See, for example, Albert Jeanneret, "La Rythmique," *La Danse*, February 1921, n.p.; André Gliger, "Jeanne Ronsay et la beauté nouvelle," *La Danse*, August 1921, n.p.; D. Strohl, "Danses gymnastiques," *La Danse*, September 1921, n.p.; Paul-Sentenac, "La Danseuse Romana et son école," *La Danse*, October 1921, n.p.; F. d'Hautrelieu, "Madame Geneviève Petit: Prêtesse du rythme," *La Danse*, November 1921, n.p., and "La Gymnastique harmonique," *La Danse*, March 1922, n.p. Albert Jeanneret was a composer and Dalcroze teacher who had studied at Hellerau; he was also the brother of the architect Le Corbusier (Spector, pp. 153n and 157).

42. Léandre Vaillat, *Ballets de l'Opéra de Paris (Ballets dans les opéras et nouveaux ballets)* (Paris: Compagnie française des arts graphiques, 1947), p. 104.

43. Marie Louise Morenté, a dancer in the corps de ballet, was among those few who opted to follow the "cours de plastique." Her letter, dated 2 December 1917, is filed with the other responses to Rouché's query, in AJ13/1206 (II), Archives Nationales.

44. Rouché, "La Danse en Russie," p. 100.

45. Olga Soutzo, letter to Jacques Rouché, 11 September [1917]. Blanche Guillemin was another who welcomed the "stimulus" of discovering "new tendencies in dance art," while choosing to continue studying with Mauri (4 September 1917).

46. Cyril W. Beaumont, *Complete Book of Ballets* (London: Putnam, 1937), p. 621.

47. Jeanine Laugier, letter to Jacques Rouché, n.d. [September 1917]. In 1925, discussing a possible teaching position at the Opéra, Bronislava Nijinska insisted that "classes

from 1 1/2 to 2 hours [were] essential" (Romola Nijinsky, letter to Jacques Rouché, 3 April 1925, AJ13/1213–1097, Archives Nationales).

48. Camille Bos, letter to Jacques Rouché, 5 September [1917].
49. Jeanne Schwarz, letter to Jacques Rouché, 13 September [1917].
50. The list is in the Fonds Rouché, Pièce 106, BN-Opéra. Those dancers who failed to respond to the questionnaire are so noted.
51. "Est-ce la grève à l'Opéra?" *L'Humanité,* 31 December 1919, p. 1.
52. In 1921, George Cecil listed the rankings for readers of *The Dancing Times* as second *quadrille,* first *quadrille, coryphées, petits sujets, grands sujets, premières danseuses,* and *étoiles* (George Cecil, "The Paris Opera Ballet," *The Dancing Times,* January 1921, p. 335).
53. Hugard, "Du Ballet classique," p. 208.
54. *Ibid.*
55. For most of the operas, see Vaillat, pp. 104–114; for the ballets and remaining operas, see the title entries in Stéphane Wolff's *L'Opéra au Palais Garnier (1875–1962)* (Paris: Slatkine, 1962).
56. Vaillat, p. 107.
57. Pasmanik also contributed to music journals, sometimes under the name of Pasmanik-Bespaloff. I am grateful to Selma Odum for the background information about her.
58. Spector, p. 235. Howarth later worked with the directors Fermin Gemier and Jacques Copeau. It would be interesting to know if Howarth is the "Mademoiselle Jasmine" who played the role of Alkippé in *Artemis troublée.*
59. Nicolà Guerra, letter to Jacques Rouché, 20 January 1918. Fonds Rouché, Pièce 166 (Guerra, Nicolà), BN-Opéra.
60. For the day-to-day repertoire during the period May–August 1922 (although not for the individual performances of the July ballet season), see the booking sheets (*feuilles de location*) in AJ13/1428, Archives Nationales.
61. "Théâtres," *Le Temps,* 11 July 1922, p. 3.
62. "Théâtres," *Le Temps,* 12 July 1922, p. 5.
63. "Théâtres," *Le Temps,* 18 July 1922, p. 4.
64. Obviously, neither Fokine nor Rubinstein was French. Guerra was Italian-born, as was Zambelli, although after nearly three decades on the Opéra stage, she had become something of a French national monument. Howarth was probably English; Pasmanik may have been Polish. The employment of foreign artists was an issue (along with demands for cost-of-living increases) in the strike of Opéra personnel that began in mid-October 1920 and lasted until the end of November. See, for instance, P. S., "Le syndicalisme à l'Opéra," *Le Temps,* 11 October 1920, p. 1. For Guerra's international career, see Francesca Falcone, "Dalla notazione alla scene: *Edelweiss* di Nicolà Guerra," *Chorégraphie,* 2000, pp. 203–236. This was part of a special issue on nineteenth-century Italian dance (*Recupero, ricostruzione, conservazione del patrimonio coreutico italiana del XIX secolo*).
65. Spector, pp. 74, 196–197, 230, 240. Spector states that Brooke was engaged before Jane Erb (pp. 205, 261). However, there is no evidence supporting this claim.

66. René Piot, letter to Jacques Rouché, n.d. [1921]. L.A.S. (Piot, René), 96, BN-Opéra.

67. Spector, pp. 156, 235, 240.

68. Vaillat, p. 107.

69. Ivor Guest, in his history of ballet at the Opéra, devotes a paragraph to the subject; Jacqueline Robinson, in her history of modern dance in France, ignores it entirely. See Guest, pp. 158–160, and Jacqueline Robinson, *L'Aventure de la danse modern en France (1920–1970)* (Paris: Editions Bougé, 1990).

70. "Sitter Out," *The Dancing Times,* May 1921, p. 638.

71. "Sitter Out," *The Dancing Times,* July 1921, p. 777.

72. A. t'Serstevens, *A la Danseuse* (Paris: Lapina, [1925]), n.p.

73. Levinson, "Le Répertoire: 'La Tragédie de Salomé,'" *La Danse au Théâtre,* pp. 26–27.

74. "Sitter Out," *The Dancing Times,* July 1921, pp. 777–778.

75. Louis Laloy, "La Musique: Quelques Réflexions sur le ballet moderne," *La Revue de Paris,* 15 May 1922, p. 426.

76. Levinson, "'En Bateau.' Le Préjugé du rythme," *La Danse au théâtre,* pp. 15–16.

77. Vaillat, p. 108.

78. Levinson, *La Danse d'aujourd'hui,* p. 452.

79. *Ibid.,* p. 456.

80. On the inside cover of the May 1921 issue of *The Dancing Times,* Daunt is shown in costume for an unidentified ballet wearing pointe shoes. In a photograph for another unidentified ballet, this one in Orientalist style, she again appears in pointe shoes. Clipping File (Yvonne Daunt), Dance Division, The New York Public Library for the Performing Arts.

81. "Sitter Out," *The Dancing Times,* March 1922, p. 502.

82. Vaillat, p. 104.

83. For photographs of various Opéra dancers, see Levinson's section on "L'Esprit de la danse classique et le ballet d'Opéra" in *La Danse d'aujourd'hui.* I am indebted to Robert Greskovic for sharing his thoughts with me on the subject of pointe work.

84. "Sitter Out," *The Dancing Times,* May 1921, p. 638.

85. Levinson, "Lettre à Mlle ***, de l'Opéra," *La Danse au théâtre,* p. 72.

86. For a review of this concert, see Levinson, *La Danse d'aujourd'hui,* p. 479.

87. Odette Joyeux, *Côté jardin: mémoires d'un rat* (Paris: Gallimard, 1951), pp. 163–164.

88. *Ibid.,* pp. 165–166.

89. *Ibid.,* p. 169.

90. Levinson, "La Danse. Epitaphe," *Comoedia,* 21 September 1925, p. 3.

91. Levinson, *La Danse d'aujourd'hui,* p. 201.

92. Myroslava M. Mudrak notes this on several occasions in her book *The New Generation and Artistic Modernism in the Ukraine* (Ann Arbor, Mich.: UMI Research Press, 1986).

93. Romola Nijinsky, letter to Jacques Rouché, 3 April 1925, AJ13/1213–1097, Archives Nationales.

RIVALS FOR THE NEW

THE BALLETS SUÉDOIS AND THE BALLETS RUSSES

In the early 1920s, the Ballets Russes faced a rival that challenged its monopoly of avant-garde ballet—the Ballets Suédois. Organized by Rolf de Maré, the new company made its début at the Théâtre des Champs-Elysées on 25 October 1920 with an ambitious program of works choreographed by Jean Borlin, the company's star. Three ballets were given on the opening night—*Iberia, Jeux,* and *Nuit de Saint-Jean*—and in the course of the season, which lasted for nearly six weeks, six new ones were added—*Divertissement, Maison de Fous, Le Tombeau de Couperin, El Greco, Derviches,* and *Les Vierges Folles.* The premiere was a glamorous affair, attended by everyone who was anyone in Paris, including Serge Diaghilev. Anxious to weigh the potential threat to his own enterprise (which was then performing in London), he braved a Channel crossing for a glimpse of the new company, which ended its season only days before his Ballets Russes was scheduled to open at the same theater.

Diaghilev had genuine cause for concern. Although the Ballets Russes had managed to survive the First World War, financially, its position was shaky. Rich Russian patrons had disappeared with the Revolution; German touring venues with the Axis defeat. For months the company had been a "turn" on the English music-hall stage, while its grand postwar comeback at the Paris Opéra early in 1920 had been marred by a two-week strike of Opéra personnel. And, compared to the fifty-odd performances of the Ballets Suédois opening season, the Ballets Russes season that followed would amount to fewer than a dozen.

Still, Diaghilev must have found some consolation in the identity—or lack of identity—of the rival enterprise. To all appearances, the new company was a knockoff of the Ballets Russes, from its name, which meant "Swedish Ballet," to its repertory, roster of collaborators, and general aesthetic approach. Indeed, most of the works presented during the troupe's maiden season recalled its Russian predecessor. *Iberia,* for instance, drew on the Spanish idiom of *Le Tricorne* (1919); *El Greco* on the painterly approach of *Las Meninas* (1916); *Nuit de Saint-Jean* on the stylized neoprimitivism of *Midnight Sun* (1916). The eighteenth-century setting of *Le Tombeau de Couperin* recalled *Le Pavillon d'Armide* (1909),

This essay was originally published in *Paris Modern: The Swedish Ballet 1920–1925,* ed. Nancy Van Norman Baer (San Francisco: The Fine Arts Museums of San Francisco, 1996).

while the Chopin music and romantic style of *Divertissement* and *Pas de Deux* invoked *Les Sylphides* (1909).[1] *Jeux,* created by the Ballets Russes in 1913 and now recreated by the Ballets Suédois, testified even more dramatically to Maré's adoption of the Diaghilev "recipe."

Not only did Maré model his initial repertory on that of the Ballets Russes, he also enlisted a number of Diaghilev collaborators. These included the composers Claude Debussy (*Jeux* and *La Boîte à joujoux*) and Maurice Ravel (*Le Tombeau de Couperin*), the painter Pierre Bonnard (who designed the scenery for *Jeux*), and the poet Jean Cocteau (who created *Les Mariés de la Tour Eiffel*). Maré also drew on key Diaghilev collaborative ideas. Rejecting the nineteenth-century "specialist" tradition, he commissioned stage designs from easel painters and music scores from symphonic composers, freelancers who formed the company's larger creative "community." He viewed ballet as a fully collaborative medium where artists met as equals and where performance served the multiple functions of art gallery, concert hall, and theatrical showcase. "Modern ballet," he wrote in 1926, "is . . . the synthetic fusion of four fundamentally divergent arts: choreography, painting, music, and literature. . . . The Swedish Ballet has always held as its principle the intimate association of the[se] four arts. . . . [which] mutually supplement one another [and] offer the possible approach to a perfect totality."[2] Finally, like Diaghilev before him, Maré used the exotica of folklore to define the national character of his enterprise. Even if a number of dancers were actually Danish,[3] the display of traditional Swedish costumes, themes, and dances in works like *Nuit de Saint-Jean* and *Dansgille* certified the company's "native" identity.

Like the Ballets Russes, however, the Ballets Suédois was preeminently a showcase for the modern. The company's scores (apart from the traditional music for its Swedish works) were either new or of recent vintage; its designs reflected current trends in painting and stage design; its choreography explored a range of contemporary idioms and styles. The organization of the company was equally indebted to Diaghilev. Not only was it an independent, privately financed entity, it was also a vehicle for its male star, Maré's protégé and lover Jean Borlin. If imitation is any measure of success, Diaghilev had good reason to be flattered by the new venture.

It had resources, however, of which Diaghilev could only dream. A millionaire, Maré poured a fortune into the Ballets Suédois. Nothing less than the best would do. The dancers wore costumes from the ateliers of Marie Muelle and Max Weldy, leading Paris costume houses, and dresses by the couturière Jeanne Lanvin. The sets were executed by Georges Mouveau, the Opéra's head scene painter. Guest conductors were sometimes brought in, and, on occasion, musical soloists and even special orchestras: one hundred musicians were hired for the opening season alone. Posters were commissioned from Paul Colin, Francis Picabia, and Miguel Covarrubias.

Moreover, to ensure the proper environment for his enterprise, Maré took a seven-year lease on the Théâtre des Champs-Elysées, the magnificent Art Nouveau theater where *Le Sacre du Printemps* had received its premiere. He founded *La Danse*, the only Paris dance magazine of the period, which chronicled the activities of the company in detail and at length, according the Ballets Russes only a fraction of the coverage. He also bought up *Le Monsieur, Paris-Journal*, a guide to goings-on in Paris, and *Le Théâtre*, a glossy monthly that merged with *Comoedia Illustré* in 1922, thus eliminating another source of publicity for the Ballets Russes, whose programs for years had appeared as inserts in the semi-monthly magazine.

The new company quickly struck out on its own. A publicity leaflet for its November 1921 season, which opened in Paris just weeks after the premiere of Diaghilev's *Sleeping Princess* in London, announced the change in direction in the provocative tones of a Dada manifesto and in terms that cast the Ballets Russes as a reactionary bogeyman:

> Only the Ballets Suédois 'DARES.' Only the Ballets Suédois represents contemporary life. Only the Ballets Suédois truly opposes academicism. ALL ACADEMICISMS. Only the Ballets Suédois can please an international public because Rolf de Maré thinks only about the pleasure of evolution. The Ballets Suédois seeks neither to be old nor to be modern; it stands beyond the absurdities mounted under the pretext of THEATRICAL ART; it propagates REVOLUTION by a movement that every day destroys convention by replacing it with invention. LONG LIVE LIFE.[4]

Between 1921 and 1924, Maré largely succeeded in edging Diaghilev to the sidelines of avant-garde Paris. Although the Ballets Russes produced a few works, including Prokofiev's *Chout* and Stravinsky's *Le Renard*, with impeccable avant-garde credentials, it was only in 1923 that Diaghilev staged a modernist masterpiece that transcended the best of his rival's offerings. *Les Noces*, probably the greatest dance work of the decade, teamed three of his closest Russian collaborators: Stravinsky, his "first son," as composer; Natalia Goncharova, as designer; and Bronislava Nijinska, as choreographer. For the most part, however, the productions of these years reveal a Diaghilev more closely attuned to the conservative temper of the Right Bank than to the dadaist atmosphere of Montparnasse. From *Aurora's Wedding* and *Le Spectre de la Rose*, high points of the 1922 season, to *Les Tentations de la Bergère, Cimarosiana*, and the series of nineteenth-century operas—Emmanuel Chabrier's *Une Education manquée*, Charles Gounod's *La Colombe, Le Médecin malgré lui*, and *Philémon et Baucis*—presented in Monte Carlo early in 1924, a significant part of the Ballets Russes repertory turned away from modernism and themes of contemporary life.

For the Ballets Suédois, by contrast, these same years were a time of frenzied experiment. Beginning in 1921, the company became a meeting ground for the most exciting young talents of Paris. A key figure in this was Jean Cocteau. An early enthusiast of the Ballets Russes, he had contributed to two of its productions, the lackluster *Le Dieu Bleu* (1912) and *Parade* (1917), a small gem that evoked the poetry of the fairground and also brought cubism to the ballet stage. Three years later, at the Comédie des Champs-Elysées, he produced *Le Boeuf sur le Toit*, an "American farce," as he described it, "by a Parisian who has never been in America"[5] set in a Prohibition-era speakeasy. The following year came *Les Mariés de la Tour Eiffel,* another tribute to the "poetry and miracle of everyday life," represented, this time, by a madcap wedding party at the most famous monument of Paris.[6] The work grew out of Cocteau's Saturday night dinners with the "faithful"—painters Jean Hugo, his wife, Valentine Gross Hugo, and Irène Lagut, writers Paul Morand and Raymond Radiguet, and the composers of the group recently baptized "Les Six"—Louis Durey, Georges Auric, Francis Poulenc, Germaine Tailleferre, Arthur Honegger, and Darius Milhaud. Nearly all contributed to *Mariés*, which had sets by Lagut, costumes and masks by Jean Hugo, music by all the members of Les Six, except Durey, and was reviewed in *La Nouvelle Revue française* by Paul Morand.[7] Passing over Diaghilev, with whom he was temporarily at odds, Cocteau offered the work to Maré, who promptly offered him a contract.[8]

Along with *Mariés*, the outstanding work of the company's 1921 season was *L'Homme et son désir*. Conceived by Milhaud and the poet Paul Claudel during their wartime diplomatic service in Brazil, the work was intended for Vaslav Nijinsky, whose dancing with the touring Ballets Russes had "so impressed" the poet that "he immediately conceived the subject of a ballet for him."[9] However, Nijinsky's dancing days were numbered, and Diaghilev, whom Milhaud approached in 1920, rejected the project. "My symbolic and dramatic ballet," the composer wrote, "no longer corresponded with the needs of the day."[10] So, Milhaud took the work to Maré, who agreed to stage it, in spite of the expense of hiring the four singers, eleven instrumental soloists, and seventeen extra percussion instruments required by the score.

"A plastic drama . . . born of the Brazilian forest," as Claudel described the ballet in a program note, *L'Homme et son désir* was a work of major significance. The subject, he wrote elsewhere, "is the theme of man trapped in a passion, an idea, a desire, and vainly endeavouring to escape, as though from a prison with invisible bars, until the point when a woman, the image of both Death and Love, comes to claim him and take him with her offstage."[11] The score was equally original, with passages for unaccompanied percussion—clashing cymbals, tiny bells, flutes of Pan—that evoked the nocturnal sounds of the forest, the ballet's primal world. However, the most striking aspect of the production was its setting, which Claudel had worked out with the painter Audrey Parr. The stage was divided into four tiers (including the stage floor) representing the different planes of symbolic action. On the uppermost tier were the Hours, a dozen women who processed across the stage for the entire duration of the action, framing it temporally and spatially. Just below was the flame-colored

Moon, and on the lowest tier, her shadow, while ranged vertically on the sides were groups of musicians. The drama unfolded at the center: Here, clad only in briefs and the body makeup that created an effect of sculptural nudity, Man endured the torments of memory and illusion that ended only with the coming of day. The mysticism that infused the work (critic Florence Gilliam spoke of "its trance-like remoteness" and "throb of hidden passion"),[12] like the organization of stage space and the use of rhythmic movement, recalled Emile Jaques-Dalcroze's experiments at Hellerau, where Claudel's play *The Tidings Brought to Marie* had received its premiere in 1912.

In 1922 came another Ballets Suédois milestone, *Skating Rink*. The work was based on a prose poem by Riciotto Canudo, who saw the rink as a mirror of contemporary life—anguished, full of carnal longing, hate, and desperation. From the incessant circling of the crowd to the frenzied lovemaking of the Madman to the sudden intrusion of his knife-wielding rival, the ballet pulsed with violence and working-class life in the raw. The score, by Honegger, was as feverish as the action, "speed[ing] along," as critic Emile Vuillermoz put it, "like the skaters' roller skates on the cement floor, . . . lit by the arc lamps and muffled by the cigarette smoke."[13]

However, as with *L'Homme et son désir*, the most striking aspect of the ballet was its design. The curtain, scenery, and costumes were by Fernand Léger, and with their bold geometric shapes, flattened perspectives, and brilliant colors, they formed an enormous abstract painting. Léger conceived the action as an interplay of moving shapes and shifting color constellations, a sequence of images that changed according to the evolutions of the dance but absorbed the dancer into the scenic landscape. "Léger does away with the dancer as a representation of human elements," wrote Maurice Raynal after the premiere. "The dancer, in his view, should become an integral part of the décor, a plastic element that will be a moving part of the décor's plastic elements." By way of example, he describes a moment in the ballet where Léger arranged the "mobile decor"—or dancers—in contrasting masses, with "ten characters *in red, moving at speed* set against ten characters *in yellow, moving slowly.*"[14] The approach was an extension of cubofuturist ideas that had circulated within the avant-garde since the early 1910s and that Diaghilev himself had toyed with during the war, not only in *Fireworks* (1917), which eliminated the dancer entirely, but also in Fortunato Depero's unrealized *Le Chant du Rossignol*, where the artist described the chief interest of the dances as being the "movement of volumes."[15]

Léger's second commission for the Ballets Suédois was *La Création du monde*, produced in 1923. Probably the most distinguished of Maré's creations, it teamed the painter with Milhaud and the poet Blaise Cendrars and drew on their common interest in African and African-derived folk forms. The ballet, which told the story of the creation through the lens of African myth, owed its genesis to Cendrars, who had recently published an account of African folk beliefs under the title *Antologie nègre*. The theme was timely. Although artists such as Picasso and Matisse had discovered African art long before the war, it was only in the immediate postwar years that it commanded widespread public attention. A number of events fueled this growing interest—Paul Guillaume's "Première Exposition d'art nègre et d'art océanien" at the Galerie Devambez in May 1919; *La Fête Nègre*, an evening of avant-garde performance organized by Cendrars and others at the Comédie des Champs-Elysées the following month;[16] Borlin's *Sculpture nègre*, presented on a program of solo works at the same theater in March 1920. In addition, there was jazz. Introduced by American soldiers toward the end of the war, it invaded music halls and dance halls, concert halls and art galleries, prompting an exodus of African-American musical talent across the Atlantic.[17]

African-derived music had fascinated Milhaud ever since his days in Brazil, and in 1922 he went to New York. The music he heard in Harlem was a revelation:

> Against the beat of the drums the melodic lines crisscrossed in a breathless pattern of broken and twisted rhythms. A Negress whose grating voice seemed to come from the depths of the centuries . . . sang over and over again, to the point of exhaustion, the same refrain, to which the constantly changing melodic pattern of the orchestra wove a kaleidoscopic background. . . . Its effect on me was so overwhelming that I could not tear myself away.[18]

These Harlem memories found their way into *Création*. The orchestra of seventeen solo instruments was the same he had observed in Harlem, while the score made "wholesale use of the jazz style."[19] Critics dismissed the music as frivolous, and worse. "The feeling one gets listening to Darius Milhaud's latest production is rage," wrote Pierre de Lampommeraye in *Le Ménestrel*. "Going back to tom-toms, xylophones, bellowing brass, and noise is not progress."[20]

Léger, for his part, went far beyond his previous experiments. In *Création*, the scenic elements themselves were mobile, while the human figure became a fully pictorial creation indistinguishable from the surrounding objects. The ballet opened with a curtain in the style of synthetic cubism that rose on three enormous deities, the gods of creation. Twenty-six feet tall, they were shifted by invisible dancers, and as they began to move, the creatures of a magical, African forest—birds, crocodiles, monkeys, insects—came to life. Finally, the first human couple was born. Masked and wearing black leotards tattooed in white, they were joined by men and women enveloped in constructions that covered everything but the feet. Transformed into moving sculpture, the "human material," as Léger would later write, "had the same spectacle value as the object and the decor."[21]

Jazz, albeit in a lighter vein, was also featured in another work of the October 1923 season: *Within the Quota*. Conceived for the American tour that began the following month, the ballet teamed two expatriates, composer Cole Porter and painter Gerald Murphy, in a tale of immigrant-makes-good that opened in the United States just as Congress was about to severely restrict immigration. Diaghilev almost certainly missed the work in Paris, but even if he had seen it, he would have detested it. "The whole of Venice," he wrote to Boris Kochno in 1926, "is up in arms against Cole Porter because of his jazz and his Negroes. He has started an idiotic night club on a boat . . . and now the Grand Canal is swarming with the very same Negroes who have made us all run away from London and Paris."[22] Although *Parade* had introduced both ragtime and the American theme to the ballet stage, Diaghilev dropped them both once they became associated with blacks. Maré, by contrast, had an abiding interest in the cultural expressions of Africa (where he had a house throughout the 1920s)[23] and the African diaspora. He made documentary films of African dance (which Borlin used in preparing *La Création du Monde*) and, after the demise of the Ballets Suédois, presented both Josephine Baker (in *La Revue Nègre*) and Florence Mills (in *Black Birds of 1926*) at the Théâtre des Champs-Elysées.

Relâche, the company's swan song, belonged even more to the world of the Paris avant-garde. Conceived by Francis Picabia, a painter close to Dada and the emerging group of surrealists, this "snapshot ballet in two acts with a cinematographic entr'acte" was practically a who's who of the international avant-garde. The music, based on children's round games, was by Erik Satie; the set, made up of 370 car headlights that dimmed and brightened with the music, was by Picabia; the film was directed by René Clair and featured cameo appearances by Man Ray, Marcel Duchamp, Satie, Borlin, Picabia, Maré, and various other artists. "*Relâche* is life, life as I love it," wrote Picabia:

> life without morrow, life today, . . . Automobile headlights, ropes of pearls, . . . advertising, music; men in evening dress; movement, play, clear and transparent water, the pleasure of laughter. . . . *Relâche* strolls through life with a great burst of laughter. *Relâche* is aimless movement. Why think?[24]

Why, indeed? As described by Maré, the action was certainly bizarre:

> [T]he curtain rose on a glittering and strange decor. . . . There were flashing floodlights that blinded the audience; a fireman who strolled about, smoking nonstop; a woman in an evening dress who made her entrance through the hall, . . . eight men in dinner jackets; games for the woman and several jumping jacks that went on until one of the latter carried her off.[25]

In the second act, the authors "trained a cannon at the audience"—posters with such provocative lines as: "Those who are discontent are authorized to clear out" or "There are some—poor imbeciles—who prefer the ballets at the Opéra."[26] Judging from the reviews, most of the critics fell into this category.

The Ballets Suédois cut a wide swathe through avant-garde Paris. Not only did the themes of ballets like *La Création du monde* coincide with the interests and favorite pastimes of its artists, but they were expressed in forms that linked the company to experiments on the artistic fringe: Léger's treatment of the performer as a "spectacle-object," for instance, recalls Georges Valmier's designs for the Théâtre Art et Action.[27] The company's visual artists received wide coverage in the avant-garde press, including expatriate journals like *transition* and the *Little Review*, which reproduced numerous works by Picabia and Léger. In September 1923, *L'Horizon*, a monthly devoted to the art of "today and tomorrow," published Cendrars' scenario for *Création*, an excerpt from Milhaud's score, along with fifteen of Léger's designs.[28]

Although Maré never formally identified the Ballets Suédois with either Dada or surrealism, the network of artists that formed the company's larger community linked the enterprise to both. At the center of this network was Nils Dardel, a Swedish painter who had settled in Paris in 1910. A close friend of Maré, Dardel had assisted him in assembling the vast collection of modern art that presaged his later commissions as an impresario. He also introduced Maré to friends like Cocteau (whose Saturday night dinners Dardel regularly attended), Léger, Satie, and the composers of Les Six, as well as to the larger Left Bank community, in whose social doings Borlin sometimes participated.[29] Although ballet held only minimal interest for this community, it did turn out for certain Suédois events. Thus, in October 1923, at the invitation-only gala where Marcel L'Herbier filmed the "riot" scene of *L'Inhumaine* (a riot actually provoked by the music of George Antheil, making his Paris debut as a composer), the audience included Picasso, Satie, Man Ray, Ezra Pound, James Joyce, Constantin Brancusi, Milhaud (who wrote the film score), and various surrealists.[30] Left Bank artists also participated in a New Year's Eve revue by Picabia and René Clair that included the last performance of *Relâche*, a sex farce called *Ciné Sketch* (with Man Ray as the Blabbermouth, Duchamp as the Naked Man, and Borlin as the Constable), dances by Caryathis (*La Belle Excentrique*, to Satie; *Le Jongleur*, to Poulenc; *Aujourd'hui*, to Auric), recitations by Yvonne George (the star of Cocteau's *Antigone*), and music by the Georgians, "the latest Jazz-band from New York."[31]

Although Diaghilev had little sympathy for the more extreme experiments of the Ballets Suédois, he was certainly not immune to its influence. Beginning in 1923, a number of artists associated with the Ballets Suédois received their first commissions from Diaghilev. This group included not only Auric, Poulenc, and Milhaud, but also Giorgio de Chirico (who designed *La Jarre* in 1924 for Maré and *Le Bal* in 1929 for Diaghilev), Henri Sauguet (who presented a short program of symphonic works at a Suédois performance in 1923 and in 1927 wrote the music for Diaghilev's *La Chatte*), and Man Ray (whose photographs would figure in Diaghilev programs). In addition to raiding Maré's "stable" of artists, Diaghilev also dipped into his stock of ideas. Although *Parade* had drawn on contemporary material as early as 1917, seven years elapsed before the settings and pastimes of the modern world reappeared in his repertory. When they did, they nearly always bore the stamp of Maré's "discoveries": *Les Biches* (1924) was composed by Poulenc; *Le Train Bleu* (1924), by Milhaud; *La Pastorale* (1926), by Auric; *La Chatte* (1927), by Sauguet. *Romeo and Juliet* (1926) had designs by Max Ernst and Joán Miró, surrealists whom Diaghilev stumbled upon only in 1926, even though both had been working in Paris since early in the decade. With its use of film and neon light, *Ode* (1928) was also indebted to the Ballets Suédois, as was *Barabau* (1925), a rustic farce set in Italy modeled on *La Jarre*.

Although the visual element dominated certain Diaghilev works of the 1920s, the Ballets Russes nevertheless remained a showcase for dance, with many talented performers and an outstanding roster of choreographers that included Léonide Massine, Bronislava Nijinska, and George Balanchine. This was not the case of the Ballets Suédois. In fact, after its initial season, dance declined in importance as an element of the company's formula, until, by 1923, the year of *Les Noces*, it had become little more than an accoutrement of the decor.

Although Maré was deeply interested in folk and "ethnic" forms of dance, he had little sympathy for ballet, which he equated with the old-fashioned productions of provincial European opera houses like Stockholm's Royal Opera. His writings on the Ballets Suédois make no reference to classical language, nor do they allude to a single work of the classical repertory. Apart from Borlin, they seldom mention any of the company's dancers and give short shrift to its choreography, concentrating instead on narrative and design. Like Diaghilev, Maré was a "hands-on" director. By his own admission, he never missed a rehearsal or performance; he dealt with backstage and administrative matters, made artistic decisions, and accompanied the troupe on all its tours.[32] The one thing he never mentions is attending company class. Although all the dancers were classically trained, few had the technical equipment of their Ballets Russes counterparts. This was partly a matter of training: standards at the school affiliated with the Royal Swedish Opera, where most of the dancers had studied, were low compared to the Maryinsky. But it was also a reflection of Maré's priorities. Unlike Diaghilev, he had little interest in developing the potential of his dancers, apart from Borlin, and no interest at all in furthering their technique. Maré never hired a ballet master (as Diaghilev did) to give company class (which was regularly conducted by Borlin), nor was he troubled by dancers who complained that they had less and less to dance. Unsurprisingly, many abandoned the company. Jenny Hasselquist, a first-rate classicist, left after a season. Carina Ari, the company's other *première danseuse,* left in 1923. One can only speculate on the part that Léger's insistence that "star performers . . . accept the role of 'moving scenery'"[33] played in that decision, but one may be sure that Maré's exclusive focus on Borlin clashed with Ari's own choreographic ambitions. Within two years of her departure Ari presented an evening-long work, *Scènes dansées.*[34]

Although the Ballets Suédois was founded as a vehicle for Borlin, it was to an even greater extent a vehicle for the mentor who formed him and led him down a path that ultimately stunted his growth as a choreographer. Under Maré's tutelage, Borlin came to regard painting as the primary source of movement ideas:

> Each picture gives birth in me to an impression that immediately transforms itself into dance. That is why I owe so much to old and modern masters. They have been an immense help to me. It is not that I have tried to copy them by making "tableaux vivants." But they awaken in me reflections, ideas, and new dances.[35]

Borlin's earliest dances belie this credo. Indeed, his first Paris concert, a program of solos that anticipated the debut of the Ballets Suédois by six months, revealed a strong debt to Michel Fokine, with whom he had studied in Stockholm in 1913–1914 and in Copenhagen in 1918, the year both were introduced to Maré.[36] Two of the numbers—*Arlequin,* a Harlequin dance to Chopin, and *Danse céleste,* a Siamese dance to Delibes[37]—were almost certainly versions of solos originally choreographed by Fokine for Nijinsky. Indeed, the "graceful spiral 'fall' in a slow pirouette" that D.-E. Inghelbrecht, who conducted the concert, remembered Borlin performing in *Arlequin*[38] came directly from Nijinsky's role in *Carnaval.* Fokine's influence could also be discerned in the reworking of "ethnic" material in *Danse tzigane* and *Danse suédoise,* as well as in the music for *Derviche*—Alexander Glazunov's "Dance of the Seven Veils"—which Fokine had previously used for Ida Rubinstein's *Salomé.* The expressiveness of Borlin's arms, remarked upon by a number of critics, was another Fokine trademark. Meanwhile, the connection with Nijinsky was underscored by a concert performance of the music for his first ballet, Debussy's "Prélude à l'après-midi d'un faune."[39]

Little is known of Borlin's travels between 1918, when he left Stockholm to work with Fokine, and 1920, when he produced this Paris concert. Accompanied by Maré, who had taken his education in hand, he spent the winter of 1919 in Spain, where he worked with José Otero and studied the Spanish dances that found their way into *Iberia.* He also traveled to North Africa. Far more intriguing is the year he is said to have spent elsewhere in Europe familiarizing himself with the dance currents emanating from Central Europe. Maré later told Bengt Hager that Borlin had studied at the Dalcroze school in Geneva, and Mary Wigman has said that he stayed with her in Zurich, where Suzanne Perrottet, Rudolf von Laban's assistant, thinks he may have come into contact with the Dadaists.[40] Even if none of this information can be verified, the evidence of Borlin's exposure to early forms of German modern dance is clear from a number of works presented in 1920 and 1921.

Although, as Hager claims, the inspiration for *Derviches* (1920) and the solo on which it was based may well have come seeing dervish dances in North

Africa,[41] a more likely source was Wigman's solo *The Dervish*. Created in 1917 for a program of *Ecstatic Dances* given at the Laban School in Zurich, the piece had many of the same ingredients as Borlin's later treatments—emotional exaltation, physical prostration, and the trance-like spinning that appeared in several of Wigman's dances of the period. Since the solo was dropped from the revised version of *Ecstatic Dances*, Borlin probably never saw the work in performance. But he could well have seen it in the studio, and he would almost certainly have seen *Idolatry*, another solo from the cycle, which Wigman performed on several occasions in the spring of 1919, wearing a straw shift that completely masked her torso and whirling until she collapsed.[42]

Both the primitivist theme of *Idolatry*, where Wigman was "a being crouche[d] in the middle of the primeval forest,"[43] and the costuming of the work suggest a link with the most interesting of the solos presented at Borlin's first concert, *Sculpture nègre*. Like Wigman, he wore a bodysuit, and although the contours of his body were revealed, his face and hands were masked by constructions that gave him the appearance of a wooden African sculpture. During World War I, Dada artists living in Zurich had organized "African Nights" at the Cabaret Voltaire, where Laban's dancers sometimes performed. In 1917, for a soiree at the Galerie Dada, five of these "Laban-ladies," as Hugo Ball recorded in his diary, appeared in a new dance "as negresses in long black caftans and face masks,"[44] while at the city's last Dada event, which took place in April 1919 and which Borlin could have attended, Suzanne Perrottet danced before a crowd of fifteen thousand in a hall that Tristan Tzara described as "already boiling in the bubbles of bamboulas."[45]

Critics who wrote about Borlin's early dances occasionally alluded to what appear to be other legacies of his encounter with Wigman—weight and stillness. "His dancing," wrote Pierre Scize, "is characterized less by virtuosity . . . than by a certain heaviness which appears to be deliberate." In *Sculpture nègre*, his body "bend[s] as if under the weight of an abominable compulsion," then slowly rises, "as if ossified by years of contemplative immobility."[46] Pitts Sanborn, referring to *El Greco*, spoke of the atmosphere of "ecstatic madness and cataleptic aspiration," while Florence Gilliam, in one of several articles praising *L'Homme et son désir*, summed up Borlin's "method of dancing" as "restricted, static, and attitudinal." Henri Béraud, who dismissed the work as "gymnastics according to the method of Professor Müller, [Borlin's] compatriot," inadvertently attested to the influence of Dalcroze.[47]

In all these works, as well as *Maison de fous*, the choreographer's goal was expression, achieved not through conventional mimicry or dance steps, but through the deployment of "action-modes"—rising-falling, bending-reaching, rotating and twisting, undulating, heaving, swaying, vibrating, and shaking—to convey emotion.[48] In *El Greco*, wrote the Swedish critic Andreas Lindblom, "The crowds, as if driven to and fro by some giant scourge, gesticulate and cry out, voiceless, writhing in impotence. The lees of the soul are stirred up and float to the surface."[49] *Maison de fous* offered another nightmare vision:

> The curtain rises on a group of lunatics. A young woman arrives. . . . Mesmerized by the devilish procession, she feels madness overcoming her and tries in vain to resist. . . . No longer in control of her actions, . . . she begins to imitate the gestures of the . . . people around her. They begin to circle faster and faster; she loses consciousness, then becomes delirious, falling prey, at last, to a dementia even more frenzied than their own.[50]

As J. Lieubal pointed out in *Comoedia Illustré*, the work "had nothing in common with the aesthetics of the Ballets Russes."[51] It did, however, explore the same terrain as Wigman's solos of demonic possession. In this and other works revealing German dance influence, Borlin adapted avant-garde movement ideas to the physical scale and theatrical resources of the ballet stage.

Although Massine had drawn on extratheatrical movement idioms in *Parade,* most Ballets Russes choreography remained firmly grounded in the *danse d'école*. Borlin, by contrast, not only incorporated such idioms into his work, but did so at the expense of both the classical and modern dance idioms on which it had previously rested. The impetus almost certainly came from Cocteau, who worked closely with the choreographer in staging *Les Mariés de la Tour Eiffel*. As Cocteau later wrote, his aim was to "rehabilitate the commonplace," what Edmund Wilson called "the droll and homely aspects of the Parisian world."[52] The work's few dances all derived from this world of familiar pastimes—the polka for the Trouville bathing beauty (a role that Borlin himself sometimes danced), the quadrille and wedding march for the guests, the two-step for the "telegrams" who looked like Tiller girls. *Skating Rink,* too, drew on vernacular idioms—the gliding and endless circling of roller skaters and the rough, sexually charged dancing of working-class *apaches*. In *Le Tournoi singulier,* Eros carried a golf club and Folly danced a blues, while in *Within the Quota,* "Everybody's Sweetheart" did a shimmy. André Levinson, who seldom had a good word for the company, criticized the dancing in this work unmercifully. The Swedes, he wrote:

> are as awkward on the dance floor as they are in a classical *ballabile*. . . . I consider it the maddest audacity on the part of the "Swedes" to pit themselves against performers of the music hall, those consummate virtuosi, flawless technicians, imbued with age-old traditions . . . who spend ten years elaborating and completing a turn. You want to make the *Immigrant* . . . a world success? Cast Nina Payne as the Jazz Baby, [Vicente] Escudero as the Cowboy, Mr. [Louis] Douglas or John as the Negro, the Catalans as the Immigrant and the Fairy. . . . Here, then, is a superb theatrical theme—the ironic and picturesque apotheosis of Americanism—reduced to a trifle. Once all aesthetic controversy is put aside, the truth hits you:

Serge Diaghilev. Photo by Jan de Strelecki. Jerome Robbins Dance Division, The New York Public Library for the Performing Arts, Astor, Lenox and Tilden Foundations.

Michel Fokine. Portrait by Valentin Serov. From Valerian Svetlov, *Le Ballet contemporain* (St. Petersburg, 1912).

George Balanchine, late 1920s. Photo by Vladimir Dimitriev. Ballets Russes souvenir program, 1929.

Lincoln Kirstein. Photograph by George Platt Lynes. The Metropolitan Museum of Art, Gift of Lincoln Kirstein, 1985. (1985.1087.15) All rights reserved, The Metropolitan Museum of Art.

Olga Preobrajenska. *Yearbook of the Imperial Theaters,* 1903–1904 Season.

Anna Pavlova. Photo by Claude Harris. Jerome Robbins Dance Division, The New York Public Library for the Performing Arts, Astor, Lenox and Tilden Foundations.

Ida Rubinstein in the "Dance of the Seven Veils" from *Salomé*. Photo by Boissonas. Valerian Svetlov, *Le Ballet contemporain* (St. Petersburg, 1912).

Tamara Karsavina and Vaslav Nijinsky in *Giselle*. Roger Pryor Dodge Collection,
Jerome Robbins Dance Division, The New York Public Library for the Performing Arts,
Astor, Lenox and Tilden Foundations.

Isadora Duncan in *La Marseillaise*. Photo by Arnold Genthe. Courtesy of Jacob's Pillow Dance Festival.

Felia Doubrovska as the Bride in *Les Noces*. Photo by James Abbé. W. A. Propert, *The Russian Ballet 1921–1929* (London, 1931).

Lydia Lopokova in *La Boutique Fantasque*. Photograph by Rehbinder. Former collection of the Stravinsky-Diaghilev Foundation.

Alexandra Danilova in *The Good-Humoured Ladies.* Collection of Kim Kokich.

whatever the contribution of its painters, musicians, and poets, the Ballets Suédois will never succeed in creating a work of art so long as its ballets are danced by the Ballets Suédois.[53]

Although Levinson's criticism of the dancers in general and Borlin in particular seems unduly harsh, neither was above reproach, even during the earliest seasons, which Levinson never saw. Referring to the "manifestos" that accompanied the appearance of the company, Reynaldo Hahn wrote in 1920: "to declare that [Borlin's] young company is 'all of the highest order,' when a majority of its members would cut a sorry figure at the dance examinations of the Paris Opéra . . . is carrying panegyric . . . too far."[54] W. J. Turner, who reviewed the company in London just after its debut, echoed Hahn's criticism of the dancers, even if he adopted a milder tone. In *Divertissement*, he wrote, they "were somewhat heavy and rather below the standard to which the best of the Russians have accustomed us." Although P. J. S. Richardson, the editor of *The Dancing Times*, had nothing but praise for Jenny Hasselquist, he felt that the technique of the company in general "would doubtless be improved had they the advantage of daily tuition from a thoroughly experienced *maître de ballet*." Of the company's star, he wrote: "M. Borlin suffers by failing to have that ballon and elevation which are so essential for the successful male dancer. As a mime he is remarkable."[55] By 1923, even Florence Gilliam, who had strongly praised Borlin's performance in *L'Homme et son désir*, acknowledged his limitations. "As a dancer he has no great versatility. Certain pleasing attitudes, a graceful sense of movement, and a few interesting steps are his only equipment."[56] In another article published that year, she singled out Kaj Smith as being a "more brilliant and . . . more varied dancer," noting that "Borlin's dance-steps are almost entirely restricted to certain attitudes and turns which he employs indefatigably in ballets of the most diverse character," a point that Levinson also made.[57] Nevertheless, unlike Levinson, she regarded Borlin as a choreographer who was "sophisticated," "gifted with imagination," and "intellectually advanced."[58]

Gilliam wrote this before the company embarked on the most experimental chapter of its history. Indeed, the works she cites again and again are those mining the expressive vein opened by his exposure to modern German dancemaking. By contrast, she had no sympathy for the "monstrous inanities" of *Les Mariés de la Tour Eiffel*,[59] and one can only assume that she would have equally disliked its descendants—*Within the Quota, Le Tournoi singulier,* and *Relâche*—not only because of their self-conscious modernity, but also because of their designs, which overwhelmed the dancing and reduced it to inconsequence. With time, Borlin himself grew resentful of this imbalance, telling Roland-Manuel, who composed the music for *Le Tournoi singulier,* "that the dancer must cease to be the sandwich man condemned to carry the great painters' advertisement boards."[60] Borlin's earliest works had eschewed design completely. However, even in ballets like *Maison de Fous, El Greco,* and *L'Homme et son désir* that incorporated visual elements, design had supported rather than undermined the dance conception. Maré's growing interest in artists like Picabia and Léger not only destroyed this balance, but also threatened to evict dance entirely from the avant-garde performance gallery that the company had become. Maré later claimed that he had dissolved the Ballets Suédois because after *Relâche* it was neither possible to turn back nor to move ahead: "*Relâche*," he wrote, "was contrary to our Nordic spirit."[61] More to the point, Maré could not go forward without transforming the Ballets Suédois into an enterprise with no role for the choreographer it was intended to serve. And because Maré had no genuine interest in ballet and had already lost millions, there was no compelling reason for him to turn back.

Compared to the Ballets Russes, the long-term contribution of the Ballets Suédois to twentieth-century ballet has been slight. The reason for this has less to do with Levinson's "persistent scorn" for the company, as Bengt Hager insists,[62] than with Maré's persistent deemphasis of its dance legacy. Ballets only survive as living entities when they are performed. After dissolving the Ballets Suédois, Maré made no attempt to revive its works. Borlin, for his part, lacked both the means and the company to do so. Abandoned by his erstwhile mentor, he tried his hand at acting, while continuing to give dance recitals both in France and abroad. With his death in 1930, the possibility of reviving any of his works vanished.

What survived of those works—designs, posters, programs, curtains, letters, photographs, press clippings—was squirreled away in a remarkable collection, all the more valuable because it remained intact. Maré, who owned the collection, housed it initially at the Archives Internationales de la Danse, which he founded in Paris in 1932, later transferring it to the Dansmuseet in Stockholm, which he opened in 1953. Drawing on these materials, he organized a few exhibitions. He also published *Les Ballets Suédois dans l'art contemporain* (1931), a limited-edition volume with more than sixty pages of photographs, fourteen color plates of designs, descriptions of the ballets (omitting the classical ones and the dances performed as divertissements), and dozens of published and unpublished statements by painters, writers, composers, and critics attesting to the importance of the company and its works. Only one dance artist—Fokine—was deemed worthy of inclusion. Although the volume was intended as a tribute and a vindication of Borlin, his contribution was outweighed by the emphasis placed on that of his prestigious collaborators. If the Ballets Suédois has been written out of dance history, it is because from early on dance was written out of the company's history by Maré himself. For all that Borlin was the troupe's initial raison d'être, his legacy existed only to the extent of its presence in the company's "collectibles." In these autographed letters and libretti, signed posters, scores, photographs, and designs, lay the true story of the Ballets Suédois. Among them, the dancers, invisible, flit like ghosts in search of a past willed to oblivion.

NOTES

1. Although Bengt Hager alludes to *Divertissement* in *Ballets Suédois (The Swedish Ballet)* (trans. Ruth Sharman [New York: Abrams, 1990], p. 19), he does not list the work among the company's productions, nor is it mentioned in Rolf de Maré's *Les Ballets Suédois dans l'art contemporain* (Paris: Editions du Trianon) or the catalogue *Cinquantenaire des Ballets Suédois 1920–1925: Collections du Musée de la Danse de Stockholm* published in 1970. *Chopin*, a pas de deux (sometimes listed simply as *Pas de Deux*), was another "classical" work mentioned by critics in reviews of the company's earliest seasons, but ignored in these publications. An (undated) program for the November 1921 season at the Théâtre des Champs-Elysées includes a *Chopin*, but since this was an ensemble work closely modeled on *Les Sylphides* (according to the program, it consisted of a "Valse," "Prélude," "Mazurka," "Etude," and "Valse brillante"), it was probably *Divertissement* under another name. The reason for the change in title may well have been the addition to the repertory in 1922 of *Divertissements* (or *Divertissement*), a potpourri of dances, including several solos, that recalls Anna Pavlova's programming. The individual items listed on programs for the 1922–1923 American tour are *Greek Dance* (Grieg), *Siamese Dance* (Jaap Kool), *War Dance* (Berlioz), *Humoresque* (Florent Schmitt), *Valse—"Dame Kobold"* (Weingartner), *Dance of the Mountain Girl* (Alfven), *Anitra's Dance* (Grieg), *Dervish* (Glazunov), *Spanish Dance* (Rubinstein), *Arabic Dance* (Grieg), *Gypsy Dance* (Saint-Saens), *Halligen, Swedish Dance,* and *Oxdance*. None of these dances are listed in the major Ballets Suédois source books.

2. Rolf de Maré, "The Swedish Ballet and the Modern Aesthetic," trans. Kenneth Burke, *Little Review*, Winter 1926, p. 24. This article appeared in the magazine's special theater issue.

3. Rolf de Maré, "Les Ballets Suédois expression d'une époque," *Les Ballets Suédois dans l'art contemporain* (Paris: Editions du Trianon, 1931), p. 27.

4. Reproduced in Bengt Hager, *Ballets Suédois (The Swedish Ballet)* (New York: Abrams, 1990), p. 27.

5. Quoted in Erik Aschengreen, *Jean Cocteau and the Dance*, trans. Patricia McAndrew and Per Avsum (Copenhagen: Gyldendal, 1986), p. 89.

6. Quoted *ibid.,* p. 99.

7. Paul Morand, "Ballets Suédois: Les Mariés de la Tour Eiffel," *La Nouvelle Revue française,* 17, no. 95 (August 1921), p. 225.

8. For a reminiscence of the group and its activities, see Chapters III ("Les dîners du samedi") and V ("Les mariés de la Tour Eiffel") of Jean Hugo's *Avant d'oublier 1918–1931* (Paris: Fayard, 1976).

9. Darius Milhaud, *Notes without Music* (New York, 1953; rpt. New York: DaCapo, 1970), p. 79.

10. *Ibid.,* p. 109.

11. Quoted in *Les Ballets Suédois,* p. 52. The English translation comes from Hager, p. 125.

12. Florence Gilliam, "Parade," *Gargoyle,* August 1921, p. 5.

13. Quoted in Hager, p. 36.

14. Quoted *ibid.*, p. 166.

15. Quoted in Melissa McQuillan, "Painters and the Ballet, 1917–1926: An Aspect of the Relationship Between Art and Theatre," Ph.D. diss., New York University, 1979, II, p. 394.

16. The centerpiece of this performance was Cendrars' *La Légende de la Création*, "transposed" by the poet from "Fang tradition." Although the piece included spoken and musical sections, it chiefly consisted of dances ("Danse de la Reconnaissance des Créatures," "Danse Guerrière de Bétsi," "Danse de la Provocation à la Divinité," "Danse de l'Arbre," "Danse Totémiste des Mpongwés, "Danse de l'Accouplement"), which were performed by Caryathis, Marcel Herrand, Djemil-Anik, Collin (or Colin) d'Arbois, Stasia Napierkowska, in addition to "Mademoiselles" Redstone and Israel. According to Jean Mollet, Djemil-Anik, who was from Martinique, appeared "completely nude, painted from head to toe by [Kees] Van Dongen," while the other dancers wore costumes with "bunches of bananas" (*Les Mémoires du Baron Mollet* [Paris: Gallimard, 1963], p. 134). Three of the numbers, which were performed on "authentic native instruments," were adapted by Honegger. The costumes were designed and executed by Janine Aghion and the painter Guy-Pierre Fauconnet; the tatoos were by Van Dongen, and the "ceremonial" was "arranged" by the painter André Dunoyer de Ségonzac and Luc-Albert Moreau. André Salmon referred to the impact of the event in an article published in *The Burlington Magazine:* "An exhibition of negro art held in a Parisian gallery at the beginning of last winter served to render familiar to the public, and to some extent popular, the interest of modern artists in the productions of African and Oceanic sculptors. . . . A *fête nègre,* as delightful as a charming Russian ballet, which was held on the occasion of this exhibition, seems to have greatly favoured the fashion but to have been of little service to the pure idea. And so although many amateurs of negro art . . . will have taken the trouble to revisit the incomparable collection at the British Museum, we cannot feel sure that each of them will see it with . . . eyes completely purified from a love of the curious and picturesque" (André Salmon, "Negro Art," *The Burlington Magazine,* 15 April 1920, pp. 164 – 165).

17. For a summary of avant-garde events on African themes, see Laura Rosenstock, "Léger: 'The Creation of the World,'" in *"Primitivism" in 20th Century Art: Affinity of the Tribal and the Modern,* ed. William Rubin (New York: The Museum of Modern Art, 1984), II, pp. 473 – 484.

18. Milhaud, pp. 136–137.

19. *Ibid.,* p. 149.

20. Quoted in Hager, p. 44.

21. "The Spectacle: Light, Color, Moving Image, Object-Spectacle," in Fernand Léger, *Functions of Painting,* ed. and introd. Edward F. Fry (London: Thames and Hudson, 1973), p. 38.

22. Quoted in Boris Kochno, *Diaghilev and the Ballets Russes,* trans. Adrienne Foulke (New York: Harper and Row, 1970), p. 222.

23. Richard Brender, "Reinventing Africa in Their Own Image: The Ballets Suédois' 'Ballet nègre,' *La Création du monde,*" *Dance Chronicle,* 9, no. 1 (1986), p. 125. Brender situates the work and treatments of the African theme generally within the larger context of French colonialism.

24. Quoted in *Les Ballets Suédois,* pp. 75–76.

25. *Ibid.,* p. 77.

26. *Ibid.,* p. 78.

27. For Valmier, see Laurence Marceillac, "Cubisme et théâtre: Les réalisations de Valmier pour Art et Action," *Revue de la société d'histoire du théâtre,* 35, no. 3 (1983), pp. 338–346.

28. "Le Théâtre de demain. Les Ballets Suédois de Rolf de Maré. *La Création du monde,* ballet nègre," *L'Horizon,* September 1923, pp. 1–2.

29. In *Kiki's Paris: Artists and Lovers 1900–1930* (New York: Abrams, 1989) by Billy Klüver and Julie Martin, two photographs show Borlin surrounded by artists at costume balls organized by the Maison Watteau, a center for Scandinavian artists (pp. 130–131) whose annual gatherings were "attended by everyone in Montparnasse" (p. 95). Among the artists identified by the authors are Moïse Kisling, Tristan Tzara, Tsuguharu-Léonard Foujita (who designed *Le Tournoi singulier* for the Ballets Suédois in 1924), Marie Vassilieff, Per Krohg, and Dardel. It is unclear how fluent Borlin was in French. According to conductor D.-E. Inghelbrecht, who worked closely with him from 1920 to 1923, composed the score of *El Greco,* and eventually married the ballerina Carina Ari, Borlin "understood and spoke little French" (*Mouvement contraire: souvenirs d'un musicien* [Paris: Editions Domat, 1947], p. 130.)

30. George Antheil, *Bad Boy of Music* (Garden City, N.Y.: Doubleday, 1945), p. 134; "Courrier des Théâtres," *Figaro,* 2 October 1923, p. 6; *Kiki's Paris,* p. 134.

31. The program for this one-time-only event is in *MGZB (Ballets Suédois), Dance Division, The New York Public Library for the Performing Arts (hereafter DD-NYPL). A photograph by Man Ray showing Duchamp with a strategically placed handful of leaves appears in *Kiki's Paris* (p. 137).

32. *Les Ballets Suédois,* p. 23.

33. Léger, "The Spectacle," p. 39.

34. Erik Naslund, "Carina Ari," *Dance Research,* 7, no. 2 (Autumn 1989), pp. 75–76.

35. Quoted in *Cinquantenaire des Ballets Suédois,* p. 39.

36. Erik Naslund, "Les Ballets Suédois," in *Les Ballets Suédois 1920–1925* (Paris: Bibliothèque Nationale de France, 1994), pp. 22, 26; Jean Borlin, letter to Michel Fokine, 17 June 1918, in *MGZM-Res (Jean Borlin Manuscripts), DD-NYPL.

37. The program for this "Concert de Danses" is in the collection of the Dansmuseet (Stockholm).

38. Inghelbrecht, *Mouvement contraire,* p. 124.

39. Another echo of the Ballets Russes in the program's musical offerings was Alexander Borodin's "Esquisse sur les steppes de l'Asie centrale," which audiences would have associated with the extremely popular *Polovtsian Dances,* choreographed by Fokine in 1909.

40. Hager, p. 12.

41. *Ibid.*

42. For Wigman, see Susan A. Manning, *Ecstasy and the Demon: Feminism and Nationalism in the Dances of Mary Wigman* (Berkeley: University of California Press, 1993), pp. 62–67.

43. Berthe Trümpy, quoted *ibid., p.* 65.

44. Quoted in RoseLee Goldberg, *Performance: Live Art 1909 to the Present* (New York: Abrams, 1979), p. 42.

45. Quoted in *ibid,* p. 48.

46. Quoted in Hager, pp. 13–14.

47. Pitts Sanborn, "The Swedish Ballet," *Shadowland,* December 1921, p. 66; Florence Gilliam, "The Swedish Ballet," *The Freeman,* 22 August 1923, p. 567; Henri Béraud, "Théâtre," *Mercure de France,* 1 July 1921, p. 192.

48. The term "action-modes" was coined by Elizabeth Selden in *Elements of the Free Dance* (1930). For its relation to Wigman's work, see Manning, pp. 43–44.

49. Quoted in Hager, p. 106.

50. *Ibid.,* p. 96.

51. J. Lieubal, "Au Théâtre des Champs-Elysées. Saison de Ballets Suédois," *Comoedia Illustré,* 20 November 1920, p. 56.

52. Cocteau is quoted in *Les Ballets Suédois,* p. 60; Wilson, in Frank W. D. Ries, *The Dance Theatre of Jean Cocteau* (Ann Arbor: UMI Research Press, 1986), p. 83.

53. André Levinson, *La Danse d'aujourd'hui* (Paris: Duchartre et Van Buggenhoudt, 1929), pp. 400–401.

54. Reynaldo Hahn, "Théâtre des Champs-Elysées. Deuxième spectacle des 'Ballets suédois,'" *Excelsior,* 10 November 1920, File 13 (Ballets Suédois), Valentine Hugo Collection, Theatre Museum (London).

55. W. J. Turner, "The Swedish Ballet," *The New Statesman,* 25 December 1920, p. 367; "The Sitter Out," *The Dancing Times,* January 1921, p. 310.

56. Florence Gilliam, "Ballet Suedois—A Unique Stage Spectacle," *Theatre Magazine,* November 1923, p. 64.

57. Gilliam, "The Swedish Ballet," *The Freeman,* p. 566. In *Skating Rink,* Levinson wrote in *La Danse d'aujourd'hui,* Borlin, "posed in 'attitude,' obstinately executed little turns en dedans, while around him the action languished, broke up, and melted away" (p. 394); in *Marchand d'oiseaux,* he "made a very graceful entrance with his two cages, then, having disposed of the cages, he posed in attitude and did some little turns en dedans" (p. 396).

58. Gilliam, "The Swedish Ballet," p. 566.

59. Gilliam, "Parade," p. 5.

60. Hager, p. 232.

61. *Les Ballets Suédois,* p. 33.

62. Hager, p. 44.

POLITICS IN PARADISE

ANDRÉ LEVINSON'S CLASSICISM

André Levinson fell in love with ballet practically as a tot. "It was in St. Petersburg, in 1891," he told an interviewer many years later. "Was it for my fourth birthday? In any case, they took me, that Sunday, to see *The Sleeping Beauty*, a *ballet-féerie*. I had grown up, so to speak, in the shadow of the Maryinsky Theater, in the charming Kolomna district, crossed by rivers and canals. . . . And it was at Ivanov's, the theater artist's confectionery, that we stocked up on *cérises ivres*, chocolates with aquavit. . . . Shall I say it? That very day, I had, however prematurely, the revelation of classical dancing."[1]

Falling in love is not a political act. Nor is the revelation of beauty or the vision of the sublime. What makes them political is what happens in the aftermath of the epiphany itself, the process whereby they acquire symbolic meaning.

In Levinson's case, *The Sleeping Beauty* marked the start of a journey that grew in time not only increasingly political but also increasingly conservative. With *Beauty* he never fell out of love. The ballet became a touchstone of his thought, the linchpin of a creative order he exalted throughout his career. Later in life, he described the work as the "most truly representative of the heroic period of the Russian ballet."[2] In the aftermath of the October Revolution, he saw it, too, as summing up the lost civilization of imperial Russia, St. Petersburg before the déluge. And he found in the form of the ballet, which was a fairy tale, a rejection of positivism and modern verities. Here, he later wrote, was "the last refuge of the departing gods, of lapsed mythologies, of gracious aristocrats now dissolved in smoke, of vanished glories and faded dreams . . . relegated by triumphant scepticism to an inglorious obscurity."[3]

At the heart of the ballet lay the abstract beauty of Marius Petipa's choreography, with its inherited language of steps and traditional lexicon of forms. This was the *danse d'école*, the "school" of classical dance, and it became the cornerstone of Levinson's thought. In the hierarchy of forms represented in Petipa's grand, multifaceted works, classical dance stood at the pinnacle. It was a lyric that sang of beauty and eternal essences, a poem that made visible the platonic world of ideas, a "system of formulae and symbols, independent of sentiment and aloof from realism."[4] From the creations of Petipa's maturity, Levinson came

This essay was originally published in the Spring 1994 issue of *The New Dance Review*.

away with two ideas that remained central to his vision of classicism. One was tradition, which he viewed as unchanging and disengaged from the present. The other was idealism, which treated the forms of the *danse d'école* as heralds of a spiritual order, transcendent and timeless. These ideas were the articles of Levinson's critical faith. Extrapolated from Petipa's enchanted world, they became the critic's universal yardstick, applied to all branches of dance and to all kinds of choreographers. If Levinson's faith never wavered, in the end none but Petipa lived up to it.

Little is known of Levinson's politics prior to 1917. In all likelihood, they were liberal. As a literary critic, he took a keen interest in contemporary authors; he wrote weekly columns for *Rech'*, an important Petersburg newspaper identified with the liberal Cadet Party; he was a Jew. But whatever his personal sympathies may have been, Levinson's writings on dance staked out a position that was anything but liberal. At a time when the tradition associated with Petipa was coming under fierce attack especially among intellectuals, Levinson appointed himself its paladin. Beginning with his very first article, he announces in the preface of *Ballet Old and New,* he "came out in 'defense and glorification' of classical dance."[5] He did so with passion and polemics, attacking the most visible proponents of what he called "the new departures in dance reform."[6] These, of course, were Isadora Duncan, who attracted a wide following among the Russian intelligentsia (which was generally hostile to ballet), and Michel Fokine, the "master-rebel" (in Levinson's phrase)[7] who led the choreographic secession within the Maryinsky. For obvious reasons, Levinson came down hardest on Fokine. His sins were legion; they even included some committed by others— the pictorialism of Ballets Russes productions like *Schéhérazade;* the use of scores like Igor Stravinsky's for *Firebird,* whose merits, Levinson claimed, "lay completely outside the realm of choreography."[8] The road elected by Fokine and his associates, he argued, could only lead to "ballet's *suicide* on the public stage."[9] Although Levinson did acknowledge the merits of designers like Léon Bakst and the shortcomings of nineteenth-century specialist composers like Ludwig Minkus, he treated virtually every departure from the methods and forms canonized by Petipa as a step down the "path of degeneracy."[10] Indeed, his sole concession to the music problem was to suggest a "more refined reorchestration of the old scores."[11]

In Russia, under Petipa, ballet had flourished. In Paris, where Levinson settled in 1921, traditional ballet was in the doldrums. Technical standards were low, production values old-fashioned; at the Opéra, where *Giselle* and *La Sylphide* had given birth to romanticism, fewer than a dozen ballets were probably in active repertory. The Opéra became Levinson's special charge. He wrote with love of its dancers, its teachers, its old ballets like *Sylvia* and *Coppélia.*[12] He also wrote— although with anything but love—of its eurhythmic dancers, whom Jacques Rouché, the Opéra's director, had hired toward the end of World War I in one of many efforts to bring the venerable institution into the twentieth century.

For the most part, the eurhythmic dancers appeared in operas with exotic settings like *Salomé* (where Mlle. Delsaux, the choreographer, also performed the "Dance of the Seven Veils"), *Antar, Hérodiade,* and *Miarka* (which featured the entire "eurhythmics class") or in dance works like the exotic *Istar* produced by Ida Rubinstein.[13] At times, they appeared in works of their own, such as the *Petite Suite* choreographed by Rachel Pasmanik and Jessmin Howarth that Levinson summed up as a "scampering of bare feet all around the music"[14] and prompted him to declare, "The renaissance of Parisian ballet will not come from Hellerau,"[15] a slap at Emile Jaques-Dalcroze. Even Léo Staats, the Opéra's in-house ballet master, succumbed to the new influence. In *Esther,* for example, the dancers wore sandals; in *Les Troyens,* they performed in bare legs. To Levinson's dismay, some of them actually liked "the outmoded childishness of Duncan-ism," as he put it.[16] So he thundered and railed against the "gymnasiarchs," until, finally, in September 1925, he reaped the fruits of his campaign: the Opéra's eu-rhythmic section was abolished.[17]

Although Levinson was formed as a critic in Russia, the years he spent in France significantly broadened his outlook. Paris in the 1920s was Europe's leading dance capital, a mecca for performers from all over the world. Levinson went to everything and wrote about it. The seeing sharpened his eye; the diver-sity saved him from parochialism. Thus, in addition to their documentary value, his writings include superb analytical essays on Spanish, Asian, and African-American styles of dancing that can still be read with profit, even if the racialist ideas informing them are outmoded.[18] Certainly, the great vogue for Spanish dancing in the 1920s owed a considerable debt to Levinson, whose writings evoked an art poised between East and West, "regenerated" by the "strange ge-nius" of La Argentina.[19] And of his contemporaries no one captured so well as Levinson the hypnotic power of Josephine Baker, whom he summed up in that wonderful phrase, "the black Venus who haunted Baudelaire."[20]

Levinson had little sympathy for "the Negro dance" itself. But he could be fair to it, finding "an intrinsic beauty" in some of its steps and "a positive grandeur" in its rhythmic "frenzy."[21] He was not always so judicious in appraising the era's avant-garde ballet companies, which like the Opéra's "gymnasiarchs" were at-tacking classical tradition from within. Obviously, the chief offender—because it was the first and because of its staying power—was Diaghilev's Ballets Russes; lesser sinners were Rolf de Maré's Ballets Suédois and Count Etienne de Beau-mont's Soirées de Paris. In *Ballet Old and New,* Levinson first sounded the theme reiterated time and again in his writings of the 1920s. Compared to the works of the classical repertory, those of the new ballet masters (exemplified, at the time he was writing, by Fokine and Vaslav Nijinsky) were "aesthetic diver-sions," "playthings of precocious snobbism and restless frivolity."[22]

Levinson did not dismiss all theatrical experiment out of hand; in *La Danse d'aujourd'hui,* he has kind words for Jean Cocteau's *Romeo et Juliette,* Alexander Tairov's *Phèdre,* and Vsevolod Meyerhold's *Pisanella,*[23] all works that were in some measure experimentalist. However, these were plays; ballets that employed the same innovative techniques were held to a different, stricter standard: they had to make visible "the things of the soul" through the "abstract sign, ideogram, and symbol" of the classical dance.[24] In short, they had to look like Petipa viewed through the symbolist prism of Mallarmé.

Few, if any, postwar choreographers measured up. Like Fokine and Nijinsky earlier, Léonide Massine, Bronislava Nijinska, Jean Borlin, and George Balanchine—the leading avant-garde ballet choreographers of the French 1920s—searched hither and yon for material. They combed both the arts of the time and the city's popular amusements. Levinson's writings include many admiring reviews of the clowns and "steppers" he saw on the music hall stage, and in the late 1920s he became an important film critic. But when borrowings from these and other genres appeared in ballet, he saw only nihilism, snobbery, and dilettantism. Of *La Création du Monde,* a Ballets Suédois work inspired by African sculpture with choreography by Borlin and designs by Fernand Léger, he wrote that it was "an aberration to engage live dancers to imitate with contorsions the formulas of exotic sculptors. One will never make a dance work by using saltatory movements to translate the conventions proper to the plastic arts."[25]

Levinson was not much kinder to Balanchine, summing up the choreography of his earliest ballets as "a clownish parody of the Classic Dance."[26] He was nearly as dismissive of *Apollon Musagète,* despite the fact, as he informed his readers, that "pure dance takes possession of the stage" in the variations and pas de deux: "I do not resign myself to accepting the choreography of Mons. Balanchine as definitive. . . . I have grasped as its intention that of 'refrigerating' classical dance, of pushing it toward the abstraction and impassiveness of geometric formulas of movement. But . . . his repertoire of steps is limited; his combinations are awkward. He tediously repeats himself and plagiarizes his previous ballets. If some groups are ingeniously constructed, certain passages, like the 'promenade' turn that Mons. Serge Lifar, a splendid and athletic Apollo, executes with each of the three Muses, verge on parody. The variations of the god have few happy details. . . . The choreographer is better inspired in the pas de deux for Mlle. [Alice] Nikitina and Mons. Lifar; here he juxtaposes the fragile elegance of the 'acrobat' with the superb vigor of the 'lifter,' for the influence of the 'acrobatic adagio' is vividly felt in the 'lifts' and the 'splits' that delight Mons. Balanchine. In *Apollon* the inadequacy, nay, the poverty of the choreography undermines the effect of the score."[27] For all practical purposes, Levinson's vision of "timeless" classicism never advanced beyond the forms perfected by Petipa in the last decade of the nineteenth century.

The "gift of creative assimilation," Levinson once remarked, "is one of the most evident characteristics of the Russian genius."[28] It was certainly a characteristic that he exemplified. From his encyclopedic knowledge, which embraced literature no less than dance, to his mastery of a dozen languages, he was a cosmopolitan intellectual of the highest order. Like so many Russians of his time and class, he was a Francophile. He wrote the language with a command that all but the most gifted native speakers might envy; he knew its history, its architecture, its poetry, its painting. But France, for Levinson, was more than a place; it was an idea, a symbol, an ideogram for that very Occident that found expression in the classicism of ballets like *The Sleeping Beauty*. Reviewing Henri Massis' book *The Defence of the West*, he wrote:

"I passionately share the devotion of Mons. Massis toward the civilization of the Occident and his militant faith in the vitality of its principles. . . . The Occident in question, that incomparable human value, is . . . neither Latinity nor even France, but rather the notion held by a French elite of the true spiritual nature of its country . . . : an ideal France, the 'Goddess France,' the eldest daughter of the Church even; the formidable duel engaged between the Catholic thinker and that Orient 'seated immensely on the coast of Night' is of an order more metaphysical than political."[29] Here is the same high idealism that Levinson brings to ballet, the same burning faith in tradition, the same passionate belief in history remade as metaphysics.

During the 1920s, ideas such as these had definite political overtones, invoking a vision of society—ordered, aristocratic, and profoundly nationalist—dear to the era's protofascists. Levinson was certainly aware of these connotations; it would have been hard for anyone to avoid them in the French intellectual climate of the late 1920s. As it happens, Levinson in emigration was deeply political, with fiercely anti-Soviet views that made their way into many of his writings. These included polemics with Western intellectuals, whom he accused of inaction and hypocrisy in the face of "the extermination of all the great class of Russian intellectuals."[30] (That many intellectuals elected to remain in the Soviet Union was of no concern to him.)

When the Soviet poet Vladimir Mayakovsky committed suicide, Levinson wrote: "In putting a bullet through his head, Mayakovsky made use of the last and only means he had of regaining the freedom that he had renounced . . . ; at the same time he bought back, at the highest price a man can pay, ten years of voluntary servitude and all his betrayals of the Muse. By this final act, unforeseen dénouement of a life without honor, he reinstated himself as a *poet* in the eyes of posterity."[31] Outraged by the article, over one hundred artists and intellectuals, including Picasso, Léger, Tristan Tzara, André Malraux, Natalia Goncharova, and Man Ray, signed a public letter expressing "shock that one of the great French literary journals should have published a libel that was only a pretext for the author to express his Russian-émigré rancor."[32]

In 1918, Levinson had come under heavy attack for criticizing Mayakovsky's *Mystery-Bouffe*, a parody of the story of Noah's ark that ended with the international proletariat entering a utopia of the machine. The attack was led by the artistic left, newly empowered by a revolution that had temporarily thrown its weight behind the avant-garde.[33] The controversy added political fuel to Levinson's stance on experiment; it also labeled certain ideas as Bolshevist. Among these was the machine aesthetic associated with constructivism. Referring to the "triumph of the machine" depicted in the second tableau of Massine's *Le Pas d'Acier,* Levinson wrote: "I abhor the underlying symbolic idea of this scene, which compels living men to imitate in idolatry the dynamism of motors, pistons, and wheels." Still, he applauded the realization as "vigorous, with several groups of dancers executing simultaneously or in counterpoint movements with the regular and imposing gestures of work."[34]

It was Nijinska who suffered most from Levinson's politics. Having passed through what he termed "the collectivist reveries of the Soviets"—a reference to her early experimental works in Kiev just after the Revolution—she created to Stravinsky's music for *Les Noces* a "'Marxist' choreography that leveled the art of the dancer while swallowing him up."[35] "To this score, so full of vitality and direct power, . . . Mlle Nijinska brought a hollow image of life, mechanical and bloodless. . . . The executants were arranged in columns or in symmetrical figures, dressed exactly alike in brown and white. These groups alternated, taking each other's places and reproducing the rhythm, going through the identical movements at the same instant. Or else they were arranged in double files, like the soldiers of a firing squad. . . . advanc[ing] in strict time [and] serving as a moving background to the isolated protagonist. . . . In the end Mlle. Nijinska herded her cowed company into an immobile group in three tiers—a sort of practicable stage property constructed with flesh and blood or an apotheosis of exhibition gymnastics. . . . In *Petrouchka* the doll tried to become a living being; in *Noces* living men are reduced to the gloomy nothingness of mannequins."[36]

In his book on *The Sleeping Beauty,* Levinson describes the corps de ballet in Petipa's works as "a complex organism moved by a single will."[37] He might have said the same of the ensemble in *Les Noces* had he viewed this through a lens other than anti-Sovietism. He might have seen in the uniformity of dress an analogy with the impersonal tutu and in the virtual elimination of plot and psychology a brave step toward resolving the "unreconciled duality" of the old ballet, "the antimony between the psychological qualities of pantomime and the ideal nature of classical dance," which in *Ballet Old and New* he called "the task of the near future."[38] He might even have discerned in the ballet's final image intimations of a spiritual order. That he could find none of these things in *Les Noces* suggests to what extent his vision of classical dance was anything but value free.

Whatever his politics, Levinson the critic is always compelling; the power of his thought, if not his actual conclusions, makes him, to paraphrase Lincoln Kirstein, one of the few critics of his time that most of us can still read.[39] In France, possibly because of his politics, his influence ended with the Second

World War;[40] indeed, his most ardent disciple, Dominique Sordet, wrote for *L'Action Française*, the fascist weekly.[41] Although Levinson is cited again and again in Kirstein's historical writings of the 1930s,[42] his principal influence in the United States has been among critics rather than historians. For all his immense erudition, Levinson's method was fundamentally ahistorical; it winged across time in search of immemorial traditions and viewed the individual as the sole, heroic agent of change. Thus, it was Argentina alone who "regenerated a dance form long cheapened and falsified by the music hall,"[43] and Taglioni, alone, with *La Sylphide*, who created ballet's "celestial calligraphy."[44] The revolutions they bodied forth, Levinson insisted, conserved rather than destroyed. "Historians ill versed on the subject of dance," he wrote in his study of Taglioni, "have sought to *oppose* the romantic and the classical dance. The antithesis is arbitrary. In reality, the new style was *superimposed* on the old. *Tradition* was the happy outcome of *revolution*."[45]

Not unexpectedly, this idea reappears in early Kirstein. In a 1934 essay published in the left-wing monthly *New Theatre*, he praises the Soviet Union for conserving the inherited forms of theatrical dancing rather than discarding them, unlike supporters of the revolutionary dance movement in the United States: "The workers need a demonstrated subject matter, a dramatized, legible spectacle, far more than they need a new *form* for its expression. A form is only a frame and a medium, call it feudal, bourgeois, or proletarian. It will be a signal service to the revolution if choreographers can give working-class content to the preceding form."[46]

Unlike Levinson, however, Kirstein accepted the inevitability of change in ballet. "Massine has taken much from Wigman's arsenal," he writes. "Balanchine's plastic [sic] stems from Goleizovsky. But the skeleton underneath is strong enough . . . to support [these] addition[s]."[47] Such additions Levinson never admitted. When Nijinska returned to the Ballets Russes in 1921, she was dismayed to find the company rehearsing *The Sleeping Beauty*. "I had just come back from Russia in revolution," she later recalled, "and after many a production of my own there, the revival of *The Sleeping Princess* seemed to me an absurdity, a dropping into the past. . . . I started my first work full of protest against myself."[48] It was not simply realism that Levinson rejected, but the idea that classical forms might originate in promptings other than those of tradition alone. Fokine, Nijinska, Balanchine—he expected them to take up where Petipa had left off, as if Petipa's own forms had existed in a vacuum, divorced from habits of feeling and the imperial surrounds that had made his great works possible. Ballet, Kirstein wrote, changes every ten years. Ballets change, Levinson would have countered, but not the classical dance. How could it? With its secret voices and celestial caligraphies, its mysteries, mythologies, and transcendent symbols, classical dance for Levinson was ultimately a metaphor, a paradise of the spirit willed into being through an act of imagination and faith.

NOTES

1. Quoted in Paolo Fabbri, "André Levinson: un poeta della danza scomparso," *Il Secolo Milano,* 16 December 1933.
2. *The Designs of Léon Bakst for "The Sleeping Princess",* preface André Levinson (London: Benn Brothers, 1923), p. 1.
3. *Ibid.,* p. 8.
4. *Ibid.,* p. 6.
5. André Levinson, *Ballet Old and New,* trans. Susan Cook Summer (New York: Dance Horizons, 1982), p. xv.
6. *Ibid.*
7. *Ibid.,* p. 1.
8. *Ibid.,* p. 47.
9. *Ibid.,* p. 48. The emphasis is Levinson's.
10. *Ibid.,* p. 48.
11. *Ibid.,* p. 47.
12. See, for instance, his chapters "La Danse à l'Opéra" and "Deux Figures de danseuses" in *La Danse d'aujourd'hui: Etudes, notes, portraits* (Paris: Duchartre et Van Buggenhoudt, 1929), pp. 189–227.
13. For a partial listing of works in which dancers from the eurhythmic unit participated, see Léandre Vaillat, *Ballets de l'Opéra de Paris: Ballets dans les opéras—Nouveaux ballets* (Paris: Compagnie Française des Arts Graphiques, 1947), pp. 104–107, 110. For documentary particulars about the various productions, see Stéphane Wolff, *L'Opéra au Palais Garnier (1875–1962),* introd. Alain Gueillette (Paris: Slatkine, 1962).
14. André Levinson, "'En Bateau'. Le Préjugé du rythme," *La Danse au Théâtre: Esthétique et actualité mêlées* (Paris: Bloud et Gay, 1924), p. 16. The review was published in *Comoedia* on 17 April 1923.
15. *Ibid.,* p. 17.
16. "Lettre à Mlle ***, de l'Opéra," *ibid.,* p. 72. The article was originally published in *Comoedia* on 26 June 1923.
17. "La Danse. Epitaphe," *Comoedia,* 21 September 1925, p. 3.
18. See, for example, "The Spirit of the Spanish Dance" (pp. 49–55), "Javanese Dancing: The Spirit and the Form" (pp. 118–124), and "The Negro Dance: Under European Eyes" (pp. 69–75) in *André Levinson on Dance: Writings from Paris in the Twenties,* ed. Joan Acocella and Lynn Garafola (Hanover: University Press of New England/Wesleyan University Press, 1991). The concept of "race," as used by Levinson, was principally a national concept, denoting characteristics inherent in and determining the cultural expressions of a "people." The idea also informs his essays on *Ausdruckstanz* ("The Modern Dance in Germany") and precision dancing ("The Girls") reproduced in the same volume (pp. 100–109 and 89–94, respectively). Race could even be a factor in the expression of personality. Marie Taglioni, he once remarked, "danced what Kant purely thought" because of the Scandinavian blood in her veins

(quoted in Lincoln Kirstein, *Dance: A Short History of Classic Theatrical Dancing* [N.Y., 1935; rpt. N.Y.: Dance Horizons, 1974], p. 245).

19. "Argentina," *André Levinson on Dance,* pp. 95–96. This article was originally published in *Theatre Arts Monthly* in October 1928. See also his essay "The Spirit of the Spanish Dance" reproduced in the same volume (pp. 49–55), his chapter "Argentina et le génie de la danse espagnole" in *La Danse d'aujourd'hui* (pp. 229–256), and his book *La Argentina: A Study in Spanish Dancing* (Paris: Editions des Chroniques du Jour, 1928).

20. "La Danse. Paris ou New-York? Douglas. La Vénus Noire," *Comoedia,* 12 October 1925, p. 2. Levinson incorporated portions of this review (including the Baudelaire reference) into the chapter "Steps nègres" in *La Danse d'aujourd'hui* (pp. 271–280) and the essay "The Negro Dance" published in *Theatre Arts Monthly* in April 1927. The latter is reproduced in *André Levinson on Dance,* pp. 70–75.

21. "The Negro Dance," p. 74.

22. *Ballet Old and New,* p. 36.

23. See, for example, *La Danse d'aujourd'hui,* pp. 406, 413–414.

24. *Ibid.,* p. 414.

25. *Ibid.,* p. 399.

26. "A Crisis in the Ballets Russes," *André Levinson on Dance,* p. 67. This essay was originally published in November 1926 in *Theatre Arts Monthly.*

27. *La Danse d'aujourd'hui,* p. 88. This appears in the chapter "Stravinsky et la danse théâtrale" (pp. 75–89). A shorter version, published in *Theatre Arts Monthly* in November 1924 (and hence without the section on *Apollon Musagète*), is included in *André Levinson on Dance* (pp. 35–41).

28. *The Designs of Léon Bakst for "The Sleeping Princess",* p. 7.

29. "Russie et Eurasie. A propos d'un livre d'Henri Massis," *Comoedia,* 24 April 1927, p. 3.

30. "La Vie étrangère. Le Martyre des Ecrivains et des Artistes russes. La 'chape de liège,'" *Comoedia,* 12 April 1924, p. 1. See also "Le Martyre des Intellectuels russes. Une lettre de M. Romain Rolland," *Comoedia,* 18 April 1924, p. 1.

31. "La Poésie chez les Soviets: Le suicide de Mayakovsky," *Les Nouvelles Littéraires,* 30 May 1930, p. 6.

32. "Autour de Maiakowsky," *Les Nouvelles Littéraires,* 14 June 1930, p. 6.

33. For accounts of the *Mystery-Bouffe* episode, see Konstantin Rudinitsky, *Meyerhold the Director,* trans. George Petrov, ed. Sydney Schultze, introd. Ellendea Proffer (Ann Arbor, Mich.: Ardis, 1981), pp. 252–259, and *Meyerhold on Theatre,* trans. and ed. Edward Braun (New York: Hill and Wang, 1969), pp. 160–161.

34. *La Danse d'aujourd'hui,* p. 70.

35. "La Danse. Où en sont les 'Ballets russes,'" *Comoedia,* 18 June 1923, p. 4.

36. "Stravinsky and the Dance," *André Levinson on Dance,* p. 41. I have made a few minor adjustments in the translation. For the French text, see *La Danse d'aujourd'hui,* p. 85.

37. *The Designs of Léon Bakst for "The Sleeping Princess",* p. 5.

38. *Ballet Old and New,* p. 81.

39. *Dance: A Short History*, p. 257.

40. In recent years, it should be noted, there has been a renewal of interest in his work by cinema as well as dance scholars in France.

41. In 1934, after Levinson's death, Sordet published a long essay on the critic in *La Revue Universelle*, a journal associated with the political right ("André Levinson et la danse théâtrale," *La Revue Universelle*, 1 December 1934).

42. See, for instance, his essay "The Diaghilev Period," published in *Hound and Horn* in 1930, and *Dance: A Short History of Classic Theatrical Dancing*, published in 1935. The Diaghilev essay is reprinted in *By With To & From: A Lincoln Kirstein Reader*, ed. Nicholas Jenkins (New York: Farrar, Straus and Giroux, 1991), pp. 103–129.

43. "Argentina," *André Levinson on Dance*, p. 96.

44. Levinson, *Marie Taglioni*, p. 40.

45. *Ibid.*, p. 23. The emphases are Levinson's.

46. Lincoln Kirstein, "Revolutionary Ballet Forms," *New Theatre and Film 1934 to 1937: An Anthology*, ed. Herbert Kline, foreword Arthur Knight (San Diego: Harcourt Brace Jovanovich, 1985), p. 219. The article was published in *New Theatre* in October 1934. Especially curious is Kirstein's description of what he calls "Balanchine's articulate program": "At present the School of the American Ballet is in a state of gestation. It is attempting on the basis of the Russian State Schools, adapted to American needs, to create an excellent troupe of dancers. This takes time and patience. Balanchine luckily has both. But in the meanwhile he has experimented. He knows ballet as 'ballet' is dead. The very word seems mortified. He has found an old word which may have a revivified meaning. Vigano, the Italian innovator of a century ago, composed ballets which he called *Choreodrame:* literally danced dramas. The idea of three ballet-divertissements in an evening is through, however persistent. Ballet as innocent amusement is far too little to demand of it. Dancing can be the equivalent of any of the other lyric or dramatic forms. Words, spoken by dancers or by an independent choir in unison, without music or with it; the greater participation of the audience as a contributory factor in heightening the spectacular tension, the destruction of the proscenium arch as an obstructive fallacy, the use of Negroes in conjunction with white dancers, the replacement of an audience of snobs by a wide popular support are all part of Balanchine's articulate program. In the rehearsal classes at the School, these ideas are becoming crystallized and closer to production. In his first choreodrame, *Tom*, based on the Stowe novel of slavery in the South, E. E. Cummings has heroically theatricalized that serious historic situation. The spectacle as realized will be more pantomime than dancing, more speech than song, more myth than ritual—but on its way to a closer realization of an enlarged drama, popular in its deep sense" (*ibid.*, p. 217).

47. *Ibid.*, p. 218.

48. Bronislava Nijinska, "Reflections about the Production of *Les Biches* and *Hamlet* in Markova-Dolin Ballets," trans. Lydia Lopokova, *Dancing Times*, February 1937, p. 617.

PART II

RECONFIGURING THE SEXES

THE TRAVESTY DANCER IN

NINETEENTH-CENTURY BALLET

More than any other era in the history of ballet, the nineteenth century belongs to the ballerina. She haunts its lithographs and paintings, an ethereal creature touched with the charm of another age. Yet even when she turned into the fast, leggy ballerina of modern times, her ideology survived. If today the art of ballet celebrates the *danseur* nearly as often as the *danseuse,* it has yet to rid its aesthetic of yesterday's cult of the eternal feminine. Like her nineteenth-century forebear, today's ballerina, an icon of teen youth, athleticism, and anorexic vulnerability, incarnates a feminine ideal defined overwhelmingly by men.

The nineteenth century did indeed create the mystique of the ballerina. But it also gave birth to one of the more curious phenomena of ballet history. Beginning with romanticism, a twenty-year golden age stretching from the July Revolution to about 1850, the *danseuse en travesti* usurped the position of the male *danseur* in the corps de ballet and as a partner to the ballerina. Stepping into roles previously filled by men, women now impersonated the sailor boys, hussars, and toreadors who made up "masculine" contingents of the corps de ballet, even as they displaced real men as romantic leads. Until well into the twentieth century, the female dancer who donned the mufti of a cavalier was a commonplace of European ballet.

In real life, donning men's clothing meant assuming the power and prerogatives that went with male identity. Cross-dressing on the stage, however, had quite different implications. Coming into vogue at a time of major social, economic, and aesthetic changes, it reflected the shift of ballet from a courtly, aristocratic art to an entertainment geared to the marketplace and the tastes of a new bourgeois public.

Thus the *danseur* did not vanish in Copenhagen, where August Bournonville guided the destiny of the Royal Theater for nearly five decades, or at the Maryinsky Theater in St. Petersburg, where Marius Petipa ruled the Imperial Ballet for a similar tenure. On these courtly stages, the male remained, even if eclipsed by the ballerina.

This article was originally published in *Dance Research Journal,* 17, no. 2/18, no. 1 (1985–1986). It was subsequently republished in *Crossing the Stage: Controversies on Cross-Dressing,* ed. Lesley Ferris (London/New York: Routledge, 1993) and in *Moving History/Dancing Cultures: A Dance History Reader,* ed. Ann Dils and Ann Cooper Albright (Middletown: Wesleyan University Press, 2001).

Where he fought a losing battle was in those metropolitan centers that stood at the forefront of the new aesthetic—Paris and London. At the prestigious cradles of ballet romanticism in these cities, the Paris Opéra and King's Theatre, he was edged gradually but firmly from the limelight by a transformation in the social relations of ballet as thoroughgoing as the revolution taking place in its art.

Unlike the theaters of the periphery, where government control of arts organization remained intact, those of the European core operated, or began to operate, as private enterprises.[1] Entrepreneurs stood at the helm, with subscribers paying all or a substantial share of the costs—even at the Paris Opéra, which continued to receive partial subsidy from the government after losing its royal license in 1830. This change in the economic structure of ballet placed the audience—particularly the key group of moneyed subscribers—in a new and powerful position. It led to a new kind of star system, one based on drawing power rather than rank, while eliminating, for purposes of economy, the pensions and other benefits traditionally accruing to artists in government employ. The disappearance of the male dancer coincided with the triumph of romanticism and marketplace economics.

The ban on male talent was not, strictly speaking, absolute. Even in the second half of the century in England and on the continent, men continued to appear in character roles such as Dr. Coppélius, the doddering lovestruck Pygmalion of *Coppélia,* parts that demanded of dancers skill as actors and mimes and could be performed by those long past their prime. Men on the ballet stage were fine, it seemed, so long as they left its youthful, beardless heroes to the ladies and so long as they were elderly and, presumably, unattractive.

Initially, then, the "travesty" problem defines itself as one of roles, specifically that of the romantic hero, who incarnated, along with his ballerina counterpart, the idealized poetic of nineteenth-century ballet. In the new era opened by the July Revolution, this aesthetic and the styles of masculine dancing associated with its expression became gradually "feminized." Scorned by audiences as unmanly, they became the property of the *danseuse en travesti,* that curious androgyne who invoked both the high poetic and the bordello underside of romantic and post-romantic ballet.

Although travesty roles were not unknown before 1789, they were rare, especially in the so-called *genre noble,* the most elevated of the eighteenth century's three balletic styles.[2] Indeed, its most distinguished exponents were men, dancers such as Auguste Vestris, who brought a supreme elegance and beauty of person to the stage and majestic perfection to the adagios regarded as the touchstone of their art. No one embodied more than the *danseur noble* the courtly origins of ballet, its aristocratic manner, and the masculinity of a refined, leisured society.

Already by 1820, the *danseur noble* appealed to a very limited public—connoisseurs and men of refined tastes. To the increasing numbers from the middle classes who began to frequent the Paris Opéra in the later years of the

Restoration, his measured dignity and old-fashioned dress betrayed, like the *genre noble* itself, the aristocratic manner and frippery of the Ancien Régime.

In the changing social climate of the 1820s, then, a new kind of gendering was under way. The men about town who formed the backbone of the growing bourgeois public saw little to admire in the stately refinements of *danseurs nobles*. Their taste, instead, ran to the energized virtuosity of *danseurs de demi-caractère* like Antoine Paul, whose acrobatic leaps and multiple spins offered an analogue of their own active, helter-skelter lives. The high poetic of ballet, the loftiness of feeling embodied by the *danseur noble,* came to be seen as not merely obsolete, but also unmanly. With the triumph of romanticism and the new, ethereal style of Marie Taglioni in the early 1830s, poetry, expressiveness, and grace became the exclusive domain of the ballerina. At the same time, advances in technique, especially the refining of pointe work, gave her a second victory over the male: She now added to her arsenal of tricks the virtuosity of the *danseur de demi-caractère.* By 1840, a critic could write, "If male dancing no longer charms and attracts today, it is because there is no Sylphide, no magic-winged fairy capable of performing such a miracle and doing something that is endurable in a male dancer."[3]

In appropriating the aesthetic idealism and virtuoso technique associated with the older genres of male dancing, the ballerina unmanned the *danseur,* reducing him to comic character and occasional "lifter." But her gain had another effect, more lasting even than the banishment of the male from the dance stage. Beginning with romanticism and continuing throughout the nineteenth century, femininity itself became the ideology of ballet, indeed, the very definition of the art. Ideology, however, turned out to be a false friend. Even as nineteenth-century ballet exalted the feminine, setting it on a pedestal to be worshipped, its social reality debased the *danseuse* as a worker, a woman, and an artist.

From the romantic era with its triumphant bourgeoisie and market ethos came the dual stigma of working-class origins and sexual impropriety that branded the woman dancer well into the twentieth century. The great ballerinas continued, by and large, to emerge from the theatrical clans that had survived from the eighteenth century, a kind of caste that trained, promoted, and protected its daughters. (Taglioni, for instance, arrived in Paris in 1827 with a brother to partner her and a father who coached her, choreographed for her, and acted as her personal manager.) The rest, however, belonged to the urban slums. "Most of the dancers," wrote Albéric Second in 1844, "first saw the light of day in a concierge's lodge."[4] Bournonville summed up the lot of the majority succinctly—humble origins, little education, and wretched salaries.[5]

Poverty, naturally, invites sexual exploitation, especially in a profession of flexible morals. (Liaisons sweeten almost every ballerina biography.)[6] In the 1830s, however, the backstage of the Paris Opéra became a privileged venue of sexual assignation, officially countenanced and abetted. Eliminating older forms of "caste" separation, the theater's enterprising management dangled before the elect of its paying public a commodity of indisputable rarity and cachet—its female corps of dancers.

Imagine for a moment the inside of the old Paris Opéra. Descending tier by tier from the gods, we move up the social scale until, finally, we stand at the golden horseshoe of wealth, privilege, and power where, in boxes three deep on either side of the proscenium, sit the pleasure-minded sportsmen of the Jockey Club.

As the Opéra's most influential *abonnés,* the occupants of these *loges infernales*—all male, of course—enjoyed certain privileges: the run of the coulisses, for example, and entry to the Foyer de la Danse, a large room lined with barres and mirrors just behind the stage. Before 1830, lackeys in royal livery had warded prying eyes from this warm-up studio. When the new regime turned the Opéra over to private management, the Foyer de la Danse acquired a different function.[7] No longer off limits to men of wealth and fashion, before and after performances it became an exclusive *maison close,* with madams in the shape of mothers arranging terms. Nowhere was the clash, evoked time and again in lithographs and paintings, between the idealized femininity of balletic ideology and the reality of female exploitation so striking as in the Opéra's backstage corridors.

The commerce in dancers' bodies was not peculiar to Paris. In London, remarked Bournonville, it lacked even the pretension of gallantry that accompanied such exchanges across the Channel. To be sure, some dancers did eventually marry their "protectors." Many more bore children out of wedlock, sending them in secrecy to distant relations or country families to be reared. Nor did marriages between dancers fare well in this atmosphere of libertinage: one thinks of the choreographer Arthur Saint-Léon, Fanny Cerrito's on- and off-stage partner, who, jealous of the gifts showered on his beautiful and brilliant wife (which he could neither duplicate nor reciprocate), left the field of battle to his competitors.[8] The association of ballet and prostitution was so pervasive that Ivor Guest in his history of ballet under the Second Empire makes a special point of noting the Opéra's good girls—model wives, midnight poets, authors of books of religious reflections. But such cases were only exceptions. For pleasure-loving Paris, dancers were the cream of the *demi-monde.*

Aesthetics today stresses the dancer's symbolic function: It views physical presence as the form of dance itself. In the nineteenth century, however, the *danseuse* was first and foremost a woman. Like her audience, she saw the task of ballet as one of charming the sensibility, not elevating the mind. Tilting her face to the *loges infernales,* flashing the brilliants of her latest protector, making up with coquetry the shortcomings of technique, she presented herself as a physical synecdoche, a dancer without the dance. For the nineteenth-century public, ballet offered a staged replay of the class and bordello politics that ruled the theater corridors.

Conventional wisdom has it that there were two sorts of romantic ballerinas: "Christians" who evoked romanticism's spiritual yearnings and supernal kingdoms, and "pagans" who impersonated its obsession with exotic, carnal, and material themes.[9] But this paradigm, invented by Théophile Gautier to describe the contrasting styles of Marie Taglioni and Fanny Elssler, is at best misleading. For no matter how patly the virgin/whore scheme seems to fit the ideology of romanticism, it ignores both the dancer's totemic reality—her position within the social order of ballet—and that troubling third who articulated the common ground of the period's balletic avatars of Eve. As an emblem of wanton sexuality, feminized masculinity, and amazon inviolability, the *danseuse en travesti* symbolized in her complex persona the many shades of lust projected by the audience on the nineteenth-century dancer.

Unlike the older genre distinctions based on body type, movement, and style, romanticism's female triptych aligned balletic image with a hierarchy of class and sexual practice. If Taglioni's "aerial, virginal grace" evoked romanticism's quest for the ideal, it also summoned to the stage the marriageable demoiselle, chaste, demure, and genteel. So, too, Elssler's "swooning, voluptuous arms," like her satins, laces, and gems, linked the concept of materialism with a particular material reality—the enticing, high-priced pleasures of a *grande horizontal.*

The travesty dancer practiced none of these symbolic feminine concealments. As shipboys and sailors, hussars and toreadors, the proletarians of the Opéra's corps de ballet donned breeches and skin-tight trousers that displayed to advantage the shapely legs, slim corseted waists, and rounded hips, thighs, and buttocks of the era's ideal figure. Like the prostitutes in fancy dress in Manet's *Ball at the Opéra,* the *danseuse en travesti* brazenly advertised her sexuality. She was the hussy of the boulevards on theatrical parade.

The masquerade of transvestism fooled no one, nor was it meant to. The *danseuse en travesti* was always a woman, and a highly desirable one (a splendid figure was one of the role's prerequisites). She may have aped the steps and motions of the male performer, but she never impersonated his nature. What audiences wanted was a masculine image deprived of maleness, an idealized adolescent, a beardless she-man. Gautier, in particular, was repelled by the rugged physicality of the *danseur,* that "species of monstrosity," as he called him.[10] "Nothing," he wrote, "is more distasteful than a man who shows his red neck, his big muscular arms, his legs with the calves of a parish beadle, and all his strong massive frame shaken by leaps and pirouettes."[11]

His critical colleague, Jules Janin, shared Gautier's prejudices: even the greatest of *danseurs* paled against the delicate figure, shapely leg, and facial beauty of the travesty dancer. Janin, however, added another element to Gautier's list of characteristics unbecoming in a male dancer—power. No real man, that is, no upstanding member of the new bourgeois order, could impersonate the poetic idealism of the ballet hero without ungendering himself, without, in short, becoming a woman in male drag. Janin's remarks, published in the *Journal des Débats,* are worth quoting at length:

Speak to us of a pretty dancing girl who displays the grace of her figure, who reveals so fleetingly all the treasures of her beauty. Thank God, I understand that perfectly. I know what this lovely creature wishes us, and I would willingly follow her wherever she wishes in the sweet land of love. But a man, as ugly as you and I, a wretched fellow who leaps about without knowing why, a creature specially made to carry a musket and a sword and to wear a uniform. That this fellow should dance as a woman does—impossible: That this bewhiskered individual who is a pillar of the community, an elector, a municipal councillor, a man whose business it is to make and . . . unmake laws, should come before us in a tunic of sky-blue satin, his head covered with a hat with a waving plume amorously caressing his cheek, a frightful danseuse of the male sex . . . this was surely impossible and intolerable, and we have done well to remove such . . . artists from our pleasures. Today, thanks to this revolution we have effected, woman is the queen of ballet . . . no longer forced to cut off half her silk petticoat to dress her partner in it. Today the dancing man is no longer tolerated except as a useful accessory.[12]

As the concept of masculinity aligned itself with productivity, the effeminate sterility of the *danseur* became unacceptable to ballet's large male public.

But in defining power as male, Janin implicitly defined powerlessness as female. In photographs of the *danseuse en travesti* posed with her female counterpart, the modern eye notes a curtailment of scale, a reduction not only in the height and girth of the masculine figure, but in the physical contrast of the imaged sexes. What is missing, above all, is the suggestion of dominance, that intimation of power that even the most self-effacing danseur communicates to his audience. In appropriating the male role, the travesty dancer stripped that role of power.

In eliminating the *danseur,* ballet turned out the remaining in-house obstacle to sexual license. With the decline of the clan, only his lust, that last bastion of power, stood between the *danseuse* and the scheme so artfully contrived by the entrepreneurs of ballet for the millionaire libertines of the audience. For what was the Opéra if not their private seraglio? Thanks to the travesty dancer, no male now could destroy the peace of their private harem or their enjoyment of performance as foreplay to possession.

In appearance, the feminine androgyne laid claim to another erotic nexus. Tall, imposing, and majestic, she added to the charm of wantonness the challenge of the Amazon, that untamed Diana who so fascinated the nineteenth-century imagination. In Gautier's description of Eugénie Fiocre as Cupid in *Néméa,* note the sapphic allusions:

Certainly Love was never personified in a more graceful, or more charming body. Mlle. Fiocre has managed to compound the perfection both of the young girl and of the youth, and to make of them a sexless beauty, which is beauty itself. She might have been hewn from a block of Paros marble by a Greek sculptor, and animated by a miracle such as that of Galatea. To the purity of marble, she adds the suppleness of life. Her movements are developed and balanced in a sovereign harmony. . . . What admirable legs! Diana the huntress would envy them! What an easy, proud and tranquil grace! What modest, measured gestures!. . . So correct, rhythmical and noble is her miming that, like that of the mimes of old, it might be accompanied by two unseen Mute players. If Psyche saw this Cupid she might forget the original.[13]

Fiocre, an exceptionally beautiful woman who created the role of Frantz in *Coppélia,* was one of the most famous travesty heroes of the 1860s and 1870s. Like a number of Opéra dancers, she shared the boards with a sister, whose shapely limbs commanded nearly as much admiration as her sibling's. By far the most fascinating sister pair of the century were the Elsslers—Fanny, the romantic temptress with the body of a "hermaphrodite of antiquity"[14] and Thérèse, her partner and faithful cavalier. For over ten years they danced together, lived together, and traveled together. On stage they communicated a veiled eroticism, while offstage their relationship suggested a feminized relic of the older clan system.

A giraffe of a dancer at 5′6″, the "majestic" Thérèse served her diminutive sister in the multiple roles reserved in an older era for the ballerina's next of kin. She handled all of Fanny's business affairs, decided where and what she should dance, and staged, without credit, many of the ballets and numbers in which they appeared. As a woman, however, Thérèse lacked the clan's patriarchal authority, while as a dancer she would always be without the wealth and power of the "protectors" who increasingly materialized behind the scenes—promoting favorites, dispensing funds, as well as maintaining dancers and their impoverished families. Indeed, one such protector, the self-styled Marquis de La Valette, who became Fanny's lover in 1837, eventually destroyed the sororial ménage: his scorn for the ex-dancer who shared her bed forced Thérèse to leave.

One expects that the likes of the Marquis de La Valette relished the sight of his Elssler girls charming *confrères* of the *loges infernales.* But one also suspects that the travesty pas de deux was not so completely unsexed as the household he ruled. Certainly, it had been neutered by the substitution of a woman for the man, but that hardly means it was devoid of erotic content. Might not audiences have perceived in the choreographic play of female bodies something other than two women competing to whet the jaded appetites of libertines? Consider Gautier's account of a duet performed by the two Elsslers:

The pas executed by Mlle. T. Elssler and her sister is charmingly arranged; there is one figure in particular where the two sisters run from the back-cloth hand in hand, throwing forward their legs at the same time, which surpasses everything that can be imagined in the way of homogeneity, accuracy, and precision. One might almost be said to be the reflection of the other, and that each comes forward with a mirror held beside her, which follows her and repeats all her movements.

Nothing is more soothing and more harmonious to the gaze than this dance at once so refined and so precise.

Fanny, to whom Thérèse has given as ever the more important part, displayed a child-like grace, an artless agility, and an adorable roguishness; her Creole costume made her look ravishing, or rather she made the costume look ravishing.[15]

Thérèse had choreographed *La Volière* (*The Aviary* in English), which like her other ballets and dances made no use of men: she cast herself in the masculine role. Yet despite the differences in their attire, what struck Gautier was the oneness of the pair: He saw them as refracted images of a single self, perfect and complete. In evoking an Arcadia of perpetual adolescence untroubled and untouched by man, the travesty duet hinted at an ideal attainable only in the realms of art and the imagination—not the real world of stockbrokers and municipal councillors.

But dancing by its very nature is a physical as much as a symbolic activity. In the formalized mating game of the travesty pas de deux, two women touching and moving in harmony conveyed an eroticism perhaps even more compelling than their individual physical charms. The fantasy of females at play for the male eye is a staple of erotic literature, a kind of travesty performance enacted in the privacy of the imagination. Ballet's travesty pas de deux gave public form to this private fantasy, whetting audience desire, while keeping safely within the bounds of decorum. For ultimately, sapphic love interfered with the smooth functioning of the seraglio as much as the obstreperous male. In the case of the Elsslers, where Thérèse seems to have animated her choreography with something akin to personal feeling, the incest taboo coded as sisterly devotion what might otherwise have been construed as love. And one cannot help thinking that the buxom travesty heroes of the Second Empire and subsequent decades flaunted an outrageous femininity to ward off the sapphism immanent in their roles. In so doing, however, ballet robbed the *danseuse* of erotic mystery.

Today, thanks to the example of the Ballets Trocadero, we are apt to think that travesty in dance inherently offers a critique of sexual role playing, but the travesty dancers of nineteenth-century ballet offered no meditation on the usages of gender, no critical perspective on the sexual politics that ruled their lives, no revelation of the ways masculine and feminine were imaged on the ballet stage. What they exemplified was the triumph of bordello politics ideologized as the feminine mystique—a politics and an ideology imposed by men who remained in full control of ballet throughout the century as teachers, critics, choreographers, spectators, and artistic directors. The advent in 1909 of Diaghilev's Ballets Russes with its dynamic new aesthetic shattered the travesty paradigm. Seeing real men on the stage in choreography that exploited the strength, athleticism, and scale of the male body simply electrified audiences, causing them to look anew at the travesty dancer. But the audience itself had changed dramatically. The new following for ballet came from the highly sophisticated milieu of Tout-Paris. The great connoisseurs, collectors, musical patrons, and salonnières of the French capital—many of whom were women—replaced the sportsmen and roués of the *loges infernales*. At the same time, a new androgynous thematic and iconography, particularly evident in works created for Nijinsky where images of sexual heterodoxy transgressed rigid categories of masculinity and femininity, regendered the ideology of ballet, ending the reign of the feminine mystique. The era of the *danseuse en travesti* had come to an end.

NOTES

1. For the dramatic changes in the organization of the Paris Opéra after the Revolution of 1830, see Ivor Guest, *The Romantic Ballet in Paris,* forewords Ninette de Valois and Lillian Moore, 2nd ed. rev. (London: Dance Books, 1980), pp. 22–25. In England, nineteenth-century ballet appeared exclusively in a commercial setting. John Ebers, a former ticket agent, assumed the management of the King's Theatre in 1820, an association that ended in bankruptcy in 1827. He was succeeded in 1828 by Pierre Laporte, who, with the exception of the 1832 season, controlled the opera house until his death in 1841, whereupon Benjamin Lumley, in charge of finances since 1836, assumed the theater's management. In the hands of this solicitor/impresario, Her Majesty's (as the King's Theatre had been renamed) entered upon an era of glory. In the 1830s and 1840s, under the management of Alfred Bunn, the Theatre Royal, Drury Lane, became another important venue for ballet. During the latter part of the nineteenth century up to the eve of the First World War, ballet lived on in the music halls, above all the Empire and Alhambra. See Ivor Guest, *The Romantic Ballet in England: Its Development, Fulfilment and Decline* (London: Phoenix House, 1954), pp. 33, 46, 83–87, 128–131; Guest, *The Empire Ballet* (London: Society for Theatre Research, 1962); Guest, "The Alhambra Ballet," *Dance Perspectives,* Autumn 1959; Guest, *Ballet in Leicester Square: The Alhambra and the Empire, 1860–1915* (London: Dance Books, 1992).

    In France, it should be noted, the commercial boulevard stage was the breeding ground for theatrical romanticism. Long before the Paris Opéra's *Robert le Diable,* usually considered the official point of departure for romantic ballet, spectacular techniques and supernatural effects were commonplace in the melodramas and vaudevilles of the popular theaters. Ballet was an important component of these spectacles. Indeed, it was at theaters like the Théâtre de la Porte-Saint-Martin, which maintained a resident troupe and regularly presented new ballets and revivals, that the aerial style of dancing associated with romanticism began to crystallize early in the 1820s. Among the talents associated with the flowering of romantic ballet at the Paris Opéra who gained early experience on the boulevard stage was Jean Coralli, who produced several ballets in the Théâtre de la Gaîté. See Guest, *The Romantic Ballet in Paris*, pp. 4–5, 13–14, 16, 272–274; Marian Hannah Winter, *The Pre-Romantic Ballet* (London: Pitman, 1974), pp. 178–179, 193–197.

2. Some instances of gender swapping prior to the nineteenth century are Marie Sallé's appearance as Amour in Handel's *Alcina* (which Sallé choreographed herself) and the three graces impersonated by men in *Platée*, Jean-Philippe Rameau's spoof of his own operatic style. The lover in disguise à la Shakespeare's *Twelfth Night* was a popular conceit that called for cross-dressing. I am grateful to Catherine Turocy for this information. For the response of the London audience to Sallé's performance, see Parmenia Migel, *The Ballerinas: From the Court of Louix XIV to Pavlova* (1972; rpt. New York: Da Capo, 1980), p. 25.

3. *Le Constitutionnel*, quoted in Guest, *The Romantic Ballet in Paris*, p. 1.

4. *Les Petits Mystères de l'Opéra*, quoted in Guest, *The Romantic Ballet in Paris*, p. 25.

5. August Bournonville, *My Theatre Life*, trans. Patricia N. McAndrew (Middletown: Wesleyan University Press, 1979), p. 52.

6. Fanny Cerrito's liaison with the Marqués de Bedmar, Carlotta Grisi's with Prince Radziwill, Fanny Elssler's with the Marquis de La Valette, Pauline Duvernay's with (among others) La Valette and Lyne Stephens, and Elisa Scheffer's with the Earl of Pembroke are a few of the romances that dot the ballet chronicle of the 1830s, 1840s, and 1850s.

7. For the changes introduced by Dr. Louis Véron at the Paris Opéra after the Revolution of 1830, see Guest, *The Romantic Ballet in Paris*, p. 28. Under Ebers, the Green Room built at the King's Theatre performed a similar function as the Foyer de la Danse, while at Drury Lane, Bunn allowed the more influential patrons the run of the coulisses. Procuresses "of the worst type" circulated backstage at Drury Lane, among them the blackmailing beauty specialist known as Madame Rachel (Guest, *The Romantic Ballet in England*, pp. 36–37, 113).

8. Migel, *The Ballerinas*, p. 218. Married in 1845 (to the chagrin of Cerrito's parents, who had hoped for a son-in-law with a fortune or at least a title), the couple broke up in 1851. Shortly thereafter, her liaison with the Marqués de Bedmar became public knowledge. When rumors began to circulate in 1844 about Cerrito's impending marriage to Saint-Léon, the ballerina's London admirers, headed by Lord MacDonald, created a public disturbance when Saint-Léon appeared onstage. During one performance, the dancer stopped before their box and with a "sarcastic grin" and an "indescribable gesture" hissed menacingly at Lord MacDonald. The word *cochon* was heard to leave Saint-Léon's mouth, a gross impertinence coming from a dancer. Saint-Léon's written apology appeared in *The Times* a few days later. See Ivor Guest, *Fanny Cerrito: The Life of a Romantic Ballerina*, 2nd ed. rev. (London: Dance Books, 1974), p. 85.

9. Théophile Gautier, "Fanny Elssler in 'La Tempête,'" in *The Romantic Ballet as Seen by Théophile Gautier*, trans. Cyril W. Beaumont (London, 1932; rpt. New York: Arno Press, 1980), p. 16.

10. "Perrot and Carlotta Grisi in 'Le Zingaro,'" *ibid.*, p. 44.

11. "The Elsslers in 'La Volière,'" *ibid.,* p. 24.
12. 2 March 1840, quoted in Guest, *The Romantic Ballet in Paris,* p. 21.
13. Quoted in Ivor Guest, *The Ballet of the Second Empire* (Middletown: Wesleyan University Press, 1974), p. 200.
14. "Fanny Elssler," in *Gautier,* p. 22.
15. "The Elsslers in 'La Volière,'" p. 24.

SOLOISTS ABROAD

THE PREWAR CAREERS OF NATALIA TROUHANOVA
AND IDA RUBINSTEIN

More often than not, the history of twentieth-century dance is framed by the polarities of ballet and modern dance. While useful in a general way, this paradigm is far from adequate when applied to the broad spectrum of turn-of-the-century dance in Europe. Especially problematic is the assumption that in European centers such as Paris choreographic activity by women was a phenomenon uniquely associated with the progenitors of modern dance.

Although women may have been a rarity at the Paris Opéra, many served as ballet mistresses at less illustrious institutions, including the Opéra-Comique, music halls such as the Folies-Bergère, which had its own ballet troupe, and theaters such as the Châtelet, which specialized in spectacle shows. Also problematic is the equating of the female soloist tradition with dancers who founded their art on an explicit rejection of ballet. While this was certainly the case of the vast majority of soloists who emerged in North America and Germany, it overlooks the appearance in France and elsewhere of soloists who began their careers as ballet dancers, performed on the ballet stage, and developed a solo repertory that was often strikingly similar to that of early modern dancers, yet also overlapped with certain ballet forms of the period. Finally, in defining the creative role of the soloist preeminently in terms of choreography, the paradigm fails to account for the many Europeans who constructed highly original personas even if their dances were frequently staged by others. Appearing in venues associated with the opera house, concert hall, and commercial theater, these soloists have been ignored by historians of ballet and modern dance alike. In part, this is because their roots lay outside the Anglo-Saxon and German worlds on which most of the modern dance literature is based; in part, too, because their careers were seldom associated with major institutions. To a greater extent, however, they have disappeared from the historical record because they fall outside prevailing conceptual categories. Belonging neither to the "modern" nor to the "ballet" camp, they exist in a nameless, invisible limbo.

Turn-of-the-century Paris was an international mecca for female soloists. Many came from abroad: Loie Fuller, Isadora Duncan, Ruth St. Denis, and Maud

This article was originally published in *Experiment,* 2 (1996).

Allan from North America; Stasia Napierkowska from Constantinople;[1] Djemilé Fatmé from Turkey, Mata Hari from the Dutch East Indies, Sada Yacco from Japan, Sahary-Djeli from the Middle East. Their repertory was as exotic as their origins. Greek, Hindu, Japanese, Javanese, Spanish, Turkish, Cambodian: their dances traversed the world, ignoring borders and often the niceties of national style as well, especially in the Salomé works that no fewer than four of them— Fuller,[2] Maud Allan,[3] Sahary-Djeli,[4] and Mata Hari[5]—presented in the decade before World War I.

Even in the case of French-born dancers such as Jane Hugard (a sometime Salomé who choreographed the premiere of Maurice Ravel's *Ma Mère l'Oye*),[6] Odette Valéry (another sometime Salomé, whose Cleopatra dance featured a live asp),[7] Ariane Hugon (who specialized in "Greek" works),[8] Régina Badet (who offered programs of "Greek" and "sacred" Indian dances),[9] and Cléo de Mérode (who favored southeast Asian as well as "Greek" styles), the flavor of their freelance repertory was cosmopolitan. Unlike the vast majority of their foreign sisters, however, they frequently started their careers as ballet dancers, often at the Paris Opéra, which gave them cachet and the beginnings of a repertory as soloists. Thus, in 1898, when Mérode, then a *grand sujet* at the Opéra, made her first solo tour, her program included the pizzicato variation from *Sylvia*, the "sabotière" from *La Korrigane*, dances in the style of Louis XV, and a "Greek" dance, originally choreographed for the ballet *Phryné*.[10] The following year, for an engagement at the Théâtre des Capucines that followed her departure from the Opéra, she augmented this program with additional Greek dances and a Javanese dance. Finally, in 1900, inspired by photographs of Ankor-Wat and the recollections of a former French governor of what was then known as Indo-China, she devised a series of Cambodian dances that were a high point of the Universal Exposition held that year in Paris.[11] Performed several times daily at the fair's "Indo-Chinese" Theater, they were among the numerous foreign and exotic attractions that made the Exposition—and the city that hosted it—an international showcase for dance.[12]

Among the female soloists who established themselves in France in the years before World War I, few were as celebrated as Natalia Trouhanova and Ida Rubinstein. Both were Russian, expatriates who offered themselves to the public as Salomés and exotic creatures of mystery. No one knew who they were or what they had done in Russia, that strange, distant country they had all but abandoned. They were perceived as self-fashioned mavericks, an identity they cultivated. For all their apparent similarities, however, the two were strikingly different. Enormously wealthy, Rubinstein could do exactly what she wanted. She performed in contexts of her own making, and combined dancing with a career as an actress. Trouhanova, by contrast, was a dance professional, who performed virtually nonstop from the time she arrived in France—around 1904— until her temporary retirement on the eve of the First World War. Together, their careers suggest the range of possibilities open to female soloists of the period, the kinds of dances that formed their repertory, and the relative openness of the categories that defined what and where they danced, and how they were received.

Natalia Vladimirovna Trouhanova was born in Kiev in 1885 into the family of the singer Vladimir Bostunov.[13] "By blood and taste," she told Jean Delion in an interview published in *Comoedia* in 1911,

> I am a cosmopolitan; my parents are French, Polish, Serbian, and Bohemian in origin. Is it to this ancestry that I owe my admiration for art works regardless of their country of origin and their differences in character? . . . Kiev is my birthplace. . . . My parents left when I was a year old, and since then I have only returned on tour. Until I was thirteen, I lived like a nomad, traveling through all the countries of Europe.
>
> My father was a remarkable artist of the opera. He taught me to read from theater libretti, and my first books were dramas and comedies. Dolls amused me only when costumed as characters for a toy theater. I even wrote plays in very bad verse. At thirteen, I entered the gymnasium . . . ,and despite the worst hardships, the greatest family misfortunes, three years later I entered the Conservatory of Moscow. I excited no one. I was considered pretty and a little silly, with an incorrigible accent of the Midi. By dint of patience and willpower, I corrected my faults; I lost my accent, and despite my turned-up nose, I played dramatic leads. During my three years at the Conservatory, I won all the first prizes. Poverty and laryngitis forced me to change careers. First prizes are a poor weapon in the struggle to live; I had great dreams, but they were dreams never to be fulfilled.[14]

In turn-of-the-century Russia, as Elizabeth Souritz has pointed out, innovative trends in dance were closely linked to drama. Although Trouhanova's future lay in dance, her professional training at the Conservatory—or, more likely, the Moscow Philharmonic Society Drama School—was as an actress. According to one account, she studied in the class of Vladimir Nemirovich-Danchenko, a cofounder of the Moscow Art Theater.[15] Classes in "movement" (or "plastique," as it usually was called) were generally part of the acting curriculum. Early on, however, Trouhanova began to study dance with Ivan Clustine, a ballet master at the Bolshoi Theater and a teacher at its affiliated school. In 1903, overshadowed by the rising star of Alexander Gorsky, he left the Bolshoi for Paris. Within a year, Trouhanova was there as well.[16]

Like most dancers of the period, Trouhanova went to work in the music halls. Entertainment was big business in the pleasure capital of Europe, and dance made up a considerable part of the fare. Several music halls, including the Folies-Bergère, the Olympia, and the Casino de Paris, had ballet troupes, as did theaters such as the Gaîté, which presented light operas and operettas, and the Châtelet, which gave spectacle plays. There were Tiller girls and Spanish dancers, eccentric dancers and fire dancers, dancers who flew and dancers who did "light" dances à la Loie. Although highbrows like Duncan pointedly refused to perform in music halls, for dancers beginning a career they were both a major source of employment and an important talent showcase. Frequented by impresarios from all quarters of the entertainment world, they were a stepping-stone to the most prestigious venues of Europe.

Trouhanova was lucky. Within a year of leaving Moscow, she was in Monte Carlo for the first of several seasons at its celebrated opera house. Engaged as a soloist, she made her debut in April 1905 as Ludovic Bréa, the artist hero of *Au temps jadis*, a "ballet-opera" on a theme inspired by an episode in Monegasque history and choreographed by Giorgio Saracco, the theater's resident ballet master. Three weeks later, she created the title role in *La Mariska*, a ballet-pantomime by Jean Lorrain that was also choreographed by Saracco. Here, in the part of the Hungarian gypsy girl, Trouhanova scored her first genuine success. Her "piquant beauty and great talent as a mime and dancer," wrote the *Journal de Monaco*, "worked wonders in the characteristic steps of the Slavic dances. No one could be wilder or more provocative than this Mariska, who was warmly applauded after each dance."[17]

Although she continued to study classical dance (one of her teachers was Madame Mariquita, the ballet mistress of the Opéra-Comique),[18] character dancing became Trouhanova's specialty. In 1906, she danced the lezginka in Anton Rubinstein's opera *Le Démon*, and a mazurka, "Pas Slave," and "Danse Russe" in *La Snegorochka*, a ballet adapted from one of Ostrovsky's Russian legends in which she played the title role. Clustine was now her regular partner; the following season he became her personal choreographer. In the revival of *Phryné*, a ballet in Greek style, he staged the "Danse Bachique" and "Danse Mystique" that later figured in her concert repertory; in Saracco's version of *Les Deux Pigeons*, in which she played the role of Gourouli, he choreographed all her dances, including their duets together. *Les Contrebandiers* and *Espada*, both produced in early 1908, were other ballets that exploited her talent as a mime and character dancer. Reviewing *Les Deux Pigeons*, a local critic noted with admiration "the expressive beauty of her face, the harmony of her movements, and the impeccable elegance of her sculptural forms." However, her talent, he added, "seems better made for character than for classical dancing, where her remarkable qualities as a mime hardly find employment."[19]

Because mime and character dance were essential ingredients of early twentieth-century ballet, Trouhanova did not lack for opportunities on the ballet stage, even if her abilities as a classicist were limited. On the contrary, the particular nature of her talent stamped her creations with an individuality that raised her above the rank and file of ballet dancers and earned her the coveted status of *danseuse étoile*. It was only a matter of time before Paris beckoned. In 1907, she performed the "Dance of the Seven Veils" in Richard Strauss' opera *Salomé*, one of the stellar events of the theatrical season. The production, which was presented by Gabriel Astruc and enjoyed the patronage of Comtesse Greffuhle, names closely associated with Diaghilev's early enterprises, was a triumph for the entire cast, including Trouhanova, who had entrusted the choreography to Clustine.[20] Unlike Maud Allan, who was then performing her "Vision of Salomé" in a revue at the Théâtres des Variétés, Trouhanova, thanks to Strauss, had entered the world of Tout-Paris.[21]

Within a month, she was engaged by the Paris Opéra. She made her debut as the priestess in Saint-Saëns' opera *Samson et Dalila,* and toward the end of the year appeared as one of the king's daughters in *Le Lac des Aulnes,* a ballet choreographed by Vanara and starring Carlotta Zambelli.[22] At the same time, she added to her concert repertory. For a gala organized by the Belgian ambassador at the Théâtre Réjane, she appeared, as *Figaro* noted, "for the first time before the public in a classical costume and on pointe."[23] These "purely classical dances" were almost certainly the "Danses romantiques" to Chopin that she performed at various functions in the summer of 1907, including the matinee organized by the fashion magazine *Femina,* where she was partnered by "her ballet master, Monsieur Clustine."[24] In all likelihood, Clustine had choreographed these dances, which may well have included the Polonaise (op. 40, no. 1), Nocturne in F, Valse Posthume, and Mazurka (op. 57, no. 3) featured on Trouhanova's 1911 concert program. A forerunner of his *Suite de danses* mounted for the Paris Opéra in 1913, they were probably inspired by *Chopiniana,* which Michel Fokine had unveiled in St. Petersburg only five months before.[25]

Between 1907 and 1911, when she presented her first full-scale concerts, Trouhanova's career demonstrated the fluidity of the categories of dance performance in a Paris that had yet to assimilate Russian notions of status and professionalism as applied to nonballetic forms of dance. In 1909, for instance, while appearing as a guest artist at the Opéra, she starred in Paul Franck's "mime-drama" *L'Apache,* revealing herself to be "a tragic mime of the first order."[26] She performed at galas and private receptions, danced a Rhapsody by Liszt at the Université des Annales, and with the celebrated Russian soprano Felia Litvinne and the orchestra of the Concerts-Rouge embarked on a summer tour that took her to Switzerland, Germany, Austria, Holland, Belgium, and various French resorts.[27] The year closed with her appearance in yet another "colossal success," the opera *Quo Vadis?* In the dances, "magnificently arranged by Mademoiselle [Jeanne] Chasles," she was a "living, sinuous Tanagra."[28]

In photographs of the period, Trouhanova seldom appears in traditional ballet dress. An exception is a picture originally published in *The Tatler:* identified as the "principal dancer at the Opéra at Monte Carlo," she wears a short fluffy tutu revealing the stocky legs and hourglass figure of an early twentieth-century ballerina.[29] Otherwise, she is typically garbed as an exotic—in turbans and Turkish trousers, caftans, veils, jeweled bras, and the long floating tunics that linked the world of the East and that of the ancients with the latest in Paris fashion, which she sometimes modeled for magazines. With a torso as sinuous as an Art Nouveau curve, long, expansive arms, beautiful hands, and the facial vivacity of an actress, she was a vision of sensuous femininity—mysterious, winning, and theatrical. No wonder critics spoke so highly of her mimetic powers and the plasticity and expressiveness of virtually everything she danced.

By 1911, she was not only a star but also a highly respected artist. Moreover, through her involvement with the composer Paul Dukas, she was becoming a propagandist for modern music. His *La Péri* was almost certainly intended to be a highlight of the "Concerts de Danse" that Trouhanova presented at the Théâtre du Châtelet in early May 1911, less than a month before the opening of Diaghilev's own season there. The programming of the two concerts blended old and new—the Chopin pieces, Liszt Rhapsody, and lezginka from *Le Démon* that she had been dancing for years; suites to Gluck, Schubert, Fauré, and various Russian composers, Carl Maria von Weber's "Invitation to the Waltz" (which audiences would hear again the following month with Diaghilev's premiere of *Le Spectre de la Rose*), Vincent d'Indy's *Istar,* which was performed in its entirety, and selections from Edvard Grieg's *Peer Gynt,* including Anitra's Dance, a staple of the female soloist repertory.[30]

Diaghilev's interest in *La Péri* was almost certainly piqued by a sense of competition: apart from *Le Dieu Bleu,* which had music by Reynaldo Hahn, his new season was notably short of French composers. "Settle definitively Dukas question," he wired Gabriel Astruc on March 25. "Four performances six thousand francs. Very important for moral effect."[31] On April 3, he telegraphed Astruc that Trouhanova was acceptable, but only if he received world performing rights to the ballet. He also claimed that Nijinsky would dance only if Dukas conducted.[32] The telegrams flew back and forth, with Diaghilev alternately threatening to cancel the production and begging Astruc for Trouhanova's contract. The surviving drafts of two such documents show that she was anything but cowed by "Big Serge." Not only did she insist upon dancing a minimum of four performances of *La Péri* and an equal number of performances of *Schéhérazade* (replacing Ida Rubinstein in the role of Zobéide), but she also insisted on retaining ownership of the production, including the scenery and costumes to be designed by Léon Bakst and the staging "arranged" by Fokine.[33] The contracts were never signed, nor was a later agreement in which Diaghilev agreed to pay the production expenses, thus guaranteeing his ownership of the materiel.[34] Still, by the middle of April, the designs were ready.[35] At this point, however, another issue arose. If Trouhanova danced the Paris premiere, Diaghilev claimed he would lose not only his best dancers but also his financial support.[36] He returned to the theme in late May, using it now as an excuse to drop the production, which was nowhere near completion: "The unanimous revolt against this intrusive ballet has now reached a climax. Karsavina refuses to come to Paris to dance alongside Trouhanova. Fokine declared yesterday that staging *La Péri* with Trouhanova would be the most idiotic thing he had ever let himself in for. . . . Benois declines all responsibility for this anti-aesthetic act. The artists are in revolt."[37]

Trouhanova, of course, was neither the first nor the last unconventional dancer whom Diaghilev either contemplated hiring or actually engaged for his prewar company. In 1909, Ida Rubinstein had created the role of Cleopatra; in 1910, that of Zobéide, a part that Roshanara, an "Indian" dancer, performed in London in 1911. In 1912, for the St. Petersburg season that was canceled when fire leveled the theater in which the company was to perform, he not only signed up Mata Hari but also went to great lengths to engage Stasia Napierkowska, a dancer from the Opéra-Comique who had initially made her mark as an "exotic" dancer; both were to appear in *Le Dieu Bleu*.[38] In 1914, the opera singer Maria Kuznetsova, who had studied with Fokine and later gave concerts of Spanish music and dance, created the role of Potiphar's Wife in *Legend of Joseph;* in London, she was replaced by the actress Maria Carmi, a star of Max Reinhardt's "wordless" spectacles. Trouhanova herself had played the role of the Nun in the London edition of *The Miracle,* one of the most celebrated of Reinhardt's mimed dramas.[39] Obviously, there was a place in Diaghilev's prewar repertory for "crossover" performers who had presence, moved well, and could mime.

In 1912, Trouhanova embarked on her most ambitious project yet—a series of ballets to modern French music. Organized by Jacques Rouché, the founder of the innovative and prestigious Théâtre des Arts, the program was a melomane's dream. There was *La Péri,* which finally saw the light of day; *Adélaïde, ou le Langage des fleurs,* which was set to Maurice Ravel's "Valses nobles et sentimentales," heard for the first time; *La Tragédie de Salomé,* to the Florent Schmitt score originally commissioned by Loie Fuller; and d'Indy's *Istar.* The choreography for the program was by Ivan Clustine, now principal ballet master at the Opéra; the orchestra of the Concerts Lamoureux was conducted by the various composers, and the sets and costumes were by George Desvallières (*Istar*), Maxime Dethomas (*Salomé*), René Piot (*La Péri*), and Drésa (*Adélaïde*), all associated with the Théâtre des Arts.

The season was both a popular and critical success. Lengthy reviews appeared in the daily papers lauding every aspect of the program, "an indelible memory," as Robert Brussel wrote in *Figaro,* "for all those who dream of a closer union between music and dance." For Brussel, this dream had come close to realization at the Châtelet:

> We have experienced both the charm of the traditional ballet, where everything is subordinated to virtuosity, and the savor of those tumultuous . . . ensembles where everything is subordinated to the fantasy of the decor. . . . In neither case does music occupy first place: the former reduces it to a machine producing conventional and facile rhythms; the latter, even when inspiring illustrious works of art, treats it . . . according to . . . laws where caprice is everything. . . .
>
> Monsieur Paul Dukas' *La Péri* was the capital piece of the performance because of the very novelty of the principle determining its composition. . . . [It] is neither a marvelously adapted symphonic piece like *Istar,* nor a tragic "mime-

drama" like *Salomé,* nor a comedy-ballet like *Adélaïde: La Péri* is a danced *lyric poem,* . . . a freely developed musical work that for the first time is intimately wed to a mimed action.[40]

For other music critics, including M. D. Calvocoressi, who had worked closely with Diaghilev during his first seasons in Paris, Trouhanova had done what the impresario had only promised—serve the cause of modern French music:

> Since the Russian dancers first came to Paris, the idea of commissioning productions from young French composers was discussed. . . . There were hesitations, disagreements, delays . . . and today it is to Mademoiselle Trouhanova that the honor falls of being the first to arrange a series of dance performances to music representing the best of the French school.[41]

The 1912 concerts were also a personal triumph for Trouhanova as a dancer. "I cannot say enough about the astonishing beauty of Mademoiselle Trouhanova's performance," wrote Brussel.

> In the course of an evening she impersonates four different heroines, . . . endowing each of them with a distinctive character, attitude, gesture, and expression. . . . She incarnates the lofty yet humble Istar, the fierce Salomé, the divine Péri, and the coquettish Adélaïde with equal mastery and equal feeling for the demands of the musical rhythm. The final scene of Salomé . . . attains the very heights of tragedy, while the slow ascent of her Péri is a tableau of ideal purity.[42]

Not everyone was quite so overwhelmed. Reviewing the season in *Mercure de France,* Henry Gauthier-Villars found the dancer's pointework and *temps d'élévation* in *Adélaïde* wanting:

> It would be reprehensible to divert Mademoiselle Trouhanova from her exciting projects, but it would be criminal to allow her to think that she possesses the well-rounded technique to accomplish them. On no account should she repeat the attempt at classical dancing of *Adélaïde;* rather, she should . . . develop the genuine qualities as a mime and tragedienne that she demonstrates in *Salomé.* . . . Harmonious attitudes, yes, but no more pointes or jumps—ever![43]

With the success of her Châtelet concerts fresh in everyone's mind, Trouhanova now accepted an engagement at the Folies-Bergère. For these "galas," which began in June, she assembled seven programs of short dances that included most of the offerings of her 1911 concerts. New, however, were Debussy's "Danse sacrée" and "Danse profane," and two pieces to Saint-Saens—his "Danse macabre" and "The Swan," which, in Paris at least, was not yet considered the property of Anna Pavlova. Interest in the season ran high. The Folies-Bergère orchestra was augmented, and the public alerted to the twice-weekly changes in program. To accommodate the personal following that Trouhanova was likely to attract, the Folies-Bergère management took the unusual step of publishing the time of her show. Supported by Robert Quinault, a young dancer from the Opéra-Comique who had replaced Clustine as her regular partner, Trouhanova was bringing art—"great art"—to the music hall.[44]

She was at the height of her celebrity. In 1913, she made a tour of Russia and Germany, danced at the Théâtre Marigny, and starred in *Narkiss,* a ballet inspired by the legend of Narcissus that was choreographed by Madame Mariquita for the casino in Deauville—where she was snapped in a swimsuit wading in the Channel.[45] That year, too, she was awarded the "first prize in plastique" by *Comoedia Illustré* in a competition that also singled out Stasia Napierkowska "for the originality of her artistic compositions."[46] The following year she returned to the Opéra-Comique, where she interpreted the title role in a reprise of *La Péri,* with Quinault as her partner, and also danced in a new ballet by Mariquita, *Le Ballet des Nations.*[47]

Trouhanova was not alone in shuttling between the opera house and the music hall and concert stage or in relying on others to choreograph the dances that she personalized in performance. Nor did she regard her movement style as an attack on ballet. Even if she had little love for the "outdated academicism," as she put it, of entrechats and jetés-battus,[48] and only modest attainments as a classicist, she was schooled in ballet and fully conversant with its idioms. She culled her early repertory as a soloist from character dances choreographed for her in ballets and in her mature repertory extended the boundaries of these idioms to accommodate orientalist styles and popular forms of mime-drama. Unlike Duncan and the vast majority of American-bred soloists, who had no experience of ballet repertory and only minimal knowledge of ballet technique, Trouhanova existed simultaneously both within and outside the ballet world. In those countries where ballet traditions were strong, elements from those traditions inevitably seeped into the soloist's art, offering both a stock of possibilities and numerous points of contact with the theatrical world. As Trouhanova's career demonstrates, the female soloist was anything but marginalized in prewar Paris. Courted and fêted, she shone brightly among the city's many stars.

Ida Rubinstein was another of those stars brightening the theatrical landscape. Born in Kharkov in 1883 to a wealthy Jewish family, she was raised in the lap of luxury. She spent her early years in the Ukraine and, after her parents died, went to live with an aunt in St. Petersburg, where she attended secondary school. The family was cultivated and eminently respectable, intermarried with some of Europe's most distinguished Jewish clans. Nothing could be more different from Trouhanova's family of wandering players.

By the early 1900s, Rubinstein had set her sights on becoming an actress. She may have gone to Germany, hoping to work with Reinhardt, and she may have spent some time in a private clinic near Paris, where her family—or at least the husband of one of her sisters—hoped to cure her obsession with the stage. The cure, assuming one took place, failed. In 1904, the year she turned twenty-one (and presumably came into her money), Rubinstein made her debut at St. Petersburg's New Theater in the title role of Sophocles' *Antigone*. The play was staged by Yuri Ozarovsky, a staff director at the Alexandrinsky Theater with whom she had studied privately, and designed by Léon Bakst, with whom she now began a twenty-year collaboration.[49] The only concession to her family was the pseudonym she adopted for the occasion—I. L. Lvovskaia. However, since the first two initials were her own and the surname a variation on her patronymic, Lvovna, the ruse must have fooled no one.

At this point, Rubinstein still had no thought of becoming a dancer. In fact, donning a crimson dress, she now auditioned—and was accepted—for a place in the three-year program offered by the Moscow Theater School's drama department. Here she studied from 1904 to 1906, receiving excellent grades in a curriculum that encompassed both academic and practical subjects. Among the latter was "plastique," a combination of mime, gesture, and expressive movement that was taught by Vasily Geltser, a former Bolshoi character dancer and one of the company's greatest mimes. By the end of her second year, however, her hopes had turned to disappointment. In a letter to Akim Volynsky, the future ballet critic and a confidant of hers in this period, she sharply criticized director Alexander Lensky, who "trains," so she claimed, "only the actress in me, not the part of me that must subsequently realize my dream." The following year, she transferred to the school's St. Petersburg counterpart, appearing in *A Winter Tale, Macbeth, Mary Stuart,* and *Richard III,* among other plays, as part of her third-year examinations.[50]

Unlike Trouhanova, who by 1905 was dancing in Monte Carlo, Rubinstein gravitated to dance at a time when new theories of movement were beginning to transform the Russian dramatic stage. Ozarovsky, with whom she remained in contact, had lectured on François Delsarte as early as 1903, and one may assume that as an aspiring actress she was acquainted with the system of "plastic motion" that Meyerhold began to explore in 1905, when it is likely that she first saw Isadora Duncan perform.[51] According to Stanislavsky, who had no love for Rubinstein (possibly because years before she had dismissed his Moscow Art Theater as "antiquated"), she managed to meet the dancer, only to be "chased away."[52] The rebuff soon had its effect. By 1906, Rubinstein was writing to her former classmate Elizaveta Iuvitskaia that in six months "all of me must be flexible: my voice, face, and plastique."[53] The following year she began to work with Fokine. She was an assiduous pupil, and by 1908 was ready to make her debut. The vehicle she chose was Oscar Wilde's *Salomé,* yet to be performed in Russia. Although the play was banned before the premiere, apparently the censors had no objection to her giving the "Dance of the Seven Veils" on a concert program at the St. Petersburg Conservatory, despite the scanty costume of beads that remained after she shed the final veil.

The dance, which was choreographed by Fokine, became a staple of Rubinstein's concert repertory. She performed it in London as well as Paris, and for a time considered dancing it with actress Vera Komissarzhevskaia's company, whose own version of the Wilde play was scheduled to open a week before Rubinstein's; indeed, the censor's ban came in response to the *répétition générale* of the Komissarzhevskaia production. Rubinstein also toyed with the idea of doing "Anitra's Dance" (to Grieg's music from *Peer Gynt*), with the intention of performing it for Komissarzhevskaia, another plan that came to naught.[54]

The choice of repertory was significant. Europe was awash in Salomés, and Rubinstein cannot have been unaware of the phenomenon. She had traveled to Western Europe on several occasions and, according to Stanislavsky, had studied "everything in France and in Germany and in Italy."[55] In November and December 1908, the Russian theater weekly *Teatr i iskusstvo* published photographs of several notable Salomés, including Trouhanova and Maud Allan, as well as Aubrey Beardsley's famous drawing; it also printed items about Odette Valéry's "Cleopatra Dance" (with an accompanying picture) and the "Eastern Dances" of Ruth St. Denis (with a photograph of her *Nautch*).[56] Although by 1908 Rubinstein was "studying," as she wrote to Komissarzhevskaia, "dance in general," she was still thinking in terms of "numbers" that could be assimilated into existing performances, explaining that because of the new stress in her training she "[could] more easily work on [Salomé] or some other dance."[57]

It is idle to speculate on the course Rubinstein's career would have taken had Fokine not persuaded Diaghilev to cast her in the title role of *Cléopâtre,* the runaway success of the 1909 season that made her an overnight star. In Russia, opportunities were few. Indeed, as suggested by at least one critic, *Antigone* may well have been intended as a stepping stone to the Alexandrinsky, a means of circumventing the auditions and rigorous training expected of actors on the Imperial stage.[58] However, even after she had completed her formal training, doors remained closed—or, at least, offers failed to materialize that she was likely to entertain. Unlike Trouhanova, she did not have to earn a living and was thus under no compunction to join a provincial company or accept roles that she felt did not show her to advantage.

In addition, she was enamoured of the theater as high art. Her letters of the time are bathed in the aestheticism and lofty idealism so typical of the era's Russian intelligentsia. Writing to Iuvitskaia in 1906, she spoke of the "miracle" she hoped to perform: "to absorb all feelings, all thoughts, to experience everything, then go to others with a full heart and exalted mind, to be mad for truth, then to sing this truth and light the whole world with my song."[59] To Volynsky, she confessed: "When I live most intensely, when the radiant future seems close to me and attainable, when everything inside me sings, I want to talk to you, to tell you how I love and believe in the theater of the future. It will burn with a fire ever bright, so fearfully bright that it must kindle all the world."[60]

In her letters to Volynsky, there are frequent mentions of an *Antigone* project, never to be realized, that prompted them to spend several months together in Greece in 1907. After returning to Petersburg, Rubinstein began to study the role of Elektra, which she may have hoped to perform with Alexander Sanin's new company or in the rose marble theater that she was said to be building in St. Petersburg "for the production of ancient tragedies and plays by Ibsen."[61] Nothing came of the project, nor of the other projects, possibly involving Ozarovsky, hinted at in her correspondence. And in the winter of 1909, something happened—whether of a professional or personal nature will probably never be known—that prompted her to seek her fortune in Paris.[62]

As the mysterious, fatal temptress of Diaghilev's *Cléopâtre*, Rubinstein was a sensation. The role, which Fokine had rechoreographed, fit her like a glove, emphasizing her exotic looks and attenuated limbs, and what Henry Gauthier-Villars called, the "prodigious art of her . . . poses."[63] Robert de Montesquiou, who now became a close friend, glimpsed "old Egypt" in her exalted beauty, and a host of ancient idols—Isis, Salammbô, Salomé, Sappho, the Sphinx, and the Queen of Sheba.[64] Robert Brussel spoke of a body made "pliant to the rhythms of Egyptian gesture," Cocteau of discerning "something of the movement of the Ibis' wings" as she stood "before the spell-bound audience, penetratingly beautiful, like the pungent perfume of some exotic essence."[65]

When the season ended, Rubinstein decided to stay in Paris "and dance," as she wrote to Montesquiou.[66] She accepted a month-long engagement at the Olympia, one of the city's best music halls, and in August made her debut in the "Dance of the Seven Veils." The program offered a variety of attractions: *Les Filles de Bohême*, a romantic ballet in three tableaux with one hundred dancers from London and Milan; a troupe of Persian funambulists; Holden's Mannikins in a puppet version of *Salomé*; and The Dog Theater, where fifty dogs performed a two-act play.[67] Rubinstein's "act" was generally applauded, although the critic for *Variety* found it "somewhat monotonous."[68] Stanislavsky caught the show and was appalled. "Her famous name," he wrote home, "stands next to a cast of dogs. . . . I have never seen anyone more naked, and vapidly naked. How shameful! The music and Fokine's staging of the Dance of the Seven Veils are very good. But she is without talent, and naked."[69] Montesquiou, for his part, returned again and again, often with friends such as the painter Romaine Brooks and the actress Cécile Sorel, who shared his enthusiasm for the "beautiful Idol" but wondered what she was doing as a "music hall caryatid," a question Rubinstein might well have asked herself, especially during the dog act.[70]

The experience was depressing for another reason. With Fokine away on holiday, she had no one to direct her or see to the choreography of new dances. For the first time, she had to go it alone. "I wanted to work yesterday after the theater," she wrote to Montesquiou, "but I was too tired to compose anything without the aide of my master. And how can I present myself before an elite public without knowing what I will do and without having rehearsed? All this upsets me very much."[71]

When the Olympia engagement ended, Rubinstein traveled to London for her debut at the Hippodrome. Again, she was to do her *Salomé* dance; her program may have included other items as well. She felt "very lonely and lost," she told Montesquiou: her debut had been put off for a week so as "to change the entire program, procure a big orchestra, and prepare the public."[72] When she finally opened, it was at the Coliseum rather than the Hippodrome, and the reception was lukewarm. Wrote the critic of *The Era*, a weekly trade paper: "There is nothing remarkably distinctive about the movements of Miss Rubenstein [sic], who is, however, supple and graceful. The enthusiasm exhibited is of a mild kind, and it is evident that the taste for dancers in classical drapery is dying down."[73] Three weeks later she was back in Paris, preparing for a November departure to America, a trip that either never took place or that she later denied.[74]

These experiences plus the realization, driven home in 1910 after her triumph as Zobéide in *Schéhérazade*, that Diaghilev had pigeonholed her as a mime and femme fatale, doubtless made her accept with alacrity the proposal that Gabriele d'Annunzio now made: to play the Christian hero in *Le Martyre de Saint Sébastien.* Her return to the drama stage was a first for Paris, which knew her only as a dancer: indeed, she had kept her training as an actress a well-guarded secret. She did not give up dancing: in 1911 she repeated her Diaghilev roles at La Scala and in Monte Carlo, and in three of the plays she presented before the war—*Saint Sébastien* (1911), *Salomé* (1912), and *La Pisanelle* (1913)— there were dance numbers that she performed to acclaim. But nothing could induce her to return to the Ballets Russes, not even the role of the Chief Nymph in Nijinsky's *L'Après-midi d'un Faune* (she later described the angular choreography as containing "not a single natural movement")[75] or Potiphar's Wife in *Legend of Joseph*, a part that had been conceived for her.[76] And she never set foot again on a music hall stage.

To an even greater extent than Trouhanova, Rubinstein's prewar career reveals a disjunction between the technique she studied in the classroom and the style of the dances she performed in public. Beginning with Fokine, she worked only with ballet teachers, including, most notably, Rosita Mauri, who conducted the "class of perfection" at the Opéra from 1898 until 1920.[77] And with the partial exception of Kurt Jooss, the preferred idiom of all her choreographers was ballet. Until the 1920s, however, she scaled her dances to her technique. Her palette of movement was limited. She had little turnout, and her feet lacked the flexibility that comes with early ballet training. Her torso, by contrast, was remarkably supple. Photographs published in England of her *Salomé* reveal the deep plunge of her backbend and the long arms that extended its curve into space.[78] The drawings by Georges Tribout inspired by her miming in

Hélène de Sparte (1912) reveal her mastery of the spare, unadorned line as well as the stillness that seemed, as Charles Batilliot wrote, to "eternalize" her "attitudes, as in ancient frescoes."[79] Finally, the footage of her "exotic" dance in *La Nave*, a film shot in Italy in 1919, confirms that she was indeed a dancer, albeit not a classical one. True, her legs do little more than patter and run. But her arms, hands, torso, and neck are fully articulate—curving, pliant, visually and rhythmically harmonious.[80] Her refinement is evident, as is the reserve that appears in many of her photographs and contrasts oddly with the public nature of her profession.

Although Rubinstein seldom, if ever, choreographed the steps of her dances, she certainly orchestrated their larger context. As both the instigator and "angel" of most of her productions, she scripted their narratives as fully as any female soloist/choreographer. She chose her roles with extraordinary care, tailoring them not only to what she perceived as her strengths but also to an exalted vision of heroism that she never abandoned. St. Sebastian was the first of several male heroes and visionaries—Orpheus, David, Amphion, Don Quixote—that Rubinstein played or conceived for herself in the next twenty-five years. Her women were cut from a similar cloth. Whether from narcissism or something akin to feminism, she created a pantheon of female heroes. Many derived from the ancient world (Phaedra, Persephone, Clytemnestra); others, such as Joan of Arc, from Christianity. There were sinners like Marguerite Gautier and voluptuaries like Sémiramis, miracle makers, madwomen, Amazons, royal mistresses, and arts patrons. As female figures, they were all in some way remarkable, and as played by Rubinstein, most of them were also autonomous, agents of fate rather than its victims, manipulators of desire rather than its objects. When Alice Pike Barney, the mother of Nathalie Barney, a leading figure in Paris sapphist circles, entrusted her daughter with a script of "Atlantis" in the hope of getting it produced at the Opéra, Barney immediately sent a copy to Rubinstein.[81]

Already in 1913, unhappy with the precariousness of life as a soloist, Trouhanova had confessed to René Bizet that she was thinking of giving up dance and becoming an actress. "Dance today for us pure dancers has become impossible," she told him.

> We drag our tutus or . . . veils abroad . . . , but are chased from the big theaters. . . . I do not belong to the Opéra and can make only occasional appearances at the Opéra-Comique or the Gaîté. The music halls no longer mount those sumptuous works of Richepin or Lorrain in which we did so many beautiful things. So what should we do? Run off to London, Russia, Germany? Rent halls at our own expense? Wait for authors to give us works? We have to live. Pure art feeds the dancer no more than the writer.[82]

In the end, Trouhanova did not make the jump to drama. However, she happily gave up her career as a dancer during World War I. She married Count

A. A. Ignatiev, the chief of the Russian military mission at the French G.H.Q. (as *The Dancing Times* put it) and, after the Russian Revolution, started a model farm with him near Paris. She resumed dancing in 1921 (to help pay the bills), appearing at the Opéra as well as in revues, and in a joint program with the Russian Kibaltchitch Chorus.[83] Despite Ignatiev's aristocratic background, he eventually returned to the Soviet Union, as did Trouhanova. A new career now opened—translating Soviet authors (including Stalin!) into French. In 1935, on a rare visit to France, she lectured on "The Reflection of New Humanity in Soviet Literature" to the Friends of the Soviet Union in Lyon.[84]

Rubinstein's fate was no less strange. In 1936, two years after she stopped dancing, she converted to Catholicism. To the Nazis, however, she remained a Jew, and when they invaded Paris in 1940, she fled to London, where she befriended Free French soldiers—especially aviators—from a suite at the Ritz. (One story has it that she managed to get olive oil for General de Gaulle, who was very fond of salads!) Returning to France after the Liberation, she gave a few performances, then gradually faded into obscurity. She sold her mansion on the Place des Etats-Unis and moved to the south of France, eventually settling in Vence. Apart from her servants and her secretary, no one knew she was there. When she died in 1960, it took nearly a month for the news to reach Paris.

As dancers, Rubinstein and Trouhanova stand outside the major successions of twentieth-century dance. However, in the decades before the First World War, their performances marked out the shifting frontiers of an art that was awakening to modernity. This awakening took many forms, and while it is tempting to edit out the minor ones, their absence skews the larger picture, eliminating much of the complexity from a process of transformation that was anything but straightforward. The striking diversity of early twentieth-century dance in European capitals such as Paris calls not only for an interpretative framework that goes beyond the simple polarities of modern dance and ballet but also for a radical revision of prevailing ideas about ballet itself.

In its turn-of-the-century avatar, ballet was not simply equated with classicism, as it is today: even on the opera house stage, it embraced mime and character dance, both fully represented in the repertory. Thus, even in its most conservative form, ballet included practices that not only eluded the extremes of academicism, but also abutted on genres that stood outside ballet. Moreover, apart from Russia, ballet in Europe was not confined to the opera house, but flourished in contexts such as music halls where novelty was at a premium. In such contexts, mimes as well as dancers of an original bent were easily assimilated: indeed, they were frequently cast in productions that otherwise featured ballet dancers. In almost every way, this was a period of fluid rather than rigid categories and boundaries. What is needed is an interpretative schema that accommodates both the diversity and complexity of the era, that can account, in the final analysis, not only for a Duncan but also for a Trouhanova and a Rubinstein, and the nameless, invisible tribe of their boundary-defying sisters.

NOTES

1. According to an article published in a London newspaper in 1911, Napierkowska was born in Constantinople to a Russian father and a French mother. Her father, an engraver, had left Russia for political reasons and settled in France, eventually obtaining a professorship at the Academy of Fine Arts in Constantinople, where his daughter was born. At the age of twelve, the family returned to France. In time, she came to the attention of Madame Mariquita, the venerable ballet mistress of the Opéra-Comique, who arranged for her to dance not only at the Opéra-Comique but also at the Folies-Bergère, where she scored a great success in the "Eastern ballet" *Les Ailes* ("Palace Theatre: A New Russian Dancer," Stasia Napierkowska Clipping File, Dance Division, The New York Public Library for the Performing Arts [hereafter DD-NYPL]).

2. Loie Fuller's production of *La Tragédie de Salomé*, with a libretto by Robert D'Humières and music by Florent Schmitt, premiered in November 1907 (Margaret Haile Harris, *Loïe Fuller: Magician of Light* [Richmond, Va.: The Virginia Museum, 1979], p. 20). This, in fact, was Fuller's second *Salomé*. Her first, a pantomime by Armand Sylvestre with music by Gabriel Pierné, was presented in 1895 at the Comédie-Parisienne.

3. Allan danced her "Vision of Salomé" at the Théâtre des Variétés in the spring of 1907. The number was part of *La Revue du Centenaire,* starring Max Dearly and Polaire and featuring "Le Palais de Danse" and "Napoleon I, the Imperial Court, and the Grand Army" among its ten tableaux ("Courrier des Théâtres," *Figaro,* 7 May 1907, p. 4).

4. Sahary-Djeli's "new and original mime-drama version" of *Salomé* was given at the London Hippodrome in March 1911. It was written by Xanrof with music by Léo Pouget.

5. Mata Hari's Salomé was a Javanese version of the "Dance of the Seven Veils" (Bettina Knapp, "Dance Archeology: Orientalia," *Arabesque,* January–February 1986, p. 13).

6. *Ma Mère l'Oye* (Mother Goose) was produced in 1912 by Jacques Rouché's Théâtre des Arts. At this time, Hugard was probably a dancer at the Opéra. An undated clipping describes her program at the Comédie-Royale as conveying "the perverse and passionate play expressed in Richard Strauss' music and the sketches of Gustave Moreau" ("'Les danses de Salomé,' par Mme Jane Hugard," Folder 25, Valentine Hugo Collection, Theatre Museum, London).

7. For photographs of Valéry as Cleopatra, see "Great Snakes Alive! Cleopatra the Charmer," *The Sketch* [Supplement], 5 August 1908, p. 8; and "Original'nyia tantsovshchitsy," *Teatr i iskusstvo,* 21 December 1908, p. 917.

8. A member of the Paris Opéra company, Hugon presented herself as a Duncan-style soloist in works such as *Vision antique* (André Arnyvelde, "Ecoles de beauté," *Je sais tout-Noël,* n.d., pp. 612–613, Folder 49, Valentine Hugo Collection). She also danced in several Théâtre des Arts productions.

9. Régina Badet made her debut at the Opéra-Comique in 1904. In 1909, she appeared on a program at the Université des Annales, where she performed "sacred dances of

India" as "reconstructed by Monsieur Bourgault-Ducoudray and arranged by Madame Mariquita" ("Le Masque de Fer," "Echos," *Figaro,* 24 April 1909, p. 1). For her article, "Danses grecques et danses modernes," see *Musica* [Noël], Folder 25, Valentine Hugo Collection.

10. A ballet-pantomime in three acts by Auguste Germain with music by Louis Ganne and choreography by Madame Stichel, *Phryné* was produced at the Casino Municipal of Royan in July 1896. The principal roles were danced by Mérode (Phryné) and Emma Sandrini (Praxitèle), supported by the corps de ballet of the Grand Théâtre, Bordeaux. Stichel made her debut at the Paris Opéra in 1881, returning to her former company in 1910 to stage the ballet *La Fête chez Thérèse* and the dances in the opera *La Damnation de Faust.* A prolific choreographer, she served at various times as ballet mistress of the Théâtre du Châtelet, Théâtre de la Gaîté-Lyrique, and Opéra-Comique. For *Phryné,* see Cléo de Mérode, *Le Ballet de ma vie,* pref. Françoise Ducout (Paris: Pierre Horay, 1985), pp. 143–145; for Stichel's career at the Opéra, see Stéphane Wolff, *L'Opéra au Palais Garnier (1875–1962),* introd. Alain Gueullette (Paris: Slatkine, 1983); for her productions at the Opéra-Comique, see Stéphane Wolff, *Un Demi-siècle d'Opéra-Comique (1900–1950)* (Paris: André Bonne, 1953); for her contributions to *La Princesse sans-gêne, Pif! Paf! Pouf! ou un Voyage endiablé, Tom Pitt, le Roi des Pickpockets, Les 400 Coups du Diable,* and *La Revue du Châtelet,* see the programs in PRO.B.87/Théâtre du Châtelet, Bibliothèque de l'Opéra, Paris. Both *Sylvia* (1876) and *La Korrigane* (1880) were choreographed by Louis Mérante. In the 1890s and early 1900s, preromantic dances, costumed in period style, were frequently performed at galas and private society events.

11. Mérode, *Le Ballet de ma vie,* pp. 214, 222–230.

12. For Sada Yacco's celebrated appearances at the Théâtre Loïe Fuller and a survey of the Exposition's dance entertainments in general, see Shelley C. Berg, "Sada Yacco in London and Paris, 1900: *Le Rêve Réalisé*" (*Dance Chronicle,* 18, no. 3 [1995], pp. 367–389). In addition to the Palais de Danse, where Christine Kerf, Maria Giuri, and Aida Boni led the company in ballets and stylized French folk dances choreographed by Madame Mariquita, many national pavilions offered dance attractions. At the open-air theater attached to the Spanish pavilion, for instance, one could see, as Cléo de Mérode later wrote, "all the dances of Madrid, Sevilla, Valencia, Salamanca, etc." (*Le Ballet de ma vie,* p. 229). At the Egyptian Theater, there were the dancers "Zohra" and "Matouka"; at the Ceylon pavilion, the "Devil Dancers"; at the restaurant La Feria, *flamencos* from Madrid, Granada, and Seville. The Javanese dancers were another popular attraction.

13. Alla Klimov and Alison Hilton, "Anna Pavlova, A Remembrance," *Dance Magazine,* January 1976, p. 44. This article is based upon Trouhanova's unpublished memoir, "The Blaze of the Footlights," in the Central State Archives of Literature and Art (TsGALI), Moscow.

14. Jean Delion, "Mlle Trouhanowa," *Comoedia,* 5 May 1911, p. 1. Although Trouhanova states that she studied at the Conservatory, Klimov and Hilton (p. 44) write that she

studied at the "Philharmonic School in the class of Vladimir Nemirovitch-Danchenko." This would suggest that she received her theatrical education at the Moscow Philharmonic Society Drama School, where the director taught in this period (Alma Law and Mel Gordon, *Meyerhold, Eisenstein and Biomechanics: Actor Training in Revolutionary Russia* [Jefferson, N.C.: McFarland, 1996], p. 18).

15. Klimov and Hilton, "Anna Pavlova," p. 44.

16. Lydia Joffe, "*La Peri:* 1912," *Dance Magazine,* April 1967, p. 41.

17. "*La Mariska,*" *Journal de Monaco,* 2 May 1905. I am indebted to the Société des Bains de Mer, Monte Carlo, for copies of programs and reviews in the SBM collection.

18. According to the caption accompanying a photograph of Trouhanova published in England during her tenure at the Monte Carlo Opera, she was one of Madame Mariquita's "cleverest and most beautiful pupils" (Mariquita Clipping File, DD-NYPL).

19. "Les Deux Pigeons," *Journal de Monaco,* 7 May 1907.

20. Robert Brussel, in a piece published on the morning of the premiere, noted that the "steps [of the dance] have been arranged by Monsieur Clustine" ("Avant 'Salomé,'" *Figaro,* 6 May 1907, p. 5).

21. The *répétition générale,* a gala event attended by the President of the Republic, took place at the Théâtre du Châtelet on 6 May 1907.

22. She danced her first *Samson et Dalila* on 12 June 1907. The premiere of *Le Lac des Aulnes,* a "ballet féerique" in two acts and five tableaux with music by Henri Maréchal, took place on 25 November 1907.

23. "Courrier des Théâtres," *Figaro,* 22 May 1907, p. 6.

24. "Pour nos abonnées: la dernière matinée de la saison," *Femina,* 1 August 1907, p. 340. Trouhanova also performed them at a soiree in the home of Baronne La Caze and at a charity matinee organized by Duchesse d'Estissac-La Rochefoucauld and Madame Nelidov, the wife of the Russian ambassador ("Le Monde et la Ville," *Figaro,* 9 and 14 June 1907, p. 2).

25. The first performance of *Chopiniana* took place at the Maryinsky Theater on 10 February 1907; the premiere of *Suite de danses* on 23 June 1913. "Cinq Pièces de Chopin" was given on 3 May 1911 at the first of two "Concerts de danse" presented by Trouhanova at the Théâtre du Châtelet. The opening Mazurka (op. 7, no. 1) was played by the orchestra as an overture.

26. "Courrier des Théâtres," *Figaro,* 11 May 1909, p. 4. The piece was given on a mixed bill at the Théâtre Michel.

27. For an announcement of this tour, see "Courrier Musical," *Figaro,* 15 June 1909, p. 7; for her appearance at the Université des Annales, where she "accompan[ied]" Jean Richepin's lecture on the czardas, see "Le Masque de Fer," "Echos," *Figaro,* 24 April 1909, p. 1; for her participation in various charity events, where she performed either *L'Apache* or unspecified dances from her repertory, see "Le Monde et la Ville," *Figaro,* 9, 13, 19, and 22 May 1909, p. 2.

28. Maurice Lefèvre, "Théâtre lyrique municipal de la Gaîté: *Quo Vadis?*" *Le Théâtre,* January 1910, II, p. 22. Based on the novel by Henrick Sienkiewicz, the opera had

music by Jean Nouguès and a libretto by Henri Cain. Jeanne Chasles made her debut at the Opéra as a *petit sujet* in 1888 and danced principal roles at the Opéra-Comique from 1899 to 1910 (Wolff, *L'Opéra au Palais Garnier*, p. 530, and *Un Demi-siècle d'Opéra-Comique*, p. 327). She choreographed the dances in Fauré's opera *Pénélope* presented in 1913 at the Théâtre des Champs-Elysées, and, according to one source, a ballet for the Théâtre des Arts. In 1920, she became ballet mistress of the Opéra-Comique.

29. A clipping with this photograph is in the Mariquita Clipping File, DD-NYPL.
30. For an advertisement listing the programs for the two concerts, see *Courrier musical,* 15 April 1911, p. 286. For last-minute changes in the first program, see "Deux Concerts de danse," *Comoedia,* 2 May 1911, p. 2.
31. Diaghilev to Astruc, 25 March 1911, GA53–1, Gabriel Astruc Papers, DD-NYPL.
32. Diaghilev to Astruc, 3 April 1911, GA53–8, Astruc Papers.
33. The contracts, which are undated, are in GA65–8, Astruc Papers.
34. This contract, which is also unsigned, is in GA65–9/10, Astruc Papers.
35. Léon Bakst, telegram to Diaghilev, 14 April 1911, GA49–1, Astruc Papers.
36. Diaghilev to Astruc, 14 April 1911, GA53–19, Astruc Papers.
37. Diaghilev to Astruc, 27 May 1911, GA51–1, Astruc Papers. In an account of the episode based on Trouhanova's unpublished memoirs, Lydia Joffe offers a number of details that contradict Diaghilev's version of events. Writing to Astruc on May 22, Diaghilev insisted that Trouhanova, "having given her word to come to Monte Carlo, never managed to do so during the entire two months we were there" (GA50–2, Astruc Papers). According to Joffe, however, this was not the case at all. "Rehearsals," she writes, "were constantly postponed. . . . Nijinsky and choreographer Michel Fokine were repeatedly 'indisposed.' Trouhanova became suspicious that Diaghilev was plotting to steal the ballet from her. . . . [O]ne day when [she] came to rehearsal she found Adolph Bolm had replaced Nijinsky as her partner. She thought it the last straw and left the company" ("*La Péri*," pp. 41– 42). Joffe also quotes Trouhanova as claiming that she had been persuaded by Diaghilev "to give up Balakirev's *Thamar*" (*ibid,* p. 41). The ballet was produced by Diaghilev in 1912.
38. Diaghilev to Astruc, 8, 14, and 16 January 1912, GA74–2/3/4, Astruc Papers.
39. For a photograph of her in this role, see *The Sketch* [Supplement], 1 November 1911, p. 8.
40. Robert Brussel, "Les Théâtres," *Figaro,* 24 April 1912, p. 4.
41. M. D. Calvocoressi, "Les Concerts de danses de Mlle Trouhanowa," *Comoedia Illustré,* 15 May 1912, p. 638.
42. Brussel, "Les Théâtres."
43. Henry Gauthier-Villars, "Musique," *Mercure de France,* 16 May 1912, p. 414.
44. "Aux Folies-Bergère: Les Galas Trouhanowa dans *la Revue de Printemps*," *Figaro,* 6 June 1912, p. 6. Within days of their premiere at the Folies-Bergère, Trouhanova "mimed" the two Debussy pieces at a soiree given by the "futurist" dancer Valentine de Saint-Point (André Warnod, "La Soirée napoléonienne chez Mme Valentine de Saint-Point," *Comoedia,* 13 June 1912; "Françoise," "Une Soirée d'art," *Femina,* 15 July

1912). I am grateful to Nancy Moore for drawing my attention to this event, yet another example of Trouhanova's penchant for border crossing.

45. René Bizet, "Les adieux à la danse de Mlle Trouhanowa," 26 February 1913, Dossier d'artiste (Trouhanova), Bibliothèque de l'Opéra; "Spectacles et Concerts," *Figaro,* 13 June 1913, p. 6; Louis Delluc, "A Deauville," *Comoedia Illustré,* 20 August 1913, p. 1024; H. Decé, "Casino de Deauville: *Narkiss,*" *Le Théâtre,* October 1913, I, pp. 20–24; "Notre Concours Photographique," *Comoedia Illustré,* 5 September 1913, p. 1051.

46. "Résultats du concours de *Comoedia Illustré* d'août 1913," *Comoedia Illustré,* 20 September 1913.

47. The reprise of *La Péri* took place on 29 May 1914; the premiere of *Le Ballet des Nations* on 9 June 1914. According to Stéphane Wolff (*Un demi-siècle d'Opéra-Comique,* p. 211), *La Péri* was choreographed by Mariquita, not by Clustine. However, her name is not mentioned in announcements of the premiere, which suggests that Clustine's choreography was largely retained. It is certainly possible that she changed some passages to accommodate Quinault, who was now dancing the role of Iskendar.

48. Quoted in Pierre Mortier, "Mademoiselle Natacha Trouhanowa," *Le Théâtre,* 1 July 1909, n. p.

49. "What a brilliant idea it was to ask Léon Bakst to do the costumes," she told an interviewer in 1913. "With his austere, peerless originality the great artist eschewed the conventions and traditions that overburdened and deformed classical figures. He conjured up from the depths of time the crude and naked spirit of those ages when Oedipus cried out and Antigone wept. He gave the human figure that acute sense of tragedy which emanates from the lines of the classics. Ever since then, Léon Bakst has never deserted me. I have an artistic compact with him which is very precious to me" ("Ida Rubinstein about Herself," *Solntse Rossii,* no. 25 [1913], p. 12, quoted in Irina Pruzhan, *Léon Bakst,* trans. Arthur Shkarovki-Raffé [New York: Viking, 1987], p. 218). Prior to Rubinstein's commission, Bakst had designed two other classical plays—Euripedes' *Hippolytus* (1902) and Sophocles' *Oedipus at Colonnus* (1904)—both produced at the Alexandrinsky Theater and directed by Ozarovsky.

50. For the curriculum, teaching personnel, and Rubinstein's grades at the Moscow Theater School, as well as her transfer to its St. Petersburg counterpart, see "Vedomosti ob ispytaniakh uchashchikhaia Dramaticheskikh Kursov 1901–1908," fond 682 (Mosk. Teatr. Uchilishche), op. 1, ed. khr. 192, TsGALI. The Volynsky letter, which is undated, also comes from TsGALI (fond 95 [Volynsky], op. 1, ed. khr. 761, l. 97–98). Vera Pashennaia in *Iskusstvo aktrisy* (Moscow: Iskusstvo, 1954) recalled that Rubinstein "wore a sumptuous crimson dress with a kind of lace that seemed enchanting, a long train, costly brilliants, and elegant shoes. I was struck by her fashionable coiffure that cascaded splendidly over her brow" (p. 19). I am grateful to Elizabeth Souritz for providing me with copies of these documents.

51. For Delsarte, see "Mikhail Yampolsky, "Kuleshov's Experiments and the New Anthropology of the Actor," in *Inside the Film Factory: New Approaches to Russian and Soviet Cinema,* ed. R. Taylor and I. Christie (London: Routledge, 1991), p. 32. Meyerhold's symbolist experiments of 1905 to 1908 are discussed in detail in Konstantin

Rudnitsky, *Meyerhold the Director,* trans. George Petrov, ed. Sydney Schultze, introd. Ellendea Proffer (Ann Arbor: Ardis, 1981), pp. 55–130. Duncan gave her first concerts in Moscow in February 1905.

52. Quoted in Rudnitsky, *Meyerhold,* p. 196.

53. Rubinstein to Iuvitskaia, n.d. [autumn 1906], fond 1958 (N.N. Gorich and E.A. Iuvitskaia), op. 1, ed. khr. 104, l. 16, TsGALI.

54. Rubinstein to Komissarzhevskaia, n.d. [spring and August 1908], fond 778 (V.F. Komissarzhevskaia], op. 2, ed. khr. l. 1–3, TsGALI. I am grateful to Elizabeth Souritz for copies of these letters. The *répétition générale* of Komissarzhevskaia's *Salomé,* which was directed by Nikolai Evreinov, took place on 27 October 1908; Rubinstein's production, which was staged by Meyerhold, was scheduled to open on November 3 at the Mikhailovsky Theater ("Khronika," *Teatr i iskusstvo,* 12 October 1908, p. 702, and 19 October 1908, p. 726). After the ban, *Rech'* announced that the "Dance of the Tsar's Daughter" (as the number was known in Russia) would be "presented in December in a private theater with the . . . same cast . . . as at the Mikhailovsky Theater ("Teatr i muzyka," *Rech',* 29 October 1908, p. 5).

55. Quoted in Rudnitsky, *Meyerhold,* p. 196.

56. "Original'nyia tantsovshchitsy," *Teatr i iskusstvo,* 21 December 1908, pp. 916–918. The *Nautch* is identified as "Palace Dance." The photograph of Trouhanova and the Beardsley drawing appeared in the November 2 issue (pp. 769 and 776 respectively); the photographs of Maud Allan and Odette Valéry in the December 21 issue (p. 917).

57. Rubinstein to Komissarzhevskaia, n.d. [August 1908], *op. cit.*

58. Ozarovsky's "specialty," wrote the anonymous reviewer for *Teatr i iskusstvo,* is "preparing actresses for classical roles at the Alexandrinsky Theater. It is almost as though he had a contract for the theater to supply in such-and-such a period so many items at such-and-such a price. And so, in order to train Mademoiselle Lvovskaia, who has means, Monsieur Ozarovsky straightway assigned her classical roles and what is more difficult ones like Antigone. The result is unfortunate: Mademoiselle Lvovskaia still does not know how to make an entrance, but she has been "prepared" for the company at the Alexandrinsky Theater and apparently for such plays as *Antigone*" ("Khronika," 25 April 1904, p. 350).

59. Rubinstein to Iuvitskaia, n.d. [autumn 1906], ed. khr. 104, l. 18.

60. Rubinstein to Volynsky, n.d. [1907], ed. khr. 764, l. 1–2.

61. "Khronika," *Teatr i iskusstvo,* 9 September 1907, p. 580. Ibsen seems to have been more than a passing whim of Rubinstein's. In 1912, she told a reporter for the *New York American,* "If I ever go to America, . . . I want to play Hedda Gabler, whom I love." (Alan Dale, "The Only Girl Who Ever Broke D'Annunzio's Heart," *New York American,* 2 June 1912, Ida Rubinstein Clipping File, Dance Division). Sanin, who directed Diaghilev's 1908 production of *Boris Godunov,* staged Rubinstein's productions of Emile Verhaeren's *Hélène de Sparte* and Wilde's *Salomé* in Paris in 1912. In the fall of 1908 Sanin produced Hugo von Hofmannsthal's *Elektra* at St. Petersburg's New Theater.

62. She alluded to this in a letter to Comte Robert de Montesquiou written in the sum-

mer or early fall of 1909: "I do not regret having suffered everything I suffered last winter; for it was in this way that I came to Paris and that I met you" (15284/129, Robert de Montesquiou Papers, Department of Manuscripts, Bibliotèque Nationale).

63. Henry Gauthier-Villars, "Opéra Russe (Châtelet)," *Comoedia,* 5 June 1909, p. 2.

64. Robert de Montesquiou, "La Dame bleue," *Figaro littéraire* [supplement], 19 June 1909, p. 2.

65. Jean Cocteau, *The Decorative Art of Léon Bakst,* trans. Harry Melvill (London, 1913; rpt. New York: Dover, 1972), p. 30.

66. Rubinstein to Montesquiou, n.d. [June–July 1909], 15333/26, Montesquiou Papers.

67. Pierre Raniz, "Réouverture de l'Olympia," *Comoedia,* 22 August 1909, p. 2. The show opened on August 21; Rubinstein's name remained on the bill until September 17.

68. Edward G. Kendrew, "Ida Rubinstein, 'Dance of the Seven Veils,' Olympia, Paris," *Variety,* 11 September 1909, Ida Rubinstein Clipping File, Theatre Collection, New York Public Library.

69. Quoted in Rudnitsky, *Meyerhold,* p. 196.

70. Sorel to Montesquiou, n.d. [September 1909], 15163/145, Montesquiou Papers.

71. Rubinstein to Montesquiou, n.d. [August 1909], 15222/17–18, Montesquiou Papers.

72. Rubinstein to Montesquiou, n.d. [September 1909], 15333/21–22, Montesquiou Papers. The Saturday before she was originally scheduled to open, it was announced that she would "present, among other items, the Dance of the Seven Veils" ("Variety Gossip," *The Era,* 18 September 1909, p. 20).

73. "The Coliseum," *The Era,* 2 October 1909, p. 21.

74. Rubinstein to Montesquiou, n.d. [October 1909], 15333/39–40, Montesquiou Papers.

75. Quoted in Bronislava Nijinska, *Early Memoirs,* trans. and ed. Irina Nijinska and Jean Rawlinson, introd. Anna Kisselgoff (New York: Holt, Rinehart and Winston, 1981), p. 406.

76. For the gestation and casting of the work, see *A Working Friendship: The Correspondence between Richard Strauss and Hugo von Hofmannsthal,* trans. Hanns Hammelmann and Ewald Osers, introd. Edward Sackville-West (New York: Random House, 1961).

77. Rubinstein to Montesquiou, n.d., 15241/50–53, Montesquiou Papers.

78. Four of these photograhs, all by H. B. Marinetti, were published in *The Sketch,* on 13 October 1909, Ida Rubinstein Clipping File, Raymond Mander and Joe Mitchenson Theatre Collection.

79. Georges Tribout, *Dessins sur les gestes de Mademoiselle Ida Rubinstein,* prof. Charles Batilliot (Paris: La Belle Edition, n.d. [1912]), n.p.

80. *La Nave* was a filmed version of a play by Gabriele d'Annunzio directed by his son in 1919. A print survives at the Museo del Cinema in Milan.

81. Rubinstein to Nathalie Barnay, 23 November [1920], NCB.C.1854, Bibliothèque Littéraire Jacques Doucet, Paris. Barnay also showed a copy of the manuscript to Jacques Rouché, the director of the Paris Opéra (Barnay to Rouché, 22 September 1920, AJ13/1207, Archives Nationales, Paris).

82. Bizet, "Les adieux à la danse."

83. "Paris Notes," *The Dancing Times,* June 1921 (p. 719), March 1922 (p. 539), April 1922 (p. 607), and July 1922 (p. 855). For a detailed announcement of the "Grand Festival de Chant et de Danse donné par le Choeur Russe de Kibaltchitch et Mme Natacha Trouhanowa," see "Feuilles de location" (May–Aug. 1923), AJ123/1431, Archives Nationales. The festival took place on 26 January 1923. The following June the chorus would take part in the premiere of *Les Noces.*

84. "Mme Trouhanowa-Ignatieff à Lyon," *Lyon-Républicain,* 17 March 1935, Dossier d'artiste (Natalia Trouhanova), Bibliothèque de l'Opéra.

LYDIA LOPOKOVA AND LES SOIRÉES DE PARIS

It was in January 1924 that Lydia Lopokova first heard of plans for a month-long season of ballets to be produced that May in Paris. Léonide Massine was to be the choreographer, Georges Braque one of the designers, and the season would take place in a legitimate theatre—not a music hall. With alacrity, Lopokova accepted Massine's offer.

The season that promised to unite "all that [was] best in painting and music" became Les Soirées de Paris. Organized by Comte Etienne de Beaumont, and with dancers from all over Europe participating, Les Soirées de Paris was one of the decade's many attempts to duplicate the success of the Russian Ballet by aping Diaghilev's post-war modernist "recipe." Beaumont himself was a long-standing friend of Cocteau, and was close to "Les Six," the group of young French composers, and a member of the Franco-American Painting and Sculpture Exhibition Association. Like Rolf de Maré's Ballets Suédois a few years earlier, Les Soirées de Paris aspired to replace the Ballets Russes at the vanguard of the Paris artistic world.

By contrast with its more distinguished predecessors, Les Soirées de Paris has remained no more than a footnote to the dance history of the 1920s. Few memoirs have recorded the drama of its creation, and its brief existence has had to be pieced together from press notices and reviews. Hence the incalculable value of Lopokova's letters to her future husband, John Maynard Keynes, now at King's College, Cambridge. Penned nightly in the full flush of rehearsals and performances, Lopokova's letters provide an eyewitness account—from a dancer's point of view—of Les Soirées de Paris, from its gestation to its less than glorious demise.

Lopokova had responded with enthusiasm to Massine's offer of a place in his new company. Artistic considerations, however, quickly gave way to financial ones in the first of the dancer's wrangles with Beaumont about money. Although, at first, he had asked her to name her "price" (20 January 1924), Lopokova was forced to take a heavy cut in her usual salary—5,000 francs less than her "lowest possible fee." A draft (the original is in French) of her letter to Beaumont on 8 February explains her position:

> Monsieur Massin [*sic*] must have told you that my regular salary in London is 100 pounds a week. Before I saw you this afternoon, my idea was that, given condi-

This essay was originally published in *Lydia Lopokova*, ed. Milo Keynes (London: Weidenfeld and Nicolson, 1983).

tions in Paris, my lowest possible fee was 20,000 francs a month (which comes to a little more than half the amount I receive in London). When you offered half of my half, I didn't know what to say. But the project and artistic ideas associated with it are very appealing, and I want to avoid difficulties about money; still, thinking of the future, it is difficult for me to lower my regular salary so much. Nevertheless, I will accept 20,000 francs for the engagement of a month-and-a-half.[1]

As preparations for the season went forward, rumors flew fast and furious between Diaghilev's headquarters in Monte Carlo and London. Despite Massine's concern for secrecy, reported Lopokova, Osbert Sitwell's "latest gossip" on 25 February was that "Big Serge" was in "such a rage" over Beaumont's project, which would coincide with the Russian Ballet's regular Paris season, that he was engaging "everyone possible with a contract *forever*":

Stas [Stanislas Idzikovsky] arrived soft as a peach with me, the Count engaged him also for Paris with Massine, he said (the Count) that Diaghileff . . . was pleading for a favour and should not engage Stas for Paris season, the Count promised, in the meantime Big Serge tried behind his back to destroy Count's season, so that now Count is furious and engages Stas for spite.

10 March

On 24 April, Lopokova was in Paris. From the outset, things seemed to go wrong:

Boulevard Raspail is hell after Gordon Square especially for sleeping. . . . The Count and Countess received me with enthusiasm, asked me for lunch with Stas. . . . The house is beautiful, and two big rooms are given for rehearsing, and all the furniture is taken away; I have a complex about my exercises; my room is too small; as for the Count's room Massine gives a lesson in the morning to thirty dancers, and to study with them is of no use. Massine looks ill and seems pleasant to everybody.

26 April

Absolutely without any strength, my legs twitch incessantly. . . . Stas begins to make difficulties . . . and asked me [for] a 100 francs.

28 April

As Lopokova was doctoring a brief illness with French cheeses and cream ("I do not dare to weigh myself"), rehearsals went ahead for the season's eclectic repertoire, which included not only dance, but two theatre pieces: Tristan Tzara's Dadaist "tragedy in fifteen acts," *Mouchoir de Nuages,* and Cocteau's "adaptation" of Shakespeare, *Roméo et Juliette.* Loie Fuller, by then a fixture of

Tout-Paris, was in charge of lighting. Eight ballets were presented. *Salade,* a commedia dell'arte "counterpoint," with music by Darius Milhaud and designs by Braque, Lopokova judged "too futuristic." *Mercure,* a series of "plastic poses," had a score by Erik Satie and designs by Picasso. *Les Roses,* a plotless "divertissement" by Henri Sauguet, featured designs by Marie Laurencin (mysteriously credited on the program as "N . . . "). For *Gigue,* a suite of courtly dances to themes of Bach and Handel, André Derain confected the "costume of a princess" for Lopokova in shades of grey, green, and blue. *Vogue,* "three danced pages" "illustrated" by Valentine Hugo, was dressed by the couturière Lanvin. With the rage for Spanish dancing at its height, José-María Sert's *Ballet Espagnol* (performed by Diaghilev's original Cleopatra, Ida Rubinstein) provided the requisite touch of Iberian colour, while a medley of "contemporary dances" by the revue star Harry Wills nodded to the jazz craze. The most popular item of the repertoire, however, was *Le Beau Danube,* a frothy evocation of the Second Empire by Constantin Guys, set to the music of Johann Strauss. Here, Lopokova added the role of the Street Dancer—later made famous by Alexandra Danilova with Colonel de Basil's post-Diaghilev Ballet Russe—to her delightful galaxy of soubrettes.

The program for the season at the Théâtre Cigale was both "advanced" and "chic," being calculated to appeal to the sophisticated taste-makers of *les années folles.* Although Lopokova was not, strictly speaking, a "classical" dancer—her strength lay in *demi-caractère* and soubrette roles—she became increasingly perturbed by the choreography, which she felt did not show her to best advantage. Her critical attitude was bound to end in emotional fireworks.

A new choreograph the Count himself! The ballet called "Vogue" [a "poem" by the fashionable novelist Paul Morand] our tableau about three minutes with a young man a young girl who is like a boy, and I the woman of the smart set. We lie on the beach in Lido and the man and the boy are "getting on" so that I must produce a vexed face and stand in the middle, showing a costume made up of miroirs (dernier cri naturally). I do all I am asked except that I cannot look jealous, not in my nature. . . . Massine does not interfere, it is not worthwhile either. A good reclame for Vogue, but perhaps I sound too sarcastic.

5 May

Massine this morning asked me an advice to give three ballets or two and a one-act play. I thought with the play is better, because his "Salade" and "Mercury" are all the same in movement, and also better to make it different from Big Serge, but of course they try to imitate him, although denying it. They should also aim at the "grand public" and not for the little groups. Big Serge always knew that. I wonder if they realize it. Older I am more critical I become.

6 May

Oh I have been through fire and water . . . as last night I came to a decision that I could not do "Vogue" ballet, and with V. and G. [Vera Bowen and her husband Garia, or Harold, Bowen] a letter was composed and dispatched. This afternoon when I saw him [Beaumont] "Did you receive my letter forgive me." The Count, "je vous déteste." So I received his answer with a smile, and now I am a free woman again.

12 May

With the opening night a few days off, nerves became frayed, and it was the dancers who bore the brunt of the shortened tempers and squabbling among the organizers:

We spent from 2 till 7 in the theatre. . . . I plead [with] Massine to have clear lights in the scene where the psychological moment develops, but he is difficult. My costume is good, but my rehearsal skirts are much better as a costume with the decor. The ballet "Salade" how I like it. [It] is with singing; music is stirring, and the decor of Braque very attractive, and the ballet is of a structure that develops like a building. The order of the programme first a play, then "Salade" then "Blue Danube." Big Serge asked for three seats.

11 May

In our company are "too many cooks" the dancers waited in the theatre to-day from 2–6 while Loie Fuller tries the light and hides all the movements of the dancers.

12 May

By now I am like theatrical rat, always in the theatre, and without end we wait, there is not one controlling voice in the situation, except the Comte's polite but weak falsetto. I think V. and G. would achieve more results for the lights than Loie Fuller, what a big fat toad; perhaps she is very clever.

13 May

Scenes and scenes, the direction now decided for me to have a wig, but it is made of black straw, and I looked ugly, so I made an unsympathetic face, they gave me another, but it is out of style with the others, too modern.

16 May

Opening night 17 May found Lopokova with her "fibres . . . in a state of perpetuum mobile"—a quaint phrase for first-night jitters. The performance, however, came off with great success, although, as she noted to Keynes, no more than a hundred people turned up at the following day's matinee. Not unexpectedly, Lopokova's letters of the next few days were concerned with the impression she had made both on friends and critics:

[M]y friends find as ever that Massine does everything to shadow me and not make me his equal, but also V. and G. think I have never looked better or danced better, and that my costume is chef d'oeuvre and big Serge can't say I am too fat. However we can't change nature of Massine, it is always twisted in the wrong direction.

18 May

Today, in the "Comoedia" is a criticism [by André Levinson] not at all stupid, but I receive hard knocks. "Lopokova conserve la candeur touchante et l'incertitude technique d'une debutante de 17 ans. Tant mieux pour la femme, tant pis pour la danseuse." You see how badly I am established in Paris.

20 May

Meanwhile, reports from the "enemy" camp began filtering back:

Last night big Serge came to the theatre, but reports are that he did not express any admiration; he sat with Nijinska and "favorite" and when Nijinska applauded he seemed dissatisfied. To-day in the restaurant Grigoriev-[T]chernicheva at the other table thought I had an unsuitable part and also irritated by the idea that Massine might have engagements in other countries. Of course their life is not a light burden, and they are terrified of any competition.

21 May

He [Beaumont] and Massine speak of nothing else but "enemies" and although to-night there is a premiere of Big Serge a certain princess will arrive to Cigale instead and that satisfies our set.

26 May

Although *Gigue* was given its first performance on 29 May, the better part of the company's energy that week was devoted to rehearsals for one of Beaumont's famous fancy-dress balls to be held on the thirty-first. Once again, Lopokova was angered by his willingness to allow Massine to upstage her:

I went to a rehearsal for that damnation ball to-morrow. Stas came into the dressing room with a newspaper . . . and it said how this charity ball includes all the amateurs society and L. Massine. As it is a thing of *charity* I absolutely want my professional name, and as Count is very busy, I left the dirty theatre. . . . Besides my costume is the same as corps de ballet and they do not take least trouble to make it better. . . . The Count must not overlook these matters, and if he does, there is penalty for him; the announcement certainly comes out of his organisa-tion. To-night I shall tell him so.

30 May

Last night I had my "conversation" with the Count, he of course pleaded not guilty that he never edited this advertising e.c. and he asks a favour to do it for him, so you see Lydochka agreeing . . . but very independent telling him that director should be a director and not overlook mishaps.

31 May

Yesterday's ball seemed very prosperous, the Count's perfect "metier." Stas and I were prosperous also in success, although we danced with a net in front of us, and Massine in another scene without it. I register facts that do not encourage me with devotion to M.

1 June

A few days later, she spent sixty francs on a ticket to see "Big Serge's ballet." Diaghilev himself was very "cool" toward her, as he "considered" whether to "embrace or not." The house, she noted, was "beautifully" dressed, and Picasso's drop curtain for *Le Train Bleu* of two giantesses bounding along the seashore, she found "moving and alive." About the performance, which included Nijinska's *Les Fâcheux*, however, she had reservations. It was "smooth and professional," "but nothing or no one stirred" her. Sounding the theme of such contemporary critics as André Levinson and Valerian Svetlov, she found herself longing "for very old fashioned ballets without abstract ideas. I want simplicity and Poetry; Massine or Nijinska choreography clever as it is have too much intellect" (5 June).

On 10 June, Beaumont's dancers found themselves once again at the beck and call of society—appearing this time before a minor royal personage for whose convenience a private performance had been arranged:

Last night we had to dance after our representation once more to an empty the-atre "Gigue" and "Divertissement" because in the middle sat the Queen of Rou-mania coming after the Opera, so when the dance was over Massine, Stas . . . and I shook the hand of the Queen. . . . Then Loie Fuller [long an intimate friend of the Queen] began her repertory with lights, that looked like insides of the stom-ach, or oysters or kinds of Easter eggs or simply eggs, and we poor worn out dancers had to wait and admire it.

10 June

Lopokova's gastronomic fantasies are to be pardoned, for the dancers must have been as hungry as they were tired. The post-performance recital capped a long day, for the company had been rehearsing a complete new program: *Les Roses, Mercure,* and a "sketch about a girl who dreams of dolls" (11 June),

Lopokova being one of the dolls. Her letters of the next few days talk of little except physical exhaustion and maltreatment. They evince none of the enthusiasm that Massine's initial proposal had excited. In fact, they are pervaded by a tone of disillusionment - not only with the enterprise itself, but also with its overall aesthetic and its pandering to fashion:

> I still work like an elephant. . . . I told Massine that he must give us one free night before Saturday to come into a normal condition, and also I have not washed myself for a week, because a hot bath wears me completely out, so I wait for the night of liberty.
>
> 12 June

> In the theatre from 2 till [8.30] for ever waiting, trying on costumes, and [have] not been able to dance with the orchestra except for 7–8 minutes. I told Massine that except [for] himself, he considered the other dancers as mud (in the Roses he does not dance), but the ballet with him he rehearsed for hours, so that musicians when tired were logical to stand up and depart. . . . To-night is the night of liberty. I shall put my worn out legs into the embrace of hot water and recite.
>
> 13 June

> Last night the "furore" of the evening was Stas. He had to repeat his variation; in it he does the same turns in the air as in the "Lac de Cygnes." I looked very well, but there is no chance for me to develop any dance, as all the pieces are too short. "Mercure" to me seems a decadence. Picasso perhaps wanted to pull the noses of the public; the colours are very good but the way they [are] brought on or executed or what they represent is beyond any measure of comprehension. It is no ballet, no parody, but somehow a stupid farce. Smart audience and success, as always on the first night.
>
> 15 June

The premiere of *Mercure* was marked by fireworks behind the curtain and in the hall. Lopokova nearly "came to blows" with Beaumont when she refused to don the "cheap," tasteless flowers of her costume. Beaumont stamped his foot. "Mum [L. L.], his stubborn adversary won the day" (15 June). Venturing into the theatre later that evening, Lopokova found herself in the eye of another artistic storm:

> *Oh* what a demonstration last night. "Mercury" being the last on the program I went into the "promenoir" to look steadily at the ballet and have a firm opinion about it. First tableau began with cries, "Vive Picasso"; the other party replies, "Vive Erik Satie". . . "En bas E. Satie et vive Picasso." After the [second] tableau pro-Picasso-sists became enormous and shouted "Vive Picasso seul, En bas E. de Beaumont les garçons, et toutes soirées de Paris." I was only a few steps away from

the young man who proclaimed this. Then the policeman rushed to him and arrested [him], the anti-Picasso group ran to his box and shouted, "En bas Picasso."

16 June

The remaining days of the Beaumont season were uneventful by comparison. The dancers continued to rehearse "to perfect ourselves or to give something to do to the Count or M." (18 June). Cherries came into season. Lydia spent forty francs on a picture of Fanny Cerrito. On 20 June the letters break off.

For Beaumont and Massine, the season was not a success. Reviews were mixed, perhaps the worst notice appearing in *The Dancing Times*. ("The corps de ballet was, without exception, the worst I have ever seen," wrote Gilson Mac-Cormack.) Houses were rarely full. The eagerly awaited engagement by the London producer Charles B. Cochran failed to materialize. Most tragically for Massine, his attempt to form a successful repertory group, at the level of Diaghilev's Ballets Russes or Rolf de Maré's Ballets Suédois, came to nought.

NOTES

1. This and the letters that follow are part of the Keynes Papers, King's College Library, Cambridge.

RECONFIGURING THE SEXES

"Ballet is woman," George Balanchine liked to say. His first star in the West, however, was a young man named Serge Lifar. Lifar, who directed the Paris Opéra ballet from 1929 to 1945 (when he was dismissed for collaboration with the Nazis) and again from 1947 to 1958, was the last of Serge Diaghilev's leading men, one of the golden boys who made his company famous. Like his predecessors, Lifar was uniquely a product of the Ballets Russes; plucked from oblivion, he was groomed by Diaghilev for stardom, launched on a path that asserted not only his preeminence within the company as an individual, but also the preeminent role within its repertory of a new kind of hero.

This hero, who first made his appearance with Vaslav Nijinsky, differed markedly from the princes of the nineteenth-century Russian repertory that formed the early dancers and choreographers of the Ballets Russes. No longer merely a consort to the ballerina or the exponent of a chivalric ideal of masculinity, he was a protagonist in his own right, projecting an image of sexual heterodoxy that left a deep imprint not only on the ballets of the Diaghilev period, but also on its audiences. From the androgynes of *Le Spectre de la Rose* (1911) and *L'Après-midi d'un Faune* (1912) to the deco gods of *La Chatte* (1927), *Apollon Musagète* (1928), and *Prodigal Son* (1929), Diaghilev's heroes traced a spectrum of male roles that transcended conventions of gender while presenting the male body in a way that was frankly erotic. Ballet after ballet celebrated its physique, dramatized its athletic prowess, and paraded its sexual availability. Among the many excellent *danseurs* who passed through the ranks of the Ballets Russes, the "ballerino" alone haunted Diaghilev's imagination.

As a type, the "ballerino" had no historical precedent, so Diaghilev, with typical invention, manufactured him from the material at hand. Nijinsky was first; Léonide Massine, Anton Dolin, Lifar, and a few lesser lights followed. For Diaghilev, they were sometime lovers, would-be sons, and muses. He made them star dancers and fashioned them into star choreographers; he shared his life with them, and his purse, and the passion, intelligence, and taste he brought to every branch of art. At a time when the memory of Oscar Wilde kept most homosexuals in the closet, Diaghilev made the Ballets Russes a venue where the public medium of ballet and the private theater of his imagination at least

This essay was originally published in *The Ballets Russes and Its World*, ed. Lynn Garafola and Nancy Van Norman Baer (New Haven: Yale University Press, 1999).

partly overlapped—a kingdom of "beautiful boys." Generous at times to a fault, cunning, quixotic, willful, and perspicacious, he used this peculiar collection of attributes to alter the course of ballet. Before him, individual dancers may have been homosexual, and homosexual individuals may have been present in the ballet audience. Still, the terrain itself remained ideologically and socially hetero-sexual. With Diaghilev, however, ballet in Western Europe no less than in Amer-ica became a privileged arena for homosexuals as performers, choreographers, and spectators. It was a feat unparalleled in the other arts, and for gay men, to use a modern term, it was a revolution. The captain of ballet modernism was a homosexual hero who did as much for the cause of gay freedom as its more celebrated advocates.

For women, however, the consequences of this revolution were mixed. If, with Bronislava Nijinska, the Ballets Russes launched a major female choreog-rapher on an international career, the company did little else to accommodate female talent, even as performers. Indeed, with the partial exception of Tamara Karsavina, the female star of the company's pre–World War I years, the balle-rina went into eclipse. She did so not only as an individual, but also as a cate-gory and an idea. Reversing the trend of nearly a century of ballet history, she became a subordinate or an appendage of the new Diaghilev hero, an absence in the poetics of ballet modernism at large.

Although the nineteenth-century ballerina was largely a creature of men, she was also a power in her own right. She dominated the stage, just as her roles dominated the ballet repertory, and she stood, in contrast to her male consorts, at the apex of the performing hierarchy, the star audiences paid to see. For cho-reographers, she was both a medium and an instrument; they gave her steps to dance and imagined characters for her to act, but it was only to the degree that she invested them with charm, eroticism, and the mystique of her own person-ality that they acquired larger meaning.

Woman, of course, was the great obsession of romantic and post-romantic ballet. She came in many guises and in many national variants. But it was in her virginal, ethereal guise, ostensibly beyond class or race, that she left the deepest mark on choreography; in the "white acts" of ballets like *Giselle, La Bayadère, The Sleeping Beauty,* and *Swan Lake,* the purity of her young womanhood was identified with an Eden of transcendent form. Even if it sprang from the mind of the prince (and that of the ballet masters who imagined it), this kingdom of the ideal belonged to the ballerina, as did the larger domain of subjectivity—poetry, loss, grief, beauty, desire, eroticism. Indeed, in its nineteenth-century form, ballet was uniquely an expression of the feminine as embodied in the ide-ology and physical presence of the ballerina.

Diaghilev's revolution dethroned the ballerina from this seemingly impreg-nable position within the dance universe. Within his company, her role was sharply curtailed; her repertory limited; her image radically transformed. At the same time, her eroticism and physical bravura were appropriated as attributes of the new male hero. If *Swan Lake* and *La Bayadère* were meditations on the mystique of femininity embodied in the ballerina, works like *Schéhérazade* (1910), *L'Après-midi d'un Faune*, and *La Chatte* (1927) celebrated the mystery of the male androgyne or the prowess of the homosexual athlete as represented by one or another of Diaghilev's golden boys.

The shift away from inherited conventions of ballet sexuality was not immediately apparent in 1909, when the Ballets Russes first appeared in Paris. Handpicked by choreographer Michel Fokine and chosen to a large extent from the "reform" wing of St. Petersburg's Maryinsky Theater, the dancers continued to be divided according to traditional categories of *emploi*. The chief division was between "classical" and "character" dancers, that is, between dancers who excelled in the academic idiom of the *danse d'école* and those who excelled in the folk-derived idioms of character work. Although this division principally rested on technical ability, it also embraced matters of style and decorum. For the classical dancer, this implied attractive physical proportions and a deportment that called for nobility and restraint; for the character dancer, it meant a freer use of the body coupled with a more overt projection of sexuality. Whether upperclass or populist, the paradigm in each case was heterosexual.

Four of the five ballets presented in 1909 adhered to this traditional paradigm. *The Polovtsian Dances* celebrated the muscular masculinity of a tribe of pre-Christian warriors and the serpentine femininity of their captive maidens; *Les Sylphides*, a poetic reverie, evoked the virginal play of ballet's traditional sisterhood. In *Le Pavillon d'Armide*, the ballerina came to life in the dream of the protagonist, while in *Le Festin*, classical and character dancers joined forces in a potpourri of preexisting dances.

Only in *Cléopâtre*, based on Fokine's earlier *Egyptian Nights*, was there a perceptible shift in the paradigm, and this, significantly, came in revising the work for Paris. The inspiration for the ballet was Alexander Pushkin's tale "Egyptian Nights," which gave birth to the first of the nineteenth century's "killer-Cleopatras" (in Lucy Hughes-Hallet's phrase)—a lascivious queen who has her lovers put to death once she has slept with them.[1] In the ballet, her victim is Amoûn, a youth who abandons the girl who loves him for a night of pleasure with the queen. In the St. Petersburg version of the work, Cleopatra was a minor seductress; her rival, Ta-hor, a passionate innocent. For Paris, Diaghilev not only enhanced the role of the femme fatale (now performed by Ida Rubinstein), but also played up the ballet's decadent elements, transforming the Egyptian queen into an idol of perverse and deadly sexuality. He had her carried onstage in a sarcophagus, wrapped in veils that slaves peeled away one by one, disclosing, as Alexandre Benois wrote, "a divine body omnipotent in its beauty."[2] At her side, crouched like a panther ready to spring, was Nijinsky, her favorite slave, half-man, half-beast, blazing with an erotic fire stoked by her beauty and cold, majestic disdain. By contrast to the thrill of this voluptuous sadism, the romance of Amoûn and Ta-hor seemed tame and irrelevant. In later ballets that explored the same ground, the romantic pretext was discarded.

Cléopâtre proved so popular that it became the matrix of numerous Diaghilev works, all of which exploited the French appetite for exoticism and several of which also exploited the theme of voluptuous sadism. In *Thamar* (1912), for instance, the legendary Georgian queen of the title plunged a dagger into the heart of her captive lover. In *Legend of Joseph* (1914), Potiphar's Wife (a role originally intended for Ida Rubinstein) towered over Joseph (a role originally intended for Nijinsky), a youthful shepherd caught in the web of a Venetian courtesan. And in Diaghilev's version of *La Tragédie de Salomé* (1913), the period's most famous nymphette, now tricked out in kiss curls, tattoos, and a huge glittering headdress, danced for an all-male cast of "Negroes" and executioners, as well as the severed head of John the Baptist. It was *Schéhérazade*, however, that laid out the theme most clearly and emblematically. Here, Rubinstein's "proud, cunning and unrestrained passion" as Zobéide and Nijinsky's "half-cat, half-snake, fiendishly agile, feminine and yet wholly terrifying"[3] impersonation of her favorite Negro slave reiterated the sexual dynamics of *Cléopâtre*. His death, which followed on the heels of a frenzied orgy, was a thrilling reminder of the wages of sexual sin at the hands of a grasping woman. As personified in Diaghilev's "killer-Cleopatras," female sexuality and female power were a deadly combination, with more than a touch of misogyny.

Not all the women of the company found such roles congenial. Anna Pavlova, who danced the role of Ta-hor in 1909, left Diaghilev at the end of the first season, miffed, among other things, at the last-minute substitution of *Les Sylphides* and *Le Festin* for *Giselle*, one of her greatest roles, at a Paris Opéra gala. That Nijinsky had received the lion's share of the season's publicity did not help matters, nor was she tempted to change her mind by the promise of the title role in *Firebird* (1910), scheduled for production the following year. Ida Rubinstein was the next to go. Most Diaghilev apologists, echoing Prince Peter Lieven, explain that she departed because she wanted to perform dance roles as opposed to mime ones, and "Diaghileff, who knew perfectly well that she was no good as a dancer, gave her a decisive rebuff, at which she took offence."[4] Given that in the nine years following her break with Diaghilev she devoted herself to acting rather than dancing, it seems likely that she was indeed "bored," as Lieven claims she told Diaghilev, with "caresses, embraces, and stabbing herself." In any event, like Pavlova, she went her own way. Other women principals came and went as well—Vera Karalli, Yekaterina Geltzer, Olga Preobrajenska, Mathilde Kchessinska, Elena Poliakova. Like Pavlova, all were identified with the classical repertory and its major ballerina roles.

Only Tamara Karsavina, who occupied a rung apart in the company, remained loyal to Diaghilev, although she never succumbed to his persuasions to quit the Maryinsky. And, for all the affection she bore him, by 1913 she had become sufficiently restive to demand a work of her own. He rewarded her loyalty with *La Tragédie de Salomé,* a work that was not only familiar to the French public from the versions produced by Loie Fuller (in 1907) and Natalia Trouhanova (in 1911), but was also sufficiently minor so as not to detract from the season's other premieres—Nijinsky's *Jeux* (1913) and his monumental *Le Sacre du Printemps* (1913). Unsurprisingly, the fillip endured for no more than a season.

Diaghilev's dethronement of the ballerina was reflected not only in the diminished importance and overt misogyny of many female roles, but also in the progressive devaluation of pointework. This, more than any other aspect of female technique, defined the ballerina; it was her exclusive province and an analogue of the idealism traditionally embodied in her roles. In the interest of historical authenticity, Fokine typically eschewed the use of pointe except in works identified with the Western past—*Les Sylphides,* which evoked romantic-era ballets like *Giselle* and *La Sylphide; Le Spectre de la Rose* (1911), which was set in the Biedermeyer period; *Carnaval* (1910), which introduced the commedia dell'arte theme within the context of a nineteenth-century masked ball. In exotic ballets or ballets set in antiquity, which, together, comprised a majority of his works for Diaghilev, its use was either proscribed or sharply curtailed.

In *Petrouchka* (1911), however, a different sort of authenticity was at stake. Here, Fokine's choreography for the Ballerina exploited the technique of pointe to parody not only the tricks of female virtuoso style but also the ballerina manners that typically accompanied it. Fokine had no quarrel with femininity; what he loathed was its expression as artifice. Even as he disavowed pointe, Fokine used arms and a newly pliant, uncorseted torso to create a more "natural" female body, one that moved freely and expansively, arching, stretching, twisting, bending, in a way that enhanced its plasticity and three-dimensionality. Although not exclusive to women, this unfettered body, with its curves and softened contours, was the basis of the "femininity" he prized in his women dancers. Even if Fokine never abandoned academic technique as a system of training, in much of his choreography, especially for women, he sought to neutralize its presence.

In Nijinsky's three works for Diaghilev—*L'Après-midi d'un Faune, Jeux* (1913), and *Le Sacre du Printemps*—the conventions of the female dance virtually disappeared. Only in *Jeux,* where the ballet's two women danced on high three-quarter pointe, were they present, albeit treated with the utmost minimalism. Although Fokine had opposed bravura effects in principle, he occasionally made use of bravura steps. Nijinsky eliminated these entirely. He virtually abandoned the duet, and with this, the system of supports by which the *danseur* had traditionally presented his partner: the men and women in his ballets almost never touched. At the same time, Nijinsky hardened the contours of Fokine's "natural" female body. In *Faune,* the female body, both individually and collectively, was little more than an interplay of angles across a two-dimensional plane, indistinguishable in shape from that of the hero, although softened, to a degree, by flowing Grecian tunics. In *Sacre*, too, men and women shared a common stance and gestural vocabulary, although at certain times, such as the ring dance that opens the second tableau, the score's only extended lyrical passage and the only dance sequence performed exclusively by women, these common gestures took on a "feminine" quality that militated against their normative unisexuality.

In *Sacre*, as in *Faune* and *Jeux*, Nijinsky grounded the choreography in a movement idiom worked out on his own body, then passed on to his dancers. In modern dance, this is standard practice; in ballet, by contrast, a highly elaborated technique, independent of the choreographer, interposes itself between the maker and the executant of a dance. Most early modern dance choreographers were women, and initially at least, so, too, were most of their dancers. The female body was thus the model and the matrix of an enterprise that was in some measure reciprocal. In Nijinsky's case, however, both the generative body and the model body were male, and whether from ignorance or inexperience or a combination of the two, he insisted on imposing them on his dancers autocratically. Obviously, in *Sacre*, he imposed them on men as well as women. But in both *Faune* and *Jeux*, his most experimental works, he was not only the "star," but also the only male presence onstage. If the female body had dominated the ideology of nineteenth-century ballet to the extent of eclipsing and, in some cases, even banishing men from the stage, in Nijinsky's ballets the male body not only claimed the stage but haunted the female bodies that shared it.

For all that Nijinsky's choreography elided traditional differences between male and female dance idioms, his ballets retained a thematic link with other Diaghilev works. Both *Faune* and *Jeux* reiterated the theme of male sexual innocence and female sexual knowledge of *Petrouchka* (1911). In *Faune*, the Chief Nymph (a role that Nijinsky initially wanted Ida Rubinstein to play, in part because of her height) dropped her veils one by one, a striptease that recalled Rubinstein's unveiling in *Cléopâtre*. In *Jeux*, the two women engaged the young man in erotic games as provocative and potentially dangerous as those of *Schéhérazade*. To be sure, none of these temptresses was a classic Cleopatra. In *Jeux*, they wore designer tennis dresses; in *Faune*, Grecian tunics of a sort favored by at least some of the ladies in Diaghilev's audience. Like the costumes, the settings—a garden in *Jeux*, a woodland clearing in *Faune*—were also shorn of exotica, as was the music, supplied in both cases by Claude Debussy rather than by the Russian neonationalist composers of *Cléopâtre* and *Schéhérazade*. In muting the overall tonality of his ballets, Nijinsky domesticated their erotics; instead of "killer Cleopatras," his women were everyday seductresses of the international elite. Diaghilev's exotic ballets typically ended in an orgy of sex. In Nijinsky's works, by contrast, the hero not only avoided sexual entanglement but also eschewed physical contact with women, as though the female body itself filled him with loathing.

Although Nijinsky left the Ballets Russes in 1913, Diaghilev sought again and again to emulate the pattern of his career. In Léonide Massine, a talented Bolshoi dancer, he found a youth worthy of his passion for mentorship, an instrument capable of realizing his ambitions. He discovered him in the turbulent months following Nijinsky's marriage, and he immediately cast him in *Legend of Joseph* in the role originally intended for Nijinsky. Although Massine had completed his studies at the Bolshoi theater school, he was far from being the technical wunderkind that Nijinsky had been. He lacked finish, which teachers hired by Diaghilev eventually supplied, as well as the ideal physical proportions and distinguished presence of a *danseur noble*. Given the nature of the Ballets Russes repertory, this hardly mattered. With his eye for talent, Diaghilev discerned in Massine not only the charisma of a future star but also the raw material of a future choreographer. In the months that followed the outbreak of World War I, Diaghilev took him to museums, introduced him to the futurists, arranged lessons with the great Italian pedagogue Enrico Cecchetti, and watched over his maiden choreographic essays with the modernist painter Mikhail Larionov. Massine was willing, able, and malleable. It was only a matter of time before he fulfilled the high hopes Diaghilev had placed in him.

From 1914, when he joined the Ballets Russes, until 1921, when he left it, Massine was not only the company's preeminent star but also the pivot on which the repertory turned. He was the Chinese conjuror of *Parade* (1917), the Miller in *Le Tricorne* (1919), and a leading player in *La Boutique Fantasque* (1919), *Pulcinella* (1920), and *The Good-Humoured Ladies* (1917)—all ballets that he choreographed. He took over Nijinsky's roles in *Petrouchka, Cléopâtre, Schéhérazade,* and *L'Après-midi d'un Faune,* thus stressing the continuity of pattern between his career and that of his predecessor. And in 1920, he choreographed a new version of Nijinsky's greatest work, *Le Sacre du Printemps.*

For all his star quality, Massine was not a classical dancer in the strict sense of the term. A superb actor (for a time he had contemplated a career on the dramatic stage), he had a strong affinity for character styles of movement, especially the Spanish dance idioms that he exploited so successfully in *Le Tricorne.* He loved the "eccentric" dance forms associated with jazz and incorporated them into his ballets, along with elements from the circus, commedia dell'arte, cinema, and other vernaculars of twentieth-century folklore. Such idioms sat well upon his body and formed the basis of his personal style as a performer and his early style as a choreographer. Both left a deep imprint on the company's dancers.

With Massine, the Ballets Russes ceased to be a classical company; it became instead a *demi-caractère* one. The transformation itself had started before the war; indeed, it dated to the company's earliest years. But it was Massine who completed the process. Although Diaghilev never abandoned classical technique as the physical basis of the company's training, with Massine, the *danse d'école* became irrelevant to the company's experiments in choreography. What was studied in class had little organic relationship with what was danced onstage, even if elements of that technique coded the work as ballet. The divorce between studio and stage was virtually complete.

Although rarely called upon to make full use of her powers as a classicist, Tamara Karsavina had remained Diaghilev's official ballerina up to the war. With the reorganization of the company that coincided with Massine's early essays in choreography during World War I, the title (now that Karsavina had returned to Russia) fell into abeyance. Although, like Nijinsky, Massine dominated the Ballets Russes as a performer, his choreography, unlike Nijinsky's, offered at least some of the women in the company (most notably Lydia Lopokova and Lydia Sokolova) roles that were meaty and challenging. But these roles and the technical idioms associated with them were rooted in the idiosyncracies of Massine's own style. For all their sterling qualities as performers, Massine's women were formed on the *demi-caractère* model of his own body. Their classical potential remained largely untapped.

It was Bronislava Nijinska who put them back on pointe. Indeed, *Les Noces*, which she choreographed in 1923, was the first ballet created for the Diaghilev company in which the entire female ensemble donned ballerina footwear.[5] Nijinska stressed the percussive rather than the aerial qualities of pointe, an approach that broke with nineteenth-century conventions. Moreover, in choosing to employ the technique in a work inspired by Russian folklore and staged to modern music (the score was by Igor Stravinsky), she also broke with Fokine's historicism. If, technically, the pointework of *Les Noces* was uncomplicated, its very use was a milestone, asserting not only its centrality to the female dance but also its adaptability as a means of expression. The following year, in *Les Biches,* a ballet with a contemporary setting, Nijinska again put all the women on pointe; now, they were flappers with the prancing strut of mannequins. This time, however, she also reintroduced the ballerina (albeit in the sexually ambiguous and somewhat ironic role of the Garçonne) and the classical pas de deux (which was not only distilled in form, but also, to a degree, treated ironically). With these two works began the "reclassicizing" of avant-garde ballet.

For all this, a tension remained between this "reclassicizing" impulse and the need to showcase one or another of the company's "ballerinos." Thus, in *Le Train Bleu* (1924), choreographed by Nijinska six months after *Les Biches* and intended as a vehicle for Anton Dolin, the gymnastics (at which he excelled) were treated as bravura turns, while the classical elements of the duets, along with their romantic entanglements, were treated as occasions for parody. The tension remained in Balanchine's works for the company as well. For the choreographer whose ballerinas would later be celebrated for the bravura and refinement of their pointework, his use of the technique in the Diaghilev period was remarkably sparing. Indeed, unlike *Les Noces* and *Les Biches,* virtually all his ballets employed pointe selectively. They did, however, employ it significantly: More than any other technical element, pointe identified the domain of the hero's female counterpart. This role, although it had a ballerina component, was ancillary rather than primary to the larger character of a work, whose theme remained embodied in the hero. Indeed, whether as the Movie Star in *La Pastorale* (1926), the Cat in *La Chatte* (1927), Terpsichore in *Apollon Musagète* (1928), or the Siren in *Prodigal Son* (1929), the female, however striking her choreography, was essentially a foil to the hero, presenting and complementing him, and showing off his attributes.

In the case of Serge Lifar, who was the star of all these ballets, these attributes included a pronounced athleticism and the striking good looks of a "beautiful boy." The athleticism was partly a compensation for his late start and patchy early training as a dancer. The good looks, on the other hand, were at least partly thanks to Diaghilev, who had arranged for his teeth to be fixed and for his nose to be straightened. Ballet after ballet celebrated the young god and his slim, muscled body, selectively bared and occasionally even stripped à la *Cléopâtre* (as in the Prologue of *Apollon Musagète* and in the next-to-last tableau of *Prodigal Son*) to heighten the sensation of its beauty. In *La Chatte,* he was borne onstage in a triumphal car formed by six youths—the very apotheosis of a deco god. The *danseuse,* when she appeared at all, was no more than an accoutrement.

Indeed, even apart from *Les Biches, Le Train Bleu,* and *La Pastorale,* all of which had contemporary settings, many ballets of the 1920s, including those with mythological or period themes, alluded to contemporary fashion. In Massine's *Zéphire et Flore* (1925), for instance, the Muses wore adaptations of flapper styles, including "chic little pork-pie hats and earrings, quite in keeping with the only Olympus they had ever known—one nearer Deauville than Thessaly."[6] In Nijinska's *Romeo and Juliet* (1926), the dancers in the rehearsal scenes wore practice clothes, and in the 1929 "redressed" version of *Apollon Musagète,* the Muses wore tunics by Gabrielle Chanel, the couturière responsible for *Le Train Bleu,* draped with scarves from Charveau.

In all these ballets, the accent was on youth and the celebration of the body beautiful. For men, this entailed revealing the body; for women, clothing it in the styles of fashionable consumption. If, in his latest incarnation, Diaghilev's hero was a boy with the physical endowments of a god, his new woman, by contrast, was a girl who looked like a mannequin. Slim, boyish, and decorative, she was a symbol of modern life as this was defined by deco luxury. Like the Bright Young Things (as flappers were known in England) who thronged Diaghilev's audience, she paraded her worth by what she wore on her back: she embodied a consumerist ideal rather than a physical one.

Chanel once said that Diaghilev did not know how to dress women. More to the point, he did not care to undress them; he kept their bodies hidden, except for the occasional revelation of skin that came with a tutu. However, what had been daring in the nineteenth century (and even the stuff of pornography) was now positively Victorian. At a time when short skirts routinely displayed the leg and tight-fitting bathing suits showed off the torso, when Paris chorus girls and specialty dancers performed their acts in G-strings, Diaghilev's women, for the most part, were as sexy as matrons. If their gilt-edged style enhanced the value of the hero, it never detracted from his desirability.

Despite his overwhelming commitment to new work, Diaghilev did not wholly eschew the traditional repertory. In 1910, he presented *Giselle;* in 1911, the first of several versions of *Swan Lake;* and in 1921, *The Sleeping Beauty* (or, as he renamed it, *The Sleeping Princess*). To mount these productions, however, he faced a problem: he needed the ballerinas his company had jettisoned. His solution (except in the case of *Giselle,* which Karsavina danced) was to import them. Like Pavlova, one of his 1911 Swan Queens, most of these imports made brief appearances in the "regular" repertory: Mathilde Kchessinska, the Maryinsky's *prima ballerina assoluta* and another of the 1911 Swan Queens, in *Carnaval;* Vera Trefilova, one of his Auroras, in *Le Spectre de la Rose* and *Aurora's Wedding.* None of them stayed with the company; even Olga Spessivtseva, the most celebrated of his Auroras and a dancer he assiduously courted, found greener pastures elsewhere—not only at the former Maryinsky Theater, to which she returned in 1922, but also at the Paris Opéra, where, in 1924, she danced the title role in its first revival of *Giselle* since the 1860s. Compared to such plum roles, what Diaghilev offered were scraps: the female lead in *La Chatte,* the Swan Queen in one or another of his truncated versions of *Swan Lake,* whose periodic dismemberments he seemed to relish. Nor did it take much discernment on her part to realize that partnering Lifar, with whom she was typically paired, was a mixed blessing. For all his courting of Spessivtzeva, Diaghilev treated her as cynically and highhandedly as he had her predecessors.

Although Diaghilev pounced on choreographic talent no matter what its sexual packaging, only his favorites reaped the full rewards of his mentorship. Indeed, without him, it is unlikely that Nijinsky or Massine, to say nothing of Lifar (whose first ballet, a remake of *Le Renard,* was produced by Diaghilev in 1929) would ever have become choreographers at all. His generosity was boundless; he gave them all the accumulated wisdom of his years and all the fruits of his broad experience, in addition to a knowledge of the arts, an appreciation of aesthetics, and an introduction to everyone who was anyone in High Bohemia. Money was no object; he paid for months of experiments in the studio and hundreds of rehearsal hours with dancers, for music by the greatest composers and for sets by the finest artists. No Pygmalion ever served his Galatea as devotedly as Diaghilev served his lover-choreographers.

Obviously, women and straight men were at a disadvantage. They might work for him, but they would never be his intimates, and although he might guide them, he would never fashion the company in their image or make them the instruments of his imagination. The progression from lover to star dancer to choreographer was a pattern that repeated itself again and again, and not only in the Ballets Russes. Both Rolf de Maré's Ballets Suédois and Comte Etienne de Beaumont's Soirées de Paris were conceived as vehicles for favorites (Jean Borlin, in the case of the Swedish ensemble; Massine, in the case of the

Soirées), who not only starred in virtually every work of their respective companies, but also supplied all the ballets for their repertories. Like the Ballets Russes, these companies were modernist in orientation and private, rather than public in ownership. Compared to institutions like the Paris Opéra, tradition sat lightly on them; as one-man shows, they were also unhampered by bureaucracy. In this, they more closely resembled modern dance companies than the traditional ballet troupes of the opera house.

In these, of course, custom militated against women as choreographers or, more correctly, as ballet masters, for it was only in the twentieth century and in companies formed on the Diaghilev model that the ballet master's choreographic function was detached from his functions as a producer, teacher, and administrator. Where women did make inroads as choreographers was in venues that lacked the prestige of a major opera house. In music halls and other stages that catered to a popular audience or lyric theaters of secondary category (at least from a dance point of view), one finds all but forgotten choreographers like Katti Lanner and Madame Mariquita. Theoretically, the avant-garde companies should have welcomed women; as enterprises enunciating a male homosexual ideology, they did not. Yet within these companies were any number of women who harbored choreographic ambitions. The most notable (apart from Nijinska, who found favor with Diaghilev partly because of her brother's claim on his affections) were Ninette de Valois and Marie Rambert, both of whom eventually formed their own companies; Carina Ari, a principal with the Ballets Suédois, who created a number of works for the Opéra-Comique; and dancers like Karsavina and Lopokova, who choreographed at least some of the numbers they performed on the music-hall stage. Indeed, the post-Diaghilev years witnessed a genuine flowering of women ballet choreographers, a phenomenon encouraged not only by the marginal status of the companies with which they were typically associated, but also by the fact that these companies, although partly inspired by the Ballets Russes, broke with its cult of the "ballerino."

If this had proved a serious barrier to the promotion of women as choreographers, its public expression, as evinced in the aesthetic practices of the company and its broader iconography, linked the larger enterprise of ballet modernism with homosexuality. Although Diaghilev made no secret of his proclivities, they were not general knowledge beyond the elite circles in which he traveled. But the image of the "ballerino," as depicted in company programs and in numerous books, photographs, and drawings of the period, made the connection with homosexuality explicit, even if the word itself was never uttered. In Nijinsky's case, the body was progressively feminized. Released from the decorum of conventional masculinity, it openly displayed its erotic attributes—a pliant, supple middle, soft, embracing arms, eyes lengthened and darkened with liner. In the drawings of Robert Montenegro, Paul Iribe, and George Barbier especially, the pose is often languid, its curves dramatized by serpentine scarves and by gestures that circle inward on the body, as if announcing its availabilty; here was a houri waiting to be taken.[7] The eroticism was heightened by designer Léon Bakst's exotic packaging and by costume elements that often crossed gender lines—harem trousers in *Schéhérazade*, a peplum skirt in *Le Dieu Bleu* (1912), tunics in *Narcisse* (1911) and *Daphnis and Chloe* (1912), body stockings in *Carnaval*, *L'Après-midi d'un Faune*, and *Le Spectre de la Rose*. Such packaging revealed the contours of the male body to an unprecedented degree, as well as expanses of flesh in the midriff and lower reaches of the neckline. At the same time, by identifying such revelations with the exotic, antique, or imaginary, Diaghilev neutralized the "danger" of their effeminacy. In contrast to Fokine, whose choreography for the company's women celebrated a "natural" body unfettered by corsets and free of ballerina artifice, Diaghilev made the very stratagems of femininity integral to the identity of his new hero.

For all his erotic charisma, Nijinsky was never conventionally attractive. Massine, on the other hand, was beautiful: dark, slender, with enormous Mediterranean eyes and the grave expression of an innocent. His beauty haunted Diaghilev, as it haunts the portraits of Massine that he commissioned from Bakst, Matisse, Natalia Goncharova, Mikhail Larionov, and other artists associated with the company as designers. Most of these portraits—like the works that a later group of artists made of Anton Dolin and Serge Lifar—found their way into company programs, making public the sitter's unique position within the Diaghilev enterprise.

Women, of course, did not vanish from company programs. However, the space allotted to them was minimal, and almost always they were depicted in roles from the repertory. For the most part, too, the images reproduced were photographs, as opposed to the line drawings and paintings that associated the representation of the favorite with the prestige of the unique art work and, more generally, with the modernism of Diaghilev's newest designers. Only in the numerous drawings made by Picasso in the late 1910s and early 1920s when he designed several company productions did women receive a share of the glamor. But what women! And what avoirdupois! If the men in his drawings have the ideal proportions and nonchalant eroticism of the youths of classical sculpture, his women—for all the charm of their ballerina manners—are as fresh and fleshy as milkmaids.

Ironically, as Picasso added pounds to Diaghilev's women, they themselves were getting thinner. "She is too fat for us," Diaghilev remarked about Lydia Lopokova in 1924.[8] And, indeed, compared to Alice Nikitina, the reed-thin newcomer whom he was then promoting as his latest female find, she did seem positively robust. By the mid-1920s, of course, the lean silhouette was high fashion, and it was only natural that Diaghilev's women, like generations of women dancers before them, would personify in some measure the elite beauty ideal of their age. In its newest incarnation, this ideal had a definite masculine component; it demanded a body as hipless and flat-chested as a boy's. Ida Rubinstein may have been slim, but her body had revealed the usual female equipment (at least until Gabriele d'Annunzio, anxious that she acquire a "man's figure" for her role as the travesty hero in his play *The Martyrdom of Saint Sebastian,* put her on the diet that made her, according to some accounts, the thinnest woman on the French stage).[9]

If, before the war, Diaghilev had feminized the male body, now he set about making the female body masculine. Thus, in 1922, when he revived *L'Après-midi d'un Faune,* he cast Nijinska in the role originally created by her brother. The experiment was not a success. However much she strapped in her breasts, she needed more than a body stocking to camouflage the fact of her sex, even if she resembled Nijinsky in physical type and musculature. Only in Massine's *Ode* (1928), and specifically in the role created by Felia Doubrovska, was the unencumbered female body allowed to be itself. Clad in tights and a leotard (the only time, apart from Nijinska's appearance in *Faune,* that Diaghilev permitted a woman of the company to wear such revealing garb), Doubrovska displayed the harmonious line and long lean silhouette of the prototypical Balanchine ballerina—along with small, but unmistakable breasts.

Unlike Nijinsky, in whom the feminine was at least partly associated with sexual passivity, Diaghilev's heroes of the 1920s wore their sexual plumage like peacocks. Beginning in 1923, when Anton Dolin briefly joined the company, and continuing throughout the years of Lifar's preeminence, the body beautiful was not only bared but its erogenous zones were also explicitly sexualized. In a remarkable series of photographs dating to the mid-1920s, Man Ray recorded the various elements of Lifar's erotic uniform—trunks (to show off the legs), belts (to dramatize the waist), laces, garters, and boots (to draw attention to the calves and knees), tunics or tunic-style tops (to reveal a midriff, a shoulder, and sometimes even a nipple). Nearly always the legs were bare. Although the display might be regarded as "feminine," the body itself—hard, muscular, athletic— was that of a sexually active, "virile" male. Indeed, in the later years of the Ballets Russes, Diaghilev discarded the trappings of fin-de-siècle androgyny that had made the effeminacy of Nijinsky acceptable. With Lifar, he revealed the homosexual as an openly gay man. No wonder the theaters where the company now performed had become a privileged gathering place for what *Vogue*'s Herbert Farjeon described, with obvious disapproval, as "velvet-voiced youth."[10]

By almost any yardstick, women in the Ballets Russes counted for less than men. In a sense they were triply disadvantaged, for, with the exception of Nijinska, their role behind the scenes did not make up for the loss of their traditional preeminence as performers or for their irrelevance to the ideology and practice of modernist ballet generally. That this occurred at a time when women were establishing a dominant presence in other forms of concert dance only emphasizes the antifemale bias implicit in Diaghilev's homosexual radicalism. The 1930s partly redressed this imbalance: The growing trend of neoclassicism demanded women of high technical accomplishment to fill both traditional and new-style ballerina roles, while a number of fledgling companies either were headed by women or associated with them as choreographers.

Nevertheless, the "ballerino" remained a force to be reckoned with. At the Paris Opéra, where Serge Lifar directed the ballet troupe for nearly thirty years, numerous works continued to foreground the hero (a role that Lifar typically reserved for himself), even to the point of eliminating women entirely (as in his 1935 revision of *Faune*). And in companies like the Joffrey Ballet, which in the 1970s and 1980s did so much to keep the Diaghilev repertory alive, or Maurice Béjart's Ballet of the 20th Century, which in the 1960s and 1970s reinterpreted works from that repertory from an openly gay perspective, the development of ballerinas has been ancillary to the celebration of male talent.

If ballet, in its female-centered variety, is about more than women, so, in its male-centered variety, it is about more than men. Liberation, in Diaghilev's book, was for men only, even when this entailed, as it often did, appropriating attributes associated with femininity. In the long run, the cult of "masculinity" offered no more than a temporary antidote to the "problem" of nineteenth-century ballet, which burdened women no less than men with the legacy of the feminine mystique and a system grounded in patriarchy. Nor did Balanchine's cult of "femininity," with its selective privileging of women as muses and of men as Pygmalions. Today, as in Diaghilev's time, full and equal citizenship in the ballet polity remains an elusive dream.

NOTES

1. Lucy Hughes-Hallett, *Cleopatra: Histories, Dreams and Distortions* (New York: Harper and Row, 1990), p. 233.

2. Alexandre Benois, *Reminiscences of the Russian Ballet,* trans. Mary Britnieva (London: Putnam, 1941), p. 296.

3. *Ibid.,* p. 315.

4. Prince Peter Lieven, *The Birth of Ballets-Russes,* foreword Catherine Lieven Ritter (London: Allen and Unwin, 1936), p. 260.

5. Although Diaghilev gave *Les Sylphides* a new title, the ballet itself, as *Chopiniana*, was first given at a Maryinsky charity performance. *The Sleeping Princess* (1921) was a revival of Petipa's 1890 *Sleeping Beauty.*

6. H[oward] H[annay], "Zephyr and Flora," *The Observer,* 25 November 1925, p. 11.

7. Apollinaire spoke of the connection between "feminine art" and the "serpentine" in one of his art chronicles of the period: "C'est cela même, la peinture féminine est serpentine et c'est peut-être cette grande artiste de la ligne et des couleurs, la Loïe Fuller, qui fut le précurseur de l'art féminin d'aujourd'hui quand elle inventa cette chose géniale où se mêlient la peinture, la danse, le dessin et la coquetterie et que l'on apella

très justement: la danse serpentine" (Guillaume Apollinaire, "Chronique d'art: Les Peintresses," *Le Petit Bleu*, 5 April 1912, in *Chroniques d'art 1902–1918*, ed. L. C. Breunig [Paris: Gallimard, 1960], p. 302).

8. Lydia Lopokova to John Maynard Keynes, 12 May 1924, John Maynard Keynes Papers, King's College (Cambridge).

9. "Starved to be a Saint; To be Gilded to be a Goddess?" *The Sketch*, 31 May 1911, in Ida Rubinstein clipping file, Mander and Mitchenson Theatre Collection (Beckenham Junction, Kent).

10. Herbert Farjeon, "Seen on the Stage," *Vogue* (British edition), 11 July 1928, p. 80. At least one Ballets Russes dancer complained (although not publically) about the influence of such iconography on the style of male dancing generally. Stanislas Idzikowski, a Polish dancer who joined the company in 1914, told Karsavina that he had left it in 1926 when the style of male dancing underwent a change: "I could not demean myself . . . by wiggling my posterior" (Stanislas Idzikowski, interviewed by John Gruen, 2 August 1974, pp. 116–117, Oral History Archive, Dance Division, New York Public Library for the Performing Arts).

CHOREOGRAPHY BY NIJINSKA

Like most women artists of her time, Bronislava Nijinska came late to her profession. She was twenty-five when she presented her first choreography at a wartime concert at the Narodny Dom—or People's House—in Petrograd. Little hinted at the importance of the occasion, described on the program as "a grand evening of vocal music and ballet by the celebrated prima ballerina-artist of the State Ballet Bronislava Nijinska."[1] Certainly, the bill wasn't promising. Musically, it consisted of a duet from *Eugene Onegin* and bits of Mussorgsky and Arensky, sung by V. A. Zelentskaia and A. M. Trostianskii. The dances, too, aimed to please, from the *Trepak* (to Rubinstein) that opened the program to *The Polovtsian Dances* (to Borodin) that closed it. Wedged between these rousing folk numbers were four other dances: *Autumn Song*, to Tchaikovsky; *Walpurgis Night* (Faun and Nymph), to Gounod; *The Doll*, to Liadov; and *Khaitarma*, to Spendiarov. The dancers were Nijinska and her husband Alexander Kotchetovsky.

The program doesn't say who choreographed any of these dances, although thanks to Irina Nijinska, we know that two of them—the solos *Autumn Song* and *The Doll*—were created for the occasion by Nijinska and danced by her. Most of the other titles have a familiar ring, however. Not that they recalled Marius Petipa or the ballets féeries of the Imperial stage. Rather, the works Nijinska liked enough to "borrow" for her first public showcase were by Michel Fokine. The most obvious of these "loans" was *The Polovtsian Dances,* which Fokine had choreographed in 1909 for the Diaghilev company and in which both Nijinska and her husband had danced. Less obvious were *Khaitarma* and *Walpurgis Night,* two of the many concert pieces choreographed by Fokine during the war years and presented at the Maryinsky Theater on charity programs. Equally telling was Nijinska's choice of Tchaikovsky as the composer for *Autumn Song,* the most important of her new solos. In 1915–1916, after neglecting his music for years, Fokine staged no fewer than four works to Tchaikovsky: *Francesca da Rimini, Eros* (to music Balanchine later used for *Serenade*), *Romance,* and *Andantino.*

Choreographically, too, *Autumn Song* owed a debt to Fokine. Nijinska taught the dance to Alicia Markova in the 1930s, and in 1953, with Markova, it was filmed for television's *Show of Shows*. A brief excerpt shows drifts and circlings

This essay was published in *Ballet Review,* 20, no. 4 (Winter 1992).

in bourrée, soft arms, fluttering wrists, and the play of curves we associate with Fokine's *Dying Swan,* which Nijinska also taught to Markova. Although she says little about the solo in *Early Memoirs,* she describes—at length—her first *Chopiniana,* which she danced in February 1909.

> The impression of this performance . . . has remained forever in my memory. For the first time I could clearly comprehend the true art in Dance and Ballet. Something was revealed to me; something was born in me and became the basis of my creative work, to influence all my artistic activity.
>
> The extraordinary choreography of Fokine that flowed into Chopin's music . . . the scenery and lighting by Benois, creating the poetic images for Fokine's interpretation of Chopin's music . . . the choreography, the decor, and the music . . . all merged inseparably into a single creation—a masterpiece.[2]

For a choreographer who would come to believe, as Nijinska wrote toward the end of her life, that "everything in ballet must be expressed only through choreography,"[3] *Chopiniana* was a revelation. Here was a ballet that was all dance—no plot, no mimicry, no tricks; a ballet in which movement seemed to fuse with the music in a flow of powerful images; a lyric sung in the choreographer's own voice. Though her mature work bore little resemblance to Fokine's, she remained ever loyal to the ideas of that first eye-opening *Chopiniana.* Like other choreographic innovators of the early Soviet period, including Fedor Lopukhov and Kasian Goleizovsky, Nijinska found the way to modernism along a road first traveled by Fokine.

Fokine was the first of many influences on Nijinska's development as a choreographer. Others I want to talk about today are folk dance, avant-garde design, her body, and Petipa. Although Nijinska gained renown as a neoclassicist, character styles of movement had a role in her work that was far from unimportant. Indeed, on the Narodny Dom program, at least three of the items—*Trepak, Khaitarma,* and *The Polovtsian Dances*—had their source in real or recreated folk traditions. By the standards of her time, Nijinska was a classical (as opposed to character) dancer. Yet her repertory included many *demi-caractère* roles, from the Street Dancer in *Petrouchka* to the Chief Polovtsian Girl in *The Polovtsian Dances.* From childhood, she had seen—and done—all kinds of dancing. At two she sat quietly in a corner while her parents taught polkas and Russian round dances to well-to-do children in Odessa; at three she took her first lessons, with a pair of Afro-American tappers, and made her first public appearance in a hornpipe. At the Imperial Theatrical School, too, the children breathed character dance. It was in the ballets they danced as students, ballets such as *The Daughter of the Pharaoh, The Nutcracker, The Sleeping Beauty,* and *Paquita,* where Bronislava and Vaslav led the mazurka in 1904. It was the specialty, too, of some of their best teachers. Among these was Alexander Shiriaev, Petipa's assistant and rehearsal master, who, with Alfred Bekefi and Andrei

Lopukhov, developed the character-dance class that later became part of the school curriculum. And it abounded in Fokine's "new" ballet. In the original version of *Chopiniana*, for instance, the moonlight pas de deux for Anna Pavlova and Mikhail Oboukhov gleamed like a rare stone among the character numbers—a polonaise, a mazurka, and a tarantella. In Fokine's quest for a freer, fresher idiom, folk-derived movement held an appeal that classical movement, increasingly rigid, conventional, and academic, did not.

Nijinsky, too, in *Le Sacre du Printemps*, found raw material for choreography in the vernacular of Russian folk dance. As historian Shelley Berg has written:

> The "harvesting" movement for the women is especially typical. The legs and feet are held parallel, with the knees slightly bent and the body folded forward at the waist. The accompanying movement usually is a gentle, pulsing, sidestepping motion, found in many folk dance styles. . . . A shuntlike skip, moving either forward or back, is another distinctive folk dance movement.[4]

The positions of the hands and arms, Berg adds, also have folk dance counterparts, especially in the Ukraine.

Unlike Fokine, who found only grace and spontaneity in folk dancing, Nijinsky made this the Ur-language of primitivism. Weighted, grounded, serving the angle rather than the curve, folk dance became a means toward the creation of a new, "objective" dance language. In this remade vernacular, however, Nijinsky asserted two key principles of classical form—generalization and objectivity—even as he struggled to create a new language of movement.

Folk material appeared early in Nijinska's work—as early, probably, as her first concert. Certainly, by the time she choreographed "The Three Ivans" for Diaghilev's 1921 *Sleeping Beauty*, she knew her business. The rousing hopak would have made her father proud. With its somersaults and tumbling stunts, it recalled the big tops where he had worked, and it was full of the jumps and squat steps for which he had been celebrated, including the spinning "millwheel" she remembered him teaching Vaslav. It was a dance, too, that Fokine might happily have claimed. With its freshness and spontaneity, it did what he thought art should do: "innoculat[e] the audience with [feeling]."[5]

Nijinska's *Snow Maiden*, choreographed for the Ballet Russe de Monte Carlo in 1942, had the same infectious charm. Wrote critic Edwin Denby:

> Nijinska's other new ballet, *The Snow Maiden*, . . . I liked very much too. It is set to an arrangement of Glazounov's *Seasons*. It has a Russian folk-tale plot about a daughter of Frost and Spring, a maiden who is cool until a shepherd wins her love at a village festival; she loves, melts, and dies in his arms. . . . The ballet, especially in its Aronson setting, gets pretty close to greeting-card art, but by some gift of vivacity and unpretentiousness its sentiment turns out to be fresh and light. . . . The

simplified Russian folk dances come off very happily too, and Danilova, as the Spring, is poetic just being carried around the stage.[6]

By contrast, in ballets like *Pictures at an Exhibition* and *Les Noces,* Nijinska's approach to folk material recalled her brother's. *Pictures,* a "ballet in nine scenes" choreographed in 1944 for Ballet International, was a stylization of Russian folk steps and village games to Mussorgsky. The ballet had a clean, spare design and Blue Blouse style costumes. Both were by Boris Aronson, an émigré, like Nijinska, formed in part by the early Soviet avant-garde. Portions of the ballet were filmed in Chicago by Ann Barzel, and in them we recognize typical features of *Les Noces*—the attention to architecture, the elongated line, and most importantly, the simplification of step and gesture. This, I think, is what makes the character work so unusual. Instead of a particular drumming walk or squat step, Nijinska gives us a generic one, pared of ornament, reduced to its basic idea. Thus, we see arms as straight as lines or as smoothly curved as tubing; we see hands clasped, clenched, or webbed. And to stylize things even more, the women dance on pointe and in parallel, rather than on half-toe and with the modified turnout typical of character dance. Nijinska leaves nothing to nature and nothing to chance; all is subordinated to a grand design.

This, of course, is clearest in *Les Noces,* her masterpiece. Produced only ten years after *Sacre,* it reveals major similarities and differences with Nijinsky's work. Among the similarities, of course, was the tendency toward abstraction, not only in the treatment of folk material, but in the elimination of narrative detail. Nijinska went much further than her brother on both counts. *Les Noces* has no divining scenes, no 300-year-old men, no ancestors in bearskins. And though it has the stamps and marching lines that Nijinsky in *Sacre* borrowed from folk dance, few of the other borrowings are that obvious. Thus, in the second tableau, when the Bridegroom's friends do a character rond de jambe from a low fondu, the step seems almost fully absorbed into the image—a kind of mechanical centipede, chugging forward like a train. With classical steps, Nijinska did pretty much the same; taking them apart, she reassembled them in a way that made them look strange. The choreography for the women uses a few common steps—jetés, pas de bourrés, little runs on pointe. But because of the way Nijinska has played with the rhythm, phrasing, and shape of these steps, they look different, remade. In other words, where a movement came from didn't matter; what was important was what happened to it. In Nijinska's work, classical and character work underwent an identical process of stylization.

Unlike the Nijinsky of *Sacre,* Nijinska wasn't looking for a new movement language. What she was after was a way of making the system of classical movement—or the classical "school," as she liked to call it—responsive to the needs of post-Petipa choreographers. To do that, however, that "school" had to be modernized, yanked into the twentieth century. Adding to the stock of inherited pas was one way of doing this. In Nijinska's ballets of the 1920s, gymnastics, acrobatics, and ballroom styles appeared side-by-side with character and classical styles. Not only did this enrich the choreography with the forms and rhythms of modern life; it also infused it with irony and in ballets like *Les Biches* and *Le Train Bleu* with the playful wit so typical of the decade.

Far harder than adding to the technique was renewing it, finding a way to make classically based dances with a modern sensibility. She believed, as she wrote in an essay published in *Schrifttanz* in 1930, that "the classical school simply is the foundation of dance. . . . One must totally sweep away useless things, but one must not disregard, or even destroy, the things that constitute the foundation, the basis of the mechanics of the art."[7] What to preserve? Throw out? Nijinska struggled to answer these questions in her early years as a choreographer. Like her brother, she was fascinated by the circle, and in a notebook from her years in postrevolutionary Kiev, there are whole pages devoted to it. But there are others, equally fascinating, that explore the diagonal and the triangle (which he didn't), and still others in which the arcs, ovals, and lines are shown intersecting in various ways or in action. Presumably, Nijinska was using these doodles to figure out something about space (the word appears in some of the captions), though a few may have been preparatory studies for some now forgotten dance. Primarily, however, their function was speculative; in these diagrams, Nijinska could imagine movement at its most utopian, as pure form, geometric and abstract. On paper, she could recreate the stage as a suprematist painting.

By contrast, her later notations look more like floor plans. There are dots for bodies, and arrows to show where the bodies have to move. You see couples, ensembles, and soloists in relation to the group. Yet even in these diagrams, generally recorded after the completion of a work, Nijinska insisted upon the geometry of her concept. She liked to link the dots, making outward fanning lines into the sides of a moving trapezoid or double diagonals into the long sides of a parallelogram. Along with this interest in linear geometry, we note her fascination with mass. Among the notations for *La Valse* is a diagram from Act I that shows two advancing lines of four couples each. You don't apprehend them as couples, but as a mass, barely furrowed by four advancing soloists. We meet these soloists again in another diagram, and here, too, we see them in relation to the group, this time, in an impenetrable diagonal. The configuration recalls Martha Graham's *Heretic*, created a year later in 1929. It also recalls something critic Edwin Denby wrote about her *Chopin Concerto* in 1944:

> The structure of the piece—like that of much of Mme Nijinska's work—is based on a formal contrast: in the background, rigid impersonal groups or clusters of dancers, which seem to have the weight of statues; in the foreground, rapid arrowy flights performed by individual soloists. One appreciates their flashes of lightness and freedom because of the weight they seem to rise over, as if the constraint of the group were the springboard for the soloist's release.[8]

"Architecture," Nijinska once said, "yes, that's always the sign of one of my ballets. But do not be misled by pictures. My ballets are not static . . . there is always movement."[9] Nijinska was talking of choreography, but she could have been referring to the pictographs scattered among her notations, especially the early ones. True, the drawings all reveal Nijinska's "architecture." But the glue that holds the bodies together is physical rather than visual—a kind of centripetal force. A sketch for the 1920 *Demons* is an early example of how she liked to force bodies together at the waist, while elsewhere pulling them apart; the straining produced a tense and dynamic image. In another unidentified drawing, she shows a line of identical stick figures driving forward like the shaft of an old locomotive. Here, too, the accent is on movement, the forward thrust of a mechanical frieze. Indeed, for Nijinska, movement was the principal element of dancing. As she wrote in one of her essays: "Movement gives life to dance. Movement alone enables the dance to affect the spectator."[10]

In the years just before and after World War I, artists like Malevich, Matisse, and Oskar Schlemmer experimented with costumes that "reconstructed" the body, transforming its natural shape. In *Night on Bald Mountain* and *Holy Etudes,* Nijinska played with a similar idea. Her sketches for *Bald Mountain* show elongated, arc-like forms; those for *Holy Etudes* round, smooth blobs. None of them are identified by sex; we don't know which blobs (if any) are male and which arcs (if any) are female. The costumes Alexandra Exter actually designed for these ballets were lighter, leaner, and more elegant. But they still played with shape, and they still played with gender. Indeed, in *Holy Etudes,* the attire for men and women was always the same: dropped-waist dresses in the 1920s, tunics (by Boris Belinsky) in the 1930s and 1940s. As Frederic Franklin, recalling the Ballet Russe de Monte Carlo revival in 1943, put it: "[Y]ou couldn't tell the boys from the girls except for the head of somebody."[11]

If Fokine, folk dance, and the avant-garde all left their mark on Nijinska's choreography, another influence was her own body. For a woman it was a unusual instrument. "She was a very strong dancer," Franklin told an interviewer, "and danced very athletically for a lady, and had a big jump."[12] "She had incomparable endurance," recalled Anatole Vilzak, who worked with her in the 1920s and 1930s, "and seemed never to be tired. . . . During a rehearsal for *Les Biches* I was having difficulty in a lift with Mme. Nemtchinova. Nijinska became so angry at my inadequacy that she lifted and carried Vera for me. I saved face by applauding her."[13] Another Diaghilev dancer, Lydia Sokolova, thought she was "a most unfeminine woman, though there was nothing particularly masculine about her character. Thin but immensely strong, she had iron muscles in her arms and legs, and her highly developed calf muscles resembled Vaslav's; she had the same way of jumping and pausing in the air."[14] As a performer, Nijinska was both versatile and charismatic, with her brother's ability to lose herself in a role. As the Hostess in *Les Biches,* wrote Sokolova, "she flew round the stage, performing amazing contortions of her body, beating her feet, sliding backwards and forwards, screwing her face into an abandoned attitude onto the sofa. She danced as the mood took her and was brilliant."[15] For critic André Levinson, she was "powerful" and "strange," a dancer "intoxicated with rhythm, . . . racing against the most breathless 'prestos' of the orchestra."[16] "It was a strange combination," summed up ballerina Alicia Markova, "this terrific strength, and yet there was a softness."[17]

It was a combination that left an imprint on Nijinska's choreography. She liked strong movement, and she liked it danced big. Her own roles were packed with jumps and beats; others she jammed full of pirouettes. She paid close attention to the way the torso was used. Choreographer Frederick Ashton, who worked with her in the Ida Rubinstein company, recalled that even the simplest movements were done with adjustments of épaulement or with the body bending from side to side. "Working with her I became saturated with movement."[18] In composing, she analyzed music in great detail and in advance and would begin by giving the dancers their counts—an indication of her excellent musical training. Indeed, as critic Pierre Michaut wrote about *Holy Etudes,* her work was "an essay in transposing musical forms into choreographic ones."[19] Toward the end of her life, she told critic Jack Anderson that she conceived her ballets as "music through the eyes. If you could close your ears you could still hear the music—you could see the music. A paradox! But a paradox close to the center of my idea of ballet."[20] There were times, apparently, when rhythm got the upper hand. In his review of *Pictures at an Exhibition,* Denby commented that "the descriptive side [of Mussorgsky's score] is very often ignored; its melodic line is ignored, too, and the rhythmic counterpoint that the dance offers is overheavy."[21] As her notations indicate, the relationship of music and movement in Nijinska's work could be quite complex. Sometimes, choreographic phrases started in the middle of musical ones; sometimes, they had different time signatures or different counts. "She had," explains Nina Youshkevitch, "what she called the 'music of the choreography,' which sometimes didn't quite correspond with the structure of the music, although it all came together."[22] For all the toughness, the "virility" that some like Margaret Severn found in Nijinska's choreography, works like *Chopin Concerto* were unexpectedly poignant; Denby spoke of the work, created in the late 1930s for the Polish Ballet, as being "tense and romantic in its emotion."[23] As with many modern dance choreographers, though few ballet ones, there was a real connection between Nijinska's identity as a dancer and her concerns as a choreographer.

Last but not least, we see in her work the influence of Petipa. As a child she appeared in many of his ballets; she carried the Lilac Fairy's train in *The Sleeping Beauty* and ant eggs in *Les Caprices du Papillon;* she was a stream in *The Daughter of Pharaoh* and an Immortal Flower in *The Magic Mirror.* (During one of the rehearsals, Petipa patted her on the head and said "bien.")[24] Even before she graduated, the magic began to wear thin. "We could not decide what was good and what was bad," she wrote toward the end of her life. Like Fokine, she was disturbed by the incongruities—geographical ethnological, and conceptual—that coexisted in Petipa's ballets. She was disturbed, too, by how they were being taught, after his forced retirement.

> N[icholas] Sergeyev, who rehearsed Petipa's ballets, gave all his attention to achieving unbroken dance lines. The corps de ballet . . . danced with all its might, without the least musical nuance, only keeping the beat to the snap of Sergeyev's fingers. Sometimes, in a solo, the dance phrase would not coincide with the music; he never noticed it. The absence of artistic programming on the part of the leaders of the St. Petersburg ballet had brought it to crisis, and us—to our condemnation of it.[25]

In another article, she speaks of her shock at learning of Diaghilev's plans to mount *The Sleeping Beauty* in 1921:

> In the early days of Diaghilev's ballet we were denying classicism and searching for new forms, almost for a new school of the dance. And then, all of a sudden, with the production of the *Sleeping Princess* we went half a century back. Diaghilev's idea in producing the *Sleeping Princess* came to me as a surprise, since it seemed the negation of the fundamental "religion" of the ballet as he conceived it, and of his searching towards the creation of a new ballet. . . . I started . . . work full of protest against myself.[26]

The ballet had been set by Sergeyev, but according to Nijinska, "Diaghilev and Bakst did not feel it possible to present *The Sleeping Beauty* to the London public in such a state. So under their guidance and with the collaboration of Stravinsky . . . I took part in this revamped production."[27] Nijinska created several new dances for Diaghilev's *Beauty*, including "The Three Ivans," the fairy tales "Schéhérazade" and "Bluebeard," and Prince Charming's variation, all credited to her on the program. But her real contribution was considerably greater. The Lilac Fairy's variation in the Prologue (staged to Sugar Plum music from *The Nutcracker*) was hers, and also the Hummingbird Fairy's (one of Nijinska's own roles). Both were classical dances, she later wrote, created "on Petipa's themes."[28]

In addition to the new dances, Nijinska made a number of other changes in the ballet as taught by Sergeyev.

> [Petipa's] mime seemed absurd to Diaghilev and myself. Therefore, the pantomime scenes . . . were done differently. I also restaged the ensembles for . . . Carabosse's entrance. In Aurora's scene with the spindle and in the awakening scene, the dancers and extras had . . . created [their] own mime . . . I tried to subordinate the staging to the music. The arbitrary pantomime of individuals was excluded, subordinated to the group choreography expressing the action onstage.[29]

In other words, the production that introduced *Beauty* to the West was already a revision of Petipa's original.

It was only later, when she had revived and rehearsed other works of his, that she came to "feel a profound respect for Petipa and the genius of his choreography."[30] "Now I am against altering Petipa's ballets," she wrote in old age. Still, she added: "The texture of Petipa's works is not dear to me; even today, I believe that everything in ballet must be expressed only through choreography, and Petipa overburdened his productions with nondance elements."[31] Toward the end of the essay, she returns to the theme:

> From our teachers we continually heard that every step in a Petipa ballet had to be part of our "school." This concern of Petipa's for the school of classical dance, in itself an idea of genius, left a greater impression on my creative work than his ballets. It fascinated me and laid the foundation for my teaching and choreographic activity. I understood that Petipa's school must not only preserve the past but also continue to develop in the future.[32]

This renewable legacy was at the heart of Nijinska's classicism. Though she loved the art of the past and would coach dancers like Markova in *Swan Lake* and *Giselle,* she had a higher regard for the language that was her native tongue as an artist. True, she spoke it differently from her teachers. But she never abandoned it. If anything, as the years passed and the Diaghilev era joined the Maryinsky in an ever more distant past, this portable legacy became ever more precious. In 1937, it gave rise to *Chopin Concerto,* possibly her finest post-Diaghilev work. Wrote George Amberg about the 1942 revival:

> The most striking impression . . . is one of impeccable style. . . . The purity of its design, the transparency of its structure, the cleanness of its movement pattern, create an effect of truly classic perfection. The restaging preserved the flawless integrity of the original version, and it also carried with it the climate of Paris and the suggestive beauty of a vanishing era. It marked a moment of creative culmination. . . . It was the absolute ballet in retrospect.[33]

It was also, we might add, a tribute to Petipa's living legacy.

NOTES

1. The program for this performance is in the Nijinska Archives. I am indebted to Nancy Van Norman Baer for allowing me to examine a copy of this program. The Nijinska Archives are now at the Music Division, Library of Congress.

2. Bronislava Nijinska, *Early Memoirs*, ed. Irina Nijinska and Jean Rawlinson, introd. Anna Kisselgoff (New York: Holt, Rinehart and Winston, 1981), p. 251.

3. Bronislava Nijinska, "The Triumph of Petipa," in *Marius Petipa: Materialy, Vospominania, Stat'i*, ed. A. Nekhendzi (Leningrad: Leningrad State Theater Museum, n.d.), I, p. 317.

4. Shelley C. Berg, *"Le Sacre du printemps": Seven Productions from Nijinsky to Martha Graham* (Ann Arbor: UMI Research Press, 1988), p. 52.

5. Michel Fokine, *Memoirs of a Ballet Master*, trans. Vitale Fokine, ed. Anatole Chujoy (Boston: Little, Brown, 1961), p. 62.

6. Edwin Denby, "De Mille's 'Rodeo'; Nijinska's 'Chopin Concerto'; Massine's 'Aleko,'" *Dance Writings*, ed. Robert Cornfield and William Mackay (New York: Knopf, 1986), p. 98.

7. Bronislava Nijinska, "On Movement and the School of Movement," in *Schrifttanz: A View of German Dance in the Weimar Republic*, ed. Valerie Preston-Dunlop and Susanne Lahusen (London: Dance Books, 1990), p. 58.

8. Edwin Denby, "Nijinska's 'Chopin Concerto'; Balanchine's 'Serenade,'" *Dance Writings*, p. 213.

9. Quoted in *Nijinska: A Legend in Dance*, KQED-TV.

10. Bronislava Nijinska, "On Movement and the School of Movement," ed. Joan Ross Acocella and Lynn Garafola, *Ballet Review*, 13, no. 4 (Winter 1986), p. 77.

11. "Bronislava Nijinska: Dancers Speak," *Ballet Review*, 18, no. 1 (Spring 1990), p. 21.

12. Quoted in *Nijinska: A Legend in Dance*.

13. Quoted in Marian Horosko, "Teachers in the Russian Tradition. Part I. Ludmilla Schollar and Anatole Vilzak," *Dance Magazine*, April 1979, pp. 70–72.

14. *Dancing for Diaghilev: The Memoirs of Lydia Sokolova*, ed. Richard Buckle (London: John Murray, 1960), p. 203.

15. *Ibid.*, p. 216.

16. André Levinson, "20 mai: Le retour des 'Ballets russes,'" *La Danse au théâtre: Esthétique et actualité mêlées* (Paris: Bloud & Gay, 1924), p. 36.

17. Quoted in *Nijinska: A Legend in Dance*.

18. Quoted in David Vaughan, *Frederick Ashton and His Ballets* (New York: Knopf, 1977), p. 30.

19. Pierre Michaut, *Le Ballet contemporain, 1929–1950* (Paris: Plon, n.d.), p. 22.

20. Jack Anderson, "La Nijinska," *The Dancing Times*, April 1972, p. 361.

21. Edwin Denby, "Nijinska's 'Pictures at an Exhibition,'" in *Dance Writings*, p. 266.

22. "Bronislava Nijinska: Dancers Speak," p. 28.

23. Margaret Severn, "Dancing with Bronislava Nijinska and Ida Rubinstein," *Dance Chronicle*, 11, no. 2 (1988), p. 341; Edwin Denby, "Nijinska's 'Chopin Concerto': Balanchine's 'Serenade,'" in *Dance Writings*, p. 213.

24. Nijinska, "The Triumph of Petipa," p. 316; *Early Memoirs*, p. 114.

25. Nijinska, "The Triumph of Petipa," p. 317.

26. Bronislava Nijinska, "Reflections about the Production of *Les Biches* and *Hamlet* in

Markova-Dolin Ballets," trans. Lydia Lopokova, *The Dancing Times,* February 1937, p. 617.

27. Nijinska, "The Triumph of Petipa," p. 317.

28. *Ibid.,* p. 318. It is unclear whether Nijinska knew the Lilac Fairy variation choreographed by Fedor Lopukhov for the 1914 revival of *Beauty* at the Maryinsky. Like Nijinska, Lopukhov reconceived what had originally been a partly mime role as a classical one.

29. *Ibid.,* pp. 317–318.

30. *Ibid.,* p. 318.

31. *Ibid.,* p. 317.

32. *Ibid.,* p. 319.

33. George Amberg, *Ballet: The Emergence of an American Art* (New York: Mentor Books, 1949), p. 58.

MARK MORRIS AND THE FEMININE MYSTIQUE

When Mark Morris was young, he toyed with some pretty nasty stuff. In *Lovey* the subject was child abuse, with Kewpie dolls as dildoes; in *Dogtown,* sexual sadism by a pack of predatory Amazons. Almost everything about the pieces seemed calculated to shock, from the perversity of the material to the violence of its treatment.

Few of Morris' works today depict these lowest rungs of a modern hell. Yet the theme of transgressive sexuality is rarely absent. In his own solos, this often takes the form of transvestism or something very close to it: mesmerizing hermaphrodites who incarnate the very essence of femininity. In *Deck of Cards,* he plays a country-'n'-western darlin' hustling at truck stops and dreaming of romance—an Isadorable in heels and an orange dress. In *O Rangasayee,* he dons the loin cloth of an Indian sage and the languor of a houri, offering him-self to the audience as a rapt ambisexual divinity. He does so again in the re-worked *Offertorium,* with buttery arms, as supple as a kathakali dancer's, that cloak the solo in feminine softness and mystery. Sometimes, as in *Jealousy,* Mor-ris parodies his own persona, with comic opera gestures so broad as to mini-mize their campiness. It's not impersonation he's after, although he's brilliant at it, but something more subversive. As in *One Charming Night,* where his vam-pire hero borrows Giselle's romantic arms and little jumps, he's out to under-mine heterosexual ideology. He does it with irony and pastiche, and a good dose of épatisme. But however much the method is postmodern, the theme itself re-flects more than fashion, appearing explicitly or implicitly in virtually all his works. Morris doesn't hate women or even heterosexuality. What he finds pro-foundly distasteful is the ideology that dance has attached to both, identifying the eternal feminine and romantic love with the art's highest expression of po-etic idealism.

Morris doesn't throw love out, only the clichés that go along with it. People make love all the time in his dances. But the couplings involve members of the same sex as often as those of the opposite, and the partnerships are constantly shifting. For Morris, this community of adventurous lovers represents an alter-native romantic ideal—love without exclusivity, long-term commitment, and only one kind of sex partner. It's a young community, still in its teens, naive, rough at the edges, a little tough. It also belongs very much to the 1980s. For

This article was first published in *Ballet Review,* 16, no. 3 (Fall 1988).

however chummy and liberated their play, Morris' new age primitives seem caught up in the idea of romance, of looking for that one true love (who never appears), of yearning for that indefinable something beyond sex (which also never appears), of hankering even after sentimental grace notes. The tension between Morris' alternative ideal and the clichés of conventional romance animates much of his recent choreography.

Included in this category is *Sonata for Clarinet and Piano,* one of the three new works presented during his May 1988 season at the Brooklyn Academy of Music. Set to Francis Poulenc's jazzy, witty music, the piece is a send-up of ballet, as naughty and provocative as anything Morris has done. If there's one work that sums up ballet's romantic idealism, it's *Swan Lake.* And if one role identifies that idealism with the eternal feminine, it's Odette. Only Morris would have the chutzpah to take on both. With his black top, lemon-colored tights, messy ponytail, and flabby middle, he certainly doesn't look like Odette. Yet from the moment he appears, sailing offstage in an imprisoning lift, he seems to embody everything about her—her fragility, her mournfulness, her yielding femininity. Morris' great scene comes in the second of the ballet's three movements, an adagio, as meditative as the blue of the star-brushed background. He enters without fanfare, a sorrowing ballerina among the red-and-black costumed corps. He has it all down: the soft, pliant arms, the gently inclining head, the modest backbends, the swooning falls that, here, in a typically subversive touch, end in a somersault. Finally, he sinks in a pool of light, downed by someone who might be Rothbart.

However much Morris pooh-poohs the ideology behind all this, he leaves the dance itself alone. The steps get their full value, and he shows us the beauty of ensemble configurations. A wedge opens into a double diagonal, then widens as the heroine, spinning like a whirlwind, rushes through—a bird flapping its wings at some unseen pursuer. In the first movement, it isn't so much Ivanov the choreography recalls, but the Balanchine of *Serenade,* in the flying entrances and exits of the duos, trios, and occasional solo figure. This is only one of many allusions to the ballet master in Morris' recent choreography. In *Vestige* (not shown at BAM), the recurring human pyramid, with a woman at the apex, brings to mind the final image of *Serenade*—an ideal of perfection to which mortals can only aspire. *New Love Song Waltzes,* his vision of new age love, pays an even greater tribute to Balanchine by appropriating music from *Liebeslieder Walzer.*

The second BAM premiere, *Fugue and Fantasy,* was less successful, although the opening section is wonderfully witty. The wit lies in the high-voltage calisthenics set, improbably, to Mozart's Fugue in C minor, K. 401. There are four dancers, and when the curtain opens they're sitting in bridge chairs, wiggling their feet, bending their torsos, clasping their hands, and doing this over and over again in a parody of Tanztheater. Morris elaborates, enlarges, and complicates these bits of material, then juxtaposes them polyphonically, matching

Mozart at his own game in a piece of inspired postmodern foolery. *Fugue* is a hard act to follow. But even on its own terms, the subsequent *Fantasy* is weak, running out of steam well before Mozart's Fantasia in C minor for Piano, K. 475, ends. The dance is a long diagonal cross, with five dancers edging in a huddle from upstage left to downstage right, then suddenly exiting. Whether friend, foe, or some figment of the imagination awaits them is unclear, and the tone—serious, with bursts of parody when the music swells—doesn't add to our understanding. There are some fine moments, however, for Keith Sabado, the dreamy innocent of the group, and the cloddish primitives who take turns with him as its leader.

Strict Songs, which also received its New York premiere at BAM, has already been reviewed in these pages. Since then, Morris has tinkered with it, eliminating the choreography's arcane gestures and heightening its buoyant athleticism. The result is a work that celebrates the prowess of the male body in a ritual as ecstatic as an Indian war dance. The piece is filled with fire images: jumps as darting as tongues, leaps that chase one another with the swiftness of flames. Yet even in its revised form, *Strict Songs* isn't completely successful. Although individual sequences build, the overall action is static, with lulls that repeatedly interrupt the momentum gathered in the other sections. For this, Lou Harrison's music is largely to blame. Inspired by Hopi chants, it has a meditative undercurrent that doesn't lend itself to dance, or at least, to the structured kind of dance Morris favors. On its own, however, the music can be hauntingly beautiful, as at BAM, where it was performed by the Orchestra of St. Luke's and the New York City Gay Men's Chorus.

Close on the heels of the BAM season came the premiere, at the end of May, of another Morris work, *Drink to Me Only With Thine Eyes,* by American Ballet Theatre. This is his third ballet, and the best new piece ABT has commissioned in many a season. Brilliantly inventive in its theatrics as well as its choreography, *Drink* uses classical steps to create an alternative to classical form—a ballet free of romantic convention and ideology. Morris begins with that time-honored genre, the piano ballet. But instead of Chopin, he gives us Virgil Thomson, and his sprightly Etudes for Piano, modernist fantasies on American tunes (a musical choice that should have landed Morris a spot in the New York City Ballet's American Music Festival). Morris' organization of the stage space is equally subversive. *Drink* has no follow spots for lovemaking or dark pools where couples rest, only a band of intense white light running across the forestage. The effect, from a visual point of view, is riveting. But it's more than a decorative device. With this ribbon of light, Morris and lighting designer Phil Sandstrom (who also lighted the works at BAM) have both delimited the space of group action and apportioned it equally among the dancers. If the piano ballet is about isolated couples and their entanglements, *Drink* is about individuals and multiple relationships within society.

Like Morris' dances for his own company, the ballet belongs to the ensemble.

There are circles, long diagonals, and horizontal crosses that bring the dancers together, then dissolve into trios, couples, and other small groupings as fluid as the bonds among the dozen men and women. The first cast included some of ABT's most interesting dancers, from principals Mikhail Baryshnikov, Julio Bocca, and Martine Van Hamel to soloists Robert Hill, Carld Jonassaint, and Kathleen Moore. Morris doesn't try to make them over. Even when he uses their torsos in unclassical ways, he seems to revel in their classical precision, pull-up, and virtuosity. His solo for Baryshnikov displays the brilliance as well as the fancifulness of the dancer's pirouettes, while that for Van Hamel—all échappés and passés relevés—celebrates her Cecchetti footwork. Even more dazzling are the trios, actually solos in counterpoint, where themes are stated, elaborated, contrasted, and transcended in Morris' finest demonstration of choreographic bravura. And throughout, there is the wit of his response to Thomson's music.

With the dancers in white (their elegant, casual sportswear is by Santo Loquasto), *Drink* is a ballet blanc. Actually, it's Morris' answer to the genre—a *Giselle* or *Swan Lake* purged of romanticism. Familiar as the steps are, they seem innocent of sentimental convention, as if Morris had plunked them onstage directly from the classroom, freeing them of the burden of history. The result is a language that seems newly invented, even though it's the vernacular of dance in the West. And not only do the steps seem freshly minted. Disclaiming hierarchy and gender, the dancers themselves seem reborn as innocents, cousins to the unspoiled primitives of Morris' own company.

By creating a purely ensemble work, Morris has gotten around the problem that marred *Esteemed Guests*, his 1986 work for the Joffrey Ballet—what to do with the ballerina. But this is not a long-term solution. Since the romantic era (with the partial exception of the Diaghilev years), the ballerina has occupied the center of ballet's poetic universe, the incarnation of its idealism. *Esteemed Guests* had a ballerina, a solitary figure reminiscent of many of Balanchine's women. But she was only a piece of classical scenery; she was there, you felt, because she had to be, not because Morris wanted her. In choreographing for his own company, Morris retains the dualism of sexual difference, even as he subverts the categories of gender. Except he reverses things; he makes the women tough and the men gentle and caring. If there is one dancer in his company who embodies the lyricism associated with the ballerina, it's not Tina Fehlandt, Morris' female alter ego, or Teri Weksler, the most conventionally feminine of his women, but Keith Sabado, a loving St. Francis. The ballerina of *Esteemed Guests* was certainly not a Morris woman. But she wasn't conventionally feminine either, and she had none of the eroticism that might have made her a lover or a love object. She was, you could say, the idea of a straight woman, without any of the attributes—save sex—of the real thing. The rich femininity of Morris' own roles was something, apparently, that he was unwilling to spare on a ballerina.

This imaginative stinting when it comes to women may well prove his Achilles heel as a choreographer, especially of ballets. Within his own company,

Morris can remake bodies at will, treating them as tabulae rasae, as new as the movement invented for each piece. But in ballet the past is harder to forget; it's in the steps, and it's bred into the dancers by long years of training. Like virtually all Morris' pieces, *Drink to Me Only With Thine Eyes* is an ironic work. To be sure, the irony is light, but only because he avoids the issue of gender and the even larger question of love. Morris is an openly gay artist, and many aspects of his work, from its treatment of gender to its use of irony, can be seen as a gay "take" on sex. At issue, however, isn't sexual preference but imaginative generosity, the quality that made Frederick Ashton, a homosexual, one of ballet's great poets of heterosexual love. Mark Morris is surely the most gifted choreographer to appear in this decade. Where he goes from here doesn't only depend on talent, however, but on the continued expansion of his imaginative universe: how well he can impart the female otherness of his own impersonations to the women of his dances.

THE LATE SNOW PRINCE

Back in the 1950s, the English publisher Adam and Charles Black had a series called "Dancers of To-Day." The books were slim and typically featured a star of the Sadler's Wells Ballet: by 1953, the list included Margot Fonteyn, Alicia Markova, Moira Shearer, Beryl Grey, Violetta Elvin, Nadia Nerina, Svetlana Beriosova, Michael Somes, and John Gilpin. Although only thirty-two pages long, the books were marvels of economy. They told you where a dancer had studied and what she had danced; indicated the milestones of her career and what distinguished her personality as a performer. They were also full of pictures, well-chosen studio portraits, stage photographs, "action" photographs, a snapshot or two taken at a party or on tour. At 7s. 6d., the books were a bargain.

Diane Solway's *A Dance Against Time: The Brief, Brilliant Life of a Joffrey Dancer* could not be more different. A biography of Edward Stierle, a talented dancer and budding choreographer who died of AIDS at the age of twenty-three, the book runs to nearly four hundred pages and, with its milking of events both personal and trivial, reduces the life of its subject to soap opera. The book grew out of an article Solway wrote for the "Arts and Leisure" section of *The New York Times* shortly after Stierle's death. Because this occurred only three days after the premiere of his second ballet, *Empyrean Dances,* and only six days after his twenty-third birthday, the story was an editor's dream. It had tragedy and glamor, gay sex and AIDS, even an all-American family gathered around the deathbed. What more could a publisher like Pocket Books want? So, the author was signed up, and the story became a book, doubtless in the hope that it would be a big moneymaker, like Gelsey Kirkland's *Dancing on My Grave.*

The result is a volume so overblown that it's easy to lose sight of its virtues. The writing, for instance, is clear and straightforward. The dialogue rings true, and the description of characters is apt. Moreover, the author has done her homework as a journalist. She has interviewed just about everyone who knew Stierle during his short life—teachers, dancers, friends, lovers, doctors, ballet masters, and choreographers, in addition to the members of his family, who gave her their full cooperation and complete access to the dancer's scrapbooks,

This essay was originally published in *The New Dance Review,* Winter 1995, as a review of Diane Solway's *A Dance Against Time: The Brief, Brilliant Career of a Joffrey Dancer* (New York: Pocket Books, 1994).

letters, diaries, and choreographic notebooks. Her diligence has left no aspect of Stierle's personal and professional life untouched.

The most rewarding pages come toward the beginning of the book, an account of Stierle's early career as a tap dancer and child model in South Florida. The last of eight children, he was the son of ethnic Catholic transplants who had left the gritty streets of North Philadelphia for the tropical sunshine of Hollywood, Florida. Here, they assimilated into a blue-collar world of milkmen, carpenters, paper hangers, plasterers, and maintenance men—jobs that Bill Stierle himself held at various times. Rose Stierle had a passion for dancing, and when her daughter Rosemarie was old enough she enrolled her for lessons at the local tap school. Little Eddie soon followed. He loved to perform, and by the time he was six he was dancing at Miami Beach hotels such as the Doral and the Fontainbleu. Commercials followed and, when he was eleven, a top prize in a Dance Educators of America competition held in New York. Before long, he had graduated to Razz Ma Jazz, a professional song-and-dance revue that played the south Florida condo, convention, and dinner theater circuit. Beyond, the lights of Broadway beckoned.

Despite its proximity to Miami, Hollywood was still small-town America. For the boys at Eddie's school, dancing of any kind was girl's stuff; sports were for boys. When Rosemarie, who had gone on to a professional stage career, prescribed ballet lessons for her eleven-year-old brother, the taunts of "faggot" turned to shoves and threats of violence. Bill Stierle was dead set against the lessons. As he told his wife, "I don't think there's a father around who doesn't associate ballet with being gay." Meanwhile, at the Liana Ballet and Ballet Concerto studios where his son took his first classes in ballet, there was hardly a boy in sight. Indeed, it wasn't until Eddie was fourteen, and a summer scholarship student at the School of American Ballet, that he found himself for the first time in a ballet class for boys. And only when he enrolled the following year at the North Carolina School of the Arts was he finally surrounded by kids just like himself.

Far from being unique, his story is all too common. For all that the history of ballet is dominated by men, at the American grass roots it remains an art identified with women. Even in sophisticated enclaves, like Santa Monica, Seattle, and, yes, Manhattan, women comprise the vast majority of teachers, and little girls, the overwhelming majority of their pupils. Ballet audiences tend to be disproportionately female, except for *The Nutcracker,* which alone brings families to the theater, dads included. Women volunteers staff company boutiques, run fundraising events, act as docents, newsletter writers, and part-time secretaries. In addition to being a women's world, ballet trades on images of femininity. From the Sugar Plum Fairies who arrive like clockwork at Christmas to the little girls who play dress-up in tutus from K-mart, ballet in the popular mind boils down to the feminine. What the "jock" is to masculinity in America, so the ballerina is to femininity, a distillation of ideas about traditional gender identity carried to their extreme.

Men in ballet have long ceased to be an anomaly. But ever since Diaghilev's day, they have been identified in the West with homosexuality. (Some claim this has always been the case, but, in my opinion, offer no convincing evidence.) The Ballets Russes brought about a rebirth of male dancing, put an end to the travesty tradition, and encouraged young men to study ballet. But because of Diaghilev's own sexual orientation and that of many of his collaborators, including his male stars, the homosexual thematic of certain ballets, and the presence by the 1920s of large numbers of male homosexuals in the audience, the reappearance of men in ballet was identified strongly with homosexuality. This was not simply a matter of perception; large numbers of homosexuals gravitated to ballet both as performers and spectators. The very marginality of ballet, especially in America, made it a safe haven.

Solway doesn't go into any of this. Like a good journalist, she keeps close to her story, explaining the difficulties Stierle encountered in terms of homophobia and dysfunctional family dynamics. This approach is typical of the book throughout. We get Stierle's story, and little more, and that story is only marginally about dance. Rather, it is one of family conflicts and reconciliations, sexual encounters and bittersweet romances, living arrangements, dressing-room conversations, doctors' visits, inspirational gurus, T-cell counts, drug therapies, rivalries with other dancers—interspersed with bulletin reports on AIDS. Stierle's dying goes on for pages. We learn who was at the bedside and how each of them reacted; what the nurses did and what the doctors did; when morphine was prescribed and when it "kicked in"; and, of course, every word the patient uttered, and to whom, in the last twenty-four hours of his life.

This isn't the only episode that sinks under the weight of talk-show trivia. Romances, too, are described in excruciating detail, and as if this were not enough, padded even further with lengthy quotations from Stierle's letters and diaries, which, unsurprisingly, reveal the characteristic self-involvement and sentimentality of a teenager. We are told again and again of his conflicts with Joffrey ballet master Scott Barnard, a demanding taskmaster who insisted upon "academic precision" and "rarely suffered disruptions lightly" in company class. Yet we never learn the kind of class he (or any of Stierle's other teachers) conducted, or why, given the diverse backgrounds and technical weaknesses of the Joffrey dancers, such rigor might have been necessary. And the author never considers that maybe, just maybe, Barnard was right to throw Stierle out of class one day when he was chattering, even if it "embarrassed" him and made him lose face before the company. No, for Solway, Barnard is simply a stickler for discipline and a man who liked to throw his weight around. He is redeemed only by his behavior in the last months of the dancer's life, when he shows his "true friendship" by cleaning up the rough spots in *Empyrean Dances*, which Stierle never could have completed without his assistance.

Solway is equally dismissive of the idea of "métier," which she likens to an exclusive "club," by which ballet dancers are assigned to the categories of *danseur noble, demi-caractère,* and *caractère,* depending on physical type. Short and stocky, Stierle was not blessed with a prince's body. He was rejected by the New York City Ballet and by American Ballet Theatre because of his physique, and was told time and again that he should set his sights on dancing with a European company, where the physical requirements were less demanding. It is hard not to sympathize with his plight; no amount of training, however excellent, could make him grow taller, even if it could improve his feet and lengthen his line. Yet as Solway herself acknowledges, the problem was not only his body. Years of tap and jazz routines had shortened his muscles and left him with a taste for tricks and razzmatazz, like the grands pirouettes and scissor leaps of his Prix de Lausanne solo *Fly From Over,* which Jennifer Dunning singled out for its "disturbing vulgarity." However much he yearned to be the "Baryshnikov of America," Stierle had little use for the niceties of technique. He was after the big effect, so if his legs were overcrossed or his line faulty, it mattered less to him than the excitement generated by the sheer force of the movement as a whole. His interpretation of certain roles, such as Petrouchka, left much to be desired. Solway quotes some of the negative criticism of his portrayal, including Anna Kisselgoff's description of Stierle's puppet as "snarling and gritting his teeth, never poignant." But she lets choreographer Senta Driver, a friend of Stierle's, have the last word. "Anna," she protested to Kisselgoff during the intermission following his debut in the role, "he has a concept. How many dancers have a concept?" As always in this book, personal considerations triumph over professional ones.

Stierle's years with the Joffrey were a period of turmoil for the company. Robert Joffrey's death, which followed the premiere of the Hodson-Archer reconstruction of *Le Sacre du Printemps,* marked the end of an era, while bringing the company close to collapse. Although Solway marks these events, she is far more interested in the gossip surrounding Joffrey's death, from AIDS, although this was never made public. Joffrey, as we know, was not the only company director to keep the disease a secret. Alvin Ailey also hushed up his condition, and like Joffrey, he did so for personal as well as financial reasons; going public could have dried up company funding during the critical period following his death. One may disagree with Joffrey's (or Ailey's) decision, but, given the precarious existence of even the most established American dance companies, one is compelled to respect it. That "outing" may have served only a minority of individuals rather than the artistic polity as a whole apparently never entered the author's mind.

Equally uncritical is her presumption of Stierle's greatness. The history of dance is full of careers that never fulfilled their early promise. Just because Stierle died young, there is no reason to assume—and considerable reason to doubt— that he would have become a dancer of major stature or a choreographer of genius. Indeed, for all the excitement generated by his performances, he had neither the technical nor artistic equipment of a young Nureyev or a

Baryshnikov. And despite his evident desire to choreograph and the fact that by the age of twenty-three he already had completed two ballets, his works revealed little of the originality of Nijinsky's *L'Après-midi d'un Faune,* Ailey's *Blues Suite,* or Robbins' *Fancy Free.* Biographers often exaggerate the accomplishments of their subjects, but one wonders whether Solway would have advanced the same claims had Stierle died of kidney failure or in a car crash—or if he had been a woman.

In a sense, the artistic questions raised by *A Dance Against Time* are beside the point, since the real subject of the book, as opposed to its setting, has little to do with dance. This, presumably, is what appealed to Pocket Books in signing up the author in the first place: the proposed volume wasn't a dance book, but a soap opera in which the star was an all-purpose victim—of his family, body, sexuality, AIDS, you name it. No greater contrast can be imagined between this antidance biography and the volumes in the "Dancers of To-day" series. For Adam and Charles Black, dance wasn't a pretext, but the raison d'être of its books, which dealt unabashedly with the art and artistry of their various subjects. And these books weren't the only dance items on the publisher's list, which also included Tamara Karsavina's *Ballet Technique,* Kay Ambrose's *The Ballet-Lover's Companion,* and the *Ballet Annual,* edited by Arnold Haskell. In other words, Black had a genuine commitment to dance and a sense of the public its books were intended to serve. Alas, Pocket Books, with its eye on the dubious mirage of big money, has neither.

WHERE ARE BALLET'S WOMEN CHOREOGRAPHERS?

Women choreographers abound in modern dance; in ballet, by contrast, they are a historical rarity. Even for the twentieth century, the names that immediately come to mind can be counted on the fingers of one hand—Bronislava Nijinska, Agnes de Mille, Andrée Howard, Ninette de Valois, Ruth Page. For the nineteenth century, there are even fewer: Marie Taglioni, whose claim to the title rests on one work, *Le Papillon;* and Katti Lanner, who choreographed the spectacular ballets that figured on the programs at London's Empire Theatre, a music hall.

Many reasons have been advanced for this absence of women choreographers in an idiom that for nearly two hundred years has been dominated by women as performers. One reason, it is said, is the codified movement vocabulary of ballet—its "stiff and commonplace gymnastics," in Isadora Duncan's words[1]—which supposedly limits the play of the imagination. Another explanation is what Susan Manning has called ballet's "sexual division of labor," which "defined choreography as a male task and performance as a female task."[2] Still another is the representational system of nineteenth-century ballet, which presented women as objects of male desire rather than as subjects in their own right.

In our day, explanations have focused on the day-to-day realities of ballet. Ballerina Karen Kain, for instance, has spoken of the unusually heavy burden that performing at the professional level imposes on women: with fewer claims on their time and energy, men can more easily try their hand at choreography.[3] Others have noted the difference in structure between modern dance and ballet classes. Where modern dance classes often include an improvisational or choreographic component, ballet classes for the most part are exclusively devoted to technique. Finally, professional training for women in ballet begins extremely early, and, unlike the training for modern dancers, seldom includes academic learning or exposure to other artistic forms. Thus, women in ballet learn to experience their bodies through the medium of a single all-embracing technique and in isolation from the larger world of ideas.

While all these explanations have some validity, they rest upon a number of dubious historical assumptions. The first is that the authorship of dances—

This essay is based on a paper given at the Institute for Research on Women and Gender, University of Michigan, on 21 October 1996.

including those of minor importance—has been generally acknowledged, when, in fact, in many eras this was seldom the case. The second is that dance-making is an activity that has always been identified with the individual choreographer, although the use of this term only became widespread in the twentieth century. The third is that choreography is preeminently an act of individual creation rather than the expression of an institutional style, as was typical in the nineteenth century. The fourth is that the choreographer is chiefly a maker of ballets, although in the past these formed only a fraction of most choreographers' total output. The fifth is that most ballet choreography was created for the opera house, as opposed to the popular stage or venues like circuses and pleasure gardens that in the nineteenth and early twentieth centuries routinely presented ballet spectacles and entertainments. The sixth is that the historical record, as this has come down to us, is an accurate reflection of reality. In terms of women, this is tantamount to saying that the only ones who choreographed are those we know about.

As I have said, all these assumptions are problematical. Based on a highly selective reading of the past, they ascribe to it the practices and prejudices of the present, while accepting on faith ballet's master narrative. This, in a nutshell, views the development of ballet genealogically, as a royal succession of choreographers of genius—Noverre, Perrot, Petipa, Fokine, Ashton, Balanchine. Because few ballets survive even the passage of a generation, such lineages are seductive, even if the order they invoke bears little resemblance to the messiness and contradictions of history. Above all, by viewing the ballet past as a succession of individuals of genius, this approach consigns most of ballet history to the dustbin. Yet it is here, in the now invisible crannies of the popular, the forgotten, and the second-rate, in the everyday chronicle of the ballet past as opposed to the selective chronicle of its most privileged institutions that women made dances. In these spaces, which even today remain largely undocumented, one finds the women choreographers of early twentieth-century French ballet.

I did not set out to unearth their forgotten history: it came to me unbidden, in newspapers, programs, books, and magazines—a history stumbled upon in search of something else. But there they were—women with names like Ariane Hugon, Jane Hugard, Mademoiselle Stichel, Madame Mariquita, Louise Virard, Adelina Gedda, Jeanne Chasles, Rita Papurello—turn-of-the-century ghosts, choreographers invisible to history although they had worked in the theater for years.

It is not my intention to offer a panorama of French women choreographers of this period. Nor is it my aim to make a case for the genius of any one individual. My goal, rather, is to situate these artists institutionally, suggest why certain venues welcomed their talents and others did not, and speculate on the reasons they vanished so completely from the historical record. I then turn to the women choreographers who emerged in the modernist heyday of the 1920s and 1930s. How did they differ from their predecessors? Under what new constraints did they labor? In what artistic contexts did they operate? Finally, and more broadly, what can we deduce about the institutional preconditions for female achievement as choreographers in ballet?

Although today her name is forgotten, in her time Madame Mariquita was among the busiest and most respected choreographers of Paris. Critics spoke of her "exquisite art"; one even dubbed her "the fairy of artistic choreography."[4] She had "imagination, talent, [and] taste," wrote Cléo de Mérode, and a "sensitivity" that made dancers "adore" her.[5] From 1898 to 1920, Mariquita was the ballet mistress of the Opéra-Comique, where she produced nearly thirty ballets and the dances in numerous operas.[6] Her tenure at the city's second opera house (where she succeeded Berthe Bernay, a former Opéra dancer and teacher at the Opéra school) climaxed a long career on the popular stage. Born near Algiers in the 1830s, she made her Paris debut in 1845 at the renowned Théâtre des Funambules, home of the mime Deburau. She danced at the Théâtre des Bouffes-Parisiens, Théâtre de la Porte-Saint-Martin, and Théâtre des Variétés; choreographed early ballets for the "Skating de la rue Blanche," a roller derby turned popular theater; served as ballet mistress of the Théâtre de la Gaîté-Lyrique and eventually the Folies-Bergère, which throughout the Belle Epoque had a ballet troupe.[7] Katti Lanner regarded her as a rival and closely monitored her doings from across the Channel. As Enrico Cecchetti observed, "Did Mdlle. Mariquita put on 'Autour de Paris' in the French capital, Katti Lanner was sure to put on 'Round the Town' in London."[8]

During her years at the Opéra-Comique, Mariquita still kept a foot in the popular theater. In 1900, for instance, she served as ballet mistress at the Palais de la Danse at the Universal Exposition. In 1908, she "arranged" the dances for *La Belle au Bois Dormant* (The Sleeping Beauty), a "*féerie lyrique*" in fourteen scenes with Sarah Bernhardt in the double travesty role of the Poet and the Prince. In 1912, she provided some of the choreography for the "galas" given by soloist Natalia Trouhanova at the Folies-Bergère. In 1919, at the Théâtre Vaudeville, she staged the first production of Debussy's children's ballet *La Boîte à joujoux* (The Toy Box), a work later produced by the Ballets Suédois. She even found time to produce the odd trifle for high society. *Narkiss,* a "story-ballet with singing," was mounted in 1913 for the Casino in Deauville.

Madame Mariquita (she was never known otherwise) was the most prolific of the era's women choreographers. When she died in 1922 close to the age of ninety, she could look back to a career spanning more than seven decades of professional activity—a remarkable feat in its own right. Despite its longevity, Mariquita's career followed a pattern typical of many women choreographers. It unfolded in many different types of venues, included long stints in the popular theater as well as engagements at provincial opera houses, and in the subsidized sector, centered at the Opéra-Comique, not the Opéra.

Compared to the Palais Garnier, the Opéra-Comique was as a stepchild of the French state. Its subsidy was substantially less than the Opéra's, and its charter precluded the production of the grand historical operas that were considered the summit of lyric art and the exclusive domain of the Opéra. Although each institution had its own ballet company, only the Opéra had an affiliated school. (One was later started at the Opéra-Comique, but subsequently closed.) Its troupe was larger and better trained, and until well into the twentieth century its senior ballerina was an *étoile* of international standing, generally imported from Italy. Beginning in the late 1880s, many of the Opéra's principal ballet masters were foreign as well: Joseph Hansen, who held the post from 1887 to 1907, was Belgian; Ivan Clustine, who served from 1911 to 1914, Russian; Nicolà Guerra, who did two stints at the Opéra between 1917 and 1929, Italian. Although artistically and economically favored, the Opéra produced few ballets in the decades before the First World War—exactly seven in the years between 1900 and 1910 (one of which, *Javotte*, had been created—by Madame Mariquita— elsewhere).[9] At the Opéra-Comique, by comparison, twice as many ballets reached the stage in the same decade—all choreographed by Mariquita. In sheer numbers (if not in technical expertise and the possession of a traditional inherited repertory), it was the Opéra-Comique and not the more prestigious Opéra that was truly a showplace for French ballet. Indeed, by 1921, according to *The Dancing Times*, "good judges of dancing [were] mak[ing] pilgrimages from all parts of France" to savor the much-esteemed offerings at the Opéra-Comique, where ballet was "a speciality of the management."[10]

These figures, however, do not fully reflect the dance activity at either of these theaters. Unlike its Italian counterpart, French opera of the second half of the nineteenth century retained the ballet scenes and divertissements that were a traditional feature of the genre. Practically every new French opera—and under their charters both the Opéra and the Opéra-Comique were compelled to produce a minimum number of new operas each season—had its requisite ballet or divertissement. Today, we tend to dismiss such efforts as "decorative" rather than "inventive" (to borrow Lincoln Kirstein's distinction between the different levels of creation in choreography).[11] This was not the view of earlier generations. For dancers and audiences alike, these ballets were an integral part of the repertory; the entire company took part in them, and they were judged by the same yardstick as independent dance works. (Indeed, in 1947, Léandre Vaillat followed up his book on the Opéra's ballets with a volume on the ballets performed in operas.)[12] Although neither the Opéra nor the Opéra-Comique offered full evenings of dance before the 1920s, full-length ballets—or, at least, works that today we would consider full-length—shared programs with operas. At the Opéra, astonishing as it now seems, *Coppélia* might be paired with *Rigoletto*, *Salomé* with *Les Deux Pigeons*. And it was not uncommon to follow a long evening of opera with a one-act ballet for a visiting star.[13]

Hence, for choreographers attached to opera houses in this period, staging dances for operas claimed as much if not more of their time than producing ballets. Mariquita seems to have been an exception to this general rule; at the Opéra-Comique the list of her ballets is longer than that of her operas. But for her colleagues, men as well as women, operas tended to predominate. The post of ballet master or ballet mistress was thus inseparable from the artistic identity of the institution to which he or she was attached. Originality was not a goal, as it would be for the choreographers of the Ballets Russes, so much as serving the repertory with skill, adaptability, and resourcefulness. Mariquita staged an amazing variety of dances during her years at the Opéra-Comique—Greek, Russian, "Hindu," Spanish, Egyptian, "French" (meaning dances in eighteenth-century style), classical, romantic—whatever the repertory needed. Although her choreography routinely was singled out for its spatial and rhythmic variety, and for "repudiating" the tutu (Cléo de Mérode's word) in favor of period costuming,[14] it was job work tailored to the task at hand rather than the expression of a personal style or vision.

In today's parlance, Mariquita was a company "man." As a ballet mistress, she taught as well as choreographed, functions that were regarded as virtually inseparable. At the Opéra-Comique, she was responsible for training the corps de ballet, proving herself, as Cyril W. Beaumont wrote, "an admirable teacher."[15] This involvement in an institution's day-to-day life was typical of pre-Diaghilev choreographers, men as well as women. Women, however, tended to work at less prestigious institutions than men; they also tended to be concentrated in the popular theater. This was true even of women who began their careers—as several did—on the stage of the Opéra and served their apprenticeship as ballet mistresses at provincial theaters.

Mlle. Stichel (as she was always known, although her real name was Louise Manzini)[16] first came to my attention when I was going through a stack of programs for the Théâtre du Châtelet in the years just before the appearance of the Ballets Russes. The theater was famous for its "féeries," huge evening-long extravaganzas that hung on a wisp of a plot and featured dozens of spectacular decors, hundreds of performers, and an array of dances. Stichel, who had made her debut at the Opéra as a petit sujet in 1881,[17] served as ballet mistress at the Théâtre de Monte-Carlo in 1891–1892, and staged the ballet Phryné at the Casino de Royen in 1896,[18] choreographed a number of these productions, including La Princesse sans-gêne (1907), Pif! Paf! Pouf! ou un Voyage endiablé (1906?), Tom Pitt, le Roi des Pickpockets (1905), and Les 400 Coups du Diable (1905). Although she was not the only woman to choreograph such fare at the Châtelet (La Petite Caporale [1909], for instance, was by Adelina Gedda, a sometime ballet mistress at Rouen's Théâtre des Arts[19] and a long-time ballet mistress at the Théâtre de Monte-Carlo), Stichel's work must have been exceptional, for in 1910 the Opéra appointed her to the post of ballet mistress. Her tenure lasted only a year, long enough, however, for her to choreograph La Fête chez Thérèse, a ballet to music by Reynaldo Hahn (who would soon compose Diaghilev's Le Dieu Bleu), and the dances for several operas including La Damna-

tion de Faust and *Salomé.* Her contribution to *La Fête chez Thérèse* received high marks from the playwright Fernand Nozière, who reviewed the premiere in *Le Théâtre:* "Madame Stichel, the new ballet mistress, has abandoned conventional groupings. She has made the dancers more natural, given them more life. The workers move freely. The guests come and go with fluidity. We no longer see lines of soldiers at drill. This is a great advance."[20]

After leaving the Opéra, Stichel did some choreography for recitalist Natalia Trouhanova.[21] What she did until 1921 I have yet to discover. In that year, however, she was busy at work, choreographing the ballet in *Boccaccio,* a light opera produced at the Gaîté-Lyrique, some dance songs for the Gaumont-Palace cinema,[22] and three works for the Opéra-Comique, where she occupied the post of ballet mistress from 1923 until 1925. During this time, she worked steadily at the Gaîté-Lyrique, supplying dances for the operettas that were now its standard fare.[23] She produced her last ballets at the Casino de Nice in 1932–1933.[24]

Another woman who occupied the post of ballet mistress at the Opéra-Comique in the 1920s was Jeanne Chasles. A former dancer at both the Opéra and the Opéra-Comique,[25] she, too, did her earliest choreography outside the subsidized theaters where she also occasionally performed.[26] In 1910, she contributed the "magnificently arranged" dances to the opera *Quo Vadis?* produced at the Gaîté-Lyrique;[27] in 1913, the dances to Fauré's opera *Pénélope,* which opened at the Théâtre des Champs-Elysées only days before *Le Sacre du Printemps.*[28] During the same period, she also choreographed a ballet for Jacques Rouché's innovative Théâtre des Arts,[29] as did Jane Hugard, who staged the dances for Ravel's *Ma Mère l'Oye.*[30] As a choreographer, Chasles displayed an unusual interest in the dance past. Her ballet for the Théâtre des Arts was to music by Lulli for Molière's play *Le Sicilien.* In 1923, for a charity event, she arranged a Renaissance "divertissement" to fifteenth-century music by Charles Lévadé;[31] two years later, for a revival at the Opéra-Comique, the dances in the third "entrée" of Rameau's *Les Fêtes galantes,* an effort that won praise no less than gratitude from critic André Levinson.[32] Such undertakings were of a piece with the remarkable collection of dance-related documents and engravings that Chasles had amassed in the years before World War I.[33]

In 1920, when Mariquita retired as ballet mistress of the Opéra-Comique, Chasles took her place. Although she continued to choreograph for the theater until 1925, she vacated the post after three years, when it went to Stichel. In 1925, Louise Virard became ballet mistress, remaining until 1932, when Carina Ari, a former star with the Ballets Suédois, assumed the post for a year. Finally, in 1933, it went to Constantin Tcherkas, a former Diaghilev star. With his appointment, the era of women choreographers at the Opéra-Comique came to an end.

Although the upper echelons of late nineteenth-century ballet continued to be dominated by men, the role of women was far from negligible. Even at institutions like the Opéra, they held important positions as teachers. Rosita Mauri, for instance, conducted the Opéra's "class of perfection" from 1898 to 1920, while

Berthe Bernay, who wrote extensively about ballet technique, taught the first and second quadrille—equivalent to the corps de ballet—for most of the same period.[34] Like the others who labored in the company's studios, they upheld the traditions of the house and a style that with the advent of the Ballets Russes became synonymous with the "decline" of French ballet.[35]

The influence of the Ballets Russes and the "free" dance of the period dealt a heavy blow to choreographers identified with the "old" ballet. Initially, however, these currents favored women, especially at the Paris Opéra, which in the years immediately after the First World War actively promoted female talent. Without exception, however, the new choreographers hailed from the Opéra's eurhythmic section, established by Jacques Rouché in 1917. Today, Rachel Pasmanik, Jessmin Howarth, Jane Erb, Clara Brook, Yvonne Franck, and Alice Bourgat are as forgotten as their female contemporaries at the Opéra-Comique. Yet, for nearly a decade and over the bitter opposition of ballet traditionalists, they challenged the prevailing sexism of the Opéra. After the section was abolished in 1925, Bronislava Nijinska briefly joined the choreographic roster. Her tenure, which was not a success, ended two years later with *Impressions de Music-hall,* in which, to the consternation of traditionalists, ballerina Carlotta Zambelli danced a Charleston. However, as occurred at the Opéra-Comique in the early 1930s, it was the appointment of a Ballets Russes star—in this case, Serge Lifar—that reinvigorated the ideology of sexism by identifying the creative principle in ballet with the male choreographer.

Although Nijinska was herself a veteran of the Ballets Russes, she was the only woman among Diaghilev's choreographers, a group that included not only Michel Fokine, her brother Vaslav Nijinsky, Léonide Massine, and George Balanchine, the company's major choreographers, but also Boris Romanov, Adolph Bolm, Thadée Slavinsky, and Serge Lifar, its minor ones. Diaghilev certainly respected Nijinska's talent; he regarded her sex, however, as a liability, a sign of the incompleteness that was the fate of the woman artist. "What a choreographer Bronia would have been," he was fond of saying, "if only she were a man!"[36]

However, sexism alone does not explain the "remasculinization" of choreography during the Diaghilev period. With the Ballets Russes, the dancemaking art was assimilated into a new ballet star system, one that centered predominantly on men. From this pool of company-made stars, Diaghilev molded a new breed of choreographer, a diva whose glamor, commodity value, and specialized, expert skills commanded power in the marketplace regardless of institutional affiliation. The emergence of this new "high-profile" choreographer brought the era of the choreographic traditionalist to an end. And because the pool created by Diaghilev was almost exclusively male, a phenomenon that should have been propitious to the promotion of women as choreographers ended up excluding them more completely than ever.

However, it was not only as choreographers that women were eclipsed. The male-centered aesthetic of the Ballets Russes explicitly challenged the identification of nineteenth-century ballet with femininity. The male body—especially the androgynous or gay male body—became the norm, and in ballet after ballet it dominated the stage, physically as well as dramatically. Just as modern painting self-consciously defined itself as "masculine" as opposed to the "feminine" culture of symbolism, so modern ballet jettisoned the cult of the eternal "feminine" born with romanticism.

The "ballet girl" occupies a special niche in late nineteenth-century French art—an image of charm, innocence, and careless désabille, wispy, floating tarlatans, and pervasive eroticism. Although women in tarlatans (which were de rigueur throughout the 1920s) continued to labor in the Opéra's studios, the gaze that had permeated this world with male desire turned elsewhere. With Diaghilev's sexual revolution and the appearance of large numbers of homosexual men in the audience, the object of male desire ceased to be the female body; it became instead the newly eroticized body of the danseur. This shift—which for obvious reasons could never be fully explicit—complicated the representation of the feminine, at times idealizing it, at others investing it with danger or neutering it. In the contesting of femininity the female body became something akin to a theater of war.

Although French institutions may have closed their doors to women in the post-Diaghilev period, the late 1920s and 1930s witnessed the emergence of several female choreographers in England.[37] For the most part, they found their voices outside elite institutions—a point of similarity with their earlier French counterparts—at a time when the English dance world was in a state of flux. Although for decades, London had boasted two resident ballet companies, both were attached to music halls. No "high art" institution existed for ballet, and the academies that offered classical training typically channeled their students into pantomimes and other forms of popular entertainment in venues where many teachers doubled as ballet masters.

The initial seasons of the Ballets Russes did not significantly alter this paradigm, although it prompted a wave of Russian dancers—including the immensely popular Anna Pavlova—to accept highly lucrative engagements at London's leading music halls. But with the return of the company after the First World War, when it was taken up by intellectuals of all stripes and acquired a broad popular following, dancers, teachers, and critics began to call for the organization of an indigenous "British ballet." By this was meant a company on the Diaghilev model, a "high art" enterprise that not only brought together the best British talents, but also represented a modernist aesthetic. During the 1920s, various attempts were made to put this into practice. But it was only in the vacuum created by Diaghilev's death in 1929 that these efforts began to bear fruit.

Like modern dance, "British ballet" was largely a creation of women. The story of Ninette de Valois and the founding of the Vic-Wells company, forerunner of today's Royal Ballet, has often been told; so, too, has that of Marie

Rambert and the Ballet Club, which later became Ballet Rambert. From these crucibles of modern British ballet emerged the dancers, choreographers, designers, and musical directors of its glory years, along with the body of works that defined the phenomenon stylistically. Of the two, de Valois was the institution builder; Rambert the gleaner and nurturer of talent; among her many "finds" were Frederick Ashton and Antony Tudor. Both women had worked briefly with the Ballets Russes—Rambert in the years just before the First World War, de Valois in the early 1920s—and been deeply marked by the experience. However, it was only after leaving the company that their organizational and mentoring gifts were revealed.

Although they made their greatest mark elsewhere, de Valois and Rambert were also choreographers. Initially, their efforts stemmed from their personal needs as performers. De Valois, for instance, created material for her early recital programs, her performances with the Lila Field company, her opera ballet appearances at Covent Garden, and all the numbers for her short-lived touring group.[38] Rambert, for her part, created most of the dances she performed as a recitalist. By the late 1920s, however, with mentoring claiming the greater part of her energies, Rambert largely abandoned choreography. De Valois, by contrast, invigorated by her exposure to the Ballets Russes and especially Nijinska's path-breaking works, now entered an intensely creative phase. Working principally with groups, she experimented with a form of expressive movement that was indebted to modernism, while remaining anchored to the technical foundation of the *danse d'école.*

Although, as teachers, both women adopted the Russo-Italian method of Enrico Cecchetti, with whom they had studied, their background embraced far more than ballet. Rambert had trained in eurhythmics at Hellerau, where she worked with Emile Jaques-Dalcroze, while de Valois, after an early exposure to "Greek" dancing, absorbed elements of eurhythmics and the gestural vocabulary associated with Central European dance. For both women, as for Nijinska during her formative years as a choreographer in post-revolutionary Russia, contact with "modern" forms of movement seems to have been the catalyst prompting them to choreograph. Not only were such forms dominated by women, but they were also forms that set a premium on dance-making. Anyone could try a hand at it, and in the marginalized spaces of amateur, semi-professional, and avant-garde performance, many did. Even if the results were unsuccessful, they revealed what Diaghilev knew from experience, that given a modicum of talent, choreography was a skill that could be learned.

Although neither de Valois nor Rambert became a choreographer of the first rank, choreography figured prominently in their vision of modern ballet. This, as Beth Genné has pointed out, was strikingly demonstrated in the name that de Valois chose for her school—The Academy of Choreographic Art. Although "operatic dancing," as ballet was generally known in England, was the basis of the curriculum, her goal was to make this serve the practice of modern choreography, not the style "of the eighties" espoused by classical teachers of the old school.

Ironically, given her admiration for Nijinska and her own professional career, de Valois did little to foster choreographic talent in women. Rambert, by contrast, nurtured the careers of two major women choreographers, Andrée Howard and Agnes de Mille, who worked with her during extended visits to London in the 1930s. Indeed, de Mille's experiments with the women of Rambert's company—a choreographic seedbed analogous in function to modern dance groups in America—provided much of the material for her all-important works of the 1940s. Designer Sophie Fedorovitch was another remarkable woman discovered and nurtured by Rambert, who teamed her with Ashton in what proved the start of a long and close collaboration. Albeit on a smaller scale, "Mim" did for women in ballet what Diaghilev had done for men.

Rambert and de Valois profited not only from the vacuum created by the demise of the Ballets Russes, but also from the crisis provoked in the London dance world by the demise of music hall ballet. In Paris, a similar phenomenon, played out on both the subsidized and popular stages, had pushed women choreographers aside. In London, because of the institutional void, the passing of the old guard represented an opportunity that women such as Rambert and de Valois could seize.

The organizations they mothered were fragile and unfunded, positioned— in the case of Rambert's company—on the fringe of the avant-garde or—in the case of de Valois'—within the embrace of the repertory theater movement. Like Nijinska's short-lived companies of the 1920s and 1930s, they existed on a pittance and played for the most part to the converted. In nearly every way, they more closely resembled American modern dance groups of the 1930s than traditional ballet companies. This would tend to suggest that the presence or absence of women as choreographers and artistic directors has more to do with resources, social practices, and institutional clout than the use of a particular movement idiom. Indeed, once Rambert and de Valois retired, the companies they founded—which by then had grown into powerful, subsidized institutions—passed into the hands of men. (A similar change took place in the directorship of the Martha Graham Company after its founder's death and in that of American Ballet Theatre after Lucia Chase's retirement.)

In ballet—as in all fields of human endeavor—power is closely tied to gender. Although women have always choreographed, in the nineteenth century they were seldom entrusted with entire productions: indeed, because their choreography usually took the form of isolated dances within a larger work (dances, moreover, that they themselves often performed), their contribution rarely was acknowledged. At the same time, those productions that were entrusted to them tended to exist in less prestigious contexts, often in conjunction with popular entertainment. Finally, as choreographers, women typically were associated with theaters that had little or no interest in choreographic innovation. Viewed by the 1920s as the perpetuators of discredited "house" styles, these women disappeared in the wake of the Ballets Russes and changes in popular entertainment. The rewriting of twentieth-century ballet history that began in the post-Diaghilev period completed the process. In beginning their chronicle of ballet in Monte Carlo in 1911, the year of Diaghilev's first residency there, Georges Detaille and Gérard Mulys necessarily eliminated the various women who had earlier served as ballet mistresses.[39] In this category was Adelina Gedda, who occupied the post for no fewer than eight seasons between 1889 and 1904.

In the post–World War I period, women choreographers emerged in spaces that were either female dominated or allied with movements associated with the intelligentsia or the avant-garde. Typically, these spaces were created by the choreographers themselves; typically, too, they began as makeshift arrangements, growing out of the classes that provided dancers for the group and helped pay its bills. The vast majority of the nearly three hundred ballet companies that exist in the United States today reveal a similar pattern. Not only are they extensions of schools, they are also for the most part headed by women, who often double as choreographers. The chief difference between these companies and those of the 1920s and 1930s is artistic. Where Nijinska or de Valois viewed technique as serving choreography, their descendants typically view choreography as serving technique. As ballet traditionalists, they are closer to the French choreographers I have discussed than to the modernists who followed.

The most important lesson to be gleaned from this is that our narratives of women's practice in ballet prior to the modern period are both partial and incomplete. Indeed, apart from the ballerinas who achieved renown on the most prestigious stages of the nineteenth and early twentieth centuries, we know next to nothing about the subject. Men, to be sure, dominated the very top of the profession. Under them, however, as teachers, ballet mistresses, and, yes, even choreographers, labored women—numerous women. The recovery of their history and that of the institutions and practices they served is crucial to the task of reimagining the ballet past.

NOTES

1. Isadora Duncan, *My Life* (New York: Horace Liveright, 1927), p. 21.
2. Susan Manning, *Ecstasy and the Demon: Feminism and Nationalism in the Dances of Mary Wigman* (Berkeley: University of California Press, 1993), p. 1.
3. In discussion with Penelope Reed Doob, "Knowing the Dance from the Dancer: A Collaborative Model for Appreciating Performance," *Border Crossings*, SDHS/ADUCC Joint Conference, Toronto, 13 May 1995.

4. "Courrier des Théâtres," *Figaro*, 6 June 1913, p. 5; "Un Monsieur de l'Orchestre," "La Soirée: *Snégourotchka* à l'Opéra-Comique," *Figaro*, 23 May 1908, p. 4.

5. Cléo de Mérode, *Le Ballet de ma vie*, preface Françoise Ducout (Paris: Pierre Horay, 1985), p. 238.

6. For the list of her productions at the Opéra-Comique, see Stéphane Wolff, *Une Demi-siècle d'Opéra-Comique (1900–1950)* (Paris: André Bonne, 1953).

7. Cyril W. Beaumont, *Complete Book of Ballets* (London: Putnam, 1937), p. 652; Ivor Guest, *The Ballet of the Second Empire* (London: Pitman, 1974), pp. 262–266, and *The Divine Virginia: A Biography of Virginia Zucchi* (New York: Marcel Dekker, 1977), pp. 163–164.

8. Olga Racster, *The Master of the Russian Ballet: The Memoirs of Cav. Enrico Cecchetti*, introd. Anna Pavlova (London: Hutchinson, [1922]), p. 167.

9. Mariquita created *Javotte* in 1896 for the Grand Théâtre in Lyon and remounted it three years later at the Opéra-Comique. The Opéra version, which entered the repertory in 1909, was choreographed by Léo Staats.

10. George Cecil, "The Opéra Comique Ballet," *The Dancing Times*, April 1921, p. 556.

11. Lincoln Kirstein, *Ballet Alphabet: A Primer for Laymen* (New York: Kamin, 1939), p. 19. This distinction appears in the entry for choreography.

12. Léandre Vaillat, *Ballets de l'Opéra de Paris* (Paris: Compagnie Française des Arts Graphiques, 1943); *Ballets de l'Opéra de Paris: Ballets dans les opéras—nouveaux ballets* (Paris: Compagnie Française des Arts Graphiques, 1947).

13. Thus, in June 1907 at the Opéra-Comique, Vera Trefilova and Nicolas Legat went on after a performance of *Carmen*, while in May 1909 at the Opéra, those who survived the five-act *Monna Vanna* could see Olga Preobrajenska in *Javotte*. "Courrier des Théâtres," *Figaro*, 4 June 1907, p. 4; 23 May 1909, p. 5. Elsewhere, as Ann Barzel documents in her fascinating article on the career of Elizabetta Menzeli, who "arranged" the dances for the world premiere of *Aida* in Cairo, dancers often appeared between the acts or in interpolated divertissements in operas lacking ballets. Like Thérèse Elssler, Elizabetta was the taller and stronger of two sisters, and often appeared in the male role, *en travesti*, opposite the lighter Elena. Both Thérèse and Elizabetta choreographed the material they danced with their sisters. Given the popularity of sister acts, which allowed women the freedom to perform—and tour—without the encumbrance of a male relative, further investigation is likely to reveal the existence of many heretofore unknown women choreographers. See Ann Barzel, "Elizabetta Menzeli," *Dance Chronicle*, 19, no. 3 (1996), pp. 278–281.

14. Mérode, *Le Ballet de ma vie*, p. 287.

15. Beaumont, *Complete Book of Ballets*, p. 652.

16. I am grateful to Jane Pritchard for this information.

17. Stéphane Wolff, *L'Opéra au Palais Garnier (1875–1962)*, introd. Alain Gueullette (Paris: Slatkine, 1962), p. 533.

18. Mérode, *Le Ballet de ma vie*, p. 144. "Madame Stichel," the dancer later wrote, "the well-known ballet mistress, arranged our ensembles and our solos with her usual precision and in a style as Greek as could be imagined."

19. "Courrier des Théâtres," *Figaro*, 13 September 1897, p. 4.

20. [Fernand] Nozière, "Théâtre National de l'Opéra: La Fête chez Thérèse," *Le Théâtre*, March 1910, II, p. 20.

21. "Tout Paris," "Bloc-Notes Parisien: Mlle Trouhanowa," *Le Gaulois*, 3 May 1911, p. 1.

22. "Paris Notes," *The Dancing Times*, November 1921, p. 97.

23. In 1923, for instance, she choreographed "Le Ballet de deux coqs" in Louis Urgel's operetta *Amour de Princesse;* in 1925, the "grand ballet" in Félix Fourdrain's operetta *La Hussarde.*

24. I am grateful to Jane Pritchard for this information.

25. According to Stéphane Wolff, Chasles made her debut at the Opéra as a *petit sujet* in 1888 and danced principal roles at the Opéra-Comique from 1899 to 1910 (*L'Opéra au Palais Garnier*, p. 530; *Un Demi-siècle d'Opéra-Comique*, p. 327).

26. In 1897, for instance, she danced a principal role in the fourth-act "grand ballet" of *Mam'zelle Quat'sous*, an "opéra-comique à spectacle" produced at the Théâtre de la Gaîté. The choreography was by Mariquita ("Courrier des Théâtres," *Figaro*, 5 November 1897, p. 4.)

27. Maurice Lefevre, "Théâtre Lyrique Municipal de la Gaîté: *Quo Vadis?" Le Théâtre*, January 1910, II, p. 22.

28. "Courrier des Théâtres," *Figaro*, 9 May 1913, p. 6.

29. The ballet, to music by Lulli, was in Molière's *Le Sicilien, ou l'amour peintre*. Francis de Miomandre, "Théâtre des Arts," *Le Théâtre*, December 1910, II, pp. 24–25.

30. *A Ravel Reader: Correspondence, Articles, Interviews*, ed. Arbie Orenstein (New York: Columbia University Press, 1990), pp. 129–130. At this time, Hugard may have been a dancer at the Opéra; in 1932, she was definitely on the payroll, although presumably as a teacher or a régisseur. A fluent writer, she contributed an essay on the Opéra, "Du Ballet classique," to the volume *Les Spectacles à travers les ages: musique, danse* (Paris: Editions du Cygne, 1932), pp. 193–212, and the preface to Gaspard Maillol's album of woodcuts of Opéra dancers, *Danseuses* (Paris: La Presse à Bras, 1932). She is identified in the Maillol album as "Jane Hugard de l'Opéra."

31. André Nède, "La Musique et la Danse: l'Assemblée au Concert," *Figaro*, 10 January 1923, p. 1.

32. André Levinson, "A l'Opéra-Comique: *Les Indes galantes," Comoedia*, 4 June 1925, p. 2.

33. Carlotta Zambelli, "Danseuses d'hier et d'aujourd'hui," *Musica-Nöel*, n.d., p. 252, Folder 25, Valentine Hugo Collection, Theatre Museum (London).

34. Bernay's books are *La Danse au Théâtre*, pref. Gustave Goetschy (Paris: E. Dentu, 1890), and *Théorie de l'art de la danse* (Paris: Garnier, 1902). She also wrote the concluding chapter on technique in Raoul Charbonnel's *La Danse: Comment on dansait, common on danse* (Paris: Garnier Frères, [1900]), and the entry "La Danse" in *Encyclopédie de la musique et dictionnaire du conservatoire*, 5 (1930), pp. 3411–3435. She began to teach at the Opéra in the 1890s and remained in its employ at least until 1914. Her 1907 to 1914 contracts with the Opéra are in AJ13/1214, Archives Nationales (Paris).

35. See, for instance, the chapter "Décadence et renaissance" in Boris Kochno's *Le Ballet,*

with Maria Luz (Paris: Hachette, 1954), pp. 121–127, and "The Decline of Ballet in the West" in Ivor Guest's *The Dancer's Heritage: A Short History of Ballet,* foreword Margot Fonteyn, 5th ed. (London: The Dancing Times, 1977), pp. 47–53.

36. Quoted in Richard Buckle, *Diaghilev* (London: Weidenfeld and Nicolson, 1979), p. 446.

37. Although Ruth Page does not figure in the following discussion since she worked exclusively in the United States, her development as a choreographer reveals many of the same patterns as British women choreographers of the period.

38. I am grateful to Beth Genné for this information.

39. Georges Detaille and Gérard Mulys, *Les Ballets de Monte-Carlo 1911–1944* (Paris: Editions Arc-en-Ciel, 1954).

PART III

DANCE IN NEW YORK

DANCE IN THE CITY

TOWARD AN AMERICAN DANCE

Dancers need a home like anyone else. As artists they need to share
the natural life of a city, like the people who knew they belong
there.

—Edwin Denby, 1944

Paris, London, and Leningrad have long given dancers a home. New York has
done so only recently. In fact, only an incurable optimist could have predicted,
when critic Edwin Denby wrote those words, that within fewer than twenty
years New York would become a Mecca to dancers from around the world.

Yet the 1940s turned out to be a watershed: the start of an era that would see
the transformation of New York from a provincial outpost to the dance capital
of the West. Between 1940 and 1965, the city witnessed an explosion in dance
activity unprecedented since the Paris dance boom of the 1920s. New companies, among them Ballet Theatre (known today as American Ballet Theatre)
and the New York City Ballet, came into being. Modern dance found a haven in
metropolitan-area universities. Broadway opened its arms to choreographers
and ushered the American musical theater into its golden age. As traditional
forms of dance became increasingly institutionalized, a new dance underground appeared. By the early 1960s, the lofts and church halls of Greenwich
Village had become the center of a revolution from whose throes postmodern
dance emerged. In no other city was dance as varied and diverse as in New York.

To some extent New York has always been a dance center. But from the 1940s
through the 1960s, it witnessed the growth of a vital dance community. This included not only dancers, teachers, and choreographers, but also critics like
Denby who laid the foundations for an American school of dance criticism, historians like Lincoln Kirstein who established the first of the city's dance archives
at the Museum of Modern Art, photographers, managers, publishers, book-
sellers, and editors—all of whom in their very different ways brought the art to

This essay was originally published in *New York: Culture Capital of the World, 1940–1965*, ed.
Leonard Wallock (New York: Rizzoli, 1988).

its public. And then there were the fans: Together they made up the world's biggest and motliest audience for dance.

The sheer growth of dance in New York in this twenty-five-year period is only part of the story. The transformation of New York into an international dance capital reflected a new aesthetic orientation, a redefining of what it meant for dance to be American. In 1940 this had been largely a matter of native themes, characters, and materials. By the 1950s, form rather than content defined "American" dance. Abstraction, evidenced above all in the work of George Balanchine and Merce Cunningham, triumphed and with it a set of values—dynamism, energy, speed, impersonality—that were attributes of the city itself. None of these elements were inventions of the time. But unlike the experiments of the European avant-garde of the 1910s and 1920s, they became the coin of an international style—exports of the newly cosmopolitan postwar city.

Modern Dance: From Politics to Myth

The 1930s was the heroic age of modern dance, and New York City the setting of the movement's epic. Here were the studios of the Big Four—Martha Graham, Doris Humphrey, Hanya Holm, and Charles Weidman—choreographers who, along with Helen Tamiris, left the deepest imprint on the new art. Here, too, were the performance venues—the Mecca Temple (since renamed City Center), the Guild Theatre, the New School, Washington Irving High School, and the 92nd Street Y—that saw the modern dance movement through its earliest years. Here, also, were the foundations, settlement houses, colleges, and presses that ensured its survival and gave it intellectual legitimacy.

As a major entertainment capital, New York was no stranger to dance. For nearly a century, visiting ballerinas and their pick-up troupes had set out from the city on cross-country tours, and Broadway's enterprising producers had "packaged" European extravaganzas like *The Black Crook* (1866) and *The White Faun* (1868) for the American market. The commercial theater, in fact, was the unlikely forcing ground of the "art dancers" who prepared the way for the modern dancers of the 1930s. Here, the matriarchs of modern dance—Loie Fuller, Isadora Duncan, and Ruth St. Denis—began their careers and gleaned some of their most important ideas. Unlike Europe, however, America entered the twentieth century without a tradition of high art. Dancers may have performed snippets of ballets created at the Paris Opéra or other bastions of institutionalized high culture, but they did so on popular stages for popular audiences. The art dancers who made their appearance around the turn of the century harbored a two-fold goal. On the one hand, they sought to create a distinctly American dance; on the other, a dance that ranked with music and literature as a high art. Although the commercial theater was the setting of their earliest endeavors, the ideology of those endeavors came from genteel movements for self-improvement—Delsarte, dress reform, diet, exercise, and back-to-nature cults—all uniquely American and with a strong feminist tinge. The combination of radical individualism and a pastoral vision of nature dominated American art dance into the 1920s.

As with painters, writers, and composers, many American dancers found Europe more congenial than their homeland. Loie Fuller and Isadora Duncan settled more or less permanently abroad, as did a host of less celebrated dancers. By the 1920s, along with the more famous literary expatriates, Paris was home to a large and varied "lost generation" of American dancers. Not everyone, however, succumbed to the allure of Europe. Ruth St. Denis, the most influential art dancer of the 1910s and 1920s, spent most of her performing years at home, touring, teaching, and converting upright citizens to the idea of an indigenous American dance. With her husband Ted Shawn, she founded the company and school known as Denishawn, through whose ranks passed Martha Graham, Doris Humphrey, Charles Weidman, and numerous other future modern dancers.

Denishawn dance, it has been said, was the most eclectic system imaginable. The basic technique was modified ballet in bare feet, the basic repertory a hodge-podge of styles from the Americas and the Far East. Exotica had long been standard popular fare. But St. Denis invested it with a mystical aura that spiritualized it. To audiences reared on the poems of Tagore, her nautches communed with the divine. Along with exotica, Denishawn purveyed a "free" style that derived from Isadora Duncan. Performed in "fleshlings," ancestors of the modern leotard, these music visualizations played on genteel, old-fashioned images of sensuous girlhood.

Although Denishawn survived until 1933, its vitality had long since been sapped by defections, as Graham and others abandoned it to investigate, as Humphrey later wrote, "movement [that] had to do with ourselves as Americans."[1] In its later years, Denishawn made its home in New York. Yet the city left no imprint on the company's brand of Americanism. This, to the end, embodied a republican vision of society—Anglo-Saxon, individualist, preindustrial.

For the Denishawn graduates who settled in Greenwich Village in the 1920s, a different reality presented itself: a city of immigrants, masses, and factories. From the first, the metropolis and the democratic ideology of its liberal intelligentsia became central to the identity of modern dance. Even before the inception of the "Red Decade," social concerns made their appearance in modern dance. Graham's *Revolt*, which premiered in 1927 (a year that witnessed huge rallies in Union Square to protest the execution of Sacco and Vanzetti), like her *Poems of 1917: Song Behind the Lines, Dance of Death*, and *Immigrant: Steerage, Strike* (both 1928), were early harbingers of a trend that would become dominant in the 1930s. These new concerns went hand-in-hand with a new kind of dance movement—spare, angular, percussive, self-consciously "difficult." "Like the modern painters and architects, we have stripped our medium of decorative unessentials,"[2] said Graham in 1930, underscoring the link between modern dance and avant-garde currents in the other arts. This New York marriage of left-wing content and vanguard form accounted for the creative vitality of 1930s modern dance and its passionate following among the city's intelligentsia.

Thanks to McCarthyism and its legacy, the impact of left-wing culture on modern dance remains an untold story. But even a quick summary of the decade's major trends suggests that few choreographers failed to respond to the era's social imperatives. In the case of Graham, Humphrey, and Hanya Holm, indictments of capitalism merged with a range of other concerns: puritanism in *Panorama* (Graham, 1935), possessive love in *New Dance Trilogy* (Humphrey, 1935–1936), timeless creative forces in *Trend* (Holm, 1937). Among the radicals associated with the Workers' Dance League (later renamed the New Dance Group), dance was a vehicle of social protest, a means of enfranchising workers as artists. Antifascism, unemployment, the Scottsboro case were favorite themes, and the league's many units took the message to union halls and workers' cultural centers from Brooklyn to the Bronx. Politically, the left-wing movement actively championed the rights of blacks. So, too, did works like Helen Tamiris' *How Long, Brethren?* (a 1937 production of the Federal Dance Theatre [FDT] that played to packed Broadway houses for forty-two performances) and, in a more practical way, the black dance units organized by the FDT, which had Humphrey, Tamiris, and Charles Weidman among its staff choreographers.

The many works on Spanish themes that followed the outbreak of the Spanish Civil War, like the growing number of pieces that celebrated American history and folkways, suggest that within the world of modern dance the Popular Front, announced by the Communist Party in 1936, did indeed realize its twofold goal of creating a broad antifascist coalition and making progressive ideas as American as apple pie. (Graham's 1938 *American Document*, for instance, wove together quotes from Lincoln's Gettysburg Address, the Declaration of Independence, and other significant documents with a score by Ray Green that was rich in American folk rhythms.) If colleges such as Bennington in Vermont, where modern dancers gathered every summer between 1934 and 1938, cemented links with genteel female culture and academe, New York's left-wing movement gave modern dance the broadest and most diverse public it would ever enjoy.

Already, by decade's end, that base was eroding. In 1939, the Federal Theatre (into which the Federal Dance Theatre had been absorbed) collapsed: a victim, like so many New Deal programs, of a political turn to the right. With the signing that year of the nonaggression pact between the Nazis and the Soviets, the Popular Front also collapsed. Both events severed modern dance from its popular audience. In 1940, moreover, New York witnessed its first McCarthy-style witch-hunt. Ending with the dismissal of alleged Communists teaching in the city's public colleges, the Rapp-Coudert hearings were a harbinger of the virulent anticommunism that accompanied the opening of the Cold War.

The country's entry into World War II also took its toll. Male dancers were called up, and with Bennington's administrator Mary Jo Shelley a WAVE lieutenant in Washington, D.C., the school that had tided the leading companies over the summer closed. The country at large had changed as well. The war put people back to work; prosperity was in the air, the Depression a memory. People wanted to be entertained. By the early 1940s, then, the institutional supports that had sustained modern dance were gone. Retreating to the studio, modern dance turned in on itself.

Nowhere was this tendency toward self-examination more evident than in the work of Martha Graham. Beginning with *Letter to the World* (1940), which explored the complex inner life of Emily Dickinson, and *Deaths and Entrances* (1943), a foray into the dark, troubled mind of Emily Bronte, introspection became the hallmark of Graham's work, a means of probing the intimate psychology of her heroines. Previously, her protagonists had been individuals who stood alone in society: the outsider in *Heretic* (1929), the virgin priestess of *Primitive Mysteries* (1931), the pioneer woman of *Frontier* (1935). Now society itself disappeared, and the wall of others, the masses who embodied fate, gave way to a dynamic of psychological necessity. Writing in 1961, composer Louis Horst, an artistic intimate and collaborator of Graham's for over twenty years, summed up the influence of "depth psychology" on her theater of the 1940s and 1950s: "Martha Graham's typical dramatic scene is laid within the mind or heart of a woman faced with an urgency of decision or action, and with the dramatis personae of the group performing as symbols of her complex emotional reactions."[3] The outer world had ceased to exist.

The two Emilys were but the first of the larger-than-life heroines brought to the stage in this second great period of Graham's career. Many had their origin in ancient myth—Medea (*Cave of the Heart*, 1946), Ariadne (*Errand into the Maze*, 1947), Jocasta (*Night Journey*, 1947), Clytemnestra (*Clytemnestra*, 1958), Phaedra (*Phaedra*, 1962); others—Herodias (*Herodiade*, 1944) and Judith (*Judith*, 1950; *Legend of Judith*, 1962)—in the Bible. From the lore of history came the quasi-mythical figures of Joan of Arc (*The Triumph of St. Joan*, 1951) and Mary Queen of Scots (*Episodes: Part I*, 1959). Artists throughout the ages have drawn inspiration from myth. But in America of the 1940s and 1950s myth seemed to fill an imaginative vacuum. In the void created by the abandonment of the socialist ideal, myth sated a need for universals, for all-encompassing explanations of the human condition.

The appearance of myth in Graham's work occurred at a critical moment in her life—the break-up (temporary, as it proved) of her liaison with dancer Erick Hawkins, her leading man since 1938, and her venture into analysis with Dr. Frances Wickes, a dedicated Jungian. Together, these explain her obsession with sexuality (which now became Graham's great theme) and with myth (now her generalizing ideology), the means of converting personal experience into universal truth. For whether Medea, Jocasta, or Judith is her subject, the works themselves almost always center on female desire, that complex phenomenon that in Graham's hands alternates between possession and submission to a powerful male. Her stage (decorated from 1944 to 1967 by sculptor Isamu Noguchi) seems a maze of sexual symbols—shafts, coils, horns, serpents, columns with protruding mounds and cylinders—among which her women seek the key to their archetypal dilemmas. Her men, forceful and sexually attractive, are equally archetypes: fathers in their power, sons in their dependence, lovers in their virility. Although Graham tells her stories from the heroine's point of view, the male fuels the drama, not because of his sensitivity—if anything, Graham's men are rough-hewn blocks of manhood—but because maleness itself, symbolized by the phallus, lies at the center of her driving obsessions. Like good Puritans, Graham's physically liberated heroines pay the price of carnal knowledge in guilt.

Although most evident in Graham's work, the displacement of social concerns by history, sex, psychology, and myth occurred in dances by many other choreographers, including those of more radical convictions. This new content did not appear overnight. Well into the 1940s, Spanish themes and American genre styles—both identified with the Popular Front—continued to inspire Doris Humphrey, Charles Weidman, Sophie Maslow, William Bales, Anna Sokolow, Jane Dudley, and José Limón. But works of overt political content became increasingly rare. (One of the last, Maslow's *Fragments of a Shattered Land* [1945], paid tribute to the struggle of Yugoslavia's partisans against the Nazis.) As the decade drew to an end on a wave of anti-Communist hysteria, social concerns, like the Communist Party itself, went underground. Neither disappeared, but just as progressive politics could only take expression indirectly, so in modern dance subterfuge became the order of the day. As critic Margaret Lloyd wrote in 1949, "the left wings [now] are all tucked out of sight."[4]

Humphrey's *Corybantic,* which premiered in 1948, was only one of several McCarthy-era works to mask politics—in this case, the disarray of the left in the wake of government witch-hunts—under a cover of allegory and myth. "The Bartok sonata that inspired *Corybantic,*" Humphrey's biographer Selma Jeanne Cohen has written, "suggested to [Humphrey] an expression of the conflict and drama of the time. An Aggressor threatens, but the Defender's group, disagreeing on how to meet the danger, panics and engulfs all in destruction. After lying apparently lifeless, they recover gradually. . . . Innocence brings tidings of peace and the group rejoices, but its celebration is excessive: 'the Defender guesses that peace will not be so simple.'"[5]

José Limón, a towering presence in postwar modern dance, was another choreographer who worked increasingly "under cover." Believing that the artist's function was to be the voice and conscience of his time, Limón created works that had their source in contemporary life, despite their historical and literary trappings. *The Traitor,* which he choreographed in 1954, took its subject from the Gospels: Judas' betrayal of Jesus. But like Arthur Miller's play *The Cru-*

cible (a chilling exposé of the Salem witch trials that was written in 1953), *The Traitor* was a veiled protest against McCarthyism, specifically the execution of Julius and Ethel Rosenberg. Pauline Koner's solo *Cassandra* (1953) had an equally political subtext. Alarmed by the activities of the era's various investigating committees (one of which called Jerome Robbins to testify that year), Koner created *Cassandra* as an indictment of right-wing hysteria.

The Cold War did not eliminate politics from modern dance. But it forced choreographers to bury their convictions in politically innocent narratives, stories only remotely connected to their underlying theme. In many instances, a curtain of incomprehensibility seemed to keep the public at bay, as if meaning itself, no matter how indirect or subtle its expression, had become suspect. Humphrey's *Night Spell* (1951) centered on a noble dream figure, tormented by nightmare visions of some vague and menacing terror, while in *Ruins and Visions*, which she choreographed two years later, reality and illusion, good and evil, innocence and guilt seemed to have lost their very identities.

Anna Sokolow, a "people's choreographer" of the 1930s, was another who turned to the darker side of the psyche in the 1950s: despair, loneliness, sexual repression, alienation. "Her dances," critic Marcia Siegel has written, "are overwhelmingly depressed, dark, alienated, sometimes violent, angry, and unresolved."[6] In *Rooms* (choreographed in 1955), Sokolow explored the private hell of eight men and women, creatures adrift, restless with pent-up energy, locked in rooms of the mind as isolated from the hum of life as the characters of a Sartre play. The optimism of the 1930s had given way to an anguished, brooding pessimism.

The emotional tension that animated the best Cold War works derived from the presence of a social subtext, a carryover, however generalized and transmogrified, from the 1930s. With time, however, the social impulse weakened. By the late 1950s, McCarthyism had destroyed the left-wing movement, depriving older choreographers of its continued sustenance and younger ones of its idealism. From an act of rebellion, modern dance had become an art of canonical forms—turgid psychological dramas, oracular pseudo-myths—and increasingly restricted content.

Such academicism was also related to another postwar phenomenon: the institutionalization of modern dance in colleges and universities. These had always supported modern dance, but with the demise of the left-wing movement, they became a crucial source of subsidy, providing teaching jobs, performance venues, and a ready supply of dancers—to say nothing of social respectability. The Juilliard School of Music (which set up a dance department in 1952), Sarah Lawrence College, Barnard College, New York University, and Connecticut College for Women (home to the American Dance Festival beginning in 1948) helped modern dance survive the Cold War. But this help had a price. Thanks to academe, modern dance grew increasingly isolated, all but ignoring the new trends emanating from New York's downtown avant-garde. By 1960, the once vital art of modern dance had become a historical relic, living, like an aging dowager, off memories of a glorious, increasingly remote past.

Ballet: From Americana to Abstraction

While the history of modern dance between 1940 and 1960 was one of gradual decline, ballet enjoyed extraordinary growth. In fact, in the twenty-five-year period that opened in 1940, New York City witnessed a minor miracle—the creation of two major ballet companies that transformed classical dancing in the city and in America at large. Ballet was no stranger to the city. As the country's theatrical port of entry, New York had welcomed foreign stars and foreign attractions for over a century, launching both on tours that went north and south, and as far west as California. Not all the visitors returned to Europe. Some, like Maria Bonfanti and Elizabetta Menzelli, stayed on in New York, opening studios that trained dancers for the commercial stage and, after the founding of the Metropolitan Opera in 1883, for the city's first resident classical company. Ballet in turn-of-the-century New York was an Italian affair. The teachers, like most of the stars imported by the Met, were Italian-born and trained, and the technique they imparted followed the canons laid down in the first half of the nineteenth century by Carlo Blasis, the great Milanese pedagogue. The Italian style, as elaborated by graduates of the academy at La Scala, emphasized virtuosity: precision in the feet, strength in the toes, speed, dynamic attack—all anathema to the first generation of art dancers.

The 1910s witnessed a surge of interest in ballet, as Russian dancers, led by Anna Pavlova and Mikhail Mordkin, brought the latest vogue in European ballet to New York. Most of the newcomers were graduates of Serge Diaghilev's Ballets Russes, the famous troupe that between 1909 and 1929 revolutionized ballet, making it more expressive and more attuned to movements in the other arts. New companies were formed, and although (with the exception of Pavlova's) most were short-lived, they sent a generation of youngsters to the barre. By 1916–1917, when Diaghilev's company paid its second visit to the United States, Russians had become important figures in the New York dance world. In the aftermath of the Bolshevik Revolution, this Russian community grew. Michel Fokine, the celebrated Diaghilev choreographer who settled in the city in 1919, and Mikhail Mordkin, a choreographer of secondary importance who arrived in 1924, were the most important of these newcomers. From their studios emerged dancers of professional caliber and a passing familiarity with the styles put into currency by Diaghilev. From the Mordkin Ballet, moreover, came the nucleus of the company that in 1940 made its debut as Ballet Theatre.

To most Americans of the 1930s, ballet was a foreign, hothouse art. Its best practitioners were Russian, its natural habitat privileged. The arrival in New

York in 1933 of the Colonel de Basil Ballet Russe, a successor to the Diaghilev company, did nothing to dispel either prejudice. Glamorously "packaged" by impresario Sol Hurok, the company stormed the city with a repertory of Diaghilev standards, a roster of Russian—or renamed Russian—stars, and an array of wealthy sponsors. For American dancers, some of whom found jobs with the company, the success of the Ballet Russe was a mixed blessing. Popularizing ballet, it dashed hopes for a native, self-sustaining art.

What that art was to be was an open question, one that remained unresolved until the 1950s. Did it mean a distinctive national repertory? Or an organization made up exclusively of American dancers? Or a style of movement peculiar to and expressive of the American character and temperament?

Among those who tried to find an answer to these questions was Lincoln Kirstein, the dilettante son of a wealthy department store family. An impassioned balletomane, avid collector, and sometime novelist, poet, editor, historian, and critic, Kirstein was only twenty-six when he invited Russian-born George Balanchine, Diaghilev's last in-house choreographer, to come to the United States and found an American ballet. The year was 1933—hardly an auspicious time. Not only was the country sunk in the Depression, but modern dance had taken hold of the intellectual imagination. Nor did Kirstein have any very clear idea of his goal or any real plan for making it a reality. As for Balanchine, a modernist formed in Petrograd and Paris, to his way of thinking art knew no boundaries. If anything, both men were out of step with the times. The American Ballet, the first of several companies created by this unlikely duo, seemed calculated to offend the progressive-minded intelligentsia. With the backing of Warburgs and Rockefellers and a repertory attuned to the neo-romantic, transcendentalist strain of conservative Paris art circles, the company was the antithesis of the social and artistic values embodied in native modern dance. When, in 1935, the American Ballet became the Metropolitan Opera's resident ballet company, the image of privilege and Parisian preciousness was reinforced.

Far more important to the immediate future of American ballet was a chamber troupe formed by Kirstein in 1936. (Balanchine, dividing his time between the Met and Broadway, was not involved.) Ballet Caravan, Kirstein later wrote, was "a pilot experiment." "Primarily it attempted to produce a new repertory by native choreographers, musicians, and designers working with national themes. . . . I hoped to summon out of the air an 'American' style from something in our atmosphere—literary, musical, theatrical. Films, vaudeville, musical comedy, the popular arts in painting and sculpture—all could serve."[7] In 1936, Americana was very much in the air, especially in left-wing circles. Kirstein was no stranger to these circles. As director (briefly) of the New York Project of the Federal Dance Theatre, as a critic for the liberal weekly *The Nation,* and as a contributor to the radical journal *New Theatre,* he was in the thick of things. With Ballet Caravan, Kirstein allied classical dancing with the populist ideology of the Popular Front. The result, akin to the celebration of American history and folkways by the era's modern dancers, became known as "Americana ballet."

Under Kirstein's unlikely aegis, American subject matter became the meat and potatoes of ballet. There were works about Indians (*Pocohontas*), gas station attendants (*Filling Station*), cowboys (*Billy the Kid*), and sailors (*Yankee Clipper*). Kirstein, in the guise now of an American Diaghilev, let his imagination roam over a catholic range of American classics. One of his unrealized schemes was *Uncle Tom's Cabin*. Others included *Br'er Rabbit*, Herman Melville's *Confidence Man*, Henry James' *Turn of the Screw*, and F. Scott Fitzgerald's story, "The Diamond as Big as the Ritz." Kirstein was not the first to adapt American lore to the ballet stage. Adolph Bolm's *Krazy Kat*, inspired by the George Herriman comic strip, had done so as early as 1922. But Kirstein's goal, unlike earlier efforts, was to emphasize the poetry of the vulgus; like Jean Cocteau, a power in Diaghilev's postwar "cabinet," Kirstein sought to "gentrify" the commonplace. Through Ballet Caravan important American artists received their first dance commissions. Many of these collaborators had spent time in Europe; and their work, a marriage of the American vernacular with Parisian modernist trends, displayed a sophistication more attuned to "uptown Bohemia" (a term coined by historian Thomas Bender) than to the radical intelligentsia. Kirstein's populism had a definitely elitist edge.

Nevertheless, Americana ballet became the rallying cry of the period's ballet radicals. Ballet Caravan collapsed in 1940. But with the birth of Ballet Theatre that year, the genre style pioneered by Kirstein developed into a genuinely American, populist form. Ballet Theatre was a choreographers' company, an alliance of diverse talents unique in its time. There were four wings—classical, Russian, English, and American—roughly corresponding to the era's major "schools," and despite shifts in emphasis (while the company was under the management of Sol Hurok, Russian influence was ascendant), the divisions remained intact during Ballet Theatre's first decade.

From the start, Ballet Theatre actively promoted American performing and choreographic talent. Initially, Agnes de Mille, a dancer with one foot in the modern dance camp, and Eugene Loring, a Ballet Caravan veteran, dominated the native wing. For the company's short-lived "Negro Unit," modeled on similar Federal Theatre Project groups, de Mille created *Black Ritual* (1940), while Loring revived *Billy the Kid* (also in 1940) and, in collaboration with William Saroyan, the hero of the Broadway intelligentsia, produced *The Great American Goof* (1940), a mixed-media satire. In 1942, de Mille went to the Ballet Russe de Monte Carlo (for which she staged *Rodeo*), and Loring left to found Dance Players, a chamber ensemble. These losses were offset by the appearance of fresh choreographic talent within the company—Michael Kidd, who created his first ballet, *On Stage!*, in 1945, and Jerome Robbins, who in 1944 gave Americana ballet its definitive form. "*Fancy Free* was a smash hit," wrote Edwin Denby in his

Herald Tribune notice of the premiere, as well as "a very remarkable comedy piece. Its sentiment of how people live in this country is completely intelligent and completely realistic. Its pantomime and its dances are witty, exuberant, and at every moment they feel natural. It is a direct, manly piece: there isn't any of that coy showing off of 'folk' material that dancers are doing so much nowadays. The whole number is as sound as a superb vaudeville turn; in ballet terminology it is perfect American character ballet."[8]

Ballet Theatre and Hurok parted company in 1945, leaving the field open to Americans. But the American ballets that now appeared differed markedly from their predecessors. No longer a celebration of native folkways, American ballet of the postwar period, like modern dance, exchanged its preoccupations with society for the psyche, with life in general for individual experience in particular. Jerome Robbins' *Facsimile* (choreographed in 1946) was inspired by an observation of Santiago Ramón y Cajol: "Small inward treasure does he possess who, to feel alive, needs every hour the tumult of the street, the emotion of the theater, and the small talk of society."[9] The original cast called for four principals—A Woman, A Man, Another Man, and a Third Man—and a corps of eighteen Integrated People. By the time this nineteen-minute ballet reached the stage (after no fewer than 138 hours of rehearsal), the corps had been eliminated along with the Third Man. The result was a knotty, introspective work: rife with suggestions of sadomasochism, misogyny, and homosexuality, Robbins' ménage à trois was a brooding exploration of contemporary sexual obsessions. Agnes de Mille's *Fall River Legend,* choreographed two years later, also had a psychosexual theme, even though the setting was thoroughly American and traditional. The gruesome story was inspired by the nineteenth-century murder case summarized in a popular ditty: "Lizzie Borden took an ax/ And gave her mother forty whacks/ When she saw what she had done/ She gave her father forty-one." In de Mille's hands, the tale became an indictment of the repressive Puritan family: her Lizzie does what Freud's patients only dream of doing.

The shift of emphasis in the treatment of American material by Ballet Theatre choreographers partly reflected the influence of Antony Tudor, the English choreographer associated with the company from 1940 until his death in 1987. Tudor's earliest ballets, created before he emigrated to the United States, had explored the nuances of social relationships. Once in America, however, Tudor recast the theme in psychosexual terms. In *Pillar of Fire,* created for Ballet Theatre in 1942, a young woman's sexual encounter with a libertine became the stuff of Puritan tragedy. The association of guilt, desire, and repression reappeared in *Undertow* (1945), where a young man, terrified by heterosexual passion, strangled a girl who made advances to him.

If Tudor prepared the ground, other factors contributed to the transformation of American genre ballet: the burgeoning interest in psychoanalysis, the feeling that art should be serious, and the final demise of Popular Front ideology with the opening of the Cold War. Born in the socialist 1930s, Americana ballet ended in the postwar Age of Anxiety—the title, in fact, of a work choreographed by Robbins in 1949.

In the 1950s, Ballet Theatre ceased to be a New York company. Not only did its seasons in the city grow progressively shorter, but increasingly the company came to regard itself as a national entity—an image enhanced by its many foreign tours conducted under the auspices of the U.S. State Department.

Meanwhile, in Gotham, a new enterprise had appeared. Lincoln Kirstein had spent World War II hunting down paintings confiscated by the Nazis. Balanchine, for his part, divided his time between the concert and the musical stage. In 1941, just before America entered the war, he created *Ballet Imperial* and *Concerto Barocco,* two of his most enduring works, for American Ballet Caravan, which toured South America under government auspices. (Nelson A. Rockefeller, Coordinator of Inter-American Affairs and an old friend of Kirstein's, arranged the tour.) Back in New York, Balanchine freelanced for the New Opera Company, Ballet Russe de Monte Carlo, American Concert Ballet, Ballet Theatre, and Ballet International, while also choreographing nearly half a dozen Broadway shows. With Kirstein's release from the army, the two teamed up again to form Ballet Society.

Organized on a subscription basis, the new enterprise was dedicated to the production of new works. Ballet Society gave its first performance at the Central High School of Needle Trades in November 1946. Like the Hunter College Playhouse, another early venue, Central High was a well-known modern dance center, home of the popular Students' Dance Recitals series directed by Joseph Mann. Later Ballet Society performances took place at an equally populist venue, the New York City Center of Music and Drama, founded in the early 1940s to bring high art, at low prices, to the city's working people. If these settings linked Kirstein's venture with modern dance audiences, other Ballet Society activities, including film screenings and exhibitions at the Museum of Modern Art and productions of chamber operas, harked back to Diaghilev's marriage of modernism and "high Bohemia." This certainly added cachet to the fledgling enterprise. But it was only when Morton Baum, City Center's managing director, invited Kirstein to form a resident company analogous to the New York City Opera that the future of Ballet Society was assured. In 1948, under City Center's "protective custody" (the phrase is Kirstein's), it became the New York City Ballet.

Ballet Society opened a new era in Balanchine's career, one that many believe to be his greatest. With a permanent company at his disposal, hardly a year went by that he did not create at least one major work. Balanchine had always been a master of styles; but in the period of stability that followed the move to City Center, the range of his production was astounding. In the 1920s, he had made a name for himself as a modernist; in the 1930s, as a neoromantic. Now, in the 1940s and 1950s, two new styles came to the fore. The first of these, which may be termed "neo-imperial," distilled the legacy of the Russian Imperial Ballet, at whose school in St. Petersburg he had studied as a child. The second—his so-called "leotard ballets"—represented an encounter with postwar America.

Balanchine always insisted that dance was an art of the present. But in his neo-imperial ballets, he created works haunted by the past, by the memory of a golden, vanished world. Not all these ballets had their source in Russian works. Some, like *Gounod Symphony* (1958) and *Donizetti Variations* (1960), invoked traditions of nineteenth-century French and Italian ballet. Others, including *Symphonie Concertante* (1947) and *Divertimento No. 15* (1956), both to music by Mozart, celebrated the civility and classical deportment associated with eighteenth-century art. But Balanchine's greatest works of the genre—*Ballet Imperial* (1941), *Theme and Variations* (1947), both to music by Tchaikovsky, and *Symphony in C* (1948), to music by Bizet—were tributes to the Russian past, meditations on the Tchaikovsky masterpieces that marked the zenith of imperial classicism.

Other companies had staged *Swan Lake* and *The Sleeping Beauty*. But they had done so with historicist fidelity, intent on reproducing a canonical original. Balanchine, always an iconoclast, created these works anew, extracting their poetry, distilling their essence in a way that acknowledged the revolution of modernism. Through his memory, we rediscover the ordered symmetries of Marius Petipa's hierarchical heavenly city, his formalized poems of love, his virtuoso combinations of steps. But where, in Petipa, these elements always appeared within the context of a story, in Balanchine, they stood naked, as pure dance, shorn of inessentials. Not that Balanchine spurned meaning, even if he did away with narrative. Rather, like the painters who first made the transition to abstraction, he fused content with the very form of these ballets. In art, as in life, Balanchine had no use for nostalgia. He desentimentalized the past, viewing it through a prism of indifference. In this sense, the speed, clarity, and complex spatial evolutions that are touchstones of his style code his paradise of the ideal as one from which he is forever banished. Such distancing belongs fully to the twentieth century. So, too, does the manner in which emotion is expressed—as contained in Balanchine as in T. S. Eliot or Piet Mondrian. Balanchine's great adagios are full of feeling. But no matter how romantic, they are bereft of sentimentality: the ideal love they portray exists only in the imagination. Here, the very discipline of form conveys the tragic sense of loss of a romantic manqué.

If Balanchine's neo-imperial ballets celebrated the power of memory, his "leotard" works—so-called because of the practice dress worn by the dancers—were rooted in the postwar present. *The Four Temperaments* (created in 1946 to music by Paul Hindemith) invented the genre. Like *Facsimile* and Graham's mythic epics, the ballet unfolded in a landscape of anxiety—stark, anguished, and sexually charged. Initially, there were both scenery and costumes, fanciful creations by Kurt Seligmann, who "swathed" the dancers, as Kirstein wrote, "in cerements, bandages, tubes, wraps, and tourniquets."[10] Each season, scissors in hand, Balanchine snipped away at the decorative appendages, until, by 1951, with the scenery gone and the dancers dressed in leotards, he had bared the very bones of his choreography. This seemed modern in a new way. Although based on the *danse d'école*, the choreography extended this traditional language with angular, percussive movements—pelvic thrusts, flexed feet, parallel positions—that recalled modern dance at its most uncompromising. Balanchine used rhythms that were jagged and complex, and in the splayed legs, sky-high extensions, and convoluted limbs of his women, he exposed the female body provocatively. From the start of his career, Balanchine had shown his inventiveness in partnering. But in these "leotard" ballets he surpassed himself, inventing supports as daring as they were physically taxing, that charted new psychological territory.

In *The Four Temperaments*, as in *Agon* (1957) and *Episodes* (1959), the greatest works of the cycle, Balanchine's theme was sex. In a broad sense this was the subject of all his ballets. (As he once said, "duet is a love story, almost.") But in the "leotard" works he gave the theme a postwar, New York twist. Like Robbins, but with infinitely greater penetration, Balanchine laid bare the anguish of sexual relationships and the ambiguity of sexual identity. With their chance encounters, mechanical pleasures, calculated seductions, and abrupt departures, his matings belong to the lore of the city. His couples cleave to each other as much from loneliness as from irrepressible attraction, cataloging in their sophisticated love games the obsessions of an era fascinated with sex and with the neurotic consequences of its repression.

In most Balanchine ballets, men play second fiddle to women. In the "leotard" cycle, however, men are often the central focus, heroes of a drama that turns on beleaguered male sexuality—Pierrot crucified on the altar of Columbine. The theme is an old one. But in Balanchine's hands, it acquires something akin to a Freudian dimension. In both *Episodes* and *The Four Temperaments* there is a moment that pits an anguished youth against a battery of female viragos. Escape is vain: their limbs trap him in a space as close as the vagina dentata. This image, appropriate to an era that made Momism a household word, suggests an ambiguity in Balanchine's attitude toward women that rarely found overt expression. In fact, one can see these ballets, along with *Agon,* as a kind of collective therapy, a "working through" of male sexual anxieties of the period. Significantly, all three works end on a note of heterosexual affirmation, a celebration of newfound harmony. In *Episodes,* the last of the series, a man and a woman face the audience holding hands, as if plighting their troth before God.

Sex and the "psychologizing" of experience were not unique to Balanchine. They emerged on the New York concert stage to fill the void once occupied by the populist styles associated with the 1930s. Balanchine's "leotard" ballets, like his neo-imperial works, were completely plotless, their meaning embedded in images as private as the keys of a secret code. As early as the late 1920s, he had toyed with abstraction. But only in the Cold War years did this become the major aesthetic thrust of his work, as if, like Robbins and the moderns, Balanchine, too, had taken refuge in the recondite.

This is not to suggest that Balanchine was a closet leftist. Far from it: No one was more patriotically American than this early Soviet "defector." But he was always attuned to the contemporary, and in the "leotard" ballets he conveyed the uncertainty and quiet anguish that clouded the artistic and intellectual atmosphere of postwar New York. After 1960, Balanchine returned to the "leotard" style only rarely. "Twelve-tone nights," at which the company's intellectual following regularly gathered, became a thing of the past. Some have attributed the shift in repertory direction to the presence in Balanchine's life of a new muse—ballerina Suzanne Farrell. But her appearance in the company, however inspiring to the choreographer, also coincided with a profound change in the city's cultural climate. With the new decade, the Cold War and its McCarthy-style committees came to an end. Youth was in the air; a young couple in the White House: New York breathed optimism and possibility.

By 1960, moreover, abstraction itself had lost its subversive intent. Canonized and copied, abstraction had become the American standard, the style par excellence of the disciples who took the Balanchine gospel to the country at large. In little more than two decades, American ballet had acquired a new and unique identity. No longer a celebration of indigenous experience, American ballet had become a sophisticated reflection of the metropolis that had nourished it.

The New Avant-Garde

By the late 1950s, modern dance and ballet had joined the Establishment. Not the same Establishment: Ballet's "home" was New York's cultivated middle class rather than academe. The effect, however, was the same. Balanchine's choreographic vitality notwithstanding, ballet, no less than modern dance, had severed itself from the avant-garde. Indeed, the very growth of ballet as an institution, reflected in the increased size of existing companies and the proliferation of regional ones, seemed to preclude experiment, to isolate the choreographer from new trends. In the 1950s, when the "old" modern dance, as critic Jill Johnston has put it, "was really beginning to look its age,"[11] a "new" modern dance emerged from the experimentalist ferment of New York's "downtown." For the most part the Establishment simply ignored what was happening. Concerts went unnoticed in the press, and only a few of the new choreographers received invitations to appear at prestigious modern dance festivals and venues. Laboring in isolation from the dance world, the rebels made common cause with the decade's avant-garde. Here, among the painters and composers of the city's downtown community, they found ideas, collaborators, and a public for their work.

Who were these new choreographers of the 1950s? Many of the names—James Waring, Katherine Litz, Merle Marsicano, Midi Garth, Aileen Passloff, Anna Halprin—are familiar only to cognoscenti. Three, however, are today celebrated internationally: Merce Cunningham, Alwin Nikolais, and Paul Taylor. Although all three began their careers under the wing of members of the Big Four—Nikolais with Hanya Holm, Cunningham and Taylor with Martha Graham—each recoiled from the narrative and Freudian-saturated dances that comprised much of modern dance in its decline. In various ways they insisted upon the importance of dance as an end in itself, an exploration of the sheer physical and personal act of moving, free of psychology, narrative, and linear development. It is easy to see the drama played out by these choreographers as an Oedipal one. It is tempting, too, to read it teleologically, or at least as the outcome of historical necessity; to a large extent, formalism remains the highest critical good in dance. But the embracing of abstraction by the 1950s avantgarde had a broader significance. Like the New York school of painters who were their contemporaries, dance artists found in abstraction a means of challenging prevailing American values without breaching the limits of acceptable political expression.

Of the choreographers who came of age in the 1950s, Merce Cunningham best exemplified this apolitical attitude. From the first, his solos went against the tide, shocking audiences used to stories and conventional musical accompaniments. Gradually, as his dances grew more complex, they came to represent a host of cultural alternatives: choice, as opposed to coercion; egalitarianism, as opposed to hierarchy; diffidence, as opposed to self-promotion; sharing, as opposed to competition; freedom, as opposed to conformity. "We represent anarchy so to speak," he told interviewer Jacqueline Lesschaeve, "a kind of individual behavior in relation to yourself doing what you do and allowing the other person to do whatever he does."[12]

The "we" refers to the larger Cunningham collective: the company of dancers that first came together in 1953 and its numerous musical and artistic collaborators. Above all, it refers to John Cage, the composer who became Cunningham's close associate in the 1940s and the guru who presided over his subsequent career. As anarchists, both rejected conventional politics. But in the company they jointly nourished, they created an ideal society that recalled the Utopian communities of an earlier America. Other institutions of the period served a similar cooperative ideal—Black Mountain College in North Carolina, where Cunningham, Cage, and several of their collaborators, including painter Robert Rauschenberg and composer David Tudor, spent long periods in the late 1940s and early 1950s; and the Living Theatre, which shared a building with the Cunningham company from 1959 to 1965. Both organizations had their share of radicals. And, like the Cunningham company, both championed forms of art that explicitly denied Establishment values. Conceived in the broadest sense,

Martha Graham in *Lamentation*. Photo by Soichi Sunami. Jerome Robbins Dance Division, The New York Public Library for the Performing Arts, Astor, Lenox and Tilden Foundations.

Cover of Anatole Chujoy's "Russian Balletomania," with a caricature by Nicolas Legat of the Russian dance writer Valerian Svetlov. *Dance Index,* 7, no. 3 (March 1948).

"The Good Fairy Bakst Leads Prince Charming Diaghileff to the Shrine of the Sleeping Princess," caricature by Edmond Dulac. *The Sketch*, 28 December 1921.

New York City Ballet souvenir program, 1958–1959.

José Limón in *The Moor's Pavane*, 1969. Photo by Daniel Lewis. Courtesy of José Limón Dance Foundation.

Pearl Primus in *Folk Dance*, 1945. Photo by Gerda Peterich. Courtesy of Jacob's Pillow Dance Festival.

Jerome Robbins and Maria Tallchief in *Prodigal Son*, 1950. Choreography by George Balanchine © The George Balanchine Trust. Photograph by George Platt Lynes. Jerome Robbins Dance Division, The New York Public Library for the Performing Arts, Astor, Lenox and Tilden Foundations.

Tanaquil Le Clercq in "*Ballade*," 1952. Courtesy of New York City Ballet Archives, Tanaquil Le Clercq Collection.

Alvin Ailey. Photo by Normand Maxon. Jerome Robbins Dance Division, The New York Public Library for the Performing Arts, Astor, Lenox and Tilden Foundations.

Suzanne Farrell and Arthur Mitchell in *Agon*, 1965. Choreography by George Balanchine © The George Balanchine Trust. Photo by Anthony Crickmay. Theatre Museum, London. V&A Picture Library.

Merrill Ashley in *Ballo della Regina*, 1978. Choreography by George Balanchine
© The George Balanchine Trust. Photo by Paul Kolnik.

Deanna McBrearty as Geoffrey Beene's Dance '93 cover girl. Photo by Andrew Eccles.

anarchism left its mark on almost every aspect of the Cunningham-Cage aesthetic: the use of time and space, the collaborative process, compositional methods—to say nothing of the social relations that supported them. Philosophically, Cunningham's work has a unity rarely found in dance.

The Merce Cunningham Dance Company stood at the crossroads of the New York school of painting and the "New York school" of music. From both came the company's major collaborators and most assiduous fans—painters like Rauschenberg, Jasper Johns, and Frank Stella; composers like Earle Brown, Christian Wolff, Morton Feldman; and, of course, Cage himself—as well as key artistic ideas. One of these was the concept of the "open field," which, as used by the Abstract Expressionists, meant that every part of the canvas existed as a potential action site: no single point was privileged. Cunningham made this notion central to his aesthetic. In his works, there is no center stage, no one spot to which the eye is coaxed, no exclusive sanctuary of soloist and star. Events take place simultaneously, and the dancers are often free to choose where they will move. "By choice," James Klosty has written, "Cunningham decentralized stage space, . . . transforming central focus into field perspective."[13]

This break with traditional spatial hierarchies had several implications. For the dancer, it meant equality; for the spectator, the freedom to choose his own experience of a dance; for the choreographer, independence from the constraints of the proscenium stage. Cunningham sought to liberate movement from the constraints of time as well as space. Traditionally, the duration of a dance was determined by its music. If the music lasted ten minutes, so did the dance. In the 1950s, Cunningham ceased to work with preexisting scores. Instead, under Cage's tutelage, he created arbitrary time structures for his dances. These structures—so many parts, so many minutes in each part—became the sole link between the dance and the music, each of which was then created independently. (Often, the first time they "met" was in performance.) Scenic adjuncts were prepared the same way.

Cunningham's "non-collaborative collaborations," as they have been called, were thus radically different from traditional collaborative ventures, in which the music supported the dance, and the décor framed it: all three derived from, and emphasized, a central idea. In a Cunningham work, the only logic was simultaneity. "What we have done," he has said, "is to bring together three separate elements in time and space . . . allowing each one to remain independent."[14] This unorthodox method of assemblage implied that each of the elements was equal. Similarly, the relationship among the collaborators was one of equality: at no point did any single voice dominate. To Cunningham simultaneity reflected a vision of life—not life in the abstract, but the bustling and busy life of the modern metropolis. "Life," he explained to historian Martin Duberman, "is all these separate things going on at the same time. And contemporary society is so extraordinarily complex that way. Not only things going on right around you, but there are all the things you hear instantly over the television, that are going on someplace else . . . that idea of separateness, of things happening even though they are separate, they're happening at the same time."[15] Despite the attractiveness of the theory, the elements did not always gel. Cage's music—especially in the 1960s, when he amplified his electronic scores to ear-splitting levels—often outraged audiences, detracting from their appreciation of the choreography. His score for *Aeon* (1962) "ran its fingers over our eardrums," wrote critic Doris Hering."[16] Less disturbing, but equally baffling, were Rauschenberg's scenic effects for the piece—magnesium flares and flashing stroboscopic lights. However admirable the idea, non-collaborative collaborations had their practical limits.

Cunningham's innovations, like Cage's, ultimately turned on the elimination of hierarchies of power from the artistic process. The use of chance procedures as a major compositional tool illustrates this in another way. For Cage, chance was a means of disarming the individual will; for Cunningham, who made his first dance with chance methods (*Suite by Chance*) in 1953, it was a way of discovering possibilities beyond his conscious reach. Tossing coins to assemble his materials, Cunningham drew up elaborate charts—for body parts, timing, placement, sequences of movement, the number of dancers, the order of a dance's various sections. If the basic movement was devised by conventional means, chance procedures of some kind almost always figured in the overall assemblage. Chance was one aspect of Cunningham's concern with "open form." The term had its source in music, and referred to compositional methods that allowed for spontaneous choices by the instrumentalist in performance. In many Cunningham works, but above all in his "Events"—evening-long performances of material culled from the entire repertory—the dancers chose the order and direction of individual movements; what material to perform, and where and with whom to perform it. Almost always, these choices were made spontaneously. "Open form" challenged the privileged role of the choreographer: the creation of a dance became a shared act, a collective activity in which the choreographer was merely the first among equals. At the same time, "open form" made it possible to adapt existing choreography to non-traditional spaces—the gymnasiums, galleries, museums, and outdoor venues where, beginning in the 1960s, the company increasingly performed.

If a politic of democratization animated almost every aspect of Cunningham's work, Cage's theoretical elaboration of that politic reflected the influence of Zen Buddhism. This, of course, found a ready hearing among disaffected artists of the late 1940s and 1950s. Like Freudianism and Jungian mythology, Zen helped fill the ideological void created by the decline of Marxism. Cage had studied with D. T. Suzuki, and at Black Mountain College he gave a complete reading of Huang Po's Doctrine of Universal Mind. In one of his conversations on Zen, recorded by the future writer Francine du Plessix Gray, Cage suggests to what extent Eastern thought justified both outward acceptance and inner resistance to the political status quo:

> In Zen Buddhism nothing is either good or bad. Or ugly or beautiful. The actions
> of man in nature are an undifferentiated and unhierarchical complex of events,
> which hold equal indifference to the ultimate factor of oneness. No value judg-
> ments are possible because nothing is better than anything else. Art should not be
> different than life but an act within life. Like all life, with its accidents and chances
> and variety and disorder and only momentary beauties. Only different from life
> in this sense: that in life appreciation is passive like listening to a sound complex
> of bird, waterfall and engine, whereas in art it must be a voluntary act on the part
> of the creator and of the listener.[17]

Zen, one suspects, justified many elements of Cunningham's work, from the use of chance to the disavowal of hierarchy, and the personal diffidence that characterized his relationships with collaborators. More important, it gave his dances an inner, meditative stillness. Rather than action, his works convey that sense of being to which, in Eastern thought, all matter aspires. Full of quiet events, they present life unwilled—relationships and encounters without drama, forethought, or consequence. Cunningham's dances provide a momentary glimpse of an ideal spiritual polity.

More than any other choreographer of the period, Cunningham was obsessed with movement for its own sake. Like most choreographers, he taught. He disliked it, but only by daily work in the studio could he get his dancers to move as he wanted. Gradually, a technique took shape, one that drew on the twin pillars of his own training—modern dance and ballet. From the first came the flexible, articulate torso and strong back that distinguished his dancers. But far more important to his technique was ballet. Above all, Cunningham style reflected the influence of Balanchine, at whose School of American Ballet Cunningham had studied and taught in the 1940s and early 1950s.

Traditional modern dance emphasized the upper body. Ballet, and Balanchine in particular, stressed the use of the legs. So, too, did Cunningham: the legs he liked moved as elegantly and expansively as classical ones. They also moved with precision. Like Balanchine, Cunningham strove for clarity: each movement had to be given its full value, its own unique meaning. Both insisted upon energy; they saw dancing not as a sequence of poses, but as continuous, energy-charged motion. And both inculcated in their dancers a sense of rhythmic variety and subtlety. Like Balanchine in the 1940s, Cunningham in the 1950s looked for openness in the body and a certain naturalness of presentation; he wanted dancers who were individuals, who revealed their personalities, not by facial expression, but by the way they moved. Still another Balanchine influence was discernible in Cunningham's partnering, above all in the "chasteness" with which Cunningham routinely presented his women. Today, techniques associated with ballet make regular appearances on the avant-garde stage. This "cross-fertilization" began early in Cunningham's career. Indeed, *Septet* (1953) is full of references to *Apollo,* one of Balanchine's greatest ballets, revived by the choreographer at various times in the 1940s. In *Septet* one also finds the slow, magnificently classical extensions that remain a central feature of Cunningham's choreography. There is more than a touch of irony in the appropriation of ballet by the exponent par excellence of radical nonconformism.

Although Cunningham did on occasion employ everyday movement, he remained firmly committed to skill—only the finest dancers could perform his work. This was not the case of his "children," the so-called Judson choreographers of the 1960s. With this new generation, the first to be known as postmodern, elitism in all its guises came under attack. Radicals of a new kind, Judson dancers belonged to the first generation of artists unburdened by the legacy of the 1930s.

The group took its name from the Judson Memorial Church, a liberal Protestant congregation on Washington Square that had long been active in reform politics and civil rights. In the late 1950s and early 1960s, the church became a thriving arts center, as progressive as the Greenwich Village community it served. There were plays, poetry readings, film screenings, exhibitions of Pop art, Happenings, and beginning in 1962, the series of concerts that put postmodern dance on the map. The choreographers were young and nearly all unknown. Yet in the dozen programs presented by the Judson Dance Theater between that year and 1964, most of today's "avant-garde Establishment"—Yvonne Rainer, Trisha Brown, Lucinda Childs, David Gordon, Steve Paxton, Meredith Monk—got its start.

"The Judson aesthetic," to quote critic Sally Banes, "was never monolithic."[18] Diversity was the keynote. "Do your own thing," that popular 1960s' slogan, could well have been Judson's motto. But however much it resisted definition, Judson did stand for certain values. One hesitates to use the term ideology; since the 1930s, few American artists have set their work in a political context. Nevertheless, taken together, the ideas of the group suggested many analogies with those of the New Left, then emerging on college campuses. Among these was the emphasis on pluralism. At Judson no single approach, no artistic "line" was privileged: each was equally valid. Another was the commitment to democratic process. Artistically, this led to methods associated with freedom—improvisation, spontaneous determination, chance; at all times, choreographers and dancers could choose among a range of options. Democracy extended to the organization of the concerts themselves. At Judson, no one was paid; responsibility was shared; admission was free.

Just as the New Left questioned fundamental aspects of American political life, so Judson asked basic questions about dance. The most basic—what is a dance?—was answered in the broadest possible way. Anything might be called a dance and looked at as a dance, even when it was the work of a filmmaker, a visual artist, or a musician. Equally broad was Judson's redefining of the material of a dance. Until that time, with very few exceptions, this had consisted of skilled or specialized movement, that is, movement generated from a particular technique. For Judson, however, any kind of movement might serve as the basis of a dance. Like the "found objects" that Rauschenberg and others routinely incorporated into their paintings, everyday movement and pedestrian activity were appropriated by Judson choreographers and framed as art.

The rejection of specialized movement as the sine qua non of a dance had obvious implications for the dancer. Rather than a skilled practitioner or an expert, anyone, theoretically, could be a Judson dancer. The workshop out of which the concert series grew included non-dancers as well as dancers. Many of the former were visual artists and musicians, members of the larger Judson community, and they tried their hand at performing no less than at choreographing. This gave performances a rough, unpolished look, a natural appearance that trained bodies can never quite achieve. Like the home-woven fabrics that decorated so many student rooms of the 1960s, a Judson dance paid greater heed to the process of production than to the display of finished craftsmanship.

Democracy also extended to performance venues. With Judson, any space, not just a traditional theater, became a potential performing area—gymnasiums, parks, churches, street corners, museum galleries, lofts. Modern dance (to say nothing of ballet) coaxed an audience to the theater. Postmodern dance made a theater wherever it could find an audience. Last, but not least, Judson democratized the body—especially the female body. Unlike Cunningham, whose dancers had a strong classical look, Judson choreographers rejected conventions of physical beauty. So long as it was interesting, any kind of body was worth watching. Judson bodies were also presented differently. Dressed in work gear—sneakers, leotards, and sweat pants—eschewing makeup and theatrical hairdos, they looked like bodies you might see on any city street. In retrospect, the Judson woman was a forerunner of the feminist style of the late 1960s.

This new image reflected a larger Judson purpose: the demystification of dance through the elimination of its theatrical conventions. This "strategy of denial" (the phrase is Sally Banes') was summed up by Yvonne Rainer in 1965:

NO to spectacle no to virtuosity no to transformations and magic and make-believe no to the glamour and transcendency of the star image no to the heroic no to the anti-heroic no to trash imagery no to involvement of performer or spectator no to style no to camp no to seduction of spectator by the wiles of the performer no to eccentricity no to moving or being moved.[19]

Where did this leave dance? Shorn of theatricality, of virtuosity, of sensuous appeal, of charm, dance became synonymous with choreography. In fact, no other generation has looked so closely and so analytically at the structure and formal compositional elements of a dance. Judson grew out of a choreographic workshop conducted by Robert Dunn at the Cunningham studio from 1960 to 1962. Dunn himself was not a dancer. A composer, he had studied with Cage at the New School for Social Research in New York and at the time was an accompanist at the Cunningham studio. Unlike Louis Horst, whose composition classes at the Juilliard School of Music and the American Dance Festival emphasized forms associated with pre-classic composers and modernists such as Arnold Schoenberg, Dunn taught the work of Cage and European avant-gardists like Karlheinz Stockhausen and Pierre Boulez. Chance and indeterminate structures played a large part in Dunn's classes, as they did in Cage's. But these were not the only influences. Dunn's classes were a microcosm of New York's avant-garde art world, and many of the ideas circulating in Greenwich Village found their way into the workshop. For Dunn, the classes were a "clearinghouse for structures derived from various sources of contemporary action: dance, music, painting, sculpture, Happenings, literature."[20]

Many of Dunn's assignments had to do with time constraints. Others involved collaborations in which personal control had to be relinquished within a semi-independent working situation. Sometimes an assignment had to do with subject matter: "make a dance about nothing special." Dunn's students, many of whom danced or took classes with Cunningham, were given wide latitude in choosing methods, materials, and structures. Discussion then focused on how these choices had been arrived at and how well the dance succeeded in carrying out the choreographer's intention. Like Cage, with regard to sound, Dunn stressed that any movement—a nod, a shake, a clap, even a sniffle, or a spoken phrase—was valid as part of a dance. Chance extended the range of possibilities, and charts outlining space, rhythm, and directional options encouraged students to give up personal quirks, to assemble movements in unexpected ways.

Structured improvisation was another technique that interested Dunn. Borrowed from jazz, improvisation was a strategy for learning to act spontaneously, for setting one's own rules within a form. Dunn's combination of analysis and permissiveness was eye-opening. As Trisha Brown later recalled, "after presenting a dance, each choreographer was asked, 'How did you make that dance?' The . . . discussion that followed applied nonevaluative criticism to the movement itself and the choreographic structure as well as investigating the disparity between . . . what the artist was making and what the audience saw. The procedure illuminated the interworkings of the dances and minimized value judgments of the choreographer, which for me meant permission, permission to go ahead and do what I wanted to do or had to do—to try out an idea of borderline acceptability."[21] Why not? was Judson's byword.

Few Judson dances survive. Conceived as experiments, most were not intended to survive; like the era's Happenings or paper dresses, the dances belonged emphatically to the present. Many caught the high spirits of the time. In *Pelican* (1963), Robert Rauschenberg, making his debut as a choreographer, roller-skated, while Carolyn Brown, Cunningham's unofficial star, danced on pointe. Accompanying the dance was a tape collage (also by Rauschenberg) that mixed march music by Handel with radio and television sounds. Here was the "factual realism" of Pop art with a vengeance. Most dances, however, took themselves more seriously. In *Trio A* (choreographed by Yvonne Rainer in 1966), dance approached the reductionist extremes of Minimalist sculpture. As Sally Banes has written, "for phrasing, development and climax, variation, character, performance, variety, the virtuosic feat and the fully extended body, Rainer [substituted] energy equality and 'found' movement, equality of parts, repetition or discrete events, neutral performance, task or tasklike activity, singular action, event, or tone, and human scale."[22]

Rainer's purpose was to expose the inner workings of a dance; structure, one could say, was its only subject. This, like the analytical emphasis of Judson generally, perceptibly narrowed the range of permissible content, channeling choreography into a direction of obsessive formalism. In a sense, minimalism, which dominated the scene until the late 1970s, severed postmodern dance from its radical roots, above all, from the populist impulse that, in various ways, aspired to repair the breach between the avant-garde and the larger human community. Only Meredith Monk and Twyla Tharp managed to bridge this gap with the public, and both, significantly, stood on Judson's periphery. The rest, and this includes Trisha Brown and Steve Paxton, the most politically minded artists to emerge from Judson, buried larger concerns in forms impenetrable to all but a small circle of insiders. If Judson was the first generation of choreographers since the 1930s to view its work politically, it never found the means to make its politics public. Therein lies its tragedy.

New York's spectacular growth as a dance capital was strongly influenced by politics—the engaged politics of the Old Left, the repressive politics of McCarthyism, and the "permissive" politics of the New Left. In one way or another, all three left their mark on dance, as they did on the other arts. But because dance was so new to American soil, their impact was all the greater, indeed critical to the very defining of dance as an American art. A theme of these pages has been the relationship of the choreographer to his audience and, in particular, the consequences for left-wing choreographers of the demise of the popular public of the 1930s. Thus far, the happiest of these consequences has not been mentioned: the renaissance of the American musical theater. Prior to the 1940s, most choreographers turned up their noses at Broadway, even if they occasionally accepted a well-paid assignment. *Oklahoma!* (choreographed by Agnes de Mille in 1943) changed this. Here was a musical that not only borrowed from ballet, but used it creatively within a popular context. De Mille's success encouraged producers, no less than choreographers, to bury the hatchet. But her success alone, like that of Balanchine, who choreographed a slew of musicals between 1936 and 1945, cannot explain one of the more startling trends of the postwar era: the wholesale invasion of Broadway by choreographers of leftist sympathies. The reasons for this seem to lie elsewhere, in many artists' desire to recapture the experience of creating for a popular audience and in the fact that Broadway, unlike Hollywood, never sought to purge its ranks of leftists. To professional blacklister Vincent Hartnett, Broadway during the McCarthy era was New York's "Great Red Way."[23]

In a sense, the American musical theater carried into the postwar period the ideology of the Popular Front. The result was a golden age for Broadway— "hits" that both lined the pockets of their investors and transformed the musical into a genuinely popular art form. Jerome Robbins and Helen Tamiris, both closely associated with the Communist Party in the 1940s (Robbins, by his own admission, was a member until 1947), were among Broadway's most prolific choreographers. Each had a string of hits. *On the Town, The King and I, Peter Pan, West Side Story, Gypsy*, and *Fiddler on the Roof* were all by Robbins; *Showboat, Annie Get Your Gun*, and *Fanny*, by Tamiris. Hanya Holm's Broadway credits—*Kiss Me Kate, My Fair Lady*, and *Camelot*—were equally impressive, as were Michael Kidd's (*Finian's Rainbow, Guys and Dolls, Can-Can, Subways Are For Sleeping*) and Agnes de Mille's (*Carousel, Brigadoon, Gentlemen Prefer Blonds, Paint Your Wagon*). With choreographers often doubling as directors, dance was an integral part of these productions—as important an element as music. The new Broadway choreography incorporated popular and concert styles: jazz, social dance, modern dance, ballet. These had been ingredients of Americana ballet. Now, having run its course on the concert stage, the genre found a new lease on life in the musical. Thus, as modern dance and ballet were becoming more esoteric and cerebral, dance on Broadway retained the directness and accessibility of earlier concert styles. Thanks in no small measure to a new wave of choreographers, postwar Broadway became the opera house of the city's small folk.

The 1960s ended this golden age. On Broadway, as in modern dance, the legacy of the 1930s had finally spent itself. But the horizon was far from gloomy. By mid-decade, a new set of institutional supports for dance had materialized in New York. Among these were Lincoln Center, which became the New York City Ballet's permanent home, and federal and state agencies—above all, the National Endowment for the Arts and the New York State Council on the Arts—that now dispensed long-overdue subsidies to a catholic range of companies. At the same time, the vast expansion of the counterculture gave renewed energy to the avant-garde, while the heightening of black consciousness established a minority presence in the city's "official" dance culture. Taken together, these developments completed the process begun in 1940. By the late 1960s, New York had become the dance capital of the world.

NOTES

1. Doris Humphrey, *An Artist First,* ed. and completed by Selma Jeanne Cohen, introd. John Martin, foreword Charles Humphrey Woodford, chronology Christena L. Schlundt (Middletown: Wesleyan University Press, 1972), p. 61.
2. Merle Armitage, *Martha Graham: The Early Years* (Los Angeles, 1937; rpt. New York: Da Capo, 1978), p. 97.
3. Louis Horst and Carroll Russell, *Modern Dance Forms in Relation to the Other Modern Arts* (San Francisco, 1961; rpt. Princeton: Princeton Book Company, 1987), p. 90.
4. Margaret Lloyd, *The Borzoi Book of Modern Dance* (New York, 1949; rpt. New York: Dance Horizons, 1974), p. 174.
5. Humphrey, *An Artist First,* p. 197.
6. Marcia B. Siegel, *The Shapes of Change: Images of American Dance* (Boston: Houghton Mifflin, 1979), p. 277.
7. Lincoln Kirstein, *The New York City Ballet* (New York: Knopf, 1973), p. 49.
8. Edwin Denby, "Fancy Free," in *Dance Writings,* eds. Robert Cornfield and William Mackay (New York: Knopf, 1986), p. 218. This review was originally published on 19 April 1944.
9. Quoted in Charles Payne, *American Ballet Theatre* (New York: Knopf, 1977), p. 145.
10. Kirstein, *New York City Ballet,* p. 82.
11. Jill Johnston, "The New American Modern Dance," in *The New American Arts,* ed. Richard Kostelanetz (New York: Horizon Press, 1965), p. 167.
12. Merce Cunningham, in conversation with Jacqueline Lesschaeve, *The Dancer and the Dance* (New York/London: Marion Boyars, 1985), pp. 162, 164.
13. James Klosty, *Merce Cunningham* (New York: Limelight, 1986), p. 12.
14. Cunningham in *The Dancer and the Dance,* p. 137.
15. Quoted in Martin Duberman, *Black Mountain: An Exploration in Community* (New York: Dutton, 1972), p. 357.
16. Quoted in Jack Anderson, *The American Dance Festival* (Durham: Duke University Press, 1987), p. 85.
17. Quoted in Duberman, *Black Mountain,* p. 349.
18. Sally Banes, *Democracy's Body: Judson Dance Theater 1962–1964* (Ann Arbor: University of Michigan Research Press, 1983), p. xvii.
19. Quoted in Sally Banes, *Terpsichore in Sneakers: Post-Modern Dance,* rev. ed. (Middletown: Wesleyan University Press, 1987), p. 43.
20. Quoted in Banes, *Democracy's Body,* p. 3.
21. Quoted *ibid.,* pp. 20–21.
22. Banes, *Terpsichore in Sneakers,* p. 44.
23. David Caute, *The Great Fear: The Anti-Communist Purge Under Truman and Eisenhower* (New York: Simon and Schuster, 1978), p. 535.

GEORGE ANTHEIL AND THE DANCE

Like many composers who came of age around the First World War, George Antheil had a long relationship with dance. Dances figured among his earliest works—the *Three Creole Dances* he wrote as a seventeen-year-old the very year the United States declared war on Germany, the *Three Spanish Dances* and *Profane Waltzes* he composed two years later, the *Ragtime Sonata* and *Shimmy* he wrote in 1923. None of these works was actually intended for dancing; they were composed for the concert hall, not the dance stage and certainly not the dance hall. Still, the fact that Antheil chose to write them at all is revealing of a great shift in thinking in the more serious quarters of the music world. What prompted this change was the Ballets Russes, and the landmark works, including Stravinsky's *Rite of Spring*, commissioned by the company's forward-looking director, Serge Diaghilev.

Music for the dance had undergone a revolution. No longer written to measure by "specialist composers," it had become the province of "serious" composers—artists as opposed to artisans. Diaghilev made it respectable to write for the ballet stage. At the same time, his Ballets Russes and modernist-oriented companies such as Rolf de Maré's Ballets Suédois proved a ready source of commissions and a launching pad to international renown. Antheil never wrote for either of these celebrated troupes. Yet as an American who spent most of the 1920s and the early 1930s in Europe, a sometime member of the Lost Generation, he was bound sooner or later to cross paths with them. And given his flair for self-promotion, the encounters were sure to be memorable.

Born in Trenton in 1900, the son of a shoe salesman, George Antheil studied music theory and composition, first in Philadelphia with Constantin von Sternberg, then in New York with Ernest Bloch. He arrived in Paris on the very day of the Ballets Russes premiere of *Les Noces*—13 June 1923; it was a balmy evening, a ticket was waiting at the box office, and Stravinsky received him warmly backstage after the performance. But fate soon brought the idyll to an end. Antheil relates the events, as an American friend recounted them, in his lively if somewhat unreliable autobiography, *Bad Boy of Music*. At the party that followed *Les Noces*, which happened to be given by that golden couple of the Ameri-

This essay is based on lectures delivered at The Cooper Union on 29 January 2000, under the auspices of The New York Public Library, and at the Antheil Festival in Trenton, New Jersey, on 21 March 2003. A slightly different version was published in *Ballet Review*, 29, no. 3 (Fall 2001), pp. 82–95.

can expatriate colony, Sara and Gerald Murphy, someone asked Stravinsky whether or not he was so terribly impressed by Antheil's compositions. With apprehension Stravinsky replied that he thought him a fine pianist but that he scarcely knew his compositions. "'Ah,' cried the American and his wife, 'that's just what we suspected, a fourflusher.'"[1] The party ended Antheil's friendship with Stravinsky.

Far more dramatic was Antheil's encounter with the Ballets Suédois. Overnight it made him nothing less than a celebrity, the *enfant terrible* of the Anglo-American avant-garde. It was a *scandale,* one of those that regularly erupts in Paris, that welcomed Antheil's debut at the Théâtre des Champs-Elysées for the opening of the troupe's 1923–1924 season, and amazingly, it was all filmed. Or was it so amazing, engineered, as it was by Margaret Anderson, the editor of *The Little Review,* for her intimate, the actress Georgette LeBlanc, whose new movie needed a riot scene?

"One day," Antheil recounted, "Margaret Anderson phoned me and asked whether I'd like to play at the opening of the Ballets Suédois—after Diaghileff's Ballet Russe the next most important social event in Paris. I said indeed I would–as who wouldn't? Everybody of importance would be present. . . . Margaret said, 'Start practicing and be sure to program your most radical works, the sonatas that caused riots in Germany.' I would go on, she added, during the early part of the program, before the ballets commenced.[2]

Antheil chose three recent works, all for solo piano: *Airplane Sonata,* which he had composed in 1921, before leaving America; the 1922 *Sonata Sauvage,* written in Germany; and a new piece, *Mechanisms,* which trumpeted its modernity in subtitles like *Mechanism Cubistic, Mechanism Interrhythmic,* and *Mechanism Elliptic.*[3] Halfway through the concert, with the cameras whirring under giant floodlights, all hell broke loose. Antheil was in ecstasy: "In the audience was Man Ray, Picasso, Jean Cocteau, Picabia, and Heaven knows who else," he wrote. "In one box alone sat James Joyce, the author of Ulysses . . . [and] in another . . . sat Léger . . . [and] Ezra Pound."[4]

"People were fighting in the aisles, yelling, clapping, hooting! Pandemonium! I suddenly heard Satie's shrill voice saying, 'Quel [*sic*] précision! Quel [sic] précision! Bravo! Bravo!' . . . Milhaud was now clapping, definitely clapping. By this time some people in the galleries were pulling up the seats and dropping them down into the orchestra; the police entered, and any number of surrealists, society personages, and people of all descriptions were arrested. . . . Paris hadn't had such a good time since the premiere of Stravinsky's 'Sacre du Printemps.' As Jack Benny would have said: 'Boy, they loved me in Paris!'"[5]

Despite its artfully contrived riot and sophisticated interiors, *L'Inhumaine,* as Marcel L'Herbier's film was called, was not a success. As the opera singer Claire (who prompts the riot), Georgette LeBlanc had none of the magnetism of a femme fatale, while Jaque [sic] Catelain, the Swedish scientist who is the victim of her coldness, seems to loathe her.[6]

Capitalizing on his newfound notoriety, Antheil announced to the press that he was working on a new piece, *Ballet Mécanique*, which he hoped to produce with motion-picture accompaniment, if he could find a collaborator. However, in a letter to his American patroness Mary Curtis Bok written in May 1924 (that is, seven months after the uproar at the Théâtre des Champs-Elysées), he described the work that was to be his fame and bane in later years as being definitely engaged for a season at the avant-garde Théâtre Bériza with "decor and staging by F[ernand] Léger, the designer of 'Skating Rink.'"[7]

Léger, who had designed the hero's futuristic laboratory in *L'Inhumaine* and both *Skating Rink* and *Creation of the World* for the Ballets Suédois, eventually teamed up with the American filmmaker Dudley Murphy to create the film version of *Ballet Mécanique*, a landmark of early experimental cinema. (This was not Murphy's first encounter with ballet; in 1922 he had worked closely in New York with Ballets Russes alumnus Adolph Bolm on the pioneering *Danse Macabre*.) But the final outcome of Léger's collaboration with Antheil was almost certainly not determined until later, no matter what the composer claimed in *Bad Boy of Music*. In its genesis, *Ballet Mécanique* was probably what its title suggests—an avant-garde ballet, cousin to such Ballets Suédois productions as *Le Marriage de la Tour Eiffel* and *Relâche*.

For reasons that remain obscure, a stage production failed to materialize. And when the music was eventually heard—at the Maison Pleyel in 1925, at the Théâtre des Champs-Elysées and the salon of Mrs. Christian Gross in 1926—it was without the Dudley-Léger film. Antheil scored his original version for sixteen pianolas, but when the master rolls were cut by Pleyel, the music turned out to be about twice as long as the film. For the U.S. premiere of Antheil's work at Carnegie Hall in 1927, there was a garish backdrop by Joseph Mullen featuring skyscrapers, noise-making machines, and a larger-than-life figure jumping off a diving board. Only in 1935 at the Museum of Modern Art—doubtless through the good offices of Lincoln Kirstein, who was interested in film almost as much as dance—were the two finally synchronized and performed together, albeit in a musical arrangement for one pianola.[8]

Antheil composed his first music for dancers in the late 1920s. By then he had left France for Germany, where he wrote incidental music for a number of plays and where his first opera, *Transatlantic*, premiered in 1930. In Vienna, he did some music for Hedy Pfundmeyr, a soloist of the State Opera Ballet and choreographer in her own right, a commission he later described as his "first music for dance," as well as sketches for a ballet called *Méditerrané*. In 1929, Helen Tamiris choreographed his *Sonatina for Radio* for a concert in Berlin only weeks after the nine-minute jazz sonata for piano had received its world premiere on the German government broadcasting station. Finally, from this same period dates the opera-ballet *Flight*, also known as *Ivan the Terrible*, an unrealized work that "involved the use of projected images rather than formal scenery."[9]

He also tried—unsuccessfully—to interest Boris Kochno in commissioning a score for the Ballets Russes. Antheil described the project to his friend, the poet Ezra Pound, after returning from summer holiday in 1927: "The Ballet, called 'Le Jour' with decor by Miró is finished. . . . I am certain that it will create a scandal, as it is unlike anything, except the Airplane Sonata, and the Death of Machines that I have ever done. Kochnow [Boris Kochno], secretary of the Ballet Russe, has informed me definitely that it will be given a tryout in November 1928, in Monte Carlo. However that is a long time, and Tschlietschieff [Pavel Tchelitchew] tells me that I shall have to keep after them to make them keep their promise. . . .

"I wish you would have another go at Sitwell to get at Diageliew [*sic*]. Don't tell him that Kochnow has made a tentative acceptance, but make him get at Diageliew, just as if nothing had happened. You can understand that if the thing is to happen . . . and the chances look very bright, that D. mustn't forget me for a moment, or leave me out of his calculations. I know . . . D. thought . . . that I had tremendous talent, but was 'too serious' for the Ballet Russe. He didn't see where he could make use of me, although he admitted that, as there were no other young men of promise, he would soon be forced to consider what he could do with me." Despite Antheil's behind-the-scenes politicking, nothing came of the commission or the ballet.[10]

A chance encounter with William Butler Yeats in the summer of 1928 led to "his first ballet opera,"[11] *Fighting the Waves*, actually one of the poet's "plays for dancers." Produced by Dublin's Abbey Theatre, it was choreographed by the future matriarch of British ballet, the Irish-born Ninette de Valois. Yeats, she recalled, "had always felt the call of movement in relation to his writings, and he felt the same draw towards music. But he did not show any active interest in music and dance as arts in their own right. For him it was the call of the rhythm of the body, and the musicality of words, the search for a fusion in a unified expression of his dance dramas, symbolic in the oneness of the mystery that surrounded his great vision."[12]

For this strange work, blending Celtic myth with the stillness of Noh, Antheil created a percussive score for orchestra that largely eschewed the use of strings. J. J. Hayes in *The Irish Times* praised the composer for "grasping the Gaelic spirit underlying the story," while avoiding the "sensationally striking. . . . The dramatic element was always present and the orchestra made clear at all times what was happening. . . . Mr. Antheil's music was eloquent in meaning and intensity."[13] For Yeats, the work was a turning point. To accommodate de Valois, who refused to speak on stage, he cut many of the speeches and put the verse dialogue into prose. The opening and closing lyrics were left unchanged, "for sung to modern music in the modern way," as he put it, "they suggest strange patterns to the ear without obtruding upon it with their difficult, irrelevant words."[14] Although at one point Yeats dismissed the play as a "mere occasion for sculptor and dancer, [and] for the exciting dramatic music of George Antheil," in performance he was overwhelmed by what the totality conveyed—"the ritual of a lost faith." This now became his ideal.[15]

In 1933, after spending most of the previous decade abroad, Antheil preturned to the United States and settled in New York. The country was mired in the Great Depression; soup kitchens fed armies of the unemployed, and tent cities filled Central Park. Still, it was an exciting time if you were a dancer or a composer. There was energy, a host of young faces, and imaginative daring; organizations were springing up, especially on the left, and audiences were growing–all this when few had a dime to spare. It was a far cry from the hedonism of Paris and other expatriate colonies of the 1920s.

Years later, composer Lehman Engel, who wrote music for Martha Graham and other modern dancers, recalled the excitement of New York in the early 1930s, when he was a student at Juilliard: "There was so much to be seen and experienced, so many people in such a variety of places. These, combined with the opportunity to create, could only have happened in New York, in our land, in our time. The discussions . . . mattered most, I think. They involved the theater, music, painting, poetry, and the dance, and they . . . caused me to think about things that had not before even occurred to me."[16]

Antheil threw himself into American life with the gusto that was one of his most endearing traits. There were concerts in Rochester, his home town of Trenton, and Yaddo, the Saratoga Springs arts colony; committee work with Aaron Copland and Wallingford Riegger; movie scores for Ben Hecht and Charles MacArthur at Paramount's Astoria studios; a performance of *Ballet Mécanique* at the Museum of Modern Art.[17]

Above all, there was his new opera, *Helen Retires*. Based on John Erskine's novel *The Private Life of Helen of Troy*, it premiered at the Juilliard School of Music in February 1934, a time when many were calling for an American opera. The book was rich in humor, and the production design, by Frederick Kiesler, was striking and unusually modern, with lights, slide projections, and even motion-picture footage creating most of the stage effects. The chorus sat onstage (as in Diaghilev's production of *Le Coq d'Or*), and the choreography for the student dancers was by Kiesler and Dalcroze expert Elsa Findlay. Arthur Mahoney, the one professional dancer in the cast, scored such a success as the Young Fisherman, that Juilliard hired him on the spot as a teacher and dance director. The opening was like a gala night at the Metropolitan, with many of the city's most distinguished musicians in the audience.[18]

In the years since *Ballet Mécanique*, Antheil had gradually abandoned the more extreme elements of his earlier modernism. By 1930, a neoromantic element could be discerned in his work; a few years later, even a touch of surrealism. At the same time, he was gradually losing interest in "pure" music. "There seems little use to writing trumpet sonatas," he told an interviewer in 1936. "The arts need to collaborate; otherwise, they become stilted, precious, playing to an ever diminishing audience."[19]

Antheil's interest in dance intensified with his return to the United States. Early in 1932, during an extended visit home, he was in touch with Doris Humphrey about using her pupils in a "little opera" he expected to complete by the middle of March. "It was a very great pleasure for us to meet you, as we always have been great admirers of your dancing, and think that it is of the greatest importance what you are doing for the American dance."[20]

The opera never materialized, but in September 1933 Antheil wrote to Humphrey about nothing less than exploring "the possibilities of a ballet here in Trenton": "The Trenton Civic Orchestra has been organized, and is . . . pretty good. . . . I have thought of using that (it is at my disposal) and the new Trenton Municipal Theater (which the city wants me to use) and with the help of the Junior League, and a number of interested people, put on a series of American ballets by American composers, with American dancers . . . a sort of Ballet Russe, so to speak, but with a poorer orchestra . . . I must admit. . . . [T]he ballets could be ordered from the young men, if they are not already written, so that they would not be too ultra difficult. . . . Princeton, the New Hope Art Colony, and Philadelphia are all nearby. N.Y. is also only 1:07 minutes away. It might be fun. What do you think? There will be no profits unless Mrs. Roebling underwrites more than she has to date, but that shouldn't stop this first chance at an unlimited orchestra and theater, and enough money for scenery and costumes."[21]

This project too never came off. But within months Antheil had encountered the patron extraordinaire who would make a place for him at the epicenter of New York's "musical ballet-opera theatre" (as he called it)[22]—Lincoln Kirstein. For Kirstein, the big adventure of his life was just beginning. On October 18, 1933, at his behest, George Balanchine had arrived in New York; less than three months later, Balanchine taught his first class at the School of American Ballet; six months after that he presented his first American ballet, *Serenade*. By 1935, the two (with financial help from Edward Warburg) had founded the American Ballet, the first of several short-lived predecessors to the New York City Ballet.

It was Lisa Parnova, a Russian-born dancer who had worked at the Cologne Opera in the 1920s and was now living in New York, who brought Antheil to the School of American Ballet in late January 1934. He played a rumba for Balanchine (so loudly that the teacher in the next studio came in to protest), and soon they were talking about a ballet. All kinds of ideas were floating around—an American ballet with a scenario by Francis Fergusson; a skating ballet set in Central Park of the 1840s; a ballet to Schumann called "The Enchanted Garden"; a Rover Boy ballet (this eventually became *Alma Mater*); revivals of works choreographed by Balanchine in Europe.

Only days before the premiere of *Helen Retires*, Antheil received his first commission—a new score for *Les Songes*, or *Dreams*, as the American version was called.[23] It was about a dancer and nightmarish figures like the Rat-Acrobat who assail her dreams. Balanchine had produced the ballet in Europe with music by Milhaud. Now, with Derain's sets and costumes at hand (they had come with him to America), he decided to revive the ballet, but with a new score.[24] A few days later, Balanchine demonstrated the dances and talked to him about timings. Within a week, Antheil was playing for the choreographer the music he had already written; it was at Lucia Davidova's and everyone was delighted; it was charming and *dansant*. By late April, the ballet was in rehearsal; by mid-May, it was nearly done. And Antheil was talking to Kirstein and Balanchine alike about other projects, including a "waltz-ballet" (which probably became *Transcendence*) and *Archipelago*, which Frederick Ashton (who had spent the winter in the United States choreographing *Four Saints in Three Acts*) took back with him to London but failed to stage.[25] By June, he was writing to Ezra Pound that even if the critics had "roasted" *Helen Retires*, a "flood of new possibilities and ideas" had followed "on the heels of the performance."[26]

Unlike most of the painters and composers associated with the Kirstein-Balanchine enterprise in these years, Antheil was closer to Balanchine than to Kirstein. Antheil's modernism struck a responsive chord in the thirty-year-old choreographer, whose days as a choreographic revolutionary lay not so far in the past. He went up to Juilliard to watch rehearsals of *Helen Retires*, and, like Kirstein, attended the premiere, and told Antheil (as the latter reported to Pound) "that I am the only composer in the U.S.A. who writes music."[27] Antheil took to dropping in at the School, which was practically around the corner from his apartment on East Fifty-fifth Street, where Kirstein as well as Balanchine were occasional visitors. In late May, all three went to see Asadata Dafora's African dance-drama *Kykunkor* at the tiny Unity Theatre on East Twenty-third Street. There was talk of Balanchine and Antheil doing a ballet on the theme of Don Juan, and even a film, an intriguing prospect given that within a couple of years both would be working in Hollywood. Still another idea was what Antheil described to Pound as "a ballet-choral work, lasting about two hours, . . . [V]ast rhythmic choruses will alternate with dances . . . and sometimes just a speaker, reciting poetry . . . and sometimes moving pictures and sometimes everything. A new musical stage form with no tenors warbling."[28]

On June 10, 1934, the School of American Ballet gave its first performance at the Warburg family estate near White Plains. Three ballets were given, all by Balanchine. The program opened with *Mozartiana* and closed with excerpts from *Dreams*. In the middle was *Serenade*, which was danced in rehearsal costume. By March 1935, when the American Ballet made its official debut at the Adelphi Theatre in New York, this most beloved of Balanchine works had costumes by Jean Lurçat, scenery by Gaston Longchamp, and a new arrangement of the Tchaikovsky Serenade in C for String Orchestra by Antheil. The composer contributed to a third ballet presented during the company's debut season. This was *Transcendence*, which had a theme by Kirstein inspired by Paganini, sets and costumes by the American painter Franklin Watkins, and music by Liszt—his Mephisto Valse and various Hungarian Rhapsodies—which Antheil both orchestrated and arranged. Although *Transcendence* did not remain long in repertory, "a faint echo" of the ballet, Kirstein was to write, survived in Balanchine's *Brahms-Schoenberg Quartet,* choreographed more than thirty years later.[29]

At the same time that Antheil was working for Balanchine, he was also working for Martha Graham. In *Bad Boy of Music,* he passes over entirely his encounter with the foremost representative of modern dance, although it produced two works and inspired an adulatory essay. How they met is unknown. Perhaps it was Lisa Parnova (who had a foot in the modern camp), or one of the many composers Antheil had met in New York. Most likely, it was Louis Horst, Graham's musical director and the composer of several of her early scores, who brought them together. Antheil found himself in good musical company. Although Graham had long used modern music, her interest in American composers was a recent development, an early expression of the nationalist impulse that culminated in *American Document.* In 1934 and 1935, her roster of composers included no fewer than a half-dozen Americans—Lehman Engel, Henry Cowell, Edgar Varèse, Paul Nordoff, Norman Lloyd, David Diamond—in addition to Horst and Antheil. Graham's commitment to new American music was unmatched by any other choreographer of the time.

For his first commission, Antheil did not write new music. *Dance in Four Parts,* a solo for Graham that premiered at the Guild Theatre in November 1934, was based on twenty-four short piano preludes from *The Woman with a Hundred Heads.* Antheil had written it the year before, inspired by a surrealist collage-novel of etchings by Max Ernst. The individual pieces varied in length and mood, with instructions like "cruel, quick," "nostalgic," and "slightly brutal"; some of the pieces were strongly percussive; others had the atonal sonorities of the composer's later neoclassic works. (Since the Graham score has disappeared, it is impossible to know which ones she used.)

Graham divided the dance into four parts—"Quest," "Derision," "Dream," and "Sportive Tragedy"—each of which she then divided into six emotionally related "moods," making a total of twenty-four short dances. The result, wrote critic John Martin in *The New York Times,* "seems oversubtle in purpose and not too well unified in form. . . . It is impossible to tell when one prelude leaves off and the next begins, and similarly where one dance theme ends and the next carries on."[30] Antheil had nothing but praise for the choreographer's use of his music: "she does it beautifully," he wrote to Mrs. Bok, "and I love it."[31]

Far more successful was Antheil's second work for Graham, *Course.* A large group composition, it was the outstanding feature of her third recital of the 1934–1935 season. Reviewing it in *The New York Times,* Martin could hardly contain his enthusiasm: "It is a completely exciting piece of work. From the first entrance of the solo figure and the group with its onrush, there is maintained a flow of swift and brilliant movement which, in spite of its variations, never pauses for an instant. The 'course' of the title is apparently . . . a series of games or contests, comparable to a race course. The seven dancers besides Miss Graham who figure prominently . . . contribute exemplary performances, . . . and George Antheil's music serves excellently as its background."[32] Alas, the score for *Course* has also been lost.

Martin was noticeably less enthusiastic about *Dreams*, which received its official premiere less than a month later. "It seems scarcely worth the labor that has been spent on it, for it is trivial in subject matter and utterly unsuited in style to the young dancers who make up the company. Certainly the abandonment of the Milhaud music was of doubtful wisdom."[33] Other critics were just as damning. Wrote Pitts Sanborn: "The phantasmagoria of 'Dreams' . . . proved to be distinctly below the Ballet's general level of achievement. The choreography was rather tiresomely conventional; the dancing . . . somewhat amateurish in its total effect, and the settings true to a French mode that arouses no excitement today. Moreover, the music, a sort of Viennese disarrangement, was ill-calculated to add lustre to Mr. Antheil's fame."[34]

The season prompted all kinds of debates. One had to do with the relative merits of ballet and modern dance. Antheil flew to the defense of ballet in an punchy article that came out in *Stage* magazine just as the Adelphi season opened. "At the moment American dancing has twisted itself into such a series of blind alleys that it is time for a little thumbing back over the exceedingly classic files. The curious thing is that, after ten years of pounding upon the theatrical boards with the heels, toe-dancing seems to come as a fresh and novel spring wind. The old ballet technique has been dusted off. Men like Massine and Balanchine have found a thousand new corners and angles to give to an already brilliant and long-perfected technique a new and Mesmeric life. How much more I prefer to see this than the heavy, already demoted *Neusachlichkeit* of the present school of American dancing. Ten years of it, and it still is short breathed, heavily Germanic, with nothing of our true pioneering spirit."[35]

The battle wasn't simply about modern dance and ballet. It was also about differing views of nationality: what it meant to be American, what was signified by the idea of an American dance, what was necessary for a cosmopolitan aesthetic like Balanchine's (or Antheil's, for that matter) to acquire an authentic American identity. There were also class issues at stake. The American Ballet was bankrolled by some very rich people, notably Kirstein (whose money came from Filene's, the Boston department store) and Warburg (whose family belonged to the international banking elite). They had connections, and they knew everyone. Kirstein brought the rich and famous to rehearsals, laying the foundation for an audience; he courted journalists (including John Martin) and talked to editors, so that by the time the American Ballet had made its debut, articles about the company and the School had appeared in such toney magazines as *Vanity Fair, Harper's Bazaar, Town and Country,* and *Vogue.*[36]

Thus, in his season round-up, when Martin questioned whether "the organization [is] to attempt the fulfillment of its original policy of developing an American ballet, or . . . to follow the direction of its present season and go on being merely 'Les Ballets Americains,'" given its audience of socialites, expatriate Europeans, and balletomanes, one feels that the company's social aura, so carefully engineered by Kirstein, repelled him far more than Balanchine's choreography.[37] In 1935, with the Great Depression still a reality, many probably shared Martin's distaste.

Finally, the season brought up questions about the nature of ballet. What kinds of stories should it tell? Did it have to tell stories? If not, how was meaning conveyed? What kinds of meaning could and should be conveyed? Diaghilev, Bronislava Nijinska once remarked, "could not readily discard the idea of a literary libretto in ballet."[38] He insisted that Ballets Russes productions have some kind of narrative, even if this was only a pretext for the dances. Once he died in 1929, however, Balanchine and others began to experiment with choreography that abjured narrative.

The most controversial of these experiments were Léonide Massine's "symphonic ballets," so called because they were choreographed to the symphonies of Brahms, Beethoven, and Berlioz. Massine was sharply criticized for plundering the symphonic repertory, but he was also taken to task for seeking to transform what John Martin called "the balanced forms and disciplined abstractions" of ballet into a personal form of expression. "The direction of these romantic, nebulously emotional, philosophical, pseudo-profound creations is the one direction above all others which the ballet must avoid."[39] Martin dismissed Balanchine's work in similar terms. Errante, he wrote, "falls . . . into the same class of cosmic nonsense as [Massine's] 'Les Présages,' which up to now has held the record for choreographic silliness."[40] Transcendence, "whether because of its training for choreographic novelty or because . . . of its . . . unsuitability to the talents of the company, remains largely incomprehensible."[41] Balanchine's ballets, he concluded, "are evidences of what someone has aptly called 'Riviera esthetics.'"[42]

Martin's criticism did not go unheeded. In the next decade, Balanchine no less than Kirstein would undergo a process of naturalization. In the case of Balanchine, this would result in nearly a score of works for Broadway and Hollywood, an exposure to popular entertainment that ultimately transformed him into an American. Kirstein, too, went his own way. In 1936, he founded Ballet Caravan, a chamber company that aimed to make ballet as American as apple pie. The themes of the ballets were American, as were the designers, dancers, and composers. Most of the ballets were forgettable, but they launched a generation of American talent, and with Billy the Kid, which had music by Copland, choreography by Eugene Loring, and a scenario by Kirstein, Ballet Caravan created one of the most important works of Depression-era Americana.

As for Antheil, in 1936 he set off in search of America, a journey that took him to Florida and New Mexico, and ended in Hollywood. He did not want to be, as he put it in *Bad Boy of Music*, "a Parisian in New York."[43] And in this realization, his collaboration with Balanchine was crucial, even as he continued to laud the choreographer's genius. By 1937, Antheil was touting Martha Graham as "the very essence of America," "one of those extraordinary *mediums* who . . . without knowing it present the mental telepathy of the race and concentrate its essence into the movements of her body."[44] The shoe salesman's son from Trenton had come home.

Like so many newcomers to Hollywood, Antheil went to work for the movies. He continued to write for *Modern Music* and for a time kept a toehold in the ballet world. When Balanchine went to Hollywood in 1937, he lived only a block away from the composer. "We are often together," Antheil reported to Mrs. Bok. "Three nights ago we played through the new Strawinsky ballet, Card Party, four hands, which Balanchine recently presented at the Metropolitan. . . . These things are good for my soul, if not for my pocket book." He was also at work on a new ballet, to be presented at the American Ballet's next Metropolitan season.[45] However, like other ballets of the late 1930s, the project came to nought.[46] Indeed, by 1939, Antheil had stopped writing music entirely, even for the movies. To make a living, he wrote a syndicated lonely-hearts column, "Boy Advises Girl"; a book of war predictions, *The Shape of War to Come,* published anonymously in 1940; and articles on the place of endocrinal glands in the human organism. With Hedy Lamarr, he patented an idea about a radio-directed torpedo.

In 1944, Leopold Stokowski conducted the premiere of Antheil's Fourth Symphony. The event marked his return to the serious music world; within months this "musical Tom Sawyer, gay, fanciful, ingenuous, self-confident, and comical," as Virgil Thomson once described him,[47] was offering his services to the Ballet Russe de Monte Carlo. "For years I have composed nothing at all," he wrote to the company's director, Sergei Denham, "it had a special psychological reason too long to go into. But now I should like to write a wonderful new ballet. And I could."[48] What almost certainly prompted Antheil to resume contact with Denham at this point was his recent appointment of Balanchine as the company's resident choreographer.

The two were soon back in touch. A few letters from Balanchine to Antheil survive from this period, and they have a jocular, even bantering tone. "Dear George," begins one dated September 13, 1945. "You reproached me for lack of promptness in answering your correspondence, well, I have reason to reproach you in turn. . . . I hear on the gossip grapevine with some alarm that somebody making a film like the one you indicate" [this was the Ben Hecht production *The Specter of the Rose,* released the following year] "is thinking of hiring a Signor Celli for a possible role. Strictly entre nous, I prefer to believe that this is just idle talk."[49] By August 1946, Antheil was writing to Denham about two possible ballets. One was *Ghost Town*, a revival of the "American folk ballet" choreographed in 1939 by Marc Platt, but with new music (the original score was by Richard Rodgers).[50] The other project was a "Creole ballet." For this, he added,

"I have already (somewhat in collaboration with Georges [*sic*] Balanchine who gave me 90% of the idea) worked out [a] little story, . . . besides collecting a vast amount of themes remembered dimly, but beautifully from my childhood."[51] Among these remembered themes may have been music from "The Creole," an orchestral work that may have been composed as early as 1919.[52]

Not only has Antheil's "little story" survived, but also a surprisingly large number of musical sketches.[53] The scenario for the "New Orleans Ballet," as he now calls it, has an unmistakable Balanchine perfume. Like his 1933 ballet *Cotillon*, it opens with a dressing scene and is set in a ballroom. But there is a cynical undercurrent, a subtle air of moral corruption that recalls the atmosphere of *Night Shadow*, or *La Sonnambula*, which Balanchine staged early in 1946. In both the hero toys with a pair of contrasting women, here, a beautiful Creole girl who is his fiancée and the beautiful quadroon servant girl who is his mistress.

In the first scene, the quadroon girl, who is identified in the score as Caroline or the "Black Creole," helps the white Creole girl to dress; at the same time she flirts with her beau, who prolongs the coquetry by rejecting the gowns modeled by his fiancée. The second scene takes place at the quadroon ball, where Caroline has arranged to meet her lover, who soon arrives and dances with her. In the last scene, and here I quote Antheil, "the Creole girl [is] being very decorously escorted home by her fiancé, never knowing that while she was dancing at the white ball, her boyfriend [was having] a wonderful time at the quadroon ball."

Why the project failed to materialize is unclear. The most likely explanation is Balanchine's departure from the Ballet Russe to join Lincoln Kirstein in founding Ballet Society, which presented its first program in November 1946. Without him the project was dead, although Antheil kept trying, unsuccessfully, to resuscitate it.[54] In fact, the ballet may have been Balanchine's project all along. This is suggested by the existence in the George Balanchine Archive at the Harvard Theatre Collection of an "original scenario" by Katherine Dunham for a "dramatic ballet in one scene" entitled "The Octoroon Ball."[55] Balanchine worked with Dunham and members of her company in 1940, when he choreographed the Broadway music *Cabin in the Sky*. The scenario almost certainly dates to this period. Dunham's thrust is fundamentally political—outrage at a system that encouraged the concubinage of beautiful young girls of mixed blood to wealthy white libertines, while forcing them to abandon the dark-skinned slaves they love. Where Balanchine's love triangle involved two women and a man, Dunham's involved two men and a woman. One can easily imagine Balanchine taking Dunham's basic plot and reversing it. Moreover, even before Antheil offered his services to Denham, there was talk of Balanchine possibly doing a ballet called "New Orleans," with music by Morton Gould.[56]

In 1950, Denham approached Antheil about a project that did materialize, although the Ballet Russe de Monte Carlo would not produce it. This was Antheil's last ballet, *Capital of the World*. The idea was born over a sumptuous lunch in honor of Ernest Hemingway at a palazzo on Venice's Grand Canal. Somehow the discussion turned to ballet and Hemingway's short story "The Capital of the World," which has as its climax a macabre scene where two Spanish boys, waiters in a *pensión* for second-rate matadors, play bullfight with a chair that has two razor-sharp meat knives strapped to its legs; Paco misses a pass; a knife plunges into his belly, and he dies. All agreed it would make an exciting ballet and should be done at the Met. Hemingway turned to a young American writer in his entourage. "'Would you like to do it, Hotch?'" Hotch would. So began a byzantine journey for A. E. Hotchner, the future author of *Papa Hemingway: A Personal Memoir*—"four harrowing, impresario-infested years," as he put it, that ended, amazingly, with both a premiere at the Met and a broadcast on national television.[57]

Hotchner wrote his scenario for Denham (whose sole piece of advice, "no cousins," sounds suspiciously like Balanchine's injunction against mothers-in-law). Denham forwarded the script to Antheil, who then contacted the writer, expressing his enthusiasm for the project. A year later the score was finished, and Antheil played it for Denham, who wept and kissed him, told him it was beyond anything he had expected, that it would open his next season at the Met. Then nothing.

Hotchner, a newcomer to the ballet world, was shocked. "Things are not conducted in the ballet world as they are in the world of writing and letters," Antheil remarked in a letter. "Writers think in terms of all sorts of rights, firm contracts, legally binding papers. To step from this world into the world of ballet, where everything is done with mirrors and where no contract I have ever signed has ever protected me an iota, is a big step."[58]

Antheil himself was no slouch when it came to plotting and scheming. As Denham procrastinated, the script made the rounds of Hollywood. At one point, director Stanley Kramer was interested, then turned it down because John Huston had announced he was doing a picture called *Matador*. There was talk of a ninety-minute television opera for *Omnibus*, the NBC series sponsored by the Ford Foundation that had already broadcast Menotti's *Amahl and the Night Visitors* and Britten's *Billy Budd*, followed by an expanded version for Broadway. At some point Denham drew up a contract, but with so many other irons in the fire, Antheil never signed it. In any event, Denham was pretty much bankrupt. At Hotchner's urging, the composer wrote to Lincoln Kirstein, now managing director of City Center, in charge of all its constituents. Kirstein was not interested, either in the ballet or in Antheil's new opera, *Volpone*. He responded that he was not in a position to commission any new works.[59] Yet in less than a month, the Center would receive a $200,000 grant from the Rockefeller Foundation "to cover the costs of creative preparatory work on new productions in ballet and opera."[60]

Kirstein's real beef was Antheil's account of Balanchine in *Bad Boy of Music*. How it must have galled him to read that working with Balanchine on his

"Parisian ballets" was what had "fulcrumed" the composer out of New York.[61] Ever one to hold a grudge, Kirstein now wanted nothing to do with Antheil, dismissing him as late as the 1970s as an "enthusiastic if disappointing collaborator," who "hardly fulfilled his early heady notoriety."[62] As a friend of Hotchner's reported, "Kirstein is much too peeved with you over your book to entertain the project in any size, shape or form."[63]

With the New York City Ballet out of the question, Hotchner sent the script to Ballet Theatre, which then forwarded it to Eugene Loring, the choreographer of *Billy the Kid*, who was now living in Los Angeles. Antheil invited him to lunch and played him the sketches. Loring loved the music but felt that extensive changes were needed for the script to work as a ballet.[64] With Hotchner's permission, they set to work on the revisions. The setting was moved from a *pensión* to a tailor shop catering to bullfighters. A love interest was introduced, along with a café scene. Once Loring had agreed to choreograph the ballet, everything fell into place: the *Omnibus* premiere in early December, the gala Met premiere just after Christmas. In what was very possibly a ballet first, the Ford Foundation's TV Workshop was underwriting the production. Antheil received $600 for his score, and a royalty of $15 for each theater presentation of the ballet—not much, even at 1950s prices.[65] And he agreed to provide two scores: one for a twenty-piece television orchestra, the other for the sixty-piece orchestra the company would have at the Met.[66] Antheil's years of experience in the movies, where composers had to work fast, now stood him in good stead.

Capital of the World was a narrative ballet in the character tradition popularized by Massine in *Le Tricorne, Gaîté Parisienne,* and many other works. Much of the action was conveyed by pantomime, and much of the choreography was in Spanish style; there was also something of the faux primitivism of so many Hemingway works, especially those set in Spain, such as *Death in the Afternoon,* which celebrated bullfighting, and *For Whom the Bell Tolls,* his powerful novel inspired by the Spanish Civil War. Paco, the hero, dreams of being a bullfighter; he is an idealist, chaste in his admiration for the coquettish Elena, kind to the wrecks who visit the tailor shop to pawn the precious suits they once wore in the bullring. The heart of the ballet is Paco's solo, a rare moment of introspection; the shaming scene that follows where he is taunted by several whores; and the fight that ends in his death. Rather than a comic hero à la Massine, Loring gives us a character with the innocence and soulfulness of the new movie heroes of the 1950s, along with a fight scene that in its intensity and in the physical closeness of the two men expresses a kind of perverse love. Roy Fitzell gave a glowing performance as Paco; Scott Douglas was a splendid Enrique, and Lupe Serrano was appropriately sexy as Elena.[67]

Virgil Thomson, long an admirer of Antheil's work, reviewed the score in his music column in the *New York Herald Tribune. The Capital of the World,* he wrote, revealed the composer "as a master [of] the choreographic musical theater. . . . Rarely have I heard music for dancing with so much real energy in it. It is no mere accompaniment for dancing: it generates physical activity on the stage, moves the dancers around. It is colorful, too, bright and dark and full of the contrasts that are Spain. Its tunes are broad and strong; its harmonic structure is clashingly dissonant; its orchestration is picturesque, emphatic, powerfully underlined, a master's score.

"Everything about the music is boldly conceived and completely effective. . . . In this ballet Antheil has found scope for his talent. That talent has ever been for clowning, for caricature. And of the art of the great caricaturists–of Hogarth and Goya and Daumier and Steinlen and Boardman Robinson–is an art always compacted of tenderness and anger, of joyful exuberance and implacable debunking, these qualities are in Antheil's music too. Never before, however, have they been so powerfully used as in this ballet. . . . Antheil's score for Eugene Loring's choreography is the most original, striking and powerful American ballet score with which I am acquainted."[68]

The response to Loring's choreography was far more mixed. In *Dance News,* P. W. Manchester complained that "Loring very rarely broke into straight choreography to tell what story there was . . . and for the greater part of the time kept his dancers strutting or tripped (according to sex) about the stage, accompanying themselves with assorted groans, laughs, jeers, coughs, screams, or the whirring of a hand-operated sewing machine."[69] For Doris Hering, writing in *Dance Magazine,* "the most absorbing moments . . . were those when the pantomime blossomed into dance—as in the seduction duet . . . and in Paco's touching solos." Like Manchester, she found the characters one-dimensional, "like bright figures in a Spanish travel poster."[70] As for *The New York Times* critic John Martin, he hated it: "The original tale, if it is to be made into a ballet at all, would demand the services of a psychological expert like Antony Tudor, who would not blanch at its sadistic undertones. But Mr. Loring has treated it rather cutely, and altogether for surface values. There is hardly a nickel's worth of dancing in it. It is diffuse, unchoreographic and undramatic, and except for outbursts of laughing, coughing, groaning (for real!) it suggests some old silent movie directed, perhaps, by Massine."[71]

Martin had once admired Massine, just as he had once admired the character tradition from which *Capital of the World* descended and to which it still partly belonged. But for Martin, as for other New York critics, the spell of Balanchine coupled with the growing presence of his New York City Ballet, made it increasingly difficult to appreciate older choreographic styles. Like Esteban Francés, the ballet's designer, who gave up painting when abstract expressionism made surrealism démodé, Balanchine's formalism, his distillation of plot and character, emotion and symbol into a dance shorn of everything but movement itself, made Loring's work seem hopelessly old-fashioned—as well as impure. Unlike a ballet by Balanchine or a painting by Jackson Pollack, *Capital of the World* could not be understood merely in terms of its form, or as an interplay of abstract properties; it was a mixed bag. In these reviews, with their Greenbergian echoes, one finds an early crystallization of the sensibility identified with the critics who came to the fore in New York during the 1960s.

Capital of the World stayed in repertory for a couple of years. Not long after the ballet went on the road, Antheil wrote to his publisher that a new commission was in the offing, on a subject he "could do particularly well."[72] Like so many of his projects, this one came to nought.

Five years later, he died of a heart attack and was promptly forgotten by the dance world. Yet he had worked with two of the twentieth-century's greatest choreographers along with several lesser ones. He had played a part in Balanchine's first American seasons and contributed to the first ballets he choreographed in America. An enthusiastic collaborator, he wrote music that revealed not only a deep understanding of theater but also an intuitive grasp of dance. Had he lived, George Antheil would have celebrated his hundredth birthday this year. Surely, the time is ripe for the dance world to remember him, to rediscover his music, and even perchance to choreograph new works to it.

NOTES

1. George Antheil, *Bad Boy of Music* (Garden City, N.Y.: Doubleday, 1945), p. 106.
2. *Ibid.*, p. 131.
3. *Ibid.*, p. 132. Unless otherwise noted, dates and titles of works follow the catalogue of Antheil's music in Linda Whitesitt, *The Life and Music of George Antheil 1900–1959* (Ann Arbor: UMI Research Press, 1983).
4. George Antheil, letter to Mary Curtis Bok, quoted in Wayne D. Shirley, "Another American in Paris: George Antheil's Correspondence with Mary Curtis Bok," *Quarterly Journal of the Library of Congress*, 34, no. 1 (January 1977), pp. 7–8. Mrs. Bok helped to support Antheil throughout the 1920s and much of the 1930s.
5. Antheil, *Bad Boy*, p. 133.
6. For a brief discussion of the film, which was released in 1924, see Eric Rhode, *A History of the Cinema From its Origins to 1970* (New York: Hill and Wang, 1976), pp. 135–137. A print is in the collection of the Museum of Modern Art.
7. Quoted in Shirley, "Another American in Paris," p. 10. Marguerite Bériza, a one-time prima donna of the Chicago and Boston operas, sponsored some of the more interesting experiments in lyric theater of the mid-1920s. Reviewing her 1925 season, *Musical America*'s special Paris correspondent wrote: "The work is often crude, for Paris theaters are not equipped for experiment, but it is always vital. With a company of singers as well as dancers, Bériza has been able to produce a series of ballets, opéras bouffes and miniature operas, which were not only novelties but successful ones. The outstanding works of her season were two ballets to modern music which has already been acclaimed in Europe and America—Francesco Malipiero's 'Sept Chansons' and Manuel de Falla's 'El Amor Brujo' (L'Amour Sorcier). . . . The setting for

['Sept Chansons'] and most of the other Bériza ballets were done by Ladislaw Medgyès, a Hungarian artist, who completed the harmony of the effect by staging the works himself" (Henrietta Malkiel, "Paris Modernists Rebel Against Outmoded Ballets," *Musical America,* 25 July 1925, p. 3).

8. Whitesitt, *The Life and Music of George Antheil,* pp. 106–107. For Lincoln Kirstein's relationship with Antheil in the mid-1930s, see below.

9. For Hedy Pfundmeyer, see Henry Gilfond, "George Antheil," published in *Dance Observer,* April 1936, p. 1; for *Méditerrané,* see Antheil's letter to Mary Curtis Bok, 1 February 1930, in George Antheil Collection, Box 1, Music Division, Library of Congress (hereafter Antheil Collection, MD-LC); for Tamiris, see Christena L. Schlundt, "Tamiris: A Chronicle of Her Dance Career 1927–1955," *Studies in Dance History,* 1, no. 1 (Fall–Winter 1989–1990), p. 72; "Antheil's Music Has Premiere in Berlin," *The New York Times* (hereafter *NYT*), 5 January 1929, p. 21; for *Flight,* see Shirley, "Another American in Paris," p. 17. The interest in projected images recalls the ballet *Ode,* designed by Pavel Tchelitchew and produced by Diaghilev's Ballets Russes in 1928.

10. George Antheil, letter to Ezra Pound, [autumn 1927], Ezra Pound Papers, YCAL MSS43, Series I, Box 2, Folder 71, Beinecke Library, Yale University (hereafter Pound Papers).

11. Gilfond, "George Antheil," p. 38.

12. Ninette de Valois, *Step by Step: The Formation of an Establishment* (London: W. H. Allen, 1977), p. 180.

13. J. J. Hayes, "A Ballet at the Abbey," *The New York Times,* 22 September 1929, sec. 9, p. 4.

14. W. B. Yeats, "*Fighting the Waves:* Introduction," in *Wheels and Butterflies* (New York: Macmillan, 1935), p. 61. Antheil's music for the overture, Fand's dance, and Fand's final dance was published at the end of this volume.

15. Judith Simpson White, "William Yeats and the Dancer: A History of Yeats' Work with Dance Theatre," Ph.D. diss., University of Virginia, 1979, pp. 122–123.

16. Lehman Engel, *This Bright Day* (New York: Macmillan, 1974), pp. 49–50.

17. For Antheil's activities in this period, see George Antheil Scrapbooks, Music Division, The New York Public Library for the Performing Arts (hereafter MD-NYPL).

18. This account is pieced together from reviews, advance pieces, and the program of *Helen Retires* in the Music Clippings File (Antheil, George), MD-NYPL. For Elsa Findlay, see *José Limón: An Unfinished Memoir,* ed. Lynn Garafola (Hanover: University Press of New England/Wesleyan University Press, 1999), p. 154, note 12; for Arthur Mahoney, see *Dancer's Almanac and Who's Who 1940,* ed. Ruth Eleanor Howard (New York, 1940), p. 70.

19. Gilfond, "George Antheil," p. 39.

20. George and Boske Antheil, letter to Doris Humphrey, 5 February 1932, Doris Humphrey Collection, Folder C324.3, Dance Division, The New York Public Library for the Performing Arts (hereafter DD-NYPL).

21. Antheil to Humphrey, 11 September 1933, Humphrey Collection, Folder C346.20, DD-NYPL.

22. Antheil to Bok, 25 February 1934, Antheil Collection, Box 1, MD-LC.

23. In a letter to Mrs. Bok written in April, Antheil claimed that the day after the reviews of *Helen Retires* had appeared, "the new American Ballet, represented by Kirstein (editor of Hound and Horn), Warburg (the financier of the new ballet), Balanchine (its guiding spirit and artistic director), and Dimitrieff came up here in a body and commissioned me to do a new ballet for them for production this year" (Antheil to Bok, 8 April 1934, Antheil Collection, Box 2, MD-LC).

24. Whether Antheil received any payment for his efforts is unclear. He later claimed, with much bitterness, that Warburg refused to pay the $400 commission he was promised. See Antheil to Bok, 17 June 1934, Antheil Collection, Box 2, MD-LC.

25. Antheil to Bok, 8 April 1934, Antheil Collection, Box 2, MD-LC. An orchestral work, *Archipelago* premiered as "Rhumba" (its subtitle) on 7 April 1935 by the General Motors Symphony Orchestra, conducted by Howard Barlow.

26. Antheil to Pound, 26 June 1934, Pound Papers, YCAL MSS 43, Series I, Box 2, Folder 74.

27. *Ibid.* On the day of the premiere of *Helen Retires,* 28 February 1934, Balanchine, Kirstein, and Warburg sent the following telegram to Antheil: "Homage and many congratulations to our friend and collaborator" (George Antheil Papers, Columbia University [hereafter Antheil Papers, CU]).

28. Antheil to Pound, 26 June 1934, Pound Papers.

29. Lincoln Kirstein, *Thirty Years: The New York City Ballet* (New York: Knopf, 1978), p. 49.

30. John Martin, "The Dance: Graham Again," *NYT,* 25 November 1934, sec. 9, p. 8. For a more detailed description of the dance, see R[alph] T[aylor], "Martha Graham," *The Dance Observer,* December 1934, p. 88.

31. Antheil to Bok, 8 January 1935, Antheil Collection, Box 2, MD-LC. Antheil first mentions Graham in a letter to Mrs. Bok written on 22 September 1934: "This season . . . I shall have more new works upon the boards than almost any other American composer. Martha Graham is presenting a rather large work of mine *The Woman With 100 Heads,* which I wrote last year in Europe, on November 8th. . . . She is known to be the very first American dancer, so this will be a rather important event" (Antheil Collection, Box 2, MD-LC).

32. John Martin, "Two New Dances by Miss Graham," *NYT,* 11 February 1935, p. 15. The cast consisted of Graham (One in Red), Bonnie Bird, Lil Liandre, May O'Donnell (Three in Green), Dorothy Bird, Sophie Maslow (Two in Blue), Lily Mehlman and Anna Sokolow (Two in Red). The program and sundry clippings can be found in George Antheil Scrapbooks, MD-NYPL.

33. John Martin, "American Ballet Opens Second Bill," *NYT,* 6 March 1935, p. 23.

34. Pitts Sanborn, "New Items on Program of Ballet," in George Antheil Scrapbooks, MD-NYPL.

35. George Antheil, "Down-at-the-Heels Ballet," *Stage,* March 1935, p. 49.

36. See, for instance, Daniel Fawkes, "The Future of the American Ballet," *Vanity Fair,* May 1934, p. 32; "An American Ballet," *Vanity Fair,* April 1935, pp. 38–39 (with "snapshots in color" by Steichen); "The American Ballet," *Vanity Fair,* January 1936, pp. 52–53 (with drawings by Dora Abrahams); Marya Mannes, "Season's Turn in

Show-Life," *Vogue*, 1 September 1934, pp. 52–53; Mannes, "Vogue's Spot-light," *Vogue*, 15 February 1935, pp. 52–53, 90; Mannes, "Vogue's Spot-light," *Vogue*, 1 April 1935, pp. 76–77, 122; "America Launches a Ballet Company," *Town and Country*, 15 December 1934, p. 31; "America On Its Toes: Balletomanes Revive a Gay New-Old Art," *Vanity Fair*(?), September(?) 1935 [in George Antheil Scrapbooks, MD-NYPL]. Photographs of Balanchine and unidentified members of the American Ballet were featured in "Beaton's Scrap-book," *Vogue*, 1 June 1935, pp. 70–73.

37. John Martin, "The New American Company's First Season Rated as a Success," *NYT*, 10 March 1935, sec. 8, p. 9. Marya Mannes spoke of this as well in her column for *Vogue*: "The Ballet audience was truly a concentration of all brilliant *chi-chi*; given over to hysterical applause, delighted gasping, and a startling lack of discrimination. It was apparently smart to laugh at the inept buffoonery of 'Alma Mater,' to clap every *entrechat*; and to weep over the colours that Tchelitchew gave 'Errante,' which were indeed exquisite and far superior to the composition itself. This same audience at a peerless performance at the Radio City Music Hall would not have lifted a finger. In justice, though, there were some in the audience who took the ballet at its worth: as a group of charming and talented youngsters working in a purely Russian convention that could give considerable optical pleasure, but that naturally needed time and fresh direction to bring it to any real importance. Of America, the only evidence is the directness and vitality of the dances, and that should be, above all, nourished. In one thing did the aesthetes and the sober-heads agree; William Dollar could be one of the leading dancers of to-day. But, as one critic pointed out the morning after the American Ballet opened, this wild applause of the fashionable is the greatest danger that promising group can know" ("Vogue's Spot-light," 1 April 1935, p. 77).

38. Bronislava Nijinska, "Reflections about the Production of *Les Biches* and *Hamlet* in Markova-Dolin Ballets," trans. Lydia Lopokova, *The Dancing Times*, February 1937, p. 617.

39. John Martin, "The Dance: Ballet Russe," *NYT*, 31 December 1933, sec. 10, p. 8.

40. John Martin, "American Ballet Makes Its Debut," *NYT*, 2 March 1935, p. 19.

41. Martin, "American Ballet Opens Second Bill."

42. John Martin, "The Dance: The Ballet," *NYT*, 10 March 1935, sec. 10, p. 9.

43. Antheil, *Bad Boy of Music*, p. 277.

44. George Antheil, "Antheil 1937," in *Martha Graham: The Early Years*, ed. Merle Armitage (Los Angeles, 1937; rpt. New York: Da Capo, 1978), pp. 72, 75–76.

45. Antheil to Bok, [June 1937], Antheil Collection, Box 2, MD-LC. At the time Antheil was living at 8163 Willow Glen Road in Hollywood.

46. A letter to Antheil from Sergei Denham dated 21 May 1939 indicates that at some point a project with the ballet Russe de Monte Carlo was in the offing, but that the composer had unaccountably failed to pursue it (Sergei Denham: Records of the Ballet Russe de Monte Carlo, Folder 1389, Dance Division, The New York Public Library for the Performing Arts (cited hereafter as Denham Papers, DD-NYPL).

47. Virgil Thomson, "Music: Our Musical Tom Sawyer," *New York Herald Tribune*, 14 February 1944, p. 8.

48. Antheil to Denham, 26 November 1944, Denham Papers, Folder 1389, DD-NYPL.
49. Balanchine to Antheil, 13 September 1945, Antheil Papers, CU.
50. *Ghost Town*, which premiered on 12 November 1939 and was set in a ghost town of the American West, had choreography by Marc Platt (Platoff), "ravishing" costumes by Raoul Pène du Bois, a future Tony award winner, and a "gem" of a backdrop by him as well. For a review of the premiere, see John Martin, "'Ghost Town' Given By Ballet Russe," *NYT*, 13 November 1939, p. 15. See also Marc Platt, with Renée Renouf, "*Ghost Town* Revisited: A Memoir of Producing an American Ballet for the Ballet Russe de Monte Carlo," *Dance Chronicle*, 24, no. 2 (2001), pp. 147–192.
51. Antheil to Denham, 3 August 1946, Denham Papers, DD-NYPL.
52. Antheil conducted the work in Trenton in 1932 ("Famous Trenton Composer Plays Here to Help Hospital," *Trenton(?) Times*, [late] February 1932, n.p., Antheil Collection, Box 2, MD-LC). According to the program, however, the piece "was conceived in 1919" ("George Antheil Fêted in His Home City," *Musical Courier*, 12 March 1932, in Music Clippings File [Antheil, George], MD-NYPL). Linda Whitesitt in *The Life and Music of George Antheil* also lists a "Creole Festival," which Antheil performed in Dresden in 1923 (p. 203).
53. Both the scenario and the sketches are in Folder 88, Antheil Papers, MD-NYPL.
54. See, for instance, Antheil's letters to Denham of 17 December 1946, 27 December 1946, and 21 September 1947, Denham Papers, DD-NYPL.
55. Correspondence, Box 14, Folder 9, Balanchine Archive, Harvard Theatre Collection.
56. John Martin, "The Dance: Ballet Russe,": *NYT*, 13 August 1944, sec. 10, p. 4; Martin, "The Dance: Notes from the Field," *NYT*, 26 November 1944, sec. 10, p. 4.
57. The genesis of the project is described in A. E. Hotchner, "Hemingway Ballet: Venice to Broadway," *New York Herald Tribune*, 27 December 1953, sec. 4, p. 3.
58. *Ibid.*
59. Kirstein to Antheil, 5 March 1953, Antheil Papers, CU. The above account is pieced together from Antheil's correspondence with Hotchner in the Antheil Papers, Columbia University. This correspondence includes not only Hotchner's letters but carbon copies of Antheil's frequent and voluminous replies.
60. Grant authorization 5316, 1 April 1953, Rockefeller Foundation Collection, R.G. 1.2 (Projects), Series 200R (U.S./Humanities), Box 392, Folder 3390, Rockefeller Archive Center, Pocantico Hills, N.Y.
61. Antheil, *Bad Boy of Music*, p. 277.
62. Kirstein, *Thirty Years*, p. 49.
63. Hotchner to Antheil, [early April 1953], Antheil Papers, CU.
64. Antheil to Hotchner, 16 September 1953, Antheil Papers, CU.
65. Samuel Lurie to Antheil, 10 November 1953, American Ballet Theatre (hereafter ABT) Records, Folder 474, DD-NYPL. "Support for American ballet came from an unusual source recently when the Ford Foundation's TV Workshop commissioned Ballet Theatre to create a new work. Ballet Theatre responded with 'The Capital of the World,' devised by Eugene Loring from a Hemingway story" ("Hemingway in Ballet," *The New York Times Magazine*, 27 December 1953, p. 38).

66. Antheil to Lurie, 19 November 1953, ABT Records, Folder 74, DD-NYPL.

67. This description is based on the revised libretto and two drafts of the television script (Eugene Loring Papers, Folders 50, 53, and 54, DD-NYPL) and a kinescope of the *Omnibus* telecast, which is also in the NYPL Dance Division.

68. Virgil Thomson, "Music and Musicians: In the Theater," *New York Herald Tribune,* 3 January 1954, sec. 4, p. 5.

69. P. W. Manchester, "Season in Review: The Ballet Theatre," *Dance News,* February 1954, p. 7.

70. Doris Hering, "Season in Review: Ballet Theatre," *Dance Magazine,* February 1954, p. 74.

71. John Martin, "Ballet Theatre Gives Novelties," *NYT,* 28 December 1953, p. 15.

72. Antheil to Samuel Weintraub, 10 May 1954, MD-NYPL.

DALÍ, ANA MARÍA, AND *THE THREE-CORNERED HAT*

In the twentieth-century rebirth of Spanish dance as a form of modernist the-ater, no work was more significant than *Le Tricorne*. Inspired by Pedro de Alar-cón's nineteenth-century comic classic *El sombrero de tres picos* (or *The Three-Cornered Hat*), it came to the stage in 1919 in an all-star production by Diaghilev's Ballets Russes. There were spectacular designs by Picasso, Spain's foremost painter, and a splendid commissioned score by Manuel de Falla, the country's leading composer. The choreography was by Léonide Massine, at twenty-two already a brilliant innovator and a connoisseur of Spanish dance.

The ballet opened in London at the Alhambra Theatre to both popular and critical acclaim. Bloomsbury was in the audience along with Spanish intellectu-als of the stature of Salvador de Madariaga, who wrote about the production for the Madrid daily *El Sol*.[1] For the first time in decades, a Spanish work, albeit one choreographed by a Russian and produced by an itinerant troupe of Russians, Poles, and various other European nationalities, stood at the epicenter of "West-ern" cultural consciousness.

Le Tricorne remained in the repertory of the Ballets Russes throughout the 1920s. In 1934, Massine revived it for Colonel de Basil's Ballet Russe, the leading successor to the Diaghilev company. With Massine in his original role as the Miller and "baby ballerina" Tamara Toumanova as the Miller's Wife, the revival, with sets and costumes from the Diaghilev original, elicited bravos from critics and audiences alike. John Martin, writing in *The New York Times*, described Massine's performance as nothing less than an "electrifying" achievement.[2]

The ballet became a favorite with the American public, and when Massine left de Basil to form a rival company with substantial U.S. backing, he sued the former colonel for legal title to the work; at that time, copyright did not auto-matically belong to the choreographer. Massine won his case, and in 1938 *Le Tri-corne*, along with its scenery and costumes, became his personal property. The following year, he teamed up with the celebrated Spanish dancer Argentinita; the result was *Capriccio Espagnol*, a rousing crowd pleaser the two had choreo-graphed, and several joint appearances in *Le Tricorne*, initially with the Ballet Russe de Monte Carlo and in the early 1940s with Ballet Theatre.

Massine's renewed interest in *Le Tricorne* on the eve of the Second World War

This essay was originally published in *Dalí and the Ballet: Set and Costumes for "The Three-Cornered Hat"*, ed. Curtis L. Carter (Milwaukee: Haggerty Museum of Art, 2000).

coincided with a boom in Spanish dance, especially in the United States. In part this was the legacy of La Argentina's trail-blazing tours of the late 1920s and 1930s, which culminated in an invitation to perform at FDR's White House in 1935 and did for Spanish dance what Anna Pavlova's earlier whistle-stopping tours had done for ballet. The outbreak of the Spanish Civil War in 1936, followed within weeks by the brutal assassination of the poet Federico García Lorca, prompted an exodus of the liberal intelligentsia and arts community. By 1940, numerous Spanish dancers and musicians had settled in New York, beginning with Argentinita, her sister Pilar López, and the guitarist Carlos Montoya. But as news items and reviews in the dance press make clear, there were Spanish dancers galore in the city. Not all of them hailed from Spain. José Fernández, a late-spring attraction at the Rainbow Room (and occasional choreographer for Ballet Theatre and American Ballet Caravan), was Mexican; his Rainbow Room partner, Monna Montes (who also doubled as a ballet dancer), was American, as was La Trianita (née Sally MacLean), who married Carlos Montoya amid a flurry of publicity, and Carola Goya (née Weller), a fixture of the Spanish dance scene for decades. As for José Greco, his name notwithstanding, he was actually an Italian raised in Brooklyn.[3] Meanwhile, in the strongly left-wing modern dance world, the war in Spain had inspired any number of dances, from José Limón's *Danza de la Muerte* to Sophia Delza's *We Weep for Spain* and *We March for Spain,* Lily Mehlman's *Spanish Woman,* Martha Graham's *Immediate Tragedy* and *Deep Song,* all choreographed in 1937.[4]

Among the real Spanish dancers who turned up on American shores in these years was Ana María. Only twenty (it was said) when she made her New York debut at the Guild Theatre in March 1940, she was a native of Madrid, a student of Pauleta Pamiés, Antonio el de Bilbao, El Estampío, and La Coquinera, and a veteran of tours that had taken her throughout Spain as well as to France, Portugal, Italy, Belgium, and most recently Cuba. For her first New York concert, she offered a sampling of her repertory—the Ritual Fire Dance from Falla's *El Amor Brujo,* flamenco and regional dances, and a "Sevilla" to music by Albéniz that she performed with José Fernández, who won plaudits from John Martin for his "aristocratic reserve."[5] About Ana María herself the critics were less enthusiastic. Although Albertina Vitak found her heel work "splendid," she thought the dancer's striking costumes were "more suitable to cabaret as were most of her numbers."[6] Walter Terry, for his part, felt that Ana María's "personal charms outbalance[d] her dancing ability. . . . She's a 'personality girl,' and if you like her personality you'll probably like her show." The audience, which was large and full of Spaniards, apparently did, for it showered her with applause and what Martin described as "enormous quantities of flowers."

After this debut (and a few other performances), Ana María did not dance in New York for eight years. Returning to Havana, she formed the Ballet Español, raised a son, and made several tours of South America. When she reappeared in New York in 1948, it was with an ensemble of twenty-three and under the management of Sol Hurok, who booked the Ballet Español into Carnegie Hall for two performances. As before, the program consisted of several divertissements, but this time it also featured the complete *El Amor Brujo,* which Ana María had choreographed and costumed; she also danced the lead part of Candelas. Despite the ambitiousness of the program and the auspicious circumstances, the reviews were discouraging. Wrote Walter Terry: "Since the stage presentation— including production, staging, lighting, choreography and dancing—did not give evidence of those standards of performance normally associated with a New York concert event, . . . detailed comment on the proceedings seems unnecessary." More positive was Miles Kastendieck, who thought Ana María "had plenty of technique to show off" but that a "dash of personality would have enlivened the whole show."[7]

Undeterred by the tepid reception, Ana María returned the following year to the Ziegfeld Theatre with her most ambitious production yet, *The Three-Cornered Hat.* Several years had elapsed since Massine's *Le Tricorne* had last been seen in New York, although he had revived the ballet in London for Sadler's Wells in 1947. This had been a coup for Ninette de Valois, the company's director, for Massine not only staged the ballet and performed his old role of the Miller (to Margot Fonteyn's Miller's Wife); he also provided the sets and costumes designed by Picasso for the original Diaghilev production twenty-eight years before. By 1949, Ana María could have had no illusions about the critical reception of her work in New York, but with Salvador Dalí designing her new *Three-Cornered Hat,* she all but announced her intention of turning the premiere into an event. In postwar New York, no visual artist was better known or enjoyed greater notoriety than Dalí.

Spanish-born, Dalí had burst on the American art world in 1932 with the first New York appearance of his work at the Julien Levy Gallery's famous—or infamous—"Surréalisme" exhibition. Dalí's painting *The Persistence of Memory,* later acquired by the Museum of Modern Art, caused a sensation; an even greater one followed in 1933 with the artist's first solo show; by 1934, when Levy gave him a second solo show, nearly half the paintings sold in three days. Dalí coveted fame, fortune, and celebrity; he courted millionaires, and he shamelessly wooed the press, especially the American press. His stunts were outrageous— landing in New York with an eight-foot-long baguette, costuming his wife as an "exquisite corpse"—his words—for a party. By 1936, when *Time* magazine put him on the cover and Bonwit Teller commissioned him to do a surrealist store window, "America," he wrote, "was prey to acute Dalinitis."[8]

Like most surrealists, Dalí did not limit his activities to the easel. With Luis Buñuel, he made those classics of French avant-garde film, *Un Chien andalou* and *L'Age d'or;* he designed fashion ads and magazine covers, illustrated numerous books, wrote essays, a bad novel, and an autobiography, *The Secret Life of Salvador Dalí,* that was published in New York in 1942. He spent the Second World War in the United States. Here, writes his biographer Meryle Secrest, "his dismembered arms, limp watches, ruined columns, pieces of driftwood, tables with women's legs, crutches and ants were helping to advertise Gunther's furs, Ford cars, Wrigley's chewing gum, Schiaparelli perfume, Gruen watches, the products of the Abbott Laboratories and of the Container Corporation of America. They were being reproduced in shop windows up and down Fifth Avenue. They inspired a Broadway show, *Lady in the Dark,* as well as a Hitchcock film, *Spellbound,* and an experimental collaboration with Walt Disney."[9] In his American incarnation Dalí certainly lived up to André Breton's disparaging moniker, "Avida Dollars."

Dalí first met choreographer Léonide Massine in Europe in the mid-1930s. But it was in New York, in 1939, just months after the artist had pushed a bathtub full of water through the window of his second Bonwit Teller display (the store had removed one of the spider-covered women without his permission) in his biggest headline-making escapade yet,[10] that *Bacchanale,* their first ballet together, opened at the Metropolitan Opera. Two other collaborations followed: *Labyrinth* (1941), based on the myth of Theseus and Ariadne, and *Mad Tristan* (1944), inspired by Wagner's *Tristan and Isolde.* Dalí also worked with George Balanchine (although André Eglevsky was credited with the choreography) on *Sentimental Colloquy* (1944), Argentinita on *Café de Chinitas* (1944), and did the original designs, which the choreographer ultimately rejected, for Antony Tudor's *Romeo and Juliet* (1943).[11]

In an essay published in the early 1950s, Oliver Smith rued that as a designer Dalí had never found a match for his "tremendous" personality. "Given collaborators with intelligence, and armed with crowbars, he might create poetic magic for the stage instead of creating a tidal wave that engulfs not only the stage production, but the audience as well."[12] His sets were dazzling indeed, fantasies writ so large they overwhelmed the human ants scurrying before them. In *Bacchanale,* the dancers made their entrances through a hole in the breast of a giant swan; in *Labyrinth,* they stepped through an opening in the naked torso of a man with a cracked skull. In *Sentimental Colloquy,* bearded, cadaverous cyclists rode across a décor painted in the style of a grid, and a fountain sprouted from a grand piano. In *Mad Tristan,* however, Dalí outdid himself. Here, wrote critic Edwin Denby, "fantastic backdrops, costumes, stage effects tumble out over the stage for half an hour in frenzied profusion . . . a proliferation of decoration no one in the world but Dali can rival." Audiences were riveted by the brilliant rendering of three magnificent horses' heads, which towered over the stage like the Mount Rushmore Memorial (as Oliver Smith thought) and parted at the end of each "act" to reveal a body descending into a grave.[13]

Dalí returned to Spain in 1948. However, before leaving the country that had been his home for eight years, he was invited by his friend Sol Hurok to attend Ana María's concert at Carnegie Hall. The artist was impressed. The two met, and Dalí proposed they stage *The Three-Cornered Hat* for the dancer's next season.[14] With its big names and international cachet, the project recalled another

Hurok initiative of the time—the 1945 Ballet Theatre production of *Firebird* designed by Marc Chagall. (In 1949, Hurok would sell these *Firebird* sets and costumes to the New York City Ballet for Balanchine's version of the work.)[15] Dalí's scenery was executed by the E. B. Dunkel Studios, which did sets for many ballet productions. Dalí supervised the scene painting and, like Picasso before him, did some of it himself.

For the critics who attended the premiere at the Ziegfeld Theatre, Dalí's contribution, as expressed by the *New York Journal-American*'s Miles Kastendieck, was "surprisingly conservative." In the *New York World-Telegram* Louis Biancolli breathed a sigh of relief: "For a change, the backdrop was almost strictly conventional in its landscape detail. No bleeding trees or melting watches of the typical Dalí canvases." Instead, there was a frieze depicting sacks of grain, a playful reminder of what the Miller does for a living, the design of a huge guitar, and a backcloth that Walter Terry in the *New York Herald Tribune* pronounced "sheer delight."[16] To the left was a white-walled Andalusian house, its red door and shuttered windows set at funny angles; beyond it stretched a dust-and-ochre landscape where sacks, as light and airy as cotton, puffed from an oversized well. The effect was playful and surprisingly evocative of the ballet's Andalusian setting, with its hot, dusty plains, mirage-like hills, and seemingly endless expanses of blue sky.

Dalí's return to Spain inaugurated what he later took to calling his classical period. But the classicism or, more properly, neoclassicism of his *Three-Cornered Hat* also harks back to Picasso's designs for the original Diaghilev production. Here, too, is the timeless cerulean sky, simple, sunbaked houses, immaculate draftsmanship, and eighteenth-century costumes inspired by early Goya. This is not to say that Dalí "lifted" his designs from Picasso, "the only Parisian," he once wrote, "who mattered to my eyes," or as he also put it, the artist he "recognized . . . alone as among my peers."[17] But he certainly knew Picasso's work, if not the actual sets and costumes (although he could well have seen a performance of the ballet in New York during the 1940s), then the designs, published in a magnificent portfolio by Picasso's art dealer Paul Rosenberg in Paris in 1920.[18] In Dalí's version, one finds the same "lavish use of bright colours in opposition to black," as art historian Douglas Cooper has described Picasso's costumes, the same bold stripes, the same very Spanish juxtaposition of *gravitas* and gaiety.[19] But there are also important differences between the two versions. Dalí's use of lime green with eggplant purple and cherry red; his dramatic expanses of black; his simplification of the decorative detailing; his playful use of constructed elements, including the "tails" of the Corregidor's dress coat—all set his work apart from Picasso's and stamp it as his own. Far from being a copy or imitation of *Le Tricorne*, Dalí's *Three-Cornered Hat* is a knowing, witty homage to Picasso's ballet.

Ana María, who danced the role of the Miller's Wife, fared less well than Dalí. Walter Terry thought her choreography was "pretty thin"; Harriett Johnson that it lacked "real characterization."[20] Still, most critics agreed that Ana María herself was dancing better than she had the previous year at Carnegie Hall and that her company was generally stronger. There was praise for the energy and teamwork of the dancers, although the warmest praise was reserved for the men and guitarist Carlos Montoya, whom she had hired (along with a full orchestra) for the Ziegfeld season.

Amazingly, given the expense and effort to which she had gone, to say nothing of the publicity value of Dalí's name, *The Three-Cornered Hat* was given only once in New York, on opening night. For the remaining two performances, Ana María fell back on tried-and-true works from her repertory, including *El Amor Brujo* (billed now as "Love the Sorcerer") and *Capriccio Español* (to Rimsky-Korsakov's well-known music). Short numbers completed each program, giving her ample opportunity to display the glamorous costumes she seems to have changed—if the press is to be believed—numerous times in a single evening.

The Three-Cornered Hat was also noticeably absent from the ten-week coast-to-coast tour that Hurok arranged the following autumn, when the company, now improbably billed as "The First Spanish Ballet Company to Tour the U.S.," played theaters, high school gyms, and college and civic auditoriums across the country.[21] In 1951, when she returned to Spain after an absence of twelve years, the work remained in repertory, and it continued to appear in company programs the following year when she toured Latin America. In October 1952, when she set out on her third U.S. tour, the work did reappear, but without the Dalí scenery, which seems to have lessened its impact. In fact, the ballet that generated most of the praise and enthusiasm on this cross-country tour was Ana María's version of *Carmen,* although some critics expressed reservations about the liberties she had taken with the plot and music. And for the first time there was mention of empty seats, which the *San Francisco News* critic, Marjory M. Fisher, attributed to the recent visit of José Greco, whose excellent company had gained a huge following since making its first U.S. tour the year before.[22] Ana María made a last appearance in the New York area under Hurok's auspices at the Brooklyn Academy of Music in 1954. Although Dalí was again listed as one of the company's designers, his ballet was not performed.

By then, Ana María seems to have had enough of the United States and New York, where she had been living since 1947, married the Cuban composer and pianist Alfredo Munar in 1951, and given birth to their daughter, also named Ana María, in 1952. But the couple's return to Cuba was not to be permanent. By 1960, they were back in New York. The following January, after a stint at the Château Madrid, one of the city's better nightclubs, the "Ballet Español Ana María" (as the company was now billed) gave its last performance at Carnegie Hall. The reviews were devastating. "If this had been the annual recital of Ana María's students in Havana or San Juan," wrote Marcia B. Marks in *Dance Magazine,* "it would have had some validity . . . but in Carnegie Hall Ana María's

Spanish Ballet turned into a talent show with limited talent and very little show."[23] It wasn't only the amateurism of the program that prompted such dismissive remarks. To American critics of the early 1960s, Spanish dance was a dying art, its practitioners "guilelessly anachronistic," as Marks described Ana María, "in this age of sophisticated sveltness and style." With the New York City Ballet, the Martha Graham company, and so many other ensembles at their creative peak, and a postmodern avant-garde fermenting downtown, Spanish dance was simultaneously a throwback to the character-style ballets of the 1930s, a genre of national dance disparaged by association with the city's growing Latin population, and a form of what used to be called ethnic dance (that is, an art thought to be expressive of a particular race). Things had come full circle since La Argentina's thrilling visits of the 1930s.

After returning to Spain, Dalí's interest in ballet waned. He did a few more productions, most notably *Gala* for Maurice Béjart's Ballet of the Twentieth Century in 1961, but not even this ostensible tribute to his wife—in the title role Ludmila Tcherina, personifying female desire, wore "two enormous flesh coloured breasts over a . . . leotard . . . so tight as to make her appear nude"[24]—recaptured the artistic excitement of his collaborations of the 1940s. Ana María and Alfredo Munar eventually settled in Miami, joining the exodus from Castro's Cuba. Meanwhile, in the decades since her *Three-Cornered Hat* disappeared in the blink of a surrealist eye, the ballet was fitfully resurrected by any number of choreographers, among them Pilar López and Antonio in the 1950s, Germinal Casado in the 1980s, José Antonio in the 1990s, to say nothing of Massine, who brought the original back to life for the Joffrey Ballet in 1969. The tale of the Andalusian miller and his flirtatious wife still exerts a spell over the imagination.

NOTES

1. Madariaga's article, "El Sombrero de tres picos," appeared in *El Sol* on 30 July 1919. It is reprinted in *España y los Ballets Russes,* ed. Vicente García-Márquez with Lynn Garafola, catalogue of an exhibition at the Auditorio Manuel de Falla in Granada, from 17 June to 2 July 1989, p. 104.

2. Quoted in Kathrine Sorley Walker, *De Basil's Ballets Russes* (London: Hutchinson, 1982), p. 35.

3. For José Fernández, see Anatole Chujoy et al., "The Ballet Theatre Arrives," *Dance,* February 1940, p. 69; "Tempo," *Dance,* May 1940, p. 5; Lincoln Kirstein, "The American Ballet in Argentina: Part II of a Travel Diary," *The American Dancer,* October 1941, p. 13; Nancy Reynolds, *Repertory in Review: Forty Years of the New York City Ballet,* introd. Lincoln Kirstein (New York: Dial, 1977), p. 69; Anatole Chujoy, *The New York City Ballet* (New York: Knopf, 1953), p. 125; Charles Payne, *American Ballet Theatre* (New York: Knopf, 1979), pp. 33, 103, 130, 362. Fernández choreographed *Goyescas*

for Ballet Theatre's maiden season in 1940, and the following year, with Lew Christensen, *Pastorela* for American Ballet Caravan's South American tour. In 1945, Lucia Chase tried to acquire *Pastorela* for Ballet Theatre but was overruled by Sol Hurok; the work was revived by Lincoln Kirstein for Ballet Society in 1947. For Monna Montes, see "Tamiment Players," *Dance,* October 1939, p. 13; Mori Fremon, "Latins in Manhattan," *Dance,* May 1940, p. 18; for her appearance with Fernández in *Goyescas,* Payne, *American Ballet Theatre,* p. 362; for Trianita, see Auricle, "Entr'acte," *Dance,* May 1940, p. 10; for Carola Goya, see Jack Anderson, "Carola Goya, 88, an Authority on Spanish Dance Forms, Dies," *The New York Times* (hereafter *NYT*), 17 May 1994, p. B8; for José Greco, see the entry by Judy Farrar Burns in the *International Encyclopedia of Dance* (hereafter *IED*), 1998. Carmen Amaya fled Spain in 1936 and, after touring extensively in South America, made her New York debut in early 1941.

4. For the response of modern dance choreographers to the Spanish Civil War, see Ellen Graff, *Stepping Left: Dance and Politics in New York City, 1928–1942* (Durham, N.C.: Duke University Press, 1997), pp. 120–121; and *José Limón: An Unfinished Memoir,* ed. Lynn Garafola, introd. Deborah Jowitt (Hanover: University Press of New England/Wesleyan University Press, 1998), pp. 79–83.

5. John Martin, "The Dance: Ana Maria in Spanish Dances," *NYT,* 12 March 1940, in *MGZB (Ana Maria Ballet Espagnol), Dance Division, The New York Public Library for the Performing Arts (hereafter DD-NYPL). Unless otherwise noted, all programs and press clippings come from this folder.

6. Albertina Vitak, "Dance Events Reviewed," *The American Dancer,* May 1940, p. 36.

7. W[alter] T[erry], "Ana Maria's New Ballet," *New York Herald Tribune,* 21 May 1948, p. 18; Miles Kastendieck, "Ballet Espanol [sic] Not Exciting," *New York Journal-American,* 21 May 1948, p. 16.

8. Salvador Dalí, with André Parinaud, *The Unspeakable Confessions of Salvador Dalí,* trans. Harold J. Salemson (New York: Morrow, 1976), p. 183. For the baguette, see pp. 178–179; for a description of the "exquisite corpse" costume, see p. 180. For Dalí's exhibitions at the Julien Levy Gallery, see the chronology by Lisa Jacobs in *Julien Levy: Portrait of an Art Gallery,* ed. Ingrid Schaffner and Lisa Jacobs (Cambridge: MIT Press, 1998), as well as Schaffner's essay, "Alchemy of the Gallery," especially pp. 34–42.

9. Meryle Secrest, *Salvador Dalí: The Surrealist Jester* (London: Weidenfeld and Nicolson, 1986), p. 189.

10. For a description of the display and the escapade, see *Unspeakable Confessions,* pp. 185–187. For another account, see the unsigned "Homage to Dalí," in *Salvador Dalí 1910–1965,* catalogue of an exhibition at the Gallery of Modern Art, New York, 18 December 1965–28 February 1966, p. VII.

11. *Bacchanale* and *Labyrinth* were produced by the Ballet Russe de Monte Carlo; *Mad Tristan* and *Sentimental Colloquy* by Ballet International; *Café de Chinitas* and *Romeo and Juliet* (which came to the stage in 1943 with sets and costumes by Eugene Berman) by Ballet Theatre. Set designs for *Romeo and Juliet* are reproduced in Ralf

Schiebler, *Dalí: Genius, Obsession and Lust* (New York: Prestel, n.d.), p. 10, and in Juan José Tharrats, *Artistas españoles en el ballet* (Barcelona: Argos, 1950), p. 25. Additional designs are in the Dance Division. Tharrats describes *Café de Chinitas* as a "flamenco scene . . . to a selection of folk dances arranged by Federico García Lorca. The work was premiered by the Ballet Theatre company in Michigan. For this ballet, Salvador Dalí painted two impressive decors, one of which, the backdrop, shows a dancer, her body transformed into a guitar, crucified on a fissured wall; from her hands, castanets riveted like nails make the blood flow, tracing the silhouette of a shawl on the wall" (pp. 40–41). Payne's *American Ballet Theatre* makes no mention of this work, although John Martin, in his review of *Mad Tristan*, refers to Dalí's "stirring, if somewhat tasteless, setting for Argentinita's 'Cafe de Chinitas'" (John Martin, "Ballet Premiere of 'Mad Tristan,'" *NYT*, 16 December 1944, p. 19). Yet another ballet conceived by Dalí in this period was *Sacrifice (A Dream of Philip II)*, later renamed *Mysteria*. For a variety of reasons the ballet was never produced, although the artist's scenario and a group of his designs have survived, the latter in the collection of Joan Flesichmann Tobin. See Malcolm McCormick, "Designing for the Ballet Russe de Monte Carlo," in *The Golden Age of Costume and Set Design for the Ballet Russe de Monte Carlo 1938 to 1944*, compiled by Kristin L. Spangenberg (Cincinnati: Cincinnati Art Museum, 2000), pp. 64–66, as well as Plates 23 and 24. In *Choreography by George Balanchine: A Catalogue of Works* (New York: Eakins Press, 1983), *Sentimental Colloquy* is credited to Balanchine, although the program identified the choreographer as Eglevsky.

12. Oliver Smith, "Ballet Design," *Dance News Annual* (1953), p. 96.
13. Edwin Denby, "The Ballet: Dali to the Hilt," *New York Herald Tribune*, 16 December 1944, p. 7; Smith, "Ballet Design," p. 96.
14. *Dalí Monumental*, exhibition catalogue, Museu Nacional de Rio de Janeiro, 25 March–27 May, 1998; Museu de Arte de Sao Paolo, Assis, Châteaubriand (Masp.), 9 June–9 August 1998 (Buenos Aires: Texoart, 1998), p. 255.
15. Payne, *American Ballet Theatre*, pp. 115–116, 139–142; Lincoln Kirstein, *Thirty Years: The New York City Ballet* (New York: Knopf, 1978), p. 106.
16. Miles Kastendieck, "Ana María Lacks Artistry," *New York Journal-American*, 25 April 1949, p. 11; Louis Biancolli, "Ballet Español Returns with Verve," *New York World-Telegram*, 25 April 1949, p. 11; Walter Terry, "The Ballet," *New York Herald Tribune*, 25 April 1949, p. 13.
17. *Unspeakable Confessions*, pp. 75, 189.
18. In 1978, Dover Publications brought out an inexpensive reprint of the original de luxe portfolio. The introduction to the Dover edition was by Parmenia Migel.
19. Douglas Cooper, *Picasso Theatre* (New York: Abrams, 1987), p. 41.
20. Terry, "The Ballet," p. 13; Harriett Johnson, "'Three-Cornered Hat' Given With Dalí Decor," *New York Post*, 25 April 1949, p 27.
21. The flyer is in the Ana María Ballet Español clipping file, DD-NYPL. For an announcement of the tour, see "Ballet Ana María Starts U.S. Tour," *Dance News*, No-

vember 1950, p. 3. The information about this and the company's other tours in the 1950s is based on the clippings in the Ana María Ballet Espagnol [sic] scrapbook at the Dance Division.

22. Burns, "José Greco," *IED*.

23. M[arcia] B. M[arks], "Ballet Español Ana María," *Dance Magazine*, March 1961, p. 23.

24. Trudy Goth, "The Dancing World: Venice," *Ballet Today*, November 1961, p. 16.

RADICAL MOMENTS

MARTHA GRAHAM CENTENNIAL CELEBRATION

Five days before the Martha Graham Dance Company opened the Next Wave Festival at the Brooklyn Academy of Music (BAM), the dancers decided to strike. The action came fourteen months after their contract had expired, with negotiations stalled by the dancers' demand for a minimum guarantee of twenty work weeks (to qualify for unemployment benefits) and by management's insistence on "givebacks" in overseas travel pay. The story hit the papers; a federal mediator was called in; a new contract was quickly signed. Two nights later the curtain went up on the New York segment of the "Martha Graham Centennial Celebration," a year-long tribute sponsored by Philip Morris and chaired by Hillary Clinton and Ambassador Pamela Harriman.

There were many ironies in the episode, beginning with the juxtaposition of public glamor and backstage penury typical, alas, of many American dance companies. The BAM season, a ten-day retrospective focusing on works from the late 1920s to the late 1950s, was billed as "Radical Graham." Not that the title referred to politics, either of the 1930s, when Graham created her first great works, or of today, when her company, for all the centenary hoopla, has trouble meeting its payroll. Like other aspects of the season, the billing was a marketing ploy to update the company's image for the stylish consumers of BAM's "Next Wave" festival.

In fact, Graham's dances, especially those of the middle and late 1930s, were genuinely radical, both in form and in content. Nor have today's choreographers given up on politics, even if they seldom take on issues like Bosnia. Only days before the Graham season began, Meredith Monk, a graduate of the 1960s avant-garde and a pioneer of site-specific works combining theater, dance, and music, presented her new *American Archeology #1* on Roosevelt Island. Set in Lighthouse Park on the northern tip of the island and in the ruins of New York's nineteenth-century smallpox hospital at the southern end, the piece wove images of the island's past into the fabric of its immediate present. With a multigenerational cast of sixty that included both amateurs (skipping children, strolling groups of oldsters) and professional singer-dancers, the first half mingled the activities of a community at play with chants paying homage to communities

This essay was published in *The Nation* on 12 December 1994.

past, while the second, which began at dusk, evoked the unfortunates—epileptics, madmen, and smallpox victims—once sent to the island to die.

Monk's radicalism permeates virtually every aspect of her work, from its subject matter, indebted to social history and multiculturalism, to its form, aimed at creating a participatory, communitarian event. Merce Cunningham's radicalism, by contrast, stems from his defiance of the marketplace, an unwillingness to accommodate the expectations of a "philistine" or untutored public that links him to the turn-of-the-century avant-garde. In the series of "Events" that inaugurated his recent season at the Joyce Theater, he showed no signs of mellowing.

Stitched together from existing pieces of choreography in an order and number that varies from performance to performance, the "Event" eschews the temporal and structural conventions of most dance works—narrative, literary symbolism, and musical "accompaniment." What it offers (like Cunningham's pieces generally) is superb dancing, especially by the women, whose legs unfold with a luminous beauty that seems beyond gravity and time. This sensuality is Cunningham's only concession to the audience. Indeed, the irony of his radicalism is that in defying the marketplace he has made his work a cult phenomenon, an art for a community of cognoscenti.

Where Monk's radicalism is rooted in the counterculture of the 1960s, Cunningham's has its origins in the late 1940s and 1950s, when his mature aesthetic took form. This, of course, was the McCarthy era, and in the hermeticism of Cunningham's work, its adamant rejection of symbolic meaning of any kind, one is tempted to see not only a connection with the Abstract Expressionists but also a political stance—the creation of a space insulated by its very inpenetrability from the incursions of politics. In the late 1930s, when Cunningham joined the Martha Graham company, socially conscious dancers were everywhere—in WPA programs such as the Federal Dance Theatre, in worker-oriented organizations such as the New Dance League, in benefit concerts for Spain and other worthy causes, in union halls, political pageants, and the companies of choreographers like Graham. The left-wing movement left a deep imprint on modern dance of the period, as did the demise of that movement, hastened by the dismantling of the WPA and the anticommunist impulse that accompanied it. Indeed, Cunningham's tenure with the Graham company, which he left in 1945, coincided with a major shift in the choreographer's aesthetic direction, as she all but abandoned the plotless group dances of her early period and embraced a form of narrative theater in which myth and psychology displaced the broad social concerns of her works of the 1930s.

This trajectory was revealed with startling clarity in the eighteen works presented at BAM. Under the artistic direction of Pearl Lang, a Graham company soloist from 1941 to 1954, the season—the best the group has offered in years—traced the choreographer's evolution over the decades of the 1930s, 1940s, and 1950s, when she stood at the forefront of modern dance and created the body of work that secured her reputation as an artist of the first rank. To be sure, there were inexplicable omissions—*Every Soul is a Circus* (1939), *Letter to the World* (1940), *Night Journey* (1947), and *Seraphic Dialogue* (1955) are those that come immediately to mind—and at least two works, both from recent decades, that should have been omitted. Nevertheless, the programming as a whole succeeded in winnowing the wheat from the chaff of Graham's sixty-odd years as a choreographer, and in identifying the significant works of her legacy that when performed with commitment and an understanding of their style—as they were this season—continue to hold meaning for audiences.

In this living canon, the works of the 1930s are of critical importance. Graham's own attitude toward them was mixed; like many artists, she preferred to look forward rather than back, to make new dances rather than tend to accomplishments past. Indeed, it was not until the revival in the late 1980s of *Celebration* and *Steps in the Streets*, dances originally choreographed in the mid-1930s and long out of repertory, that contemporary audiences had their first, riveting glimpse of early works that showed Graham in full command of her resources as an ensemble choreographer. In *Heretic* (1929) and *Primitive Mysteries* (1931), the patterns and groupings revealed her already keen grasp of the dramatics of gesture and space, although the limited vocabulary of movement and the focus in both on a central protagonist (a role that Graham assigned to herself) showed her experimenting with the tools of a craft that she had yet to master fully. The early 1930s were an intensely creative period for Graham, and with each new work she added both to her mastery of the stage and to the body of movement material that became the foundation of her technique. This technique developed in tandem with her choreography. In *Celebration*, the jumping sections called for a sharp percussive attack that propelled the body into the air with the powerful verticality of a skycraper. In *Steps in the Street*, almost the entire group section was performed in contraction, that is, with percussive movements in the torso that weighted the body and gave it a "modern," angular line. Throughout these years, Graham's company—or "group," as it was called—consisted entirely of women. Their bodies were big and immensely strong, with powerful thighs and hips that jutted through the long jersey dresses with the purposeful motion of a machine. Like the workers depicted in murals of the period, Graham's women were megaliths with the prowess of social heroes.

Celebration is a dance of joy. *Steps in the Street*, by contrast, is haunted by the specter of fear, by a menace that makes automatons of the social polity, strange, misshapen creatures scrambling across the stage in legions at once terrifying and poignant. *Steps* was choreographed in 1936, and it is not hard to see in its vision of mechanized humanity a critique of fascism. Indeed, Graham had turned down an invitation to perform at the Olympic Games held that year in Germany, citing the fact that several of her dancers were Jewish. At the same time, the revival this season of two other sections from *Chronicle*, of which *Steps* was initially part, indicates the profound ambiguity of her feelings about the collective. In *Heretic*, she had pitted this against the individual; in *Primitive Mys-*

teries, shown it as a sisterhood united in devotion to its priestess. In "Prelude to Action: Unity—Pledge to the Future," which now follows *Steps*, she abandoned these simplistic formulas. Her collective of demonic vestals is both a mirror and an interlocutor of the protagonist; their bodies exude the same hypnotic power, the same physical passion, the same will to master and subdue. Dressed in black, they appear at first as incarnations of evil, furies deaf to the pleas of the figure in white caught in the tightening vise of their swooping, circling patterns. But she is no victim or Madonna weeping at the cross. In the force and thrust of her movements and in their extraordinary scale (a performance by Terese Capucilli that was nothing short of magnificent), she dominates the stage. The thrilling dynamism of these Amazon bodies, magnified by the choreography's spatial and rhythmic tensions, which seem to contest the leader's power even as they assert it, show Graham at the very peak of her powers as an ensemble choreographer.

Like her 1937 solo *Deep Song*, one of numerous dances of the period inspired by the Spanish Civil War, *Chronicle* revealed the pervasive influence of the antifascist movement even on choreographers labeled in the radical press as "bourgeois." Although Graham herself stood at the margins of the radical dance movement, several of her dancers, including Anna Sokolow, Sophie Maslow, and Jane Dudley, performed and choreographed under its aegis. With titles like *Time is Money* (Dudley), *Two Songs About Lenin* (Maslow), and *The Strange American Funeral* (Sokolow), their works were overtly political. Typically, they drew on the movement idiom of modern dance, while also experimenting with a number of devices—spoken texts, popular entertainment forms, characterization, narrative elements—that subsequently found their way into mainstream works. Graham's 1938 *American Document*, for instance, included quotations from the Declaration of Independence, the Emancipation Proclamation, and writings by Jonathan Edwards, featured characters like the Native Figure (an Indian girl), and employed a quasi-narrative format derived from the minstrel show—all of which enhanced the "readability" of what was in effect a Popular Front vision of American social history. In the next half-dozen years, she continued to experiment with these devices: *Every Soul is a Circus* (1939), *Punch and the Judy* (1941), and *El Penitente* (1940) drew on popular entertainment traditions; *Letter to the World* (1940) quoted from the poetry of Emily Dickinson; *Appalachian Spring* (1944) evoked the dances and hymns of American folk culture. In content no less than form, these works were indebted to the Popular Front's romance with Americana.

"Accessibility," however, had a price. The incorporation of narrative buttressed the role of the soloist while diminishing that of the collective, even in works that celebrated popular culture. With Graham's discovery of myth, a theme that first surfaced in her 1944 *Herodiade*, and her growing obsession with the psychosexual aspect of male-female relationships (prompted in part by the failure of her marriage to Erick Hawkins), the collective as such virtually disappeared from her work. Where it did appear, as in the 1947 *Night Journey,* based on the story of Oedipus, its role was secondary to the drama taking place among the soloists; in others, like *Dark Meadow,* its function was purely decorative. By the late 1940s, the Amazon sisterhood of the previous decade was no more than a memory.

This shift in Graham's aesthetic concerns had many sources. Those most often cited are the presence of men in her company beginning in 1938 and her growing interest in nonlinear forms of narrative, especially those associated with the theatrical traditions of the Far East. But neither can account for the utter displacement of social themes by psychosexual and mythic ones. To explain this, one must look to the broader cultural context of the period, and specifically to the McCarthyite climate of fear that muted the expression of radical ideas or buried them in codes, ostensibly apolitical, but understood by those in the know. Thus, two of choreographer José Limón's seminal works of these years—*The Moor's Pavane* (1949) and *The Traitor* (1954)—turned on the theme of betrayal, although their narratives derived, respectively, from Shakespeare's *Othello* and Judas' betrayal of Jesus in the Gospels. Just as Cunningham drew a curtain of impenetrability across his works, so Graham in hers created an inner landscape of the mind in which sex, psychology, and myth—the postwar imaginary, one might say—sated the need for universals created by the loss of socialism's generalizing ideology. As in *Clytemnestra* (1958), the last of her great theater pieces, where the events of the tragedy, from the sacrifice of her daughter Iphigenia to the slaying of her husband Agamemnon, are relived as memory, so in all the works of the postwar period the action occurs outside time and place in the subjective realm of the imagination.

Graham's journey from the engagement of radical politics to the disengagement of radical individualism was easily the most remarkable lesson of the BAM season. The reasons for this were two-fold: the presence of so many works from the critical decades of Graham's career, and the success of the centennial artistic advisors—Pearl Lang, Ethel Butler, Jane Dudley, Stuart Hodes, Peggy Lyman, and Sophie Maslow—in making those works come alive. Graham's style changed over the years, and it is a measure of the achievement of these company veterans that her idioms, beginning with the "prehistoric" technique of early works like *Chronicle,* were rendered with commitment and stylistic fidelity. Thus, one can only assume that the misguided decision to recostume and add men to the cast of *Celebration* was made not by the veterans who restaged it, but by the company's present artistic director Ronald Protas. With the women now in backless dresses and the newly added men in harem trousers by Donna Karan, the accent is on sex rather than sisterhood, glamor rather than simplicity. This new version of *Celebration,* doubtless intended to appeal to the yuppie audience courted in recent years by the company's management, is nothing less than a travesty of the original.

The contrast between public glamor and private penury dramatized by the walk-out of the Graham dancers is not unique to the Graham company, but reflects the declining public for mainstream forms of dance. The reasons for this are too complicated to analyze here: suffice it to say that chasing an upscale audience is not the solution. As the plight of the dancers revealed all too clearly, the irony of "Radical Graham" was that its radicalism remained confined to the stage.

WRITING ON THE LEFT

THE REMARKABLE CAREER OF EDNA OCKO

I first met Edna Ocko in the early 1980s. She was my mother-in-law's best friend from college days, someone who wrote about dance in the 1930s and took a dim view of critics since. My husband was a little in awe of Edna, and the first time she came to the house, I was told to cook an extra pound of pasta because Edna was coming. To my amazement, she was almost as tiny as my grandmother. We had a lot of pasta left over.

Edna Ocko, or Edna Meyers, as we knew her, was a formidable woman. She had been a Communist in the 1930s and remained at heart a member of the Party, bonded by decades of friendship to the comrades-in-arms of her youth. She was punchy and articulate, with strong opinions and political convictions that never wavered even when she was named as a communist by Jerome Robbins before the House Un-American Activities Committee in 1953. She was also a first-rate dance critic who knew the difference between art and propaganda, could tell good choreography from bad, and wrote with verve. She was a crack editor, with a nose for a story, who understood intuitively how to balance different voices and views: unsurprisingly, her best days as a dance journalist coincided with the Popular Front, which embraced liberals and leftists alike. Finally, she was an intellectual, curious, well-read, stimulated by ideas, who counted even balletomanes like Lincoln Kirstein among her colleagues.

In 1993, I did a public interview with Edna for the conference "Of, By, and For the People." She was eighty-five and nervous about appearing in public, so to allay her fears and also to familiarize myself with her life, I had two lengthy conversations with her at her home. The conference interview was never taped. Luckily, I had the presence of mind to tape these preliminary conversations. What follows, including the unattributed quotations, is from this material.

Edna Ocko was born in New York City in 1908. Her father was a cigarmaker, an ardent left-winger and an activist in one of the era's most progressive unions. She grew up in Harlem, where many immigrant Jews then lived. It was a musical household. Her mother sang, and her brother Bernard, who eventually became a professional musician, played the violin. Edna, for her part, studied piano. Her

This was originally given as part of a tribute to Deborah Jowitt at the October 2001 CORD Conference held in New York City. It was subsequently published in *Dance Research Journal*, 34, no. 1 (Summer 2002).

first contact with dance came when a friend of the family took her to a recital by Isadora Duncan, probably during World War I:

> I was a little girl, and I was immediately taken by the music, which was very exciting to me, and, of course, I was taken by the flow of the dance. That was my first introduction to dance.

Music was Edna's entry into the dance field. While still a student at Lydia Wadleigh High School, she began to play for Sophie Berensohn and Mathilda Naaman, pupils of Bird Larson. She took her pay in the form of dance classes. She "studied everything," except ballet. "Dancers liked me to be their accompanist because I understood the movements, so I could make up music that would be appropriate for the movement, and then I could get free lessons."

Edna entered Hunter College in 1925. She majored in English, joined poetry and music societies, and discovered Marx.

> The left-wing was proselytizing. I remember they said why don't you read . . . *The Communist Manifesto?* . . . So I went to the 42nd Street library. . . . I read it and I cried. I remember crying in the reading room; it was the most beautiful thing I had ever read. . . . So that's how I got involved.

Although Edna strongly sympathized with the left, she wasn't a "joiner." She didn't march in demonstrations (as her father did), even for Sacco and Vanzetti, whose politically motivated execution in 1927 for a robbery they didn't commit was a turning point in the history of the American left. Her interests were music and "the" dance, as she called it. She saw everything she could:

> I loved dancing; I loved the movement of it and the rhythm of it, and I loved the fact that they were using modern music. I saw ballet, but that seemed stultified to me; it didn't have the same appeal that the rhythmic quality of the dance had for me, which I loved, because it was connected to music.

In 1929, Ocko graduated from Hunter with honors. She received a substitute teacher's license, and from 1930 to 1935 taught English in New York City high schools—a good job in those terrible years of the Depression. She continued to write and to play for dance classes. Then, in 1931, she began studying with Hanya Holm at the newly opened Mary Wigman school. She had a scholarship and no longer had to barter her services as an accompanist. She could be "serious" about dancing, and the experience gave new direction to her life. At the Wigman school, she found students who shared her political sympathies. It was the Great Depression; there were tent cities in Central Park, and long lines outside soup kitchens. Talk of revolution was in the air, and the Soviet Union, with its visionary rhetoric and Five-Year Plan, seemed a beacon of hope. The New Dance Group was founded in February 1932 by six "young, eager, talented dance students who had become dissatisfied with their training in the bourgeois dance schools," wrote Nadia Chilkovsky (as Nell Anyon) in the program for the group's first anniversary recital:

> They looked with distaste and even anger at the attempt of the bourgeois dancers to make the subject matter of the dance abstract. They began to oppose the attempt of the bourgeois dancers to isolate the subject matter and technique of the dance from the actual lives of the dance students; they felt the great need for a new orientation toward the masses of workers who had never had an opportunity either to dance themselves or to attend recitals of dancers. Above all, they felt the new impulse toward mass dance that would treat of the problems of the workers.
>
> This outlook found us experimenting in group dance. We attempted to make our dances a result of the improvisation of an entire group who were working each in his own manner but all following a common direction and purpose. The emotional and ideological content of the dances came from situations in our own lives and in the lives of workers around us—in their shops, in their homes, and in their daily struggles against the ruling class.[1]

Their slogan was "The Dance is a Weapon," their goal to bring modern dance to the masses. Their first headquarters was a donated room in the Central Opera House, and it was here that Edna, as a member of the group's Dance and Editorial Committee, found her true calling.[2] "Basically, I was an organizer," she told me. The New Dance Group grew by leaps and bounds. Office workers, school teachers, shop workers, housewives, and college students poured into the organization, and within six months a "lay" group was formed. Meanwhile, working-class organizations in the "hinterlands" of Brooklyn, the Bronx, and Harlem kept up a continuous demand for performances at union halls and political rallies.[3]

Teaching was a major activity. "Lessons for ten cents an hour, with a political discussion thrown in gratis," was how Edna later described the Group's classes.[4] Classes consisted of three hour-long sessions: one hour for technique, one for creative work on subject matter suggested by the Group's "Educational Committee," and one for a meeting that included "discussion of technical and political problems."[5] Intermediate and advanced students were eligible to join one of several performing groups, and anyone could propose an idea for a project to the Dance Committee. Leadership was collective. "There is no one dance choreographer, or director," Edna told readers of *New Theatre* in 1934.[6] The Group sponsored social activities, including membership meetings with folk dancing, and lectures, on subjects like the origin of the revolutionary dance, and even had a children's section.[7] Any technique was acceptable. "Within six months we began to teach tap dancing and ballet. Anna Sokolow started a group and taught Graham technique. Then we had someone . . . teaching Duncan. . . . We taught whatever a teacher was willing to teach." The Group also sent teachers out to trade unions. "It was part of our beliefs," said Edna, "that the masses have a right to culture, that the proletariat has a right to the best of culture, and we thought we were the best of culture."

With the founding of the Workers Dance League late in 1932, the radical dance movement acquired an organizational structure. "We heard there was a . . . group of dancers [in Philadelphia] . . . doing the same thing we were," Edna told me. "And we decided, . . . let's . . . get all these left-wing dance groups together, so we formed the . . . Workers Dance League." Early members of the League included the New Dance Group, Harlem Dance Group, and Red Dancers, several union-sponsored groups (N.T.W.I.U. Dance Group and Office Workers Union Dance Group), groups sponsored by recreational organizations (Nature Friends Dance Group) and youth groups (Junior Red Dancers and American Youth Federation Dance Group).[8] (Later members included the New Duncan Group and the Modern Negro Dance Group, founded by Hemsley Winfield.) In 1933, the League sponsored a National Spartakiad, the first of several events that signaled its emergence as an influential New York presenter of modern dance. By 1935, with some fifty groups outside New York affiliated with the League (now renamed the New Dance League), "the workers' dance movement of New York," as Edna wrote in *New Theatre*, "[had become] a national movement."

> Approximately a half million people attended dance recitals in the year 1934–1935. Of these, more than ninety per cent came to see New Dance League performances, or the New Dance League went to them. . . . When one remembers that the modern dance has had, of all the arts, the most limited appeal, and therefore the most indifferent audience, these facts take on even more significance.[9]

Edna was in the thick of it. "I organized a great many things. I organized organizations. . . . The Workers Dance League, the New Dance League—I was behind them." She was full of ideas. One was for a 1935 concert called "Men in the Dance" that was sponsored by the New Dance League and the magazine *New Theatre*, of which she was the dance editor. "We were really interested in men," a point borne out by the fact that the New Dance Group early on had a men's section.[10] "And . . . there were men in the dance. We had José Limón, Charles Weidman and his group, Paul Draper, Bill [William] Dollar, Roger Pryor Dodge. . . . [W]ith dancers like that, we had a program." Much to Edna's surprise, the two performances sold out in the first couple of days. "It took me a long time to figure out why. . . . Back then, we were very innocent about homosexuality."

Even if the dancers weren't paid (although the accompanists were), concerts cost money. "[S]omeone must have paid for something," Edna told me.

For instance, when we rented a theatre to give a performance, I didn't put up the money for it. I didn't pay the accompanists. I didn't write the checks. I don't know who wrote the checks. And this is really true. I was very innocent; I always thought it was paid for by the advance sale of tickets. Which is very possible. . . . But I didn't know. And I was a very trusted member, so I would have thought I would have known, but I didn't know. They had 2,000 members in the Workers Dance League. That's a hell of a lot. And they paid dues.

The numbers were phenomenal. In December 1935, for a recital to benefit the International Labor Defense, "Carnegie Hall was packed to the rafters."[11] Earlier in the year, for a program of group and solo dances presented by the Workers Dance League at the Center Theatre for the benefit of *The Daily Worker,* the Communist Party daily newspaper, "standing room was sold out for the first time in the history of Radio City."[12] No wonder Ralph Taylor, in reviewing the "Men in the Dance" concert for Louis Horst's *Dance Observer,* felt compelled to denounce the League's "total bankruptcy." "The 'New' Dance League," he wrote, "is nothing but a commercial concert agency which welcomes anyone and everyone providing they are willing to contribute their talent, time, and energy—gratis—to help garner the shekels for a 'program against War, Fascism and Censorship.'"[13] In fact, the revolutionary dance movement represented a challenge to the hegemony of modern dance as this was exemplified by the Bennington School of the Dance, with its relatively privileged student body of college girls from Middle America and physical education teachers. The dance community that Edna helped propel into being was heavily Jewish, with roots in New York's immigrant ghettoes and ties to its avant-garde theater, music, and art communities.

In the 1930s, the Communist Party was not a clandestine organization. Communists ran for office and sometimes were elected. Beginning in 1935, when the Party line shifted to the Popular Front, communists were encouraged to make common cause with liberals. The changing nomenclature of the Dance League reflects this political shift, as did the emphasis on anti-fascism, which largely supplanted the proletarian line of the early 1930s. The New Dance Group danced at Communist Party events, including gatherings at Madison Square Garden attended by thousands. "To break the monotony of all the speeches," noted Edna,

we would give a dance; they welcomed us, and we welcomed them, because it gave us an audience. . . . At such events we danced under the auspices of the Communist Party, but it was understood that we were the New Dance Group. Later, when the New Dance League was formed, we would give concerts in big halls and many groups would appear; . . . that's when we got Graham and Humphrey-Weidman to perform with us.

The left, Edna explains, was "a force" in the dance field "because it brought a receptive, enthusiastic audience to a dance world that was pretty effete and closed in on itself."

> At this time there was a big upsurge in the arts, and it was mainly connected with the fact that there was an audience for the arts that hadn't had access to them. This audience wouldn't go to the Guild Theatre, for instance, to see a dance recital by Martha Graham, but if we gave a concert at the Hippodrome, they came. Not only because we offered a broad spectrum of dancers, but because it was not expensive. The audience narrowed down when it became expensive; they couldn't afford it.

Early on Edna realized that her usefulness to the dance field lay in activities other than performance. Her work as an organizer was an acknowledgment of this, as was the writing and editing that became increasingly important as the decade advanced. A selection of her essays and reviews, edited by Stacey Prickett, was published in 1994,[14] but this is only the tip of the iceberg. Edna was a prolific writer, publishing in both the left-wing and mainstream press, and she wrote under a half-dozen names—Edna Poe, Skrip, Elizabeth Skrip, Marion Sellars, Eve Stebbins, Frances Steuben. Even Edna Ocko, her maiden name, was something of a pseudonym, since as a teacher she used her married name, Edna Meyers. (She had married the musician, film critic, and documentary filmmaker Sidney Meyers in 1930.) One reason she wrote under pseudonyms was to keep her teaching job. But it wasn't only fear of the Board of Education that accounted for the multiple identities. "I really think . . . I adopted different names . . . so that I could go to the same recital more than once." Another reason, surely, must have been the problem of wearing so many hats simultaneously. If Edna was a mover-and-shaker of the revolutionary dance movement, someone who made it happen, she was also its critic and public advocate. Editors were happy to look the other way. "[T]here was very little competition. I was literate; I was . . . able to talk a good line, and I was one of the few people who really knew the dance field."

Her writing was remarkably free of cant, and she was very clear about her loyalties:

> My responsibility to the dance field was to make sure that the people who read . . . whatever magazine I was writing for developed a point of view that would be catholic, in the sense of being able to accept dances, if they were good, no matter what their content was. . . . I was not unscrupulously partisan. I was more interested in good dancing. I felt that the proletariat deserved the best. . . . We were radical in the sense that we believed that change had to take place, that it shouldn't be commercial but had to be artistic. . . . We were generous, I think, toward the bad dancers in the field, if they had the right ideas, but we never praised them only for the right ideas.

As a critic, Edna could be tough. Reviewing a Workers Dance League concert in 1934, she praised the organization for its "ability to appeal not only to thousands of workers and intellectuals, but actually to invoke continued encouragement and praise from bourgeois as well as proletarian critics." But she criticized the League for "expos[ing] itself to attack from all quarters if, either through lack of artistic forces or lack of self-imposed discipline, it permits a recital of the calibre of the first appearance of revolutionary dance groups this season. . . . The recital was not only ill-advised artistically, but unfortunate from the technical end as well."[15]

Because she knew the field inside out, she knew that only a minority of the revolutionary dance groups were professional:

Groups like Edith Segal's Red Dancers were agit-prop groups. They were dancing because they liked to dance, but they were not professional dancers, whereas people in . . . the New Dance Group were all studying dancing someplace else— with Hanya Holm . . . or Martha Graham . . . [or] the Humphrey-Weidman group. These were the more professional dancers; the dancers in Nature Friends and a lot of other groups studied dancing only with us. . . . [T]hroughout the country there was the same split between amateur and more professional groups.

Edna often alluded to this split in her reviews. "As it now stands," she wrote in 1935,

only two groups, the New Dance Group, and the Theatre Union Dance Group, are creating dances that rightfully belong on the *concert* stage. The Red Dancers and the Nature Friends, while they are to be commended for their sincere efforts, are not only unsuited technically for recital work, but as a matter of fact are creating, not concert dances, but a commendable variety of agit-prop dance. . . . On the concert platform, . . . where . . . a large part of the audience is composed of intellectual and bourgeois elements, these dances have neither subtlety of theme, nor richness of form to commend them, and the more developed dance audience finds these dances both crude and wearisome.[16]

Edith Segal was Edna's bête noire. "I never publicly trounced Edith Segal," she told me, "but I knew she wasn't a good dancer; she was an agit-prop person." In fact, Edna was always critical of Segal. Of *Black and White,* one of Segal's most popular dances, Edna wrote in 1935:

Put any negro and white performer on the stage, show them struggling under similar conditions, show their initial enmity and their final heroic handclasp and fist salute, and you have ideal conditions for applause. *Black and White,* by the Red Dancers, recreates a slogan in pantomimic movement, but surely no one can claim for it an imaginative or original approach to the negro question, despite the fact that it evokes lusty applause.[17]

However much Edna applauded the sentiments, good propaganda was not automatically good art.[18]

Still, she felt that the "infusion of revolutionary ideology" into modern dance was salutary. Unlike Martha Graham and other modern dancers of the early 1930s, the revolutionary dancers did not shy from depicting the world around them. Rather they embraced it, finding in the turbulence and cruelty of contemporary life both a ready source of material and a new expressive content. Revolutionary ideology also prompted "valuable experimentation in form."[19] The use of improvisation as a choreographic tool was widespread. Music was abjured. Many dances were set to poems or had verbal accompaniment, a practice that anticipated by several years Martha Graham's innovative use of text in *American Document*. Reviewing the Workers Dance League solo dance concert in 1934, Edna singled out Jane Dudley's *Time is Money* and Miriam Blecher's *Three Negro Songs:*

> *Time is Money,* to a poem by S. Funaroff, was one of the most exciting dances of the evening. Dance image after image succeeded one another until an electrifying picture of speed-up, suicide, misery, and factory exploitation emerged. Here the revolutionary demands of the poem created a new form, similar to Eisenstein's, in its pictorial explosiveness and brilliant juxtaposition of associate and dissociate imagery. A simpler but equally effective use of words was utilized by Miriam Blecher in her three poems.[20]

Edna also wrote for mainstream publications, including the *New York Post.* She had a column in *Cue* magazine, and was paid "either five or ten dollars for a review," which was "a lot of money" in the mid-1930s, compared to what she made at *The Daily Worker* or *The New Masses*—nothing. She wrote with a lighter touch for *Cue* than the left-wing press and could be devastatingly funny:

> It was a dance recital! There were twenty-one musical numbers and ten "dances." We wish there had been thirty-one musical numbers. Vivienne Butler performed at Town Hall Saturday evening, February 20th. We haven't recovered yet. She counted flower petals in *D'Apres Watteau,* was a metronome in *Metronome,* slapped around at an imaginary mosquito in *I Danced with a Mosquito,* dusted furniture in *Dutch Cleanser Girl,* and most of the audience walked out after *Water Lily,* when Miss Butler was a Water-Lily.[21]

In 1934, Edna became the dance editor of *New Theatre,* a left-wing monthly devoted to theatre, dance, music, and film. She did some of her best writing for

New Theatre, and built the dance pages into one of the magazine's liveliest sections and a force in the dance world. She had a stable of writers, including Edith Segal, Blanche Evan, Paul Love, and Mignon Verne, a founder of the New Duncan Dancers.

> I couldn't disown the bad dancers, and I couldn't praise them. But if they wrote about other dancers or if they wrote about themselves, they would have articles in *New Theatre*. . . . Remember, people are very eager to put forward their point of view. So if they were asked to write about themselves—even if they had to do it for nothing, as they all did—they jumped at the chance.

Martha Graham and Doris Humphrey were among the many dancers and choreographers who contributed to *New Theatre*. "I asked them to talk about dancing. They didn't have to talk about the revolution." There were articles about wage scales for dancers, men in the dance, music for the dance, revolutionary dance forms, and a surprisingly large number of articles about ballet— about Massine by Irving Deakin, the Fokine ballets by Blanche Evan, Nijinsky's tragedy by Lydia Nadejina,[22] and any number of articles by Edna's most gifted "discovery"—Lincoln Kirstein.

She didn't remember when or how they met. There is a story about a dinner in November 1934 when she spotted a major ideological flaw in a scenario he had written. She visited the School of American Ballet, where she saw a rehearsal of *Mozartiana* and Kirstein tried to interest her in the ballet as a form. She told him that someone had called him an enthusiast; he countered that he was also a dilettante. "Well, don't boast about it," she rejoined, which sounds just like the Edna I knew. In the elevator, Edward W. W. Warburg, of the great Jewish banking family, made disparaging remarks about her appearance.

By then Kirstein was writing for her. His first article was "Revolutionary Ballet Forms," in which he asserted that "the destruction of the proscenium arch . . . , the use of negroes in conjunction with white dancers, the replacement of an audience of snobs by a wide popular support are all part of Balanchine's articulate program"[23]—a measure of how close Kirstein had drawn to the left. Other essays followed—"The Dance as Theatre" (in which he defended ballet against modern dance), "James Cagney" (in which he called the Hollywood tough "the best young male actor in America"), "A Museum of Ballet" (in which he criticized the de Basil Ballet Russe for failing to offer the "fresh and creative experience" of the old Diaghilev company), and "Dancing in Films" (in which he concluded that "The camera as an eye for dancing is as yet more unstudied than misunderstood").[24] These were not casual pieces of work, but articulated ideas that reappeared in Kirstein's work for decades.

For all their differences, Edna and "Lincoln," as she always called him, had certain things in common. Both were young, and they were advocates, eager to get their ideas across to the public. They were also intellectuals. They read books and thought about them. Edna had an "encyclopedic knowledge of . . . dance, past and present," wrote *New Theatre* editor Herbert Kline in a memoir.[25] Kline may have found this daunting, but how it must have appealed to Kirstein. Like other left-wing intellectuals of the time, she read *Hound and Horn,* which he had founded, "because it had things to say about the arts [a]nd was . . . left of center." In November 1936, an unsigned notice in *New Theatre* announced that contrary to rumors and even "positive statements to the effect," it was not planning to "sponsor a dance magazine."

> There is a definite and crying need for a magazine, international in scope, to deal with all phases of the art, and its interrelation with theatre and film. Such a magazine, to include translations and reprints of hitherto unavailable material, historical and analytical articles, illustrative material ranging from action photographs to stage designs for theatre dances, creative material including libretti and scripts of various sorts—in short, a periodical of permanent, rather than topical interest, modeled perhaps after the *Archives Internationales de la Danse.*[26]

The magazine was to be a quarterly, and Irving Deakin, Lincoln Kirstein, Paul Love, Paul Magriel, and Edna Ocko were mentioned as being members of the tentative editorial board. For the moment nothing came of their plans. The following year, *New Theatre* folded, and in 1938, after a visit to the Soviet Union, Edna became the editor-in-chief of *TAC,* an arts monthly published by the Theatre Arts Committee. When this ceased publication in August 1940, Edna moved away from the dance field. But in 1942, the magazine that she, Kirstein, and the others had dreamed of founding came to fruition with *Dance Index.* Except that now, with Edna not involved and the first round of anti-Communist hearings underway, the politics associated with its gestation vanished. *Dance Index* would exist under the unofficial auspices of the Museum of Modern Art.

Edna kept a low profile in the late 1940s and early 1950s, when McCarthyism was decimating the left. By 1953, when she was publically named before HUAC by Jerome Robbins,[27] she had been doing public relations work for the Albert Einstein College of Medicine and other educational and charitable institutions for a decade. She returned to school in 1957, earning a master's degree in remedial reading, a doctorate in counseling, and her New York State certification as a psychologist. She remained an intellectual of the left. Her dissertation was a study of "disadvantaged Negro boys," and she worked for over twenty years at the Northside Center in Harlem, first as a reading specialist, then as chief psychologist. She taught at City College from 1967 to 1980.[28]

Edna mellowed with age. "You know, I separated my political leanings from my aesthetic feelings," she told me. "If they danced well, if they did something that was expressive, I liked them, regardless of whether they were politicized or not." But, she added, "they became political." Edna never lost her punch.

NOTES

1. Nell Anyon [pseud. of Nadia Chilkovsky], "What is the New Dance Group?" First Anniversary Recital, New Dance Group, 26 March 1933, p. 3.
2. *Ibid.*, pp. 4, 12.
3. Judith Delman, "The New Dance Group," *Dance Observer,* January 1944, p. 8; Edna Ocko, "New Dance Group," *New Theatre,* November 1934, p. 29.
4. Edna Ocko, "Of Leotards and Lenin," p. 1, unpublished mss., collection of Edna Ocko Meyers.
5. Ocko, "New Dance Group," p. 28.
6. *Ibid.*
7. Delman, "The New Dance Group," p. 8; Anyon, "What is the New Dance Group?" p. 5.
8. Midi Gordon, "The Workers Dance League," in First Anniversary Recital, New Dance Group, 26 March 1933, p. 6. For a list of the League's affiliated dance groups and an announcement of the forthcoming National Sparakiad, see p. 15.
9. Marion Sellars [pseud. Edna Ocko], "The Revolutionary Dance Achieves a Mass Audience," *The Daily Worker,* 12 December 1935, p. 7.
10. Ocko, "The New Dance Group," p. 28.
11. Elizabeth Skrip [pseud. Edna Ocko], "Dance: A Notable Recital," *The Daily Worker,* 19 December 1935, p. 5.
12. Elizabeth Skrip [pseud. Edna Ocko], "World of the Dance: Outstanding Program by Dance League," *The Daily Worker,* 20 February 1935, p. 5.
13. R[alph] T[aylor], "Men in the Dance," *The Dance Observer,* Summer 1935, p. 64.
14. See "Reviewing on the Left: The Dance Criticism of Edna Ocko," selected and introd. by Stacey Prickett, in *Of, By, and For the People: Dancing on the Left in the 1930s,* ed. Lynn Garafola, *Studies in Dance History,* 5, no. 1 (Spring 1994), pp. 65–103.
15. Elizabeth Skrip [pseud. Edna Ocko], "World of the Dance: Workers Dance League in Group Recital," *The Daily Worker,* 27 December 1934, p. 5. This is a review of a Workers Dance League concert give on 23 December 1934 at Town Hall.
16. Edna Ocko, "The Dance League Recital," *New Theatre,* February 1935, p. 25. Ocko was reviewing Workers Dance League concert given at Town Hall on 23 December 1934.
17. *Ibid.* She was even more critical of Segal's *Tom Mooney,* a solo "whose use of a poem was over simplification to a point of crudity" (Edna Ocko, "The Dance," *New Masses,* 4 December 1934, p. 30). This was a review of a Workers Dance League recital of seven artists in revolutionary dance solos, presented under the auspices of *New Theatre,* at the Civic Repertory Theatre on 25 November 1934. For a more judicious appraisal of Segal's work, see Ellen Graff, *Stepping Left: Dance and Politics in New York City, 1928–1942* (Durham: Duke University Press, 1997), chap. 2 ("Dance is a Weapon"). For a charming memoir of Segal in the early 1980s, see Deborah Jowitt, "A Lifetime of Art on the Left," *The Village Voice,* 6 July 1982, in *The Dance in Mind: Profiles and Reviews 1976–83* (Boston: David Godine, 1985), pp. 267–272.
18. From the start, African-American students were welcomed at the New Dance

League, according to Edna. However, they were a "minority." "There was really no prejudice. . . . The thinking around the Communist Party was very important for all of us who grew up wanting to be decent human beings."

19. Elizabeth Skrip [pseud. of Edna Ocko], "World of the Dance: Outstanding Program by Dance League," *The Daily Worker*, 20 February 1935, p. 5. For Ocko on Graham's eschewal of the contemporary, see "Whither Martha Graham," *New Theatre*, April 1934, p. 7.

20. Edna Ocko, "The Dance," *New Masses*, 4 December 1934, p. 30. This is a review of the Workers Dance League solo dance concert at the Civic Repertory Theatre on 25 November 1934.

21. Eve Stebbins [pseud. of Edna Ocko], "The Dance," *Cue*, 27 February 1937, p. 45.

22. See Louise Mitchell, "Wage Scales for Dancers," *New Theatre and Film*, April 1937, pp. 32–33 *et seq.;* Ezra Friedman and Irving Lansky, "Men in the Modern Dance," *New Theatre*, June 1934, p. 21; Elie Siegmeister, "Music for the Dance," *New Theatre*, October 1935, pp. 10–11 *et seq.;* Irving Ignatin, "'Revolutionary' Dance Forms," *New Theatre*, December 1935, p. 28–29; Irving Deakin, "Massine," *New Theatre*, November 1936, pp. 27–28; Blanche Evan, "The Fokine Ballets," *New Theatre*, September 1935, p. 26; Lydia Nadejina, "Nijinsky's Tragedy," *New Theatre*, September 1934, p. 27. In September 1935 and in November 1936, Sol Hurok took full-page advertisements in *New Theatre* for the "Ballet Russe de Monte Carlo" (as the de Basil company was sometimes referred to), a measure of how important he regarded its readership.

23. Lincoln Kirstein, "Revolutionary Ballet Forms," *New Theatre*, October 1934, p. 14.

24. Lincoln Kirstein, "The Dance as Theatre," *New Theatre*, May 1935, pp. 20–22; "James Cagney," *New Theatre*, December 1935, p. 14; "A Museum of Ballet," *New Theatre*, June 1936, pp. 20–21 *et seq.;* "Dancing in Films," *New Theatre*, September 1936, pp. 11–13. Kirstein wrote the Cagney essay under the pseudonym Forrest Clark.

25. *New Theatre and Film 1934 to 1937: An Anthology,* ed. with commentary by Herbert Kline, foreword Arthur Knight (San Diego: Harcourt Brace Jovanovich, 1985), p. 199.

26. "A Dance Quarterly?" *New Theatre*, November 1936, p. 28.

27. For a transcript of Robbins' testimony, see *Thirty Years of Treason: Excerpts from Hearings before the House Committee on Un-American Activities, 1938–1968,* ed. Eric Bentley (New York: Viking, 1971), pp. 625–634. For a discussion of this episode in Robbins' life, see Greg Lawrence, *Dance with Demons: The Life of Jerome Robbins* (New York: Putnam, 2001), pp. 199–211.

28. Most of this biographical information comes from Edna's resumé dated September 1980.

DOLLARS FOR DANCE

LINCOLN KIRSTEIN, CITY CENTER, AND THE ROCKEFELLER FOUNDATION

In October 1952, when Lincoln Kirstein became managing director of New York's City Center, few U.S. foundations supported the arts, except on a limited and sporadic basis. Seven months later, this was to change dramatically. The decision by the Rockefeller Foundation's Division of Humanities to appropriate $200,000 to City Center "toward the expenses of creating new productions in opera and ballet . . . during the three-year period beginning July 1, 1953"[1] opened a new era in arts funding. With fully half the sum allocated to the Center's resident dance company, the New York City Ballet, this was the first grant awarded to an American dance ensemble by a leading philanthropic institution. It was also the first specifically earmarked to underwrite creative work, and hence a milestone in the history of American dance patronage. Within the dance community, however, the episode remains all but unknown, in large measure because of Kirstein's own silence about it. In *Thirty Years: The New York City Ballet,* his "diary" of the company and its predecessors, he makes no mention whatever of the grant or of his tenure as City Center's Managing Director—this in a book trumpeting any number of notable "firsts." The episode fares no better in Nancy Reynolds' *Repertory in Review: Forty Years of the New York City Ballet* or Bernard Taper's *Balanchine: A Biography,* which both ignore it.[2] Yet between 1953 and 1956, Rockefeller largesse helped underwrite nearly a dozen operas and ballets, including *The Nutcracker.* Although the company's relationship with the Ford Foundation, which began in 1959, is far better known, the Rockefeller Foundation actually predated it by several years.

Kirstein's connection with the Rockefellers went back to the early 1930s when he served on the Advisory Committee of the Museum of Modern Art. But of all the clan, it was Nelson A. Rockefeller, the future New York governor, to whom he felt the closest. The two shared a passion for art, and their correspondence is filled with references to paintings, shows, and Saturday afternoon visits to galleries. Less than a year after the School of American Ballet opened its doors in 1934, Rockefeller wrote his first check for the fledgling academy—$300—to pay a needy student's tuition for a year.[3] In 1937, he donated 100 shares of Interna-

This essay was originally published in *Dance Chronicle,* 25, no. 1 (2002).

tional Paper and Power Company preferred stock, which the board voted to sell and use to maintain on full scholarship "twenty outstanding dancers" for two years;[4] he also lent his name to the American Ballet's Stravinsky Festival, a gala occasion that helped raise money for the School's Scholarship Fund.[5] Finally, in 1941, following his appointment as Coordinator of Inter-American Affairs (CIAA), he sent the Balanchine-Kirstein company, now renamed American Ballet Caravan, on a good will tour of Latin America with a total government-paid subsidy of $141,922.04.[6] After Rockefeller's death in 1979, Kirstein, "visibly overcome with emotion," as *The New York Times* reported, dedicated the evening's program of the New York City Ballet to the man he described to the audience as a "wonderful patron."[7]

Founded in 1913 with an endowment of $182 million, the Rockefeller Foundation was among the country's outstanding philanthropic institutions, closely identified with medical research and with education.[8] Controlled by an independent board of trustees and administered by a professional staff headquartered in Rockefeller Center, it awarded grants to universities, research institutes, and other agencies. The arts were virgin territory for the Foundation in the late 1940s. Nelson Rockefeller may have written Ballet Society a $5,000 check in 1948 (he had just declined Kirstein's invitation to join the City Center board),[9] but as John Marshall, director of the Foundation's division of humanities, cautioned Newbold Morris, chairman of the Center's board, the Foundation was distinct from the "personal interests of Mr. Rockefeller." Marshall also warned "that there was little likelihood of direct assistance from the RF to the Center."[10] Still, by 1949, Morton Baum, chairman of the Center's Executive Committee, was making a case for funding. "The creative works of our serious composers and choreographers," he wrote, "are rotting for want of an opportunity of performance." "Until such time as the governmental authorities take cognizance of this situation, our Board of Directors feels that the Foundation might well undertake to meet the situation."[11] The proposal Baum outlined—$75,000 each to the Center's constituent opera and ballet companies to underwrite new work by American artists or in an American idiom—was virtually identical to Kirstein's three years later.

In the interim, the Foundation warmed to the idea of funding the arts. In April 1949, Ballet Society received a $2,500 grant toward the completion of the book *The Classic Ballet,* with most of the money being used to pay the artist Carlus Dyer and the writer David Vaughan, whose contribution was uncredited.[12] Two years later, the Foundation awarded its first substantial grant to an arts organization, the New Dramatists Committee, for $47,500.[13] Finally, on 14 May 1953, the Board of Trustees gave its final approval to a grant of $200,000 for City Center. The three-year grant, which was to be used exclusively for the creation of "new productions . . . under the direction of Mr. Lincoln Kirstein" was to be divided equally between the New York City Ballet and the New York City Opera, with $100,000 allocated for the first year, $60,000 the second, and $40,000 the third.[14]

With $200,000 to spend, Kirstein leapt into action. He was a whirlwind with a cause—the people's theater of City Center. In a letter to Nelson Rockefeller, he referred to City Center as the richest theater in the world in terms of its ability to produce new work and even compared it to the Museum of Modern Art in the 1930s.[15] He made lists, innumerable lists, of operas to be revived, composers to be commissioned, ballets to be choreographed, premieres to be scheduled. In January 1953, he sent Marshall a memorandum with his proposed budget for the 1953–1954 season. It included productions of Stravinsky's opera *The Nightingale* (last seen in the United States in 1928), Paul Hindemith's opera *Cardillac* (unproduced in the United States), and a new American opera on the scale of Virgil Thomson's *The Mother of Us All*. As for ballet, here, too, the accent was on the modern. There was *Souvenirs*, to a commissioned score by Samuel Barber; Stravinsky's *Pulcinella;* an all-British *Pocahontas* with choreography by Frederick Ashton and music by Benjamin Britten; a one-act *Don Juan* to a new score by Harold Shapero. Surprisingly, given his emphasis on the contemporary and the American, Kirstein listed two full-length ballets to nineteenth-century music, *The Nutcracker* (to Tchaikovsky) and *A Midsummer Night's Dream* (to Mendelssohn).[16]

To be sure, the list would change—many times. By the end, however, it included some of the decade's most adventurous new operas—*The Tender Land* by Aaron Copland, *The Saint of Bleecker Street* by Gian-Carlo Menotti, and *Panfilo and Lauretta* by Carlos Chávez. As for the ballets, *Pocahontas* and *Don Juan* quietly vanished. So, too, did *A Midsummer Night's Dream* and *Pulcinella* (although Balanchine later staged both works). Rockefeller monies partly underwrote *The Nutcracker, Ivesiana, Roma, Pas de Dix,* and *Western Symphony,* all by Balanchine; *Con Amore* by Lew Christensen, *Souvenirs* by Todd Bolender, and *The Concert* by Jerome Robbins; they were also used to commission music from Stravinsky (for a work tentatively titled *Apollo the Architect* or *Finale*), Hindemith (for *Kleinzach,* another work that was never produced), and Harold Shapero (for a work, also unproduced, that was initially called *Promenade* and later *The Golem* and that first Balanchine and then Robbins was to choreograph). Other projects that failed to materialize were a revival of Virgil Thomson's opera *The Mother of Us All,* an opera by William Schuman called *An American Tragedy,* and three ballets to be choreographed by Robbins—*Ritual,* to music by Copland; *Portrait,* to music by Roy Harris; and an untitled work to Prokofiev.[17] It was a distinguished list, and an ambitious one, worthy of Diaghilev not only in the combination of popular and "difficult" offerings, but also in the catholic vision of modernism, both in its European and American variants. No wonder there were misgivings in the Foundation's genteel corridors about Kirstein's imperial visions. "The chief trouble with Kirstein," commented Wallace K. Harrison not without justification, "[is] that he tends to make plans so large that they can not be carried out."[18]

The Rockefeller grant did not go unnoticed in U.S. dance circles. Indeed, even before it was approved, the Connecticut College School of the Dance, home of the American Dance Festival and a leading venue for the study of modern dance, had approached the Foundation for funding. In January 1953, Charles B. Fahs, Director of the Division of Humanities, spoke privately with *The New York Times* dance critic John Martin, seeking his views on the merits of the Connecticut College program and "the ballet group at the City Center."[19] Martin's opinion of both was high. However, it was not until 1955 that the Foundation awarded the college a three-year grant of $33,400 to support the scholarship program, help pay faculty salaries, and enable new works to be commissioned. (A second grant, for $40,000, followed in 1958.)[20] One can only speculate as to Kirstein's role in this episode, if any. A confirmed classicist, he retained until the early 1960s a grudging respect for certain practitioners of modern dance, including Martha Graham (who choreographed a section of *Episodes* in 1959), Martha Hill and Doris Humphrey (with whom he served for several years on the ANTA Dance Panel),[21] and Merce Cunningham (who staged *The Seasons* for Ballet Society in 1947). Graham (as well as Ballet Theatre's Lucia Chase) sat with him on the short-lived committee that met in 1958 to discuss the formation of a Lincoln Center Ballet Company, which would subsume existing dance companies and include two subdivisions, one oriented toward classical dance, the other toward modern dance.[22] However, the fact remains that during Kirstein's tenure at City Center, modern dance never gained a foothold there. Nor did rival ballet organizations unless they were foreign. Indeed, the instability of Ballet Theatre in the 1950s was at least partly owing to the drain of personnel as well as dollars, including Rockefeller dollars,[23] to the New York City Ballet.

The New York City Ballet was born in the virulently Cold War atmosphere of the late 1940s, when a decade of hearings, loyalty oaths, and blacklisting had decimated the left-liberal culture of the New Deal. In this atmosphere, as Baum pointed out, requests for government funding of the arts were apt to recall "the unfortunate experience of the Federal Theatre Project during the Depression."[24] In other words, to most U.S. Congressmen, funding smacked of socialism. The demise of the New Deal was still a vivid memory, nowhere more so than at City Center, which had its origin in the orchestra developed through the Federal Arts Project and a president (Newbold Morris) who had been the Project's New York director.[25] The mandarins who staffed the Rockefeller Foundation had no love of socialists (or communists) of any stripe, but like the CIA "elite" spying for freedom on the front lines of Europe, they sought to distance themselves from the yahooism and anti-intellectualism of McCarthy's populist crusade at home.[26] For them, arts funding was acceptable so long as it was unbesmirched by New Deal politics and could be enlisted in the service of the Cold War. This did not keep Charles B. Fahs from ordering political checks on Kirstein and other key City Center figures. Unsurprisingly, the investigation turned up a host of "questionable" associations. Kirstein had signed a call for a convention of American revolutionary writers in 1935; was a sponsor and member of the board of directors in 1946–1947 of Peoples Songs, Inc. (an organization "declared subversive" by the House Un-American Activities Committee); and had signed an open letter in 1939 "calling for greater unity of the anti-fascist forces and strengthening of the front against aggression through closer cooperation with the Soviet Union."[27]

Marshall, Kirstein, and their colleagues were sophisticated men, well aware that arts funding policies in the United States were out of step with those of postwar Europe, West as well as East. They knew, too, that in European intellectual circles, American culture was viewed as little more than mass-market movies and bubble gum. The new music, dance, and painting that had transformed the landscape of American art since the 1930s was totally unknown. The New York City Ballet made its first tour abroad in 1950. However, it was in 1952, when the company embarked on a five-month trip that included performances at the Berlin Festival, Edinburgh Festival, and the Paris Opéra—this as part of the huge CIA-funded arts festival "Masterpieces of the Twentieth Century"— that the company's modernist "recipe" was shown to be an exemplary export, easily pressed into the service of liberal Cold War ideology. A memorandum aimed at getting the Foundation to put up the air fare for yet another European tour (which it eventually did) struck just the right note: "The New York City Ballet Company is universally recognized as the greatest organization of its kind in the Free World."[28] Russell L. Riley, director of the State Department's International Educational Exchange Service, in a letter to Newbold Morris, described the company's tours as a "contribution to the objectives of the Department's educational exchange program, particularly in helping to change the widespread foreign opinion that American values are almost completely materialistic. Reports from abroad show that its performances have left the impression of an artistic excellence . . . representative of the high cultural standards of this country."[29] Even more rhapsodic was an account (intended for the Foundation's annual report) of the company's visit to Trieste, then a battleground between East and West, in 1953:

This was the period of Communist-inspired anti-Western riots in the Free City; there was hesitation on the part of the ballet-management to send the young dancers into what might have developed into a combat zone. The Trieste appearances were historic; even the Communist press had only praise for this artistry of the Americans. The Mayor of the Free City, Gianni Bartoli . . . awarded each dancer with the Medal of Honor of Trieste, and affirmed that the presence of the company had done much to enhance the prestige of the West at a trying time.[30]

In January 1955, Kirstein resigned from both the City Center board and the managing directorship. After many clashes, his relationship with Joseph Rosenstock, the director of the New York City Opera, had unraveled, and now, with Rosenstock's contract up for renewal, he sought to replace him with Gian-Carlo

Menotti. Unfortunately, Kirstein miscalculated the extent of his support, and instead of dismissing Rosenstock the board voted to renew his contract.[31] With this incident, Kirstein's career as a producer came to an end. The Rockefeller Foundation grant had enabled him to continue the Diaghilev-style collaborations and repertory model that he had put into practice both with Ballet Caravan in the 1930s and Ballet Society in the 1940s. It had inspired him to imagine a City Center that was virtually a blueprint for what later became Lincoln Center, an institution housing all the performing arts as well as professional training facilities. As early as 1952, he confided to John Marshall his "intention to build at the Center both producing and training facilities. . . . K knows of some interest on the part of Schuman, as Director of the Juilliard School, in disposing of its uptown property to Columbia and moving the School into a midtown location, where it would be closely associated with production and performance. . . . Also, . . . K has had encouraging conversations with Robert Moses about the possibility of better housing for the Center, which might include these training facilities."[32]

Over the years, Kirstein had done his best to get Nelson Rockefeller to join the City Center board. In 1954, he redirected his efforts to Nelson's brother, John D. Rockefeller 3d. In June, Baum formally invited John D. to join the board and serve on the Finance Committee. Enclosed with his letter was a six-year development plan for "an ideal City Center, embodying a large auditorium for musical theater (opera, ballet, light-opera), a dramatic theater, and a concert hall," and "incorporat[ing] existing schools of the performing arts (for music, dance and theater) in a professional conservatory, supervised and protected by Columbia University."[33] Rockefeller never joined the board. But Kirstein's plan for an "ideal City Center" did not fade away. Instead, it became the working model for the committee headed by Rockefeller and with Kirstein as one of its members that began to meet in the following months "to explore the feasibility of an artistic set-up that would take in ballet, concerts, chamber music, drama, light opera and perhaps educational programs, as well as opera and symphony." By December 1955, when *The New York Times* picked up the story, "an eighteen-block area north of Columbus Circle had been earmarked for demolition under the city's urban renewal program, and both the Metropolitan Opera and the New York Philharmonic had committed themselves to the project."[34] Kirstein did far more than simply shepherd the New York City Ballet to Lincoln Center; very likely he dreamed up the whole scheme.

In the years following his resignation, City Center remained the company's home. However, once it appeared that Rockefeller was prepared to include the New York City Ballet as a full-fledged constituent of Lincoln Center, Kirstein made no secret of his willingness to sever the company's ties with City Center. As early as December 1955, he was denying (at least to John Marshall) that any "legal tie" existed between the two organizations. "If K and Balanchine were to decide to move to the new center for the arts, City Center would have no legal hold on them, nor as far as K can see, on the company. There might have to be some adjudication as to properties—scenery and costumes."[35] By the spring of 1957, when the idea of a Lincoln Center dance company as distinct from the New York City Ballet was beginning to take shape, the Foundation's president, Charles B. Fahs, spoke to Kirstein about the "progress he had made in broadening . . . Ballet Society."

> K indicated that he has hesitated to add to his Board of Trustees for fear of restricting his own flexibility and committing himself to people of whose real interest and abilities he is not completely confident. CBF asked whether . . . it would be possible . . . to set up a committee under the sponsorship of Ballet Society which might request and allocate a general fund for production costs of new dance creations on the pattern of the original grant to the New York City Center but not limited either to the New York City Center Ballet or to ballet in general? Conceivably a fund of $100,000 a year might provide a useful stimulus . . . not only for the City Center Ballet but possibly also for Ballet Theatre and some of the modern dance groups. . . . With some reservations K seemed much taken by this concept, even though CBF pointed out that he had no assurance that he could get support for it here and that CBF's mentioning it did not mean that it would necessarily be impossible to get help directly for Ballet Society.[36]

Obviously, Fahs was trying to push Kirstein into adopting a less combative attitude toward his "rivals," a category that included pretty much everyone in the dance world except the New York City Ballet. And he strongly implied that the Foundation would be willing to fund Ballet Society if the monies were distributed more equitably than before.

This was a course Kirstein chose not to follow. By 1959, a new "angel" had appeared on the horizon—the Ford Foundation. Unlike the Rockefeller Foundation, it was prepared to ignore the claims of other institutions, while funding those closest to Kirstein's heart—the School of American Ballet, which now became a truly national organization, and the New York City Ballet, which in 1963 received the lion's share of a $7.7 million grant, the largest until then in the dance field.[37] Ford largesse made it possible for Kirstein and the New York City Ballet to claim—and ultimately control—the New York State Theatre. But a little over a decade before, at an even more critical juncture, Rockefeller largesse had enabled the young company to prosper by adding substantially to its repertory and international acclaim. Although dance funding during the 1950s generally has received little attention,[38] it was during this crucial decade that the basis was laid for the combination of academic, foundation, and government sponsorship that remains a hallmark of the U.S. system of financing dance. In the creation of this system, the Rockefeller Foundation's pioneering grant to City Center was of crucial, if unacknowledged importance.

NOTES

1. Grant authorization 53064, 14 May 1953, Rockefeller Foundation Collection, R.G. 1.2 (Projects), Series 200R (U.S./Humanities), Sub-series (City Center), Box 392, Folder 3390, Rockefeller Archive Center, Pocantico Hills, New York. Unless otherwise noted, all citations are to material housed at this archive.

2. See Lincoln Kirstein, *Thirty Years: The New York City Ballet* (New York: Knopf, 1978); Nancy Reynolds, *Repertory in Review: Forty Years of the New York City Ballet,* introd. Lincoln Kirstein (New York: Dial, 1977); and Bernard Taper, *Balanchine: A Biography,* rev. ed. (Berkeley: University of California Press, 1996). The episode is discussed at length in Martin L. Sokol's *The New York City Opera: An American Adventure* (New York: Macmillan, 1981), ch. 15.

3. Edward M. M. Warburg, letter (copy) to Nelson A. Rockefeller, 8 October 1934; Rockefeller to Warburg (copy), 10 October 1934; Warburg to Rockefeller, 11 October 1934, Rockefeller Family Collection, R.G. 2, Series (Educational/SAB), Box 37, Folder 251. During the School's early years, Warburg was the president, Vladimir Dimitriew the vice-president and director, and Kirstein the secretary-treasurer. For the overlapping social and professional ties among the members of Kirstein's circle in the late 1920s and 1930s, including their ties with the Museum of Modern Art, see Nicholas Fox Weber, *Patron Saints: Five Rebels Who Opened America to a New Art 1928–1943* (New York: Knopf, 1992).

4. Rockefeller to Warburg (copy), 8 and 13 January 1937; Vladimir Dimitriew to Rockefeller, 16 January 1937; Kirstein to Rockefeller, 18 January 1937, Rockefeller Family Collection, R.G. 2, Series (Educational/SAB), Box 37, Folder 251.

5. Warburg to Rockefeller, 3 February 1937; Rockefeller to Warburg (copy), 5 February 1937, Rockefeller Family Collection, R.G. 2, Series (Educational/SAB), Box 37, Folder 251.

6. "The American Ballet Caravan" [report], p. 1 (Rockefeller Family Collection, R.G. 4 [NAR/Personal Projects], Series F966, Box 101, Folder [Lincoln Kirstein/Ballet Caravan]). The company also enjoyed subventions from local governments in Brazil, Chile, Peru, Colombia, and Venezuela. The Brazilians, for instance, put up $7,500 for two weeks in Rio and one in Sao Paulo (Lincoln Kirstein, "Draft of a Preliminary Report Concerning the Tour of the American Ballet Caravan in South America, June–September 1941," 9 September 1941, p. 5, Rockefeller Family Collection, R.G. 4 [NAR/Personal Projects], Series F965, Box 100, Folder [Lincoln Kirstein]). The souvenir program, which was edited by Monroe Wheeler, was made possible by an additional grant from Rockefeller's office ("Brief of report from Lincoln Kirstein, Re. Contract No. NDCar-50, effective March 17, 1941," 14 June 1941, Rockefeller Family Collection, R.G. 4 [NAR/Personal Projects], Series F966, Box 101, Folder [Lincoln Kirstein/Ballet Caravan]). In addition to American Ballet Caravan, the CIAA sponsored the Yale Glee Club, an exhibition of contemporary U.S. art arranged by the Museum of Modern Art, Chicago White Sox catcher Moe Berg (on a bat-and-ball

tour), and two Spanish-language motion pictures by Walt Disney. For a discussion of these and other projects launched by Rockefeller during his CIAA career, see Cary Reich, *The Life of Nelson A. Rockefeller: Worlds to Conquer 1908–1958* (New York: Doubleday, 1996), pp. 214–222.

7. "Tribute to Rockefeller Staged by City Ballet," *The New York Times*, 31 January 1979, sec. 3, p. 19.

8. Reich, *Rockefeller*, pp. 11–12.

9. Kirstein to Rockefeller, 30 May 1948; Rockefeller to Kirstein (copy), 3 June 1948; and Kirstein to Rockefeller, 4 June 1948, Rockefeller Family Collection, R.G. 4 (NAR/Personal Projects), Series F1428, Box 145.

10. John Marshall, report of an interview with Newbold Morris, 5 October 1948, Rockefeller Foundation Collection, R.G. 1.2 (Projects), Series 200R (City Center), Box 392, Folder 3390.

11. Morton Baum, letter to John Marshall, 12 January 1949, Rockefeller Foundation Collection, R.F. 1.2 (Projects) Series 200R (City Center), Box 392, Folder 3390.

12. "Grant in aid to the Ballet Society, Inc.—toward the completion of a book, *A Model of the Classic Dance*," RA H 4937, 14 April 1949; Kirstein to John Marshall, 14 November 1950 and 12 February 1951, Rockefeller Foundation Archives, R.G. 1.2 (Projects), Series 200R, Sub-series F2766, Box 296, Folder (Ballet Society/Dance Manual/Lincoln Kirstein). In the book's acknowledgments Kirstein wrote: "Above all she [Muriel Stuart] wishes to thank David Vaughan, the young English dancer and choreographer, who emigrated to New York to study in the School of American Ballet and to aid in the final revisions of this text" (*The Classic Ballet: Basic Technique and Terminology* [New York: Knopf, 1976], p. vii). In fact, his role, Vaughan told the present writer, was far greater; he did not simply revise the text but actually wrote (with Stuart) the step and movement descriptions that comprise the heart of the book.

13. Preliminary resolution approving grant to City Center, 1 April 1953, Rockefeller Foundation Archives, R.G. 1.2 (Projects), Series 200R, Sub-series (City Center), Box 392, Folder 3390.

14. Grant authorization 53064, *op. cit.*

15. Kirstein to Rockefeller, 1 February 1952, Rockefeller Family Collection, R.G 4 (NAR/Personal Projects), Series F965, Box 100, Folder (Lincoln Kirstein, 1933–1966).

16. Kirstein to Marshall, 26 January 1953, Rockefeller Foundation Archives, R.G. 1.2 (Projects), Series 200R, Sub-series (City Center), Box 392, Folder 3391. In a letter to Charles B. Fahs, Director of the Division of Humanities, written prior to receipt of the grant, Kirstein mentioned a number of possibilities that lack of subsidy precluded exploring. Among them was a production of *A Midsummer Night's Dream*, with music by Virgil Thomson after Mendelssohn, choreography by Balanchine, and the dancers playing speaking as well as dancing roles (Kirstein to Fahs, 14 November 1952, Rockefeller Foundation Archives, R.G. 1.2 [Projects], Series 200R, Sub-series [City Center], Box 392, Folder 3391).

17. Kirstein to Marshall, 21 August, 8 and 14 September 1953; to Malcolm Gillette, 12 and

26 January 1954, 13 January 1955; Rockefeller Grant Report, Fall Season 1955, Rockefeller Foundation Archives, R.G. 1.2 (Projects), Series 200R, Sub-series (City Center), Box 392, Folders 3392, 3393, 3394, 3396, 3398–3401.

18. EFD, report of a conversation with Wallace K. Harrison, 15 April 1953, Rockefeller Foundation Archives, R.G. 1.2 (Projects), Series 200R, Sub-series (City Center), Box 392, Folder 3392.

19. Fahs, report of an interview with John Martin, 26 January 1953, Rockefeller Foundation Archives, R.G. 1.2 (Projects), Series 200R, Sub-series (City Center), Box 392, Folder 3391.

20. Jack Anderson, *The American Dance Festival* (Durham: Duke University Press, 1987), pp. 40, 48.

21. Kirstein served on the ANTA Dance Panel from 1955 until January 1960, when he resigned. For a list of the panel members during this period, see Naima Prevots, *Dance for Export: Cultural Diplomacy and the Cold War,* introd. Eric Foner (Hanover, N.H.: University Press of New England/Wesleyan University Press, 1998), pp. 147–149.

22. See, for instance, the minutes of the second Advisory Meeting on [sic] the Dance, 11 February 1958, Lincoln Center for the Performing Arts Archives.

23. In April 1954, Marshall asked John Martin for his opinion of both Ballet Theatre and the Ballet Russe de Monte Carlo, since "a question ha[d] been raised about RF aid to both companies and M's comment was that it would be literally scandalous for the RF to give them its support. Neither company can stand comparison with the New York City Center Company" (Marshall, report of a interview with John Martin, 21 April 1954, Rockefeller Foundation Archives, R.G. 1.2 [Projects], Series 200 R, Sub-series [City Center], Box 392, Folder 3394). An unsigned memo circulated internally explained in greater detail the case against Ballet Theatre: "In the case of Ballet Theatre, the application sent us is virtually prima-facie evidence of the company's uncertain future. We are asked to provide for what amounts to total deficits of over $400,000 a year. We are told that the sources from which this company earlier met its deficits have now dried up. The general impression in informed circles is that it is about to go out of existence" ("Current requests for aid to ballet companies," 22 April 1954, *ibid.*).

24. Baum to Marshall, 11 April 1949, Rockefeller Foundation Archives, R.G. 1.2 (Projects), Series 200 R, Sub-series (City Center), Box 392, Folder 3390.

25. Marshall, report of interview with Newbold Morris, 5 October 1948, Rockefeller Foundation Archives, R.G. 1.2 (Projects), Series 200 R, Sub-series (City Center), Box 392, Folder 3390.

26. For an excellent discussion of the CIA's infiltration of postwar Europe's cultural elite, see Frances Stoller Saunders, *The Cultural Cold War: The CIA and the World of Arts and Letters* (New York: New Press, 2000).

27. Unsigned memorandum written on behalf of Charles B. Fahs, 23 March 1953, and response from A.M. dated 24 March 1953, Rockefeller Foundation Collection, R.G. 1.2, Series 200R, Sub-series (City Center), Box 392, Folder 3391. It should be noted that the memorandum requested the addressee to "check on . . . names" associated not

only with City Center but also with the American Shakespeare Festival (which received a Foundation grant either late in 1953 or early in 1954) and the Connecticut College School of the Dance (virtually the entire faculty). Unfortunately, the attached response deals only with the City Center names. Kirstein's FBI files detail other left-wing associations, such as speaking in 1947 at a Cultural Freedom and Civil Liberties conference sponsored by the Progressive Citizens of America, declared a Communist front; calling for a national convention of American revolutionary writers in 1935 and subsequently being a member of the Communist-dominated League of American Writers. The FBI ran its last check on Kirstein in March 1985, when he was invited to the White House to receive an award. In addition to the files at the Washington office of the FBI, there are files at the FBI's branch office in New York.

28. "Memorandum: New York City Ballet: Proposed European Tour, 1953," n.d. [18 August 1953], Rockefeller Foundation Archives, R.G. 1.2 (Projects), Series 200 R, Sub-series (City Center), Box 392, Folder 3392. This unsigned memorandum was attached to John Marshall's account of a meeting with Kirstein in which he expressed "considerable distress about his unexpected inability to secure $50,000 needed for transportation costs of the Ballet Company of New York City Center in a remarkable European tour definitely scheduled for the autumn, during which the Company would appear at most of the leading opera houses of Europe. Expenses in Europe are fully covered by local guarantees, but transportation costs simply cannot be earned. Until quite recently, K had what he supposed a firm agreement with one of his friends that the friend in question would meet those charges. Now, quite unexpectedly, the friend has found himself unable to do so."

29. Riley to Morris, 8 October 1953, Rockefeller Foundation Archives, R.G. 1.2 (Projects), Series 200 R, Sub-series (City Center), Box 392, Folder 3393.

30. "The New York Ballet Company," unsigned and undated memorandum attached to a letter dated 1 February 1954 from Kirstein's secretary, Josephine Cerasani, to Miss Magee of the Rockefeller Foundations Office of Publications, Rockefeller Foundation Archives, R.G. 1.2 (Projects), Series 200 R, Sub-series (City Center), Box 392, Folder 3394. Elsewhere, the memo states that the grant enabling the company to take its third trip to Europe came from the Rockefeller Brothers Fund.

31. For Kirstein's clashes with Rosenstock and the events that prompted his resignation, see Sokol, *The New York City Opera*, ch. 15. See also see Marshall's interview with Kirstein, 26 February 1954, copies of Kirstein's letters to Rosenstock, 15 February 1954, and Dr. Leopold Sachse, 12 February 1954, Rockefeller Foundation Archives, R.G. 1.2 (Projects), Series 200 R, Sub-series (City Center), Box 392, Folder 3394. After his resignation, Kirstein told Charles B. Fahs that "He had never had the full artistic control which we assumed he had at the time of our original grant. While he recognized the feelings of other directors that his plans would increase the cost of the City Center overhead, he had also felt that with high-quality productions additional support could be found. He felt that the difference between his theoretical powers and the actual situation in which policy was determined by Morton Baum had reached the point where it was undignified for him to continue with the title, managing direc-

tor" (Charles B. Fahs, report of an interview with Lincoln Kirstein, 31 January 1955, Rockefeller Foundation Archives, R.G. 1.2 [Projects], Series 200 R, Sub-series [City Center], Box 392, Folder 3396). Kirstein was far less circumspect in discussing his resignation with the press. "If one sees the City Center as a money-making concern," he told Howard Taubman of *The New York Times*, "I see the City Center as a money-spending concern. If we had the highest artistic principles, we would get the money" (Howard Taubman, "City Center Director Quits in Policy Fight," *The New York Times*, 28 January 1955, pp. 1 *et seq.*).

32. Marshall, report of an interview with Lincoln Kirstein, 8 October 1952, Rockefeller Foundation Archives, R.G. 1.2 (Projects), Series 200 R, Sub-series (City Center), Box 392, Folder 3391.

33. Baum to John D. Rockefeller 3d, 3 June 1954 and attached "Development Program: 1954–1960," attached to Marshall's report of an interview with Kirstein, 21 June 1954, Rockefeller Foundation Archives, R.G. 1.2 (Projects), Series 200 R, Sub-series (City Center), Box 392, Folder 3395.

34. Harold C. Schonberg, "Rockefeller 3d Will Direct Study of a Lincoln Sq. Center for Arts," *The New York Times*, 1 December 1955, pp. 1 *et seq.*

35. Marshall, report of an interview with Lincoln Kirstein, 6 December 1955, Rockefeller Foundation Archives, R.G. 1.2 (Projects), Series 200 R, Sub-series (City Center), Box 392, Folder 3397.

36. Fahs, report of an interview with Lincoln Kirstein, 12 March 1957, Rockefeller Foundation Archives, R.G. 1.2 (Projects), Series 200 R, Sub-series (City Center), Box 392, Folder 3398–3401.

37. Allen Hughes, "Ford Fund Allots 7.7 Million to Ballet," *The New York Times*, 16 December 1963, p. 1. For an overview of the Ford–New York City Ballet relationship, see Anne Barclay Bennett, "The Management of Philanthropic Funding for Institutional Stabilization: A History of the Ford Foundation and New York City Ballet." Ph.D. Diss., Graduate School of Education, Harvard University, 1989.

38. An exception is Prevots' *Dance for Export.*

PARALLEL LIVES

ALVIN AILEY AND ROBERT JOFFREY

They could not have been more different. Robert Joffrey was white, Alvin Ailey black. Where Joffrey made a cult of the ballet past, Ailey loved the dance vernaculars of African-Americans. Yet, even more striking than their differences were their similarities. Near contemporaries, both were gay men who died of AIDS in the late 1980s. Both were the founding directors of dance companies that bear their names, companies synonomous with the sexy, adventurous, and populist spirit of the 1960s. Yet the men who conceived them, nursed them to adulthood, and denied they had AIDS to protect them remain an enigma. Why, in a society that views dance almost wholly as a female activity, did they become dancers? What influence did racism and sexual orientation have on their careers? How did the companies they fathered serve as a vehicle of creative self-expression? What were the wages of success?

Jennifer Dunning's *Alvin Ailey: A Life in Dance* and Sasha Anawalt's *The Joffrey Ballet: Robert Joffrey and the Making of an American Dance Company*[1] go a long way toward answering these questions. Of the two, Dunning's is the more satisfying, a work by a longtime critic of *The New York Times* that unravels the complicated weave of Ailey's private and professional life with knowledge, skill, and tact. Anawalt's book, the first by this California-based dance writer, is considerably less expert. Not only can it be glib, it often loses sight of its subject. At the same time, the book touches on issues related to gender, funding, and the role of criticism that Dunning skirts.

Born in 1931, Ailey was the adored only son of a woman married and abandoned by age eighteen, who washed, cooked, and cleaned in one Texas town after another before heading to Los Angeles in 1941. Dunning eloquently resurrects these early years—not only their grinding poverty, rootlessness, and pervasive fear of violence, but also the warmth of family and faith. She evokes the one-room Mount Olive Baptist Church where Ailey was baptized, and the magic of the ceremony itself, with deacons wading in the water, children wrapped in white sheets, and the pastor's wife singing "I Been 'Buked and I Been Scorned"—all relived in his joyous signature work, *Revelations* (1960). And she

This essay was originally published in *The Nation* on 24 February 1997.

conjures up the hot music, pulsating bodies, and raunchy atmosphere of the era's Dew Drop Inns that Ailey commemorated in countless works beginning with *Blues Suite* (1958).

If Texas formed him, it was Los Angeles that made Ailey an artist. In its theaters and nightclubs he discovered black idols, from Pearl Bailey, Billie Holliday, Lena Horne, and Duke Ellington, who became his favorite composer, to Katharine Dunham, whose lush, lavish, all-black *Tropical Revue* thrilled him. It was in Los Angeles, too, that Ailey took his first dance class. Inspired by Carmen de Lavallade, a classmate at his mostly black high school and the cousin of Janet Collins, the Metropolitan Opera's first black ballerina, he found his way to Lester Horton, a white modern dance maverick with a flair for theatrics and an open-door policy toward blacks.

In tracing Ailey's career, Dunning sheds a much-needed light on racism in the period's dance world. Although most ballet companies excluded blacks, modern dance, which even during the Cold War retained a social conscience inherited from the 1930s, did not. Like many black dancers, Ailey studied ballet with Karel Shook and modern dance at the New Dance Group; he appeared with Anna Sokolow's company and played an Israeli soldier in the 1955 edition of Sophie Maslow's Chanukah Festival at Madison Square Garden. And he danced on Broadway. With de Lavallade as his partner, he made his debut in *House of Flowers* (1954), an all-black musical starring Pearl Bailey and featuring an astonishing line-up of black dance talent, from Geoffrey Holder to Arthur Mitchell. But even if choreographers like Helen Tamiris, Michael Kidd, and Hanya Holm pushed for hiring black dancers in "white" shows, Broadway was the most segregated quarter of the dance world until well into the 1960s.

In 1958, Ailey gave his first independent concert with the nucleus of his future company. In the rehearsal studio "there was . . . a sense of mission," writes Dunning. Although companies like Martha Graham's might have been integrated and all-black shows like *Jamaica* were a gold mine for performers, Ailey's goal was to create a genuine home for black dancers and a haven for black dance. This did not necessarily preclude dancers of other races, but meant the number had to be kept to a minimum. It also meant a repertory company that would fulfill Ailey's own choreographic ambitions while showcasing work by other black choreographers.

In the pick-up company of friends that performed with Ailey at the 92nd Street Y, Jacob's Pillow, and the Delacorte Theater in Central Park, no one was paid. Ailey scrounged for costumes and rehearsal space, usually dipping into his own pocket. What kept the company going, apart from sheer love of dance, was the Westside YWCA, which turned over its entire second floor practically rent free, and the State Department, which underwrote the company's first foreign tour in 1962 and a number of subsequent ones. Still, for long stretches the company could not afford to perform in New York. "One of the most surprising aspects of our senior modern-dance companies," wrote *The New York Times* dance critic Clives Barnes in 1968, "is that they can appear in extensive seasons in Europe, but at home it appears that they are not wanted on the cultural voyage."[2]

Dunning gives a good sense of the company's growing pains in the middle and late 1960s, when "dance was becoming an increasingly professionalized field of activity" and dancers "had begun to insist on their rights as professionals." With no business know-how, a chronic shortage of cash, and a host of back bills, bad checks, and missing receipts, managing the company's finances was a nightmare. It was only in the 1970s, when the National Endowment of the Arts developed programs to shore up financially weak institutions, that the Alvin Ailey American Dance Theater became a fully professional company, although it could never free itself of deficits.

Still, the first half of the 1970s were balmy times. With stars like Judith Jamison, hits like *Masekela Language* (1969), *Cry* (1971), and *Night Creatures* (1975), long seasons at City Center, booming audiences, and federal arts dollars, AAADT moved to the front ranks of national dance companies. But stress began to take its toll. As Ailey's choreographic output diminished, he seemed to grow harder; he drank too much and spent much of his spare time with street people—drug dealers and hustlers among them. Finally, in 1979, when the dancer Joyce Trisler, a friend of thirty years, was found dead in her apartment, possibly from suicide or an accidental overdose, Ailey fell apart. He commemorated her death in *Memoria,* a dance of lyric grandeur, and with heavy bouts of drugtaking. There were public incidents, and he soon landed at Bellevue. Although he eventually pulled himself together, his most creative years were over.

Dunning treads lightly over this last decade. With the company now a resounding success (even if critics complained of its commercialism) and Ailey himself covered with honors, the story ends triumphantly. The description of his final months with AIDS, like the account of his death with his mother at his side, has more than its share of bathos. The author might have speculated more profitably on the nature of his choreographic legacy, its relationship to the tradition of black dance and its influence on young black choreographers. And a brief word on how racism and the cultural separatism that remain facts of American life justify the continued existence of all-black companies would have been useful.

If Dunning shies from such issues, Sasha Anawalt raises them with gusto. The impact of homosexuality on artistic policy, the mirage of the perfect ballet body, the politics of criticism, drug use among dancers, ballerinas having babies, shortsighted funding policies, minority dancers in ballet, control of artistic policy, and struggles with the board—all these and more turn up in *The Joffrey Ballet.* Unfortunately, they are seldom explored in depth, partly because the book's strictly chronological approach all but precludes thematic analysis, but also because of the author's spotty knowledge of dance history, which keeps her from understanding the broad implications of much of what she recounts.

Still, as the first detailed chronicle of the Joffrey company, the book is an important addition to the literature of American dance in the 1960s and 1970s. Not only does it trace season by season the development of the Joffrey's many-faceted repertory, it also introduces the numerous personalities who passed through the company as dancers, choreographers, administrators, and board members. Far more than the New York City Ballet, which by the mid-1950s had become almost exclusively a platform for George Balanchine's choreography, the Joffrey Ballet was a crossroads for many tendencies. There were "pop" ballets, mostly by Gerald Arpino, Joffrey's personal and professional partner; historical revivals of the Ashton and Diaghilev-era works that were Joffrey's passion; "crossover" ballets by postmoderns such as Twyla Tharp and Mark Morris. With Ailey, Balanchine, Paul Taylor, and Jerome Robbins included in the repertory, the Joffrey Ballet offered a remarkably broad spectrum of twentieth-century dance.

Behind this quite extraordinary achievement was Robert Joffrey, the son of an Afghan khan who immigrated to America, opened a chili parlor in Seattle, and married his cashier, an amateur violinist from Italy. Anawalt reconstructs this story, like most of Joffrey's childhood, from interviews. Born in 1928, he began dancing as a kid, horrifying his father and, like so many boys, keeping his lessons a secret. At sixteen, he fell in love with Arpino, and at eighteen, headed east with him to New York. He studied at Balanchine's School of American Ballet; with Alexandra Fedorova, a veteran of the early Ballets Russes; and with modern dancers such as Gertrude Schurr and May O'Donnell, both Graham alumnae. From the start, his viewpoint was remarkably open-minded. He was also unusually receptive to dancers whose bodies did not fit the mold. Although this would change somewhat in later years, his company was never a physically homogeneous entity.

Like the Ailey company but a few years earlier, the Joffrey Ballet began with a concert at the 92nd Street Y. Then the dancers piled into a red-and-white Chevrolet and made the first of the endless tours that became the company's bread and butter. In the move toward professionalization in the 1960s, Rebekah Harkness played a key role. Her Standard Oil millions meant paychecks for the dancers at full union scale and six-hour Equity workdays. Works were commissioned from Ailey (*Feast of Ashes*, his first work for ballet dancers), Brian Macdonald, Fernand Nault, and others. Her patronage was anything but disinterested. Harkness liked to meddle, at one point hatching a plot to oust Balanchine from Lincoln Center, at another to merge Joffrey's school with the Metropolitan Opera's. Finally, she dropped the company and formed her own.

With money always in short supply, mayhem and insecurity were everyday facts of life. But there were other forces behind the constant flux that no amount of government funding—the Joffrey was a privileged beneficiary of NEA dollars in the 1970s—could stay or reverse. Anawalt describes wholesale dismissals, radical shifts in repertory, walkouts by embittered principals, unproven youngsters brought to the fore. She makes no attempt to link these recurring episodes or to explain why Joffrey may have provoked them. Was it to avoid the claustrophobia of repetition? To allay a feeling of unworthiness so deeply rooted as to be unconscious? Was he a power freak, a patriarch and a Saturn to his unruly brood? Or was he just plain persnickety? Sadly, the author never enters the workshop of his soul.

This is especially unfortunate because of the enthusiasm and enormous research that has gone into this book. Anawalt has talked to just about everyone who knew Joffrey, slogged through mountains of clippings and correspondence, dug up programs and school records, and put together a complete list of Joffrey productions that is reason enough to keep this book handy. However, unlike Dunning, Anawalt fails to control her sources and her subject. Long quotations from interviews clutter the story, throw it off course, and give a conversational tone to the writing that often trivializes it. The volume begins and ends as a biography, yet Joffrey himself is often buried under an avalanche of material about the company and the dance world at large.

Reading these books, I found it hard to avoid nostalgia for a time when dances were made on a shoestring and companies lived on faith. Of course, life was cheap then, and part-time jobs easy to find. In today's world, dancemaking is a tough, professional game, involving big money, high risks, and widespread underemployment. No art has been harder hit than dance by the high cost of urban space, and no art has suffered more from cuts in public funding. So one reads these books marveling that so much was possible on so little, and pondering the unexpected virtues of smallness.

NOTES

1. Sasha Anawalt, *The Joffrey Ballet: Robert Joffrey and the Making of an American Dance Company* (New York: Scribner's, 1996); Jennifer Dunning, *Alvin Ailey: A Life in Dance* (New York: Addison-Wesley, 1996).

2. Quoted in Olga Maynard, *Judith Jamison: Aspects of a Dancer* (Garden City, N.Y.: Doubleday, 1982), p. 111.

REVELATIONS

For some years now, the Alvin Ailey American Dance Company has presented a month-long December season at New York's City Center. This year, as always, the company drew huge houses, filling not only the orchestra and mezzanine of the old Shrine Temple, but even the second balcony, which an increasing number of dance attractions now close off because of falling attendance. Even the New York City Ballet's *Nutcracker,* a moneymaker since the 1950s and as much a part of Christmas in the city as the tree in Rockefeller Center, had empty seats this season, albeit many fewer than for the company's repertory programs.

Meanwhile, Ailey was turning people away. At curtain time, the lobby was jammed with a cross-section of the city's middle class, black as well as white, including many young people. This racial mixture is the most notable aspect of the Ailey audience. What makes the phenomenon all the more remarkable is that Ailey is an "uptown" company, performing at a big Manhattan theater and charging relatively high ticket prices.

A key to AAADC's success lies in courting audiences that live outside the wealthiest Manhattan neighborhoods. Another is its stature as an artistic organization. Growing out of the unpaid "group" assembled by Ailey in the late 1950s, AAADC has developed over the years into a major national company, with thirty-one dancers, works by a host of choreographers, a "junior" ensemble, and an affiliated school. Although Ailey's own works, which include *Revelations,* the company's signature piece, make up an important part of the repertory, this season was typical in offering works by nearly a dozen other choreographers, from Jerome Robbins and John Butler, who have worked extensively in ballet, to Garth Fagan, Donald Byrd, and Jawole Willa Jo Zollar, African-American artists with distinctive styles and movement idioms.

In size, the mixed character of its repertory, and the scale of many productions, Ailey more closely resembles a ballet company than a modern dance one. *Revelations* uses nearly two dozen dancers, while *Memoria* has a cast of forty-one, including twenty-six students from the Ailey school. Moreover, even in works that incorporate postmodern elements—like Zollar's *Shelter,* a piece about homelessness, and artistic director Judith Jamison's *Hymn,* which has a text written and performed by playwright Anna Deavere Smith—"readability" is always a concern. Also, like ballet, AAADC seduces its audience with specta-

This essay was originally published in *The Nation* on 17 April 1995.

cle. Production values are high, as is the technical expertise of the dancers; both can draw audible gasps from the public.

Finally, AAADC is mindful of tradition. Almost from the start of his career as a choreographer, Ailey had a strong sense of roots, of legacies to be acknowledged and preserved. At his school, the techniques of Lester Horton and Katherine Dunham—both formative influences on him—are part of the curriculum, "so that," as he says in his autobiography, *Revelations,* "these ways of moving will not be lost." Horton, a maverick in Los Angeles dance circles from the late 1920s until the early 1950s, trained an extraordinary group of black concert dancers in the years after World War II, including Ailey, Carmen de Lavallade, Janet Collins, and James Truitte. At a time of pervasive racism, Horton's Dance Theatre was a fully multiracial ensemble where blacks enjoyed equal footing with whites and where casting was color-blind.

Horton's technique, which stressed falls, pelvic movements, and fluid motion, became the basis of Ailey's; its eloquence pervades the lyrical sections of *Revelations.* Stylistic eclecticism was another Horton legacy. Ailey's vocabulary incorporated elements from black vernacular dance as well as jazz and the Afro-Caribbean idiom popularized by Katherine Dunham. Later, it would include ballet steps as well. Musically, too, Ailey drew on both African-American and modern "high" art traditions. *Revelations* was set to spirituals; *Night Creature* and *The River* to Duke Ellington; *The Lark Ascending* to Ralph Vaughan Williams; *Choral Dances* to Benjamin Britten.

Like Dunham in the 1930s and 1940s, Ailey had an abiding sense of obligation to the culture of black America. Over the years, practically every African-American choreographer of note was represented in his repertory, beginning with Dunham and Pearl Primus, the founding "mothers" of black concert dance. For Talley Beatty and Donald McKayle, who belonged to the generation that followed them, the Ailey company was both an ongoing source of commissions and a showcase for older works, such as Beatty's *The Road of Phoebe Snow* and McKayle's *Rainbow 'Round My Shoulder,* both of which grew directly out of the black experience and might otherwise have vanished.

Even before the late 1960s, when Ailey first hired a number of white and Asian dancers, white choreographers such as John Butler, Lucas Hoving, and Joyce Trisler had choreographed for the company. In the 1970s, their number grew with the inclusion of works by Anna Sokolow, Pauline Koner, Ted Shawn, and José Limón, reflecting Ailey's vision of his company as being a repository of the classic works of modern dance as well as a source of new ones. In his early years in New York, Ailey had danced with Sokolow as well as Sophie Maslow; another Martha Graham company veteran, Pearl Lang, directed his school. Like Graham herself, all had welcomed black dancers in their companies. Just as he never lost sight of his roots, so Ailey never forgot those who had treated black artists with respect.

Still, as revealed in his newly published autobiography, the last years of Ailey's life were clouded with bitterness. Drugs, which precipitated a major breakdown in 1980, certainly heightened the sense of futility that overwhelmed him at times. But far more crushing was the burden of running a dance company, even a successful one, without the security of long-term funding. Prior to the establishment of the National Endowment for the Arts, most dance companies existed outside the commercial marketplace. Concerts were done on a shoestring, and no one was paid. In one way, however, Ailey was lucky. The Cold War was still on, and the campaign for civil rights had moved into high gear. To allay criticism abroad of America's racial system, the State Department sent black artists to politically sensitive areas like Africa, the Far East, and the Soviet Union. Although touring for propaganda was both prestigious and lucrative, it failed to keep the company afloat at home. In 1970, when a tour of the Soviet Union fell through, Ailey was forced to disband the company; it was only resurrected when the State Department decided to send it to North Africa.

The increase in monies from NEA in the 1970s did not so much stabilize companies like AAADT as encourage them to expand and professionalize. As dancers went on payroll and administrative staff was hired, expenses mounted. Although AAADT was extremely successful, earned income did not suffice to meet costs. The difference had to be covered by grants. The catch was that NEA grants tended to be given for the creation of new works, rather than for general operating expenses, and increasingly in the form of matching grants. Large-scale fundraising became essential, along with professional management. Meanwhile, the spiraling inflation of the 1970s made budgets difficult to contain, and deficits grew.

Ailey hated to beg for money. He also hated the controls, as he viewed them, imposed by an increasingly cost-conscious management that robbed him of intimate contact with his dancers and, by extension, of any impetus to choreograph. Productions had to be planned at least a year in advance, so even when he had an idea for a new work, the idea died, or he lost interest in it, before it was possible to begin working in the studio—or so he said.

Increasingly, too, he spoke with bitterness about the continuing racism in ballet. Despite the existence of the Dance Theatre of Harlem, he once remarked, "nothing has changed. We have black kids at the school studying ballet and I know there is no chance of getting them into classical companies." Since then, certain changes have taken place, especially among regional companies. Still, only the Miami City Ballet can be considered a genuinely multiracial ensemble, featuring as it does a large contingent of Latin Americans and Americans of Hispanic descent, along with non-Latino whites and blacks. As for American Ballet Theatre and the New York City Ballet, the country's major national companies, they remain overwhelmingly white. That ballet companies received a disproportionate amount of the funding for dance was, in Ailey's view, simply another instance of racism.

For all the cutbacks of recent years, some black groups, like Garth Fagan

Dance (whose *Griot New York* was recently aired on PBS's *Dance in America* series), have done well. Under Judith Jamison, moreover, AAADT has gone from strength to strength, not only weathering Ailey's death in 1989 but also broadening the repertory to encompass younger African-American choreographers, including Fagan and Jawole Willa Jo Zollar (one of the founders of the Urban Bush Women), whose works lie outside traditions close to Ailey.

However, the most spectacular African-American success story of the late 1980s and 1990s has been Bill T. Jones. Black, gay, and HIV-positive, he has achieved the kind of recognition that few dance artists ever receive—a MacArthur "genius" award, news magazine cover stories, commissions from prestigious opera companies, a *New Yorker* profile by Henry Louis Gates, Jr. With the New York premiere last November of *Still/Here*, his multimedia piece about AIDS, Jones has also become the season's choreographer *célèbre*, thanks to dance critic Arlene Croce's vitriolic attack on the work.

Still/Here grew out of "survival workshops" conducted by Jones with victims of what the press material describes as "life-threatening illnesses." The interviews were videotaped, and portions spliced into the work, providing its much-publicized "testimonials." As it turns out, Jones' treatment of these is remarkably cavalier, even in the first half, where the walking patterns of the dancers suggest the ritual of a mourning collective. Not only does he fragment the images of his witnesses, depriving them of voices even as he projects their faces on the set's half-dozen screens, but with his banal and intrusive questioning, he also undermines the power of their words; one woman, for instance, never gets to finish her story about learning that she was HIV-positive. And after the first telling, he trivializes even that version by cutting, distorting, and recycling it as a virtually unintelligible sound bite.

Overshadowed by video clips and Kenneth Frazelle's music (sung at one point by Odetta), the choreography is of minor interest. Jones has little sense of structure, and little feeling for the physical logic of a phrase. Whatever expressiveness seems to reside in his choreography comes from the dancers, especially the women, whose gestures convey the pathos of loss and physical dismemberment that the men, instruments of Jones' anger, fail to provide. This anger is the prevailing motif of the second, chaotic half of the work, where blinking images, a deafening sound score, and aggressive, nonstop movement not only dwarf the human drama, but also preclude any expression of empathy. The trouble with *Still/Here* is not that it puts its "victims" onstage, but that it trivializes and betrays them.

The weaknesses of the work were apparent to many critics. But the celebrated *New Yorker* article by Arlene Croce began with the proud affirmation that she chose not to review—or even attend—*Still/Here*, since "by working dying people into his act, Jones is putting himself beyond the reach of criticism."[1] Nonetheless, Croce went on to attack not only Jones and "victim art" (which she saw his piece as exemplifying), but also NEA funding policies and the cultural politics of the 1960s (or at least her version thereof). The intensity of her screed may have derived in part from the appearance a month earlier of Gates' profile of Jones, *The New Yorker*'s first dance-related piece in years that appeared without the imprimatur of its dance critic.

Although Croce's attack on the "blackmail" of "dissed blacks, abused women, or disfranchised homosexuals"[2] has been hailed by conservatives as a leading critic's sudden awakening to the perils of multiculturalism and the politicization of art, it actually reflects her longstanding political conservatism and hostility to most black dance. Indeed, in the late 1970s, when she served on an NEA panel, Jones had been one of her favorites, precisely because, as she writes, "he seemed to be uninterested in conforming to the stereotype of the respectable black choreographer,"[3] an allusion, as her reviews of the period make clear, to Ailey, whose "'cultured' folk art" and "solemn conservatory-dance pieces"[4] she never tired of attacking. Nor has Croce refrained from using epithets that some might consider racist—"Mighty Mouse,"[5] for Gen Horiuchi, the New York City Ballet's only Japanese-born dancer; "dancing lobster,"[6] for (black) Ailey dancer John Parks; the "Herbert Ross Chair of Talmudic Choreography,"[7] for the Jewish-American choreographer of films and musicals.

Croce has long insisted that political concerns have no place in art. She even criticized George Balanchine, the choreographer she most deeply admires, for having his dancers come onstage with candles after Martin Luther King's assassination. "[T]heater, she once wrote, "can't speak in the sentimental ... colloquialisms of 'people' theater (peace vigils, marches, love-ins, encounter sessions etc.) without becoming by that much less a place of art and by that much more a place of worship."[8] This, from the critic who had previously declared that "ballet is ... a kind of aestheticizing church."[9] Obviously, some churches are more acceptable than others.

Croce's desire to insulate art from everyday concerns is a familiar aesthetic stance. However, in her case, it leads to a complete denial of the social conditions under which the production of dance takes place. Thus, while criticizing Ailey fundraisers for selling the company on the basis of its "multiracial character" and "native populism"—"in short, as a cause for good liberal Americans"[10]— she nowhere deals with the historical segregation of black dancers and choreographers. Nor, in her generally commendatory reviews of the Dance Theatre of Harlem does she mention that although by the mid-1970s the company had demonstrated "that black Americans [could] dance ballet as well as white Americans,"[11] the point was apparently lost on the vast majority of ballet companies.

That this is now no longer wholly the case is at least partly due to the multicultural policies of the arts bureaucracy that Croce also attacks in her nonreview of *Still/Here*. Not that she addresses the issue of racism. Rather, following the lead of conservatives like Robert Brustein, Lynn Cheney, and Hilton Kramer, she insists that under pressure from NEA and the private funders who "knuckled under to the community- and minority-minded lobbies," "disinterested art has become anathema." Instead, she discerns a "blatant bias" for utilitarian or socially useful art, whose "ideological boosters" turn out to be the usual left-wing suspects, descendants of the political crusaders of the 1960s—"against Vietnam, for civil rights"—and the "proletarian" 1930s, "when big-government bureaucracy began."[12] And like the pseudo-populist politicians still smarting over the Mapplethorpe episode, she attributes Jones' success to the "campaigns of the multiculturalists, the moral guardians, and the minority groups."[13] As if Jones lacked the chutzpah and opportunism to take care of himself.

There is nothing "neo" about Croce's conservatism. Although neither her entry in *Who's Who of American Women* nor the biographies on the dust jackets of her books mention it, she spent most of the 1960s on the staff of conservative magazines, becoming a senior editor of William F. Buckley's *National Review* in 1966. Although she contributed articles about movies, plays, and ballet, her interests were not purely aesthetic. She wrote a laudatory piece about the Parents and Taxpayers Coordinating Council (PAT), a grassroots organization opposing racial integration of the New York City schools during Senator Barry Goldwater's 1964 presidential campaign, and another piece denying that the John Birch Society was truly Christian; she also covered the conspiracy trial of Benjamin Spock (or "Dr. Quack," as she once referred to him) for aiding draft resisters.[14] Among her other contributions were comic verses ridiculing the Great Society and theater people concerned with the depredations of the Ku Klux Klan. She was also an editor of *Rally*, an obscure conservative publication aimed at college students, which had the distinction of predicting an upsurge of student conservatism at Columbia University on the eve of the greatest student uprising in American history.[15] In *National Review*, during the years that Croce was associated with it, one finds the same hatred for radicals, "philistines," and government bureaucrats, the same disregard of social concerns, the same inflammatory rhetoric, and the same thinly disguised racism as in her attack on Jones and "victim art." Her criticism is anything but politically neutral.

As the dean of American dance critics, Croce is hardly a voice crying unheard in the wilderness. Her views carry weight because of both what she writes and where she writes. She has served on funding and foundation panels, and despite her distaste for universities as hotbeds of feminism, multiculturalism, and Marxism, has lectured at centers of "political correctness" such as Berkeley. She has influenced a generation of dance critics, teaching them not only how to see dance, but also how to think about it. She has used the idea of disinterestedness to isolate the aesthetic act from the social circumstances that surround it, and identified excellence with the patrician elitism of old-style conservatism. For Croce, there is little room for black dance that is not a carbon copy of the white dance she esteems as art.

Despite this and for all the recent cuts in funding, black dance is thriving. Its forms are as diverse as its techniques, and although shared in many cases with those of white concert dance, often identify issues that are quite different.

Moreover, thanks to the Ailey company's strong commitment to a diverse repertory, a mainstream outlet exists for African- American choreography that is important historically or representative of new trends. Finally, to a degree unmatched by any white enterprise, the audiences for black dance are racially mixed, even though the public for more experimental work remains largely white.

One troubling note within this generally cheerful picture is ballet, where African-Americans remain heavily underrepresented both professionally and at the elite training academies. The combination of economics and social practice that lies behind the prevailing tokenism requires concerted action on the part of funders as well as critics. The enterprise of ballet is intimately tied to its ideology as an art. No one who loves it can afford to remain "neutral."

NOTES

1. "Discussing the Undiscussable," *The New Yorker,* 26 December 1994/2 January 1995, p. 54. The essay is reprinted in Croce's *Writing in the Dark, Dancing in "The New Yorker"* (New York: Farrar, Straus and Giroux, 2000), pp. 708–719.

2. "Discussing the Undiscussable," p. 55.

3. *Ibid.,* p. 56.

4. "Standing Still," in *Afterimages* (New York: Knopf, 1977), p. 29.

5. "Singular Sensations," *The New Yorker,* 24 June 1985, p. 90.

6. "Standing Still," in *Afterimages,* p. 27.

7. "Sylvia, Susan, and God," *Ballet Review,* 1, no. 1, p. 6.

8. "Folies Béjart," in *Afterimages,* p. 384.

9. "Sylvia, Susan, and God," p. 10.

10. "Standing Still," p. 28.

11. "Faces of Harlem," in *Afterimages,* p. 58.

12. "Discussing the Undiscussable," p. 56.

13. *Ibid.,* p. 60.

14. Arlene Croce, "Backlash in New York: PAT vs. Board of Education," *National Review,* 22 September 1964, pp. 816–817; "Is Robert Welch's Doctrine 'Christian,'" *National Review,* 9 August 1966, p. 762; "The Boston Happening," *National Review,* 18 June 1968, pp. 599–602; A[rlene] C[roce], "The Spockery of Dr. Quack, *National Review,* 3 November 1964, p. 944; A[rlene] C[roce], "LBJ Walks at Midnight," *National Review,* 1 December 1964, p. 1046; A[rlene] C[roce], "There's a Civil Right for Ev'ry Light on Broadway," *National Review,* 20 April 1965, p. 314.

15. Stephen A. Stertz, "The New Right at Columbia," *Rally,* November 1967, p. 13.

DANCE THEATRE OF HARLEM AT THIRTY

In 1969, a year after the death of Martin Luther King, Jr., Arthur Mitchell, the country's leading African-American dancer, founded the Dance Theatre of Harlem. A Harlem native and graduate of New York's High School of Performing Arts, Mitchell was a principal dancer with the New York City Ballet, which he had joined in 1955, quickly becoming one of the most interesting of the company's neoclassical princes. His goal in forming DTH was both to prove that black dancers "could do ballet" and to provide them with an outlet to perform.

DTH was not the first all-black ballet company, but it came into existence at a time when civil rights was still a galvanizing idea and large-scale monies for ballet were available from both the Ford Foundation and the National Endowment for the Arts. Unlike its short-lived predecessors, such as the First Negro Classic Ballet (founded 1947) and the New York Negro Ballet (1954–1959), DTH was well-positioned not only to survive but to flourish.

All the signs were propitious. The company's cofounder was Karel Shook, Mitchell's own ballet teacher and mentor to scores of black dancers. On the board sat George Balanchine and Lincoln Kirstein, the artistic director and patron extraordinaire respectively of the New York City Ballet, and among the benefactors were Peabodys, Rockefellers and Plimptons—names long associated with philanthropy for blacks. The Ford Foundation subsidized the company's affiliated school, which functioned as both a neighborhood arts center and a professional training academy. DTH gave its first extended engagement at Jacob's Pillow in 1970, made its official debut at New York's Guggenheim Museum in 1971, and soon afterward shared the stage at a New York City Ballet gala. Among DTH's early repertory were Balanchine classics like *Agon* and *Concerto Barocco*, the rights given free of charge by the choreographer.

Dancers flocked to the company's Harlem studio. For black ballet dancers, the 1960s were not a good time. True, John Jones had danced with Jerome Robbins' short-lived Ballets U.S.A., and Christian Holder and Gary Chryst were rising stars of the Joffrey Ballet. For black women, however, opportunities were limited for the most part to guest appearances in works outside the standard repertory. Thus, in 1960 Mary Hinkson appeared with the New York City Ballet in Balanchine's *The Figure in the Carpet* and in 1966 with American Ballet Theatre in Glen Tetley's *Ricercare*. The previous year, ABT had engaged no fewer

This essay was originally published in *The Nation* on 3 January 2000.

than four black women—Judith Jamison (later Alvin Ailey's muse), Carmen de Lavallade, Cleo Quitman, and Glory Van Scott—for Agnes de Mille's *The Four Marys*. None left with a contract. As Jamison would discover during her brief tenure with the Harkness Ballet, few roles were deemed suitable for a black woman.

Over the years, DTH underwent many changes. The neoclassicism that initially linked it stylistically to the New York City Ballet declined in importance. There were forays into the nineteenth-century repertory (most notably, a "Creole" *Giselle* set among pre–Civil War free blacks in the Louisiana bayous), revivals of early twentieth-century works (including Bronislava Nijinska's *Les Noces* and *Les Biches*) and later Americana classics such as Agnes de Mille's *Fall River Legend*, Ruth Page's *Frankie and Johnny*, and Valerie Bettis' *A Streetcar Named Desire*. And, increasingly, there were dramatic ballets (such as William Dollar's *The Duel* and John Butler's *Medea*) and works by black choreographers, including John Alleyne, Garth Fagan, Robert Garland, Geoffrey Holder, Louis Johnson, Alonzo King, Vincent Sekwati Mantsoe, Dwight Rhoden, Billy Wilson, and Mitchell himself.

DTH was born at the height of the dance "boom" when grants were plentiful and touring earned a big chunk of the company's income. Then came the Reagan years. Government and foundation funds dried up; costs rose steeply; audiences, hit by recession, down-sizing and rising ticket prices, declined. In 1990, faced with a projected $1.7 million deficit, DTH laid off all fifty-one dancers as well as other personnel for six months. American Express and the Lila Wallace-Reader's Digest Fund came to the rescue with $1 million each. But even with the economies DTH now undertook—foregoing expensive productions (such as its acclaimed Nijinska program), focusing on the new, "contemporary" works that tour sponsors wanted—by 1995 it was forced to reduce its fifty-two dancers to thirty-six, not enough to perform *Giselle* or its popular *Firebird* without being augmented by students. The use of apprentices and nonunion "floaters" was behind the 1997 walk-out that ended with the dancers being guaranteed only thirty weeks of work during the second contract year. Today, even as the dance world recovers from the effects of Reaganomics, stability continues to elude DTH.

This fall DTH celebrated its thirtieth anniversary with a two-week season at New York's City Center, its first appearance in midtown Manhattan in five years. Dozens of company "alums" were on hand, and there were balloons and cheers when they took a bow onstage after the last performance. Alas, the season itself was less festive. With thirteen principals and eight soloists (fewer than one-third the number of musicians hired for the season), the company's dance ranks are much depleted. "Guest artists"—retired former company members—shored up the roster, along with a corps of twenty-three student/apprentices from the DTH school. Equally diminished is the repertory. The nineteenth- and early twentieth-century classics are gone, along with the early Americana works.

Only a smattering of Balanchine remains. Mostly there are works of recent vintage by black choreographers that seem designed to prove that DTH is really black, that it can "dance black" and wow a black audience—in other words, perform the dances of African, Caribbean, or vernacular inspiration that black audiences will pay to see. This is a far cry from Mitchell's founding vision.

Typical of this market-driven trend is Robert Garland's new *Return*, a glitzy work to songs by James Brown and Aretha Franklin that looks like a music video danced on pointe. Another is *South African Suite*, presented in a expanded version this season, which has wonderful music by the Soweto String Quartet and choreography (by Mitchell, Augustus Van Heerden, and Laveen Naidu) in which everyone struts their stuff in sleek workout wear. More interesting is Dwight Rhoden's *Twist*, the season's other premiere, which combines fabulous spectacle (lighting and projections by Michael Korsch) and contemporary energy. Dramatically, the piece has its flaws; it goes on too long and needs dynamic variety. But it does challenge the dancers, not because they have to work in other idioms, but because Rhoden wants them to look like classicists. Although trained as a modern dancer, he revels in the stretched feet, harmonious line, and clean footwork that create a ballet "look."

In the 1970s and 1980s, DTH scrupulously maintained its Balanchine repertory. Now, only *Prodigal Son*, in which Duncan Cooper gave an exciting performance as the Son, was danced with an understanding of the choreography and its style. (Cooper, a real dramatic talent, was also outstanding in the revival of Michael Smuin's Native-American epic, *A Song for Dead Warriors*.) *Bugaku*, a Japanese-inspired court ritual led by the retired Ronald Perry, one of the original company's most accomplished technicians, and Simone Cardoso, another former DTH member, was an embarrassment. As for *The Four Temperaments*, of the present company, only Donald Williams, who danced the role of Phlegmatic with elegance and a fine, understated passion, displayed an understanding of the ballet's style, a combination of postwar "cool" and nervous intensity.

Thirty years after its founding, the mission of DTH is very much up in the air. In 1999 it is no longer necessary to prove that blacks can dance classical ballet, nor is DTH the only venue where classically trained blacks can dance. There are any number of major U.S. companies with black principal dancers, and the opportunities continue to grow, especially for men. The fact that this is today the case is a measure of DTH's accomplishment both in developing black talent and in making a place for it in ballet.

Over the years, DTH has also developed a substantial black audience, a notable achievement given that the ballet audience, even in places like New York, remains heavily white. For the most part, however, this new public is not a ballet or even a dance audience. It is an audience for *black* dance, and it wants to see work that looks black, that shows a little bit of "attitude," takes a cook's tour of the African diaspora, or does a classy version of MTV or Broadway—the kind of dance the Alvin Ailey company has made its trademark. For this overwhelmingly middle-class and upper-middle-class audience—itself largely a product of the post–civil rights era—race is not so much a physical attribute as a cultural identity. In a sense, the cultural tastes of the DTH audience make it increasingly difficult for the company to maintain a classical identity.

Rather than catering only to these tastes, Mitchell might want to make good on the idea that DTH has become, as its publicity states, "a multicultural institution." By this I mean expanding the company's artistic or cultural profile beyond its current largely racial identity. Although DTH would remain a company committed to developing black dancers and black classical choreographers, its "black" works would be merely one part of a much broader repertory embracing a small number of nineteenth-century classics and a larger number of twentieth-century ones. In other words, DTH should remake itself as a truly national company along the lines of the old Joffrey Ballet or the current Miami City Ballet, with its mixture of Hispanic-oriented works and classical repertory.

To do this, however, DTH needs dancers with solid training and strong technique. This season much of the dancing was depressingly mediocre. Although Kellye A. Saunders and Andrea Long turned in some excellent performances, few of the women have the technical equipment to join even the corps de ballet of a major national or regional company. This does not speak well for the teaching that takes place in the DTH studios.

In a century that has seen history-making ballet companies fold in less than a decade, surviving thirty years is quite an accomplishment. By now, Mitchell knows pretty much everything there is to know about running a company. It's what he does best—what he did in the years before DTH became an institution that had lost its raison d'être but that nobody could allow to founder. Maybe the time has come for him to return to the idea that inspired him so long ago, to recreate his vision of a company of magnificent black classicists.

AMERICAN BALLET THEATRE

1989

Ever since 1920, rethinking *Swan Lake* has been a Soviet pastime. In that year, Alexander Gorsky restaged the work in "Stanislavskian" style, jettisoning the old choreography and inventing the Jester. Thirteen years later, Agrippina Vaganova created a "romantic" version, with Odette as a mysterious dream girl and Odile as the daughter of a landowner. In 1937, Asaf Messerer rid the Bolshoi version of mime; in 1950, Konstantin Sergeyev did the same for his Kirov recension, which centered on the tribulations of Siegfried. Three years later, Vladimir Bourmeister partly restored Tchaikovsky's original musical sequence; two years after that, Lyubov Serebrovskaya used the composer's original score in full. In 1958, Fedor Lopukhov revived the 1895 Maryinsky version, mime and all, while in 1969, Yuri Grigorovich dropped the first-act peasants. In 1984, Rudolph Nureyev—a Soviet artist under the skin—made the Tutor, who doubled as Von Rothbart, the center of a homoerotic drama with Siegfried.

American Ballet Theatre's new *Swan Lake*, conceived and partly rechoreographed by Mikhail Baryshnikov, belongs to this Soviet tradition. Baryshnikov has tinkered with virtually every aspect of the ballet, and like his Soviet contemporaries and predecessors, he has done so in the hope of freshening it up and modernizing it. His version fails on both counts. Rather, with the exception of the new fourth act, animated by a vision absent from the rest of the ballet, his *Swan Lake* strains after novelty to the point of losing artistic coherence.

Practically all Baryshnikov's departures from traditional Western productions have Soviet precedents. He has restored much of Tchaikovsky's original music, including the Pas de Six, apportioned now to the Act IV pas de deux, Odile's new first variation, and the Mask and Sword Dances in Act III. He has deleted most of the mime, although he has kept the passage in Act II where Odette tells the story of her enchantment. He has substituted courtiers for peasants in Act I and outfitted the men in harlequin wear—an allusion to the Jester in Soviet versions. And, in releasing the swans from Von Rothbart's spell, he has given the ballet a happy ending.

Like his counterparts at the Kirov and Bolshoi, Baryshnikov also has chipped away at the vernaculars that coexisted with classicism in nineteenth-century

This review was originally published in *Dance Magazine* in October 1989.

ballet. The Act I genre dances are gone, replaced by a ballabile for courtiers in classical style. He downplays the narrative by deleting whole sequences, including the Tutor's flirtation with the peasant girl. He has kept the mime roles but emptied them of content. The Tutor ambles, waves his arms, and retreats to the sidelines. The Queen Mother, as svelte as a maid, hands Siegfried his bow and vanishes.

In trimming the narrative, Baryshnikov also thins out the drama. Siegfried's disenchantment with life—his unease at marrying, his attempt to find solace in simple pleasures, his readiness to set off in quest of the ideal—is conveyed only fitfully, as though the plot of the ballet were incidental to its theme. This, Baryshnikov told *The New York Times*, is "that life is never what you think it is." At several points in the ballet, masks are donned. But instead of sharpening the contrast between reality and illusion, they appear as isolated gestures, unrelated to the ballet as a whole.

For the most part, Baryshnikov has left Act II alone. But, as in Act I, the changes he has made lessen the drama. At one point in the old ABT version, the swans gathered in a flock on the right, while Siegfried and his hunters, on the left, made ready to shoot. Odette flew in and, placing herself at the head of the flock, opened her arms in a gesture of protection. That moment is gone. Now, following the Kirov version, the swans form a double line, the "tunnel" through which Odette rushes to the footlights. There is no facedown with the hunters, no heroic gesture of sisterhood. Throughout, in fact, Baryshnikov sacrifices drama to design, the experience of present passion to a memory of love frozen in time. Like the Kirov's version, Baryshnikov's Act II fails to convey a sense of tragedy.

His Act IV, by contrast, overflows with feeling. The choreography is new, and certainly at odds with the rest of the ballet. But it possesses a vision that is missing elsewhere, as if this were the only act that held genuine meaning for him. The theme is romantic—and profoundly Soviet: the release of the enchanted polity through an act of trust. In most *Swan Lakes*, Siegfried and Von Rothbart slug it out. Here, Von Rothbart wilts as the lovers plight their troth—a slow walk in the shadow of death to the lakeside. With their suicide and the tyrant's unmasking, the enchained collective is transformed; under a beam of radiant light, it sheds its classical demeanor, moving for the first time like natural beings. In this, the ballet's most poignant scene, Baryshnikov has created a perestroika parable: a statement of hope in the face of stifling authoritarianism.

Alas, the choreography falls short of the conception. As in the traditional Kirov version, the scene belongs to the ensemble. But Baryshnikov has broken up the linear patterns and, with caracoles and wedges and circles, created a sisterhood bonded in anticlassical ritual. The steps themselves are few—bourrées, piqué arabesques, walks—and almost entirely uninflected, as if the imagination that served him as a dancer were alien to him as a choreographer. In Act I, he employs a slightly richer palette. But the enchaînements come straight from the classroom, and the comings and goings reveal little feeling for the dramatic or psychological potential of the stage. Neither convincing as pastiche Petipa nor consistent with the choreography elsewhere, Baryshnikov's contribution merely adds to the ballet's stylistic amorphousness.

Design might have given ballast to the production. But PierLuigi Samaritani has elected a time-traveling solution that only compounds the incongruities of the choreography. The setting for Act I is leafy and pastoral, a symphony in mauve recalling Watteau; the lakeside scenes take place under the brooding arches of a ruined cloister; Act III, in a ballroom hung with tapestries, deep red and medieval in design. The costumes are equally a hodgepodge: mauve-toned milk-maid and harlequin wear in Act I; mid-nineteenth-century-length tarlatans in the swan scenes (and for Odile); Renaissance dress and contemporary debutante wear in Act III. Some of the color choices are inexplicable: the use of kelly green as a decorative highlight in Act I; its juxtaposition with Ulster orange in the czardas in Act III. Equally puzzling is the rationale behind Samaritani's sexual grotesques—the Queen Mother, a seductive witch in hot pink and gold, and Von Rothbart, an owl-headed macho in a black leather codpiece.

Baryshnikov's swan song as ABT artistic director, the production is a measure of his achievement in the past decade. The male ensemble is nothing short of superb—noble, airborne classicists, with a clear understanding of nineteenth-century style. The male soloist ranks are also bursting with talent, from Wes Chapman and Ricardo Bustamante, accomplished cavaliers with a genuine romantic presence (promoted after the season to principals), to Gil Boggs, John Gardner, Jeremy Collins, Danilo Radojevic, all dashing in the ballet's new divertissements. When it comes to female classicists, the ranks are thinner, although Christina Fagundes, flowing and ever-gracious, and Deirdre Carberry, unmatched in the bounce and precision of her allegro, stand out in the Peasant pas de trois.

The problem lies in the ballerina ranks, increasingly segregated by age and Kirov-style typecasting. On one side stand the displaced "seniors," Martine van Hamel and Cynthia Gregory, whose performances, scheduled late in the season, had all the fire and passion of the old *Swan Lake*. On the other are Baryshnikov's protégées Susan Jaffe and Christine Dunham, coached to the hilt in the artful plastique and dynamic deadness that are Kirov trademarks. Although Jaffe's Odette had ravishing moments, Dunham's uninflected phrasing drained the role of even decorative interest.

Alone among the younger ballerinas, Amanda McKerrow (inexplicably cast only at matinees) has found the key to the ballet. Her Odette is both a testament to classical beauty and a lyric of unrequited love—grave, poignant, with moments of pure passion. Her developpés breathe with the hope of womanhood; her lifts aspire to the empyrean. And when, at the end of Act II, she flings herself into Siegfried's arms, she does so with a wildness that registers a protest against destiny along with triumphant love. She brings the same warmth to *Bal-*

let Imperial, where she seems the very embodiment of Balanchinean memory—an Odette, an Aurora summoned from the wreckage of the past through the sheer radiance of her technique.

Most of the season's other revivals and new works (those by Twyla Tharp are reviewed separately) reinforced the division in the ballerina ranks. For Gregory, *Prodigal Son* briefly returned to the repertoire (with Radojevic as an edgy, forceful Prodigal), while for van Hamel there was *The Garden of Villandry,* a slight work about an Edwardian ménage à trois choreographed by Martha Clarke, Robert Barnett, and Felix Blaska. Van Hamel also made richly textured debuts in two character roles. The first was Lady Capulet in *Romeo and Juliet*—a woman of ripe sexuality, torn between sympathy for a daughter and anger at losing a lover. In Martha Graham's *Appalachian Spring,* performed at the ABT-Graham gala, her Pioneer Woman was the very salt of the earth—open, generous, full of quiet dignity. (Why ABT has chosen to take Graham's *Diversion of Angels* into its repertoire, rather than the ever-fresh *Appalachian Spring,* is a mystery.)

The ballerina who suffered most this season from Baryshnikov's pigeonholing was Alessandra Ferri; apart from two *Romeo and Juliets* and two *Don Quixotes,* she had almost nothing to do. Yet there are many repertory slots she could fill, from the Glove-Seller in *Gaîté Parisienne* (remember her French ballerina last year in *Gala Performance?*) to any of the roles in *Les Sylphides.* One would like to see her in Balanchine works: *Ballet Imperial,* the second movement of *Bourrée Fantasque* (Dunham, who now dances the part, misses the romanticism), either of the leads in *Stravinsky Violin Concerto.*

This ballet—and the Balanchine repertoire generally—needs smartening up. Although the male corps looks splendid, the female ensemble remains sluggish. In the second Aria, only McKerrow conveys the vulnerability of a woman making a gift of her nakedness, although the recipient of her gift, the ever-grandstanding Andris Liepa, seems largely indifferent to it. (Would that Bustamante, so poignant in the second lead at another performance, had been her partner.) Elsewhere, the casting is equally troubling. Cheryl Yeager, consistently teamed with Julio Bocca in *Theme and Variations,* has bounce but none of the smoothness and romantic presence that make his all too few appearances something to look forward to. Deirdre Carberry may have the technique for the opening movement of *Bourrée Fantasque,* but she misses the wit, and she certainly lacks the figure for a short bobbing tutu. As for *Ballet Imperial,* with its cartoon St. Petersburg decor and interfering skirts, it remains an eyesore.

Ironically, the company's strength lies where it has traditionally—in the *demi-caractère* ranks. Kathleen Moore goes from triumph to triumph. Her Hagar in *Pillar of Fire* has gained in complexity and depth; anxiety, hunger, pain, loneliness, guilt—all are there now. In *Gaîté Parisienne,* she gives us a Flower-Girl who's pure commedia—a candy-cane Columbine with the bounce of a Kewpiedoll. (In her debut in the same role, Marie-France was little more than a pouty coquette.) In *La Sylphide,* Amy Rose also added to her glories, with an Effie full of joy (how she loves to dance that reel!) and the pathos of a wounded bird. The same performance also witnessed Shelley Washington's debut as Madge—a wild, immensely physical portrayal, full of theatrical power. Of the new Tharp dancers, Washington alone seemed at ease in a classical setting. As the Master of Ceremonies in *Swan Lake*, Jamie Bishton and Kevin O'Day looked distinctly uncomfortable, while as Tybalt in *Romeo and Juliet*, the latter undermined a strong dramatic presence by the small-scale naturalism of his gesture. The hero of the season was Victor Barbee—chilling and virile as Von Rothbart; passionate and masterful as Tybalt; quietly ardent in the second movement of *Bourrée Fantasque*, alas, one of the few romantic roles within his technique.

Clark Tippet, the company's in-house choreographer, came up with two new pieces this season. Neither had great originality, but like his *Bruch Violin Concerto No. 1* of last year, each revealed the pleasure he takes in his dancers and the respect he has for their classical vocabulary. *Rigaudon*, the more ambitious of the two, is part Balanchine and part baroque, with a fine opening section that nods to eighteenth-century style—pulsing relevés, beats, the weaving patterns of a contredanse—without attempting to duplicate it. The piece loses steam in the middle trios and duets, which go on too long and show an excessive fondness for upside-down lifts. In *Some Assembly Required*, Tippet fares considerably better. A duet for Amanda McKerrow and John Gardner, an unlikely pair of truck-stop lovers, the piece capitalizes on its dancers—their homespun American looks, unexpected sexiness, technical virtuosity. At the same time, it calls for an edgy tension that plays against the "niceness" of their usual personas.

Apart from Tharp's *Everlast* and *Bum's Rush*, *Assembly* was the only "down-home" item in the season's repertoire. As such, it made you think—about where ABT is headed, about the prospects for an American classicism that, while indebted to Balanchine, also acknowledges its *demi-caractère* inheritance. In a season that gave us a "Soviet" *Swan Lake* and, with Andris Liepa, a Soviet headliner with neither the sensibility nor the accomplishment for the roles he was privileged to play, one can only welcome the appearance of Tippet, a choreographer—however modest his talent—who respects ABT's dancers for what they are and understands their heritage as Americans. In his desire to remake ABT in a Kirov image, Baryshnikov has forgotten the truth of that New York saying: You can take the girl out of Brooklyn, but you can't take Brooklyn out of the girl.

AMERICAN BALLET THEATRE

2001

The best thing about ABT these days is how Kevin McKenzie is bringing along the company's gifted young dancers. Gillian Murphy's extraordinary debut in *Swan Lake*—she is a ballerina in all but title now—and her newly cemented partnership with Marcelo Gomes testify to McKenzie's success in identifying future principals and understanding what they need to develop. Murphy, who received her training at the North Carolina School of the Arts, commands a prodigious technique. She is a distinctly American phenomenon, with the scissor legs, articulate pointework, and fleetness one associates with dancers reared in the Balanchine tradition. At the same time, she has the strengths that come from training with a more traditional emphasis—placement, line, port de bras, épaulement, even a huge Plisetskaya leap. She can turn on a dime. As an Odalisque in *Le Corsaire*, she did three and even four turns—with time to spare. This season, as Odile, she did triple and double attitude turns and a deep renversé so slow it seemed to halt the flow of time; then she whipped into the fouettés with a triple, followed by singles and doubles. Her dynamics are thrilling. And what power in her leg as it lifts forward, circles into second, moves around to arabesque, then sweeps up into a penchée. And this was only her debut.

Murphy does not dance with "soul," nor does she "act." She finds her way into a role through the music. As Odette she *was* the music, following it, yielding to it, fleeing it, plumbing its depths. The dancing said it all, freshly, spontaneously, in the here and now. But also impersonally. This is not an Odette to warm the heart or tug at the emotions. As Siegfried, the Brazilian-trained Marcelo Gomes is fire to her ice. He is dark where she is fair, ardent where she is cold, a romantic hero come to win his lady. He has the proportions of a ballet prince, as well as the demeanor. One is struck by his utter ease in classical movement, as though this were a language he speaks not only fluently but also naturally. He is blessed with line, flexibility, and elevation, expressive, unmannered arms, a light effortless jump, and wonderful turns; even in the most bravura passages he never sacrifices elegance. Finally, he is a marvelous partner, who gives Murphy a womanliness that other partners (including Angel Corella, unsuccessfully paired with her in *Don Quixote*) seem unable to elicit. Their *Theme and Varia-*

This essay was originally published in *Dance View,* 18, no. 4 (Autumn 2001).

tions together was charged with eroticism, yet so pure, so technically accomplished, and musical that one experienced the ballet as something abstract, a thrilling distillation of Petipa and *The Sleeping Beauty.* Technically Gomes may not be quite at her level yet, but their partnership is that rarity, a meeting of true artistic minds.

Another exciting partnership this season paired Julie Kent and José Manuel Carreño. Their *Giselle* was one of the best I have seen in years, freshly imagined and emotionally compelling, yet faithful to the spirit and form of this most traditional work. Both are magnificent dancers. They are also marvelous actors, who can infuse the most classical gesture with the throb of human life. In the first act, they have completely rethought the narrative episodes, breaking them down, fleshing them out, emphasizing the dramatic logic, clarifying the details. The surprise encounter of the lovers at the start of the ballet is played almost in slow motion. Dancers, of course, are always touching. But I have never seen the touching that is part and parcel of these scenes take on so strong an emotional coloring, express so clearly the desire experienced by the protagonists. Not a step is changed in the choreography. What is new is the dramatic specificity, the focus, the detail. In her solo, Giselle looks at Albrecht, gestures to him, as if she were dancing for him alone. Yet they remain fully a part of the ballet's community, protagonists of a collective drama revitalized by their presence. The contrast between the lovers and Hilarion, as played by Ethan Brown as a rube disdained, lurking as an outsider on the periphery of village life, could not be greater. It's hard to feel much sympathy for him, or the fate awaiting him in the ballet's intensely romantic second act, a last night of love before the separation of eternity. As ideal mates in this distilled poem of love, Kent and Carreño were superb. Both are great classical stylists, with beautiful line and open, expressive port de bras; both are musical and immensely generous collaborators. There are times when a single impulse seems to propel them through the air, when a single mind seems to be shaping a step or magnifying the scale and dynamics of a phrase. Nothing is overstated or done solely for effect. The idea of classicism— clarity, proportion, harmony—is always uppermost, and even when executing the most bravura passages they stay in character. One leaves the theater elated and purged, released from a genuine cathartic experience.

The success of a *Swan Lake* or a *Giselle* depends on more than its principals. In *Swan Lake,* the Act I pas de trois, beautifully coached by Kurt Petersen, has become a showcase for dancers headed for the top. Once a haven for Russians, ABT is now a magnet for Latins. They come from all over the Spanish-speaking world, and with their strong classical training and easy relationship with the audience, they have largely overshadowed the Russians. The strongest trio this season featured Erica and Hermán Cornejo, a brother-sister pair from Argentina, and Xiomara Reyes, a Cuban-trained soloist who joined ABT after dancing in Europe. Seldom have I seen a threesome better matched. Each has a marvelous jump (although Hermán's elevation—he seems to jump as high as he is tall—

is phenomenal), clean footwork, strong turns, flexibility, and an engaging personality. The Cornejos were twinned again as the gypsy couple in *Don Quixote*, where Hermán gave free rein to his fantasy in the air, and his sister danced with exuberance. Soloist Anna Liceica, who began her training in Rumania and completed it at the School of American Ballet, also danced the pas de trois, and with her big jump and strong turns (all her piqués were doubles) made a fine partner for Joaquín De Luz, an elegant stylist from Spain; the weak link in the trio was Anne Milewski, who lacks the strength for the increasingly demanding roles she is receiving. Liceica looked very much in command in the peasant pas de deux in *Giselle*, where she was partnered by Marcelo Gomes; her variation was beautifully calibrated, with pirouettes that slowed to a perfect ending, although her extensions occasionally sacrificed beauty of line to height.

A product of Washington's Kirov Academy, Michelle Wiles is an anomaly—an American who dances more like a Russian than ABT's own Russians. Tall, blond, and long-limbed, she has the strengths and weaknesses of traditional Russian training. The pluses include her open, expansive port de bras, majestic balances, and slow, serene adagio. On the minus side, she has little speed; her footwork needs greater clarity, and she is not particularly musical. Although she was cast this season in contemporary works as well as in Balanchine's *Theme and Variations* (which did not show her to advantage), most of her growing repertory is in nineteenth-century classics—Moyna in *Giselle*, a solo Shade in *La Bayadère*, the Dryad Queen in *Don Quixote*, Diamond in *The Sleeping Beauty*, one of the "big" Swans in *Swan Lake*—roles that she filled out, imparting an imperial, if studied, grandeur to their choreography. While grandly scaled, her Myrta was less successful. Stiff rather than imperious and curiously remote from the Wili sisterhood that surrounds her, Wiles has yet to find her way into the role, the most dramatically challenging of her career.

Upholding the honor of Russia on ABT's increasingly Latin-dominated roster are Irina Dvorovenko and her husband and excellent partner, Maxim Belotserkovsky. They are now big stars, with endorsements and a *Dance Magazine* cover to their credit, and their every appearance brings out New York's Russian-speaking community, which applauds them wildly. Both hail from Kiev, where they received their training and made their professional debut. Of the two, Dvorovenko is more intriguing, a brilliant virtuoso dancer, with the sky-high extensions of the current crop of Russian ballerinas, coupled with speed, strength, and (for a Russian) unusually articulate pointework. There is nothing she cannot do. She turns like a top, jumps like a gazelle, is equally at home in adagio and allegro, and sets the stage a-sizzle with personality. Yet whatever note she strikes—spectral, seductive, petulant—her acting is one-dimensional. In the first act of *Giselle*, who could fail to admire her huge jumps, the extraordinary elevation of her ballottés? But who could admire the smug look on her face after she sat down, the way she fiddled with tempi and ignored everyone on stage except her husband, who happened to be Albrecht? And what is one to make of the kewpie doll-vamp of her mad scene? In Act II, everything—poetry, style, drama—was sacrificed to technical effects: freakishly high extensions, excessively slow tempi, excessively fast tempi, split jetés, overhead lifts, all of which elicited deafening applause.

Dvorovenko is ambitious, hard-working, and smart. She is here in America to stay, and, unlike some Russians, she has partly remade herself. Last year, for instance, she acquitted herself admirably in the revival of Twyla Tharp's *Push Comes to Shove*, where she almost seemed to mock her own ballerina mannerisms. In ABT's new production of John Cranko's *Eugene Onegin* (of which more later), there were moments when she seemed to lose herself in the role of Titania, to plunge deeply into her character, to approach it freshly and with imaginative engagement—even to downplay the technical fireworks. It could well be that Titania was the first emotionally demanding role she had to do on her own, without the coaches, without the hallowed interpretation of generations before her. Still, it was in *Don Quixote,* that old Russian chestnut, that Dvorovenko scored her biggest triumph this season. From her first entrance, she lit up the stage, a real spitfire, full of fun and totally alive. She jumped higher and moved faster than ever, and used her fan with a playfulness that recalled Makarova, although without the latter's wit. Dvorovenko never sits on her heels; she carries her weight forward like Balanchine's proverbial boxer, ready to take off—the secret of the speed and dynamic attack that sets her dancing apart from that of most Russians. Alas, in this and virtually every other ballet she danced this season, she could not resist the hard sell. She makes no distinction between artistry and bravura, revels in tricks, and sees nothing wrong with exploiting them shamelessly.

How different is the company's senior Russian ballerina, Nina Ananiashvili. In *The Merry Widow,* she gave the wealthy Pontevedrian widow Hanna Glawari— a role she shared with Dvorovenko—heart as well as glamor, sadness as well as beauty, longing as well as abandon. She has a face made for tragedy, expressive arms, and beautiful hands. Everything about her is refined. As Aurora in the Wedding act of *The Sleeping Beauty* (performed on an all-Tchaikovsky mixed bill), she was gracious and regal, with the long, singing line that was once a touchstone of Russian lyrical style. Her hand gestures in the second variation were as light as gossamer with all the charm of a traditional Russian dance—no one today performs them quite like that. And what nobility she brought to the first arabesque that ends the ballet. Here was a true Russian artist.

Another senior ballerina in whom the idea of service runs deep is Amanda McKerrow. From her earliest performances she was something of an anomaly, a ballerina who was artless, even plain, with no tricks or hard sell. She was affecting as Cinderella, above all in the opening solo in Act III, where her small frame and utter lack of pretension fit the ballet's character like a glove. With Vladimir Malakhov out for much of the season because of injury, her Prince was Ethan Stiefel, a less than ideal match, given his youthful exuberance and generally wooden acting. (When Malakhov did return, it was to partner Susan Jaffee in one of the most mismatched *Nutcracker* pas de deux I have ever seen; his leg was often higher than hers.) Stieffel's boyish élan served him well in *Tchaikovsky Pas de Deux*, invigorating McKerrow, giving a happy innocence to his spectacular technical feats in the variations. Stieffel also partnered her in *Swan Lake*, where his immaculate technique shone in the variations, although, here again, he seemed emotionally constrained, uncomfortable in the role of ballet prince that Malakhov, for instance, inhabits so easily. McKerrow, by contrast, glowed with a deep contentment. Seldom has her Odette seemed so unworldly or her Odile so ravishing; seldom has her technique seemed so pure.

Cuban-trained Xiomara Reyes, who joined ABT this year as a soloist after dancing with the Royal Ballet of Flanders, is a happy addition to the company's roster. Petite and vivacious, with a light, airy jump, she has the gift of naturalness on stage and a talent for characterization that recalls Alessandra Ferri. In the role of Valencienne, the second female lead in *The Merry Widow*, Reyes was delicious, a flirt with a heart of gold who loves her aging husband almost as much as she adores her handsome lover. She brings little touches to the part, like patting her hair when the perfectly coiffed Hanna appears or jumping up to dance at the ball, and she is alive to everything that goes on around her. She really looks at her partner and responds to him. Best of all she puts her heart into the drama. There is a moment in Act III when her husband, Baron Mirko Zeta, played by that consummate actor Victor Barbee, now one of the company's ballet masters, finally realizes how things stand with his wife and Camille de Rosillon, the French attaché who is her lover. Other casts turn the scene into a farce. But Barbee and Reyes give it genuine pathos, and in the end the three go off together in a quiet, unexpected act of love. In John Cranko's *Onegin*, new to the repertory this season, she was a splendid Olga—frivolous, but also girlish, a sprite who dances for joy. Reyes is an exceptionally musical dancer, with the speed and pristine footwork of today's best Cuban dancers. She can pull out all the technical stops, and does so without the grand russki manner. Her Lensky was Angel Corella. Technically, she was fully his equal, while both physically and emotionally she complemented him (far better than Ashley Tuttle, with whom he is frequently paired): their pas de deux was a poem of young love. Might a *Giselle* or a *La Sylphide* be in the offing?

Born in Uruguay and trained at the North Carolina School of the Arts, Maria Riccetto is another dancer who seems headed for the top. Tall and rangy, with the Balanchine-inflected techique of an American dancer and the sunny personality of a Latin, she was a solo Shade in *La Bayadère*, a friend in *Giselle*, a Flower Girl in *Don Quixote*, the White Cat and Silver in *The Sleeping Beauty*, the Italian Princess in *Swan Lake*. Her big chance came in *Onegin* with the role of Olga, the ballet's second female lead. Although technically she met its challenges, artistically she was too young for the role; compared to Malakhov's Lensky, burning with romantic ardor, she looked like a kid. Still, I admire McKenzie's willingness to gamble on young talent. He has good instincts, and often his bets pay off, if not immediately then in the long term. Sascha Radetsky (who is American despite the name and a real heart throb in the movie *Center Stage*) is another corps dancer adding solo and demi-soloist parts to his repertory, with good reason: a fine classicist, with a buoyant jump, a natural feeling for gesture, and a relaxed stage presence, he gets better every time you see him. This season he was a Toreador and a Gypsy in *Don Quixote*, one of the Neapolitan leads in *Swan Lake* and one of its two Rothbarts. He also danced Blue Bird, doing full justice to its flying jumps and beats, and partnering Elena Shelkanova, his less than ideal Princess Florine, with gallantry. Other casting gambles that worked included Joaquín De Luz as the Jester in *Cinderella* and lead Pontevedrian dancer in *The Merry Widow*, roles that displayed not only his extraordinary bravura (as the Jester he did six pirouettes that stopped dead in passé relevé, then came down) but also his gift for infusing steps with character. Finally, a word about Jerry Douglas, an African-American newcomer to the corps who was a last-minute replacement as the Jester in *Cinderella;* with his classical proportions and princely demeanor, he is a talent to watch.

McKenzie can bring dancers along, but he can also let them get out of hand. He has done nothing to discipline Dvorovenko; one suspects that so long as she sells tickets and receives critical accolades, her antics will be tolerated if not actually encouraged. Certainly, in the case of Paloma Herrera, the baby wonder of some years back, the policy backfired. Although her *Cinderella* and the Rose Adagio she danced on the Tchaikovsky program were technically competent, they lacked the sparkle of her early performances; for whatever reason she seems to have lost her way. Probably the most egregious failure of artistic discipline this season occurred in *Cinderella*. Julio Bocca, whose career as a premier danseur is coming to an end, gave a truly hilarious performance as the simpering Stepsister, batting her baby browns, primping, flying, falling, fussing over her petticoats. But it was all interminable, the slapstick, the shenanigans, the sadism (which is in the plot, not an invention of the performers), the business that becomes busier with every performance, intruding ever more intrusively on the narrative.

McKenzie's strengths lie in the studio. However, as artistic director, he also has a large say in repertory, although I wonder how much of the decision-making really lies with the ABT board. Certainly, the decision to all but proscribe mixed bills (one of which was an all-Tchaikovsky program) from the Met season was a marketing strategy, one that seems to have paid off, at least in terms of box office. But where was one to find the "product," the multi-act narratives that the ABT audience apparently is dying to see? Nineteenth-century ballets are few, but those with strong male roles are fewer. Yet this, apparently, is the litmus test that traditional ballets must pass. Hence, the reworking of traditional ballets along the lines of *Le Corsaire*, which has numerous male roles (some converted from mime roles) with virtually interchangeable bravura variations. This was the model for McKenzie's tasteless reworking of *Swan Lake,* in which the female choreography was left pretty much intact, while male roles were either added (like the hyper-active Jester) or beefed up (like Rothbart, a seducer in black leather). (When the ballet premiered, there was even a variation for Siegfried in Act II; this was soon cut.) The "new ballet" that began with Fokine in the early 1900s explicitly rejected the multi-act formula. Virtually all new ballets created during the first half of the twentieth century were one-act works, although they sometimes co-existed in a repertory that included versions of the older full-length "classics." It was only in England, home of the West's re-invented classical tradition (Beth Genné's article about this in a recent issue of *Dance Research* is fascinating), that the creation of new full-length ballets was actively encouraged. (The Soviets, for quite different reasons, encouraged them as well.) These narratives, which might be called "neotraditional," had all the trappings of their nineteenth-century predecessors—stories, pas de deux, big ensemble numbers, at least one ballerina heroine, along with much-enhanced roles for men. They also had lots of stuff—costumes, sets, props—and big production values. Having exhausted the stock of Kenneth McMillan ballets and eschewed Frederick Ashton's longer works, ABT has turned to their British successors. It would be hard to say which is worse—Ronald Hynd's *The Merry Widow* or Ben Stevenson's *Cinderella.* With its Prokofiev score, the latter is certainly more pretentious. But like *The Merry Widow,* it is a narrative that collapses under the weight of its own inconsequence. Scenes go on interminably, with endless repeats and drawn-out "business" (not that traditional mime is used). The settings (*Cinderella*'s are by David Walker, *The Merry Widow*'s by Desmond Heeley) are totally without imagination, and the costumes are vulgar. *Cinderella*'s, which come from the Houston Ballet, included the kind of tutus with sparkles that five-year-old girls drool over.

John Cranko comes out of this British tradition as well. However, his *Onegin,* which entered the ABT repertory this season, is in a completely different category. Indeed, it is a happy acquisition for the company. The original designs by Jürgen Rose have been duplicated, and they are beautiful, full of atmosphere, evoking the period and the people of Pushkin's Romantic-era poem like a genre painting. Cranko choreographed the ballet in 1965 for the Stuttgart Ballet, and it quickly became a favorite on the company's U.S. tours. Then, the tours stopped, and the ballet vanished, until a couple of years ago, when the Stuttgart returned with it to New York. Seen again after so many years, *Onegin* seemed a throwback to a time when spectacle had yet to become synonymous with stuff and artistic unity was something to which collaborators still aspired. There are wonderful ensemble dances, waltzes, khovorods, and a peasant number in which couple after couple leaps across the stage, exits, then returns en masse, crossing to the other side—a thrilling escalation of effects. The narrative is always clear; we know what happens, when, and why—without recourse to mime or interminable "business." The characters too are always clear—Tatiana, the ballet's impetuous heroine; her flighty sister, Olga; Olga's fiancé Lensky; his brooding friend, Onegin, with whom Tatiana falls in love; Prince Gremin, the elderly relation she marries. There are spectacular pas de deux, above all for Tatiana and Onegin, full of complex partnering, dangerous tosses, and the kind of gymnastic lifts that wowed the West in the 1950s on the first Bolshoi tours. And there is a magnificent role for a ballerina. Julie Kent was all fire-and-ice as Tatiana, flush with passion for Onegin in Act I, crushed by his rejection in Act II, glowing with voluptuous maturity in Act III. She plays the last scene brilliantly—the agony, ecstasy, and consciousness of choice, the final, wrenching separation from Onegin. Who would suspect that she had such depths of passion in her? Her Onegin was Robert Hill, who has the hewn face and gravitas of a young Abraham Lincoln. But the heroic gesture comes hard to him, and the romantic role does not sit easily. Still, he was a fine complement to Kent and handled the difficult partnering effortlessly. By contrast, the second-cast Onegin, Giuseppe Picone, seemed even colder and more self-absorbed than his character, which he played as a diabolic Svengali. His fumbles in the pas de deux with Dvorovenko, his Titania, were all too evident. Although a fine addition to the repertory, the production needs to "season." At times the pace seems a little sluggish and the stage business a little blurred, as though we are seeing a dress rehearsal rather than the finished ballet. A special mention should be made of Georgina Parkinson's detailed acting and authority as Madame Larina, Tatiana's mother.

Since the ABT management appears to view mixed bills as box-office death, the "contemporary" program was given right at the beginning of the season, when houses tend to be thin. On the bill was Twyla Tharp's *The Brahms-Haydn Variations* (choreographed for the company a year ago), and two new works, Paul Taylor's *Black Tuesday* (which premiered at Washington's Kennedy Center), and *Gong*, by Mark Morris. Unlike most people, I liked *Black Tuesday*. Set to songs from the Depression and with splendid lighting by Jennifer Tipton evoking life in the streets under the old New York "Els," the work has a sobriety— a darkness—more attuned to modern dance than the usual hoopla of an ABT season. This was not a show-stopping piece, although it did showcase dancers like Stella Abrera, Elena Cornejo, and Adrienne Schulte, a member of the corps who is just beginning to receive small roles. In "Brother, Can You Spare a Dime?" which brought the ballet to an end, Ethan Stiefel gave a fine performance, as though being a Depression-era hobo gave him permission to enjoy the swivels and leaps and spins he does so effortlessly. *Gong* was another fine work, a ballet that is unapologetically balletic, yet unmistakeably by Mark Morris. The music, by Colin McPhee, has its roots in Java, long a source of inspiration for the choreographer, but confined here to prayer poses and the like, and the looming forms projected on the cyc like huge shadow puppets. Seen from above, the work looks even better than from the orchestra. The opening is stunning, a pale purple circle containing the line of dancing figures set on a deep purple floor. The circle motif is reiterated in Isaac Mizrahi's pancake tutus, which add their own lush tones—lime green, aqua, purple, mahogany, wine. And from above (where I sat one night because I couldn't get a press ticket), one can really savor the freedom with which Morris uses space, the way he keeps it alive and full of visual interest, whether the dancers are circling in a manège or spinning offstage as a group, chaining à la Balanchine, or performing a slow, slow adagio against a backdrop of shadows. Like a number of Morris works, *Gong* has a meditative center.

Last and certainly least among the new works was *The Pied Piper*. This was the brainchild of Louis G. Spisto, the company's former Executive Director, who spoke about its gestation in a Works & Process program at the Guggenheim Museum. Indeed, it was Spisto who brought John Corigliano's score to the ABT board, the answer, so he claimed, to its prayer for a story ballet for kids. What could be better than the Pied Piper? Spisto may have aspirations of imitating Diaghilev, but he hasn't a clue of what appeals to kids. This *Pied Piper* was totally untheatrical, with an incoherent scenario cobbled together by Mark Adamo and choreographer David Parsons, and a stage so dark that one kept expecting the lights to come up. (They didn't.) There were rats galore, human-size and mechanical puppets by Michael Curry that scurried everywhere. There were animations by Michaela Zabranska that turned the town of Hamelin into a dead ringer for the expressionist Flanders imagined by Robert Edmond Jones for Nijinsky's 1917 *Tyl Eulenspiegel;* more striking was the opening, with its flickering stars and psychedelic sunrise. Parsons is a modern-dance choreographer much in demand by ballet companies. Unfortunately, he has only a passing knowledge of virtuoso technique and ballet character work. For the Piper, danced by Angel Corella, he choreographed spins and more spins, leaps and more leaps, an aerobic workout but not much else. He did no better with the ensemble dances, which an old pro like Freddy Franklin could have staged in an afternoon. And despite the masked faces of the townspeople and the stylized costumes by Ann Hould-Ward, no evidence of stylization could be discerned in the choreography. This was an expensive production, and a great deal of money was spent on promoting it. The fact that the ballet was a dud probably did more to end Spisto's career at ABT than his expense account and alleged mistreatment of company employees. The lesson to be drawn from this fiasco can be summed up as follows: God spare us from Diaghilevs who know nothing about dance.

DANCE FOR A CITY

FIFTY YEARS OF THE NEW YORK CITY BALLET

In 1949, in a special issue on the city, *Holiday* magazine noted that New York was "on the way to becoming the artistic center of the world." Museum attendance was booming; several opera troupes were thriving in addition to the Metropolitan; of "considerable importance," too, was jazz. But the great change since the First World War lay in public attitudes toward ballet. Thanks to the New York City Ballet, depicted in performance at the City Center for Music and Drama, "ballet," in the words of the author, Robert M. Coates, "has become firmly rooted in New York life."[1] Amazingly, the company that had brought about this renaissance was only six months old.

The New York City Ballet was the last of several companies founded by George Balanchine and Lincoln Kirstein in a partnership that spanned fifty years and initially, at least, experienced more failures than successes. The new company made its debut on October 11, 1948, at City Center, a barn of a theater on West Fifty-Fifth Street known until only a few years before as the Mecca Temple; it was a Monday, not a promising day in terms of box office, but unavoidable because it was the only night the house was dark. On the program were three remarkable ballets—*Concerto Barocco, Orpheus,* and *Symphony in C.* All were by Balanchine, and all became signature works of the new company. All remain in repertory to this day.

During NYCB's sixteen years at City Center, Balanchine created an extraordinary body of work and many of his greatest ballets. He nursed to maturity a brilliant roster of ballerinas and extended the boundaries of ballet technique. And he gave definitive form to a synthesis of the classical legacy inherited from St. Petersburg's Imperial Ballet, where he had trained, and the experimental impetus of Diaghilev's Ballets Russes, where he had served his choreographic apprenticeship.

Balanchine was no stranger to New York in 1948 when NYCB became a constituent member of the City Center of Music and Drama. He had come to the city fifteen years earlier at the invitation of Lincoln Kirstein to found, as Kirstein

This essay was originally published in *Dance for a City: Fifty Years of the New York City Ballet,* ed. Lynn Garafola, with Eric Foner (New York: Columbia University Press, 1999).

wrote, "an American ballet."[2] He arrived with impressive credentials—nearly five years with the Ballets Russes, stints with the Royal Danish Ballet, the fledgling Ballet Russe de Monte Carlo, his own short-lived Les Ballets 1933. Only twenty-nine years old, he had more than one hundred dances and ballets to his credit. However, with fascism on the rise and the European economy sunk in depression, the future looked dim, especially for artists left stateless, as Balanchine had been, by the Russian Revolution. He accepted Kirstein's invitation with alacrity.

Even younger than his protégé, Kirstein was equally prolific. In 1927, while still a college student, he had founded *The Hound & Horn*, a literary review dedicated to modernism, and, in 1928, the Harvard Society for Contemporary Art. By 1930, he was on the junior advisory committee of the Museum of Modern Art, where he subsequently curated a controversial show on American mural art and organized a Soviet film archive and the country's first dance archive. And even before Balanchine's arrival, he had published his first book, the novel *Flesh Is Heir*, which described Diaghilev's funeral cortège gliding across the Venice lagoon to the island cemetery of San Michele—a prescient image, for Kirstein's career as a ballet director would be modeled largely on Diaghilev's.

Between 1933, when Balanchine arrived in the United States, and 1948, when the New York City Ballet was founded, he and Kirstein created not one but several companies, in addition to the School of American Ballet (SAB), which soon became a ready source of dancers. Their first company, the American Ballet, debuted in 1935 with *Serenade*, then, as resident ballet company of the Metropolitan Opera, mounted a haunting opera-ballet version of *Orpheus and Eurydice* (1936) and a Stravinsky Festival (1937), after which the Met terminated the engagement and the American Ballet collapsed. The second company, Ballet Caravan, was really a Kirstein vehicle, an experiment in creating a repertory that was American in theme and modernist in form, a means of associating ballet with the country's emerging avant-garde, through the collaboration of visual artists like Paul Cadmus (*Filling Station*, 1938) and Ben Shahn (*Tom*, unproduced); composers like Elliott Carter (*Pocahontas*, 1936), Paul Bowles (*Yankee Clipper*, 1937), and Aaron Copland (*Billy the Kid*, 1938); librettists like Glenway Westcott (*The Birds of Audubon*, unproduced) and e.e. cummings (*Tom*); and photographer George Platt Lynes.

In 1941, as American Ballet Caravan, the Balanchine-Kirstein companies pooled their repertory and personnel for a good-will tour of Latin America arranged by Kirstein's former MOMA colleague Nelson A. Rockefeller, an early supporter of SAB and now President Roosevelt's coordinator of Inter-American Affairs. For this tour, Balanchine created two of his most enduring works, *Ballet Imperial* and *Concerto Barocco;* in its later "undressed" form, *Barocco* became a NYCB signature work. Like its predecessors, American Ballet Caravan was short-lived. Kirstein was drafted, as were some of the company's male dancers.

Balanchine returned to Hollywood and to Broadway, where he had worked intermittently since the 1930s, adding to a string of "hits" that began with *On Your Toes* (1936). Commissions from Ballet Theatre and the Ballet Russe de Monte Carlo added to Balanchine's growing reputation, while introducing him to future NYCB stars, including Maria Tallchief and Diana Adams.

In 1946, when he and Kirstein teamed up again, instead of a formal company, they set up Ballet Society, a "non-profit educational organization for the advancement of the lyric theatre by the production of new works"[3] that was organized as a subscription society. Most of the money came from Kirstein, who had received a substantial inheritance, and most of the new ballets were by Balanchine, including the seminal *The Four Temperaments*. But the programming consisted of more than ballets. There were operas (Maurice Ravel's *L'Enfant et les Sortilèges*, Gian-Carlo Menotti's *The Medium* and *The Telephone*), films (Jean Cocteau's *Beauty and the Beast*), and both "ethnic" and modern dance works (among the latter, Merce Cunningham's *The Seasons*), all of which suggests the breadth of Kirstein's interests as a producer and his continued faith in modernism. Other members of the Ballet Society team were conductor Leon Barzin, who became NYCB's longtime musical director, and lighting designer Jean Rosenthal, a veteran of the Mercury Theatre who lit the company's productions until the 1970s, while among the designers were a number of second-generation surrealists—Kurt Seligmann, Corrado Cagli, Joan Junyer, and Estebán Francés, a Catalan painter who did many NYCB productions. The subscribers included not only members of the city's artistic elite, but also many practicing artists and, among the dancers, a surprising number associated with modern dance.

Apart from offices on Fifty-Sixth Street, Ballet Society had no home. Rehearsals took place at the School of American Ballet, and performances at rented venues, including Hunter College and the High School of Needle Trades, which had a modern dance series. It was at one such rented space, City Center, that Morton Baum, chairman of the Center's executive committee, happening to see an early performance of Balanchine's *Orpheus* (1948), experienced the *coup de foudre* that prompted him to invite the company to become a constituent of the theater, joining the New York City Opera and City Center Orchestra. The encounter was a fluke and a lifesaver that rescued the company from economic collapse. Opened in 1943 by Mayor Fiorello La Guardia, City Center was owned by New York City and heavily supported by unions, then central to the city's political and cultural life. It had a popular-price ticket policy ("top" in 1948 was $2.50) and a large working-class and lower-middle-class audience. This audience NYCB tapped and in the early years partly catered to, even as it retained and built upon the knowledgeable public associated with Ballet Society. The result was an audience of unparalleled breadth and sophistication that eventually included most of the New York School of poets—Frank O'Hara,

John Ashberry, Kenneth Koch, among others—and an eclectic group of visual artists, from Joseph Cornell and Edward Gorey, to Willem de Kooning, Howard Kanovitz, and Eugene Berman.

This diversity helps explain the extraordinary richness of the NYCB repertory during the City Center years. Although the fledgling company had inherited a number of works from Ballet Society (as well as the American Ballet and Ballet Russe de Monte Carlo), new ones were needed to prosper and grow. Under Kirstein's dynamic leadership, the company embarked on an ambitious program of revivals and premieres, which recalled Ballet Theatre (later American Ballet Theatre) during its most creative period of the early 1940s. Many were by choreographers other than Balanchine, including several Ballet Caravan or American Ballet veterans—Todd Bolender, who revived *Mother Goose Suite* (1948) and choreographed *The Miraculous Mandarin* (1951); Lew Christensen, who revived *Jinx* (1949) and *Filling Station* (1953); Ruthanna Boris, who choreographed *Cakewalk* (1951) and *Kaleidoscope* (1952); and William Dollar, who choreographed *Ondine* (1949) and *The Duel* (1950).[4] There were also Britons among the group—John Cranko, who choreographed *The Witch* (1950), which had designs by Dorothea Tanning and premiered during the company's first season at Covent Garden; Antony Tudor, who revived *Lilac Garden* (1951) and choreographed *Lady of the Camelias* (1951) and *La Gloire* (1952); and the great classicist Frederick Ashton. For many people, critic Anatole Chujoy would later write, Ashton's *Illuminations* (1950), a series of "danced pictures" suggested by Rimbaud, was one of the works that "justified the existence of the New York City Ballet."[5] Ashton also choreographed *Picnic at Tintagel,* which was designed by Cecil Beaton, as were *Illuminations, Lady of the Camelias,* and Balanchine's one-act version of *Swan Lake* (1951). Finally, there was Jerome Robbins, who, in 1949, as Kirstein later wrote, "cast his lot with us."[6] As Associate Artistic Director, a position he held for the next decade, Robbins brought a distinctive note to the company's artistic identity. Indeed, apart from Balanchine, he was the only choreographer whose works found a permanent place in the NYCB repertory.

As for Balanchine himself, he was at the height of his creative powers during the City Center years. In 1948 he had turned forty-four; he had gone from company to company, and seen most of his works—and most of the companies that had produced them—vanish. Now, for the first time, he had a company with a home and a future. True, at first, the company was small, the seasons short, and the finances strapped. But with the expansion of the school, which now had a full-fledged children's program and such outstanding teachers as Felia Doubrovska and Anatole Oboukhov, there was an ever-growing supply of well-trained talent. In time the seasons lengthened. There were tours—continental ones throughout the United States, with long stays in Chicago, Los Angeles, and San Francisco, and far-flung ones that took the company to Europe, the Far East and, finally, in 1962, under the auspices of the State Department, to the Soviet Union, where Balanchine, after an absence of thirty-eight years, was welcomed like a returning prodigal. And very quickly, thanks to Kirstein's indefatigable proselytizing and personal stature, to say nothing of his deeply ingrained sense of civic service, the company acquired a public profile, a distinctive New York identity. There were gala occasions (the premiere of Ashton's *Picnic at Tintagel*, for instance, took place before the British Ambassador and other dignitaries) and fundraising benefits, *Time* and *Holiday* magazine cover stories, and pictures of NYCB dancers in Central Park.[7] And, in 1953, Kirstein, now managing director of the whole of City Center, secured from the Rockefeller Foundation the first of the big foundation grants that would not only shore up the company financially but give it a cachet enjoyed by no other American dance group.

With the company's newfound stability, Balanchine went into high gear. Like the chef he sometimes described himself as, he cooked up something for everyone. The accent, to be sure, was on the modern. He streamlined ballets like *Concerto Barocco* and *The Four Temperaments*, eliminating the scenery (designed by Eugene Berman and Kurt Seligmann respectively) and replacing the costumes (which they had also designed) with tunics and leotards that were stylized versions of ballet practice clothes. This dramatic transformation removed these works from their original neoromantic and surrealist contexts, relocating them in a timeless, anonymous present.

In *The Four Temperaments, Agon* (1957), and *Episodes* (1959), Balanchine's most celebrated "leotard" ballets of the time, that present was partly a metaphor for postwar New York. All three unfolded in a landscape of anxiety: they were anguished and sexually charged, with rhythms borrowed from jazz and percussive movements from modern dance, and matings fraught with loneliness, empty pleasure, and erotic tension. In the brilliantly inventive *Agon* pas de deux, the tension between the partners was magnified by the fact that Arthur Mitchell was black and Diana Adams white: this was the first duet by a major choreographer for a racially mixed couple. Other ballets invoked the city more directly. These included *Ivesiana* (1954), a darkly atmospheric work, which hinted at rape ("Central Park in the Dark") and brilliantly depicted a young man's sexual humiliation ("The Unanswered Question"), and Robbins' *Age of Anxiety* (1950), which was inspired by Auden's poem of the same name, accompanied by Oliver Smith's blow-ups of the Flatiron Building, and "haunted," as critic Doris Hering wrote, "by the inspired melancholy and looming protectiveness of the big city."[8]

Race was a veiled presence in Robbins' first ballet for the company—*The Guests*. With a commissioned score by Marc Blitzstein, it began, as Robbins later explained, as a "ballet [about] competition among people who worked in a department store. It turned out that the winners [were] a black and a white. But the more we worked on it, the more we . . . [got] away from specifics."[9] Eventually, it became a semi-abstract study of what Doris Hering described as "the bitter problem of social stratification and snobbery and its effect upon two young people."[10] Other works followed, and they too revealed an attentiveness to the era's characteristic social and psychological concerns. In *The Age of Anxiety,* there was a "Colossal Dad," represented, in critic John Martin's words, as "a gigantic figure from childhood imagination, a sort of wizard on stilts."[11] In *The Cage* (1951), which Robbins described as a "contemporary visualization" of the second act of *Giselle,* a community of barbarous Amazons strangled men in a frenzy of primal hate so shocking that the ballet was briefly banned in the Netherlands as "pornographic."[12] There were jazzy ballets, such as *The Pied Piper* (1951) and *Interplay* (1952); there was *Afternoon of a Faun* (1953), a work of understated eroticism set in a contemporary ballet studio, and *The Concert* (1956), a hilarious spoof of culture seekers and their daydreams. And onstage was work by some of the best designers working in the American theater—Boris Aronson, Oliver Smith, Irene Sharaff, and Jean Rosenthal.

In this period, Robbins was a riveting presence as a dancer. In *Bourrée Fantasque* (1949), where Balanchine first teamed him with Tanaquil Le Clercq in what became a truly inspired partnership, Robbins was as "agile as a leprechaun and twice as mischievous," in the words of critic Walter Terry.[13] In 1950, when Balanchine revived *Prodigal Son* for the first time since its premiere twenty-one years before, he chose Robbins to be the Biblical hero. "Here was a performance to wring your heart," wrote John Martin after the premiere. "It is dramatically true and it touches deep; there is not a movement that is not informed by feeling and colored by the dynamism of emotion."[14]

Le Clercq was more than a partner for Robbins (and with her long legs and girlish build a prototypical Balanchine ballerina); she was also a muse. Robbins was fascinated by her coltishness and sense of fun, which he exploited to great effect in *The Pied Piper,* where she did a wild Charleston and even chewed gum. He was intrigued by her banked sexuality, which he used in *Afternoon of a Faun,* pairing her with Francisco Monción, whose dark good looks added to the ballet's erotic tension. And he incorporated her zaniness into the role of the screwball ballerina in *The Concert.* After she was struck down with polio in 1956, Robbins made no more ballets for the company until the late 1960s. In 1957, he choreographed *West Side Story,* and the following year formed his own company, "Ballets: U.S.A.," which mostly toured abroad. Only in 1969 did he return to NYCB.

At the same time that Balanchine was testing the aesthetic boundaries of ballet, he was also producing crowdpleasers. One was *Swan Lake* (1951), which Morton Baum had suggested because, in Kirstein's words, it would "attract customers"[15]—which it did. But not even Baum could have anticipated the moneymaking potential of *The Nutcracker* (1954), the company's first full-length ballet, which premiered exactly two weeks after the twelve-tone *Opus 34* and has never gone out of repertory. Balanchine's was not the first American production of *The Nutcracker*. But it was the first to become popular Christmas entertainment, and, as the company and innumerable imitators were to discover, a source of earned income that carried them through the entire year. At the same time that Balanchine was remaking *Swan Lake* and *The Nutcracker*, he was also distilling the legacy of the past into works that were completely new. Innumerable ballets of the City Center years—*Symphony in C* (1948), *Sylvia Pas de Deux* (1950), *Scotch Symphony* (1952), *Valse Fantaisie* (1953), *Raymonda Pas de Dix* (1955), *Allegro Brillante* (1956), *Divertimento No. 15* (1956), *Gounod Symphony* (1958), *Donizetti Variations* (1960)—paid homage to the Russian, French, and Italian traditions he had imbibed as a youth. Updated by the speed, complexity, and plotlessness of the choreography, these traditions now shed their period identity, entering Balanchine's timeless paradise of the ideal. Here was grand ballet in a post-narrative mode, a magnificent display of the eloquence of the academic vocabulary, extended, technically refined, and rigorous to a degree previously unknown in this country—or anywhere else.

Another important vein that Balanchine mined during these years was neo-romanticism, sometimes with a surrealist undercurrent. The combination first appeared in *Le Bal* (1929), left its perfume on *Cotillon* (1932), and reappeared in *La Valse* (1951), one of the most enchanting and mysterious of Balanchine's ballets, a work "permeated," as critic Anatole Chujoy wrote, "with the spirit of the romantic period of the 1830s and . . . with the sense of futility which pervaded Europe . . . when Ravel wrote the music."[16] Photographer George Platt Lynes caught some of the enchantment, and it lingers in Karinska's tulle-skirted ball gowns. Although, by this time, Balanchine was turning away from designers, his relationship with Karinska remained close. He loved her tutus, with their short, "powder-puff" skirts, masterful craftsmanship, and exquisite detail, and although his dancers were not the first to wear them, they became an NYCB signature. Like Pavel Tchelitchew, who designed several ballets for Balanchine in the 1930s and early 1940s, including *Orpheus and Eurydice*, and George Platt Lynes, who photographed Balanchine's work for nearly twenty years, Karinska enjoyed his confidence and worked with him on a genuinely collaborative basis. She was one of very few artists to do so.

In *Liebeslieder Walzer* (1960), Balanchine did away with the surrealist trappings of *La Valse*. *Liebeslieder* was the most romantic of ballets, a homage to the waltz and the amazing fecundity of Balanchine's imagination, a ballet about passion and the myriad subtle ways it gets expressed—all told as pure dance. The work was in parts: for the first, set in a nineteenth-century drawing room, Karinska designed long satin ballgowns; for the second, set under a galaxy of stars, dresses of shimmering tulle. Hailed, in critic Andrew Porter's words, as "one of the sublest, most delicate, and most beautiful ballets of our age,"[17] the work occupies a very special place in the NYCB repertory.

In addition to these major veins, Balanchine cultivated a number of minor ones. There were remakes of twentieth-century classics such as *Firebird* (1949), which had scenery and costumes by Marc Chagall and catapulted Maria Tallchief to stardom; modern narratives such as *Orpheus* (1948), which had a commissioned score by Igor Stravinsky and designs by sculptor Isamu Noguchi, and Balanchine's Diaghilev-era ballets *Apollo* (1928) and *Prodigal Son* (1929); there were gay, spirited frou-frou such as *Bourrée Fantasque* (1949) and *Western Symphony* (1954), and high-stepping extravaganzas such as *Stars and Stripes* (1958). And, as if this were not enough, Balanchine even choreographed an original full-length ballet, *A Midsummer Night's Dream* (1962). It was a record of unparalleled achievement.

Meanwhile, the company was rapidly expanding. In 1948, it was little more than a pick-up troupe with advanced students from SAB filling the corps; two years later, when it went to London (a season that David Webster, General Administrator of Covent Garden, said would either "make" or "break" the company),[18] there were fifty-three dancers, all on payroll; by 1965, when it returned to the British capital, the number had jumped to about sixty-five. Equally dramatic was the lengthening of the company's home seasons. In 1949, the company performed at City Center for exactly four weeks; in 1955, for eleven; in 1960, for thirteen. Salaries had begun to rise, although even in the late 1950s a week's rehearsal pay was less than unemployment compensation. But rents were low, and neighborhoods like Yorkville abounded in cold water flats that dancers could afford, once they came to New York. And come they did. Although New Yorkers dominated the corps (and the children's divisions at SAB) well into the 1960s, most of Balanchine's principal dancers of the 1950s were from elsewhere: Maria Tallchief from Oklahoma; Francisco Monción from the Dominican Republic; Nicholas Magallanes from Mexico; Melissa Hayden and Patricia Wilde from Canada; Diana Adams from Virginia; André Eglevsky from Moscow via Paris; Allegra Kent, from California; Violette Verdy from France; Erik Bruhn from Denmark. What made NYCB so much a New York phenomenon was precisely this cosmopolitanism. NYCB belonged to the metropolis that was the cultural capital of the Western world.

Most of NYCB's first generation of principals came from Ballet Theatre and Ballet Russe de Monte Carlo. They were strong performers, but few were outstanding classicists. Under Balanchine's tutelage, the women, especially, were transformed, remade as speedy, athletic virtuosos, with the best feet and turnout in the business, and pointes like steel.

The NYCB ballerina of the 1950s was among Balanchine's greatest creations. Supple and long-limbed, she had the look of a greyhound. The city's energy infused her dancing, which was as fleet as New York's famously rushing crowds, as dramatically scaled as its skyline, as modern in line as its avant-garde. She had style as well as technique, and a personality that expressed itself through the clarity and articulation of the movement, rather than older conventions of self-presentation. When future NYCB principal Suki Schorer came to New York in 1959, she was "astonished at the way the New York City Ballet danced. That was how I wanted to move—that quickly, that slowly, that grandly, that clearly, and especially, that beautifully."[19] And much to Balanchine's astonishment, after much hard work she did.

By the early 1960s, many changes were underway. In 1955, articles about plans for a new music center in the Lincoln Square area were beginning to appear in *The New York Times*, a project in which, as Kirstein told the paper, he and Balanchine were "strongly interested." Soon, Kirstein was appointed to the committee headed by John D. Rockefeller 3d to study the feasibility of what was now described as a "performing arts project" that "would take in ballet, concerts, chamber music, drama, light opera . . . as well as opera and symphony."[20] Four years later, the Ford Foundation commissioned Ballet Society to conduct a survey assessing the professional standard of ballet schools throughout the country. At the same time, it awarded Ballet Society a grant of $150,000 for scholarships that would bring students from outside the New York region to the School of American Ballet.[21] The creation of Lincoln Center and the channeling of Ford Foundation largesse would have broad implications for the company in the decades to come.

In 1964, the New York City Ballet left the former Mecca Temple on Fifty-Fifth Street and moved to its present home at Lincoln Center. The move symbolized the company's coming of age as an institution and was a tribute to its international stature. Although still in its adolescence, NYCB stood across the plaza from the Metropolitan Opera and the New York Philharmonic, among the city's most august cultural institutions. After the cramped quarters at City Center, the New York State Theater, the first theater built specifically for dance, was like a palace. Designed by Kirstein's friend, architect Philip Johnson, to Balanchine's specifications, it had a huge stage, a practice room as big as the stage floor, comfortable dressing rooms, and state-of-the-art equipment. Conceived as a national arts showplace as well as an urban renewal project, Lincoln Center was backed by a broad coalition of banking, real estate, and political interests that met in the person of Nelson A. Rockefeller, governor of New York State from 1958 to 1973 and, in Kirstein's words at the NYCB tribute following his death, a "wonderful patron."[22]

From the start, the project was plagued with controversy. Although the neighborhood marked for demolition had more than its share of oldtimers living on fixed incomes and a growing population of impoverished newcomers from Puerto Rico, it was far from the slum described in the Center's promotional literature. Painters lived there (including, at one point, Robert Indiana, who designed one of the Center's inaugural posters), and it was teeming with small businesses and even larger commercial establishments, such as the twelve-story Kennedy Building on the site of the New York State Theater. In a vain effort to stop the demolition, which threatened to oust some five thousand families and hundreds of merchants in the city's biggest redevelopment project yet, lawsuits were filed, and demonstrators took to the streets with baby carriages and slogans like "Shelter Before Culture." But the U.S. Supreme Court gave the project a green light, and in June 1958 the city turned the thirteen-block site north and west of Columbus Circle over to Lincoln Center for the Performing Arts and the project's other "non-profit" beneficiaries—Fordham University and the American Red Cross. While John D. Rockefeller 3d's blue-ribbon committee of architects struggled over plans for the performing arts complex, the bulldozers moved in, and on May 14, 1959, amid a crowd of twelve thousand, President Dwight D. Eisenhower broke ground for the Center on two square blocks of leveled plain.[23]

Internally, too, the Center was riven by politics. From the start, Kirstein, who had wanted a theater for years, supported the project. The Met had no objection to including NYCB in the complex (early on, in fact, it was suggested that the company "supply" the Met's "ballet requirements" instead of having "separate permanent ballet groups").[24] It did, however, have strong objections to the New York City Opera, City Center's other major constituent, demanding, at one stage of the negotiations, that NYCO "refrain from producing grand opera of the production magnitude [of] *Aïda, Faust,* [and] *Macbeth,*" that it give priority to the Met in scheduling Italian operas "of modest production" and "smaller Mozart operas," and that it drop from its season repertory any contemporary opera in English the Met might chose to produce.[25] Kirstein, with his strong sense of loyalty and public service, refused to break ranks. "I was in at the start of the organization of Lincoln Center," he wrote to Newbold Morris, chairman of the City Center board, on March 27, 1961, "and only resigned from the Board of Directors when I realized that Messrs. [Anthony A.] Bliss and [Charles M.] Spofford were dedicated to the destruction of the City Center as the only possible competitor for the Met at such a time as rising costs would mark the distinction between the rich man's house and the poor man's house impossible for the ultimate control of the Met." In a letter to Nelson Rockefeller, he struck a similar populist chord, calling the project "a real-estate development handled by able bankers, lawyers and insurance agents, in which art would only receive a more hygienic facility." He warned that if City Center did not retain its independence as part of the new entity, he and Balanchine would "withdraw those dancers who wish to stay with us and find funds to operate elsewhere."[26] He never had to carry out his threat. In the end a deal was brokered, and City Center received full control over the New York State Theater.

By the time this controversy reached the press, it was linked to another, equally divisive issue. Who was to represent dance at Lincoln Center? For Kirstein, the answer was obvious—the New York City Ballet. For others, including Martha Graham and Lucia Chase, who, with Kirstein, Doris Duke, William Kolodney, and William Schuman (among others), met regularly in 1958 as members of the Center's Advisory Council for the Dance, this was far from self-evident. Indeed, much of the discussion in the Council's meetings centered on the need to form a single, expanded Lincoln Center Ballet Company, which would subsume existing companies and might include two subdivisions, one oriented toward classical dance, the other toward modern dance:

> A unified, overall organization for the Dance is, therefore, a subject the Council must consider. In this connection Miss Graham had pointed out that a ballet training foundation was important in the field of Contemporary Dance, and Mr. Kirstein had added that the techniques of the Ballet had expanded and absorbed much from Modern Dance. . . . The repertoire outlook will probably be a blend of the old and the new and must satisfy the public's demand for what Mr. Kirstein referred to as "invention."[27]

The Balanchine/Graham *Episodes,* which came to the stage the following year, may well have exemplified the kind of relationship the committee had in mind.

At the same time, as Philip Johnson's designs and Lincoln Center's promotional literature make clear, the new theater was intended to serve multiple functions. A full-page ad in a 1960 issue of *The New Yorker* described it as a place "you will come for operettas, music festivals and dance programs. And also to see great foreign companies like England's Old Vic, the *Comédie Française,* and the Kabuki Dancers of Japan."[28] Johnson's preliminary designs, now at Columbia University's Avery Library, made provision for blocs of seats to be removed or closed off in all parts of the house. Thus, the larger hall Kirstein wanted for ballet could also accommodate attractions best served by a smaller one.

In 1964, William Schuman, now president of Lincoln Center, turned the populist argument against City Center. As Allen Hughes reported in *The New York Times:*

> Mr. Schuman, who truly wants the New York City Ballet at Lincoln Center very much, also wants the same kind of competition in dance as there is among orchestras and other musical media in Philharmonic Hall and as he says there will be among opera companies when the new theaters for these arts are opened. He said specifically . . . that he felt Lincoln Center should have both the New York City Ballet and a "more eclectic" company or companies. . . . For very nearly 15 years at City Center, there have been no appearances by any American dance company except the New York City Ballet.[29]

Hughes went on to contrast this with the varied attractions booked by Lincoln Center into the New York State Theater during 1964–1965. In addition to NYCB, these included the Royal Danish Ballet, Chilean National Ballet, American Ballet Theatre, and two evenings of modern dance presented by the New York State Council on the Arts.

The controversy over the New York State Theater only deepened resentments in a dance world already divided over the Ford Foundation's decision in 1963 to award $7.7 million—the largest sum ever allocated to dance—to the New York City Ballet, the School of American Ballet, and six companies, including two in existence for less than a year, with close ties to NYCB. Modern dance was excluded, as well as ballet companies such as American Ballet Theatre and the Joffrey Ballet. Of the $5.9 million earmarked for NYCB and SAB, a little under half went to the company to strengthen its financial and administrative resources; similar "stabilization" grants would follow in the next fourteen years. The money for the School, actually two separate grants, was to enlarge the faculty, underwrite teacher training seminars, and increase the number of scholarships for advanced students living outside the New York area.[30] The scholarship program, which transformed SAB into a truly national institution, would, in time, alter the character of the company, transforming it from a microcosm of New York to a reflection of the country at large.

The New York State Theater opened on April 23, 1964. It was a star-studded occasion. Governor Nelson Rockefeller himself did the honors, telling Balanchine, "It's all yours, George. Take it from here."[31] In more ways than one it was his; as Kirstein's old friend, architect Philip Johnson, told *Newsweek*, "I did the house with Balanchine in mind. . . . It is really a theater for ballet. It is a sparkle in red and gold, with an old-fashioned lyre shape. It is both splendid and luxurious."[32] On the program was a scene from *Carousel* performed by the Music Theater of Lincoln Center (a short-lived company directed by Richard Rodgers), *Allegro Brillante* (led by Maria Tallchief and André Prokovsky), and *Stars and Stripes* (led by Jacques d'Amboise and Patricia McBride). A champagne reception followed on the Promenade. The second half of the program was broadcast live over CBS. Camelot had come to Lincoln Square.

The company itself had become high chic. Even before the move to Lincoln Center, Jacqueline Kennedy would drop in for an occasional performance, causing John Martin to remark: "Hardly a man is now alive who can recall another First Lady ever having gone to the ballet simply for the pleasure of it." Balanchine was invited to the White House, as were several of his dancers. They went to the Soviet Union under the auspices of the State Department, and on their return heard Mayor Robert F. Wagner declare "New York City Ballet Day." For all the glamor, they retained a link with the community around them. They danced for "slum children," Long Island schoolchildren, and maximum-security prisoners at the Clinton State Correctional Facility in Dannemora. They gave lecture-demonstrations at New York City junior and senior high schools, and a month after Martin Luther King Jr. was killed in 1968, mourned his memory in Balanchine's *Requiem Canticles*.[33] They were chic, but with a sense of service and *noblesse oblige*.

"The Big Time," as Kirstein put it, tapped a new audience for NYCB. In 1966, at the behest of the Ford Foundation, a subscription system was introduced, the first by a major American dance company. With four tickets for the price of three, it was really a bargain, and the public was quick to respond; when the spring 1966 season opened, the company had a $500,000 box-office advance, the largest pre-sale of tickets it had ever enjoyed.[34] Critics were quick to note changes in the NYCB audience. Wrote Harris Green, the music critic of *Commonweal:*

> When the City Center moved its ballet and opera to . . . the New York State Theater, it hurled itself into a subscription drive so desperate and indiscriminate in its search for large chunks of assured cash that it bombarded people who'd never had any interest in the arts with junk mail. . . . As a result, the New York City Ballet (the only Lincoln Center institution ever to be headed by a supreme creative genius) draws audiences so innocent they rarely bring Violette Verdy before the curtain for more than one bow.[35]

Dale Harris, writing in *Saturday Review,* put it a little differently: "The poets and painters whose support and critical judgments gave such excitement to the old days at City Center—not to mention a sense of artistic community—seem to have disappeared."[36]

Kirstein, for his part, reveled in the change. "For 35 years," he told Anna Kisselgoff in 1971, "I fought to be the Establishment. . . . Now we're the enemy and I'm delighted."[37] Still, the Big Time was expensive. In 1964, only months after moving into the New York State Theater, the dancers signed their first year-round contract. Sets had to be refurbished, and in some cases—*The Nutcracker* being one—redesigned. Maintenance costs were higher at the new theater, and running expenses more than four times what they had been at City Center. A 1965 Ford Foundation grant defrayed some of these expenses.[38] But it could not contain the upward spiral set in motion by the move. It was not simply a matter of rising costs, or the double-digit inflation of the 1970s, but the breakdown of the old City Center financial structure and the failure of large amounts of federal funds—on which so much of the dance boom seemed to ride—to materialize on a sustained basis. The year 1966 witnessed the first of numerous strikes by the musicians of the NYCB orchestra. At stake, in addition to salaries (which in the early 1970s were still higher than the dancers') were employment issues—the size of the orchestra, the number of performances per week, the number of weeks guaranteed each year. Beginning in 1966, when the Joffrey Ballet became a constituent of City Center, performing at the Fifty-Fifth Street house, the NYCB orchestra also played for the Joffrey. However, in 1973, City Center, now facing a $2 million deficit (partly because of NYCB's 1972 Stravinsky Festival), severely curtailed its support of the Joffrey, making the company's two six-week seasons financially untenable. (The Ford Foundation, which gave City Center two $500,000 interest-free loans to help deal with the crisis, specified that the money be used exclusively for the New York City Opera and the New York City Ballet.)

That fall, for the first time in NYCB history, the company's eighty-three dancers went on strike, demanding that they be guaranteed work or pay for the full fourteen-week season, something management could not guarantee because the ballet orchestra, which was still without a contract after three months of negotiation, refused to give management a full no-strike pledge. Along with a substantial pay hike, the musicians wanted compensation for loss of work through the curtailment of the Joffrey's season. They struck again in 1976, this time demanding an increase from twenty-five to forty weeks of guaranteed work. After a month, the musicians gave in. "The demise of the City Center is what all these strikes are about," NYCB's lawyer, Alan Jaffe, told *The New York Times*. "Until the mid-1960's, there was more musicians' work provided by the City Center. When that work died out, the musicians felt they had lost employment and they looked to the parent companies—the City Opera and City Ballet—to replace that." Exacerbating the situation was City Center's decision in 1975 to limit its sponsorship to those "parent" companies. Finally, there was the realization that federal monies would never amount to more than what Hilton Kramer called a "minor (if . . . crucial) role" in keeping NYCB and City Center functioning.[39]

Whatever else was happening, the company itself was flourishing. Thanks in large part to the Ford scholarships, a new generation of ballerinas had come to the fore, teens with the slim-hipped sexiness of a Pamela Tiffin or Twiggy. As in the country at large, the accent was on youth. Senior ballerinas left in a huff, or found themselves warming the bench, while the youngsters—"rookies," *Newsweek* called them—got all the "juicy" parts.[40] But for Balanchine, who celebrated his fiftieth birthday in 1964, the new breed kept his juices flowing. "I need dancers more than they need me," he acknowledged.[41] If few of the ballets created after the move to Lincoln Center measured up to the masterworks of the City Center years in terms of originality, his exploration of technique (something he claimed only to "apply") remained unparalleled. If anything, during the last fifteen years of his active choreographic life, he took classical movement to dizzying heights of virtuosity, fantasy, and inventiveness that have never been matched.

The grandest tribute to this new generation of dancers was *Jewels,* a plotless, full-length ballet inspired, so Balanchine said, by a visit to the Fifth Avenue jeweler Van Cleef and Arpels. Produced in 1967, each "act" had a gem as the basis of its color and design scheme, as well as Karinska's magnificent costumes. But the real jewels of the work were its ballerinas—Violette Verdy, Mimi Paul, Sara Leland, and Suki Schorer in the haunting, mysterious *Emeralds;* Patricia McBride and Patricia Neary in the brashly sexy *Rubies;* Suzanne Farrell, partnered by Jacques d'Amboise, in the stately, imperial *Diamonds,* a summation of the great Russian tradition of *ballets blancs.* A meditation on the different faces of Eve, *Jewels* was testimony to Balanchine's absolute mastery of the most complex and varied forms of choreographic beauty.

It was Farrell, Balanchine's great Muse of the 1960s and the Dulcinea for whom he revived the idea of *Don Quixote* (1965) nearly twenty years after he had first conceived and then discarded it, who came closest to expressing his ideal; she was swift, strong, musical, obedient, a virtuoso with the sensuality of a woman and the purity of a nun. More than any other ballerina, she embodied the "new" Balanchine style; her dancing had the speed and precise footwork of dancers of the 1950s, but also an expansiveness and amplitude that matched the larger scale of Lincoln Center. As a dancer, she loved taking risks; she would try anything, even the seemingly impossible, thus becoming a collaborator in the fullest sense of the word in Balanchine's technical experiments. Onstage, she lived in the moment, tackling each phrase with a spontaneity that made it new, no matter how often she danced it. She was Balanchine's spiritual daughter, as well as a child of the 1960s, and she left her mark on a generation of American dancers.

Farrell left the company in 1969. The action was precipitated by her marriage to NYCB soloist Paul Mejía, and although Balanchine allowed her to leave, it diminished his appetite for choreography. Indeed, in the next three years, apart from *Who Cares?* (1971), a light-hearted tribute to Broadway showgirls of yore, the quality of his work fell off, and critics were quick to pounce on his much re-vised *Firebird* (1970) and *PAMTGG* (1971) (whose music Clive Barnes dismissed as "almost too trivial for elevator music")[42] as evidence of his declining powers.

Implicit in the criticism, not all of which was fair, was a comparison with Jerome Robbins, who had rejoined NYCB in 1969 after an absence of more than ten years. *Dances at a Gathering* (1969), which premiered less than two weeks after Farrell's departure, was almost universally praised. Nancy Goldner called it a "masterpiece"; Barnes "a cross between *Liebeslieder Walzer* and Tudor's *Dark Elegies*."[43] Deborah Jowitt analyzed its air of naturalness:

> The vocabulary is balletic, rich and immensely clever, but made to look simple by Robbins's beautiful way of shaping phrases. Preparations are never obtrusive; girls arise almost invisibly onto pointe, as if such an action were the natural consequence of drawing breath. Contemporary ideas about art have freed Robbins to be romantic in a way that choreographers contemporary with Chopin were not ready to be. Not for them the irregularities, asymmetries, open forms that give *Dances at a Gathering* its air of naturalness and inevitability.[44]

The works that followed *Dances*—*In the Night* (1970), *The Goldberg Variations* (1971), and *Watermill* (1971)—all ventured into new terrain. *In the Night* was an exploration of the pas de deux to four of Chopin's noctures. *Watermill,* which had music of Teiji Ito, was a daring experiment with stillness and arrested movement. *The Goldberg Variations* offered the challenge of a score that—at 100 minutes long and with thirty variations all in the same key—almost defied realization. These works brought new life to the company at a critical moment in its existence.

By 1971, however, a project was in the offing that would usher in the final era of Balanchine's life—the 1972 Stravinsky Festival. This was not the first festival that Balanchine had dedicated to Stravinsky (in 1937 the American Ballet had offered one at the Metropolitan Opera), nor was it the only festival of the period to single out a composer. (In 1975, Ravel was so honored; in 1981, Tchaikovsky.) But Balanchine's relationship with Stravinsky was different. His music for *Apollo*, which Balanchine first encountered in 1928, was a turning point in the choreographer's life; it taught him to clarify, distill, and reduce; for the first time, as he later put it, he "dare[d] to not use all my ideas."[45] Over the years, Balanchine choreographed numerous works to the composer's music, from popular classics like *Firebird* and *Le Baiser de la Fée* (1937) to commissioned masterpieces such as *Orpheus* and *Agon*. No composer was closer to him; with no composer did he collaborate so willingly and with such happy results. The Stravinsky Festival opened just over a year after Stravinsky's death in 1971. It was an extraordinary achievement, stretching the company to the limit, and, with a half-million-dollar price tag, daring as well. More than thirty works were given, including twenty new ones. Balanchine himself choreographed no fewer than nine of the premieres, of which three, *Violin Concerto*, a throwback to the angst-ridden "leotard" ballets of the 1950s, *Duo Concertant*, a duet that celebrated the union of music and dance, and *Symphony in Three Movements*, a paean to the new female athlete spawned by feminism, were major additions to the repertory. Robbins, John Taras, Todd Bolender, Richard Tanner, John Clifford, and Lorca Massine choreographed the rest. It was a truly magnificent tribute to the composer.

In the company's City Center days, the house was seldom full. By the 1970s, audiences were packing the New York State Theater. During the Stravinsky Festival, nary a ticket was to be had. Balanchine had long rejected the star system (it was expensive and detracted from the choreography) and had turned a deaf ear to the pleas of Soviet defectors to create ballets for them. Still, by the 1970s, he was beefing up the company's roster of danseurs. All the new men came from abroad: Jean-Pierre Bonnefous (later Bonnefoux) from the Paris Opéra Ballet, Helgi Tomasson from Iceland (via the Harkness Ballet and Joffrey Ballet), and Peter Martins from the Royal Danish Ballet. Martins, who joined NYCB on a permanent basis in 1970, was tall and handsome, with the nobility of an Apollo—one of his most celebrated roles—and the technique of a cavalier. With Suzanne Farrell, who returned to NYCB in 1975, he formed an inspired partnership that Balanchine nurtured in new works and by frequently casting them together in old ones. Two years later, Martins choreographed his first ballet, *Calcium Light Night*, and was teaching company class; by 1981, when he joined the roster of NYCB ballet masters, he was widely regarded as Balanchine's heir apparent. Audience favorite though he may have been, Martins was never a box-office draw like Mikhail Baryshnikov, whose much-publicized defection from the Kirov Ballet in 1974 had made him an international superstar. Four years later, amid much fanfare, Baryshnikov left American Ballet Theatre, with its star salaries and repertory of nineteenth-century "classics," to join NYCB. He spent little more than a year with the company. He danced many new roles, but because of poor health, Balanchine never created a ballet for him, although they worked closely on a revival of *Prodigal Son* that subsequently was televised. However disappointing the interlude may have been for Baryshnikov, for NYCB it was box-office magic; for the first and only time in its history, sold-out houses became a common occurrence.

Although NYCB audiences were never bigger than during the 1970s, when the dance boom was at its height and PBS was introducing the company into upscale living rooms across the country, the company's hometown was changing dramatically. Two decades of suburbanization and migration from Puerto Rico and the American South had brought about a great shift in the city's population and economic base. In 1975, New York City nearly went bankrupt. Crime was up, the Bronx was burning; Martin Scorsese's *Taxi Driver* and, a little later, Tom Wolfe's *Bonfire of the Vanities* captured the national imagination. New York had become Fort Apache, the symbol par excellence of the "inner city" and the ills afflicting urban America. Overnight, it seemed, the city's glamor had gone. Everywhere, that is, except at NYCB. "Everything is beautiful at the ballet," Cassie sang throughout the 1970s in Michael Bennett's long-running musical *A Chorus Line*. And, so, to many New Yorkers the company became a kind of refuge from the city, a sanctuary that night after night expressed an ideal of urban culture under siege on the streets.

No work summed up this sense of glorious escapism more than *Vienna Waltzes* (1977). It was grand and glamorous, with seventy dancers and costumes that called for yards of Karinska's finest white silk. In the final tableau, mirrors multiplied the number of swirling couples until it seemed as if they would spill over into the real world, banishing its ugliness. The ballet was a tremendous hit (even *People* magazine did a spread on it!),[46] but it was not the only culminating work of Balanchine's last years. In *Ballo della Regina* (1978), he celebrated the consummate virtuosity of Merrill Ashley; in *Chaconne* (1976), the heavenly partnership of Suzanne Farrell and Peter Martins.

For all the glorious dancing, an era was drawing to a close. "I cannot wait," Balanchine had said in the 1960s, referring to the two years it allegedly took for a ballerina to get back into shape after childbirth.[47] Now, as he entered his seventies, the ticking of the biological clock grew more insistent. He had always reveled in youth; now he pushed it to the breaking point, leading to devastating injuries that probably could have been avoided. Anorexia had become a cause for concern, and feminists such as Suzanne Gordon, influenced by the women's health movement, singled out the cult of extreme thinness associated with the ideal Balanchine physique as a cause of its rapid spread among ballet dancers.[48] Education was also a problem; at a time when increasing numbers of Americans were attending college, many NYCB dancers, in a throwback to the 1940s and 1950s, didn't have a high school diploma. And by 1980, they were again threatening to strike; as dancer Toni Bentley put in her memoir *Winter Season,* "we only want enough money to pay the rent."[49]

On April 30, 1983, after a long illness, Balanchine died at Roosevelt Hospital, only blocks from the New York State Theater. His death was front-page news; telegrams poured in from politicians and celebrities from all over the world. The company performed as scheduled that night, and the SAB annual workshop went on at the Juilliard Theater. But the dancers and many in the audience were in shock. With Balanchine's death, Jerome Robbins and Peter Martins became the company's joint artistic directors or, as they were called in NYCB parlance, "co-ballet masters in chief."

Together, they shepherded NYCB through the transitional period that followed Balanchine's death. It was not an easy time for the company. Many dancers left. Those who stayed found the change in management style unsettling. For years Balanchine had attended to every aspect of their lives down to the color of their eyeshadow; now they had to make those decisions for themselves. "Balanchine was our father," Lourdes Lopez told Deborah Weisgall in 1996. "He taught you how to live. With Peter, you simply learn to dance."[50] Backstage, most of the old faces remained, but Martins, who took charge of the day-to-day running of the company, could hardly fill the void created by Balanchine's absence. Only thirty-six and still performing (he retired from the stage at the end of 1983), he was more of a peer than a "boss" to his fellow dancers. Moreover, despite thirteen years in the company and the trust Balanchine had placed in him, not everyone viewed him as an unimpeachable authority on the master's works when differences of interpretation inevitably—and increasingly—arose.

Far graver was the question of who owned the Balanchine repertory. Although this was the core of NYCB's identity, the choreographer had willed it to fourteen legatees, including friends, dancers, and a former wife, without specifying its future relationship to the company. Already reeling from the impact of Balanchine's death, the NYCB board and administration now had to deal, as Bernard Taper wrote, with "the possible loss of the ballets that justified the company's existence. How could they program a season or plan for tours when at any moment their repertory could be pulled out for under them or extortionate fees demanded? And what might happen when the legatees passed their ballets on to others—to their heirs in turn, or possibly to exploitative entrepreneurs?"[51] Once the estate was settled, two of its three principal legatees, Barbara Horgan, Balanchine's long-time personal assistant, and former principal dancer Karin von Aroldingen, established The George Balanchine Trust, into which they and several other legatees deposited their rights. There were threats of legal action on the part of the NYCB board, terrified of losing proprietary right to the ballets, and threats by Barbara Horgan of revealing to the world at large the board's exasperating shenanigans, of which the press, amazingly, was unaware.

Strenuous negotiations followed, culminating in a five-year licensing agreement between the company and the trust. Under the terms of this 1987 agreement, the company, for a blanket fee, received the right to perform any or all ballets owned or represented by the trust. When the agreement expired in 1992, it was promptly renewed.[52]

Criticism of Martins' leadership did not surface immediately. Indeed, in the years just after Balanchine's death, he was treated by the press as the true, apostolic heir, a golden boy who could do no wrong: "Prince of the City Ballet" Newsweek called him in a 1983 cover story marking his retirement from the stage.[53] The backlash was as bitter as the honeymoon had been sweet. Balanchine had not only created a company and a repertory; he had also formed a generation of critics for whom the experience of his ballets as danced by the members of his company was a crucial source of intellectual identity and a basis for aesthetic judgment. For many of these critics, and the junior colleagues influenced by them, Martins was destroying—both willfully and inadvertently— Balanchine's priceless legacy.

Most of the criticisms had a grain of truth. His casting was often misguided; he sacrificed emotion to architecture, allowed the technical level of the company to slip, played favorites, and failed to develop the artistic potential of many dancers, especially women. As the decade progressed, however, the tone grew sharper, the language more virulent, and the forecasts of doom more apocalyptic. NYCB was no longer Balanchine's company; it was no longer their company; under Martins, who assumed full artistic control when Robbins retired in 1990, a new aesthetic had entered the muscle memory of the dancers and transformed works full of vitality into museum pieces. Critics for whom Balanchine could do no wrong—and by the 1970s, they were legion—rushed to protest the betrayal. Like Peter, his Biblical namesake, Martins had denied his Lord and must pay the price. The reviews do not always make for pleasant reading.

Whatever his flaws as an artistic director, Martins has kept the company going. ("Basically, I've kept the ship from sinking," he once said.)[54] In truth, his accomplishment is far greater than the holding action he describes. Simply put, he has succeeded in transforming what was basically a one-man operation— that is a company serving, in the manner of a classic modern dance ensemble, Balanchine's vision of dance—into a repertory organization closely associated with that vision but not identical to it. Few companies are able to make that transition. Many fold; others founder in the search for new direction; still others find the past a burden. "I'm interested in keeping Balanchine ballets as he would want them to be seen," he told Anna Kisselgoff in 1984, "not to make them look stylistically preposterous in 10 years. . . . Choreography has certain advantages. You can bring it right into your time and it will still be that choreography."[55] From the start, Martins had no interest in erecting a temple to Balanchine, in transforming the company into a museum of fossilized masterpieces.

Although Martins has certain choreographic preferences, he has largely subsumed his artistic identity to the needs of the company. He choreographs to schedule and, whether the result is good, bad, or indifferent, he delivers on time and close to budget. Whatever the slot, he manages to fill it; he has done big works and pas de deux, ballets to traditional music and "contemporary" pieces—a skilled composer of dances in the tradition of European ballet masters.[56] And he has kept the dancers coming. To be sure, the School, since 1991 in magnificent new premises in Lincoln Center's Rose Building, continues to supply new blood. But it is Martins, as the company's artistic director, who must nurse it through the ranks. Although his way of doing this is certainly open to criticism, his accomplishments are also undeniable. He has presided over a distinguished roster of principals, from Merrill Ashley, Kyra Nichols, and Darci Kistler, all largely, if not entirely, formed by Balanchine; to Wendy Whelan, Heléne Alexopoulos, Jock Soto, Peter Boal, and Albert Evans, all largely, if not entirely formed by Martins. A dancer's life is notoriously short. Fifteen years after Balanchine's death only a handful of the company's dancers had ever worked with him. The rest had left, most quietly; others, like Suzanne Farrell and Merrill Ashley, with flowers and fanfare.

The New York City Ballet was not alone in undergoing a transformation in the 1980s. The city itself was in the throes of major changes. In midtown and around Wall Street a new generation of skyscrapers was springing up—huge, postmodern boxes attesting to the triumph of Reaganomics and the globalization of capital. Real estate was booming, and up and down Broadway luxury housing for singles and high-priced health clubs were swallowing up dance studios. (In 1993, the studios at Broadway and 82nd Street that once housed the School of American Ballet would be taken over by Barnes and Noble for one of its superstores.) A new generation of millionaires descended on New York, but dance, it turned out, was seldom high on their list of philanthropies. The dance boom had long ended. Audiences fell off, as well as traditional gift-giving, as foundations poured money once earmarked for the arts into education and health, replacing government cutbacks. Public funding of the arts plummeted, and what remained increasingly went to programs and institutions uncontaminated by the label of "high art." Meanwhile, Christian fundamentalists, boasting new political muscle and a hotline to the conservative wing of the Republican Party, crusaded against homosexuality, the National Endowment for the Arts, and other cultural evils.

At the same time, in the studios and galleries of "downtown," a new generation of artists had come to the fore. Most had started out in the 1960s or early 1970s, and by the 1980s had become hot items in the booming art market and at the Next Wave Festival held annually at the Brooklyn Academy of Music. In dance, critics bemoaned the dearth of ballet choreographers, and funders embraced "crossover" projects, which typically paired a modern dance choreographer with a ballet company, as the solution. The 1980s, too, saw the invention of MTV, and the rock-dance "commercials" that influenced not only a generation of teen viewers but also young concert choreographers. At the same time, postmodernism—ironic, detached, conceptual, enamoured of technology, pastiche, popular culture, and theory—emerged as the era's unifying stylistic tendency.

Balanchine's choreographic revolution was rooted in the modernism that swept the arts before and after the First World War. His favorite composer was Stravinsky, who, more than anyone except possibly Schoenberg, epitomized that movement in music. He had only limited interest in "serious" American composers, apart from Ives, and he tended to equate jazz with the show tunes he had encountered on Broadway. This was not the case of Martins. Beginning with his first ballet, *Calcium Light Night* (1977), which was set to Ives, he revealed a sympathy with the city's "downtown" energies—its street rhythms, punk styles, unsentimentality, and postmodernism. And beginning with Heather Watts, his first Muse, he identified this "contemporary" style with dancers whose restless energy, high-voltage attack, athleticism, and quirky body and bearing struck him as profoundly American. Although he has staged a number of ballets to older music, his preference is for twentieth-century composers, especially Americans: Michael Torke, Charles Wuorinen, John Adams, Philip Glass, Wynton Marsalis. In the fifteen years since Balanchine's death, more new ballet scores were commissioned by NYCB than in the preceding thirty-five. However different his taste, Martins has remained deeply loyal to a key tenet of Balanchine's artistic credo—the integral connection between contemporary music and dance.

The American Music Festival, which opened almost five years to the day after Balanchine's death, underscored the company's goals in a typically NYCB way. In the space of three weeks, no fewer than twenty-one world premieres were given, many to commissioned scores, several with guest conductors, and all to music by Americans. To drive home the company's identity as a creative enterprise, each of the festival's ten programs had a front curtain designed by a major contemporary artist; among the roster of painters were Keith Haring, Julian Schnabel, Susan Rothenberg, and Francesco Clemente. For the first time since the company's earliest years, the work of living artists—as opposed to the "specialist" scene painters favored by Balanchine in his later years—shared the stage with NYCB dancers.

In addition to seven ballets by Martins, the festival presented works by nearly a dozen other choreographers, including several NYCB dancers and members of the company's extended "family." More surprising was the decision to open the company's doors to "outsiders," such as William Forsythe, the controversial expatriate director of the Frankfurt Ballet, and three well-known modern dance choreographers: Paul Taylor, Lar Lubovitch, and Laura Dean. "Everybody is talking about the big difference between modern dance and classical ballet," Martins told journalist Diane Solway. "It's ridiculous. It's all about music and dancing. It's the same language with a different dialect. I don't look down upon modern dance. . . . It has inspired me in many ways. If I didn't find it important and if I didn't feel it gave me something, I wouldn't have invited them." At the same time, he affirmed the continuing tradition of NYCB avant-gardism: "This company is about creation and experimentation. . . . Classical ballet will always be the basis [of our work], but it's important not to exclude everything else and become stifled. This festival is about going with the times and fitting in and finding your way."[57] Although only a handful of the new works entered the permanent NYCB repertory, the festival revealed that Martins was neither afraid of venturing into new choreographic terrain nor intent on making the company his personal choreographic instrument. The biennial Diamond Projects, which he has used to encourage in-house talent as well as outsiders—John Alleyne, Ulysses Dove, Kevin O'Day, among others—versed in both classical and modern dance, underscore his commitment to new work in a contemporary vein.

Although Martins prefers to work this vein himself, he is also adept at neo-traditional choreography, as he first demonstrated in his 1981 remake of *The Magic Flute*, a hundred-year-old ballet by Lev Ivanov. Ten years later, he staged *The Sleeping Beauty*, thus bringing to fruition a dream long cherished by Kirstein no less than Balanchine, who had danced in the ballet as a child in Russia and even staged the "Garland Waltz" in 1981. With a $2.8 million price tag, the production was lush. The scenic designs by David Mitchell recalled Chenonceaux and other fairytale châteaux of the Loire Valley; the costume designs by Patricia Zipprodt were set in the seventeenth and eighteenth centuries, as was the original ballet. There were a half-dozen Auroras and as many Lilac Fairies and Princess Florines, revealing the depth of classical talent in the company, while, as Carabosse, Merrill Ashley and Lourdes Lopez revealed an unexpected flair for character acting. As for the choreography, it was streamlined, "cut and trimmed," as critic Laura Shapiro wrote, "so skillfully it's now an efficient two acts, with Petipa's beloved choreography at the center of the action, looking fresh and handsome." Shapiro also noted, however, that in this pared-down version, "perhaps inevitably, Martins has sliced out the emotional core of the ballet."[58] For Kirstein, who conceived the overall style, closely supervised the designs, and wrote an essay for the gala program, the production was a throwback to his days as an impresario. Fittingly, *The Sleeping Beauty* was Kirstein's swan song.

Although Martins has refrained from turning NYCB into a museum, he has paid ample tribute to its rich choreographic past. Works by Balanchine and Robbins (until the latter's death in 1998, new ones as well as existing ones) continue to form the lion's share of the company's active repertory. He has restored certain "lost" ballets, such as Balanchine's *Gounod Symphony,* and mounted the Robbins Festival that was a highpoint of the 1990 season. But Martins' greatest feat as custodian of the NYCB past was the 1993 Balanchine Celebration. "The Balanchine Celebration is more than big," wrote *Dance Magazine:*

> With seventy-three ballets performed over an eight-week period, it is massive. It is also totally unprecedented. Although many companies have paid tribute to the chief architects of their repertoires, none have attempted festivals on as grand a scale. . . . Spanning more than fifty years of his career as a choreographer and including both acknowledged masterpieces and lesser works, the NYCB tribute is like the Picasso and Matisse megashows mounted in recent years by the Museum of Modern Art—a major retrospective of a twentieth-century creative giant.[59]

The Balanchine Celebration was an enormous success. Fans came from far and wide, as did the dancers who performed at the marathon closing night gala. Balanchine may have belonged to New York City, but the reach of his influence was international.

Under Martins, certain aspects of company life have changed dramatically. "It's a new world," he said in 1996. "You don't have to hide your boyfriends and girlfriends. The kids are getting married, they are going to college, they're having babies."[60] Where Balanchine discouraged his dancers from continuing their education, more than half the members of today's NYCB are enrolled at Fordham University, whose downtown campus is across the street from the New York State Theater. Balanchine did not want his ballerinas having babies: by the mid-1990s, the company had several ballerina mothers, including Martins' own wife, Darci Kistler. Today's NYCB dancers are more concerned about health-related issues, including nutrition and injury prevention, than their predecessors; more apt to grapple with the problem of career transition even before their dancing days are over; more likely to take charge of their careers and have lives outside the studio. The nunlike existence that Balanchine extolled in his later decades has become a thing of the past.

The packed houses of the late 1970s and early 1980s belong to the past as well. NYCB is not the only "high" art enterprise to find its audiences dwindling, nor the only one in search of solutions. According to the company's market research department, the average NYCB ticket buyer is white, female, well-to-do, has a successful career, decides on her own to make the ticket purchase (even when she is married), lives in Manhattan or Bergen County, and started seeing the company on a regular basis in the 1970s. She is a concerned citizen, who writes letters to the company about issues ranging from the use of fur to investments in South Africa. And like many supporters of the city's elite cultural institutions, she is aging. There are many reasons for this decline in the ballet-going public—the low birthrate of baby boomers, who failed in a sense to reproduce themselves; the migration of senior citizens to Florida and other sunny climes; the cultural philistinism pervasive in many quarters of the city's new elite; AIDS, which devastated the arts, media, and fashion worlds; what some perceive as the company's diminished social clout on the party circuit.[61] But there are other reasons as well. Ticket prices have risen steeply. In 1976, a seat in the orchestra cost $10.95; in 1983, $23.00; today, it goes for $60.00 (or $80.00 at a "peak" *Nutcracker* performance)—far outstripping the rise in consumer prices.[62] In fact, apart from the very uppermost reaches of the house, there are no seats for the price of that 1983 orchestra ticket. The result has been to price much of the potential audience out of the market, identifying the company's public with the wealthiest segments of society. The fact that much of the company's advertising has been targeted to young white professionals only underscores this. Yet NYCB, like New York's other major cultural institutions, exists in a city that has become a magnet for immigrants, and heavily nonwhite.

Fifty years after its founding, the New York City Ballet can look back to a half-century of unparalleled accomplishment. In virtually every way it has transformed the landscape of American ballet. As the instrument of Balanchine's imagination, it has created a body of work of a magnitude and depth unparalleled in the history of twentieth-century dance. It has enhanced the stature of ballet as an art form and the status of dancers as artists. It has raised technique to dizzying heights of virtuosity and defined an American classical style. It has seeded innumerable companies, supplying them not only with distinguished repertory but also with gifted dancers, choreographers, and artistic directors. In all but name, only NYCB is the country's national showcase for ballet.

Now, perhaps, as America rediscovers the virtues of its urban polities, it is time for this national company to come home, to renew its covenant with the city itself. For, however much the New York City Ballet belongs to the country at large, it is above all a citizen of New York. The city birthed it and baptized it, gave it life, energy, and the means to realize its founders' vision. Who knows? The ever-changing kaleidoscope that is New York could well be the key to the company's future.

NOTES

1. Robert M. Coates, "Friend to the Arts: New York is Becoming the Capital of Culture," *Holiday*, April 1949, pp. 131, 135.
2. Kirstein to A. Everett Austin, Jr., 16 July 1933, in *I Remember Balanchine: Recollections of the Ballet Master by Those Who Knew Him*, ed. and introd. Francis Mason (New York: Doubleday, 1991), p. 115.
3. *The Ballet Society, 1946–1947*, vol. 1 (New York: Ballet Society, 1947), p. [4].
4. More surprisingly, given her long association with Ballet Theatre, Kirstein asked Agnes de Mille to stage a work for NYCB. After much delay, she sent him the scenario for *Rib of Eve*, but in November 1952, just before it was scheduled to go into production, the project was canceled because of a severe financial crisis affecting all the con-

stituents of City Center. De Mille and Kirstein had known each other since the 1930s and met regularly throughout the 1950s, when both served together on the ANTA Dance Panel. For Kirstein's correspondence with de Mille, see Agnes de Mille Papers, Folder 650, Dance Division, The New York Public Library for the Performing Arts.

5. Anatole Chujoy, *The New York City Ballet* (New York: Knopf, 1953), p. 242.

6. Lincoln Kirstein, *Thirty Years: The New York City Ballet*, rev. ed. (New York: Knopf, 1978), p. 122. Forty years later, when he resigned from the company, Robbins said: "I joined the New York City Ballet in 1949 for a single purpose: To work for and with George Balanchine" (quoted in Anna Kisselgoff, "Jerome Robbins Is Resigning as Co-Director of City Ballet," *The New York Times* [hereafter *NYT*], 6 November 1989, p. C13).

7. For the opening of *Picnic at Tintagle*, see John Martin, "Ashton's 'Picnic' Has Its Premiere," *NYT*, 29 February 1952, p. 19. The cover stories were "Ballet's Fundamentalist," *Time*, 25 January 1954, pp. 66–74; J. Kobler, "Exciting Rise of Ballet in America," *Holiday*, November 1952, pp. 106–113. A photograph published on 18 May 1952 in the *New York World-Telegram and Sun* showed fifteen of the company's women, most in tutus from *Symphony in C*, posing in a lunge fourth around the sundial in Central Park. The caption read: "An outdoor tuneup for the ballerinas of the New York City Ballet Company. The place—Central Park. Note the hands of the dancers and how they draw toward the center girl." *New York World-Telegram and Sun* Collection, Prints and Photographs Division, Library of Congress.

8. Quoted in Nancy Reynolds, *Repertory in Review: Forty Years of the New York City Ballet*, introd. Lincoln Kirstein (New York: Dial, 1977), p. 109.

9. Quoted *ibid.*, p. 94.

10. Quoted *ibid.*

11. Quoted *ibid.*, p. 109.

12. Daniel Schorr, "Disputed Ballet Wins an Ovation," *NYT*, 4 July 1952, p. 9.

13. Quoted in Reynolds, *Repertory in Review*, p. 101.

14. Quoted *ibid.*, p. 104.

15. Kirstein, *Thirty Years*, p. 122.

16. Quoted in Reynolds, *Repertory in Review*, p. 118.

17. Quoted *ibid.*, p. 209.

18. Kirstein, *Thirty Years*, p. 113.

19. Suki Schorer, *Balanchine Pointework*, ed. Lynn Garafola, with an afterword by Robert Greskovic, *Studies in Dance History*, no. 11 (1995), p. ix.

20. "City Center Eyes Move to Project," *NYT*, 29 October 1955, p. 13; Harold C. Schonberg, "Rockefeller 3d Will Direct Study Of a Lincoln Sq. Center for Arts," *NYT*, 1 December 1955, p. 1.

21. Jennifer Dunning, *"But First a School": The First Fifty Years of the School of American Ballet* (New York: Viking/Elisabeth Sifton Books, 1985), p. 111.

22. "Tribute to Rockefeller Staged by City Ballet," *NYT*, 31 January 1979, sec. 3, p. 19. Rockefeller also had a hand in the construction of the Performing Arts Center in Saratoga Springs, a five-thousand-seat auditorium that beginning in 1966 became

the company's summer home. In 1960, the company dedicated *Panamerica*, a "program of new choreographies . . . to music by eight Latin American composers," to Rockefeller for "his many past instances of support of artistic interchange between the Americas" (John Martin, "Ballet: Dedicated to the Governor," *NYT*, 21 January 1960, p. 28).

23. With seven daily newspapers, these events were covered extensively and from many different points of view. The single best collection of clippings, promotional material, and photographs is at the Lincoln Center for the Performing Arts Archives (hereafter LCPAA). Robert Indiana recalled the neighborhood in "Biography of a Poster," a short essay in the souvenir program for the April 1964 inaugural performances at the New York State Theater.

24. "Report on Survey to Determine Feasibility of Creating and Operating a Performing Arts Center in New York City—To the Exploratory Committee for a Performing Arts Center," p. 8, LCPAA. This confidential, undated report was by the engineering firm Day & Zimmermann, Inc. For Kirstein's interest in a new theater, see Franz Schulze, *Philip Johnson: Life and Work* (New York: Knopf, 1994), p. 187; and Martin L. Sokol *The New York City Opera: An American Adventure* (New York: Macmillan, 1981), p. 167.

25. Sokol, *New York City Opera*, p. 169.

26. The letter to Morris is quoted in Sokol, *New York City Opera*, pp. 170–171; the letter to Rockefeller on pp. 171–172.

27. Minutes of second Advisory Meeting on [sic] the Dance, 11 February 1958, p. 3, LCPAA.

28. "What Lincoln Center will mean to you: Progress report on New York City's new 'neighborhood of the immortals,'" *The New Yorker*, 9 April 1960, p. 139.

29. Allen Hughes, "Centers Collide: Control of New York State Theater Disputed by Culture Combines," *NYT*, 11 October 1964, sec. 2, p. 13.

30. Allen Hughes, "Ford Fund Allots 7.7 Million to Ballet," *NYT*, 16 December 1963, p. 1; "Ford Grants Stir Dance Comment," *NYT*, 17 December 1963, p. 49; Allen Hughes, "Ballet Grants: Ford Foundation Grants Raise Many Questions," *NYT*, 22 December 1963, sec. 2, p. 11. For an overview of the Ford-NYCB relationship, see Anne Barclay Bennett, "The Management of Philanthropic Funding for Institutional Stabilization: A History of Ford Foundation and New York City Ballet," Ed.D. diss., Harvard University, 1989.

31. Quoted in Kirstein, *Thirty Years*, p. 183.

32. "House of Balanchine," *Newsweek*, 8 April 1963, p. 88. According to Johnson, he had only "one boss" on the project—Kirstein. Thus, it was Kirstein, with Johnson, who decided to trade a full stage house for the Promenade. As the architect explained to Sharon Zane, who interviewed him for the Lincoln Center for the Performing Arts Oral History Project: "[B]ackstage was a requirement, but there was no room for a backstage [and] a great reception hall. . . . So . . . Lincoln and I just made that decision." Amazingly, Balanchine was not consulted about the orchestra pit. After it was

done, according to Johnson he "took one look at it . . . and said, 'Get those seats out of there and get me a decent orchestra pit!'" As for the so-called "continental seating" (meaning without a center aisle) in the orchestra, a recommendation of seating consultant Ben Schlanger, it was a design "never . . . done before or since." Finally, on the subject of the hall's much-criticized accoustics: "Lincoln and I, leaning toward the dance, didn't pay too much attention to the opera acoustics. . . . [F]or dance, it doesn't really make that much difference." See pp. 34, 50, 82, 88, 92 of the transcripts, at LCPAA. The interviews took place in August and September 1990.

33. John Martin, "Ballet: Revised Program," *NYT*, 22 March 1961, p. 38; "Mayor Lauds Balanchine, Kirstein and Ballet Company," *NYT*, 6 December 1962, p. 55; Nan Robertson, "Ballet a Delight to Slum Children," *NYT*, 7 February 1960, p. 61; "Free Concerts on L.I. for Schoolchildren," *NYT*, 2 February 1966, p. 22; "City Ballet Group Appears at Prison," *NYT*, 26 July 1971, p. 32; "Ballet Talks Begin in 30 City Schools," *NYT*, 18 February 1964, p. 26.

34. Clive Barnes, "Dance: A Bright Omen," *NYT*, 26 March 1966, p. 14.

35. Harris Green, "That Subscription Crowd Must Go!" *NYT*, 7 June 1970, sec. 2, p. 24.

36. Dale Harris, "Balanchine: The End of a Reign," *Saturday Review*, 15 July 1972, p. 47.

37. Anna Kisselgoff, "City Ballet's 'Arrival' Delights Kirstein," *NYT*, 17 June 1971, p. 48.

38. Allen Hughes, "New Contracts for Christmas," *NYT*, 6 December 1964, sec. 2, p. 21; Harold C. Schonberg, "City and Lincoln Centers in Battle Over State Theater," *NYT*, 8 November 1964, sec. 2, p. 12; Theodore Strongin, "City Center Gets $3.2 Million From Ford Fund," *NYT*, 18 November 1965, p. 59.

39. For the 1966 strike, see Richard F. Shepard, "Musicians Strike the City Ballet," *NYT*, 15 November 1966, p. 52, and "Talks Broken Off in Ballet Strike," *NYT*, 16 November 1966, p. 52; Louis Calta, "Musicians Ratify Pact with Ballet," *NYT*, 17 November 1966, p. 56. For City Center's 1973 financial crisis and the 1973 dancers' strike, see "Fund Cut Curtails Joffrey's Fall Season" and Mel Gussow, "Ford Fund Lends City Center a Million," *NYT*, 19 March 1973, p. 46; Emanuel Perlmutter, "On Eve of Its 25th Year, the City Ballet Goes on Strike," *NYT*, 14 November 1973, p. 47; "Disputes Mar Cultural Season"; and Linda Greenhouse, "Center Faces Unending Deficit," *NYT*, 14 November 1973, p. 47; Clive Barnes, "Dance: One of the Strangest Strikes to Hit the Arts," *NYT*, 25 November 1973, sec. 2, pp. 17–18; Richard Severo, "City Ballet Ends Strike of 25 Days," *NYT*, 9 December 1973, p. 41. For the 1976–1977 strike, see Emanuel Perlmutter, "Current Strike At City Ballet Perils Season," *NYT*, 29 December 1976, p. 22; "Ballet Cancels Season as Musicians Reject Mediator Plan to End Strike," *NYT*, 18 January 1977, p. 1; Emanuel Perlmutter, "Musicians End City Ballet Strike; Short Season May Open Tuesday," *NYT*, 23 January 1977, p. 1. For Jaffe's remarks, see Anna Kisselgoff, "Troubles of the City Ballet—and the Cultural Cost," *NYT*, 23 January 1977, sec. 2, p. 22; for Kramer, see his article, "The Quest for Funds to Keep the Arts Lively Goes On," *NYT*, 15 November 1973, p. 54.

40. "'I Cannot Wait,'" *Newsweek*, 25 October 1965, p. 100.

41. Hubert Saal, "Making Balanchine Happy," *Newsweek*, 13 January 1969, p. 54.

42. Quoted in Reynolds, *Repertory in Review*, p. 280.

43. Nancy Goldner, "Dance," *The Nation*, 16 February 1970, p. 189. Barnes is quoted in Reynolds, *Repertory in Review*, p. 262.

44. Quoted *ibid.*

45. Quoted in Bernard Taper, *Balanchine: A Biography*, rev. ed. (Berkeley: University of California Press, 1996), p. 100.

46. Sally Moore, "A Ballet is Born," *People*, 4 July 1978, pp. 74–81.

47. "'I Cannot Wait,'" p. 100.

48. Suzanne Gordon, *Off Balance: The Real World of Ballet* (New York: Pantheon, 1983).

49. Toni Bentley, *Winter Season: A Dancer's Journal* (New York: Random House, 1982), pp. 64–65.

50. Quoted in Deborah Weisgall, "The Company He Keeps," *NYT*, 21 April 1996, sec. 6, p. 28.

51. Taper, *Balanchine*, p. 402.

52. *Ibid.*, pp. 404–407.

53. Walter Clemons, "Prince of the City Ballet," *Newsweek*, 26 December 1983, pp. 56–63.

54. Quoted in Diane Solway, "City Ballet Moves to an American Beat," *NYT*, 24 April 1988, sec. 2, p. 1.

55. Quoted in Anna Kisselgoff, "Peter Martins Talks About New Role as City Ballet's 'Daddy,'" *NYT*, 25 January 1984, p. C17.

56. Kirstein in the entry on "choreography" in *Ballet Alphabet: A Primer for Laymen*, first published in 1939, made a useful distinction between "different levels of creation." "Choreography," he wrote, "may be interpretative or decorative, or more importantly, inventive and creative. To 'interpret' or illustrate music, or to decorate a stage with period revivals, however charming, is less interesting than the creation of lyric drama where dancing may not necessarily be a sole end in itself, but where it can be preeminently an arrangement of ideas particularly suitable to expression in dance terms" (*Ballet Bias and Belief: "Three Pamphlets Collected" and Other Dance Writings of Lincoln Kirstein*, ed. and introd. by Nancy Reynolds [New York: Dance Horizons, 1983], p. 311). Following this distinction, Balanchine was an "inventive" or "creative" choreographer, Martins an "interpretative" or "decorative" one.

57. Quoted in Solway, "City Ballet."

58. Laura Shapiro, "Reviving a Reverie: 'Sleeping Beauty' Bows," *Newsweek*, 13 May 1991, p. 71.

59. Lynn Garafola, "Ten Years After: Peter Martins on Preserving Balanchine's Legacy," *Dance Magazine*, May 1993, p. 40.

60. Quoted in Weisgall, "The Company He Keeps."

61. Monique P. Yazigi, "City Ballet Opening: Of Redecorating and a Rivalry," *NYT*, 30 November 1997, sec. 14, p. 6.

62. According to the Bureau of Labor Statistics, the consumer price index for New York City was 176.3 in 1976, 288.6 in 1983, and 500.1 in mid-1998.

PART IV

STAGING THE PAST

PRICE-TAGGING DIAGHILEV

The atmosphere in the London galleries of Sotheby Parke Bernet last May 9 bristled with excitement. From the podium, Sotheby director Julian Barran smoothly coaxed the bidding upward at £5,000 a stroke. Opened on his left were three scrapbooks once belonging to Lady Juliet Duff, a friend of Serge Diaghilev and a benefactor of his Ballets Russes. In minutes these albums would fetch the highest price in this record-breaking $1.1 million auction of ballet material from the collection of Serge Lifar.

At Sotheby's, a nod is all it takes to make your bid. As prices mounted far above the £50,000 to £80,000 estimate regarded by many as exorbitant, only the high-rollers in the packed gallery dared set their glasses straight or pat a wayward strand of hair. But when the bidding reached and quickly passed the £100,000 mark, even the cautious leaned forward in their seats. At £135,000 ($207,900 at Sotheby's rather inflated exchange rate of $1.54 per pound), the hammer finally rapped the podium. Like the rest of the audience, I was thrilled, stunned, and drained.

The gold-edged albums in which Lady Juliet had pasted Ballets Russes clippings, drawings, and original Baron de Meyer photographs were among many items that stirred controversy in last May's Sotheby sale. In fact, since 1968 when theater auctions became a semi-annual feature of the fusty showrooms on New Bond Street, no event has so roused the genteel world of ballet collecting as Sotheby's Lifar spectacular. On both sides of the Atlantic, dealers, collectors, and librarians buzzed: prices were too high, much of the stuff was "trash," the market would go haywire if everything sold. Events proved the naysayers both right and wrong.

With auction houses vying for prestige collections, acquiring Lifar's was a coup. Diaghilev's "primo ballerino" of the middle and late 1920s, Lifar remains one of the few living links to the Ballets Russes. He was George Balanchine's first Apollo and Prodigal Son, a star who brought to the stage the charisma of Nureyev, the looks of a matinee idol, and a technique that belied his late start in Bronislava Nijinska's Kiev studio. Collaboration with France's Nazi occupiers during World War II clouded his reputation, especially in the United States, but in his years as *premier danseur* of the Ballets Russes and Paris Opéra Ballet,

This article was published in *Dance Magazine* in October 1984.

which he directed from 1930 to 1944 and 1947 to 1958, Lifar proudly—some would say too proudly—donned the mantle of Nijinsky.

Many items in the Sotheby collection evoked those glamorous years when Diaghilev, generous to a fault to those he loved, showered art works and Savile Row suits on his protégé. A full-length oil by Pedro Pruna, who designed the 1925 sailor ballet *Les Matelots*, commemorates the Adonis who swam on the Lido under Diaghilev's jealous eye. Another 1925 portrait, a pen-and-ink drawing by Picasso dedicated to Lifar, shows the young dancer at the barre in Monte Carlo where artists and devotees of the Ballets Russes gathered each spring in anticipation of the Paris season.

Even before Diaghilev's death in 1929, Lifar had amassed a fine collection. But many items in this sale and others that have brought Lifar's Diaghilev treasure-trove to the auction block in recent years have a more questionable pedigree—as Lifar himself admits in his autobiography *Ma Vie*.

No sooner had Diaghilev died in Venice than his closest confidants broke into the Paris apartment where the impresario had stored his vast private collection of books, letters, musical manuscripts, and art works. What they failed to remove in suitcases through the tradesmen's entrance, Lifar, thanks to the generosity of well-wishers, bought back from the French government. His plea that Diaghilev's legacy be kept intact touched many hearts. Several items in the Sotheby sale, including Lady Juliet's scrapbooks and the working drawings by Diaghilev's scene painter, Prince Alexandre Schervachidze, were presented by their owners to Lifar.

Whether or not he deserved their trust is doubtful, for over the years he has scattered that legacy to the winds. As early as 1933, Lifar, who had learned the art of high living at Diaghilev's side, sold 173 of his finest pieces to Hartford's Wadsworth Atheneum when he found himself short of cash. (The museum has millionairess Barbara Hutton to thank for its remarkable find; she refused to pay Lifar's hotel bill during a less-than-triumphant New York season.) In 1975, Lifar consigned to Sotheby's in Monte Carlo Diaghilev's fabulous library, over 800 items that included books printed in 1564 by Ivan Fedorov, the Gutenberg of Russia, first editions of Pushkin, Lermontov, Gogol, and Dostoevsky, and rare journals, almanacs, and monastic imprints. (Harvard University purchased about one-eighth of the collection for its library.)

This year's sale on May 9 brought representatives of major theatrical libraries to London along with some of the world's richest collectors of Diaghileviana. The latter went away with their arms full; the others scrambled for what their strapped budgets could afford.

Consider the endowment-poor Dance Collection of the New York Public Library. It had hankered after Christian Berard's trio of set and costume designs for Massine's *Seventh Symphony* and positively lusted for the letter written by a grief-stricken Stravinsky only nine days after Diaghilev's death—items, however, priced far beyond its means. Not that the library came away empty-handed. Its André Derain letter with a flower doodled from an ink blot and the artist's account of a toothache evokes the informality of Diaghilev's relationships with many collaborators. Another purchase, a 1910 letter from the management of the Paris Opéra, complements the library's Gabriel Astruc Collection, that rich fund of material about the prewar Ballets Russes. Fascinating, too, is a small Balanchine drawing inscribed "to the Genius Prodigal Son" in which the choreographer famed for the slenderness and pointework of his ballerinas depicted a footless Lifar with the thighs and belly of an earth mother. At $4,312, it cost the library dear.

The London Theatre Museum also parted with an imposing sum to enrich its treasury of Diaghilev costumes. For the magnificent Picasso creation worn by Léonide Massine as the Chinese Conjuror in *Parade,* the museum, which for years has been searching for a permanent home, spent a record $40,040, four times more than the previous high set by Alexandre Benois' Petrouchka costume in 1980. It also bought, at nearly double the catalogue estimate, Pedro Pruna's charming drawing of Diaghilev's mid-twenties' trio of stars—Lifar, Alice Nikitina, and a sensitive, introspective Anton Dolin.

With prices pegged so high, Sotheby's spared no expense in publicizing the sale. Its catalogue was lavishly illustrated. With Lifar on hand, an exhibition of selected items opened in March at London's Royal Festival Hall, traveled north to Glasgow, then crossed the Atlantic for a week-long show at Sotheby's elegantly minimalist galleries in New York City. The night before the sale, champagne flowed on New Bond Street as buyers, press, and others with the requisite gilt-edged invitations crowded the showrooms for a last glimpse at the collection.

Sotheby's gamble paid off, with unprecedented sums changing hands even for items without claim to originality. Consider the unfinished "Portrait of Nijinsky," a copy by the Studio of Léon Bakst, which cost the Library of Congress $46,200. Or Alexandre Benois's portrait of Nijinsky as Petrouchka, one of many whipped up by the artist over the years, which a woman in a pink cardigan bought for $23,100. Or those delightfully wicked backstage caricatures of Diaghilev and his court, dashed off time and again by Jean Cocteau long after he published the originals in 1923, which sold at two and even three times their estimated value.

Names, however, don't always guarantee a sale, and in the morning session, barely half the art works and memorabilia changed hands. A diminutive, overpriced design by Max Ernst for the curtain of Diaghilev's 1926 *Romeo et Juliette* and a long, skinny watercolor project by Joan Miró for the same work—both rare graphic evidence of Diaghilev's controversial "surrealist" ballet—did not sell. Nor did Georges Yakulov's fascinating model for the Constructivist setting of Diaghilev's 1927 *Le Pas d'Acier,* priced at an inflated $30,800 to $46,200.

Nor did buyers seem inclined to spend their dollars on those plaster legs, feet, and faces of balletomane necrophilia. Wandering through the Sotheby showrooms the night before the sale, I nearly cried into my champagne glass before the cast of Nijinsky's foot, squat, pathetic testimony to decades of idleness and pain, which rested in a display case next to Pavlova's leg. Moving on, I gazed for a last time at Diaghilev's death mask, trying to imagine the restive genius behind the powerful, sensuous face and the relationship of that face to the battered silver-backed brushes and ivory manicure set of his traveling case. At once, the vanity and willfulness of the man came alive; one saw him standing before the dressing-table mirrors of those hundreds of hotel rooms to which art and ambition had propelled him for over twenty years. No amount of money can reopen the eyes of a death mask or conjure life from a hairnet, and one felt grateful that these unsaintly relics remained unsold.

Despite the publicity such items attracted, the meat of the sale lay elsewhere: in those things that added luster to Diaghilev's greatness and the accomplishments of his enterprise. The manuscripts sold in the afternoon paid tribute to that forceful genius who wrested ballet from the periphery of the European mind to its artistic center by summoning the era's greatest talents, combing the modern world for ideas, and bringing a formidable knowledge of the arts to every aspect of production.

Just how great a role Diaghilev played in masterminding artistic policy, especially in the years during and just after World War I when modernism displaced symbolism as the company's dominant aesthetic, was by far the most exciting discovery of the sale. With Dr. Stephen Roe, Sotheby's staff musicologist, I examined the manuscript of *La Boutique Fantasque*, that frothy toyshop ballet that so enchanted London in 1919. Who was the composer? Gioacchino Rossini, who wrote the nineteenth-century piano pieces on which the score was based? Ottorino Respighi, the orchestrator, who added a handful of connectives? Or Diaghilev, who assembled the music for the ballet from numerous compositions, pruned bars and passages, changed chords, keys, and tempi, corrected Respighi's additions, and wrote notes to himself like, "Don't forget that all the chords must approximate stylistically the *old* Rossini of *Barber* [*of Seville*]"?

Boutique was one of several "pastiche" ballets produced in the years 1917 to 1920. Scholars have regarded *Pulcinella*, Igor Stravinsky's 1920 "remake" of music by eighteenth-century Italian composer Giovanni Pergolesi, as a turning point in musical modernism's rediscovery of the past. But from the 1917 dating of the *Boutique* manuscript, it seems that Diaghilev, rather than his protégé, spearheaded the move toward that intriguing blend of tradition and experiment which gave rise to the post-Armistice phenomenon of "period modernism."

Priced at $10,780 to $13,860, the *Boutique* manuscript did not sell. But many other examples of Diaghilev's musicianship did, including the Tchaikovsky score for the 1921 production of *The Sleeping Princess*. Of all the items in the sale, however, it was Diaghilev's music library that took one's breath away. A treasure-trove of over 800 items—printed music, manuscripts, books, programs, libretti, and pamphlets—this extraordinary collection dispels forever the notion of Diaghilev's being no more than a musical dilettante.

Here, annotated in Diaghilev's own hand, are the Russian operas he mounted in 1913–1914 that created such a furor in London: Mussorgsky's *Khovanchina* and *Boris Godunov*, Borodin's *Prince Igor*, Rimsky-Korsakov's *Nuit de Mai* and *Le Coq d'Or*. Here, too, are reams of items, including a manuscript thought to have been copied by Diaghilev himself, documenting the intensity of his researches during the wartime years of artistic transition, those compositions by Pergolesi, Paisiello, Cimarosa, and Scarlatti that became the basis of a half-dozen ballets. And, here, finally, are the marked-up scores of the French operas Diaghilev brought to the stage of Monte Carlo in 1924, often untouched by the youthful composers called in to prepare the versions for performance. For the first time, scholars can assess Diaghilev the musician.

Purchased by the Library of Congress for a relatively modest $80,800, Diaghilev's music library will find a good home in Washington. So, too, will a number of other fine items, including Diaghilev's 1926–1929 notebook, the first edition of the piano score of Serge Prokofiev's ballet *Chout,* and several chatty letters by the composer to his theatrical mentor that complement the library's Prokofiev holdings in the Vernon Duke Collection.

Like many of the letters sold at Sotheby's, these reveal the paternal streak warming Diaghilev's friendships with young artists. "How right you are," wrote twenty-year-old Francis Poulenc in a burst of candor, "to proscribe literature from the choreographic work; calling on great poets only proves the point. Braque, moreover, said to me the other day, 'Isn't it already too much to have three—choreographer, painter, and musician; if you have to add a writer, then all unity is suppressed.'" Not only youngsters benefited from Diaghilev's guidance. Senior composers like Erik Satie also sought his advice. "What shall I do with the Andantino?" he asked when his arrangement of *Le Medecin malgré lui* encountered a snag. "And how shall we deal with those flute and bassoon things? I'd like to see you about this. . . . That Scene VII troubles me a bit. Can you enlighten me?"

What would the socialist from the red-belt Paris suburb of Arcueil have thought of the stocky American millionaire who paid $2,464 for his note? This Harvard-educated collector, who prefers to remain anonymous, spent a small fortune at the sale, beginning with Lady Juliet Duff's scrapbooks, purchased as a gift for his alma mater. And with what booty he came away: letters by Debussy, Ravel, Falla, Satie, and Stravinsky, Debussy's manuscript of *Jeux*, Poulenc's *Les Biches,* Cocteau's *Parade,* and much more. With Harvard's friend and the Library of Congress accounting for well over half the sale's $1.1 million tally, Sotheby's, not surprisingly, has decided to hold one of its semiannual theatrical sales in New York.

One might have thought that the saga of Serge Lifar's collection ended with the hammer's final rap on May 9. Only two days after the sale, however, the *Quotidien de Paris* reported that Lifar was donating to the Paris Opéra yet another portion of his astonishing collection. Like an aging ecdysiast, Lifar expertly holds the limelight by shedding his treasures one by one, tantalizing the audience with the promise of assets still to be revealed.

TRACKING DOWN *LE TRAIN BLEU*

Time was when only eccentrics thought that ballets weren't butterflies and twentieth-century classics deserved a place in the repertoire. Today, for better or for worse, reviving those classics has become a growth industry. All around the country, "lost" works are reappearing: Vaslav Nijinsky's *Le Sacre du Printemps* (Joffrey Ballet), Léonide Massine's *Gaîté Parisienne* (American Ballet Theatre) and *Le Beau Danube* (Joffrey), Bronislava Nijinska's *Rondo Capriccioso* (Dance Theatre of Harlem) and *Le Train Bleu* (Oakland Ballet), Michel Fokine's *Paganini* (Tulsa Ballet Theatre), George Balanchine's *Mozart Violin Concerto* (Tulsa), uncut version of *Apollo* (Miami City Ballet), and *Cotillon* (Joffrey)—the list goes on and on. Clearly, a trend is underway.

Of course, resurrecting dances past isn't new. Petipa did it (his revivals kept *Giselle* and *La Fille Mal Gardée* alive long after they had vanished in France). Diaghilev did it (with *The Sleeping Princess*). Even Balanchine, who coined the butterfly metaphor, did it, with *Coppélia, Raymonda, The Nutcracker,* and *Swan Lake.* But today's revivalists view their task rather differently from yesterday's. Where Petipa and Balanchine felt free to cut, change, and add to the choreography, today the idea is to create a replica of the original, even when this means stripping away details that accrued during its performance life.

As an attitude toward the past, such historicism is new. Also new is the interest in works belonging to the twentieth-century repertoire. Apart from Ballet West's 1985 revival of Bournonville's *Abdullah* (and, in England, the Royal Ballet's new *Nutcracker* and *Swan Lake*), the past currently in vogue goes back no further than the Diaghilev period. As the twentieth century wanes, and one after another of its choreographic greats bites the dust, a run has started on the works of the Ballets Russes and its immediate successors.

The trend is welcome, because it adds to our knowledge of the past. But it is also troubling, because it rests on assumptions whose application to dance is problematic. One is the existence of a fixed original; a second, that this can be duplicated; a third, that accuracy alone is a guarantee of historical truth. Today, two contrasting definitions of authenticity seem to be abroad—one about the letter of the choreography, the other about its spirit.

It's the spirit that triumphs in Oakland Ballet's reconstruction of *Le Train Bleu,* the third of Bronislava Nijinska's works to enter the company's repertoire

This article was published in *Dance Magazine* in April 1990.

and the first restaging of the 1924 beach ballet since the choreographer revived it (as *A Orillas del Mar*) for the Teatro Colón in 1926. Artistic director Ronn Guidi doesn't claim the ballet is a carbon copy of the original. (The program credits the choreography as being "after Nijinska.") But as reconstructed by the choreographer's daughter Irina Nijinska and dance historian Frank W. D. Ries, this *Train Bleu*—if not identical to what audiences saw in Paris in 1924—is true to Nijinska and the spirit of the 1920s. Just as important, it works as theater.

The reasons for this are many, and they suggest what goes into a good reconstruction. One is documentation. Although never notated or filmed, *Le Train Bleu* left one of the fullest production records of any Diaghilev-era ballet. First, there were Jean Cocteau's librettos, four complete versions of them. The ballet was both a spoof of Riviera beach games and a loving send-up of music-hall styles; in the poet's detailed notes for the action, both are marvelously conveyed. Typical is the opening of the first scene (in my translation from the French):

> Tarts. Gigolos. Sunbathing. The gigolos run (in place) and do rapid physical gymnastics, while the tarts, in groups, assume the pretty poses of color postcards. What the ridiculous gestures as a whole have to convey is the illusion of an operetta chorus when the curtain rises.

Equally vivid is Cocteau's description of the opening of scene 5:

> The tarts and gigolos shake the cabanas and lock them with a key. The male swimmer and female swimmer get angry and raise their heads through the skylights. Dance around the cabanas. Stop. The whole band stands still and looks up. (Grimacing because of the sun.) A shadow covers the scene—an airplane. To follow it with their eyes, the tarts and gigolos arch backward and bump one another. (Here, everyone should put on sunglasses for a moment . . .)

Though Cocteau never describes the dances, he gives a full account of the ballet's mimetic action.

In her initial version of the choreography, Nijinska discarded much of this pantomime. Cocteau, who saw the ballet shortly before it opened in Paris, was incensed at what he regarded as a betrayal of his ideas. With Diaghilev's approval, he marched into the studio and ordered her to cut some of the dances and substitute pantomime scenes instead. At the dress rehearsal, all hell broke loose, and the ballet was further restaged. In the midst of this mayhem, Diaghilev, his assistant Boris Kochno, and régisseur Serge Grigoriev sat scribbling the last-minute changes on a copy of the score.

Amazingly, this score has survived—the closest thing to a choreographic record of the ballet. Not surprisingly, given the haste with which they were scribbled, the notes are in a cryptic shorthand: "TN," for instance, stands for "tennis racket," "BG" for "Beau Gosse" (a leading character), "dr" for "right," "cc" for "Charlie Chaplin." One of the most fascinating entries details a moment in the "sports duet" for Beau Gosse and the lady Tennis Champion, Nijinska's own role—"gl continuez de SB pd pois," which Ries translates as "glissade, continue to fish dive in *Sleeping Beauty*" (a reference to the now famous pirouette-cum-fish-dive sequence interpolated by Nijinska in the grand pas de deux of Diaghilev's 1921 production of the ballet). In *Le Train Bleu*, as in *Les Biches*, Nijinska parodied romantic love by exposing the conventions that Petipa had used to represent it.

In addition to recording choreographic changes, the score also contains notes about lighting. These are all in Diaghilev's hand—the others were written by Grigoriev and Kochno—and are rare documentary evidence of the interest he took in this aspect of production. The notes aren't technical: "brilliant," "last rays of sunset," "in silhouette." Mostly, they evoke an atmosphere, the changing tonalities of a Mediterranean afternoon.

Two other finds completed the ballet's documentary record: Nijinska's notes (far less complete than those for other ballets) and nearly thirty performance photographs taken during the London season. Together, the sources added up to a rich cache of material. But even with all this documentation, the specifics of the choreography remained hazy. Missing from the pictures and descriptions was the physical memory of movement, the thing that makes a reconstruction dance.

Although Bronislava Nijinska died in 1971, Ries managed to interview several survivors of the original production. With Anton Dolin, the original Beau Gosse, he pieced together most of the choreography for the ballet's star role—handstands, back flips, and other acrobatic stunts wittily juxtaposed with steps from the male bravura vocabulary. (Much to Ries's amazement, Dolin later altered the choreography when he staged some of the dances for Kevin Haigen in the early 1980s.) Lydia Sokolova, the original Perlouse, was also still around, and with "wonderful coquettishness," she mimed for Ries not just her own bathing belle role but Nijinska's, which she had understudied. Leon Woizikovsky, who had danced The Golfer, a pipe-smoking playboy modeled on Edward, Prince of Wales, was another of the ballet's four principals who added to Ries's stock of "physical" memories.

Reconstructing the ensemble choreography was more difficult. Few of the half-dozen corps dancers Ries interviewed remembered what they had danced, and the principals remembered only isolated sequences. Putting his imagination to work, Ries scoured the motion picture sources of the period for clues. He found them in Mack Sennett's famous Bathing Beauties and in newsreels of the Folies-Bergère. From movies, too, came some of the missing links in the principals' choreography. The wiggle Woizikovsky half remembered turned up in newsreels of the Prince of Wales. And in films of Marjorie Moss and Georges Fontana, the ballroom couple Cocteau had taken Nijinska to see in Monte Carlo, Ries found the Cranko-style toss Sokolova describes in her memoirs.

These borrowed connectives may or may not have appeared in the original choreography. What Ries claims, and Irina Nijinska seconds, is that they are true to the style of the original. This style, as critics of the time noted, was heavily indebted to the music hall, so much so that, to some, the identity of ballet itself was in jeopardy. ("To imitate is to abdicate!" was how André Levinson put it.) In other words, the popular entertainments that were source material for the reconstruction were also source material for the original.

Unlike *Les Noces* and *Les Biches*, where Nijinska had full charge of the choreography, *Le Train Bleu* is a work that only fitfully conveys her vision. An abstractionist, she held that movement rather than narrative was the source of dance meaning, and during her tenure with the Ballets Russes, she struggled, as she later wrote, to "negate . . . the literary libretto" and create "a pure dance form." In *Le Train Bleu*, however, she was paired with an artist who was not only a wordsmith but a master of the gestural commonplace, an artist who viewed movement not as an end in itself but as a form of wordless speech. Thus, throughout the ballet, the flow of the choreography is interrupted, stayed by mimetic "bits" that cut off phrases and emphasize their function as illustration. Ries didn't invent these "bits"; they were central to Cocteau's vision of the ballet. But, ultimately, I feel they weaken it, not because they're dull—far from it—but because they keep crowding out the dance. Cocteau may have fancied himself a choreographer, but as his contribution to *Le Train Bleu* makes clear, he used movement like a stage director.

Chic, witty, and up-to-date, *Le Train Bleu* was the quintessential flapper ballet. It remains so in Oakland's reconstruction. From Chanel's russet-and-wine swimsuits and Henri Laurens's cubist cabanas to the exaggerated posturings of the gigolos and professional beauties, everything has been restored with exemplary care. It's a care that's worn lightly, without curatorial reverence. And this, I think, is the key to the ballet's success; it's not a museum piece. Like the original, Oakland's *Train Bleu* belongs fully to the theater—to the artists past and present who created it and to the audiences now taking it to heart.

MASSINE

In the 1920s and 1930s, no choreographer was more celebrated than Léonide Massine. Born in Russia in 1895 and trained at the Bolshoi, he was "discovered" by Serge Diaghilev, who made him the star of his Ballets Russes and the choreographer of works such as *Parade* (1917) and *Pulcinella* (1920) that launched the vogue for modernist ballet. An international personality who later starred in the film *The Red Shoes,* Massine did the first American *Rite of Spring* (1930), with Martha Graham as the Chosen Maiden, and innumerable revues for showmen like C. B. Cochran and S. L. Rothafel. T. S. Eliot, who followed Massine's career on both the ballet and music-hall stage in the 1920s, called him "the greatest actor whom we have in London." By the 1930s, when Massine created his plotless "symphonic" ballets, he was widely regarded, in critic Edwin Denby's words, as "the master choreographer of today."

In the ensuing decades, Massine's reputation plummeted, especially in the United States. Although lip service continued to be paid to his historical importance, few of his ballets were actually performed. Since the late 1980s, however, interest in Massine has sharply risen. Two of his symphonic ballets—*Les Présages* in 1989 and *Choreartium* in 1991—have returned to repertory, prompting critics on both sides of the Atlantic to call for a reappraisal of his work. With the publication of Vicente García-Márquez's *Massine: A Biography,*[1] their call has been answered. The first critical reassessment of Massine's art, the book reconsiders his long and productive career, tracing its sources, weighing its accomplishments, and speculating on the reasons for its near total eclipse. With passion and authority, García-Márquez reclaims for Massine a central place in the history of twentieth-century dance.

To a degree unmatched by his contemporaries, Massine weaned ballet from its nineteenth-century past. Although the technical basis of his choreography remained the *danse d'école,* Massine's movement idiom was explicitly modern. Early critics spoke of its angularity, dynamism, intricate footwork, and sophisticated use of rhythm; later ones of its innumerable nuances of body movement. A single work might juxtapose character, classical, and "free" dance styles; others explored flamenco and vernacular forms such as jazz. His ensembles were intricate and often epic in scale, with groups disposed in vast contrapuntal masses that created the effect of an "action montage," one of several debts to

This essay, with a different title, was originally published in *The Nation* on 18 December 1995.

film. An admirer of modern art, he worked closely with Picasso, Matisse, Henri Masson, and Chagall, who respected him as an artistic equal. For García-Márquez, Massine was the leading architect and exponent of ballet modernism.

More controversially, García-Márquez sees Massine's symphonic works as defining "the 1930s aesthetic of pure dance as the essential element of ballet." This view challenges the usual idea that pure dance—or abstraction—emerged as a prevailing aesthetic in ballet only in the 1940s and that it was preeminently associated with neoclassicism, especially the works of George Balanchine. García-Márquez makes a good case for reconsidering this formulation, even if he goes too far in equating the plotlessness of the symphonic ballets and their suppression of mimetic elements with the abstraction that was the choreographer's stated goal.

Still, his argument is a salutary reminder that abstraction in ballet was not the invention of a single choreographer or in its earliest manifestations necessarily tied to an aesthetic of pure dance. Indeed, in pioneering works such as Vaslav Nijinsky's *Rite of Spring* (1913), Bronislava Nijinska's *Les Noces* (1923), and Fedor Lopukhov's *Dance Symphony* (1923), abstract elements were embedded in narrative, musical, or symbolic frameworks that contextualized the dance and gave it extra-choreographic meaning. Moreover, as Nijinsky's work revealed most dramatically, abstraction did not preclude the use of movement idioms other than ballet.

With their symbolic themes and allegorical characters, Massine's symphonic works were abstract to the extent that their philosophical connotations were absorbed into the shapes, groupings, and patterns of the choreography. With the exception of *Choreartium*, however, it was not Massine's intention to abjure such connotations, to make dances that were only about dance. In *Rouge et noir,* which premiered in 1939, "Massine summoned the anguish of the age," writes García-Márquez. He quotes the French critic Pierre Michaut, for whom the ballet's "abstraction hid . . . a political allegory: the dramatic crushing of helpless nations . . .—Abyssinia, Austria, Czechoslovakia. . . . Woman . . . who survives, symbolizes the spirit that prevails and cannot be defeated."

Like many European artists, Massine spent the Second World War in the United States. The period was a turning point in his career. Although he worked constantly, he produced nothing to compare with his best ballets of the 1930s. Moreover, as America's most celebrated dance émigré, he suffered the brunt of attacks by critics and others who viewed the presence of Russian stars as hindering the development of an indigenous American ballet. (Sol Hurok, who managed Ballet Theatre, operated on the not altogether mistaken belief that Russians sold tickets.) Nor did it help that Massine's ballets on American themes were noticeably weak.

Especially ferocious was the campaign waged against Massine by Lincoln Kirstein, who dismissed his work as kitsch. "Massine," wrote Kirstein, "has a right to embellish the old music-masters, but it is scarcely a creative act when he does so. It is, pure and simple, an inferior art, the art of illustration." Denby added mockery to the criticism: "If one took [Massine] seriously, he would be guilty of murdering the Beethoven Seventh, the Scarlatti, and even tender little Offenbach. . . . There is of course no reason for taking Massine seriously; he doesn't mean to murder." By the 1960s, when Massine's ballets had virtually ceased to be performed, such barbs were all that remained to define him for a new generation.

The shift in postwar taste toward classical and neoclassical styles only partly explains why Massine's works disappeared so quickly and completely from view. More important was the demise of the so-called "international" companies—touring ensembles descended from Diaghilev's original Ballets Russes and identified with the children of the White Russian diaspora—that had witnessed the creation of his greatest ballets. Once these companies vanished, Massine's works—major as well as minor—ceased to have an outlet, while the performing tradition associated with them died. By the 1960s, few dancers could do justice to his ballets on the rare occasions when they were revived.

García-Márquez met Massine in 1978, a year before his death. Like so many others, he fell under the spell of Massine's penetrating gaze and aloof, commanding presence. Yet even after spending weeks with Massine at his island retreat in Italy, the author found the inner man impenetrable, masked by the impersonality that compelled admiration of him as an artist but also chilled his relationships as a man. "Any question," he writes, that hinted at a personal dimension, or might call for a personal opinion . . . was simply disregarded."

This diffidence, the author suggests, had its origins in Diaghilev's "aggressive fusion of . . . brilliance with sinister deviousness." Diaghilev certainly fostered Massine's gifts as a choreographer, but he did so less from altruism than a desire for his own self-fulfillment. In artistic matters, Diaghilev exacted absolute loyalty; privately, he demanded total subservience, sealing his power with sexual conquest. Massine responded with the diffidence that became an armature; he also, as it turned out, preferred women to men. In his marriages (there were four of them) and untold dalliances, he recapitulated the dynamics of his relationship with Diaghilev, treating women as instruments of pleasure so long as they remained compliant and accommodated themselves to his personal and professional needs.

The author deals tactfully with this aspect of Massine's life, although he is clearly troubled by Massine's self-centered behavior, which amounted at times to extreme cruelty. Indeed, it is hard to imagine how anyone less detached than Massine could have spent months on the road living in a trailer with both his mistress and his wife—as the choreographer did in the 1930s while touring the United States. Even in the ballet world, where unconventional relationships have long been tolerated, this celebrity ménage à trois has become something of a legend.

For all his qualms about the private man, the author never questions Massine's towering stature as an artist. Like most choreographers, Massine had his share of failures. However, he also created works that perceptibly altered the shape of his art. Thanks to García-Márquez (who died two years ago, just after completing the manuscript of this book), Massine's central place in twentieth-century ballet is assured.

NOTES

1. Vicente García-Márquez, *Massine: A Biography* (New York: Knopf, 1995).

HETERODOXICAL PASTS

Since the ascendancy of Mikhail Baryshnikov, American Ballet Theatre has mostly eschewed the genre of character ballets. Once, these formed a cornerstone of the company's identity, a model for choreographers intent on making ballet a contemporary, American art. It wasn't classicism they were after, although from Agnes de Mille to Jerome Robbins they gave their allegiance to the *danse d'école*. What they wanted to reinvent was a secessionist tradition that had its origin in Diaghilev's Ballets Russes. This tradition—of one-act works rich in drama and historical texture—was Michel Fokine's legacy to the West. His successor, Léonide Massine, often gave it a comic flavor—characters as broad as cartoons and situations bordering on farce. If American ballet choreographers of the interwar years had a model, it wasn't Petipa, whom they barely knew, but these two Diaghilev "stars," whose works filled the repertories of the era's great touring companies.

Baryshnikov has never taken to this Western phenomenon. His native roots lie in classicism, his adopted ones, in neoclassicism. Although Fokine and Massine were Russian-born, both spent the interwar decades in the West, and their ballets, with the exception of Fokine's *Les Sylphides,* never became a part of Russia's living dance memory. Baryshnikov has refurbished ABT's repertory with what he knows best: Petipa's classics and Balanchine's "neoclassics," in addition to works by several postmoderns. He has paid homage to Antony Tudor, although none of the revivals, including the most recent staging of *Pillar of Fire,* has been fully convincing. But he has steered clear of the other choreographers associated with the company in the 1940s. Thus, his decision last season to revive Massine's *Gaîté Parisienne* and Tudor's *Gala Performance* and to produce Agnes de Mille's *The Informer* represents a sea change of sorts, a long-overdue acknowledgement of the heterodoxical tradition that nurtured ABT, and American ballet generally in the 1930s and 1940s.

Newly dressed by couturier Christian Lacroix and redesigned by Zack Brown, *Gaîté Parisienne* created the season's biggest splash at the Metropolitan Opera House. The ballet itself is one of Massine's lesser efforts, a rehash of themes from *La Boutique Fantasque* and *Le Beau Danube. Gaîté* takes place in a frou-frou wonderland, a Second Empire café done up in bordello plush and funky gilt with a postcard-pretty Eiffel Tower in the distance. We're in gay Paree

This essay was originally published in *Ballet Review,* 16, no. 3 (Fall 1988).

in the good old days, when men were men and girls were girls and everyone was naughty to Offenbach. The composer's melodies from *La Vie Parisienne, Barbe-Bleue,* and *La Belle Hélène* accompany the hanky-panky: a Flower-Girl who's after a Peruvian who's after a Glove-Seller who's after a Baron (these two finally get together), as well as "cocodettes" and can-can girls, dukes, dandies, and soldiers who're after everyone else. *Gaîté* is chock-full of the naughtiness Omaha and Wolverhampton used to imagine happened in Paris.

Like a cartoonist, Massine draws his characters with broad strokes. Maids scrub; waiters whisk the tables with napkins; La Lionne struts; the Peruvian dashes like a hotspur; the Baron inclines with dignified ardor over the hand of the Glove-Seller. There's no drama or development here, only types as familiar as the stock characters of the commedia. Yet with the right dancers, these types can take on flesh and blood, becoming actors of a human comedy. For Massine's dancers, characterization was a two-way exchange in which they detailed and polished what he sketched.

Revivals seldom duplicate this imaginative collaboration, and ABT's *Gaîté,* staged by the choreographer's son Lorca, is no exception. Not that the production is lifeless: there's too much bustle for that. But it doesn't get at the heart of the ballet—its innocence, which keeps the sex from getting dirty, and its romance, which appears transfigured by classicism. Overloaded with saucy smiles and postures so exaggerated they border on the grotesque, this *Gaîté* goes for belly laughs.

In the various casts, not all the dancers succumbed to the prevailing vulgarity. Some managed to keep their manners, to say nothing of their individuality, which they stamped persuasively on their characters. As the Flower-Girl, Amy Rose bubbled with the joie de vivre she brings to all her roles. Massine's Flower-Girl is a minx, but Rose makes her lovable, good-humored even when the chips are down, as carefree as a butterfly when they're not—a whore with the proverbial heart of gold. Jennet Zerbe is another of the company's young individualists, and she, too, found the substance in a role others merely skimmed. Her La Lionne is more than a knock-'em-dead beauty. Elegant, with a playful smile on her lips, she's a fascinating femme du monde, one of those women who ruined hearts and had fortunes squandered on them: Zerbe makes us understand why. But the performance that really brought this *Gaîté* to life was Julio Bocca's Peruvian. This was the part Massine created for himself, and it is full of the eccentric movement and comic detailing that he excelled at. Yet so completely has Bocca reimagined the role that you forget about Massine entirely. This is a Peruvian tickled pink to be in Paris, who's rushed straight from the station, without even dropping off his suitcase, gunning for a night on the town. He's a masher, of course, and makes love to all the girls. But he goes about it with such shameless gusto that you forgive him; he's an innocent abroad, sowing his wild oats. Bocca is a classicist, yet he makes the eccentricities of Massine's choreography—

the snakey legs, commedia jumps—seem completely natural, the speech of a happy-go-lucky Latin.

For people who saw *Gaîté* in the 1940s, Alexandra Danilova's Glove-Seller was unforgettable. Her waltz with the Baron was the ballet's high point, a classical gem that shone over the *demi-caractère* dances that surrounded it. The choreography itself is unremarkable, although in its frankness and the simplicity of its means—turns, arabesques, sailing lifts—it seems a nosegay of romance. Danilova always danced this choreography straight. That is, she left off being a soubrette and became the purest of dancers, letting the line of her arabesques and the harmony of her lifts do the talking. Neither Susan Jaffe nor Cheryl Yeager, the season's Glove-Sellers, managed this transformation. Both remained what they had been throughout—knowing, coquettish Parisians. Lacroix, alone, seems to have gotten the point. Of all his costumes for the women, only the Glove-Seller's is free of exaggerated frippery.

The waltz is the ballet's only intimate moment as well as its only quiet one. André Levinson once described Massine's choreography as a perpetuum mobile. In *Gaîté*, the stage is packed with action: brawls and polkas, marches and can-cans—as fast-paced as a Broadway show. At almost every point, a half-dozen activities go on simultaneously. While the men brawl, the women bustle in the background; while the women circle, the men doodle about inside. The can-can that brings the ballet to its rip-roaring climax is nonstop busyness, with twirling rockettes and swaying spectators who clap in time to the music. As in Cunningham's dances, the activity has no focal point. But where Cunningham uses simultaneity to reeducate the eye, Massine employs it to create pseudo-events that camouflage the thinness of the choreography. Steps are few—piqué turns, the odd developpé, some balances. An idea is presented, then reiterated, but almost never elaborated or developed. The phrase itself has no internal shading, no little dramas packed into the interplay of movement and music. Massine just follows the oom-pah-pah of Offenbach's charming banalities.

When *Gaîté* had its premiere in 1938, it reunited Massine and Comte Etienne de Beaumont in an attempt to repeat the success of their *Le Beau Danube*, another naughty ballet set in the 1860s. Beaumont's designs for *Beau Danube*, like his sets and costumes for *Gaîté*, lovingly recreated the past. ABT threw out Beaumont's designs, and in step with the times, went postmodern. Zack Brown's decor is as delectable as fancy gift wrapping, and with its polka dot bows and bright red curtains, recalls the past without attending to the niceties of period style (the Eiffel Tower he centers on the backdrop is an anachronistic joke, presumably). Christian Lacroix forgets about the past entirely, turning the stage into a marzipan fantasy, as up-to-date as the fashions of ABT's gala first-night *Gaîté* audience at the Met. As he did with the clothes that he showed at his Paris collection last spring, he makes the women of the ballet into little girls, with short bouncey skirts, and bows, flounces, doilies, and rosettes that are as fanciful as the frills of a party dress. His palette runs the gamut of ice cream colors: raspberry reds, pistachio greens, lemon yellows, plum purples, licorice blacks, strawberry pinks. And the way he combines them—black-and-white polka dot stockings under yellow-and-black striped skirts over red-and-white polka dot blouses. His can-can dancers are a seven-year-old's Halloween dream.

Lacroix's designs are a fantasy on a theme of the past. But they are also deeply erotic, at least when it comes to women. Again and again, he plays peekaboo with their privates. When the can-can girls hoist their legs aloft, we see a frilly triangle surrounded by pink thigh. The cocodettes show us their frilly bottoms, while nearly all the girls have knees as fetichized as those of Eric Rohmer's heroine; only a Frenchman would dress his Lolitas in knee socks. Even La Lionne has her skirt hoisted up in front, a touch as wanton as the déshabille of a grande horizontale. The effect isn't naughty in the old-fashioned way. The girls aren't grown-up, and the expectations they arouse aren't ones you satisfy in a corner bistro. What Lacroix has done—brilliantly—is update the naughtiness. Instead of sex, he's given us some very classy kiddie porn.

The success of Lacroix's fashion statement notwithstanding, *Gaîté* raises a larger question. Why was this ballet produced? It's hardly Massine's best, even among his comic works, and in choreographic invention, it pales beside *La Boutique Fantasque*, which he created for Diaghilev in 1919. *Boutique*, moreover, had real importance. With designs by André Derain, music by Rossini, and a book taken from *Die Puppenfee*, *Boutique* reinvented the period ballet as sophisticated modernist entertainment. Shuttling in style between past and present, the work did what ABT's *Gaîté* only pretends to do: modernize a hackneyed period piece. It did so, moreover, without recourse to fashion, that false friend that can make this year's hit dress look passé six months later. (Lacroix's fall collection, for instance, has exchanged the *Gaîté* flamboyance of his previous one for simpler effects.) But even *Boutique* isn't the ballet ABT should have revived. Massine's stature as a choreographer ultimately rests on the symphonic ballets he created in the 1930s, such works as *Les Présages, Choreartium, Symphonie Fantastique,* and *Nobilissima Visione* (also known as *St. Francis*) that have gone out of repertory, although films exist and the dancers who could restage them are alive and well. But perhaps this is asking too much of ABT. Claims of history rarely triumph over those of the box office, and in reviving *Gaîté* ABT probably intended nothing more ambitious than bringing suburbanites and CEOs to the theater. If this is the case, the decision paid off; financially, ABT had its best New York season ever, and in the reshuffling of programs during the course of the season the number of *Gaîté*s was doubled.

The other major revival was Antony Tudor's 1938 *Gala Performance*, a welcome addition to the roster of works by the company's choreographer emeritus. A piece of charming foolery set principally to Prokofiev's "Classical" Symphony, the ballet is a minor work. But it discloses a facet of Tudor's personality very different from the poet of memory and psychological nuance we know from

Lilac Garden and *Pillar of Fire.* In *Gala Performance,* we meet Tudor, the ballet parodist, a gentle spoofer of classical conventions, styles, and personalities. The period is Edwardian; the setting, the stage of a frumpy theater (Hugh Stevenson designed the original production); the protagonists—to give the ballerinas of this production their original names—La Reine de la Danse (from Moscow), Le Déesse de la Danse (from Milan), and La Fille de Terpsichore (from Paris). The ballet opens showing the corps and the divas preparing backstage behind a closed curtain where coryphées and divas make last-minute preparations for a performance; then the scene shifts to the performance itself—a trio of solos where the divas perform their tricks. The fun ends as the rivals take their calls. Tudor has said that he became a ballet choreographer because of the pointe shoe. In *Gala Performance,* he confesses his delight at just about everything else to do with ballet, from its backstage rituals to its most hackneyed costumes and steps—the banality behind the magic.

As always with Tudor, the choreography is rich in dramatic detail. In quick strokes, he sums up each of his divas: the flamboyant Muscovite, in red, practicing her bows; the imperious Milanese, in midnight blue, slapping her dresser when the mirror drops; the coquettish Parisienne, in pink, fluffing her tarlatan. The coryphées are little gems. Adjusting a hairpin or straightening a bodice, they're as shabby and bored as Degas' petits rats. In the first scene, they do most of the dancing, a last-minute warm-up of échappés, tendus, pirouettes, and frappés made over by Tudor into a poem of the everyday. In the second scene, setting up each diva's solo, they are utterly winning. All pretty arms and mincing pointes, they troop the stage in foursomes that are a triumph of inspired silliness.

For each of his divas, Tudor has choreographed a parody of the major classical styles. The Russian turns and turns and turns, from preparations that go on forever and with eyes that never leave the audience—a mockery of de Basil's spinning teens. The Italian, despite a birdcage and feather duster on her head, is never less than stately. Her entrance for her solo takes at least a minute, and when she starts to dance, after a nod to the conductor, she minds—and mocks—her Blasis style: faultless balances, waist-high arabesques, low attitudes, arms strictly en couronne. The French ballerina is as bubbly as champagne, a soubrette who blows kisses to the audience between dainty pas de chats.

Of the performances seen in the various casts, only Alessandra Ferri's fluffy, joyous Parisienne seemed fully in tune with the choreography. Mostly, this was because she played things straight, without exaggeration, as if she had leap-frogged over time to the Met. The role itself, however, is the easiest of the diva parts to get a handle on. In the Russian ballerina's solo, there are a number of disconcerting moments: the way the body lurches over the arms in pirouettes, the way fingers trail the ground in bows—touches that vulgarize the spoof. How much of this is Tudor's doing is hard to say. Cyril W. Beaumont, for one, could not make up his mind whether the original was "intended to be serious or to be a burlesque," and concluded that the ballet teetered dangerously be-tween the two.[1] The ABT production was staged by Sallie Wilson. But even with this sensitive Tudor interpreter at the helm, the Russian ballerinas overplayed the comedy, Leslie Browne to the point of caricature. Even more perplexing in this production is the Italian ballerina. Maude Lloyd, who first danced the role, has described the character as grand and "rather elderly." "She moved very slowly as if she might plop if she moved too fast."[2] As danced by Susan Jaffe, however, she seems as cold and rigid as a corpse.

The Informer, by Agnes de Mille, isn't a revival. But it could be. A folk drama set in rural Ireland during the "time of troubles," the work—like *Rodeo* or the "dream ballet" in *Oklahoma!*—stands as a reminder of Fokine's pervasive in-fluence on American choreographers of the 1940s. With its Celtic songs and Irish dance forms, expressive crowds and movements used as mimetic speech, *The Informer* is a textbook illustration of the famous "principles" set down by Fokine in 1914.

De Mille plots her story with economy. The first scene introduces the pro-tagonists: a happy-go-lucky Girl, the cocky Young Fighter who loves her, and the jealous Wounded Veteran who turns his rival in. De Mille sketches them handily. The Girl does a sprightly clog dance; the Young Fighter tosses her a rose from behind his ear; the Wounded Veteran skulks in the shadows. The scenes that follow evoke the drama's larger world, a community as tight-knit and in-tolerant as a peasant clan. The beauty of these episodes lies in the ensembles—their bold shapes and big designs, as simple as those of a folk dance, yet always animated. In Scene 5, the women grieve, hunched over with the solidity of primitive wood carvings, while the Girl circles, punching the air in gestures as poignant as screams. There are several intimate moments, and like the group episodes they achieve their effect through simple, purely dance means. In what turns out to be their farewell duet, the Girl and the Young Warrior exchange sweet-nothings by the call and response of their tapping feet, while in her duet with the Wounded Veteran, the guilt of betrayal weights their lifts with somber gravity.

In many respects, *The Informer* is old-fashioned. It's high-minded, as dances now rarely are, and it has a political edge, as if de Mille were talking not just about yesterday's "troubles," but those of Ireland today. But it's also old-fashioned in another way: de Mille's masterful control of her medium. This, ultimately, is what makes the ballet refreshing and, at moments, compelling. At a time when few choreographers can put together a convincing narrative, move masses around the stage effectively, or come up with an imaginative pas de deux, she demonstrates how much skill counts for in a dance work.

The ballets of the interwar years went out of vogue with the triumph of Bal-anchine's neoclassicism. But not all these works deserve to be lost. Many were good, not great perhaps, but good enough on their own terms to deserve a place in the repertory. In this country, moreover, they played a critical role in the

Americanizing of ballet, providing the models imitated by virtually all our home-grown choreographers, including those who later went down other paths. Reviving ballets isn't easy, and it certainly isn't cheap. Choices have to be made. All the more reason, then, to separate the wheat from the chaff, to come up with works that are worthy in their own right and representative in terms of the past. What companies like ABT sometimes forget is that nothing less than ballet's living history rides on their choices.

NOTES

1. Cyril W. Beaumont, *Supplement to Complete Book of Ballets* (London: Putnam, 1942), p. 129.
2. Maude Lloyd, "The Psychological Space of Antony Tudor," panel discussion at the Dance Critics Association conference, New York, 18 June 1988.

TIME-TRAVELING WITH THE KIROV

In 1999, the Kirov Ballet greeted the new millennium by reviving *The Sleeping Beauty. Beauty* was a very old ballet. It had come into the world in 1890, when the Kirov was called the Imperial Ballet and St. Petersburg, its home, was still the capital of tsarist Russia. It never went out of repertory. To be sure, by the 1990s the ballet didn't look the way it had in 1890 or even the 1950s. Much of the human padding had disappeared—the scores of dancers, "supers," and children that made nineteenth-century ballet a forerunner of Cecil B. De Mille's colossal spectacles. The sets and costumes were different. Scenes had been cut, dances dropped or significantly altered, and nearly all the mime eliminated. And, with every generation, the style of the dancing and the bodies of the dancers had changed.

The goal of the new *Sleeping Beauty* was to go back to the original, to rub away the tarnish of a century to reveal the gold of choreographer Marius Petipa's greatest work. The original costume designs, by the director of the Imperial Theaters, Prince Ivan Vsevolozhsky, were unearthed in the St. Petersburg Theater Museum, along with the original set designs. Tchaikovsky's original score existed, and, amazingly, a set of notations that recorded much of the choreography. These notations, which had ended up at the Harvard Theatre Collection, made the reconstruction possible.

This summer, the Kirov returned to New York's Metropolitan Opera House with another "archaized" classic, *La Bayadère.* Choreographed by Petipa in 1877, revived by him in 1900, and notated shortly thereafter, *La Bayadère* has never enjoyed the popularity of the Tchaikovsky trio—*Swan Lake, The Sleeping Beauty, and The Nutcracker.* In part this is due to its lackluster score, by Ludwig Minkus, a Viennese-born "specialist" composer who spent years in Russia and wrote the music for numerous ballets. The sets and costumes were equally old-fashioned, the work of in-house artisans rather than easel painters or professional designers. There were seven decors, by four master craftsmen in the employ of the Imperial Theaters, representing a pictorial tradition that stretched back to the baroque theater of the seventeenth century. The accent was on sumptuousness—a rajah's palace set in a splendid tropical park, huge gilt idols, porticoed temples, a Himalyan mountainscape, stuffed tigers, rich costumes, a bejeweled

This essay was originally published in *The Chronicle of Higher Education* on 11 October 2002, with the title "A Romanov Veneer at the Kirov."

398

elephant on wheels—rather than on visual unity, harmony, or taste. By 1900, an incipient design revolution was underway in Russia, yet no sign of it appeared in *La Bayadère*.

A ballet in four acts and seven scenes with apotheosis, *La Bayadère* was a compendium of late nineteenth-century choreographic practices. There were dramatic scenes based largely on pantomime, such as the encounter of the two lead women in Act II, when Nikiya almost stabs her rival with a knife. There were processionals when masses of dancers converged on the stage making it teem with humanity in the great human pageant that made nineteenth-century spectacle ballet so popular not only in Europe but also in America. There were character dances, performed in heeled slippers, and classical ones, performed in pointe shoes. There were innumerable divertissements, including "Indian dances" that had nothing to do with India but featured lines of women with fans and parrots, as well as slave girls, demons, and diminutive "blackamoors"—actually children in dark body make-up—in set pieces that could easily have found a place in the era's better music halls.

The libretto, written by Petipa and Sergei Khudekov in 1877, was also rooted in its time. Set in faraway India, the ballet relates the tragic story of the *bayadère*, or temple dancer, Nikiya and her doomed love for Solor, a prince who abandons her to marry the Rajah's daughter, Gamzatti. Jealous of her rival, Gamzatti orders Nikiya killed. But Nikiya reappears to Solor in a dream, in the scene known as the "Kingdom of the Shades." The ballet ends with the destruction of the temple as Solor and Gamzatti are about to wed.

"I am amazing," Petipa wrote in his diary in 1904. He was then eighty-six, with a seemingly undiminished appetite to choreograph. One senses that appetite in the profusion of classical dances in *La Bayadère*, especially in the variations that were Petipa's special pride and that he whipped up at the drop of a hat. Variations were showpieces, capsule distillations of virtuoso technique that showed off whatever the dancer was best at—turns, balances, big jumps, small jumps, hops on pointe. They had nothing to do with the plot and everything to do with applause. Because they were irrelevant to the narrative, they were frequently shuffled, replaced, removed, or updated. Gamzatti's fouetté turns, for instance, were added after the 1877 original, as it was only in the 1890s that Russian ballerinas began to perform them. Mathilde Kchessinska, the 1900 Nikiya, "owned" her last-act variation, which meant that no other ballerina was allowed to dance it. Olga Preobrajenska, who played Gamzatti, and Nikolai Legat, who replaced the fifty-six-year-old Pavel Gerdt as Solor in the *pas d'action*, had the right to choose their own variations. The absence of choreographic integrity was mirrored in the musical text. On every count but one, *La Bayadère* epitomized what critics soon would be calling, disparagingly, the "old ballet."

That exception was the "Kingdom of the Shades." Here was Petipa's vision of classical heaven—forty-eight moonlit women in white (thirty-two in the version the Kirov brought to New York) entering one by one on a ramp and winding forward, all the while performing a simple arabesque phrase with the slowness and deliberateness of ritual. They are the ghosts of Nikiya conjured up by Solor's fevered imagination (he has been smoking opium to allay his feelings of guilt), a vision of enchanted sisterhood and ethereal femininity. Eventually, Nikiya herself appears—in white like the others, all-forgiving, all-loving, beyond desire, tragedy, and time. The "Shades" is perhaps the greatest of nineteenth-century *ballets blancs*—the "white" acts born with Romanticism when the hero glimpsed his unattainable love among white or pastel-skirted sylphs, wilis, naiads, and other night creatures. Unlike the *pas d'action*, which advanced the narrative, the *ballet blanc* stood outside the story; it was a pure dance sequence, one, moreover, in a single idiom from beginning to end. In this respect, it was a forerunner of the plotless dances associated with twentieth-century choreographers such as Bronislava Nijinska and, especially, George Balanchine. Indeed, in his 1942 *Concierto de Mozart* for the Teatro Colón, Balanchine quietly "borrowed" the opening signature phrase of the "Kingdom of the Shades."

The disjunction between the seemingly timeless Shades and the rest of *La Bayadère* helps to explain the ballet's checkered history. In the choreographic secession that culminated in Diaghilev's Ballets Russes, a company that only performed in the West, the emphasis was on works identified with Russia's "new ballet" rather than the "old ballet" exemplified by Petipa. Diaghilev did not wholly ignore the nineteenth-century repertory. Between 1909 and 1929, the company danced *Giselle, Swan Lake,* and *The Sleeping Beauty* as well as fragments of *The Nutcracker* and *Raymonda.* But except for a sole—uncredited— "Shades" scene staged in Paris in 1926 by Nicholas Sergeyev, *La Bayadère* failed to establish a niche in the Western repertory. Later in the 1930s, Sergeyev, the veteran Maryinsky rehearsal director who had left the Soviet Union in 1918 with the notated scores of twenty-four ballets and the dances of twenty-four operas, staged *Giselle, Swan Lake, Coppélia, The Nutcracker,* and *The Sleeping Beauty* for Sadler's Wells, but not *La Bayadère,* which was perceived as too old-fashioned to be a "classic."

Thus, when the Kirov brought the "Shades" to London and New York in 1961, it was hailed not only as a masterpiece but also as a major addition to the nineteenth-century repertory. Two years later, Rudolf Nureyev, who had defected on that 1961 tour, staged the "Shades" scene for Britain's Royal Ballet, the first Western company to dance it. In 1974, another Kirov defector, Natalia Makarova, staged it for the American Ballet Theatre. Belatedly, the scene became part of the Western classical tradition.

Meanwhile, back in St. Petersburg, which became Petrograd at the start of World War I and Leningrad in 1924, the ballet continued to be danced throughout the 1920s. But the tinkering had already started. In 1919, Act IV was deleted because of the scarcity of stagehands; in 1926, when Marina Semyonova made her debut as Nikiya, the mime was trimmed, especially in Act I. Finally, in 1941,

Vladimir Ponomarev and Vakhtang Chabukiani assembled the ballet's definitive "modern" text. In this version, too, the ballet ended with the "Shades," while most of the Act IV *pas d'action* was now transferred to Act II. The already abbreviated mime scenes were slashed, and the costumes reinterpreted to bare a little more flesh. Solor's role was significantly beefed up, and in 1948, the Golden Idol was turned into a virtuoso part.

This version, with the addition of a newly choreographed fourth act, formed the basis for Makarova's production of the full ballet in 1980 for ABT and Nureyev's in 1992 for the Paris Opéra. In both instances, the ballet was redesigned. ABT's production, by PierLuigi Samaritani, was especially handsome, combining visual harmony and decorative splendor within a traditional illusionist framework. It was a far cry from the Victorian dowdiness—however opulent—of Petipa's stage.

Given the shortcomings of the 1900 *Bayadère*, why bring it back? In a panel sponsored by the Lincoln Center Festival, the Kirov company's artistic director, Makharbeck Vaziev, linked the production, like the old-new *Sleeping Beauty*, to a widespread cultural impulse to excavate and reconstruct the past, to restore familiar works to the pristine state of an original. "This is our theater, our culture," he told the audience. Returning to the source, like cleaning an old master, can often be a good thing. The Kirov's *Don Quixote*, based on Alexander Gorsky's 1900 revision of the 1869 Petipa original, sparkled in its refurbished sets and costumes by Alexander Golovin and Konstantin Korovin, easel painters in the forefront of the new movement in scenic design whose work Petipa dismissed in his memoirs as "decadent." Gorsky's vibrant crowd scenes, bustling with life and impressionist patches of color, did away with Petipa's carefully arranged lines and symmetrical groups, revealing the influence of Stanislavsky and the Moscow Art Theater. Yet the production retained what must be the oldest of Petipa's dream scenes, older even than the "Shades," judging from the simplicity of the step vocabulary for the corps of dryads, among whom the Don sights his now transformed Dulcinea. Unlike Petipa's remake of *La Bayadère*, Gorsky's revisions of *Don Quixote* not only modernized the ballet but also strengthened it dramatically.

Kirov history did not stop in 1900, as its current repertory, with a few notable exceptions, might suggest. There are any number of works from the early decades of the twentieth century that I would love to see performed—ballets by Nicolas and Sergei Legat, Michel Fokine, and above all Fedor Lopukhov, whose plotless 1923 *Dance Symphony: The Magnificence of the Universe,* set to Beethoven's Fourth and with a young George Balanchine in the cast, was a modernist landmark. In varying degrees, these choreographers broke with the conventions of nineteenth-century "grand ballet." But apart from ill-conceived revivals of Fokine's *Schéhérazade* and *Firebird* (created for the Ballets Russes, not the Imperial Ballet) and the staging of several Balanchine works, efforts to reclaim the company's revisionist legacies are rare. Even the Kirov's Balanchine repertory has a traditional bent, underscoring the choreographer's debt to Petipa rather than his experimentalism. The fact is that the Kirov has chosen to restore only works created or refurbished prior to 1910, as if the experimentalist impulse itself were politically suspect, and modernism discredited by its association with the Russian Revolution, which many artists initially supported. However worthy the Kirov's desire to reconnect with a suppressed history, its view of this history is definitely limited. Despite the mantra of needing new repertory, the Kirov seems far happier with works like *The Sleeping Beauty* or *La Bayadère*, entertainments par excellence of the Romanovs.

Under Valery Gergiev's artistic direction, the Kirov has pursued a similar policy of sprucing up nineteenth-century Russian operas by removing their Soviet patina. Because of the existence of written texts, this is less problematic in opera than in ballet. Moreover, while most Petipa ballets continued to be danced in their original sets and costumes right up to and even after the Revolution, many operas, especially those of the Russian repertory, were designed or redesigned in the early twentieth century by Golovin and other innovative scenic artists. Some, including *Boris Godunov*, were reconceived by directors such as Meyerhold. This means that opera productions regarded today as "traditional" may well date no further back than the 1900s or 1910s.

Petersburgers always considered their city different from other Russian urban centers—more cosmopolitan, European, aristocratic—however shabby and provincial it might appear to outsiders. In their hearts they never called it Leningrad, just as the Kirov Theater was always the Maryinsky. Today, more than ever, the city flaunts its Romanov legacy—the palaces, art collections, and cultural institutions built, like the city itself, by Peter the Great and his Imperial heirs. From the start, ballet in Russia was bound up with the state. In the old days, the money came from the tsar, and many early dancers were serfs. After the Revolution, the government continued to pay the bills, and ever since the Cold War the company has been a player in the game of international politics. Initially, it toured for communism. Now it tours for free enterprise and to earn its keep. It has friends in high places, and raises money abroad through a network of trusts, foundations, and Friends of the Maryinsky Theater, which has branches in Europe and the United States. A major donor is Alberto Vilar, the Cuban-born millionaire opera and ballet philanthropist. For the city's three hundredth anniversary in 2003, the Maryinsky is planning not only a ballet festival in St. Petersburg and a "unique gala concert" at Tsarskoe Selo (where the tsar had his summer residence) but also a "magnificent ball" in the throne room of Catherine the Great's palace. Obviously, the notion of aristocracy extends to more than what takes place onstage.

Hence the importance of sprucing up the Kirov's bread-and-butter repertory. By refurbishing its *Beautys* and *Bayadères*, the company is transforming them into objects that can be marketed as novelties, but without the risk of staging something new. And by giving these ersatz novelties a Romanov veneer, the company confers on them an aura of social privilege that dovetails both with marketing strategies abroad and the elite tourism that top-of-the-line Petersburg restaurants and hotels are pursuing at home. Before 1917, the Imperial Ballet was insulated from the demands of the market because the tsar paid for everything. Now the idea of tsarist privilege is being used to promote ballets whose artistic validity and box office justification are questionable. Time traveling is not an artistically disinterested phenomenon, not solely a means to reconnect with the past, but also a marketing strategy, with only a limited number of buyers and only a finite number of old masters left to restore.

MYTH OR MEMORY?

SOLOMON VOLKOV'S *PETERSBURG*

No city holds quite the sway over the balletomane imagination as St. Peters-burg. We speak of its Maryinsky Theater as the temple of classicism, although ballet was neither invented there nor confined to its stage. In fact, like the city itself, the Maryinsky—and the image of classicism that it invokes—is the stuff of myth, a lost paradise of art shrouded by time and eternalized by memory, human and often unreliable.

Solomon Volkov's *St. Petersburg: A Cultural History*,[1] which traces the city's history from the time of Peter the Great to the so-called era of stagnation under Brezhnev, reinforces this myth, claiming for St. Petersburg a place in the history of arts and letters that many Westerners will find exaggerated. Indeed, Volkov, a Petersburger by birth, exemplifies the obsession with the "mythos" (his word) cultivated by poets, writers, philosophers, and historians almost from the moment the city rose from the swamps of the Gulf of Finland.

As defined by Volkov, this "mythos" manages to encompass just about every-thing identifying St. Petersburg with the privileged realm of high art. The clas-sical facades of the city's palaces, the statues dominating its public squares, the canals weaving through the city like a recollection of Venice announced from the start Petersburg's special status as an elite outpost of the West. At the same time, what the author calls the Petersburg "text"—the literary works, paintings and drawings, music, and theatrical productions created in and about the city—confirmed its "special place on Russian soil and in Russian history" (xiii). A sense of impending cataclysm and "searing" nostalgia (xv) for Peter's lost par-adise added a tragic dimension to the mythology in the final decades of tsarist rule, when the city became a major industrial center.

The twentieth century saw these "premonitions" of cataclysm and loss become a reality. The city, writes Volkov, was "ravaged by terror and hunger, underwent three revolutions, and suffered a siege unparalleled in modern history. It ceased to be the capital of the country and lost its best people, its self-respect, its money and power, and, finally, its glory. By the middle of the twentieth century the Petersburg mythos was submerged. One could only surmise its existence, as if the city had become another Atlantis" (xv).

This essay, with a different title, was originally published in *Ballet Review*, 24, no. 3 (Fall 1996).

Amid the "bizarre but beautiful ruins" and a present cloaked with fear, a new myth was in the making: that of "Petersburg as martyr, the symbol of Russia's tragic fate and of its hope for a phoenixlike rebirth." For Volkov, the heroine of this martyred metropolis is the poet Anna Akhmatova, "the keeper of the sacred flame, the mourner for the victims of the revolution, for Petersburg's lost grandeur" (xvii). For those like Volkov who view Russia's 1917 Revolution as an unmitigated disaster, the reinstatement in 1991 of the city's historic name, St. Petersburg, was a triumphant vindication of its culture. For the first time in three-quarters of a century, he writes, the "barbarous" division between the "metropolitan" and émigré exponents of Petersburg culture had ended (xx).

Although *St. Petersburg* purports to be a serious work of cultural history, the story that Volkov tells is highly personalized. Unsurprisingly, given the nature of his previous books—*Testimony* (1979), a volume of "memoirs" allegedly told to him by Dmitri Shostakovich, *Balanchine's Tchaikovsky* (1985), based on conversations with the choreographer, *From Russia to the West* (1990), with the violinist Nathan Milstein, and *Joseph Brodsky in New York* (1990), another volume of "conversations"—the volume is studded with stars and filled with anecdotes. No cultural history of St. Petersburg would be complete without Pushkin, Dostoievsky, Tchaikovsky, Akhmatova, Brodsky, Blok, Meyerhold, Balanchine, Shostakovich, and Diaghilev. But by defining culture in its narrowest, most elite sense, Volkov offers an extremely partial view of Petersburg artistic life, which, throughout the tsarist period, was not only dependent upon but also deeply shaped by the artistic, intellectual, and educational institutions of the state.

This limitation notwithstanding, in hands other than Volkov's the book could have been illuminating. However, his method, if this is the word for the celebrity "chat" and anecdotes that comprise much of the narrative, ultimately trivializes the subject, while overloading it with half-digested facts and empty generalizations.

In chapter 3, which deals with the opening decades of the twentieth century, Volkov covers the territory with the briskness of a gossip columnist. Everyone who was anyone in Silver Age Petersburg turns up in these pages—colorful figures like the newspaper magnate Solomon Propper, who owned *Birzhevye novosti* (Stock Exchange Bulletin); the poet Zinaida Gippius, who was known as the "decadent Madonna," smoked "long, scented cigarettes" (168), and, with her husband Dmitri Merezhkovsky, received Petersburg's symbolists at midnight; Mikhail Artsybashev, whose novel *Sanin* was damned by critics, censured for pornography, and circulated by underground "Saninist" clubs; Anastasia Verbitskaya, whose novel *The Keys to Happiness*, featuring a barefoot dancer à la Duncan who dies after six volumes because she is "powerless before love," sold thirty thousand copies; Zinaida Serebryakova, the niece of Alexandre Benois, who painted nude self-portraits with titles like "Bather"; Akhmatova, who married the poet Nikolai Gumilov, had an affair with Modigliani, and whiled the nights away at the Stray Dog, an artist's cabaret.

Among the trivia, however, Volkov does scatter the odd gem. Talking about the Stray Dog, where Ilya Sats wrote the score for *The Goatlegged,* a ballet produced at the Liteiny Theater in 1912, Volkov relays a conversation with Fedor Lopukhov assessing the merits of the work and its choreographer, Boris Romanov:

> "Very daring, borderline pornography. It was a much more revealing spectacle than *The Afternoon of a Faun* with Vaslav Nijinsky," Lopukhov replied thoughtfully. "But Romanov was a very talented man. He experimented with free dance à la Isadora Duncan. And he found a beautiful dancer who wasn't even a professional. She was very, very sexy." (191)

Romanov's gorgeous star, it turns out, was Olga Glebova-Sudeinkina, the wife of the painter and stage designer Sergei Sudeikin, who left Olga for the actress Vera de Bosset, who later married Igor Stravinsky. Olga was a charmer as well as a beauty. Her recipes for enthralling men lead Volkov to Mathilde Kchessinska, the Maryinsky's long-reigning *prima ballerina* and another of the era's great femmes fatales. Sandwiched between the gossip about her colorful love life is a fascinating excerpt from a 1912 review of *Le Talisman* by Akim Volynsky:

> Her demonic artistry sometimes gives off an icy chill. But at other times Kchessinska's rich technique seems like a miracle of a real, high art. At moments like that the audience bursts into wild applause and crazy cries of delight. And the black-eyed she-devil of ballet endlessly repeats, to the bravos of the entire hall, her incredible pas, her blindingly glorious diagonal dance across the stage. (192)

Volynsky was not alone in finding a connection between Kchessinska's onstage and offstage personalities. The director of the Imperial Theaters, Vladimir Telyakovsky, also linked them. Her performances, he noted in his diary, were a triumph of "vulgarity, triteness, and banality." He hated her "too short costume, fat, turned-out legs and open arms, expressing total self-satisfaction, an invitation to an embrace" (193). At another point, he described her as a "morally impudent, cynical, and brazen dancer, living simultaneously with two grand dukes and not only not hiding it but on the contrary, weaving this art as well into her stinking, cynical wreath of human offal and vice" (194). No wonder the young followers of Fokine—to say nothing of the choreographer himself—regarded the ballerina as an enemy of true art.

Despite a mention or two of grim factories, swelling population, and literacy rates (at seventy percent, the highest in Russia), Volkov seldom strays from Petersburg's gilded world of leisured, cultivated refinement. Although he was born long after that golden age vanished, he looks back on it with the nostalgia of a dispossessed heir. Referring to the "intensely intellectual atmosphere" of Vyacheslav Ivanov's salon, where Akhmatova gave her earliest poetry readings, he quotes a memoirist whose tragic sense of loss he clearly shares:

> We quoted the Greeks by heart, took delight in the French Symbolists, considered Scandinavian literature our own, knew philosophy and theology, poetry and history of the whole world. In that sense we were citizens of the universe, bearers of the great cultural museum of humanity. It was Rome at the time of the fall. We did not lie, but rather contemplated the most refined that there was in life. We were not afraid of any words. We were cynical and unchaste in spirit, wan and inert in life. In a certain sense we were, of course, the revolution before the revolution—so profoundly, ruthlessly, and fatally did we destroy the old tradition and build bold bridges into the future. But our depth and daring were intertwined with a lingering sense of decay, the spirit of dying, ghostliness, ephemerality. We were the last act of a tragedy. (178)

The tragedy, or course, was the 1917 Revolution, which brought violence, hunger, and chaos to Petersburg and the removal of the government to Moscow. The city emptied, as thousands left for the countryside in search of food, and thousands of others—the educated and privileged for the most part—went into emigration. Now, in the West, a new mythos of Petersburg rose, that of "the New Atlantis that sank beneath the sea in the stormy twentieth century" (249). This "powerful" mythos, which Volkov describes as "basically musical and balletic at its roots," was "initially planted right after the Bolshevik revolution by Diaghilev and his colleagues," and subsequently elaborated by the émigrés such as Balanchine, Stravinsky, and the novelist Vladimir Nabokov (249). That Diaghilev and Stravinsky had settled abroad long before 1917 is an inconvenient fact that the author prefers to ignore.

Although the ballet territory that Volkov covers is mostly familiar, some of his assertions are bizarre. He claims, for instance, in connection with *The Sleeping Beauty,* that Petipa "was drawn to Tchaikovsky's music by its nostalgic character" (260); that of the more than eighty ballets choreographed by Fokine "only a few were preserved intact" (261); that Diaghilev "became an émigré not of his own volition," but because "the logic of circumstances led him to it" (262), an idea that Diaghilev, whose will was nothing less than titanic, would certainly have found amusing. He also states that for Balanchine, as for Akhmatova, Shostakovich, and Brodsky, "Petersburg always remained the leading creative symbol and impulse" (XXII).

His evidence for this is shaky. Much of it, in fact, hinges on the "special role," as he puts it, of émigrés from Petersburg in the development of neoclassicism. Within this group, he places not only Balanchine and Stravinsky, whose embrace of neoclassicism predated *Apollon Musagète* by almost a decade, but also Alexandre Benois, whom Volkov identifies as the "main theoretician of Russian artistic neoclassicism" (317), although Benois himself typically described his sensibility as that of a *passéiste*.

Diaghilev's neoclassicism is equally problematic. Although his production of *The Sleeping Princess* certainly paid homage to Petersburg, the same cannot be said of *Les Noces* or *Les Biches*, nor of the retrospective cycle of operas and ballets inspired by the French *grand siècle*. Moreover, throughout the 1920s, Diaghilev produced numerous works, including several choreographed by Balanchine, in which neoclassical elements were either absent (*Barabau*, for instance) or (as in *Prodigal Son*) so closely blended with other influences as to elude categorization.

Finally, even among overtly anti-Soviet émigrés such as Stravinsky and André Levinson, neoclassicism was more than a correlative of anti-Sovietism, as Volkov maintains it was in Russia; rather, as Levinson's admiration for Maurice Barrès and other Western conservative thinkers suggests, it had overtones linking it to the reactionary right on the rise throughout Europe in the 1920s. Balanchine himself kept aloof from politics. However, this was not the case of Serge Lifar, his first Apollo and Prodigal Son, who collaborated with the Nazis during World War II, or Nicholas Nabokov, a cousin of the novelist and the composer of Diaghilev's ballet *Ode*, who during the same years helped organize the Voice of America. The influence of Russian émigrés on the Cold War policies of Western governments was not, as Volkov maintains, "negligible" (330).

It was in the United States, where Stravinsky, Balanchine, and Vladimir Nabokov ultimately settled, that the Petersburg branch of modernism abroad, as Volkov calls it, "flowered gloriously" (326). The 1960s, he contends, were "especially receptive" to this flowering. Stravinsky and Nabokov were at the height of their popularity, while books such as Robert K. Massie's *Nicholas and Alexandra* and James H. Billington's *The Icon and the Axe* focused the attention of large audiences on the city itself. As for Balanchine, his role and influence had become "very prominent." Although most critics are likely to regard the 1960s as the decade when his choreography assumed its definitive American guise, it was then, Volkov insists, that Balanchine "succeeded in combining disparate aspects of the Petersburg mythos into a single iconic image that had an enormous impact on the perception of Petersburg traditions by the American, and ultimately, the world audience" (327).

To support this amazing contention, Volkov might have cited *Don Quixote*, which had music by Nabokov and was one of the few Balanchine works of the period that could be described as expressing the "Petersburgian idealism" that Vadim Gayevsky identifies as one of Petipa's "main themes" (258). Volkov, however, in a typical disregard for chronology, leaps back in time to the 1930s and 1940s, when Balanchine, in works such as *Serenade, Mozartiana* (identified as one of the first ballets he choreographed in America, although it was actually done in France for Les Ballets 1933), and *Ballet Imperial*, "revived the Petersburg aura of Tchaikovsky's music, which had waned significantly by the middle of the century" (329). As it happens, Balanchine did come to terms with Petipa's legacy in those decades, and with the nostalgia that infuses both *Serenade* and *Ballet Imperial* with poignant romanticism, although in other works of the period, such as *Theme and Variations* and *Symphony in C,* he offered a joyous vision of paradise regained. But even in the earlier ballets, the tragic element stems at least as much from the sense of impending personal loss as from a sense of cultural loss, from the apprehension that the dream of perfect union embodied in their pas de deux is doomed to end with the final pose. Volkov's final point, that it was Balanchine's production of *The Nutcracker* that "made the fantasic city of Tchaikovsky-Balanchine homey and familiar to Americans" (330), is as muddleheaded as the author's other grand claims of the "happy match" (331) between Petersburg's modernists and America.

Far more interesting than Volkov's fantasy of Petersburg transplanted to the Hudson is his account of Balanchine's Petrograd years. Although Yury Slonimsky and Elizabeth Souritz have covered most of this ground, Volkov adds detail to the picture by drawing on his conversations with Balanchine. Especially fascinating are the pages Volkov devotes to the formalist literary critic Viktor Shklovsky, whose 1922 article on ballet Balanchine remembered with pleasure sixty years later. The article, which predated Fedor Lopukhov's plotless *Dance Symphony* by almost a year, reads in part:

> The Russian classical ballet is an abstract matter.
> Its dances are not depicting a mood or illustrating something. Classical dance is not emotional.
> This explains the pathetic and silly nature of the old ballet librettos.
> They were barely needed. Classical *pas* and their combinations existed according to the inner laws of art.
> Classical ballet is as abstract as music, the dancer's body does not determine the construction of a step so much as serve as one of the loveliest of abstractions itself. (290)

Shklovsky's manifesto struck a responsive chord in the young Balanchine. He met with the critic, talked to him, and attended several of his lectures. "It was difficult listening to Shklovsky," he told Volkov in 1982,

> because he kept getting sidetracked. But his article on ballet was another matter. It was written like a poem. And it seemed very important right away. I was young then and I wanted to be progressive. And who was I then? "Ballet boy," "dancer-prancer"—we were always called names. People didn't take us seriously. That's why I am so grateful to [Levky] Zheverzheyev [Tamara Geva's father]. He introduced me to all these modern things through the back door, so to speak. The front door was closed to people like me. (291)

Among those who scorned ballet was the poet and playwright Vladimir Mayakovsky. "I adored him," Balanchine told Volkov,

but he didn't pay any attention to me. He didn't understand a thing about ballet. . . . The artists came to Zheverzheyev's, had tea, talked. They mocked ballet: "it's funny," "no one needs it." You see, whenever I read that in the newspaper or a magazine, I got very upset. I was ashamed: why was I bothering with something so useless? But then I saw those people at Zheverzheyev's. And I thought, well, they may be geniuses, but they're not gods. They are still men. And they don't understand ballet. That's why I was so happy when I read Shklovksy's article. . . . Shklovsky was also a very progressive, very left person. But he wrote of the ballet with respect, not trying to kill it off. He explained why ballet didn't need complicated plots. And why you could dance without "emotions." And it was written clearly and simply—not like the muddled and verbose articles on ballet by Volynsky." (291–293)

Given the controversy that followed the appearance of *Testimony,* the now-discredited volume of memoirs that Volkov claimed to have written with Shostakovich, one necessarily wonders about the veracity of the "conversations" and "reminiscences" quoted by Volkov throughout *St. Petersburg.* Did Balanchine and Akhmatova really say what Volkov says they did? Did Fedor Lopukhov really bump into him one day in the 1960s and spend twenty minutes explaining the glories of Theater Street, telling him that "when you walk down this street to the theater, the columns of the buildings literally start to dance" (255)? Did Volkov personally witness, as he claims he did, the run-in between choreographer Leonid Yakobson and Leningrad's cultural bureaucrats that prompted Yakobson to call them "idiots" (506)? Or are these and the countless other remarks quoted verbatim throughout the book actually Volkov's own reconstructions, adapted to the subject at hand and personalized to serve the needs of the narrative?

One questions Volkov's veracity all the more readily because of his sloppiness about details. He gets many little things wrong—the premiere of *Petrouchka* (on at least two occasions given as 1910 rather than 1911); the venue of Diaghilev's 1907 Russian concert series; the year of an excerpt from Petipa's diary. He says that Diaghilev's production of *The Sleeping Princess* was a commercial failure in Paris, where the ballet was never performed, and that in 1922 Benois was the head of *Mir iskusstva,* although the journal, which was founded and edited by Diaghilev, had gone out of existence nearly twenty years before. For someone who speaks of craft and professionalism as exemplary Petersburg traits, Volkov's cavalier treatment of facts shows that even among Petersburgers these virtues are not universal.

Although Volkov has lived in the United States for two decades, he seems surprisingly unaware of Western sources, including several that would have bolstered his arguments, such as John Bowlt's study of the *Mir iskusstva* group, Laura Engelstein's analysis of Russian "boulevard" fiction, and Roland John Wiley's book on Tchaikovsky. Although much of the dance discussion centers on Western phenomena, Volkov, with a few notable exceptions (Arlene Croce's *Afterimages*, Lincoln Kirstein's *Dance: A Short History of Classic Theatrical Dancing*, and Richard Buckle's *George Balanchine, Ballet Master*), relies solely on Russian sources—the reason for so many errors in his references to the Ballets Russes. Moreover, Volkov has the irritating habit of citing works in Russian versions even when English translations exist. This is particularly egregious in the case of Fokine's memoirs and Benois' volumes of reminiscence, which were published in English long before they appeared in Russian. Equally annoying is the nomenclature adopted by the book's translator, Antonina W. Bouis, for titles such as Alexander Blok's play *The Fairground Booth* (or *The Puppet Show*), which for some reason she calls *The Fair Show Booth*. And after twenty years in the United States, Volkov should know, even if his translator does not, that the women in *La Bayadère* are "shades," not "shadows."

St. Petersburg is published by the Free Press, a trade house that in recent years has built a strong right-wing list, including *The Bell Curve*, Irving Kristol's *Neoconservatism*, and Dinesh D'Souza's *The End of Racism*. From an ideological viewpoint, one can hardly imagine a better match of author and publisher; indeed, parts of Volkov's book are little more than a Reaganite screed against the "evil empire." Just as Volkov fails to understand how Petersburgers allowed the renaming of their city as Petrograd during World War I, so he finds it impossible to explain why members of the intelligentsia supported the Revolution in 1917, except on the grounds that they were "starry-eyed," naive, or opportunistic. Class hatred is equally beyond his ken, although without it the violence that accompanied the Revolution is hard to explain. He ignores entirely the misery in which a majority of Russians lived, even in Petersburg, with its teeming slums of have-nots; all that awakens his sympathy is the plight of the city's dispossessed elite. One is reminded of Thomas Paine's celebrated response to Edmund Burke's lament over the fate of Marie Antoinette: "He pities the plumage, but forgets the dying bird."

In the construction of historical memory, what is forgotten is no less important than what is remembered. Volkov's "great tradition" is a perfect example of this. Indeed, as he uses the term in connection with ballet, it consists of exactly four individuals—Petipa, Fokine, Lopukhov, and Balanchine. Such a view is not only partial but deeply parochial, reducing the history of ballet to a Petersburg–New York axis that just happens to follow the author's trajectory as an émigré. In fact, for all Volkov's concern with the transplanting of the Petersburg "mythos" abroad, he is silent on the single most important enterprise to accomplish this in ballet. If Maryinsky classicism has rooted itself in the West, it is less because of Balanchine than because of Ninette de Valois, who, in the 1930s, with Nicholas Sergeyev, the Maryinsky's former chief régisseur, produced the full versions of *Swan Lake, The Nutcracker, Giselle,* and *The Sleeping Beauty* that made a place for these ballets in the international repertory. For all the claims to universalism, Volkov's "great tradition" represents a highly partisan view of the ballet past, one that excludes every major figure of the post-Diaghilev era apart from Balanchine.

Since the 1950s, of course, Balanchine has been a towering presence in ballet. But nowhere, even in this country, where his influence has been greatest, does he comprise the whole of ballet, just as Petipa, for all that his works constitute most of the nineteenth-century repertory danced today outside Denmark, is less than the sum of ballet as this existed in Europe and America one hundred years ago. The Maryinsky may well have been the crucible of major developments in twentieth-century ballet, but it was by no means the only breeding ground of change. To ascribe, as Volkov does, the renewal of ballet in the West to a single Petersburg source is to deny the multiplicity of "native" traditions that over the years have shaped and reshaped its identity. The history of ballet, no less than that of poetry, painting, or music, is far more than the memory of a fabled golden age seen through the distorting lens of cultural nostalgia.

NOTES

1. Solomon Volkov, *St. Petersburg: A Cultural History,* trans. Antonina W. Bouis (New York: Free Press, 1995).

American Ballet Theatre *(continued)*
391–97; *Swan Lake* production, 333–35;
technique, 335–36; 2001 review, 338–46
American dance, 52. *See also* Modern dance;
New York City
American Dance Festival, 252, 308
American Document, 234, 263, 290, 300
American Express funding for dance, 330
American Music Festival of NYCB, 367–68
An American Tragedy (Schuman), 307
El amor brujo (Falla), 43, 278–79, 282
L'Amoureuse Leçon, 87, 102n12
Ana María, 277–83; critical reviews, 278–79,
281–83; *The Three-Cornered Hat,* 279,
281–83
Ananiashvili, Nina, 341
Anawalt, Sasha, 317, 319–21
Andantino, 194
Anderson, Jack, 200
Anderson, Margaret, 257
Anitra, 68
Annenkov, Yury, 81n29
Annie Get Your Gun, 254
L'Annonce faite à Marie, 39
Antar, 93, 95, 127
Antheil, George, 114, 256–71; American Bal-
let commissions, 261–63, 273nn23–24;
Ballet Russe de Monte Carlo activities,
266–69; Ballets Suédois performance,
257; *Capital of the World,* 267–71; collaboration with Balanchine, 261–63, 266,
273n23; collaboration with Denham,
266–69; collaboration with Graham,
263–66, 273n31; collaboration with
Léger, 258; collaboration with Loring,
270–71; collaboration with Tamiris, 258;
collaboration with Yeats, 259–60; critical
reviews, 269–70, 273n23; decade abroad,
256–60; Hollywood work, 265–66; influence of Stravinsky, 256–57; Kirstein
patronage, 261–62; modernism, 260–61;
operas, 260–61; return to United States,
259; views on Balanchine, 268–69; writing and inventions, 266
Antique Theater, 70
Antonio, José, 283
Antonio el de Bilbao, 278, 283
L'Apache (Franck), 152
Apollo. See Apollon Musagète (Stravinsky)

Apollon Musagète (Stravinsky), 49, 407–8; as
Apollo, 20, 42, 50; Balanchine's choreog-
raphy, 362; Ballets Russes (Diaghilev)
production, 179, 187; Levinson's views,
128; Miami City Ballet production, 383;
New York City Ballet production, 354
Appalachian Spring (Copland), 52, 290, 336
L'Après-midi d'un faune (Debussy), 48; Bal-
lets Russes (Diaghilev) production, 55,
179, 181, 183–84, 185, 190, 191; choreogra-
phy, 160; New York City Ballet produc-
tion, 352
Archipelago, 262, 273n25
Archives Internationales de la Danse, 120
Argentinita, 277–78, 280, 284–85n11
Ari, Carina, 115, 189, 220
Arlequin, 116
The Armchair (Panfilov), 9
Aronson, Boris, 197, 352
Arpino, Gerald, 319
Artemis troublée, 93, 94
Ashberry, John, 350
Ashley, Merrill, 363, 366, 368, plate
Ashton, Frederick, 223, 262; New York City
Ballet production, 307, 350, 351; views on
Nijinska, 200; writing on Petipa, 12
Astafieva, Serfima, 68
Astruc, Gabriel, 57, 151–52, 153
Auric, Georges, 50–51, 110, 114–15
Aurora's Wedding, 109, 188
Au temps jadis, 151
Autumn Song, 194
Avant-garde ballet. *See* Modern ballet
Avant-garde dance, 245–54; Judson chore-
ographers, 250–53; minimalism, 253;
music composition, 252; Nijinska's role,
198–99; *Parade,* 40, 42, 73–74; Pop-art
influence, 253; *Relâche* (Satie), 51, 75–76,
113–14; use of abstraction, 246–47; use
of ballet technique, 249–50
Aveline, Albert, 87, 102n12
Aveline, Louis, 59

Bacchanale, 280, 284–85n11
Badet, Régina, 149, 163–64n9
Bailey, Pearl, 318
Le Baiser de la Fée (Stravinsky), 49, 50, 362
Baker, Josephine, 113, 127
Bakst, Léon, 17, 55, 89; designs for Diaghilev,

39–40, 41; designs for Rubinstein, 58; erotic design elements, 190; film of ballet, 66; Levinson's views, 126; Paris Opéra production, 43, 99; portrait of Massine, 190; Rubinstein production, 157, 167n49
Le Bal, 353
Balakirev, Mily, 48
Balanchine, George, 307, 347–65, plate; American Ballet Theatre production, 340; American dance, 232; apprenticeship under Diaghilev, 347; artistic vision, 134n46; ballerinas, 186–87, 191, 192, 244, 363–64; Ballet Russe de Monte Carlo activities, 266–67, 349; Ballet Society activities, 242–45, 261, 267; Ballets Russes commissions, 115; Ballet Theatre activities, 349; borrowings from the past, 400; Broadway works, 349; choreography, 186–87, 221; collaboration with Antheil, 261–63, 266, 268–69, 273n23; collaboration with Dalí, 280; collaboration with Graham, 357; collaboration with Kirstein, 261–62, 347–49; collaboration with Stravinsky, 49–50, 362; collaboration with Tchelitchew, 353; critical reviews, 128, 131, 301; Dance Theatre of Harlem productions, 329, 331; death and legacy, 364; early NYC work, 239, 242–45, 261; erotic dance elements, 42, 244–45; The George Balanchine Trust, 364–65; Harvard archives, 267; heroic male roles, 186–87; Hollywood activities, 266; honoring of Martin Luther King, Jr., 326, 358; influence on Cunningham, 249–50; Joffrey Ballet repertory, 319; Kirstein's views, 131, 134n46; leotard ballets, 243–45; Levinson's views, 128, 131; Martin's reviews, 265; modernism, 351, 409–10; movement style, 41; neoclassicism, 242–43, 265, 407–8; Petipa's influence, 243, 409–10; relationship with Karinska, 353; revisions of dances, 20; set designs, 243–44; Stravinsky festivals, 49–50, 361; training, 347; tributes from Mark Morris, 206; use of lighting, 44; views on abstraction, 409–10; views on narrative in ballet, 265; Volkov's views, 407–12; writings on Petipa, 12. *See also* New York City Ballet

Bales, William, 236
Ball, Hugo, 117
Balla, Giacomo, 72, 73
Ballade, plate
Ballet Caravan, 239–40, 242, 265, 348
Ballet Club, 223–24
Le Ballet des Nations, 156
Ballet Español, 278–83
Ballet Imperial, 408–9; American Ballet Caravan production, 348; American Ballet Theatre production, 335–36; Balanchine choreography, 242, 243
Ballet International, 284–85n11
Ballet Mécanique, 257, 260
Le Ballet mécanique (film), 68
Ballet Russe de Monte Carlo (Denham): Balanchine's choreography, 266–67; collaboration with Antheil, 266–69; critical reviews, 301; Dalí set designs, 284–85n11; funding, 314n23; tours, 304n22
Ballet Society, 242–45, 267, 349; design, 349; funding, 306, 355; populism, 242. *See also* New York City Ballet
Ballets Russes (Diaghilev), vii, 17; archive collection values, 377–82; conservative topics, 109, 115; costumes, 187–88; dancers, 56, 62–63, 68–70, 144–45, 179–91, 377–78; debut, 39; eroticism, 41–42, 180–84, 191; film careers of dancers, 68–70; film references, 73–75; films of ballet, 66; financial considerations, 107; Fokine's ballets, 47–48; formation, 47; French influence, 48, 50–51; homosexuality, 179–91, 212, 222; imitations of, 42–43; influence of film, 72–78; influence on American ballet, 238–39; influence on choreography, 221–22; influence on French dance, 58–60, 100; influence on Rouché, 86–87; Levinson's views, 127; male-centered aesthetic, 144–45, 179–92, 193n10, 212, 221–22; Massine's experimental work, 185–86; modernity, 38–44; new music, 45–52, 256–57; 1913 season, 54–60, 63–64; *Ode*, 76–78, 84n72; Paris Opéra performances, 90, 103n36; recreations from the past, 400; role of ballerinas, 180–84, 186, 188, 190–91; Rome years, 72; Rubinstein's roles, 158, 159, 181–82; Russian

Dance Symphony: The Magnificence of the
Universe, 388, 401, 410
Dance Theatre of Harlem, 324, 326, 329–32;
audience, 331–32; classic revivals, 383;
funding, 329, 330; repertory, 329–31;
thirtieth-anniversary season, 330–31
Danilova, Alexandra, 77, 173, 393, plate
D'Annunzio, Gabriele, 58, 68, 160
La Danse (magazine), 109
Danse céleste, 116
La Danse de l'acier, 73
"Danse macabre" (Saint-Saëns), 155–56
Danses Concertantes (Stravinsky), 50
Danse suédoise, 116
Danse Tzigane, 116
Dansgille, 108
Danza de la Muerte, 278
Daphnis and Chloe (Ravel), 48, 90; Ballets
Russes (Diaghilev) production, 55, 190;
Paris Opéra production, 94; parodies
of, 70
D'Arbois, Colin, 122n15
Dardel, Nils, 114
Dark Meadow, 291
The Daughter of Pharaoh, 14, 33n20, 46, 61,
63, 200
Daunt, Yvonne, 93, 95–98, 106n80
Davidova, Lucia, 262
Deakin, Irving, 301, 302
Dean, Laura, 367
Deaths and Entrances, 235
De Basil, Colonel W., 277, 301
Debussy, Claude, 48, 50, 155-56; music for
Paris Opéra production, 94; reaction to
The Rite of Spring, 57
Deck of Cards, 205
Deep Song, 278, 289
De Kooning, Willem, 350
Delaunay, Robert, 77
Delaunay, Sonia, 77
De Lavallade, Carmen, 318, 323, 330
Delibes, Léo, 46, 86, 99
Delion, Jean, 150
Delsarte, François, 157
Delsaux, Mlle., 127
De Luz, Joaquín, 340, 343
Delza, Sophia, 278
De Mille, Agnes, 69, 79–80n14, 330; Ballet
Russe de Monte Carlo Rodeo, 240; Ballet

Theatre performances, 240; Broadway
activities, 253–54; choreography, 215,
224, 241, 253–54, 370–71n4; folk drama,
396; New York City Ballet activities,
370–71n4; Oklahoma!, 253
DeMille, Cecil B., 69, 79–80n14
Le Démon (Rubinstein), 151, 153
Demons, 199
Denby, Edwin, 198, 231, 240–41, 387, 389
Denham, Sergei, 266–69
Denis, Maurice, 57–58
Denishawn, 233
Depero, Fortunato, 72, 73, 81–82n35, 111
Derain, André, 42, 173, 379, 394
Der Freischütz (Weber), 57
Derviches, 107, 116–17
Design. See Modern design in ballet
Desvallières, 154
Detaille, Georges, 225
Dethomas, Maxime, 86, 89, 154
Les Deux Pigeons, 91; Paris Opéra produc-
tion, 93; Trouhanova performance, 151
Les Deux vieilles gardes (Delibes), 86
De Valois, Ninette, 189, 215, 222–24, 411–12;
choreography for Yeats's work, 259;
Sadlers Wells's directorship, 279
Diaghilev, Serge, x, plate; archives and collections, 377–82; artistic vision, 56; art-
work, 8; Ballets Suédois competition,
107–8; Ballets Suédois influence, 114–15;
childhood, 3–10, 45–46; choreographic
experiment, 9, 40–41; collaboration
with Depero, 72, 81–82n35; collaboration
with Prokofiev, 50; collaboration with
set designers, 39–40, 44, 44n3; collaboration with Strauss, 60; collaboration
with Stravinsky, 49; collaborators, 108,
381; compositions, 46, 380–81; constancy
of the score, 21; death, 5; dramatic emphasis, 40; education, 3, 6, 46; emigration from Russia, 407; family background, 5–8; film, 66–67, 76, 78–79,
82n37; firing of Nijinsky, 60; formation
of the Ballets Russes, 47; gallery exhibition in Perm, 4–5; "The Good Fairy
Bakst Leads Prince Charming
Diaghileff . . . ," plate; hiring of soloists,
154; homosexuality, 179–91, 212, 221–22;
Imperial Theater production, 46; influ-

Lifar, Serge, 179, 187, 190; Ballets Russes (Diaghilev) performances, 188; choreography, 188, 221; collections, 377–82; costuming, 191; in *Ode*, 77; Paris Opéra appointment, 43, 99, 192; political activities, 408

Lilac Garden, 350, 395

Lila Field company, 223

Lila Wallace-Reader's Digest Fund, 330

Limón, José, plate; composers, 45; political engagement, 236–37, 291, 296; Spanish-influenced dance, 278; works produced by Alvin Ailey American Dance Theater, 323

Lincoln Center for the Performing Arts, 254, 310, 355–58; New York State Theater, 311, 355–56, 372–73n32; populist vision, 357; Rose Building, 366

Lista, Giovanni, 73

Liszt, Franz, 62

Liteiny Theater, 70

The Little Humpbacked Horse, 19, 33n20, 46, 61, 63

Liturgie, 8

Litvinne, Felia, 47, 152

Litvinov, Maxim, 7

Litz, Katherine, 246

Living Theater, 246–47

Lloyd, Margaret, 236

Lloyd, Maude, 396

Lloyd, Norman, 45, 263

Lloyd, Ruth, 45

London Coliseum, 160

Long, Andrea, 332

Longchamp, Gaston, 262

Lopez, Lourdes, 364, 368

López, Pilar, 278, 283

Lopokova, Lydia, vii, 190, plate; choreography, 189; fees, 171–72; film of *Dancing Grace*, 74–75; Les Soirées de Paris, 171–78

Lopukhov, Fedor, 12, 195–96; abstraction, 388, 410; choreography, 204n28; Kirov productions, 401; response to Fokine's *Les Préludes*, 62; on Boris Romanov, 406; *Swan Lake* production, 333; Volkov's views, 411

Loquasto, Santo, 208

Loring, Eugene, 240, 265, 269–70

Lorrain, Jean, 151

Love, Paul, 301, 302

Lovey, 205

Lubovitch, Lar, 367

Lugné-Poe, Aurélian, 86

Lully, Jean-Baptiste, 87, 90, 99

Lurçat, Jean, 262

Lyman, Peggy, 291

Lynes, George Platt, 348, 353

MacArthur, Charles, 260

MacCormack, Gilson, 178

Macdonald, Brian, 320

MacLean, Sally, 278

Madariaga, Salvador de, 277

Mad Tristan, 280, 284–85n11

Maeterlinck, Maurice, 86

Magallanes, Nicholas, 354

The Magic Flute, 368

The Magic Mirror, 14–20, 34n42, 200

The Magnificent Cuckold, 40

Magriel, Paul, 302

Mahoney, Arthur, 260

Maïmouna, 93, 94

Maison de Fous, 107, 117–18, 119

Makarova, Elena, 22

Makarova, Natalia, 400

La Maladetta, 91, 94

Malakov, Vladimir, 341–42

Malevich, Kasimir, 40, 61

Malipiero, Gian Francesco, 43

Malraux, André, 129

Ma Mère l'Oye (Ravel), 43, 86–87, 88, 89; Hugard's choreography, 59, 87, 149, 163n6, 220; Rouché production, 59, 101nn8–9, 163n6

Mamontov (Savva) Private Opera, 17

Mann, Joseph, 242

Mannes, Marya, 274n37

Manning, Susan, 215

Man Ray. *See* Ray, Man

Mantsoe, Vincent Sekwati, 330

Manzini, Louise. *See* Stichel, Madame

Maré, Rolf de, 43, 51; African themes, 113; Ballets Suédois, 107, 115–16, 120; collaborations, 108, 114; documentary films, 113; newspaper and magazine holdings, 109; use of film in ballet, 75–76. *See also* Ballets Suédois

Staats, Léo *(continued)*
  Paris Opéra productions, 93, 94, 96, 97,
    99, 101n8, 102n16, 226n9
Stanislavsky, Konstantin, 157, 158, 159, 401
Stars and Stripes, 354, 358
Stella, Frank, 247
Steps in the Streets, 289–90
Stevenson, Ben, 344
Stichel, Madame (Louise Manzini), 59,
    164n10, 216, 219–20, 226n18, 227n23
Stiefel, Ethan, 341–42, 345
Stierle, Edward, 210–14
Still/Here, 325–27
Stockhausen, Karlheinz, 252
Stokowsky, Leopold, 266
The Stone Flower (Prokofiev), 50
Stowitts, Hubert, 101n8
The Strange American Funeral, 290
Strauss, Johann, 173
Strauss, Richard, 60, 62
Stravinsky, Igor, 307; collaboration with Bal-
    anchine, 49–50, 362; collaboration with
    Diaghilev, 49; emigration from Russia,
    407–8; festivals of work, 49–50, 361; in-
    fluence on Antheil, 256–57; Levinson's
    views, 126; modernity, 38; modernization
    of others' works, 42; neoclassicism,
    407–8; New York City Ballet commis-
    sions, 307; *Les Noces,* 256–57; *The Rite
    of Spring,* 57
Stravinsky Violin Concerto, 49–50, 336, 362
A Streetcar Named Desire, 330
Strict Songs, 207
Strindberg, August, 86
Students' Dance Recitals series, 242
Subways Are For Sleeping, 254
Suclpture nègre, 112
Suite by Chance, 248
Suite de Danses, 59, 152
Surovshchikova, Mariia Sergeevna, 26, 37
Suvorin, Aleksei, 20–21
Suzuki, D. T., 248
Svetlov, Valerian, 55, 176, plate
Swan Lake (Tchaikovsky), 11, 14, 25, 46–47;
    American Ballet Theatre production,
    333–44; Balanchine's one-act version,
    350, 352–53, 383; Ballets Russes (Diaghi-
    lev) production, 180, 188, 400; Imperial

Ballet production, 61, 63, 333; Paris pro-
    duction, 55; parodies, 70; revivals in the
    West, 18; Royal Ballet production, 384;
    Sadler's Wells production, 400; Samari-
    tani's design, 335; de Valois/Sergeyev
    production, 411–12
Les Sylphides: American Ballet Theatre pro-
    duction, 336–37; Ballets Russes (Dia-
    ghilev) production, 181, 182, 192n5; as
    Chopiniana, 20, 48, 61; New York pro-
    duction, 69; Théâtre des Champs-
    Elysées frescoes, 57; use of pointe, 183
Sylvia, 46, 91, 164n10; Mérode performance,
    149; New York City Ballet production,
    353; Paris Opéra production, 93, 94, 126
Symphonie Concertante, 243
Symphonie Fantastique, 394
Symphony in C, 243, 347, 353, 409
Symphony in Three Movements (Stravinsky),
    50, 362

TAC (monthly), 302
Taglioni, Marie, 132–33n18, 139, 141, 215
Taglioni chez Musette, 94
Tailleferre, Germaine, 110
Tairov, Alexander, 70–71, 127
Le Talisman, 406
Tallchief, Maria, 349, 354, 358, plate
Tamiris, Helen, 232, 234; Broadway work,
    254; collaboration with Antheil, 258;
    racism in dance, 318
Tanner, Richard, 362
Tanning, Dorothea, 350
Taper, Bernard, 305, 364
Taras, John, 362
Taylor, Paul, 246, 319, 367
Taylor, Ralph, 297
Tchaikovsky, Peter, 21, 46, 194
Tchaikovsky Pas de Deux, 342
Tchelitchew, Pavel, 42, 80–81n23, 259; col-
    laboration with Balanchine, 353; *Ode*
    scenario, 76–78, 84n72
Tcherina, Ludmila, 283
Tcherkas, Constantin, 220
Tchernichva, Lubov, 62
Technique: eurhythmic dance, 85, 90–100;
    Fokine's views on naturalism, 67–68; in
    modern ballet, 56; modern modifica-

ABOUT THE AUTHOR

Lynn Garafola is a dance historian and critic living in New York City. She is the author of *Diaghilev's Ballets Russes* and the editor of many books including *André Levinson on Dance: Writings from Paris in the Twenties* (with Joan Acocella), *The Diaries of Marius Petipa, Rethinking the Sylph: New Persectives on the Romantic Ballet, José Limón: An Unfinished Memoir,* and *The Ballets Russes and Its World.* A former Getty scholar, she has curated several exhibitions, including *Dance for a City: Fifty Years of the New York City Ballet* at the New-York Historical Society. She is the former editor of the series *Studies in Dance History* and a senior editor of *Dance Magazine.* She teaches at Barnard College/Columbia University.